POLITICS, PARTIES, & PRESSURE GROUPS

POLITICS,

PARTIES,

& PRESSURE

GROUPS

FIFTH EDITION

By V. O. KEY, JR.

HARVARD UNIVERSITY

Thomas Y. Crowell Company

NEW YORK / ESTABLISHED 1834

FIFTH EDITION

10

Copyright © 1942, 1947, 1952, 1958, 1964 by
Thomas Y. Crowell Company, Inc.
All Rights Reserved

Designed by Laurel Wagner

Library of Congress Catalog Card Number 64-11799

Manufactured in the United States of America
ISBN 0-690-64785-9

PREFACE

THE FOURTH EDITION of this book reflected a fairly drastic revision of the preceding version. This, the fifth edition, does not diverge in general outline from the fourth. Seldom does a fifth edition differ markedly from a fourth. Nevertheless, several thousand amendments, excisions, and other alterations cumulate into an extensive revision in detail. Insofar as seemed useful the analysis takes into account political events since the publication of the last edition. Moreover, the revision embodies insofar as practicable the findings of recent scholarly inquiries. The large research output by students of American politics during the past decade makes it less feasible to approach bibliographical comprehensiveness than it was at the time of the first edition. To make space for newer materials, citations to a goodly number of older items have had to be omitted. Those who use the footnotes as a bibliographical guide, hence, will find earlier editions useful in supplementation of this version.

I must record my indebtedness to those who have called my attention to passages meriting correction or clarification, chiefly students who have read the book through no choice of their own. Their comments have been quite helpful. I am also obliged to David Mayhew for assistance in the preparation of some of the tables and charts. It scarcely seems necessary for the author of the fifth edition of a book explicitly to claim credit for its errors and shortcomings. Yet a sensitive regard for prefatory conventions moves me to acknowledge that responsibility, an assertion of culpability unlikely to be questioned.

Cambridge, Massachusetts   V. O. KEY, JR.

To L. G. K.

CONTENTS

II THE PARTY SYSTEM

III   PARTY STRUCTURE
AND PROCEDURE

I V   PARTY AND

THE ELECTORATE

A NOTE FROM THE PUBLISHER

After completing his work of revision on this edition of Politics, Parties, and Pressure Groups, *V. O. Key, Jr., was stricken with an illness that unhappily proved to be fatal. As with all who knew V. O., we deeply admired him as man and scholar, and we regard as exceedingly privileged the years of our association with him.*

1.

THE NATURE

OF POLITICS

GOVERNMENT is a universal, if not always an admirable, feature of society. The most primitive tribes and the most industrialized nation states have their governing processes. Whatever the religion, the race, the color, or the stage of technological development of a people, they need some sort of governing apparatus. Threats from enemies outside require the management of men and resources for defense—and perhaps for aggression. Maintenance of domestic peace and tranquillity requires means for keeping order and for settling disputes. In short, without governmental authority to provide for the common defense and to maintain domestic order, human society could scarcely exist, even though utopians dream of that day of human perfection when government shall be forever dissolved.

Government, though universal, is also diverse. The task of governing may be performed by the elders as an incident to their paternal and priestly functions; or it may be carried on by a clearly differentiated, specialized organization. The range of governmental functions may be narrow or broad. Government's main concern may be the resolution of squabbles between citizens; or its activities may extend from the education of children, through the management of the economy, to the care of the aged. The holders of authority may be few or many. Government may act at the caprice and whim of the rulers, or it may operate in accordance with constitutional standards. It may exploit the many for the benefit of the few; or the few for the benefit of the many.

1

However diverse the processes and forms of governance may appear, tribal chieftains, tyrants, ruling aristocracies, and chief executives of modern republics have something in common: they possess authority; they exercise power. Their success depends on their skill in the fulfillment of their roles as holders of power; the demands of those roles, to be sure, differ greatly from time to time, from situation to situation, from culture to culture.

Government must cultivate a cheerful and willing obedience. Yet its armory of ultimate sanctions includes powers over property, liberty, and life itself. The ubiquity of the relationship of governor and governed, of ruler and ruled, leads students of politics to single out power as the basic characteristic of that human behavior of interest to them. Who exercises power? For whose benefit? In what manner? To what ends? According to what principles, if any? By what right? Such questions occupy the philosophers of politics. They are also the concern of prime ministers, presidents, and princes.

Politics as Power

These observations give an uncommonly broad connotation to the term "politics." They equate politics with governance, with the process and practice of ruling. In everyday usage politics may be taken to cover only such matters as the battles of the Republicans and the Democrats, low and unprincipled humbugging of the people, skillful negotiation, or all the incomprehensible things "they" do in Washington. For the moment, let the term apply more broadly to workings of governments generally, their impact on the governed, their manner of operation, the means by which governors attain and retain authority. So defined, politics encompasses phenomena dealt with in courses of study ranging from police administration, to constitutional law, to international relations. Through all these and other aspects of the governing process runs the common thread of power.

WHAT IS POWER?   If the essence of politics lies in "power," precise definition of that term is in order. Often power is regarded as if it were a substance that could be poured into a keg, stored, and drawn upon as the need arises. A person has or does not have power. Wall Street has power. The labor barons have power. The inner ring of Democratic (or Republican) politicians has power. A clique of businessmen and military bureaucrats runs the country.

Such notions of power as a substance in a keg, something a person does or does not have, convey a truncated conception of the reality of power. These usages describe only a single aspect of certain relationships among human beings. Politics as power consists fundamentally of relationships of superordination and subordination, of dominance and submission, of the governors and the governed. The study of politics is the study of these relationships. George E. G. Catlin, an English political theorist, defines "politics as a study of the act of control, or as the act of human or social control." [1] In a similar vein Harold D. Lasswell, an American political scientist, says, "The study of politics is the study of influence and the influential." [2] To comprehend politics one must look not only at the man who draws power from a keg, so to speak, but at the relation between him and those whom his actions may affect. In this relationship lies the essence of politics.

Sociologists in their concept of "role," which is a bit recondite, come close to this view of politics as power. Within the political system many types of individuals possess influence or the right to command. Their positions come to be clothed with customary duties whose fulfillment evokes relatively predictable responses from those affected. No matter who fills the position, or role, about the same responses may be expected. Thus, pick at random a moderately intelligent individual with quick reflexes and good eyesight, drape him with a policeman's uniform, and put him to directing traffic. Matters will probably proceed as if our man were a duly sworn officer. By virtue of the role, that is, the actions expected of such an individual and the responses expected from all concerned, he might be said to possess power. Yet when he fills a role he occupies a position as an actor in a system of human relationships. The political order in a sense consists of a system of such patterned roles, from the players of which specified behaviors are expected by others. A president, no less than a policeman, fills a role. Or, it might be said, he possesses power by virtue of the office he holds.

If one views power as relational, he must hasten to reject some of the popular connotations of the term "power." The word carries by implication its own adjectives and may suggest unlimited authority. In fact, the power relationship may vary from brute force to the most gentle persuasion. Nor should the term "power" be allowed to conjure up solely visions of commands coming from "above." The power relationship is reciprocal, and the subject may affect the ruler more profoundly than the ruler affects the subject. As Lasswell puts it, "Power is an interpersonal situation; those who hold power are empowered. They depend upon and continue only so long as there is a continuing stream of empowering responses." [3] Nor should description in terms of power be taken as a contention that all political activists are motivated solely, or even primarily, by a drive for power. Yet the leader of the most holy cause, if he is successful, is tied to many people by relationships of power. Obviously political power (in the keg sense of the term) is

---

[1] *A Study of the Principles of Politics* (New York: Macmillan, 1930), pp. 68–69.

[2] *Politics* (New York: Whittlesey House, 1936), p. 1. See also R. A. Dahl, "The Concept of Power," *Behavioral Science*, 2 (1957), 201–15.

[3] *Power and Personality* (New York: Norton, 1948), p. 10.

something more than an end in itself, though for many practitioners of politics the deference that accompanies the achievement of positions of leadership may be deeply satisfying.

STRUCTURES OF POWER   Though political power in the relational sense ultimately distills down to the relations between individuals A and B, the isolated political act takes on a fuller meaning when regarded in the framework of the totality of political relations within the society. A working political system consists of a multiplicity of these individual relationships which, collectively, tend to be organized or shaped into characteristic forms.

Political speculators, from Aristotle on, have occupied themselves with the classification of states according to differentiations in their structures of power. That is, they have sought to identify the types of patterns of relationships of political power. Familiar is the overly simple classification of constitutions—or structures of political power in our terminology—into monarchies, aristocracies, democracies, which groups regimes according to the number of persons holding authority—one, few, or many. An additional characteristic of power relationships enters into the classification when tyranny is differentiated from monarchy, oligarchy from aristocracy, mob rule from democracy. Authority may be exercised with justice and with restraint or arbitrarily and capriciously, whether vested in one, the few, or the many. Such categories do not necessarily picture the real world of governance, for each regime has its peculiarities. One dictatorship may be a tyranny in the ancient sense, another not, and a third may differ from both. Instead of being separable into sharply differentiated classes, political systems differ in degree, and one category gradually shades off into another.

Democracy, Self-government, and Power

An observer of politics aware of the many kinds of power structures that have existed through history, or even over the globe at a particular time, has no difficulty in picturing political phenomena in terms of power. He may arrive at a generalization of the sort stated by Gaetano Mosca, an Italian political theorist:

> In all societies—from societies that are very meagerly developed and have barely attained the dawnings of civilization, down to the most advanced and powerful societies—two classes of people appear—a class that rules and a class that is ruled. The first class, always the less numerous, performs all political functions, monopolizes power, and enjoys the advantages that power brings, whereas the second, the more numerous class, is directed and controlled by the first, in a manner that is now more or less legal, now more or less arbitrary and violent.[4]

[4] *The Ruling Class* (New York: McGraw-Hill, 1939), p. 50.

The idea of a ruling class grates on democratic ears. The citizen of a democracy may assert that Mosca's generalization describes a system unknown to him. Indeed, the theory of democracy inverts the ancient relationships of authority and proposes that power rest in the people who govern themselves. The rulers become identical with the ruled. The conception of politics as a system of power relationships clashes with such doctrines as that of "popular self-government," the idea of the "general will," and the belief in government "of the people, by the people, and for the people."

Yet even the most casual observer of democratic processes finds difficulty in observing the transmutation of the popular will into statute. He quickly sees that some people have much more of a voice in what government does than do others. He has no difficulty in discerning that not all democratic orders are cut from the same cloth. A democracy may have within it a touch of aristocracy; it may have a dash of tyranny; and on occasion it may be powerless to act. Even so, political regimes classified as democratic, despite their individual peculiarities, possess characteristics that differentiate them from tyrannies, from dictatorships, and from aristocracies. Those characteristics relate to the organization of the power structure, to the manner of exercise of authority, and to ends sought through government. The most appropriate analytical approach is to assume that certain patterns in the structure and dynamics of political power are more or less peculiar to democratic orders and to seek to identify those special characteristics rather than to assume that the power analysis is inapplicable to democratic systems.

SUCCESSION TO AUTHORITY IN DEMOCRACIES   Democratic systems have evolved a characteristic solution of the problem of succession to posts of authority—a basic question that vexes all sorts of regimes. Hereditary monarchies left the matter to a biological lottery which, at times, worked well enough. Hereditary aristocracies had much the same solution. Quite as often one set of rulers replaced another by coup d'état or by revolution. Modern dictatorships confront no new problem when the dictator nears senility and the issue of succession demands attention. How to accomplish transfers of authority without serious disturbances in the life of the state has been a topic for political speculation through the ages. The democratic solution is to fill the principal posts of authority by elections. A working system of elections cannot, of course, be created by fiat. Probably elections may come to be used to determine succession to authority only with a cultural habituation to such a technique, under circumstances of general agreement on a broad range of issues both substantive and procedural, and doubtless in association with other factors neither well understood nor easily defined. Nevertheless, a major accomplishment of the architects of democracies has been the contrivance of orderly modes of succession to places of authority.

The democratic formula goes beyond the question of succession in its ancient form. It not only provides a means for filling posts of authority when

they become vacant; it assures that they will become vacant at frequent intervals without either the messiness of a beheading or the inconvenience of
a revolution. The democratic technique for the determination of succession
is thus combined with a method for the termination of the life of a government. An election poses the questions whether the ruling clique shall be
continued in power and, if not, by whom shall it be succeeded. Democratic
orders merge into a single ritual a substitute for older techniques of determining the heir to authority and a functional equivalent for the varieties of
ways by which peoples rid themselves of unwanted rulers.

CONSULTATION AND CONSENT IN DEMOCRACY   Ex-
ercise of authority in democratic orders is characterized by a deference to the
ruled, which is associated with techniques for consultation with the people or
their representatives and with means for the expression of popular consent to
governmental action. The relations involved in consultation and in obtaining
consent became by historical transformation also means for holding governments accountable for their past actions. In a way, democratic doctrine prescribes that the people ought to get what they want no matter how wrong-
headed they may be. Those charged with governance may educate, persuade,
or assume the risk of making decisions that turn out to be unpopular or
else yield precisely to what the people wanted but were unaware of until
they had lived with it for a while. Deference to the wishes of the ruled does
not mean deference to the will of each individual—which would amount to
anarchy. Most commonly democratic doctrines accord authority to popular
majorities, though the theorists often spin out limitations of one kind or
another on the majority. Whatever their exact form, democratic ideas, in
their insistence on the consent of the ruled, differ sharply from theories that
legitimize authority by such doctrines as the divine right of kings.

A corollary of the doctrine of consent and of the practice of deference to
the ruled is freedom for expression of dissent from the actions of authority,
with the expectation that protests will be heard and, if not heeded, at least
considered and not followed by reprisals. Monarchs, to be sure, heard petitions, but in democratic orders freedom of dissent is associated with the
right to join with others in efforts to seek redress by ousting the government
—through electoral means. The people may not really govern themselves, but
they can stir up a deafening commotion if they dislike the way they are
governed—all of which points to the somewhat relaxed nature of the power
relations of democratic regimes.

DISPERSION OF POINTS OF AUTHORITY IN DEMO-
CRATIC ORDERS   A closely related characteristic of democratic
orders—or at least of the American democratic order—is a wide dispersion
of power (in the sense of a substance in a keg). Actual authority tends to be

dispersed and exercised not solely by governmental officials but also by private individuals and groups within the society. Moreover, the power structure tends to be segmented: authority over one question rests here and over another, there. All this contrasts with the model of a clear and rigid hierarchial pattern of power. On one matter the President's decision may govern; on another, the wishes of the heads of a half-dozen industrial corporations will prevail; on a third, organized labor or agriculture will win the day; and on still another, a congressionally negotiated compromise completely satisfactory to none of the contenders may settle the matter. Even the journalists may cast the deciding vote on some issues. Thus the locus of power may shift from question to question and even from time to time on the same question. "Power in America," says David Riesman, "seems to me situational and mercurial; it resists attempts to locate it in the way a molecule, under the Heisenberg principle, resists attempts simultaneously to locate it and time its velocity." [5]

Dispersion of power inevitably brings with it competition among centers of power, a behavior not limited to democratic orders, though perhaps in democratic orders that competition occurs under different ground rules, over a broader range of matters, and with different consequences than in nondemocratic regimes. In some eras the rivalry among dispersed centers of power and influence becomes so salient that the entire political process is interpreted as one of the reconciliation of their conflicts. John Dickinson observed:

> The task of government, and hence of democracy as a form of government, is not to express an imaginary popular will, but to effect adjustments among the various special wills and purposes which at any given time are pressing for realization.
>
> Almost the whole range of political problems are problems of what may be called adjustment—of devising ways and means to curb particular "wills" or "interests," and thus clear the track for the realization of other wills and interests in fuller measure. This is the task of governmental decisions ranging in importance from where to locate a new street or sewage-disposal plant to whether or not to go to war. Government, from this point of view, is primarily an arbitrator, and since practically every arbitration must result in giving to one side more of what it thinks it ought to have than the other side is willing to admit, every governmental act can be viewed as favoring in some degree some particular and partial "will," or special interest. It is therefore meaningless to criticize government, whether democratic or not, merely because it allows special interests to attain some measure of what they think themselves entitled to. The question is rather whether it allows the "right" side, or the "right" special interest, to win; and the "right" special interest means only the one whose

[5] *The Lonely Crowd* (New Haven: Yale University Press, 1950), p. 252.

will is most compatible with what we, as critics, conceive to be the right direction for the society's development to take.[6]

A POLITICS OF LIMITED OBJECTIVES?   Perhaps, too, a democratic politics must be, in the short run, a politics of limited objectives. That is, given the mode of managing succession to authority and the related characteristics of democratic orders, what are the limits of change that will be tolerated through electoral and representative procedures without the invocation of force in defense by those adversely affected? Democratic procedures seem to operate on the expectation that changes in the short run will be comparatively narrow, that the "outs" will not be liquidated or deprived of their liberty, at least not without due process, and that all concerned will live to fight it out again in another campaign.[7] This point sometimes appears in the form of the contention that a democratic order can operate effectively only on the foundation of a widely shared consensus. That consensus defines the limits of political conflict, and those who advocate measures outside that range may expect to be treated roughly.

If the limitation of political conflict to tolerable bounds requires that democratic politics be a politics of limited objectives in the short run, it may also be, paradoxically, that a durable democratic order must rest on a presupposition of unlimited objectives over the long run. The mystique of democracy nourishes a belief that the wrongs of today, persistent though they may seem, will be corrected in some remote tomorrow. Any regime that struggles for stability must implant such expectations in the minds of its people. Yet democratic doctrine seems especially adapted to the encouragement of such a faith, for it contemplates an evolving system in which the dispossessed of today may hope to become the top dogs of tomorrow.

While other significant characteristics of democratic power systems could be set out, these suffice to suggest the bewildering skein of power relations within a modern democratic society as well as something of their nature. Government controls yet is itself controlled. Private centers of power influence, even command, both private individuals and government. Dispersed centers of power interact with each other, all in a most complex and kaleidoscopic manner.

[6] "Democratic Realities and Democratic Dogma," *American Political Science Review*, 24 (1930), 291–92.

[7] It would be erroneous to conclude that those in office in the United States never jail political opponents. Some prosecutions look extraordinarily like attempts to take advantage of the technicalities of the law to discourage the opposition. They only illustrate the point that bills of rights have broad significance for the workings of the political system quite apart from their bearing on the liberty of the citizen who is not a partisan activist.

Institutions of Democracy

Associated with these characteristics of a democratic system of authority are institutions congenial to the fulfillment of the requisites of such an order. Nondemocratic regimes have their executives, their courts, their councils, and even representative bodies of a sort. Democracies supplement that traditional apparatus of government with instrumentalities that link the governed more closely with the governors and facilitate the management of succession to authority, the reconciliation of the claims of competing points of authority, and the consultation of the governed. Such machinery alone is not the whole of a viable democratic order; considerable civic education and human adaptation must occur to permit the mechanism to operate. Even the institutions themselves are not built overnight. They are the product of long evolution, of trial and error, of not a little blind groping—all tutored by purpose and aided by an occasional deliberate choice that turns out to be fortunate in its consequences.

No single type of institutional apparatus is requisite to a democratic order, although elements common at least in name appear in most systems that purport to be democratic: political parties, elective representative bodies, other popularly chosen officials, and electoral systems. Yet each of these institutions may differ from nation to nation. Moreover, they combine in each situation to produce a more or less unique whole, a system in which the function of each part is conditioned by its place in relation to the other elements of the specific order.

POLITICAL PARTIES   Political parties constitute a basic element of democratic institutional apparatus. They perform an essential function in the management of succession to power, as well as in the process of obtaining popular consent to the course of public policy. They amass sufficient support to buttress the authority of governments; or, on the contrary, they attract or organize discontent and dissatisfaction sufficient to oust the government. In either case they perform the function of the articulation of the interests and aspirations of a substantial segment of the citizenry, usually in ways contended to be promotive of the national weal.

In more than a poetic sense political parties are lineal descendants of two sorts of groups that recur in the annals of governance: those that conspire to overthrow the government and those that rally around to defend and maintain the regime. The party system sublimates that ancient conflict into behaviors no more bellicose than the oratory of an election campaign. To regard the party of the outs of the moment as akin to the old-time rings of conspirators banded together to overthrow the government may seem farfetched, and their kinship may be more analogical than genealogical. Nevertheless, political parties in combination with other institutions and procedures (all in the context of appropriate behavior patterns acquired by both the citizenry and the leadership echelons) provide means for handling the problem of succession to authority more or less peacefully. Whether the party system constitutes the only way in which succession may be arranged presents another type of question. Democratic orders seem to have discovered no other technique for the purpose, although at some times, especially in smaller units of government, party systems are most rudimentary.

REPRESENTATIVE BODIES   The institutional paraphernalia of democratic orders commonly includes some sort of representative body or bodies, with, at times, other elective officials as well. Consultative councils representative of the interests within society antedated the rise of modern democracies, but their place in the governmental system came to be altered as they were linked to the electorate through the party system and elections. That linkage developed concurrently with the rise of democratic ideologies, which defined new roles for representatives: they became, at least according to some theories, agents and advocates of their constituents. Whatever norms guide the actions of representatives in a particular system, the apparatus of representation symbolizes the consultation of the governed, and its actions tend to be regarded as equivalent to the command of the popular majority if it had the capacity and inclination to command. Of equal significance may be the role of representative bodies as conduits for the communication of popular discontent with the operations of government and as forums for the expression of dissent.

ELECTORAL PROCEDURES   The practices and procedures of popular elections may be regarded as another democratic institution, which is intertwined, of course, with the system of parties and representation. Elections alone do not make an order democratic. Dictatorial regimes have their plebiscites, which reflect a fraudulent deference to the potency of the ideology of democracy. Characteristically the electoral practices of democracies are associated with party systems which propose to the electorate a choice, as well as with a general disposition to accept the verdict of the count of heads. The march of millions of people to the polls constitutes a dramatic symbolization of the ideas of democratic theory. On occasion, to be sure, the voters may act as puppets manipulated by small groups of willful men; or the electorate may be swayed by demagogues bent only on duping the people; or ballots may be a flimsy cover for a cohesive army of plunderers. Withal, over the long pull, elections in a democracy mark great turning points in public policy, express mass approval of actions taken, set limits to the course of governmental policy, and ratify the work of governments or cast them into oblivion or dishonor.

NONPARTY ASSOCIATIONS AND GROUPS   In the give-and-take between government and governed, the formal apparatus of government may be supplemented by a system of private associations, which, in the United States, are called pressure groups. These associations may perform a representative function by communicating the wishes of their members to public authorities; or they may bring "pressure" to bear upon the government. The same groups may be consulted by government. They may even exercise forms of private authority which differ little from governmental authority. At times their influence on the actions of formal government may be so potent that they in fact control the exercise of public authority. In other instances they may perform creative functions in the contrivance of proposals for public policy. Pressure groups may be in alliance with a political party, and they often seek to influence the outcome of elections.

OTHER LINKAGES OF GOVERNMENT AND CITIZENRY The more or less formalized features of the structure of power relations are supplemented by other kinds of interaction between government and governed. While these cannot be neatly classified or characterized, in general they consist of communications between official and citizen which occur in a context of official concern about public attitudes. Governments infrequently undertake measures of great import without attempting to estimate the probable public reaction. That estimate may rest on intuition or on systematic appraisals of the public mind. The flow of mail from citizens to representatives and to executive and administrative offices constitutes another link between citizen and government. The ruminations and reports of the journalists are perused in official quarters and may touch sensitive spots and have their effects on public action. None of these types of interaction between government and governed is peculiar to democratic orders, yet for their maximum development, conditions associated with democratic regimes (for example, freedom of press, the right of petition, protection against official reprisal for expression of protest) must prevail to some degree.

Other Aspects of Power

Most of this book will be devoted to an analysis of the American version of these institutions and practices of democracy: political parties, pressure groups, elections, and representation. The student should be warned, however, that these methods of developing more or less rational consent to the course of governmental action by no means cover all the complexities of the American—or any other—regime. Democratic institutional forms and procedures can operate only within an appropriate matrix of public attitudes and beliefs —a proposition amply demonstrated by many abortive attempts to transplant democratic institutions to unsuitable environments. Furthermore, the governing process as a whole from time to time employs techniques far removed from the democratic methods of give-and-take between government and governed. Democratic forms may serve as a screen for tyranny or for gang rule, at least within restricted areas and for short periods of time. Such techniques of governance, which have a way of becoming mixed with the conventional methods of democracy, deserve brief mention in this introductory conspectus of the nature of politics.

CUSTOM   The means for the development and maintenance of the customs of a people form an essential element of the political system, though their function as such is not often explicitly recognized. Politically relevant customs include a considerably wider range of behavior than narrowly political conventions. Thus, by custom the members of the electoral college cast their votes for the candidates named by the national convention of their political party. By custom Senators may invoke the right of "senatorial courtesy" and cause the Senate to deny its consent to certain appointments by the President. Beyond such customs connected with the institutions of government are politically relevant attitudes shared by the mass of the people. Though such attitudes profoundly affect the actions of government, their identification presents no little difficulty. Important on the American scene are such attitudes as the disposition to compromise; the willingness to accept the outcome of elections; the insistence on "fair" procedures, at least for those playing the game within the accepted limits; the tendency to frown on excessive and arbitrary authority; a comparatively weak sense of class identification together with a relatively strong sense of identification with the community as a whole; a moderate reverence for politicians. All such attitudes and the related customary behaviors may be regarded as equivalent to the political element of the anthropologist's concept of culture.[8]

A political order enlists for its maintenance and perpetuation all the mechanisms for the dissemination and inculcation of attitudes and beliefs and all the means for their transmission from generation to generation. The school, the church, the family, the press, radio and television, literature, patriotic ceremonials, and other institutions and practices mold the oncoming generation and re-enforce the faith of the old. In modern societies the school system, in particular, functions as a formidable instrument of political power in its role as a transmitter of the goals, values, and attitudes of the polity. In the selection of values and attitudes to be inculcated, it chooses those cherished by the dominant elements in the political order. By and large the impact of widely accepted goals, mores, and social values fixes the programs

[8] Gabriel Almond has developed the concept of political culture in his "Comparative Political Systems," *Journal of Politics*, 18 (1956), 391–409.

of American schools. When schools diverge from this vaguely defined direc-
tive and collide with potent groups in the political system, they feel a pressure
to conform.

The ideal of equality of opportunity vests in the American educational
system another function of deep significance for the political order. In a
rigidly structured society vertical mobility is apt to be slight: the sons and
daughters of each social class "inherit" a status. The offspring of favored
classes enjoy special opportunity, including access to education, and are
apt to constitute most of the favored classes of the next generation. The sons
and daughters of the less-favored classes, even though potential geniuses, are
likely to remain in the status to which they were born. The philosophy of
American education proclaims that each young person shall have an educational opportunity to develop fully his abilities—a doctrine that is part and
parcel of democratic theory. Jefferson, hence, was not out of character as a
democratic theorist when he proposed an educational system to skim off at
various educational levels persons of genius and provide further training for
them at public expense. "The object," he said, "is to bring into action that
mass of talents which lies buried in poverty in every country, for want of
the means of development, and thus give activity to a mass of mind, which,
in proportion to our population, shall be the double or treble of what it is
in most countries." Such a doctrine, revolutionary in its day, provides a
basis for an educational system that serves as something of an escalator for
the social system. Even though upward mobility is in substantial degree an
article of faith rather than a fact, the faith has a real political significance.

VIOLENCE AND FORCE   Democratic standards exclude reliance
on force and violence in domestic politics. Indeed, a great accomplishment
of democratic orders consists in their contrivance of substitutes for force.
Yet even in democratic orders violence and the threat of violence play a
part.[9] In political conflict the use of violence is almost always an underlying
potentiality. If the stakes are not deemed fundamental, if deeply cherished
values are not at issue, if the customs discourage resort to force, adjustments
through pacific means may be acceptable to the contenders. Yet the circumstances under which only pacific means are used are transient and may be
easily upset. Furthermore, nonviolent methods for the settlement of political
conflict sometimes work because of the threat of violence in the background.

Although the actual employment of violence in our society is frequent
enough, the saber more often exerts its influence without being drawn. Regimes are always prepared to defend their positions with force if the need

[9] On the political role of force, see C. E. Merriam, *Prologue to Politics* (Chicago:
University of Chicago Press, 1939) ; James Marshall, *Swords and Symbols* (New York:
Oxford University Press, 1939).

arises. Armies have their domestic potentialities as well as their foreign uses.[10] On the other hand, those groups that deem themselves insufferably oppressed may cease to be satisfied with debate and resort to arms. While social reform has at times been accelerated by the fear that "there might be a revolution," modern military technology makes revolt an unfruitful endeavor. Tenuous is the line between conditions under which arbitration of differences by discussion brings acceptable results and the conditions under which violence flares up. However the line is drawn, the content of the category of issues soluble only by the sword constantly changes. Issues that at one time generate bloody internal dissension are settled at another time by means no more sanguinary than parliamentary debate.

The American order has had its share of violence. One great sectional dispute, that over slavery, could be terminated only by war. Incidents of violence punctuate the long history of employer-employee relations, with aggressors on both sides. For many decades employer force, either in the hands of company militia or allied public police, contributed significantly to the maintenance of the status of the employing groups. Workers, when they could, met force with force. Ultimately public authority commanded other modes for the solution of employer-employee differences. Similarly, violence and the threat of violence have fixed in no small measure the status of the Negro. Lynchings, the threat of lynchings, and threats of violence have formed a part of the bundle of sanctions, official and private, that maintain the dominance of white over black in the South.[11]

ECONOMIC SANCTIONS   Not infrequently the formal mechanisms of political power are supplemented by economic sanctions or persuasives, often pecuniary in form. The actions of government in arbitration among competing centers of power may merely formalize bargains driven with dollars behind the scenes. Or money may aid mightily in the organization of popular support. Bribery and bread and circuses have an ancient, if not honorable, political lineage. The essence of the economic sanction in the power relation consists in the use of things of material value to cement support or to control. The accord of public honor and the compulsions of public duty govern some men while more mundane considerations move others.

No taxonomy of economic sanctions of political significance need be

[10] Thus, in 1934 at a time of widespread unrest, the Assistant Secretary of War, Harry H. Woodring, advocated a larger army to "cope with social and economic problems in an emergency" and to provide "secret insurance against chaos." Quoted by Merle Curti, *Peace or War* (New York: Norton, 1936), p. 266.

[11] See Robert Hunter, *Violence and the Labor Movement* (New York: Macmillan, 1914). Peltason records that in 1896 "one Negro was lynched every 56 hours; few citizens, black or white, raised a voice in protest." Even in the 1950's, in Mississippi the occasional murder of a Negro assertive of his constitutional rights produced no inconvenient consequences for the murderer. See J. W. Peltason, *Fifty-eight Lonely Men* (New York: Harcourt, Brace, 1961), p. 248.

attempted here, but the moral opinion of the community divides economic sanctions into those regarded as corrupt and those treated as correct. In the first category belongs bribery. In some political conflicts the greased palm may cast the deciding vote. While enduring political systems are not built by bribery, it has in one form or another played a potent role in public decisions in many confused, disorderly, and rapidly changing social situations. By definition, bribery can occur only in those relations in which private individuals seek to influence the holders of formal authority. Yet at times bribery is difficult to distinguish from political extortion in which holders of authority exact a price for their action or inaction.

In American localities from time to time, impressive power structures—virtual dictatorships—have been constructed by corrupt techniques. The tolerance of prohibited lines of commerce—gambling, prostitution, and other trades catering to tastes beyond the law—is sometimes regarded as simply a result of bribery and nothing more. Yet these arrangements also may tie to the political leadership groups powerful in electioneering and fruitful as a source of funds for political warfare. In the total political context a bloc is built into a dominant political coalition. The informal award of valuable "licenses" to pursue illegal endeavors parallels in its effects the use of public jobs, purchases, contracts, and other material perquisites to gain the support of particular elements of the community.

The line separating the corrupt from the correct is tenuous indeed. Material advantages and expectations of material advantage occupy no small place in the construction of political coalitions and in the maintenance of systems of power. From the normal actions of government some groups receive preference; others suffer disadvantage. The motives behind such actions may be both disputed and obscure. A work-relief program may be denounced as a calculated move by venal men to purchase the vote of the shiftless, or it may be praised as a humanitarian act to alleviate the hardships of those destitute through no fault of their own. And it may be a little of both. In any case, the forms of material benefit at the disposal of government multiply with the expansion of governmental functions: tariffs to industry, subsidies to farmers, privileges to licensed activities in a variety of forms, benefits to the aged and the incapacitated, privileges to the users of the public domain —to mention only a few. Policies on all these and other such matters affect the relations of power within the society.

These introductory pages outline a conception of politics to serve as a setting for the more detailed analyses that follow. The general drift of the argument has been that politics should be equated with governance in its broadest sense. So commodious a definition has its pedagogical disadvantages since American usage commonly attributes a narrower meaning to the term "politics." Yet perhaps a better understanding of the institutions of American politics may be gained by examining them, and speculating about them, against a backdrop of such a general conception of the nature of the political process.

To equate politics with governance brings within our definition all types of governments. The analysis has identified the salient characteristics that differentiate democratic regimes from other sorts of power structures in order better to place democratic systems in the family of governments. These features include such matters as the democratic solution to the problem of succession to power; the assumption that government should operate on a foundation of popular consent; the expectation of extensive consultation between governors and governed; freedom of dissent and criticism; the dispersion of points of authority and centers of initiative within the system; and, in general, an extensive practice of give-and-take between governors and governed.

The democratic organization of authority includes certain institutions appropriate to the characteristics of democratic governance. The most conspicuous are political parties, pressure groups, election procedures, and representative bodies. Their workings by no means encompass the totality of governance. A man from Mars studying the process of American governance would bring within his purview the workings of the civil courts in the adjudication of private rights, the application of the criminal laws, the operations of the administrative regulatory authorities, the functions of the great administrative departments, and a variety of other activities of government. In our focus on the institutions more or less peculiar to democracy—pressure groups, political parties, and related agencies—we should not be unmindful that we are dealing with only a segment of the governing process.

I

PRESSURE GROUPS

A principal instrumentality of democratic politics, as the introductory chapter pointed out, is the system of political parties. A foundation for consideration of the American party may be laid by an inspection of pressure groups. At bottom, group interests are the animating forces in the political process; an understanding of American politics requires a knowledge of the chief interests and of their stake in public policy. The exercise of the power of governance consists in large degree in the advancement of legitimate group objectives, in the reconciliation and mediation of conflicting group ambitions, and in the restraint of group tendencies judged to be socially destructive. Hence, an examination of pressure groups and of the interests from which they arise throws light on the materials that politicians must manage, on the problems with which they must cope.

The most common basis for group action is economic. As the authors of The Federalist *long ago concluded,*

> *the most common and durable source of faction has been the various and unequal distribution of property.*

17

Those who hold and those who are without property have ever formed distinct interests in society. Those who are creditors, and those who are debtors, fall under a like discrimination. A landed interest, a manufacturing interest, a mercantile interest, a moneyed interest, with many lesser interests grow up of necessity in civilised nations, and divide them into different classes, actuated by different sentiments and views.[1]

Economic motivation does not explain all. The Federalist, in an un-Marxian manner, pointed to other bases of group interest, such as "zeal for different opinions concerning religion, concerning government, and many other points, as well of speculation as of practice; an attachment of different leaders ambitiously contending for pre-eminence and power." And, when all else is lacking, "the most frivolous and fanciful distinctions" are sufficient to excite the "most violent conflicts." Whatever the bases of group action may be, the study of politics must include an analysis of the objectives and composition of interest groups within a society.

A striking feature of American politics is the extent to which political parties are supplemented by private associations formed to influence public policy. These organizations, commonly called pressure groups, promote their interests by attempting to influence government rather than by nominating candidates and seeking responsibility for the management of government. The political interests of agriculture, for example, may be advanced through lobbying and propaganda activities of pressure groups, such as the American Farm Bureau Federation. Such groups, while they may call themselves nonpolitical, are engaged in politics; in the main theirs is a politics of policy. They are concerned with what government does either to help or to harm their membership. They do not attempt to assume, at least openly, the party's basic function of nominating candidates and seeking responsibility for the conduct of government,

[1] *The Federalist,* No. X.

although the division of labor in the political system between parties and pressure groups is not always clear-cut. Pressure groups may campaign for party candidates and may even become, in fact if not in form, allied with one or the other of the parties. Yet by and large, pressure groups, as they seek to influence the exercise of public power, play a distinctive role: they supplement the party system and the formal instruments of government by serving as spokesmen for the special interests within society.[2]

[2] For a general survey of pressure-group activity, see D. C. Blaisdell, *American Democracy under Pressure* (New York: Ronald, 1957). For a theoretical analysis of group role, see David B. Truman, *The Governmental Process* (New York: Knopf, 1951), ch. 2.

2.

AGRARIANISM

THE STRUCTURE of political power may be pic-
tured as a more or less unstable equilibrium among competing interests—in
our times the accent has been on instability. Or, to change the figure and
shift the focus of attention, the politician might be regarded as a person
riding a bicycle on a tight rope and juggling an indeterminate number of
irregular objects, each moving through an unpredictable orbit. Whether the
figure precisely fits the phenomenon, the political equilibrium among social
groups is from time to time disturbed. One class or group becomes discontented with existing conditions, and the processes of politics go into operation to create a new equilibrium. The politician finds himself in the middle
—and belabored from all sides—as he seeks to contrive a formula to maintain peace among conflicting interests.

Examination of the role of agriculture in American politics will account
for one major unit in our galaxy of political interests; it will also illustrate
the manner in which maladjustments develop in the relations among great
groups of the population. Disturbances that produce deprivation or a sense
of injustice generate movements for redress which often find ultimate expression in the statute books. The reactions of American agriculture to the
changes it has undergone constitute a striking indication of the political
problems that flow from a drastic alteration in the position of a major sector
of the economy.

Agriculture in American Life: Long-term Trends

The gradual cumulation of the effects of secular changes dating approximately from the Civil War has profoundly altered the position of agriculture in American politics. The proportion of rural people in the total population has sharply declined—a change that has been accompanied by loss of political position to the cities. Furthermore, changes in the economy have, in special degree, subjected the farm population to the impact of economic fluctuations and created the practical necessity for novel types of public policy.

RURAL REAR-GUARD ACTION   Adaptation of the political system to the marked decrease in the proportion of rural population remains yet to be completely accomplished. Although by 1960 the proportion of the population living on farms had declined to 9 per cent, the influence of agriculture remains far greater than might be expected from its numerical strength. Census after census has recorded the movement of people from farms and the growth of cities, yet rural dwellers have fought a stubborn rear-guard action to delay full political recognition of the fact that America, once predominantly agrarian, has become predominantly industrial.

In their endeavors to retain their position, farmers have been able to draw on a tradition that ascribes special moral values to farm people. Rural attitudes and rural people, so the belief has been, constitute the reality and the strength of America. Thomas Jefferson asserted that farmers were "the chosen people of God, if ever He had a chosen people"; cities were "essentially evil" and "ulcers on the body politic." These ideas did not die with Jefferson, and partly from the strength of such notions agriculture has enjoyed a strategic advantage in politics. Rural overrepresentation in legislative bodies also contributes concretely to the maintenance of a powerful farm influence which manifests itself in legislation favorable to rural dwellers generally, as well as to farmers.

MARKET SHRINKAGE AND TECHNOLOGICAL ADVANCE
Trends in the division of population between country and city brought a relocation of the centers of major political influence. Yet other long-term changes in the position and nature of agriculture gradually created the economic circumstances productive of modern agrarian political problems. The net effect of one set of these changes was that there came to be too many acres in cultivation and too many people trying to make a living by farming. The export market for farm products declined after 1900 except for temporary wartime spurts in demand; it required the produce of 27,000,000 fewer acres to meet export requirements for the period 1935–1939 than for 1925–

1929. Long-term dietary changes operated to the disadvantage of some classes of farmers and to the advantage of others. Decline in flour and potato consumption has been notable. Another market for farm products disappeared with the replacement of the horse and mule by truck and tractor. Between 1918 and 1953, about 70,000,000 acres formerly used to produce food for draft animals became available for other uses.

The effects of these market losses were partially offset by population increases, but meanwhile farmers were becoming more efficient producers. Technological advances—mechanization, increased use of fertilizers, improved cultural practices, better insecticides, upbreeding of farm plants and animals —brought, at first gradual, then startling, increases in productivity per farm worker. In 1820 one farm worker produced enough for himself and three other persons. By 1920, this figure had risen to nine and by 1945, to 14 other persons.[1] In the 1940's productivity grew extremely rapidly. In 1950, on the average, a single farm worker produced 50 per cent more than he had a scant 20 years earlier. The trend continued in the 1950's. In 1960 the average production per acre of farm land was one-fourth greater than it had been in 1950.

So long as population grew rapidly enough to offset market shrinkages and increases in productivity, farming was an expanding business, even though it was becoming proportionately less important in the total economy. Yet since 1910 the farm-labor force has declined absolutely as well as relatively. From 1920 to 1955 the farm population dropped by about 10,000,000, almost one-third of the 1920 total. From 1950 to 1959 alone population living on farms declined by 15 per cent. These population adjustments, though, encounter friction, and the lag in the transfer of population from farms complicates the problem of coping with those farm problems that would exist even if there were not too many farmers.

COMMERCIALIZATION OF AGRICULTURE   Another long-term alteration in the character of agriculture—more significant for the modern political ills of the farmer than other changes in the nature of agriculture—has been the commercialization of agriculture. In the good old days, not so many decades ago, the farmer and his family subsisted in considerable degree on the produce of the farm. Moreover, the major factor in production was labor: the labor of the farmer and his family. To the extent that the farm productive unit was self-contained, it was insulated from the forces of the market.

Gradually farmers came to devote themselves more and more exclusively

[1] S. E. Johnson, "Technological Changes and the Future of Rural Life," *Journal of Farm Economics*, 32 (1950), 225–39. See R. A. Loomis and G. T. Barton, *Productivity of Agriculture, United States, 1870–1958* (Washington: Department of Agriculture, Technical Bulletin No. 1238, 1961).

to the raising of crops to be sold in the market. Dependence of the farmer on the market made him subject to all the storms of the economic system generally. When the price of wheat fluctuated in Minneapolis, the farmer in North Dakota was affected. When the price of hogs dropped in Chicago, the impact struck in Iowa. A sag in the price of milk in New York City was quickly felt on the upstate dairy farm.

Commercialization of agriculture also subjected the farmer to the impact of market fluctuations on items he came to purchase for his own consumption and for use in production. Wage rates, the price of tractors, and the cost of gasoline are links that have tied the commercialized farmer far more closely to the economy than was his predecessor, who plowed with horses and mules and relied on himself and his family for human labor. In short, the farmer gradually became an entrepreneur who invests, hires, and manages. The farm manager with his account books, his payrolls, and his capital equipment tends to replace the free and independent tiller of the soil who could afford to be radical and on occasion breathe fire. As a businessman, even an industrialized farmer, he comes to feel a common interest with the business community generally.

These fundamental alterations in the farmer's place in the economy occurred earlier in some areas than in others. They affected the producers of some commodities before they reached the producers of others. Yet the key to the understanding of recent farm politics in the United States lies in an appreciation of the peculiar position of agriculture in the economic system as a whole. The farmer came to be vulnerable to the stresses of the economic system generally, though he acquired in the process no weapons for economic self-defense. When overproduction and lower prices threaten, business groups may with some success act together to curtail production and safeguard themselves without the interposition of government. Millions of independent agricultural producers find such concerted action impossible; hence they enter politics to seek their "fair" share of the national income.[2]

Cycles of Agrarian Discontent: The Nature of Political Movements

While the long-term changes in the relation of supply and demand for agricultural products have necessitated painful adjustments in farm plant and labor force, more significant in the stimulation of agitation about the farm question have been the special effects of economic fluctuations on agriculture. The commercialization of farming—and the decline in reliance on farm out-

[2] Attempts do occur to organize farmers to advance their cause by withholding their produce from market until prices are raised. This sort of "collective bargaining," advocated in recent years by the National Farmers Organization in the Midwest, never gets anywhere.

put for subsistence—linked the farmer to the economy and subjected him to the blows of the business cycle. Yet the consequences went further: owing to the peculiar workings of the economic system, downswings of the business cycle strike the farmer far more severely than other sectors of the economy.

A factor of great significance in the setting off of political movements is an abrupt change for the worse in the status of one group relative to that of other groups in society. The economics of politics is by no means solely a matter of the poor against the rich; the rich and the poor may live together peaceably for decades, each accepting its status quietly. A rapid change for the worse, however, in the relative status of any group, rich or poor, is likely to precipitate political action. Depressions have been closely associated with intensification of farmers' political activity. Agrarian agitation, at times boisterous and disturbing to the conservative elements of society, has not occurred at a uniform pitch. It has had its dull periods and its shrill points correlated somewhat with variations in the fortunes of farmers. Though the entire story of agrarian discontent need not be recounted here, episodes can be used to illustrate the recurring pattern of economic maladjustments that generate popular movements to demand rectification of supposed injustices.

ECONOMIC ADVERSITY AND THE GRANGER MOVEMENT
The Granger movement was an early example of the relations between economic deprivation and political unrest. The Grange reached its peak strength in the 1870's and served as a vehicle for the expression of agrarian discontent in the corn- and wheat-growing region embracing the upper Mississippi Valley from Ohio to the western rim of settlement in Kansas and Nebraska— a relatively newly developed area, devoted in special degree for the time to the production of crops for market. In the late sixties and early seventies falling prices, caused mainly by the reduced demand following the Civil War, brought distress to western farmers. They blamed chiefly the railroads, the bankers, and monopolies for their plight. Of these misdoers, the railroads bore the brunt of Granger protest, and the movement bore fruit in early legislation to regulate railroad rates. The railroads, however, were not left with the entire blame: commission men and other middlemen were accused of taking an unduly large slice of the farmer's dollar; high rates of interest and the difficulties of meeting payments on heavy mortgages directed antagonism also toward the holders of mortgages.

Founded in 1867, the Grange, or the Patrons of Husbandry, had only a slow growth until the early 1870's when the pinch of economic adversity tightened. During 1873, the year of the panic, and 1874 the organization spread rapidly and at its peak had about 750,000 members. Although the Grange extended into many states, the most highly organized region was the quadrilateral from Ohio to Dakota Territory, to Kansas, to Kentucky, to Ohio.

The Grange declared itself to be a nonpartisan organization. Instead of attempting to nominate and elect candidates under its own banner, it employed those methods now known as pressures. Both the state Granges and the National Grange adopted resolutions on proposed legislation; delegations were sent to present to legislatures the Grange's views; candidates for public office were asked to indicate their stand on measures of interest to farmers.

During 1875–1880 the Grange suffered a sharp decline in membership. In the period 1880–1900 other farm organizations and movements succeeded it in the center of public attention. They rose and fell and left little in the way of lasting organizational apparatus, but the Grange persists to this day.

AGRICULTURAL DEPRESSION AND FARMER AGITATION, 1921–1952   Drops in prices and economic activity hit farmers more harshly than they do other types of producers. In contrast, in boom times the prices of farm products rise to exceptionally high levels, to the temporary advantage of farmers. Industrial prices, that is, the prices that farmers must pay for commodities they consume and use in production, are relatively sticky while the prices for farm commodities are highly variable. While a complex of factors accounts for this difference in price variability, a major cause rests in the contrasting organization of the agricultural and non-agricultural sectors of the economy. Relatively small numbers of industrial producers operate in ways to minimize price fluctuations, a result that may come about even in the absence of collusion in price fixing. Participation in farm production, on the other hand, of millions of producers, along with other factors, creates circumstances that make the prices of farm products far more responsive to changes in supply-demand relationships.

The characteristic behavior of farm prices reflects itself in the graph in Figure 2.1, which shows the index of farm prices as a percentage of the index of prices paid by farmers since 1910. In effect, the figure shows the variations in the purchasing power of the prices of farm products. In World War I, farm prices raced upward far more rapidly than did the prices paid by farmers. In 1917 a bale of cotton would buy more fertilizer or more farm implements than it would have bought in 1914. After the shrinkage of war-induced demand, the curve drops quite rapidly, and in the sharp depression of 1921 farmers enjoyed a position of severe disadvantage in dealing with their suppliers. As the graph moves across the page, a substantial recovery may be noted in the midtwenties, only to be followed by the deep trough of the Great Depression.

Economic deprivation suffices to generate political discontent. Yet the fact that economic distress affects the farmer more severely than it does the nonfarm producer contributes a special quality to agrarian political demands. When the curve in Figure 2.1 falls far below 100 per cent of parity, a demand arises to restore parity, to work toward a "fair" level of income for a sector

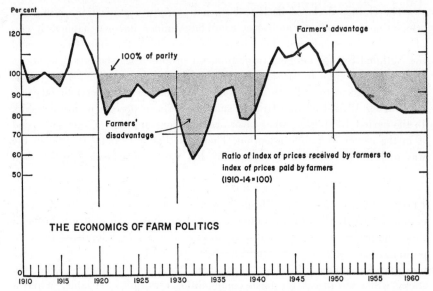

Figure 2.1   Ratio of index of prices received by farmers to index of prices paid by farmers (1910–1914=100), 1910–1962

of society subjected to unavoidable hazards by the workings of the economic system. Whether the concept of parity is defensible as a measure of fairness may be doubted, but its political appeal cannot be denied.

The precipitous decline in the economic position of agriculture after World War I, which may be seen in Figure 2.1, set the stage for the modern system of farm lobbying. The American Farm Bureau Federation became the principal means for the expression of farmer grievances in the 1920's. The Federation developed in close association with the county-agent system, which had been formed to disseminate among farmers the findings of agricultural research carried on by the land-grant colleges and the United States Department of Agriculture. The Smith-Lever Act of 1914 had provided federal grants to state extension services, under the supervision of the land-grant colleges, which, in turn, made arrangements with county authorities to employ county agricultural agents.

In order to better reach farmers with practical instruction in farming methods, local associations of farmers were formed, often by the county agents. The name "farm bureau" happened to be applied to an early association created as a unit of a chamber of commerce. On occasion the members of the bureau contributed to the salary of the county agent, and generally a close relation prevailed between the agent and the bureau. In due course, county farm bureaus federated into state farm bureau federations, and in 1919 delegates from 31 states met in Chicago to create a national federation of these state farm organizations. Formation of small groups of farmers to facilitate the demonstration of new farming methods had set in motion forces that led to the formation of the American Farm Bureau Federation, an organization that was to become extremely effective in advancing the cause of the farmer.

The Federation set to work by establishing a legislative office in Washington and by defining its mission in blunt and straightforward terms: "First, to ascertain definitely, by referendum or otherwise, the farmers' attitude on pending legislation affecting agriculture; second, to thoroughly inform members of Congress concerning the farmers' legislative needs and requests; and, third, to report to the membership fully concerning the support or lack of support of individual congressmen." The Federation followed through, and in 1921 and 1922 the agricultural bloc virtually wrested control of Congress from the party leaders. That bloc, a coalition of Senators and Representatives of both parties from agricultural districts, was formed "as a result of a series of helpful conferences at Farm Bureau legislative headquarters." [3] They agreed upon a program of measures, and Congress passed bills to control grain exchanges, to regulate packers and stockyards, to increase appropriations for construction of rural highways, and to increase tariffs on farm products.

Though the measures adopted by Congress under the spur of the farm bloc were helpful, the disadvantage of the farmer, in terms of the relationship between agricultural and industrial prices, continued to prevail. Agrarian spokesmen pointed to the tariff protection long enjoyed by industry and asserted that national policy compelled American farmers to produce food and fiber at ruinously low prices. The McNary-Haugen bill was brought forward as a means for reducing the gap between industrial and agricultural prices. The original bill was rejected by the House in June, 1924. Another version was defeated in 1926. Although backed with enthusiasm by the cornbelt states, the bill fell before the combined opposition of the Northeast and the South. In February, 1927, however, the bill, further modified, won congressional approval only to meet with executive veto. Again, in May, 1928, still another version of the bill was passed, and was again rejected by the President.

The midwestern farm states carried their battle into the 1928 Republican convention and threatened rebellion against domination of the party by industry and finance. They failed to persuade the convention to commit itself to the McNary-Haugen plan, but Hoover, triumphant in 1928, came into office committed to "do something" about the farm problem. Congress, at a special session in 1929, created the Federal Farm Board with a mandate

[3] O. M. Kile, *The Farm Bureau Movement* (New York: Macmillan, 1921), p. 188. For a full account of political ferment among farmers in the early 1920's, see James H. Shideler, *Farm Crisis, 1919–1923* (Berkeley: University of California Press, 1957).

to "promote the effective merchandising of agricultural commodities in inter-state and foreign commerce, so that the industry of agriculture will be placed on a basis of economic equality with other industries." Congress appropriated $500,000,000 for the Board to buy and sell surpluses to stabilize prices, but the efforts of the Farm Board were doomed to fail. The Board recognized "control of excessive production as absolutely essential" to improvement of the status of the farmer, yet all that it could do was to urge voluntary restraint to hold production to the limits necessary to maintain higher prices.

Though the Farm Bureau Federation did not openly endorse the Democratic presidential candidate in 1932, its president, Ed O'Neal, declared: "We must elect those who are true friends of agriculture, those who will pledge themselves to carry out our program." Roosevelt favored a large part of the Federation's program; farmers had no difficulty in identifying their "true friend." In 1933, Congress speedily enacted the Agricultural Adjustment Act, legislation agreed upon by farm leaders. The act declared "the present acute economic emergency" to be, in part, "the consequence of a severe and in-creasing disparity between the prices of agricultural and other commodities, which disparity has largely destroyed the purchasing power of farmers for industrial products." The policy of Congress was to "re-establish prices to farmers at a level that will give agricultural commodities a purchasing power with respect to articles that farmers buy, equivalent to the purchasing power of agricultural commodities" before World War I. The means for achieving this end consisted of limitations on cultivated acreage which it was hoped would reduce agricultural output and thereby raise farm prices.

The Agricultural Adjustment Act of 1933 was the first of a long series of governmental actions whose object was to move toward "parity" for the farmer. Most of the legislation sought to influence farm prices by control of production, by stimulation of consumption, or by loan or purchase operations. Acreage limitations were employed from time to time, sometimes in associa-tion with government purchase and storage programs at prices higher than would have been obtained on a free market. Among the measures to increase consumption, the school-lunch program was conspicuous, though disposition through foreign aid also played a role.[4]

All such measures brought only limited relief. The demands induced by World War II lifted the prices of farm products above parity. Stimulation, rather than limitation, of production became the order of the day, and the administrative mechanisms built up in the 1930's were used to guide produc-tion into desired lines. The Korean War prolonged the enlarged demand for farm products, but its termination was quickly followed by a renewed con-cern about ways to control production and to maintain farm income.

[4] See John D. Black, "The McNary-Haugen Movement," *American Economic Review*, 18 (1928), 405–27; Theodore Saloutos and John D. Hicks, *Agricultural Discontent in the Middle West, 1900–1939* (Madison: University of Wisconsin Press, 1951); C. M. Camp-bell, *The Farm Bureau and the New Deal* (Urbana: University of Illinois Press, 1962).

EISENHOWER'S FARM SLUMP   The proposition that gyra-
tions in farm income tend to be associated with variations in the political
temperature of the farmer finds further illustration in the intensification of
debate on farm policy in the years after 1952. A decline in demand for farm
products, together with surpluses built up by increased agricultural efficiency
and by the stimulation of price supports, caused a fall in farm prices beginning late in 1952. (See Figure 2.1.) Net realized income from agriculture in
1955 was 24 per cent less than in 1951, a shift that did not set well with
farmers who saw other sectors of the economy enjoying a high level of prosperity.

The Eisenhower Administration initiated, under Secretary of Agriculture
Ezra Taft Benson, a program looking toward the liquidation of agricultural
surpluses and the reduction of the levels of farm price support, measures
calculated to encourage a downward movement of agricultural output and a
cityward movement of farm population. As farm price declines continued,
midwestern farmers in particular became more vocal in their unhappiness. In
the 1954 congressional elections the Republican vote sagged most noticeably
in farming areas most seriously affected by price declines. In 1956 a Democratic Congress, with the aid of Republicans from farm states, adopted a high-
support farm bill only to have it vetoed by the President. Yet the Administration, fearful of the potential repercussions in the farm regions, then adopted
policies far more favorable to the farmer than it had evidently originally
intended. Those policies did not suffice to prevent, in 1956, a loss of several
Republican House seats or a decline in Eisenhower's popular vote in farming
districts west of the Mississippi. Republican troubles continued in the farm
belt in 1958; Republican Representatives often became casualties of farm discontent, even when they had opposed their party leadership in its farm policy.[5]
Heightened concern prevailed within Republican leadership circles about
their party's stand on the farm question as the presidential election of 1960
approached. They need not have worried; farmers, predominantly Protestant, seemed to forget about their economic problems—at least for the duration of the campaign.

FROM SPONTANEOUS MOVEMENT TO CRYSTALLIZED
INTEREST: PERMANENT MOBILIZATION   One moral of the
preceding recital is that movements of political protest tend to develop when
a sector of the population regards itself as unjustly treated or as the victim
of circumstances. For 50 or 60 years after the Civil War, farmers' movements
tended to sweep the country at times of economic crisis, developing more
or less spontaneously in response to frustration and deprivation. Once the
vicissitudes that gave birth to the agitation disappeared, the organization

---

[5] See T. V. Gilpatrick, "Price Support Policy and the Midwest Farm Vote," *Midwest
Journal of Political Science*, 3 (1959), 319–35.

formed to carry the movement withered. When the pain left, the farmer quit squawking and went back to the plow.

The alternation of vitality and feebleness in farm organization has apparently been replaced by a permanent mobilization for political action; organizations of farmers maintain a continuous alert. This development of farm organizations parallels the growth of collective endeavor in all sectors of American society. The character of modern public policy requires that farm organizations—like tariff lobbyists and public utility legislative representatives—give unremitting attention to the actions of government. Instead of a slumbering, rustic giant roused only by depression and adversity, farm organizations, well organized and competently led, maintain an interest in public policy as keen and continuous as that of any business or labor group. In a sense, public policy—by creating public bounty and by making the income of agriculture in part a matter of political decision—has given farmers a powerful incentive to join together in cohesive organization.

The broad objectives of farm organizations have been stated in terms of the achievement of a principle of fair treatment for a disadvantaged sector of the economy, but often their operations have had the odor of the old-style tariff lobby. Nevertheless, farmers, given the way the economic system operates, occupy a peculiarly vulnerable position. Their troubles have been magnified by the problems of adjusting the farm plant and labor force to the reduced scale dictated by the new agricultural technology. Even were that adjustment out of the way, the perverse refusal of the economic system to solve everything automatically in accord with the rules of classical economics makes it most improbable that the farm problem will soon evaporate. Despite the forbidding administrative and economic problems involved in governmental interposition, farm spokesmen will probably for a long time continue to invoke the aid of government to maintain what they regard as an equitable status for agriculture. If wages and salaries fluctuated as widely and as erratically as farm prices, a more general understanding of the forces productive of agricultural support policy would prevail.[6] Nevertheless, farm legislation is plagued by a difficulty common to many types of public intervention in the economy. Once government acts, it generates a vested interest in the new policy. The policy gains thereby, if not immortality, an enormous capacity to resist attempts to modify it once the grievous circumstances that gave it its initial justification change in character or in the severity of their impact.

[6] For treatments of governmental policy toward agriculture, see D. C. Blaisdell, *Government and Agriculture* (New York: Farrar & Rinehart, 1940) ; M. R. Benedict, *Farm Policies of the United States, 1790–1950* (New York: Twentieth Century Fund, 1953) ; Lowry Nelson, *American Farm Life* (Cambridge: Harvard University Press, 1954) ; Lauren Soth, *Farm Trouble* (Princeton: Princeton University Press, 1957).

Cleavages within Agriculture: Farm Spokesmen

Platform drafters appeal to the farmers, and political orators allude to the sterling virtues of their rural constituents, but only in a poetic sense can one speak of "the" farmer. The agricultural population constitutes no homogeneous block of voters with like political interests and aspirations. Conflicts in party loyalties and divergencies in economic interest divide agriculture into many segments, each with its own special concern about public policy. Though farmers may respond warmly to those candidates who succeed in building an image of themselves as genuine friends of the farmer, only on a very few issues do most farmers share a common interest.

Producers of different crops often have different problems. Tobacco farmers, dairymen, and citrus growers have little in common, and each group pursues its own ends. One class of farmers may produce the raw materials for another, and their political objectives may clash, as when dairymen and poultrymen of the Northeast protest against high support prices for feed grains. Often competition between different types of farmers spills over into the political arena, as in the fight between dairymen and growers of oil-bearing products over legislative discrimination against oleomargarine. The varying positions of commodities with respect to the world market bear on the political orientation of their producers. Thus, dairymen advocate protectionist measures to block cheese imports.

Farm producers differ widely in the scale of their operations, a factor that generates political differences within the agricultural population. Though no farm is big as economic enterprises go, large-scale farms, which numbered 103,000 or 2.8 per cent of the 3.7 million commercial farms in 1950, accounted for slightly more than one-fourth of the value of farm products sold. Large family-scale farms, 10.3 per cent of all commercial farms, were responsible for another one-fourth of the value of farm products. Thus, less than 15 per cent of the farms produced one-half of the marketed farm products. At the other end of the scale, smaller farms making up 43 per cent of all commercial farms accounted for only 10 per cent of the value of farm products sold. These lifeless figures conceal extremes of wealth and poverty not without political significance. Perhaps unfortunately, one of the factors of political significance is that those who have get more; federal farm legislation benefits chiefly the larger farmers.

Many differences among agricultural producers are reflected in the structure of farm organizations. A goodly number of associations formed along commodity lines advance the cause of their memberships. Illustrative are the American Cranberry Growers Association, the American Livestock Association, the American Sugar Cane League, the National Apple Institute, the

National Beet Growers Federation, the American Pork Producers Association, the National Cooperative Milk Producers Federation, and the National Wool Growers Federation. Farm organizations shade over into associations in which food processors have a hand, and it is not uncommon for leaders of food-processing industries to adorn their ears with wisps of straw and attempt, with some success, to camouflage themselves as farmers to gain legislative advantage.

The great general farm organizations loom larger in the public eye than do specialized farm groups. They are the National Grange, the American Farm Bureau Federation, and the National Farmers' Union; each attempts to cover the nation though none succeeds. Each is equipped with the customary organizational apparatus—annual national meetings, designed to be representative of the membership, together with the necessary executive and administrative staffs—to determine the wishes of the membership and to direct pressure, at the appropriate times, upon Congress and other national governmental agencies.[7]

NATIONAL GRANGE   In its early days the National Grange, with its belligerent radicalism, aroused anxieties in Wall Street, but it has become a comparatively conservative farm organization. It pictures itself as "the oldest and largest farm organization in America and the only Farm Fraternity in the World." It is a "social, educational and economic force, plus a neighborly and community building agency." It places emphasis, according to its literature, "on moral and spiritual idealism. It is a fraternity with a beautiful ritual." Founded as a fraternal order, the Grange retains its ritualistic forms. Its chief officer is the National Master while the supreme authority in ritualistic matters is the Assembly of Demeter, presided over by the High Priest of Demeter.

The Grange, with about 750,000 affiliated farm families, draws about two-thirds of its membership from Ohio, New York, Pennsylvania, and the states of New England. The Pacific Coast states account for one-sixth of its membership. National Grange policies, on the whole, reflect the views of the rural Northeast and the interests of farmers advantageously situated in relation to rich domestic markets.

The Grange early manifested lukewarmness toward New Deal programs to control agricultural production, primarily, it may be supposed, because Grange members did not have so much to gain thereby as did southern and midwestern farmers whose views were represented by the Farm Bureau Federation. The resolutions and literature of the Grange long had a timbre not unlike Republican campaign speeches, but the Grange, like the Republican party, eventually altered its tone. As federal farm programs became firmly

[7] For a survey of farmers' organizations, see Wesley McCune, *The Farm Bloc* (Garden City: Doubleday, Doran, 1943). See also his *Who's Behind Our Farm Policy?* (New York: Praeger, 1956), a discussion of business organizations interested in farm policy.

established, the Grange developed policy proposals of its own, proposals that varied with the circumstances and took into account the special problems of its membership.

Its movement in policy put the Grange, in 1961, in accord with the broad outlines of President Kennedy's farm program, which proposed a commodity-by-commodity approach to production policy as well as a high degree of farmer participation in program formulation. Grange leaders had harsh words for the Farm Bureau's "falsehoods and distortions" in its "frantic efforts" to defeat "reasonable" farm legislation. While its farm policy objectives tend to be more restrained than those of the Farmers' Union, the Grange recoils from the Federation's goal of ultimate abandonment of governmental farm programs.

At one time the Grange aligned itself firmly with protectionist manufacturers on foreign trade policy; it demanded repeal of the Reciprocal Trade Agreement Act. Eventually the Grange came around to a position of advocacy of reduction of barriers to international trade and of measures to regain foreign markets for American farm products. Trade unions find little favor with the Grange, which opposes "all efforts of labor unions to organize farmers or farm workers." [8] The Grange took some credit for blocking repeal of the Taft-Hartley Act, and it has recommended enactment of "right-to-work" laws by the states. Though the Grange sees a place of usefulness for labor unions to "offset the power of organized or big industry and finance," its detailed views on labor policies can give little comfort to labor organizations.

AMERICAN FARM BUREAU FEDERATION   The American Farm Bureau Federation, with a tinge of arrogance, asserts that it is the voice of the farmer. A powerful voice it is indeed, but it speaks principally for the corn and cotton farmer. Almost one-half of its family membership of about 1,600,000 is in the Midwest and over one-third in the South. From the circumstances of its origin in local groups of farmers organized by the county agents, it developed and continues to maintain close relationships with the land-grant colleges and their state extension services. In a sense the Federation speaks for a coalition of cotton, corn, and the agricultural services associated with the land-grant colleges. Its great legislative success in the 1930's resulted in part from the fact that it brought the South and the Midwest into alliance, a problem that had plagued the agrarian politicians of the 1920's. Maintenance of the coalition of cotton and corn requires development of Federation programs acceptable to both regions, a task that at times creates serious internal stresses in the organization.

[8] The official historian of the Grange, its High Priest Emeritus, concludes that with erratic weather, insect pests, and other such problems the farmer has "all the headaches he can possibly bear" without adding that of organized labor. C. M. Gardner, *The Grange —Friend of the Farmer* (Washington: The National Grange, 1949), p. 170.

Though comparative measurements of political strength are hazardous, the Farm Bureau is certainly the most powerful of the three general farm organizations. Any legislative or administrative measure, concludes the historian of the Bureau, "that is opposed by the AFBF is not likely to get far. On most agricultural matters, except possibly some highly specialized cooperative or crop matter, it is not too much to say that unless AFBF actively supports it the chances of its success are slight." [9] To make known its views, the Federation employs able leaders and pays them well. It maintains a research staff to aid it in reaching its decisions; through its "department of information" it educates the general public as well as its own membership.

In presenting the views of the farmer to Congress, Federation officials are guided by resolutions voted by the annual convention, which is, of course, closely guided by Federation officials. They employ the usual methods of testifying before congressional committees, interviewing Congressmen, and stirring up pressure on statesmen in their home districts. By enlisting the support of its affiliated state and county organizations, the Federation can, when the occasion demands, turn enormous pressure on Congress. Its Washington representatives watch the legislative process and guide the strategy of battle.

The Federation promotes the cause of the more prosperous farming classes of its midwestern and southern constituency with great zeal and ability. The types of measures appropriate to that cause differ from time to time. The Federation had an influential hand in the formation of the early New Deal agricultural legislation and collaborated closely with the Department of Agriculture. In the early 1940's, however, it came into conflict with the Democratic Department of Agriculture. The bases of conflict were complex. One factor was simply rivalry for farm leadership, but more fundamental was a difference over the means to be employed to maintain farm income— and over what farmers' incomes were to be maintained. In 1946 Allan Kline, of Iowa, became president of the Federation, at which time it moved toward a policy of flexible price supports at a lower level, a doctrine that made a good deal of hard economic sense but which incidentally would hasten bankruptcy for the smaller, less-efficient farmer. The Federation strongly, and successfully, opposed in 1949 the Brannan plan, a proposal by the Democratic Secretary of Agriculture, which placed emphasis on "parity income" rather than "parity price" and included features of benefit to consumers of agricultural products.[10]

With the election of Eisenhower, the Federation again came to enjoy close relations with the Department of Agriculture. Its friends occupied high posts

[9] O. M. Kile, *The Farm Bureau Federation through Three Decades* (Baltimore: The Waverly Press, 1948), p. 389.

[10] Reo M. Christenson, *The Brannan Plan: Farm Politics and Policy* (Ann Arbor: University of Michigan Press, 1959).

in the Department, and the Administration's farm legislative recommendations generally followed lines congenial to it.[11] In turn, the Federation supported Eisenhower in his 1956 dispute with the Democratic Congress over farm legislation. It by no means proposed that government abandon agriculture to the free market; rather it advocated flexible price supports which could be managed to adjust production downward and to avoid the accumulation of surpluses. In keeping with its large-farmer orientation it argued, in connection with the soil bank program, that "no limits be placed on the amount that the individual producer may earn or receive under the plan," in contrast with the Grange view that the larger farming enterprises should have to look out for themselves without government aid. In short, during the 1950's the Federation appeared as an organization dedicated to the ultimate liquidation of governmental controls over agricultural production. In the meantime, though, the Federation is prepared to take what it can get. Thus, in 1962 it had a hand in killing Kennedy's proposal to put teeth into agricultural production control and thereby assured that grain growers would continue profitably to build up surpluses at public expense.

In its general position the Federation has probably sided with the implacable economic trends that will triumph in the long run. Whether public policy can, or should, long offset the technological developments making it difficult for small farmers to exist was debatable if not questionable. Yet in taking its position the Federation leadership ran counter to the short-run interests of many of its members, aroused charges that it misrepresented the farmers, and strained the unity of the organization. The southern wing of the Federation remained cool toward flexible supports, and some southern state federations took public stands in opposition. Even in its midwestern strongholds, rival, and perhaps fly-by-night, farm organizations arose to present a contrary view.[12]

An early indication of the emerging big-farmer orientation of the Federation was its successful campaign to kill the Farm Security Administration,

---

[11] See C. M. Hardin, "The Republican Department of Agriculture—A Political Interpretation," *Journal of Farm Economics*, 36 (1954), 210–27. On Republicanism among Farm Bureau members in Wisconsin, see L. D. Epstein, *The Wisconsin Farm Vote for Governor, 1948–1954* (Madison: University of Wisconsin, Bureau of Government, 1956).

[12] The role of the Farm Bureau hierarchy in the agricultural discontent of the middle 1950's suggests an animadversion on the function of organized groups in restraining as well as in representing their membership. Under some conditions, an extensive, powerful, and politically sophisticated group leadership structure may restrain the reflex actions of the rank and file against adverse circumstances. In the absence of an operating group structure and hierarchy, leaders of the moment may fan the flames of discontent of a disadvantaged class of persons. A long-established leadership, however, may take a more restrained position because of its estimate of what is feasible by way of remedial action, and perhaps because of a tendency of well-organized hierarchies to become somewhat conservative. Mobs act differently from disciplined regiments. In a broad sense, the organizational apparatus of private groups may, under some circumstances, serve as an instrument to govern—to restrain—in quite as great a degree as it may be an instrument of agitation.

a unit of the Department of Agriculture born in early New Deal days to re-habilitate low-income farmers. It reached a class of farmers neglected by the principal programs of farm credit and production management. Moreover, it concerned itself with the wages and working conditions of farm workers, even migratory workers upon whom farm proprietors with heavy seasonal labor requirements were especially dependent. Early in 1942 the Federation launched a barrage which was instrumental in the liquidation of the Farm Security Administration. The Federation has scarcely been a zealous supporter of later agencies with related objectives, such as the Farmers' Home Admin-istration.

A feature of Federation policy has been its vigorous attempt to establish and maintain itself as the predominant, if not the sole, spokesman for the farmer. At least a color of truth pervades the cynical observation that the Federation fights for the Iowa corn grower and speaks for the southern cotton planter, but most of all it looks out for the American Farm Bureau Federa-tion. Before the extensive development of agricultural administrative ap-paratus in the 1930's, the principal agencies dealing with farmers were the state extension services connected with the state land-grant colleges. Com-monly the Federation and the state colleges were joined together in informal alliance to their mutual advantage. Administrative actions by the federal Department of Agriculture that by-passed the state colleges aroused the opposition of the Federation, which saw farm programs moving into the hands of organizations less susceptible to its influence. It reacted with special vigor against direct federal consultative and service relations with groups of farmers, apparently on the basis of the doctrine that only it should speak for farmers.

The Federation has been impatient with the Soil Conservation Service which deals directly with local soil conservation districts. It has urged that the Service's functions be devolved upon the state extension services, and in 1953 administrative actions by Secretary Benson were attacked by the National Association of Soil Conservation Districts as calculated to bring the soil conservation program within the orbit of the state extension services and the Farm Bureau. A system of county land-use planning committees by which the Department of Agriculture proposed to consult with farmers on the form and administration of agricultural programs met a quick death as the Federation moved in on the appropriations committee. Farm Bureau leaders, perhaps mindful of the Federation's origins in official stimulation, regarded these and other measures as designed to create new and competing organizations of farmers. We will, the president of the AFBF said, "crack down on any group that will do that." [13] At one stage the Federation even

[13] The story of the influence of the Federation on the administrative structure of farm programs is long and involved. See Grant McConnell, *The Decline of Agrarian Democracy* (Berkeley: University of California Press, 1953); C. M. Hardin, *The Politics of Agri-culture* (Glencoe: Free Press, 1952); William J. Block, *The Separation of the Farm Bureau and the Extension Service* (Urbana: University of Illinois Press, 1960).

proposed that important farm programs be placed in control of state committees to be appointed "from nominations by the State director of extension
after consulting with State-wide farm organizations." In some states, such
a policy would have constituted virtual delegation of public authority to the
Farm Bureau.[14]

On issues outside the agricultural sphere, the Federation often takes a
stand parallel to that of the principal business groups. On labor questions
it tends to throw its weight with business, and some state federations have
spearheaded movements for legislation to restrict organized labor. In 1956
it supported the elimination of national control of the field price of natural
gas. In 1960 it defended the depletion allowance in the taxation of oil and
gas production. On such matters peripheral to agriculture, Federation leaders
at times come perilously close to converting their organization into a tool
of business without much regard to the concern of farmers in the issues at
stake. On the other hand, the Federation looks to business for support on
farm issues and may feel obliged to reciprocate.

NATIONAL FARMERS' UNION   The National Farmers' Union
is differentiated from other farm organizations by its tradition, its ideology,
its program, and the location of its membership. Founded in Texas in 1902
by men who had been active in the Farmers' Alliance, the Union carries on
the tradition of old-fashioned, militant agrarian radicalism. Its membership
centers in such Great Plains states as Oklahoma, Nebraska, and the Dakotas,
and strong state affiliates exist in Wisconsin, Minnesota, Montana, and Colorado. The geography of its membership makes the politics of wheat an important item on its agenda, and the special uncertainties of farming on the
western rim of arable land find reflection in its outlook.

The ideas of the cooperative movement occupy a prominent place in the
Union's political creed, and at times internal debate has been spirited on the
issue of the relative emphasis to be given the development of cooperatives as
against legislative advancement of the cause of the farmer. The more extreme
pronouncements of the Union contemplate the ultimate replacement of private
enterprise by cooperatives as the "only means by which the potential abun-
dance of this Nation may be made available to all its people and by which
true democracy may be maintained and safe-guarded." In keeping with its
doctrines, the Union has sponsored cooperative terminals, elevators, insur-

[14] The abiding jurisdictional jealousies of the Farm Bureau Federation may be a specific manifestation of a general tendency of organized groups to seek to monopolize the
right to organize and speak for particular constituencies. When governmental agencies,
for example, set up advisory committees that represent unorganized as well as organized
segments of particular industries, trade associations often utter hypocritical protests about
dictatorial inclinations to ignore the recognized and established spokesmen of business.
Illustrative of the same phenomenon is the ill-concealed antipathy of the American Legion
toward other groups of veterans. Jurisdictional anxieties are by no means limited to labor
unions.

ance enterprises, creameries, and agencies for the purchase of farm supplies and the sale of farm products.

The Union advocates measures to encourage and protect the owner-operated, family farm. It opposes the "factory farm" and commercialized agriculture. Its faith in farming as a "way of life" brings it into conflict with the Farm Bureau Federation which tends to regard farming unsentimentally as a way to make money. On other matters also, it has opposed the Farm Bureau. In 1956, for example, it advocated high and rigid price supports while the Federation supported the Republican Administration's flexible price-support program. In 1961 it backed President Kennedy's farm program which the Federation opposed.

A remnant of the drive toward farmer-labor collaboration of the Populist days remains in the program of the Union. It maintains friendly relations with labor organizations and participated actively in the movement for the adoption of the Employment Act of 1946. It does not begrudge labor's gains. It supported the Brannan plan, a widely discussed scheme proposed by President Truman's Secretary of Agriculture, which would have both maintained farm income and given urban consumers farm commodities at prices fixed by the market. The Union acclaimed the plan as "an historic advance in agricultural policy-making because it grows out of and recognizes the great truth that each group in our society depends upon all the others and that governmental programs must serve fairly the needs of all groups." Farm Bureau leaders take a more jaundiced view of most measures that might benefit urban consumers.[15]

Given its traditional strain of reformism—attachment to the family farm, opposition to monopoly, advocacy of cooperatives, friendliness to labor— the Farmers' Union in recent decades has been on the Democratic side of the fence. Republican politicians and leaders of competing farm organizations have not been above charging that the Union's native American radicalism amounted to un-Americanism.[16]

FARM WORKERS   Organization of agriculture has been limited mainly to farm owners and managers. Agricultural labor and farm tenants have not found their political voice through organization. The IWW made an early attempt to organize farm labor. It claimed in the years 1916–1918

[15] See W. P. Tucker, "Populism Up-To-Date: The Story of the Farmers' Union," *Agricultural History*, 21 (1947), 198–208.

[16] In 1950, in a published letter, the executive secretary of the Utah State Farm Bureau Federation asserted that Democratic Representative W. K. Granger, a candidate for re-election, had exhibited an animosity toward all "farmers' organizations except the Communist-dominated Farmers Union." The Union and its adjunct, the Farmers Union Service Corporation, sued the Utah State Farm Bureau and won $25,000 in damages. Representative Granger had introduced a bill that would have compelled complete separation of the Farm Bureau and the State Agricultural Extension Services, a step strongly opposed by the Farm Bureau Federation.

a membership of 18,000, chiefly casual workers in the corn and wheat belts, for its Agricultural Workers Organization. Within a few years the IWW practically disappeared. In the early thirties the Southern Farm Tenants Union came into existence, in part to resist the imposition of a disproportionate share of the adjustments involved in crop reduction upon tenants and sharecroppers. It also made attempts to obtain better pay for seasonal agricultural workers, but its strength was limited and its small membership was concentrated mainly in Arkansas. In 1946 the Union, now called the National Agricultural Workers Union, became an AFL affiliate. The most vigorous attempts to organize farm workers have occurred in California, but they have by and large failed. In 1961 the AFL-CIO dissolved its Agricultural Workers Organizing Committee which had been conducting a fruitless and expensive organizing campaign in California.

The problems of farm workers do not seem to yield to the methods applicable to those of industrial labor. Moreover, the heavy need for seasonal labor in agriculture creates a migratory labor force exceptionally susceptible to exploitation as well as difficult to organize. Migratory workers, because they are migratory, lack the political capacity for self-protection enjoyed by relatively immobile groups of laborers. Farm organizations have thrown their weight, generally with success, against legislative proposals for the protection of migratory workers. They, too, support arrangements for the importation of seasonal Mexican labor, a measure that both assures a relatively cheap labor supply and keeps down the wages of native farm workers.[17]

In most instances in which farm workers have been organized effectively enough to attempt to strike, they have been suppressed with a ferocity that would make even the most reactionary industrialist blush with shame. In addition, farm organizations have often succeeded in excluding farm labor from the benefits of labor legislation, such as unemployment insurance, workman's compensation, and wage and hour rules. "We vigorously support," resolved the Farm Bureau Federation in 1960, "the agricultural, retail, service, and seasonal exemptions of the Fair Labor Standards Act." The Bureau also "strongly opposes any proposal that would eliminate or severely restrict the opportunity of farm boys and rural youth of ages 13 to 16 to obtain farm employment." In some instances farm organizations have obtained exemptions in the application of labor legislation to such processes as canning, packing, and the operation of creameries, matters essentially industrial in nature.

UNITY AND DIVISION AMONG FARMERS. This brief review of the major general farm organizations should make it clear that agriculture cannot be regarded as a unit either politically or economically. Dis-

[17] See Robert D. Tomasek, "The Migrant Problem and Pressure Group Politics," *Journal of Politics*, 23 (1961), 295–319.

tinctions of objective founded on economic interest are supplemented by contrasts in broad political ideology which find reflection in the programs of farm groups. Farm organizations seldom unite for legislative purposes. Under special circumstances they may join in coalition, as in the lobbying of the principal farm organizations, save the Farmers' Union, in World War II for special treatment under price-control policies. More typically, the major farm organizations urge upon Congress conflicting programs.

The Genesis and Course of Political Movements

The preceding discussion has served to indicate some of the political concerns and characteristics of agriculture, an important though declining element of the American political complex. The analysis has, moreover, been designed to go beyond the specific example and to point toward ideas of utility in the understanding of the political process generally.

Political systems may exist in a stable, even static, form over long periods. The holders of power are unchallenged; the allocation of rights, privileges, and benefits remains acceptable on all sides; every man knows his place and keeps it. In modern states so serene a political condition does not prevail for long. The equilibrium—the balance, the ordered course of affairs, the established pattern—is disturbed from time to time by some change that generates discontent. Such dislocations tend to set off movements in demand of a correction of the balance or for the creation of a new order. Discontent may find expression through a political movement, a more or less spontaneous rising of the people concerned, or it may be manifested in the intensified activities of existing organized groups. The farmers' movements, sketchily surveyed here, merely exemplify this more general pattern of maladjustment, agitation, and governmental action.

What is it that sets off political agitation, that brings demands for governmental action, that arouses groups, even stimulates the creation of new groups, to clamor for attention and for greater consideration in the decision-making processes of the community? In the example chosen, agriculture, particularly certain segments of it, had suffered severe economic deprivation. This change in circumstances generated discontent and led to demands for political remedies. It would be wrong to contend from this instance that all political movements are set in motion by a change in objective external conditions or by material deprivation. Yet some new element must be introduced into a situation to stimulate resort to political action. That new element may be an economic change, which dislocates pre-existing relationships; it may be a threat to a status already enjoyed; it may be mass frustration in any one of a variety of forms.

The frequency with which alterations in economic circumstances ignite political agitation gives rise to the theory that economic factors underlie all political activity. It seems clear, however, that other factors may be influential in the setting into motion of movements leading to a new political equilibrium. New scientific discoveries, for example, may direct attention to conditions hitherto unperceived, or may point to possibilities previously unknown, and be instrumental in stimulating political action. Discovery of immunization against certain diseases by vaccination and other methods, for example, laid the basis for political crusades for compulsory, universal vaccination. An idea, or ideal, may be a factor of great force in movements leading to the reshaping of public policy. How is one, for example, to explain the movements for the expansion of manhood suffrage? The woman suffrage movement? Or what single factor was at the bottom of the prohibition movement? Or why does a movement begin at a particular time rather than earlier or later? A concrete condition may exist over long periods, and at some particular moment unrest flares up to redress a long-standing wrong. Simple explanations of the origins of political disequilibrium must be regarded with reserve.

The introduction of a new element creating demands for a readjustment in the social situation does not invariably lead to political agitation. In one situation discontent may lead to legislative action and in another it may work itself out in the nonpolitical sphere. In the 1920's certain leaders, such as President Coolidge, counseled the unhappy farmers to abide by the operation of beneficent economic laws. They meant that farmers producing at high cost should reduce their costs, produce something else on their lands, or seek a livelihood in industry; that agriculture should adjust itself to the changed situation by the inexorable process of bankruptcy for high-cost producers. The farmers refused to or could not take that course of action, and governmental remedies were sought. Harold Lasswell says: "Although political movements begin in unrest, all social unrest does not find expression in political movements. Under some conditions, a community which is visited by plague may pray; under other conditions, the community will demand the retirement of the health commissioner." [18] To use a less remote example: at one time when unemployment increased, a citizens' committee would solicit funds to maintain a soup line for those in distress; now pressure is brought on public authorities to increase the appropriation for unemployment relief. In one culture drought-stricken farmers may pray for rain; in another they may petition Congress to appropriate for the installation of irrigation works. Thus the content of the governmental sphere changes.

When conditions are ripe for the rise of a political movement, a leader may come on the scene with a remedy. It is essential that the functions of leadership, agitation, and education in political movements be perceived. Before there can be a political movement, the persons making up the move-

[18] "The Measurement of Public Opinion," *American Political Science Review*, 25 (1931), 311–36.

ment must be conscious of a common cause, a common injury, a common goal. How is this consciousness created? Fundamentally by the sharing of experience; and leaders, agitators, propagandists furnish the channels for the communication of a consciousness of common interest. The agitator thus serves as a medium both for cementing together those with a common concern and for expressing that concern. The leader converts the mutterings at the crossroads, in the taverns, and wherever men gather, into a movement; that is, a joint effort by a considerable number of persons to influence the course of events. Often, would-be leaders misjudge the timeliness of their actions and elicite no response to their offer to lead. In such instances the time is not at hand to convert the discontent of scattered individuals into a cohesive movement.

As a sense of common cause grows a remedy is evolved. For the agrarian unrest after World War I, the McNary-Haugen bill served as a goal. As a rallying cry for his movement, Dr. Townsend evolved the "Townsend Plan"; Henry George, the "Single Tax"; William Jennings Bryan, free coinage of silver at sixteen to one. As movements become more complex many measures may be brought under the canopy of a single slogan: the "New Deal"; the "full-dinner pail"; the "return to normalcy." For effective agitation, the most complex measures must be reducible to simple slogans. The remedy around which a political movement is rallied need not be workable. In fact, the remedies advocated by messiahs often are, as the saying goes, "snares and delusions." Yet the expression of discontent is symptomatic of need for readjustment; even if the proposed therapy is futile the pressure may compel the government to devise a substitute treatment. For example, the Townsend Plan, which proposed $200 a month for every person over 60, was claimed by all the experts to be unworkable, but the pressure of Dr. Townsend's movement helped bring about the enactment of the Social Security Act, with a different method of caring for the aged. At times movements operate to dissipate frustrations by the mere expression of discontent, or they are worn down by the resistance of existing institutional patterns. In some instances —notably American municipal reform movements—discontent is blotted out by the enactment of an ordinance that symbolizes success for the movement but has no perceptible effect on the course of events.

Not uncommonly an element of a movement is a diagnosis that blames all the misfortunes of the affected group on some convenient scapegoat: the railroads, the Jews, Wall Street, the capitalists, union bosses, municipal bosses. These diagnoses have simple, dramatic qualities and, therefore, a high propaganda value. Yet they may be incorrect and may result in grave injustice, in uncontrollable outbursts of political discontent. Nonrational sorts of political disturbances characterized by a high concentration of attention to the devil in the situation may also be quite futile in alleviating the maladjustments that started all the commotion in the first place.

In the course of their growth, movements usually acquire an organizational apparatus and recruit a secretariat or a bureaucracy. Once the movement achieves its immediate objective, it may disappear, though its institutional machinery often gains virtual immortality. The movement may evolve into an organization that grasps new issues and new causes to keep itself alive. Most pressure groups, in fact, originate in an effort to cope with some immediate problem and then persist as an organization to deal with new matters of concern to the membership.[19]

The foregoing discussion of the natural history of political movements suggests that one of the principal tasks of those who govern is to identify and deal with maladjustments that give rise to social discontent and political movements. The skill and insight with which a politics of prevention is followed will determine whether those who govern will continue to govern. Social maladjustments tend to be neglected until they give rise to strong movements in demand of action; in rare instances all the techniques of social research are brought into play to observe, foresee, and plan thoroughly to meet rising problems. Those who govern may choose to wear down by delay and obstruction rather than deny or suppress. More often they do not have the wit to see that corrective measures are in order; otherwise the personnel of governments would not change so frequently.

[19] For discussions of the nature of social movements, see R. M. MacIver, *Social Causation* (Boston: Ginn, 1942); Hadley Cantril, *The Psychology of Social Movements* (New York: Wiley, 1941); Rudolf Heberle, *Social Movements* (New York: Appleton-Century-Crofts, 1951).

3.

WORKERS

INDUSTRIALIZATION has been at the root of most of the great domestic political issues in the United States since the War between the States. The rise of manufacturing and the development of associated financial, transport, and distributive organizations generated changes of profound political significance. The expansion of new economic interests brought struggles for a redistribution of political power; and with the erection of mighty structures of private industrial power came demands from disadvantaged groups for governmental redress of grievances. Agrarian protest movements that swept the country in the latter part of the nineteenth century failed to stay the hand of the new colossus of finance and industry. After the turn of the century, in the Progressive movement and in Woodrow Wilson's crusade for the "new freedom," the middle classes and the small entrepreneur fought only a delaying action against the same antagonist.

In the battle for power in the state the worker has proved to be, at least potentially, the strongest force loosed by the process of industrialization. The growth of industry in the United States thrust into numerical preponderance a working class sharply distinguished in status from the farmer and the small entrepreneur. In the main without property, this class found itself arrayed against those possessing title to this world's goods. With its resources limited to skills of mind and of muscle, it occupied a situation of great insecurity. Without cash reserves, its very food and shelter were dependent on the vagaries of business conditions that determined the regularity of the pay envelope. Since he was almost powerless as an individual, the only mode for defense and offense open to the industrial worker was collective action.

The American industrial laboring class emerged in an ideological climate superficially hospitable to political action. Doctrines of political equality and of the right of self-government seemed to pave the way for the new toiling masses to grasp power and to mold the state to suit their wishes. Moreover, while American workers were increasing in number, socialist ideas were blossoming around the globe. Heady doctrines were being proclaimed: workers should unite and take what was justly theirs. Furthermore, if they merged the ideas of socialism and democracy, they would not have to take what they wanted—all they had to do was to vote for it. He who would understand politics in the large may ponder well the status of labor: a numerically great force in a society adhering to the doctrine of the rule of numbers, yet without proportionate durable political power as a class.

Political Consequences of the Emergence of New Occupations

When in a liberal-democratic state substantial numbers of people begin to earn their living in a new way, it is fairly safe to predict that a redistribution of political power will occur. The emerging group seeks a share in political power mainly for the purpose of altering public policies that were designed to meet the needs of the old order. If the new group becomes a substantial proportion of the population, radical shifts in political power may take place, and the framers of public policy may come to be preoccupied with an entirely new set of problems.

OCCUPATIONAL CHANGE AND THE POLITICAL EQUILIBRIUM   The occupational and status changes associated with industrialization in the United States since 1870 brought large segments of the population into the wage-earning class. As this group expanded, it demanded alterations in the political order; and as it grew in numbers, its demands were heard more respectfully. By 1870 as many persons were employed in manufacturing and in related pursuits as in agriculture. Industrial employment continued to increase rapidly, while after 1910 farm employment steadily declined. Underlying these trends were many changes in ways of life, changes both obvious and subtle, that created new political needs and new factors in the process of politics.

Although industrialization created a large new class of wage earners, the conditions under which the industrial working class emerged were such that a relatively feeble class consciousness developed. This frailty of the sense of class membership affects profoundly the role of labor in politics. To constitute a politically effective group, individuals must share common aspirations and antipathies. It may be contended that the interests of all wage earners are the same; but, until workers as individuals believe this to be true, there can be no crystallized consciousness of common cause, and, hence, no labor solidarity in action.

Radical differences in the sense of class attachment are associated with variations in skill among wage earners. Many workers do not regard themselves as members of a "working class"; they feel, rather, an attachment to the middle class. A striking cleavage in attitude prevails between factory workers and white-collar workers. Among manual workers like differences, though not so wide, prevail. Evidence on the general point has been reported by Richard Centers from the results of a poll of a national sample on the questions: "If you were asked to use one of these four names for your social class which would you say you belonged in: the Middle Class, Lower Class, Working Class, or Upper Class?" [1] The results, which show striking differences between white-collar and manual workers, were as follows:

	Upper Class	Middle Class	Working Class	Lower Class
White-collar	2%	61%	34%	0.6%
Skilled manual	2	26	71	1
Semiskilled	1	14	83	1
Unskilled		18	75	7

Workers, thus, do not uniformly share a sense of class consciousness. To an extent varying among different subgroups of workers, they identify with the middle class. Other cleavages also cut through the wage-earning class. Economic competition among workers sometimes manifests itself in jurisdictional disputes among trade unions, which are often as bitter as conflicts between employees and employers. National, religious, and racial differences project themselves into the labor movement. Rivalries between workers of different national origins are not uncommon. Skill groups are sometimes divided among Jewish and Gentile unions; Catholics as a matter of religious principle oppose socialist tendencies within unions. In some industries and in some localities the Negro has presented a special problem in union organization, although since 1935 a gradual reduction in union discrimination against Negroes has occurred.

[1] *The Psychology of Social Classes* (Princeton: Princeton University Press, 1949), p. 86. Other studies indicate that the form of Centers' question probably affected the distribution of responses, that is, that with a different question form a smaller proportion of persons would have identified themselves with the "working class." See Neal Gross, "Social Class Identification in the Urban Community," *American Sociological Review*, 18 (1953), 398–404. Among persons who are in fact working class, those psychologically identified with that class are more frequently Democratic than are those who regard themselves as middle class. See Heinz Eulau, *Class and Party in the Eisenhower Years* (New York: Free Press of Glencoe, 1962); Oscar Glantz, "Class Consciousness and Political Solidarity," *American Sociological Review*, 23 (1958), 375–83.

INCOMPLETENESS OF LABOR ORGANIZATION   The frailty of class consciousness among American workers, and other factors as well, are reflected in the slow growth of labor organization and in the fact that many workers remain even yet unorganized. In 1960 union membership accounted for only about one-fourth of the total civilian labor force, which included many categories of workers not readily susceptible to organization, such as household workers, farm workers, and professional and technical workers. Some industries are, of course, almost completely unionized, while in others extremely few workers belong to unions.

Factors peculiar to individual trades or industries have affected the rate of growth of unions. The union movement, for example, made headway among the skilled crafts long before it became established in the mass-production industries. Industries characterized by small operations were organized before those in which huge firms dominated. In addition, certain broad conditions have from time to time stimulated spurts of unionization generally. Of special interest from the political viewpoint has been the extraordinary growth of unionism at times of widespread unrest. Unions grew rapidly in the early 1880's when both farmers and workers were agitated about the operation of the social system. Similarly, in the 1930's the growth of unions occurred under circumstances of disenchantment with the workings of American institutions. The great sit-down strikes of the 1930's had about them at least a tinge of the revolutionary. Other periods of marked expansion of unions have occurred when sharp increases in the price level coincided with a scarcity of labor.[2] A rising cost of living gave incentive to organization, and the scarcity of labor gave bargaining leverage to unions. Illustrative are the upward jumps in union membership during World War I and World War II.[3] In this century the most marked union growth has occurred in periods when government looked benignly on the labor movement, and these were eras of Democratic control of the national government, a factor which probably contributes to the broadly pro-Democratic orientation of organized labor.

OBSTACLES TO THE POLITICAL ASSIMILATION OF EMERGING GROUPS   A newly emerging group faces a different problem as it seeks power in a society than does a declining group that attempts

[2] See John T. Dunlop, "The Development of Labor Organization: A Theoretical Framework," in R. A. Lester and Joseph Shister, *Insights into Labor Issues* (New York: Macmillan, 1948), pp. 163–93; Joseph Shister, "The Logic of Union Growth," *Journal of Political Economy*, 61 (1953), 413–33.

[3] For data on trends in union membership, see Irving Bernstein, "The Growth of American Unions," *American Economic Review*, 44 (1954), 301–18, and "The Growth of American Unions, 1945–1960," *Labor History*, 2 (1961), 131–57. For information on individual unions, see *Directory of National and International Labor Unions in the United States*, an occasional publication of the U. S. Bureau of Labor Statistics.

to retain its influence. A new group meets the resistance of those already on the ground who share their power only grudgingly. A new group is likely to challenge the cherished values of the old order; an old group merely has to defend what is regarded as right, proper, and respectable. The older holders of power control the instruments of government and may use them to resist, to suppress, to weaken the newcomers, who may be regarded even as revolutionaries who would upset the ancient order.

In the long history of attempts to unify the American working classes, time and again labor suffered reverses as it collided with the reigning ideologies and interests. In his interpretation of the American labor movement, Selig Perlman places great emphasis on the strength of the institution of private property and the incompatibility of the objectives of organized labor with private property. Whether labor seeks its ends by political means or by bargaining, its objective is to restrict the control of the employer over his property.[4] The claims of labor have to a considerable degree been on matters that employers have been most reluctant to yield, and in this attitude employers have often been able to ally with themselves substantial proportions of the general public. For decades the demand for collective bargaining and for union recognition was met by private armies, sometimes supported by police and troops. When the National Labor Relations Act of 1935 guaranteed the right of collective bargaining, employers' resistance did not evaporate overnight. Sabotage of the law was widespread.

To carve out a place for itself in the politico-social order, a new group may have to fight for a reorientation of many of the values of the old order. Early unions were assailed as anarchist or socialist. Eventually they became accepted, only to have the cry of communism raised against them. Organized labor is still regarded with hostility by substantial segments of society, and some of its practices find little acceptance among the public generally. Moreover, many labor leaders even yet live under a psychology of siege: they believe, not entirely without reason, that industrial leadership merely tolerates unions or that business would, given a fighting chance, attempt to crush unionism. Nevertheless, during the past half-century organized labor established itself fairly securely as an element of the social system. Organized labor amounted to something less than an instrument for "all the toiling masses," but it came to exercise great influence on many public questions and to possess a veto, if not the affirmative power of decision, on others.

IS INDUSTRIAL LABOR PAST ITS PEAK?   If there is validity in our general proposition that the emergence of new types of occupational groupings tends to bring alterations in the pattern of political power, it may be that occupational changes have been, and are, in the making which will have far-reaching political consequences. The proportion of factory

[4] *A Theory of the Labor Movement* (New York: Macmillan, 1928), ch. 5.

workers in the total labor force has long since ceased increasing. Great growth has occurred in technical, clerical, administrative, and sales personnel. Among manual workers larger proportions are now skilled and semiskilled; and the census category of "skilled workers" conceals upgrading in the character of work performed and in the status of workers.

Projections of these trends suggest that by 1975 white-collar workers will exceed blue-collar workers in number. The full effects of these occupational shifts will materialize only slowly, yet they may be of basic importance for the American polity. The proportionate increase in professional, administrative, and other white-collar occupations augurs for a strengthening of middle-class Republicanism, unless white-collar workers develop a tendency to unionize. The probable consequences of the rise in income, educational level, and status of blue-collar workers are not so clear. The result could be an intensification of a union-oriented political outlook among these workers rather than a conversion to a middle-class outlook.[5] Nor should the possibility of the rise of a militant unionism in industries now unorganized be ruled out, even though the proportion of the civilian labor force unionized remained fairly constant from 1945 to 1960.

Government of Trade Unions

Persons interested in acting together to gain political influence, to improve their economic status, or to accomplish some other joint end do not rise spontaneously as one man and in unison shout their demands. A segment of society that seeks to improve or defend its status usually works through a relatively elaborate organization, which formulates and expresses its wishes. This machinery for collective action constitutes a group government strikingly similar to that of the state itself. An examination of the organization of American labor will throw light on its characteristics that are significant for political action and will also illustrate problems of organization and leadership common to all private groups. Moreover, even a cursory inspection of the government of labor will suggest fundamental questions about the role of private organizations in the process of governance broadly defined.

In both their formal structure and their more subtle patterns of behavior, the governments of private groups resemble the apparatus of the state. Private groups have their parliaments, their cabinets, their administrative agencies, and their courts. They have, too, their taxes, their crimes, their systems of group education, their procedures for purging dissident elements. As they strive toward group consensus, private groups operate an internal politics

[5] It is among more highly skilled workers that the sharpest sense of union identification seems to occur. See A. S. Tannenbaum and R. L. Kahn, *Participation in Union Locals* (Evanston: Row, Peterson, 1958).

not unfamiliar to the observer of the politics of the state. Although it might be supposed that the objectives of private associations, *vis-à-vis* the state or other groups, would be self-evident, they seldom are. Generally conflicts of interest, of ideology, of aims exist and must be settled if the group is to go forth united to fight its battles.

AFL-CIO: A CONFEDERACY   When in 1955 the American Federation of Labor and the Congress of Industrial Organizations merged as the AFL-CIO, newspapers dilated on the powerful creation of the act of unity. The realities differed from the dispatches. The AFL-CIO, like its predecessor organizations, is a confederacy of national and international unions; and confederations are notoriously weak. The constituent units of the AFL-CIO, such as the Auto Workers, the Bricklayers, the Rubber Workers, and the Machinists, enjoy states' rights with a vengeance. Each "national and international union is entitled to have its autonomy, integrity and jurisdiction protected and preserved." Moreover, the AFL-CIO constitution recognizes that its affiliated national unions have the right of secession. In short, the common interests of national labor organizations—with the exception of a few independents, such as the Mine Workers and the railroad brotherhoods —suffice to cause them to associate together but not to establish a powerful central government over themselves.

The biennial convention of the AFL-CIO is its "supreme governing body" and might be compared with a parliament or, perhaps more accurately, a conference of ambassadors. Representation of the constituent national unions varies roughly with their membership. The convention hears reports from the AFL-CIO functionaries, elects officers, and adopts resolutions. The executive council functions somewhat as the cabinet of a parliamentary government. It consists of the president and the secretary-treasurer along with the 27 vice presidents of the AFL-CIO. The vice presidents are, in turn, usually presidents of their respective national labor organizations.

The president and the secretary-treasurer preside over the Washington headquarters of the AFL-CIO, but they, as the officers of a confederation of labor baronies, operate within a sphere restricted both constitutionally and practically. The AFL-CIO governmental superstructure was built in the tradition of union autonomy of the older AFL. Yet the AFL-CIO constitution also took a few hesitant steps toward a greater centralization of authority, which represented also a projection of trends in the older organizations.[6]

Indicative of constituent autonomy in the AFL was the consideration by its 1940 annual convention of the problem of cleansing some of its member unions of racketeers. The principle of "states' rights" limited the convention to a condemnation of racketeering union leaders and to a direction to the

[6] On the amalgamation of the AFL and CIO, see A. J. Goldberg, *AFL-CIO, Labor United* (New York: McGraw-Hill, 1956).

executive council to use its "influence" to bring about a house cleaning in the unions concerned. By 1953 AFL constitutional doctrine had moved a long distance and its convention took the "revolutionary" step, as some labor leaders termed it, of expelling the International Longshoremen's Association from the Federation. In 1956 the ILA failed to convince the AFL-CIO that it had cleansed its ranks of racketeers, but in 1959 the AFL-CIO regarded the ILA as sufficiently reformed to re-admit it on a provisional basis. In 1961, at the end of its period of probation, the ILA again became an affiliate in good standing. Another illustration of the AFL doctrine of autonomy is provided by a debate in the 1944 convention on the question of discrimination against Negroes by some of the constituent unions. What could the Federation do about it? The answer was that each national and international union was "clothed with autonomous authority to formulate, shape, and administer its own affairs."

In principle, the CIO operated on the same confederate principle as the AFL. In its early days the CIO central headquarters exercised considerable power because many of its newly formed unions depended on subsidies from the parent body. As the new unions developed strength and sources of revenue, they became autonomous. Yet the CIO national leadership took strong action against several of its internationals which were dominated by communist factions. These unions were expelled, and the CIO financed organizing committees to recruit workers in the industries concerned into new unions with an untainted leadership.[7]

These centralizing trends affected the new AFL-CIO constitution. Unions dominated by communists, fascists, or other totalitarians are ineligible for membership, and the aim is to "protect the labor movement from any and all corrupt influences." A committee on ethical practices has the duty of assisting the executive council in keeping the organization free of communism and corruption; and a committee on civil rights has a similar duty to assist in bringing about as soon as possible conformity with the principle of non-discrimination. Yet the ultimate power of the AFL-CIO over its constituent unions is expulsion, which could be followed by an organizing campaign to woo the unionists concerned away from their old leaders, at best a costly and difficult process. Fundamentally, the rule of autonomy continues to prevail. The AFL-CIO can expel a union, but expulsion of a large union may hurt the AFL-CIO more than it does the expelled union.

Soon after the AFL-CIO was formed, those labor leaders concerned about corruption in the constituent nationals began to breathe life into the new committee on ethical practices. An obvious target for the committee was the Teamsters' Dave Beck, who, early in 1956, responded to a reporter's inquiry whether the committee had considered having him on the carpet:

[7] See Max M. Kampelman, *The Communist Party vs. the C.I.O.* (New York: Praeger, 1957).

"I don't know and I don't give a damn. We're an autonomous union and nobody's going to tell us how to run our affairs." [8] The AFL-CIO discovered that Beck was right; it could not tell him or his successor, James Hoffa, how to run the union. In 1957 the AFL-CIO expelled the Teamsters, but Hoffa's union grew in strength and Hoffa evidently grew in the affections of his members. On the other hand, the AFL-CIO had greater success in forcing the reform or removal of leaders charged as being corrupt in at least some of the smaller nationals that came under the scrutiny of its committee on ethical practices.[9]

As might be surmised from this description of its structure, no little effort must be devoted to the task of keeping the AFL-CIO from flying apart. Yet sufficient unity may be maintained at the top level of labor organization to perform certain essential functions. A primary function is the formulation and advancement of the political objectives of labor before Congress, within the administrative agencies, and in campaigns. Beyond this the national machinery needs, as a matter of public relations if for no other reason, to police its constituent units insofar as it can. Finally, the top leadership can attempt to settle jurisdictional conflicts among unions. These disputes strain the bonds of AFL-CIO unity as nationals threaten to secede unless their jurisdictional demands are met. This chronic rivalry, in 1961, developed into a crisis that led to an amendment to the AFL-CIO constitution creating new procedures for the arbitration of interunion disputes by the Executive Council.

CONSTITUENT UNITS OF AFL-CIO   The constituent units that enjoy "states' rights" within the AFL-CIO are about 130 national unions formed on either craft or industrial lines. Among the giants are the Auto Workers, the Machinists, the Steelworkers, the Carpenters, and the Electrical Workers. Each of these nationals claims over 750,000 members. Most of the national unions, though, are relatively small; 40 per cent of the AFL-CIO nationals enroll less than 25,000 members each. Less than 5,000 belong to such nationals as the Bill Posters, the Broom and Whisk Makers, the Coopers, the Flight Engineers, the Glass Cutters, the Siderographers, and the Train Dispatchers. About 50 nationals manage to get along without affiliation with the AFL-CIO. Notable among the independents are the Teamsters and the Mine Workers.

Each of the nationals is in turn built upon a base of local unions, of which there are probably 75,000 to 80,000 in the country. The local may be formed on a plant basis in an industrial union or it may consist of the crafts-

---

[8] *Wall Street Journal*, February 14, 1956.

[9] Philip Taft asserts that expulsion has effects when members at the local level revolt against corrupt practices. See "The Responses of the Bakers, Longshoremen and Teamsters to Public Exposure," *Quarterly Journal of Economics*, 74 (1960), 395–412.

men, for example, plasterers, within a locality. While the details differ from union to union, each national has a governing apparatus of its own. Ordinarily a national convention, consisting of representatives from the locals, is the top governing authority. The convention elects the national's president, and he usually works with an executive committee or board. The presidents of the large nationals are in the public eye as the major labor leaders of the country, and they commonly exert great influence in the councils of the labor movement as a whole.

While the relationships between the national headquarters of a union and its locals vary from union to union, the government of the typical national would probably be described by the political scientist as unitary. The national union superstructure historically developed to supplement and to make effective the operations of independently formed locals. The geographic mobility of goods had made futile the bargaining efforts of scattered independent locals, and the geographical mobility of labor likewise created problems for the local. The national union gradually emerged and acquired varying controls over locals in the admission and disciplining of members, the calling of strikes, compliance with contracts, wage policies, work rules, and the like. In some situations the national may take over the management of a local; in others, it may review actions by locals, such as disciplinary measures. Over the long run the authority of the nationals has grown both to prevent abuses and to permit effective bargaining over large areas.[10]

DEMOCRACY AND OLIGARCHY IN LABOR ORGANIZA-TION   The governmental apparatus of labor as a whole resembles representative institutions generally. The formal line of mass control moves from the local to the national to the AFL-CIO in a pattern not unfamiliar to students of government. Yet in private, as in public, organizations the constitutional prescriptions do not necessarily coincide with actual institutional workings. In fact, the internal governments of unions range from the most tightly controlled oligarchy—perhaps an occasional tyranny—to a system closely approximating a competitive two-party system. Spectacular instances of corrupt and boss-controlled unions have attracted attention to the internal politics of unions. Amidst assertions that all is dictatorship or that all is a sweet and reasonable democracy, there should be no mistake: the hierarchies of labor organizations, whether accountable or not accountable in specific

---

[10] The basic structure of organization, be it craft or industrial, is scarcely adaptable to the political needs of labor in state and local spheres. The state federations of labor developed to fill this gap. Local unions, whatever their national connection, could affiliate with their state federation of labor, which performed primarily political and lobbying functions on state matters. The CIO organized structurally similar state industrial union councils. Both AFL and CIO had arrangements for similar coalitions or alliances within cities. The AFL-CIO merger brought a consolidation of these state and local coordinating bodies.

situations, wield an authority over their members, as do all quasi-governmental institutions.

Before the merger, the national conventions of the AFL commonly were smoothly managed by the controlling oligarchy of leaders. A statement at the 1936 AFL convention by the late Charles P. Howard, president of the International Typographical Union, could have been used to describe many AFL and CIO national conventions: "During the years I have been a delegate to conventions of the American Federation of Labor I have observed the strongest cohesion in a controlling group for the purpose of determining every question from election of officers to selection of the city in which the convention is to meet the following year." Doubtless, as the AFL-CIO merger shakes down into a stable organization, its biennial convention, despite its formal role as the "supreme governing body" of AFL-CIO, will also operate decorously under the guidance of the official clique.

That such a national convention should be under firm control should occasion no astonishment. The dominance of the official leadership may be observed in national gatherings representative of all sorts of private associations. The lack of conflict within the convention may result not only from the power of the leadership, but may come also from the compromise of differences in advance. Nevertheless, the stability of labor leadership assured by the bureaucratic pattern of succession at times produces an inflexible and unimaginative top echelon. The formation of the CIO came in part from a breach between the old-guard oligarchy of the AFL and militant leaders who advocated a vigorous organizing campaign in the mass production industries. The processes of advancement had not brought leaders to the top who were capable of contriving policies to command the support of the entire labor movement.[11]

Within each national union, the oligarchy of professional union workers tends to manage politics. The existence in the International Typographical Union of two parties that regularly compete for control of the organization is exceptional. Even such an election as that of the United Steel Workers in 1957 when David J. McDonald drew only two-thirds of the votes in his bid for re-election is unusual. More generally the "organization slate" for national offices runs without opposition. Philip Taft reports that slightly more than 80 per cent of 764 officers chosen by seven unions over the period from 1910 to 1944 were unopposed in the voting. Uncontested elections are no necessary indication that a leadership is unresponsive to the sentiments of its followers; that fact may merely result from an assiduous cultivation of the membership. Yet ample citation may be made of instances in which union leadership has maintained its position by chicanery or violence. Some leaders

[11] See Walter Galenson, *The CIO Challenge to the AFL* (Cambridge: Harvard University Press, 1960).

have "dissolved parliament" for long periods—the officers of the Tobacco Workers called no convention from 1900 to 1939; the Marine Cooks' and Stewards' Union held no convention for the first 44 years of its existence. In contrast with the oligarchical control of the nationals, a lively competition often occurs for office in locals.

Union hierarchies represent the union member in negotiations with employers, but union hierarchies also govern the union member—within the range of union powers and subject to varying degrees of "popular" control by the member. Conduct of the collective business of the union requires discipline. To refuse to go out on a strike, to work for less than the agreed wage, to violate the union's working rules may defeat the common purpose. Further, discipline is required to enable union leadership to fulfill its commitments to those employers with whom it makes agreements.[12] In a sense union hierarchies have edged into the process of industrial administration and have a hand, through bargaining, in the formulation of policy on promotions, transfers, layoffs, fringe benefits, methods of production, and other such matters. In the application of these rules the union hierarchy may also make itself heard. If we regard the process of governing as the imposition of rules of behavior, unions in reality govern as well as agitate. And the caricature of a business agent dragging off the job workers reluctant to strike is matched by instances of business agents exhorting exasperated workers to restrain their tempers and stay on the job.[13]

THE LANDRUM-GRIFFIN ACT AND UNION GOVERN-MENT   That union hierarchies exert an authority over the union member cannot be denied. For unions to perform the functions they do, that authority needs to exist. The problem is the control of its exercise to prevent abuses. Union leaders at times have retained their power by fraud and strong-arm methods. On occasion they have embezzled union funds. They have betrayed their membership by signing "sweetheart" contracts—for a price from the em-

[12] Thus, the United Mine Workers has levied fines against the treasuries of locals that engaged in unauthorized work stoppages. See R. A. Lester, *As Unions Mature* (Princeton: Princeton University Press, 1958), p. 32.

[13] The following items have been helpful in the above synthesis: Jack Barbash, *Labor Unions in Action* (New York: Harper, 1948) ; A. L. Gitlow, "Machine Politics in American Trade Unions," *Journal of Politics*, 14 (1952), 370–86; Herbert Harris, *Labor's Civil War* (New York: Knopf, 1940) ; Will Herberg, "Bureaucracy and Democracy in Labor Unions," *Antioch Review*, 2 (1943), 405–17; Philip Taft, *The Structure and Government of Labor Unions* (Cambridge: Harvard University Press, 1954) ; Lloyd Ulman, *The Rise of the National Trade Union* (Cambridge: Harvard University Press, 1955) ; Seymour Lipset, *et al., Union Democracy* (Glencoe: Free Press, 1956) ; William M. Leiserson, *American Trade Union Democracy* (New York: Columbia University Press, 1959) ; Joel Seidman, *et al., The Worker Views His Union* (Chicago: University of Chicago Press, 1958) ; S. Barkin, *The Decline of the Labor Movement* (Santa Barbara: Center for the Study of Democratic Institutions, 1961).

ployer; or they have used their power to call strikes as leverage for extortion from the employer. These and other abuses have prevailed, though not so generally as might be supposed from the newspapers.[14]

That a competitive internal politics necessarily assures rectitude, responsiveness, and fairness from a group hierarchy is doubtful.[15] Nevertheless, Congress has worked on the assumption that the ills of labor unions would be healed by a bit more democracy in their internal operation, a condition it attempted to bring about by the Landrum-Griffin Act of 1959. That act sought to assure certain "political" rights to union members, such as the right to vote in union elections, to nominate candidates, and to speak about the business of the union. (In some unions those who had backed opposition candidates had been expelled, sometimes for "conduct unbecoming a union member.") The act also required reports by unions of their financial transactions, including loans to officers and to business enterprises, a measure calculated to throw the light of publicity on shady financial practices. (Or to lay a groundwork for prosecution of those officials who fail to report such practices.) The statute also limited the power of national unions to assume control of locals. And it required that officers of nationals must be elected at least every five years by secret ballot and that officers of locals must be elected at least every three years. It remains to be seen whether the statute will lead to marked alterations in the internal politics of unions. The law does create ways of dealing with the thugs and thieves in the labor movement. It is, though, probable that union politics will continue to be in the main an oligarchical, one-party politics.[16]

UNION GOVERNMENT AND POLITICS   The political demands of the labor movement are developed through and expressed by this complex and cumbersome organizational apparatus. The tenuous unity of the elements of the machinery reflects the diversity of interests and outlook of the American industrial working class and suggests the difficulties in the mobilization of industrial labor for electoral activity. Labor organization has its peculiarities, yet it is also an example of a more general phenomenon. Pressure groups, whatever their composition, develop instruments for formulating their political views and for expressing them to public authority. In the process power tends to gravitate to the professional leadership of the group, and as organizational hierarchies acquire continuity a stable and orthodox group outlook comes to be established.

[14] See Senate Report No. 621, 86th Cong., 1st sess. (1960), and Senate Report No. 1417, 85th Cong., 1st sess. (1959), being reports by the McClellan committee on abuses within unions.

[15] See C. P. McGrath, "Democracy in Overalls: The Futile Quest for Union Democracy," *Industrial and Labor Relations Review*, 12 (1958–59), 503–25.

[16] See Philip Taft, "The Impact of Landrum-Griffin on Union Government," *Annals*, 333 (1961), 130–40.

Political Ideology of Labor

The circumstances conditioning the formation of American labor organization contributed to the creation of the peculiar political ideology of the American labor movement. That ideology rejected the socialist formula for improvement of the worker's lot by nationalization of industry and followed a line of *laissez faire* fundamentally like that of American business. Yet over the past half-century the ideology of labor, like that of most other sectors of society, has undergone modification.

TRADITIONAL DOCTRINE OF AFL   Over a long period the AFL insisted about as vociferously as business that the true doctrine was that of *laissez faire:* let the state leave labor alone; it would care for itself through organization, collective bargaining, and the strike. Government intervention was frowned upon, since it might deprive labor of its freedom to employ the economic weapons at its command. The Federation supplemented its strict *laissez-faire* policy when employers made effective use of the state to combat labor unions. In 1906 it proclaimed "Labor's Bill of Grievances," which demanded, among other things, the exemption of labor unions from the antitrust laws and a cessation of the use of the injunction in labor disputes. Even here the Federation did not seek the positive aid of the state; it merely desired that it be freed from state coercion so that it might fight out its battle with employers on more even terms.[17]

In other legislative demands the Federation sought only negative governmental assistance. Labor might ask that immigration be restricted, that Chinese be excluded, that convict labor not be used in competition with free men; but it wanted to be left free to determine the essential items of the labor contract—wages and hours—through bargaining with the employer. In situations in which collective bargaining was not a suitable method, the Federation asked for positive legislation for the benefit of certain classes of workers, such as government workers. It also urged legislation for the benefit of groups under some special handicap, such as women, children, and seamen.

A marked change in union political philosophy first appeared in the railroad brotherhoods, not affiliated with the AFL, and the railroad unions of the Federation. When the government undertook to regulate railroad rates and thereby to determine the income from which wages could be paid, it was inevitable that the railroad unions would need to exert their political strength to advance their cause. The strategic importance of railroads in the economy

[17] Gerald N. Grob, *Workers and Utopia* (Evanston: Northwestern University Press, 1961), ch. 8; Philip Taft, *The A.F. of L. in the Time of Gompers* (New York: Harper, 1957).

made railroad strikes matters which government could not consider as private disputes. The government had to take a hand in their prevention and settlement. Moreover, the strike was less effective in dealing with great railroad corporations than in negotiating with small employers. The hostility of the railroads after World War I made it difficult for labor even to maintain the right to organize without governmental assistance. Simple reliance on "economic power" was not enough for railroad employees. Their political strength and activity have been reflected in a long series of legislative acts, including the Railway Labor Act of 1926 which guaranteed to them the right to organize. Yet the railroad unions only modified rather than reversed the doctrine of *laissez faire*. They flirted with the idea of government ownership of the railroads but wound up with a government guarantee of the right to exist and to bargain.

Despite the railroad labor deviation, the AFL doctrine of *laissez faire* persisted beyond the day of its usefulness. Dogmas, philosophies, and ideas have a strength of their own. The comparative conservatism of the traditional AFL doctrine rested also on factors other than the strength of a tested doctrine of the past. The building trades, as Professor Taft has pointed out, long played a significant part in the formation of Federation policies. These unions, not faced by the necessity of coping with the power of giant concerns, "felt they had nothing to gain from government intervention in economic matters." [18] A deeper consideration may well be that during its history the American labor movement has had to resist attempts by single-taxers, anarchists, socialists, communists, and others to capture it. Sometimes results disastrous for labor came from such intrusions, and labor leaders adopted as protective coloration a fervent affirmation of the dominant ideologies of the society. Some observers attribute the coolness of the American labor movement toward socialism in part to the influence of the Roman Catholic clergy.[19]

MODIFICATION OF AFL DOCTRINE   After 1930 the AFL modified its traditional position in some respects but retained a hard core of its ancient doctrine. The extraordinary persistence of the doctrine of *laissez faire* appeared vividly in the hesitance of the Federation to endorse the principle of unemployment insurance. The 1930 convention voted down a proposal to do so, and in 1931 the executive council again recommended against unemployment insurance. The workers, the resolution stated, "are being asked by the promoters of compulsory unemployment insurance in the United States to yield up their birthright, to practically surrender in their struggle for liberty, by enactment of legislation deliberately calculated to give the employ-

[18] Philip Taft, "Labor's Changing Political Line," *Journal of Political Economy*, 45 (1937), 637–38.

[19] See Marc Karson, *American Labor Unions and Politics, 1900–1918* (Carbondale: Southern Illinois University Press, 1958).

ers increased control over the workers." In 1932 the Federation finally endorsed the principle of unemployment insurance.

While the AFL came to support other social welfare legislation also, it continued to assert a central interest in the maintenance of the widest practicable range of freedom to exert its economic powers through bargaining. Bargaining may raise wages, improve working conditions, and shorten hours, but workers are concerned about a great many other things. In time the AFL manifested a broader interest in the promotion by legislation of matters beyond the job focus. By 1939 William Green, president of the AFL, could say: "We now seek benefit for the workers and all our fellow men by the use of either direct economic strength or legislation as the situation demands. Neither alone can suffice." [20]

IMPACT OF THE CIO ON LABOR IDEOLOGY   The older political ideology of the AFL flowed logically from the doctrine of job unionism. At bottom the older political objectives concentrated on the establishment of the right of unions to exist, to bargain, to strike, and to promote the interests of organized workers by economic weapons. Once this framework of rights was established, the task of the union was to improve the condition of its members by its own strength here and now and not to venture forth on quixotic political crusades for the working classes generally or for ends with no immediate bearing on wages and working conditions.

Upon this hallowed doctrine the CIO had a powerful impact, yet the collision left intact at least the heart of the traditional faith. The maintenance of the basic right to exist for the industrial unions of the CIO required a far more benevolent government attitude toward organized labor. Giant corporations could not so readily be coerced by the strike and threat of strike as could the smaller employers with whom AFL unions had characteristically dealt. In a sense the CIO was a creature of the New Deal. Both the circumstances of its birth and the necessities in the formation of industrial unions gave its leadership a sharp awareness of the uses of its political allies.

In its concern with legislation of general interest to workers, the CIO introduced an intensity and range of activity alien to the AFL. The younger CIO leadership, liberally sprinkled with intellectuals, attempted far more to improve the status of the working classes generally by legislation than did the old-time leadership of the AFL. The CIO came, in fact, to be interested in about every major government policy: budgets, foreign trade, the level of domestic investment, the rate of interest—these and other matters affect the health of the economy and the CIO worried about all of them.

Over time the differences between the political doctrines of the AFL and CIO narrowed. The *laissez-faire* doctrine of reliance on bargaining strength

[20] William Green, *Labor and Democracy* (Princeton: Princeton University Press, 1939), p. 67.

eroded as it came to be recognized that the right to bargain itself might depend on government protection. Beyond this, both unions moved toward the view that the proper functions of a union extended to the promotion of legislation for benefits beyond matters of wages and working conditions. Yet, on the fundamental question of the character of the economic system, the dominant labor ideology did not challenge the established order. Neither CIO nor AFL questioned, as Selig Perlman put it, "the basic management mandate independent of government or labor." That is, the owner remains the boss, no matter how much he may be hedged about by agreements through bargaining. "It is this," continues Perlman, "which marks off the American labor movement from most other national movements; it is a labor movement upholding capitalism, not only in practice, but in principle as well." [21]

CHANGING SCOPE OF LABOR LOBBYING   Through time the scope of labor's lobbying activities has changed as has the political ideology of labor. Throughout its history it has manifested the keenest interest in proposals to restrict the use of the power of the state against labor and to protect the right of organized labor to exist. In an earlier day legislation to outlaw "yellow dog" contracts and to limit the issuance of injunctions in labor controversies received enthusiastic support. Great efforts went into the lobbying campaigns for the National Labor Relations Act and subsequently against the Taft-Hartley Act. Although legislative matters affecting the existence and mode of operation of labor organizations continue to receive highest priority, lobbying effort now also goes to the support of measures to improve the status of the worker by legal action. This broadening of interest occurred in the 1930's, with the CIO taking the lead and the AFL moving, slowly and reluctantly, in the same direction.

Individual internationals have their particular legislative axes to grind on job-connected proposals. The Bricklayers have an abiding interest in housing programs. The Miners are lukewarm toward hydroelectric power developments and favor conservation of oil and gas. The Watchmakers become more exercised about Swiss competition than do the railroad brotherhoods. The building trades support building codes that may promote both the public safety and employment for their members. The Teamsters favor restraints to hamstring railroads in their competition with trucks for freight.

Any national convention of labor expresses views on a wide range of matters: foreign policy, civil rights, education, the postal system, the condition of colonial aborigines—no problem is beyond the purview of organized labor. Yet the adoption of a resolution does not necessarily set the legislative committee to working on the question in the lobbies of Congress. Energies tend to be concentrated on those measures of most immediate concern. Old-

[21] "The Basic Philosophy of the American Labor Movement," *Annals of the Am. Acad. of Pol. and Soc. Sci.*, 274 (1951), 57–63.

time labor leaders mildly object to the expansion of the agenda of labor resolutions. The grand chief engineer of the Brotherhood of Locomotive Engineers observes that the rail unions have escaped some types of criticism because they have not tried "to tell everybody how to run the country from State Department policy on down."

Political Tactics of Organized Labor

Labor adapts its political strategy and tactics to its political ideology, which gives first priority to the maintenance of the right of labor to organize and to play a role in the determination of working conditions through collective bargaining. Improvement of the lot of the toiling masses generally through direct governmental action occupies a distinctly secondary place on labor's agenda. Given its doctrinal position, labor's political objectives are comparatively narrow and its political tactics are tailored accordingly. In short, organized labor does not seek responsibility for running the country. It wants to maintain the right to exist—and to keep others from using the government to push it around. The major shifts in tactics and the chief upsurges in political activity of organized labor have been either responses to threats to its right to exist or efforts to remove legal limitations on its operations.

REJECTION OF A LABOR PARTY   In the setting of the American two-party system and the American political tradition, the political strategy consonant with the limited political objectives of labor consists in working within the major parties and in lobbying for legislative action. Although a few old socialists dream of the day when trade unions will form a new political party, labor organizations themselves, with a few local exceptions, have stuck to their knitting and rejected the notion of a labor party. In the American Federation of Labor, Samuel Gompers firmly established the doctrine that it was inexpedient for labor to attempt to form an independent political party to seek control of the government. In 1906 he pointed out that to advance through a labor party would require waiting "until labor elects a majority of the legislature and a governor and then a President of the United States, who shall appoint the justices of the Supreme Court. I am afraid we are going to wait a long time! Trade unionists don't propose to wait so long to secure material improvement in their conditions." [22]

LABOR'S NONPARTISAN DOCTRINE   The principle that guides the AFL-CIO in its campaign efforts is the so-called nonpartisan doc-

[22] Samuel Gompers, *Labor and the Common Welfare* (New York: Dutton, 1919), p. 128.

trine. Under this principle not only does labor reject the idea of a labor party; it also rejects the alternative of affiliation with either major party and dedicates itself to rewarding its friends and punishing its enemies, whatever their party affiliation may be. The American Federation of Labor developed the nonpartisan doctrine under both the leadership of Samuel Gompers and the impact of experience. Gompers' favorite formulation of the policy was that labor should be partisan for principle and not for party. Partisanship for principle, of course, resolves itself into partisanship for candidates who concur with labor's principles, and Gompers asserted ". . . we must make manifest that we have political power and that we intend to use it." The CIO adopted the same doctrinal position.

The nonpartisan doctrine fits the political facts of life in congressional and state legislative campaigns. Labor has friends and enemies in both parties. The AFL-CIO Committee on Political Education can, on the basis of legislators' records, separate the sheep from the goats. Both its predecessor agencies, the CIO-PAC and the AFL-LLPE, prepared prior to each congressional campaign analyses of the voting records of Senators and Representatives on measures of interest to labor. These records form a part of the basis for endorsement by the union agencies responsible for political action.

In practice, the campaign efforts of organized labor are not uniformly distributed in support of all its friends or in opposition to all its enemies. Campaign resources are allocated according to the necessities of the moment. Intensive efforts may be made in support of outstanding friends who are faced by strong opposition. In some states or districts incumbent candidates are so firmly entrenched that support of friends is superfluous or opposition to enemies futile.

Application of the nonpartisan doctrine to presidential campaigns has been somewhat less straightforward than to legislative campaigns. The first endorsement of a presidential candidate by an AFL convention occurred in 1952 when Adlai Stevenson received the nod. Prior to that time the convention had been held after the presidential polling, and the labor view had been expressed by means less formal than convention endorsement. Samuel Gompers in association with other ranking labor leaders supported Bryan in 1908, Wilson in 1912 and 1916, Cox in 1920, and La Follette in 1924. The AFL avoided "official" endorsement of presidential candidates, although its president and other leaders might in their "personal" capacities endorse a candidate. In 1948, for example, most of the members of the AFL executive council, "in their private capacities," became members of the "AFL Committee for Truman." The CIO executive board in both 1948 and 1952 endorsed the Democratic presidential candidate. In 1956 the AFL-CIO general board endorsed Stevenson and Kefauver, although that move was opposed by a handful of labor leaders including Dave Beck of the Teamsters and Maurice Hutcheson of the Carpenters. In 1960 the AFL-CIO executive council supported Kennedy and Johnson. Those critics who deplore the descent of labor organization into the political mire make too much of the new practice of formal endorsement of presidential candidates. The situation was not ambiguous in the good old days. In 1916, Sam Gompers, in his "private" capacity, asserted: "If the men of labor have to depend upon what is promised by the Republican Party in this campaign, God save them. That is all."

The top leadership of organized labor as a whole has been on the Democratic side, although on occasion individual nationals and internationals have endorsed Republican presidential candidates, as the Teamsters did in 1960. Only a few Republican senatorial and congressional candidates win labor endorsements under the nonpartisan doctrine. Thus, in 1960 union financial support went to 194 Democratic House candidates but to only six Republican House candidates. Yet organized labor continues to assert, and to some degree to maintain, an independence of party. In the rhetoric of labor conventions warnings recur that the Democrats may not be sure of labor support unless they deliver. Nevertheless, given the alternatives offered to organized labor in recent decades, the nonpartisan policy makes of labor, as one of its leaders has remarked, "nonpartisan Democrats."

A few local deviations from the nonpartisan doctrine need to be noted. In some states and localities trade unions have played a role in the organization of labor parties. The principal surviving example, the Liberal party of New York, rests chiefly on the support of the Ladies Garment Workers, and continues to exist probably in part because it does not operate like a conventional party. It usually nominates as its candidates persons who are also the nominees of a major party, ordinarily but not invariably the Democratic. The vote for the Democratic candidate "on the Liberal line" of the voting machine may provide the margin for victory. New York's election laws, by permitting nominations by more than one party, create the legal conditions necessary for the maintenance of an unusual type of party. The marriage of convenience between labor and the Democratic party takes other forms in other places. In Michigan the Democratic party began to come out of the doldrums as labor organization grew and the Democratic organization was heavily infiltrated by labor leaders. In Minnesota trade-union leaders take their place in Democratic councils. The more common relation is one of informal collaboration as occasion requires and circumstances permit. Union officials are often recognized by a place on the national convention delegation. Around 200 unionists attended the 1952 Democratic convention as delegates or alternates.

EPISODES IN LABOR POLITICAL ACTIVITY   The nonpartisan doctrine is a standing principle of organized labor, but the magnitude of the efforts devoted to campaigns varies considerably from time to time. These variations find partial explanation in the primacy in labor's program of the maintenance of the right to organize—of freedom to exist and to operate as trade unions. Bursts of political activity and serious reconsiderations of the political role of labor have tended to occur when organized labor has been threatened. At times its right to exist has been under attack; at other times its freedom to operate has been challenged.

The extensive use of injunctions against labor unions and the application of the Sherman Antitrust Act to labor organizations helped to spur the AFL to political activity after the proclamation of its 1906 Bill of Grievances. The AFL formed its Labor Representation Committee to campaign for the election of friendly Senators and Representatives. Although by modern measures the campaign efforts were small in scale, the AFL conventions regularly heard reports of defeats and victories. The AFL claimed some credit for the 1910 Republican loss of the House of Representatives. Eventually, in 1914 the Clayton Act prohibited the issuance of injunctions by federal courts in labor disputes "unless necessary to prevent irreparable injury to property or to property right . . . , for which injury there is no adequate remedy at law." Labor leaders hailed the act as the "Magna Carta of Labor," though they had not reckoned that the courts would interpret it to change but little the status of the injunction in labor disputes.

In the years after World War I organized labor fought a losing political battle. The postwar reaction brought a determined effort to weaken, if not to destroy, labor organization. In the roaring twenties the injunction and all the other weapons in the employer armory were brought into play. The reaction went so far that in 1924 the AFL could find no reason to favor the presidential candidate of either major party and supported therefore the independent candidacy of Robert M. La Follette. Evidently the unhappy experiences of the 1920's left the AFL leadership shell-shocked. The political activities of labor seemed weak until the CIO initiated its energetic political program.

The National Labor Relations Act of 1935 guaranteed to employees the right "to form, join, or assist labor organizations, to bargain collectively through representatives of their own choosing, and to engage in concerted activities, for the purpose of collective bargaining or other mutual aid or protection." This legislation, with its promise of the use of the power of the state in defense of the right of unions to exist, was to provide a rallying point for labor political activities. In 1936, the Democratic Administration, under powerful attack from those who wished to repeal the act, found an ally in Labor's Nonpartisan League, a subsidiary of the CIO. The new industrial unions in a sense owed their creation to a friendly government, and they exerted themselves to keep it friendly.

In World War II labor lobbyists resisted, with varying success, legislative proposals to limit the operations of unions, all justified by their sponsors on the ground of the necessity of uninterrupted war production. In 1943, after the firmer legislative line toward labor stemming from the congressional elections of 1942 became apparent, the CIO formed its Political Action Committee, which campaigned zealously for the Democratic ticket in 1944. AFL political activity meanwhile continued less conspicuously and less energetically, but the congressional elections of 1946 set in motion forces that led to a much more determined effort to mobilize the political strength of organized labor. Republican triumph in the congressional elections of that year was so complete that the "friends of labor" were unable to muster enough votes to block the passage of the Taft-Hartley Act over the veto of President Truman. That act modified the Labor Relations Act of 1935, to the disadvantage of unions. Among some of its supporters, it was regarded as the first step toward the "complete elimination of governmental labor relations agencies" and the correction of "other errors of government initiated during the 1930's," such as the Social Security Act and the Fair Labor Standards Act.[23]

The threat to organized labor in the Taft-Hartley Act, as well as the fear of a general postwar reaction, stimulated labor political action. In 1947 the AFL created a political subsidiary, Labor's League for Political Education, to propagandize the labor viewpoint and to support candidates friendly to labor. It became an important source of finance for candidates supported by the AFL and collaborated informally with the CIO-PAC with which it was ultimately to be merged as COPE—the Committee on Political Education—of the united AFL-CIO. The threat, real or supposed, to organized labor in the Taft-Hartley Act gave common cause to the AFL and CIO and doubtless contributed to their eventual amalgamation.

As the debate on the Taft-Hartley Act wore on, the political alignment of organized labor became clearer. Truman's victory in 1948 on a pledge to repeal the Taft-Hartley Act may have put an end to the hope in some quarters that labor might be put in its place. Yet Truman was unable to fulfill his campaign promise. Nor did Eisenhower fulfill his commitment to bring about modifications in the act. As his first term unfolded labor leaders became more and more certain that they could not do business with a Republican Administration. They rallied to the Democratic cause in 1958, and Republican casualties in the congressional elections were numerous. The proposal of "right-to-work" laws in several states and Republican support of these measures stimulated zealous union efforts in the campaign.[24] Legislation enacted by the new Congress made labor leaders doubt that they had really won the election. Nevertheless, in 1960 most of them were to be found still in the Democratic ranks.

ORGANIZATION OF POLITICAL ACTION   Labor organization, since it evolved to meet other needs, is not designed to perform campaign

---

[23] Fred A. Hartley, Jr., *Our New National Labor Policy* (New York: Funk & Wagnalls, 1948).

[24] See, for example, John H. Fenton, "The Right-To-Work Vote in Ohio," *Midwest Journal of Political Science*, 3 (1959), 241–53.

functions effectively. The confederate character of labor organization leaves autonomy to individual national and international unions, and almost invariably a few national presidents are conspicuous exceptions to the general Democratic orientation of labor leadership. In its 1952 resolution of endorsement of Stevenson the AFL convention emphasized "that the affiliated unions . . . and each and every one of their members are free to make their own individual political decisions without any compulsion on our part." Conspicuous in the exercise of this autonomy have been a few national leaders of the building trades. In the lower reaches of the labor hierarchy Republican deviation is more frequent, and Republican candidates can ordinarily round up a committee of union officials to endorse them, although commonly its members will be less prominent in the labor movement than those aligned with the Democrats.

Apart from the confusion induced by division among its top leaders, union organization can only most awkwardly be used to mobilize workers as voters. The accidents of history that vetoed attempts to organize all workers —skilled and unskilled whatever their craft or industrial pursuit—of particular geographical areas into single unions assured for labor a low political organizational potential. Workers are grouped into unions formed along craft, shop, plant, or industry lines, a structure ideal for bargaining with employers. Such an organization cannot readily be focused on union members in precincts, districts, or other geographical areas for the purpose of agitation and stimulation of voting. To this administrative difficulty must be added the fact that different unions have different traditions of political action.[25] Some are more militantly led than others. Some have a more direct concern with the outcome of a particular election than others. Even without such variations the coordination of the campaign efforts of different unions with members in a particular locality is a taxing operation. When it is attempted, confusion and conflict are not uncommon. Nor did the unification of the top levels of labor in the AFL-CIO alter this problem of organizing at the precinct level. The mechanisms for the communication of the advice of top leaders to the rank and file are imperfect.[26]

EFFECTIVENESS OF MOBILIZATION OF LABOR VOTE

What of the effectiveness of labor organizations in the political mobilization of their members? In presidential politics for several decades union members

[25] The content of union periodicals may be a rough index of this variation. In the first eight months of 1960, 43 per cent of the content of *UAW Solidarity* was "political"; only 3 per cent of the content of the *American Photoengraver* was so classified. See F. R. Shedd and G. S. Odiorne, *Political Content of Labor Union Periodicals* (Ann Arbor: University of Michigan, Bureau of Industrial Relations, 1960).

[26] In May, 1952, 70 per cent of a national sample of union members told Elmo Roper's interviewers that they had never received any literature from the union about candidates nor had any one from the union called at their home to talk about candidates.

have leaned Democratic. The proportion of union members supporting the Democratic ticket has changed from time to time. From slightly over 80 per cent in 1936, it declined to around 60 per cent in 1952.[27] These gross figures, of course, conceal other variations. On the average, members of the CIO unions have voted Democratic in higher degree than have persons affiliated with AFL unions. The solidarity of the labor vote doubtless also varies widely from union to union and from place to place.

What labor organizations have had to do with the Democratic orientation of unionists presents another question. The influence of organization is not solely an influence of its leadership. Group pressures of all sorts commonly bring a person's political orientation into conformity with that of his associates. Union members, for example, usually vote Democratic in higher degree than do otherwise similar but unorganized workers. That difference may be caused by factors other than organization, but it has been established that those individuals most active in unions—by attendance at meetings and by participation in other union activities—are more likely to be Democratic than are the less active members of the same union.[28] In other words, men who spend time around the union hall are apt to be indoctrinated with the politics of the activists in the union.

Whether a labor vote exists that can be delivered by labor leaders is in a way a nonsense question. The influence of labor leaders over their members probably differs enormously with time and circumstance and in each instance is so intermingled with other influences as to be beyond measurement. Given the traditional partisan attachments of workers, the labor leadership could not shift many votes from a popular Democratic President to a Republican candidate.[29] The factors making for labor voting solidarity—the exertions of labor leadership and other factors as well—may be of most effect when questions of concern to workers as workers are salient. In 1948, with memories of the Taft-Hartley Act fresh and with anxieties about a possible economic let down, labor leadership probably had far greater influence than it did in 1952 when nonlabor questions were to the fore. In other instances the contribution of labor organization to the outcome may consist more in getting voters to the polls than in influencing the direction of the vote. Probably the influence of labor leadership can be most marked in direct primaries that involve contestants relatively unknown to the electorate.

Union members, like the rest of us, manage to get along with a multi-

[27] Dr. Gallup's estimates of the Democratic percentage of the presidential vote in union households were: 1952, 61 per cent; 1956, 57 per cent; 1960, 65 per cent.

[28] Bernard Berelson, *et al.*, *Voting* (Chicago: University of Chicago Press, 1954), p. 49; Harold I. Wilensky, "The Labor Vote: A Local Union's Impact on the Political Conduct of Its Members," *Social Forces*, 35 (1956), 111–20.

[29] In 1940 John L. Lewis endorsed Willkie. Irving Bernstein found no evidence that the action moved many workers into the Republican ranks; see his "John L. Lewis and the Voting Behavior of the C.I.O.," *Public Opinion Quarterly*, 5 (1941), 233–49.

plicity of loyalties which assume changing priorities in the monitoring of our behavior. Membership in a union does not mean that a person is invariably governed in voting by his interest as a union member. Moreover, labor leaders compete with others for the vote of union members. Substantial numbers of union members regard politics as outside the proper sphere of union activity, and larger numbers prefer to be informed of candidates' views of concern to the union rather than to be told how to vote. Yet the influence of labor organization should not be dismissed as of no import because labor endorsed candidates do not invariably win. Organization doubtless re-enforces the loyalties of the hard core of labor votes. At times labor leaders manage to get to the polls a larger vote than would be cast without their efforts. And on occasion their exertions may account for victory.[30]

Private Bureaucracy and Political Inertia

The earlier discussion of the specific problems of agriculture led to the consideration of a much broader question: the process by which deprivations and dislocations of many sorts and many origins set off movements in demand of redress, adjustment, or even overthrow of the old order. In this chapter a similar sequence prevails. Organized labor has occupied the center of the stage, but its analysis points to a political phenomenon in which many sorts of organizations share: namely, the role of organized groups in the maintenance of stability or the status quo. This resistance to disruption of the ordered course of things is thus the antithesis of the general pattern of behavior touched on in the preceding chapter.

The stabilizing role of the private group may readily be perceived if it is recognized that private organizations and groups, as well as officials, govern. At least this is so if to govern is to set norms of behavior—what may not be done, what may be done, and how it shall be done—and to penalize deviations from those standards. That groups perform these functions is a commonplace of social science. The informal group, though it may lack officers, constitution, or other badges of being, may evolve its own etiquette

[30] The following titles are useful on union political action: Alfred Braunthal, "American Labor in Politics," *Social Research*, 12 (1945), 1–21; Fay Caulkins, *The CIO and the Democratic Party* (Chicago: University of Chicago Press, 1952); Morton Leeds, "The AFL in the 1948 Elections," *Social Research*, 17 (1950), 207–18; Avery Leiserson, "Organized Labor as a Pressure Group," *Annals*, 274 (1951), 108–17; Arnold M. Rose, *Union Solidarity* (Minneapolis: University of Minnesota Press, 1952); H. Rosen and R. A. H. Rosen, *The Union Member Speaks* (New York: Prentice-Hall, 1955); Joel Seidman, "Organized Labor in Political Campaigns," *Public Opinion Quarterly*, 3 (1939), 536–654; Arthur Kornhauser, *et al.*, *When Labor Votes* (New York: University Books, 1956); Nicholas A. Masters, "The Organized Labor Bureaucracy as a Basis of Support for the Democratic Party," *Law and Contemporary Problems*, 27 (1962), 252–65.

of action and its own set of values and may possess means for their enforcement—means ranging from a mere frown to ostracism.

As private groups become crystallized into formal organizations their function of governance becomes more visible. The constitutions, governing machinery, and codes of fair competition of trade associations bear many of the earmarks of the apparatus of the state, and in the nebulous areas around the fringes of the antitrust laws they exercise powers like those of the state.[31] Professional associations with their codes of ethics and their committees on professional conduct bear a close resemblance to the law-giver and the police court. Churches command the obedience of their communicants and hold over their heads the threat of everlasting punishment. Labor unions have their codes and their means for penalizing action unbecoming a union member. Corporations, a special sort of group, have their structures of authority over hundreds of thousands of workers; their power may extend to vast resources, and its exercise may have wide ramifications within the economy.

Such functions of governance, it may be said, are "nonpolitical." Even so, they are certainly politically relevant. Moreover, the governing function of private groups shades over almost imperceptibly into realms undeniably political or governmental. Groups often strive to control the exercise of public power or to obtain delegations of public authority. Notable instances occur among professional and semiprofessional associations which often obtain, in form or in fact, the authority to set standards for entry to the profession and to fix rules for the conduct of its practitioners. This tendency has brought the suggestion that the medieval guild is, to a degree at least, re-asserting itself.[32] In effect, the action of the private association becomes sanctioned by state authority. Or an underworld syndicate may obtain, through arrangements with the police, the power to "license" slot machines and to see that those operators not meeting its requirements are raided. Private groups not only set norms of conduct; they perform "service" functions similar to those of the state. Labor unions have their own welfare or social security systems, and corporations tax their stockholders for the support of charities in favor with the corporate management.

Quite apart from the formal governmental structure, if our contention is correct, the social system is bound together by an intricate network of governing relationships developed in the life of private groups. The broad

---

[31] Consider the system of promulgation of uniform rates by associations of insurance companies prior to the case of the *South-Eastern Underwriters*. Adherence to privately fixed rates was induced by refusal to re-insure the risks of nonmember companies, severance of relations with agents writing insurance for nonmember companies, and exclusion from the privileges of membership, which were real, of those concerns not in compliance with the association's rules. See "The Regulation of Insurance Rates," *Columbia Law Review*, 47 (1947), 1314–32.

[32] See J. A. C. Grant, "The Guild Returns to America," *Journal of Politics*, 4 (1942), 303–35, 458–77; Francis P. DeLancey, *The Licensing of Professions in West Virginia* (Chicago: Foundation Press, 1938).

political significance of this system—if, indeed, it may be called a system—seems plain enough. The system—the established way of doing things—constitutes a powerful brake on political change. Those who agitate for a new order invariably encounter the resistance of the old order which exists, in considerable degree at least, in the revered values more or less firmly anchored in group life. These patterns of behavior, traditional modes of action, group norms, or social equilibria—the concept employed in their description may not matter—possess a powerful capacity for their own perpetuation and resist movements that would disturb them.

The role of the group in the creation and maintenance of norms—and the direct political significance of it all—may be made more explicit. Doctrines or norms of special durability seem to be those propagated and perpetuated by group processes. The AFL, as has been noted, became devoted to a *laissez-faire* doctrine, and the strength of its adherence to that doctrine provoked grave debate on whether to endorse unemployment insurance even when millions of workers were jobless. It seems clear that group leadership and group processes function both to create group norms and to induce conformity. Group program and group policy do not emerge in finished form from a womb of determinism. Thus, the long persistence of the strength of the high-tariff policy in the American business community came in part from processes that generated a "public opinion" within business groups and even induced many elements of business to acquiesce in policies clearly to their immediate disadvantage. Or, the leadership of the American Medical Association manufactured a policy on health insurance and made it extremely bad form for a physician to dissent from the official line. The group defines norms, establishes patterns of behavior, and tends to exert its powers for their maintenance, often beyond their usefulness. Political movements that would alter the prevailing relationships must overcome the resistance of orthodox doctrines embedded in the working habits of group life.[33]

A significant element in the stabilizing and braking function of private associations may be their hierarchical leadership which tends to be renewed by co-option. The self-perpetuation of the collective leadership of private associations was illustrated by the persistence in power of the oligarchies of labor organizations, yet the patterns of succession to leadership in other private organizations are not conspicuously dissimilar. The nature of the renewal of the personnel of hierarchies probably contributes to the stability

---

[33] These are not, to be sure, the only factors that make the way of the innovator hard. Some time ago Machiavelli observed: "And it ought to be remembered that there is nothing more difficult to take in hand, more perilous to conduct, or more uncertain in its success, than to take the lead in the introduction of a new order of things. Because the innovator has for enemies all those who have done well under the old conditions, and lukewarm defenders in those who may do well under the new. This coolness arises partly from fear of the opponents, who have the laws on their side, and partly from the incredulity of men, who do not readily believe in new things until they have had a long experience in them." *The Prince*, ch. 6.

of group doctrine. When advancement depends on the decision of those already in the charmed circle, a premium is likely to be placed on conformity and orthodoxy. The "elder statesmen" with ideas of another day hold onto their power and make life difficult for the "young Turks." The prevailing attitudes tend to be perpetuated. Hierarchies have an immortality of sorts; one man may be replaced but the organization goes on forever. Thus in armies, navies, labor organizations, civil services, universities, corporations, trade associations, and all sorts of private groups, co-option to the top often helps perpetuate the group orthodoxy.[34] And the doctrines and views of the leadership, whose existence is required by the necessities of group life, may become removed from the sentiments of the rank and file. Internal conflict that results in a turnover in private group leadership may have significance for the politics of the state as a whole.

[34] Over the long run the increased collectivization of human activity (whether under corporate, voluntary association or government auspices) may create inflexibility in the social system in that larger and larger proportions of human decision fall within the purview of fewer and fewer hierarchies, each characterized by the inflexibilities induced by the gyroscopic effect of co-option. Offsetting tendencies occur, to be sure, in the conscious recognition of the need for external inspection and criticism, as in management surveys, and in attempts to institutionalize innovation, as in industrial research.

4.

BUSINESS

BUSINESSMEN are a heterogeneous lot. The president of a life insurance company seeks safety in investment. The wildcat operator bets his fortune that oil will flow from a hole in the ground. Both are businessmen. The corporate bureaucrat, managing a railroad organization encrusted with traditional practices, and the management expert, guiding an automobile manufacturing company animated by an innovative spirit, are both businessmen. The steel magnate who espouses the inflexible views typical of heavy industry and the clothing maker who has anxieties about the disposable income of consumers call themselves businessmen. The barbershop proprietor, the manager of far-flung chain-store enterprises, the corner grocer, the broker, the gadget maker, the shoe manufacturer, the undertaker, the tulip bulb importer—all these and many others are "businessmen."

The variety of interests suggested by this enumeration might mean that discussion of "the businessman" in the political process would be a bootless undertaking. Perhaps one might better treat particular classes or types of businessmen, for their interests are diverse and sometimes in conflict. Easy generalizations that businessmen believe this or that conceal a more complex reality in which variation in opinion prevails among different groups.[1] Nevertheless, a network of common interest pulls the business community together on major issues when its security is threatened. Party lines, sectional lines, and religious lines rarely divide businessmen when their common interests

---

[1] On occasion diversity of interests within a single corporation may either neutralize it or make the determination of its policy on a particular issue difficult. See L. A. Dexter, "Where the Elephant Fears to Dance Among the Chickens: Business in Politics? The Case of du Pont," *Human Organization*, 19 (1960–61), 188–94.

72

are in peril. Within the business community powerful factors operate to bring conformity. Unanimity is rare, but a predominant business sentiment usually crystallizes and makes itself heard on major issues affecting the group as a whole.

With the decline in the importance of agriculture, the preponderance of American wealth came to be controlled by businessmen. The power of wealth in politics is an age-old phenomenon. The holders of wealth, whatever its form, have great stakes in the outcome of the political struggle; they also have time to devote to political maneuver or money to employ others to do so. The power wielded by business in American politics may puzzle the person of democratic predilections: a small minority exercises enormous power. Agriculture, a waning sector of the economy, occasionally fights a rear-guard action against business. Labor assaults the business citadel from time to time with varying degrees of success. Yet, withal, business retains a position of potency in public affairs.[2]

Rise of Industry and Trade: Dynamics of Political Disequilibrium

In a static society the process of politics—of governing—is likely to be dull and uneventful. Since a major function of politics is the mediation of relations among groups of people, so long as there is no material change in the size, character, or aspirations of the major interests in a society the political pot remains at a low temperature. When the nature of relations among groups changes significantly, adjustments in political arrangements occur. The old rules of the game no longer serve. Maladjustments generate demands for new laws and new policies appropriate to the new circumstances. Individual acts of government—legislation, administrative actions, judicial decisions—constitute episodes in the continuing quest for an equilibrium among interests in society.

BUSINESS: GENERATOR OF IMBALANCE AND READJUSTMENT   While the sources of disturbance of the old order are legion, business has been prolific in producing disruptions of established group relationships. Paradoxically businessmen belligerently proclaim their conservatism yet consistently act as dedicated radicals. It was they—not the orators of the soapbox—who set in motion the forces that overturned the hallowed ways of our tranquil past. When the spirit of innovation roams the land, politicians must busy themselves in the adjustment of the institutions and laws to the new order. In America the great innovator has been the businessman; the

[2] For a brief historical survey, see T. C. Cochran, *The American Business System, 1900–1955* (Cambridge: Harvard University Press, 1957).

secondary consequences of his actions fatten the statute books and lengthen the administrative codes.

The obvious impact on the political order of technological innovation scarcely needs to be spelled out. The effects of each of many technological developments in communication, transportation, and manufacture eventually permeated the entire society and were followed, as the night the day, by the contrivance of regulatory standards, procedures, and instruments. Apart from such consequences of technological change, two other major developments associated with business merit special attention. The rapid growth of business changed the relationships between business and other social groups and raised ultimately the question of who should rule. In addition to the growth of business, radical changes in the internal nature of business occurred. Changes in the scale of business operation, in the nature of business rivalry, and in the structure of power within business drastically disturbed pre-existing relations between business and employees, business and customers, business and investors, and among different categories of businessmen. And these disturbances stimulated demands for redress, as well as the ingenuity of statesmen in the search for solutions.

BUSINESS EXPANSION IN THE NATIONAL ECONOMY

In a gross sense the roots of the remaking of the political order may be traced to the growth of the place of business in the national economy. From the beginning the power of business has been considerable. Yet business did not attain its full flowering until after the Civil War. The southern planter aristocracy, built on a foundation of slave labor and the cotton gin, was to hold sway until put to rout by the alliance of northeastern business and northwestern free agriculture in the Civil War, the outcome of which Miriam Beard calls "the victory of American business over plantocracy." [3]

After the Civil War the trend toward a more highly industrialized society continued unabated; and with it came, not without friction, a marked shift in the balance of political power. In 1870 slightly over one-half of the gainfully employed were engaged in agriculture, fishing, and forestry, and far fewer in manufacturing. The ratios gradually shifted, and by 1960 less than one-tenth of the civilian labor force found employment in agriculture.

The rapid growth of business, in comparison with other sectors of the economy, produced political changes both large and small. Eventually it raised the question whether business, instead of agriculture, was to govern the country. That question, a common interpretation holds, was settled by the election of 1896, which marked the triumph of business over the last great attempt of agriculture to assert its vanished sovereignty. Once the location

[3] *A History of the Business Man* (New York: Macmillan, 1938), ch. 24.

of decisive power became unequivocally clear, government dedicated itself to the execution of the agenda of business.[4]

ORGANIZATIONAL INNOVATION   Apart from the expansion of business, which alone sufficed to compel governmental preoccupation with the problems of business, American businessmen have proved to be great innovators in the organization of economic activity. They made it both feasible and profitable to conduct business enterprises of unprecedented hugeness. In the construction of giant concerns and in the contrivance of working relations among them business acquired a degree of independence from the invisible hand of Adam Smith. As business groups gained a power not sensitively subject to control by competitive forces, the traditional relations among groups of people were rudely disturbed. Large plants, at times virtually monopolizing the demand side of particular labor markets, altered the relations of employers and workers. Firms or combinations of firms capable of driving an isolated competitor to the wall brought new relations among businessmen in individual lines. Associations of firms able to dominate the market for a raw material put suppliers at a disadvantage. Suppliers who organized the market to dominate many small customers upset other relations. From these and other innovations in business organization sprang the political pyrotechnics that burst around "big business" for decades.

The organizational revolution in American industry began in a movement of corporate merger and consolidation around the 1880's. The process of consolidation moved with special rapidity from 1897 to 1903 and from 1925 to 1929. The earlier period saw the emergence of such noted corporate names as United States Steel, International Silver, United Shoe Machinery, American Can, Eastman Kodak, International Nickel, and International Harvester. Often the formation of such concerns had been preceded by a bitter competitive struggle which eventuated in a merger to establish "order" in an industry rent by price wars.

The degree to which the movement toward concentration of control within industry has proceeded is warmly disputed by the experts on these matters, and the measurement of the extent of concentration represents no mean technical problem. According to one estimate, by 1933 the 200 largest nonfinancial corporations controlled "approximately 19 to 21 per cent of the national wealth." In 1950, according to an estimate by the Federal Trade Commission, the 200 largest manufacturing companies accounted for 40.3

[4] The extraordinary growth of the American economy has probably had other consequences of profound significance for the polity. An expanding economy creates new pelf, new places of power, new outlets for ambition in contrast with a stagnant economy in which a limited number of places of prestige are refilled as the old retire. Had the energies devoted to economic development been dedicated to squabbles over the division of fixed resources, the United States would have had a most turbulent politics.

per cent of the total value of product of all manufacturing industries. Whatever the exact extent of concentration may be, there can be no doubt that the organizational revolution has brought a radically new business structure. Instead of the atomized economy of many firms revered by the classical economists, an "organizational economy" has come to prevail.[5] In this new economy the great corporation becomes in a sense something of a government in itself.[6] The giant concern gains power over its suppliers and its customers, not necessarily by the attainment of a monopoly position, but at times by its size alone. Groups of corporations may act in concert through habit and the dictates of a strategy of survival rather than by old-fashioned conspiracies in restraint of trade. In short, managerial inventiveness created an economic organization the nature of which is both complex and disputed by the specialists.[7] Yet the political consequences of the new business organization are plain enough. The erection within the social system of new points of economic power drastically altered the relationships among many categories of persons and brought new and continuing political problems.[8]

Business Regulation: Intergroup Mediation

The upthrust of new types of business and of new business organizations radically altered the relations between groups within the nation. The old legal principles no longer governed these relations to the satisfaction of all concerned. The political system was called upon to mediate among social groups to maintain both the peace and a rough equity in the relations of men. While there developed numerous new types of group relations with their associated problems, several patterns arose with special frequency. The growth of large enterprises created new frictions commonly described as between big business and the public; on closer inspection, they often turned out to be frictions between two sorts of businesses, as railroads and shippers. Persistent

[5] The phrase is Calvin B. Hoover's. See his "Institutional and Theoretical Implications of Economic Change," *American Economic Review*, 44 (1954), 1–14.

[6] See Adolph Berle, Jr., *The 20th Century Capitalist Revolution* (New York: Harcourt, Brace, 1954).

[7] The literature is voluminous. Samples include Walter Adams (ed.), *The Structure of American Industry*, 3d ed. (New York: Macmillan, 1961); D. E. Lilienthal, *Big Business: A New Era* (New York: Harper, 1953); T. K. Quinn, *Giant Business: Threat to Democracy* (New York: Exposition Press, 1953); Edward S. Mason, *Economic Concentration and the Monopoly Problem* (Cambridge: Harvard University Press, 1957); Edward S. Mason (ed.), *The Corporation in Modern Society* (Cambridge: Harvard University Press, 1959).

[8] The creation of great corporations also displaced many economically independent middle-class persons, once regarded as the backbone of democracy, and substituted middle-level corporate bureaucrats, a group with less concern about politics. Andrew Hacker argues that this removes from politics a class of people who had earlier been "prime participants" and thereby weakens the democratic process. See his *Politics and the Corporation* (New York: Fund for the Republic, 1958).

maladjustments arose in the relations of employers and workers, which set off a continuing debate over the principles that should guide those relations. Among different types of business, conflicts developed that led to demands for governmental intervention by one or the other of the contending groups.

In the broad variety of governmental actions bearing on business—and the affairs of business pre-empt an impressive proportion of the pages of the legal codes—no discernible thread of doctrinal consistency exists, save perhaps that business seeks to maintain the maximum freedom of action. Business, not unlike labor, likes to be left alone except when it needs government help. In some instances the business objective requires insistence on an unmixed doctrine of *laissez faire.* In others business demands the strictest governmental regulation of business—often, but not always, the other fellow's business. In a third type of situation the cause may be best promoted by government subsidy or aid. Under other circumstances, business may welcome regulation that mitigates the hazards of competition. Despite the extraordinary diversity of their political actions, business spokesmen expound more or less uniformly a philosophy of *laissez faire:* free competition, free enterprise, and the "American way." But this is an orthodoxy of ritual rather than of practice. In their actions businessmen pragmatically advocate state intervention today and nonintervention tomorrow. To catalog all the actions of government that mix into business and all the projections of business into government would require an encyclopaedia. A few categories of public policy will illustrate the broad theme that business regulation involves in considerable degree the mediation of intergroup cleavages created by the rise of industrialism.

RESISTANCE TO LABOR LEGISLATION   For a half-century or more a central concern of organized business has been legislative proposals calculated to improve the lot of labor. These proposals—originating in the main from organized labor—have been a prime factor in bringing business competitors together in organizations for common defense. Most of the major types of labor legislation have been, at least in their earlier stages, opposed with vigor by most business organizations. And the political role of business in this field has been in the main to delay rather than to prevent action. Once it loses the battle, business gradually learns to live with the new order.[9]

In its opposition to public intervention in the relations between employer and worker, organized business had the tactical advantage of being the defender of the orthodox political and economic doctrines. Doctrines of individual rights over property, individual freedom, and individual responsibility pervaded the laws. New laws violated the ancient truths, or so it was argued. A workman's compensation act, for example, would make an employer finan-

---

[9] See R. E. Lane, *The Regulation of Businessmen* (New Haven: Yale University Press, 1954).

cially responsible for injuries suffered by a worker through his own obtuse carelessness around obviously dangerous machinery. A ten-hour law would deprive both workers and employers of their freedom to fix by contract a longer workday. Unions indulged in practices that would limit the liberties of both worker and employer.

The wall of business resistance was first breached in situations in which strong humanitarian appeals could be brought to bear. Legislation to compel the elimination of hazardous conditions in factories came early as did industrial accident compensation laws. Laws limiting the hours of work of children preceded acts to prohibit child labor. On these and other related topics states enacted considerable legislation, but it was not until the Great Depression that advocates of labor legislation made spectacular headway. The 1929 crash and its aftermath drove business for a time from its dominant position, and new legislation radically altering the relations of business and labor was enacted. Of all this legislation, that guaranteeing to labor the right to organize and imposing on business an obligation to bargain most significantly altered the structure of the social system. After the revision of this legislation by the Taft-Hartley Act of 1947, organized business and organized labor maintained a stalemate, each capable of preventing the other from bringing about major changes in the statute. Yet there should also be mentioned laws fixing maximum hours and minimum wages, establishing systems of unemployment insurance, and a variety of other measures, all made politically possible by the depression and constitutionally legitimate by the new reading of the Constitution by the Supreme Court in the shadow of crisis.

POLICY ON MONOPOLY AND COMPETITION   The development of giant business organizations in a setting of economic individualism has made salient in American politics issues of monopoly and competition. Often the advocates of the application of public restraints against big business have been smaller businesses injured by the competitive tactics of the giants. The task of politics has been to achieve some more or less just balance between such groups. The consuming public, though never well organized, may also be regarded, at least symbolically, as a party to the political disputes involving the place of business within the economy.

The orthodox public policy on monopoly and competition is clear enough. The Sherman Antitrust Act of 1890 declared illegal contracts, combinations, and conspiracies in restraint of trade among the states. The Federal Trade Commission Act of 1914 made unfair methods of competition in interstate commerce unlawful. On the whole, business proclaims the soundness of the principles of free, competitive enterprise, yet at almost every session one business group or another implores Congress to grant exceptions to the general proscription of combination. These prayers have brought results in numerous instances, and the politics of administration of antitrust legislation also produces variations in the impact of the law.

One class of exemption from antitrust policy is sought fundamentally to legalize arrangements to minimize competition among producers. A striking instance occurred in the congressional debates from 1948 to 1950 over the question of policy toward basing-point pricing. Actions by the Federal Trade Commission, upheld by the Supreme Court after long litigation, had brought collusion in pricing through the use of the basing-point system within the prohibitions of the Clayton Act. The application of this principle to the cement industry stirred uneasiness in other industries with basing-point systems. (When used for collusive price fixing, the system involved the publication of prices at basing points, which were usually producing points, and an understanding among producers that the price at any consuming point would be the nearest basing-point price plus freight to that point. A contractor would have to pay exactly the same amount for a barrel of cement whether he bought it from the plant across the street or from one 200 miles away.) A great hue and cry followed from business groups that the law was uncertain, that it had become illegal to compete through the absorption of freight, that the bureaucracy was persecuting business. In fact, the law was a bit too certain. Nothing in the decisions prohibited the absorption of freight, in the absence of collusion to fix prices, and if bureaucracy was persecuting business it was doing so in the fulfillment of its sworn duty. Although the proponents of the exemption bill pushed it through Congress, the President vetoed it.[10]

In another category are modifications of antitrust policy designed to limit the exercise by large enterprises of their competitive advantage over lesser businesses. Important in this type of legislation are acts designed to maintain established channels of distribution, that is, to protect wholesalers and retailers against new and stronger competitors. Illustrative is the Tydings-Miller Act of 1937, an act adopted at the behest of retailers, principally druggists, to exempt certain price-fixing arrangements from the prohibitions of the Sherman Act. Associations of druggists had long sought to limit competition by department stores and other price-cutting outlets and had boycotted manufacturers whose products were available to retail price cutters. The druggists hit upon the idea of the state fair-trade law which permitted manufacturers to contract with retailers to fix retail prices on their products; that is, it was not only "unfair" but could be made illegal for the chain druggist or the department store to sell Pond's Cold Cream at a lesser price than the neighborhood drug store.

These state fair-trade laws were held illegal as applied to goods sold in

[10] For an account of the basing-point controversy, see Earl Latham, *The Group Basis of Politics* (Ithaca: Cornell University Press, 1952).

interstate commerce, and the National Association of Retail Druggists took the lead in pressuring Congress to grant an exception to the antitrust laws. Department stores, mail-order houses, and cut-rate retailers generally were unable to amass sufficient strength to defeat the druggists and allied retailers before Congress. In due course though, state fair-trade laws were held void or fell of their own weight before the competitive strength and ingenuity of discount houses and other new style distributors. Yet at almost every session of Congress some group of retailers hopefully advocates new legislative action to limit their competitors. The objective turned up in 1962 in the guise of a "quality stabilization" bill; the contention was that the bargaining power of giant distributors compelled manufacturers to reduce quality as they were squeezed on prices.

Another instance of legislation concerned with competition in distribution is the Robinson-Patman Act, which arose from the competitive pressures placed on wholesaling by chain stores and other mass distributors who could bypass the traditional distributive channels. By dealing directly with the manufacturer the mass distributors not only diverted business from wholesalers; they also obtained price concessions that put their retail competitors at a disadvantage, a factor not unconnected with the independent retailer support for the bill. Counsel of the United States Wholesale Grocers' Association drafted the original bill, but the propaganda presented the measure, not as a wholesalers' measure, but as a boon to the small, independent retailer, an individual high in the affections of the American politician. The legislation as enacted recognized the justice of differentials in prices by manufacturers to different types of customers but also sought to prevent mass distributors from abuse of their power of bargaining with manufacturers.[11]

All these are merely episodes in the continuing process of mediating between bigness and those groups affected or threatened by it. The conflicts arise on many fronts and in many forms. Nor is the problem solely, or even primarily, a legislative problem, for questions of competition and monopoly are fought out before the administrative tribunals and the courts in the general policy framework fixed by whatever Administration is in power.

REGULATION BY LICENSE   Another field of government regulation may be conveniently defined by its administrative technique. In several important areas of the economy enterprises operate under license, permit, or a certificate of public convenience and necessity granted by state or federal authority. Commonly specified conditions must be met to obtain and retain the right to do business. As the new technology developed some types of enterprise turned out to be, or at least were thought to be, natural monopolies. The protection of consumers from monopoly power was sought by conditional

[11] For an analysis of legislation on distribution, see Joseph C. Palamountain, Jr., *The Politics of Distribution* (Cambridge: Harvard University Press, 1955).

licenses—for example, a municipal franchise to a gas company might fix rates and other conditions of service.

Special types of political behavior seem to be associated with regulation by license. Genetically the animus of this sort of legislation is to control monopoly, but it may also create monopoly or semimonopolistic rights. Business groups may become vocal defenders of some aspects of the regulation to which they are subjected; they favor the obstacles to new entrants to the field inherent in the regulatory process. In a sense, regulation tends to breed pressure groups. All those subject to a regulatory law share a concern about the substance of the law and the manner of its administration, and they organize to articulate that common interest. Moreover, rivalry between different groups of businesses operating under different regulatory statues often takes a political form in that each jealously watches the range of action permitted to the other.

The enterprises that operate under license issued in one form or another by federal, state, or local governments are mainly public utilities. They include most types of transportation—railroads, buses, truck lines, and air transport. Important energy sources are on the list: producers and distributors of electric power, gas distributors, interstate gas transmission lines, and hydroelectric generators operating under license from the Federal Power Commission. Financial institutions such as banks, insurance companies, savings and loan associations, and credit unions exist under the state or federal charter. Communications concerns—telephone, radio, television, and telegraph —operate under public permit which carries with it both privileges and responsibilities. Systems of proration in the production of petroleum have a kinship to regulation by license. State control of race-track gambling is usually exercised through licensing.

The patterns of business politics induced by the licensing technique differ somewhat with the type of industry concerned and with the stage of development of the industry and its regulation. In the early stage of the development of television, for example, individual promoters maneuvered for licenses, that is, for the grant of a privilege of considerable value since only a few television stations can operate in a single locality. As individual rights become settled, the television industry as a whole develops a common interest and a common front in dealings with the Federal Communications Commission and Congress on matters of policy affecting the industry.

For some industries a major advantage accrues through the restriction on entry to the business that is incidental to regulation. Usually at the initiation of regulation all firms in the business are granted certificates of public convenience and necessity; newcomers have to negotiate an administrative hurdle to go into business, and often the hurdle is high. Highway transport, for example, long resisted the initiation of regulation, but important elements of the industry saw the possibility of eliminating "cutthroat" competition by a restriction of entry to the business and by the fixing of rates by public authority. The major airlines similarly grew under the protection against competition from new lines afforded by the regulatory procedure, and they defended their sheltered position with determination against fringe competitors such as the nonscheduled carriers and all-cargo lines.[12] Established banks similarly use their influence to discourage the chartering of new competitors. In all these and other similar lines of business, regulation with the aim of advancing the public interest can readily be subverted to promote the interest of the regulated.[13] And it often is.

Occasionally the conditions under which regulated enterprises are permitted to do business restrict them unduly in their competition with another group of businesses. The legal standards that limit intergroup rivalry become the subject of political dispute. Thus, truckers and railroads compete for traffic, but they also compete politically over the terms of public regulation. The Association of American Railroads and the trucking associations maintain a running battle over questions of regulation. In 1961, for example, the railroads stirred their workers and even the model railroad clubs to aid them in resisting the demands of the truckers and their workers that federal rate policies be revised to block railroads from competing effectively for "piggyback" freight.

SUBSIDIES AND SERVICES   Business manifests an odd ideological ambivalence. Almost any session of a major business organization will at one point endorse a resolution denouncing government bounty, and at some later stage it will express discontent with the services rendered to industry by government. It may even resolve that the national defense or some other worthy objective justifies a subsidy for this or that business endeavor. And there may indeed be such a justification.

Subsidies appear in a variety of forms. Direct subsidies, simple payments from the treasury, are relatively few, those to shipping remaining a prime example. Subsidies to airlines are largely concealed in costs of airports and aids to air navigation. Programs for the stockpiling of defense materials, while not subsidies in form, tend to guarantee a market for producers of some imperishable commodities. Government insurance or guarantee, as of home mortgages, may be a subsidy and attract the strongest support of the industrial groups affected. Legislation for accelerated tax amortization has from time to time resulted in heavy subsidies—interest free loans—to those concerns fortunate enough to obtain certificates under the laws. The protec-

---

[12] See U.S. House, Committee on the Judiciary, 85th Cong., 1st sess., Report of the Antitrust Subcommittee Pursuant to H. Res. 107 on Airlines (Washington: Government Printing Office, 1957).

[13] See Walter Adams and Horace M. Gray, *Monopoly in America: Government as Promoter* (New York: Macmillan, 1955); Marver Bernstein, *Regulating Business by Independent Commission* (Princeton: Princeton University Press, 1955).

tive tariff, of course, amounts to a subsidy, at least under certain conditions.

A business group may naturally regard with a cold eye what it considers a subsidy for a competitor. The railroads, for example, manifest no ardor for river-and-harbor appropriations. The railroads, the coal operators, and the United Mine Workers, thus, staved off the St. Lawrence Seaway for many years. Electrical utilities decry, and perhaps exaggerate, the subsidy element in public hydroelectric power as "creeping socialism," but they can reconcile themselves to the acceptance of an almost free, perpetual supply of energy at the hands of a government that permits private exploitation of publicly owned falling water.

TAXATION   A surface agreement prevails among business groups on tax policy. All of them believe that taxes are too high, but that agreement dissolves instantly when the question of what changes ought to be made in tax policy arises. The Chamber of Commerce of the United States and the National Association of Manufacturers have long advocated greater reliance on sales taxes and a lesser dependence on income taxes, a view widely held among business organizations though exceptions exist. The National Retail Dry Goods Association has opposed sales taxes.

The extraordinary complexity of the tax system—with particular excises on particular commodities, with tariffs on individual items, with other types of taxes limited to specified types of business—operates to create among many groups a differentiated interest in tax legislation. Truckers pressure legislators to keep trucking taxes low (and to shift road costs to passenger automobiles). Movie theater owners seek reductions of the admissions tax. Distillers resist increases in the excises on spirits, and brewers oppose beer taxes. As many groups as there are specific duties or excises on products maneuver to obtain favorable action. Associations of insurance companies are stirred by threatened changes in the taxes on their business. Petroleum companies defend the depletion allowance. One special privilege generates pleas for similar treatment for others. Large corporate users of inland waterways, great exponents of free enterprise all, steadfastly oppose the establishment of user charges in the form of taxes on tugboat fuel, a proposal regarded benevolently by the railroads.

INDUSTRY AND MILITARY POLICY   As the "cold war" persists, a new type of business concern about public policy has come to overshadow lobbying about the older business issues. The great weapons makers, their trade associations, and their allies in the military services do battle to influence defense—and thereby procurement—policy. Plane makers and missile manufacturers vie. Rival missile producers stir a clamor in the press in an attempt to affect congressional decision. Shipbuilders try to see that defense policy redounds to their advantage. Once the broad outlines of policy are set, the scramble for the allocation of contracts among companies and localities enlists the best efforts of Senators and Representatives concerned about the economic impact of administrative decisions on their localities. The size of the stakes of the game makes the old politics of public works look like a politics of the picayune, and, indeed, procurement activity on so great a scale raises fundamental issues about the utilization of resources and the geographical distribution of productive endeavor. The simple notions of purchase by competitive bid do not solve those issues. Inevitably the representation of defense suppliers becomes one of the major industries in Washington. Officials of the Pentagon, besieged on all sides, complain of the costs of the many associations of defense contractors, which, in one way or another, find their way into bills for defense equipment. And, President Eisenhower, on the eve of his retirement, warned the country of the dangers in the power exerted by the new military-industrial complex.

COMPLEX LINKAGE OF GOVERNMENT AND BUSINESS These examples provide only meager suggestion of the nature of the tangle of relationships that has developed between business and government. These relationships, complex and chaotic though they may be, add up to a working system in which organized groups, private centers of power, play a basic role. At times their leaders may be animated by the most stubborn and immediate self-interest; at others, they may be animated by more noble motives. Yet as they pursue their ends they are certain to come into conflict with each other and with nonbusiness sectors of the society. When the collisions of free groups intolerably damage the public, the state intervenes to fix the rules of the game. A private enterprise system must by its nature be also a system of state intervention.

Spokesmen of Business

The foregoing recital conveys some conception of the diversity of political and economic objectives among business groups. The intricacies of political and economic relations create an endless number of clusters of firms, each with its own common concern and common enemies. Business is crisscrossed by divisions that set this category of enterprises off against that. The roster of business organizations reflects this diversity of business as well as the joining propensities of the American businessmen. Associations of business firms number in the thousands. About 2,000 national organizations—including 1,800 trade associations—employ 30,000 association executives and assistants in their common causes. State, regional, and local trade associations account for another 11,000 business organizations, while about 5,000 local chambers of commerce were estimated to exist in 1961. The Chamber of Commerce of the United States attempts to speak for the nation's business as a whole.

Almost every line of industrial and commercial activity has its association. The enumeration of a few organizations will suggest their variety: the American Petroleum Institute, the National Coal Association, the Associated General Contractors of America, the National Canners Association, the Distilled Spirits Institute, the American Cotton Manufactures Association, the National Lumber Manufacturers Association, the American Iron and Steel Institute, the American Newspaper Publishers Association, the National Fertilizer Association, the Automobile Manufacturers Association, the Pin Manufacturers Institute, the National Retail Dry Goods Association, the American Federation of Retail Kosher Butchers, and the American Bankers Association.

Obviously these and hundreds of other business associations differ widely in their size, resources, and objectives. Some of them have staffs and budgets of considerable size, wheras in other instances one man manages a stable of associations. Some organizations are short-lived; others have existed for over 75 years. Nearly every organization claims to represent its industry as a whole, yet in almost half of them nearly 50 per cent of the cost is borne by a handful of members. Most business associations center their objectives on the narrow interests of their industries. The National Terra Cotta Manufacturers Association concerns itself with a far narrower range of public policy than does the Chamber of Commerce of the United States.

Most of the organizations perform functions other than public education and political activity. They exist for the exchange of technical information. They conduct research. Some trade associations appear to have been formed mainly to limit competition in one way or another. Nearly all business associations represent the industry before legislative committees and other public authorities when public action is desired or when public action threatens to impinge unfavorably on association members.

CHAMBER OF COMMERCE OF THE UNITED STATES   The most conspicuous spokesman for business is the Chamber of Commerce of the United States. It is a federation of other business organizations—state and local chambers of commerce, trade associations, and societies of businessmen not organized for private purposes—over 3,000 in all. Unlike trade associations which may only incidentally be concerned with public policy, the major function of the Chamber is to speak for American business on issues of public policy. It cannot, however, take a stand on all issues of concern to all types of business. Its policy declarations are on matters "national in character, timely in importance, and general in application to business and industry." Given the conflicts of interest on particular issues among the diverse membership of the Chamber, it can speak with forthrightness chiefly on those broad issues on which business as a whole, or at least two-thirds of those voting at the annual meeting of the Chamber, have a common interest and a common view. On some issues it often takes a vague position, not unlike many planks in party platforms; on others, it is silent. The Chamber cannot fight, say, the issues peculiar to the rolling pin manufacturers, but must attempt to limit itself to issues of general concern. The necessity of seeking a formula acceptable to all on general issues sometimes gives the Chamber's pronouncements a tone of statesmanship—that is, a consideration of the interests of the nation as a whole—in contrast with the attitudes of organizations that promote the narrow interests of a homogeneous industrial group. By the same token the Chamber has its internal disputes about the issues on which it should speak, its constituent groups attempting to commit it to the defense of their special cause. Thus, in 1956 the chemical industry successfully maneuvered to postpone action on policy recommendations in support of United States participation in the Organization for Trade Cooperation.

Although a referendum procedure is available, the Chamber's policies are usually adopted by its annual meeting on the basis of committee recommendations. These resolutions, which remain in effect for three years, are codified annually for the information of all concerned. The annual collection of Chamber pronouncements fills a booklet of 150–200 pages.[14] So comprehensive a statement cannot be readily summarized, but random excerpts will indicate its tone. The Chamber regards itself as "wholeheartedly committed to private enterprise in preference to government enterprise." While the Chamber does not reject all government interference in the economy, it generally urges the reduction of the scope of government control and opposes the initiation of new controls. Thus it urges voluntary health insurance and opposes compulsory medical and hospital insurance. It regards the extension of credit by federal agencies as a "menace to the private enterprise system in general and to chartered banking in particular." It advocates elimination of the federal price regulation of natural gas producers. It favors provision of off-street parking by private capital without hindrance or competition by government.

On labor policy the Chamber subscribes "to the right of employees to organize and bargain collectively whenever such action is the result of their own free and uncoerced choice." It opposes the union shop and advocates prohibition of sympathetic strikes and the outlawing of mass picketing. It contends that monopolistic practices by labor organizations should be subjected to legal controls just as employers are restricted. It argues for respon-

---

[14] See the current year's pamphlet, *Policy Declarations of the Chamber of Commerce of the United States* (Washington). The Chamber's outlook is put with less restraint in *Economic Intelligence,* a weekly leaflet, than it is in its full-dress resolutions.

sibility of labor organizations for injuries to persons and property through breach of contract or other unlawful acts. The Chamber tends to favor state rather than federal action. "The states and the local school districts should accept full responsibility for the financing of public schools." Regulation of "insurance should continue to be a function of the states." The states should have maximum freedom to establish labor relations law. Federal supervision of state unemployment compensation agencies should be subjected to "restraint and review." The Chamber supports "the dual system of federal and state-chartered banking."

Although the annual meetings of the Chamber serve as sounding boards for the views of business, its work is not limited to these sessions. It maintains a staff at its headquarters in Washington to conduct research to serve as a basis for the deliberations of its committees and to make known the views of organized business to Congress and to administrative agencies. Its committees analyze issues as they arise. Its publicity staff prepares news for release to the daily press and to specialized journals. Its official organ, *Nation's Business*, presents the Chamber's views to the membership and to the public. During congressional sessions its staff follows closely the work of Congress and keeps the membership informed on legislative developments.[15]

NATIONAL ASSOCIATION OF MANUFACTURERS One of the most articulate organs of business is the National Association of Manufacturers, formed in 1895 to promote the cause of trade and commerce by aiding in the passage of legislation and by other means.[16] Like the Chamber of Commerce, this association has a heterogeneous membership and must concentrate its efforts on those matters in which its membership has common cause. Yet since the NAM has a much less varied membership than the Chamber, it is a more zealous and hard-hitting organization. Probably the greatest source of cohesion for the Association is an antipathy to organized labor, though this has become less marked as the decades have gone by.

After 1932, when the question of the place of organized labor became more salient, the NAM exerted itself in a propaganda campaign to sell to the public the symbol of "free enterprise," an important component of which was opposition to increased power of organized labor. The fact seemed to be that a relatively small number of employers financed and used the NAM as a vehicle to resist the rise of labor strength. For a time the views of the NAM were so extreme that it probably had only a negative influence on legislation; its endorsement of a bill might be a kiss of death. "Of 38 major

[15] For analyses of the Chamber, see H. L. Childs, *Labor and Capital in National Politics* (Columbus: Ohio State University Press, 1930); J. W. Prothro, *The Dollar Decade* (Baton Rouge: Louisiana State University Press, 1954).

[16] On some of the earlier political activities of the Association, see H. H. Wilson, *Congress: Corruption and Compromise* (New York: Rinehart, 1951), ch. 2.

legislative proposals enacted into law between the years 1933 and 1941, the NAM opposed all but 7." [17]

Important elements of the NAM eventually concluded that the country could not be won to its point of view, and gradually the professed policy on labor was altered. The Association shifted to the position that collective bargaining could be tolerated under certain regulations and limitations. Even that shift involved sharp dissension within the NAM; in 1946 a minority of the NAM board, representative of large and powerful industries, "favored outright repeal of the Wagner Act, the Wage and Hour Act, and the Norris-La Guardia Act." [18] The NAM finally conceded that government might intervene in labor-management relations and then contended for limitations and procedures on the bargaining process. In the Taft-Hartley Act of 1947 Congress adopted largely, but not completely, the lines of action urged by the NAM.[19] In the succeeding years the NAM met labor's demands for relaxation of restrictions of the Taft-Hartley Act, with proposals of its own for tighter limitations on labor, some of which gained acceptance in the Landrum-Griffin Act.

NAM spokesmen usually take a gloomy view of the trend of events as they expound their gospel. In 1955 its president told the assembled NAM at its Congress of Industry that the United States was "well on the way to the achievement of a Communist state as blueprinted by Marx." NAM propaganda manifests a sense of deep conviction, if not of stridency, as it opposes federal centralization and, indeed, the expansion of governmental authority generally.

OTHER BUSINESSWIDE ORGANIZATIONS   Though the Chamber of Commerce and the NAM are the most conspicuous spokesmen for business, other organizations articulate shades of opinion within the business community. One of the more important of these is the Committee for Economic Development, incorporated in 1942. The CED represented a sharp departure in its outlook from that of the NAM. It seems evident that a group of business leaders came to the conclusion that both big business and big government were here to stay, that the policy of obstruction which had characterized the more vocal organs of business was self-defeating, and that business had a responsibility to propose rather than merely oppose. The CED undertakes to develop through "objective research and discussion" recommendations which will contribute to maintenance of employment, increasing productivity and living standards, and greater economic stability. It attempts

[17] A. S. Cleveland, "NAM: Spokesman for Industry?" *Harvard Business Review*, 26 (1948), 353–71.

[18] R. W. Gable, "NAM: Influential Lobby or Kiss of Death?" *Journal of Politics*, 15 (1953), 253–73.

[19] H. A. Millis and E. C. Brown, *From the Wagner Act to Taft-Hartley* (Chicago: University of Chicago Press, 1950), chs. 8–10.

to bring about public understanding of its recommendations to these ends but leaves the lobbying to others.[20]

With the aid of a research advisory board composed of leading economists, the CED studies problems it regards as of national interest. On the basis of these studies, committees of business executives struggle with the issues of policy and formulate recommendations. The Committee's attempt to fuse the expertise of the economist with the outlook of businessmen has resulted in policy statements that contribute in a responsible way to the solution of broad economic issues. It may well be that the declining proportion of romanticism, that is, a belief that the clock could be turned back to 1925, in the policies of the older business organizations can be attributed to the precept of the CED.

From time to time promoters enlist support in the business community for campaigns in fierce advocacy of extreme viewpoints. Old business organizations tend to develop decorous manners. Other, more or less one-man organizations, give vent to the accumulated frustrations, deep anxieties, sharp animosities, and partisan inclinations of some businessmen. They could be regarded, not as organizations, but as privateers operating under letters of marque granted by businessmen. In the 1930's the Liberty League, a club of disillusioned millionaires, fought the New Deal with more zeal than effectiveness. In the 1940's the Committee for Constitutional Government carried the torch. Its stated function was "educating the public on principles of constitutional liberty and economic freedom." Few of the policies of the New Deal and Fair Deal seemed to coincide with these principles, and the Committee operated in effect as an unacknowledged auxiliary of the Republican party. The magnitude of the Committee's work is suggested by the fact that in a period of about four years it mailed from eight to ten million pieces of literature under the frank of friendly Congressmen.[21] Many of the backers of the Committee could be found in 1957 lined up in support of the Campaign for the 48 States, an organization that sought, among other things, to limit the federal power of taxation and thereby to make futile lobbying for "socialist" causes such as aid to education.

While the viewpoints of business and of sectors of business are propagated by general business organizations and trade associations, few businesses leave to such groups sole responsibility for the promotion of their political interests. Most of the great corporations, and many of those not so great, retain Washington law firms or other specialists to represent them in legislative matters. Many legislative and administrative policy decisions have a

[20] For the story of the CED, see Karl Schriftgiesser, *Business Comes of Age* (New York: Harper, 1960).

[21] A goodly number of the most extraordinary reactionary propaganda organizations have been able to feed on business contributions. At times it has seemed that surely there was no crackpot who had failed to find a group of businessmen willing to support his "educational program" or to sponsor him as a radio commentator.

policy impact so particular and of such import that prudent corporations will see that their specific concern is forcefully communicated to those with the power of decision.

DIVERSITY AND UNITY   Although different segments of business are often arrayed in opposition, these fissures within the business class do not prevent the maintenance of an impressive business solidarity on broad political questions. The differences between shipper and carrier, between manufacturer and distributor, and between businesses of different regions are fought out in continuing skirmishes, but on the larger issues these differences tend to be subordinated to a greater unity.

One factor in the maintenance of this broad class unity consists in the disciplinary power of business organizations. The tendency of groups to develop norms of conduct and to bring the membership into conformity finds no clearer exemplification than in the workings of business groups. While nonpolitical in their aims, they impose a partisan orthodoxy on their members far more effectively than do trade unions. The regimentation of the trade association, the board of directors, the Rotary Club, the chamber of commerce, or the country club brings the deviant into line with the political mores of the group—or at least keeps the dissenter quiet. Only the most hardy soul would express Democratic views at a session of the NAM.[22]

Moreover, the operation of business associations—and of the hierarchies of corporations—creates a network of relations that ties together the scattered business leadership of the country. It is almost as if the business leadership were in a continuous political caucus. Conventions, committee sessions, board meetings, and corporate staff conferences, with their interlocking and overlapping memberships, build a system of face-to-face relations knitting the business community together. The airplane and the corporate expense account bring literally thousands of businessmen into conference every day, and they in turn have their relations back home with the less mobile elements of the business community. Such a communications system permits quick dissemination over the country of the views of the bellwethers and results in an almost continuous mobilization of business for political action.[23]

[22] See G. Mennen Williams, "Can Businessmen Be Democrats?" *Harvard Business Review*, 36 (1958), 102–6.

[23] In recent years many corporations have instituted programs for training their employees in practical politics and for encouraging them to run for office or to participate in other ways. Both the Chamber of Commerce and the National Association of Manufacturers have developed materials for courses in political action. Corporate public affairs programs are often billed as nonpartisan civic endeavors; the intent, though, is probably more usually on the order of that expressed in 1959 by the president of American Can: to oppose "powerful forces which are seriously undermining our political and economic system." George Meany, president of the AFL-CIO, welcomed business interest in politics: ". . . maybe it will help us get more workers interested in doing their real duty as citi-

Quite apart from the conformity induced by the fear of the frowns of one's fellows, pecuniary relations within the business system may discourage dissent. The concentration of business in large corporate organizations estab-lishes a large number of dependency relations (deposits in banks, retainers for attorneys, orders for suppliers, advertisements for newspapers, and the like) which may be used to purchase acquiescence or to penalize deviation. Let a vulnerable manufacturer espouse unbusinesslike views, and he may discover that he has become an undesirable credit risk and that his customers are seeking other sources of supply. The intricate network of relationships within business creates mechanism for punishment as well as reward. Yet so effective is the system of business indoctrination that the cruder sanctions rarely need to be applied.

Business and Public Opinion: Aggression and Restraint

The politics of business involves far more than lobbying for or against legislation and mixing into election campaigns. Businessmen are a small minority highly vulnerable to political attack. They labor under serious political handicaps. They lack the strength of numbers. Moreover, their posi-tion lacks the moral authority that inheres in the cause of the sturdy agrarian yeomanry or the horny-handed toiler of the factory and foundry. To protect the broad status of business and to advance its cause businessmen have to depend on something other than their votes. They have to use their wits—and their money—to generate a public opinion that acquiesces in the enjoyment by business of its status in the economic order.

The politics of business, thus, must encompass a range of activity outside the limits of that ordinarily denominated as political. One phase of this ac-tivity includes aggressive attempts to mold the attitudes of both the general public and special publics. To gain public favor business associations and corporations employ in large numbers public-relations experts, those masters of the verbal magic that transmutes private advantage into the public good. While propaganda to win friends for specific legislative proposals or to make enemies for schemes opposed by business is important, of more fundamental

zens." For handbooks for businessmen, see W. H. Baumer and D. Herzberg, *Politics Is Your Business* (New York: Dial, 1960); J. J. Wuerthner, Jr., *The Businessman's Guide to Practical Politics* (Chicago: Regnery, 1959); Albert Newgarden, *The Business Man in Politics* (New York: American Management Association, 1959). Michael D. Reagan argues that the boomerang effect makes it hazardous for corporations to go into electoral politics; they are better advised to restrict themselves to the politics of policy. "The Seven Fallacies of Business in Politics," *Harvard Business Review*, 38 (March–April, 1960), 60–68. See also Andrew Hacker and J. D. Aberbach, "Businessmen in Politics," *Law and Contem-porary Problems*, 27 (1962), 266–79.

significance is the continuing propaganda calculated to shape public attitudes favorably toward the business system as a whole or toward particular types of business. The assiduous dedication of effort to the capture of public favor lays a foundation of good will on which business groups may build in their attempts to obtain particular legislation or to obstruct undesired governmental actions.

The necessity of courting public favor carries with it, however, another type of business political behavior—at least if we define political broadly enough. The possibility of molding public opinion to conform with business ideologies has its limits, and a concern with public attitudes may compel business groups to alter their policies so that they can be sold to the public. Self-restraint, induced by anticipations of environmental reaction, may change the policy of the business group, particularly those groups dominated by a few concerns. The pursuit of some business policies, it may come to be recognized, will result in disfavor and perhaps in the eventual adoption of regulatory legislation at the behest of injured groups. The threat or possibility of governmental action may alter business behavior into a pattern more readily defensible in the forum of public opinion.

EARLY DISREGARD OF PUBLIC OPINION   Intense and continuing business concern about public attitudes is a comparatively recent development. The new industrial giants emerged from a competitive order in which the individual businessman, beset by competitors on all sides, exercised little power over his fellow man. Under these conditions a man's business could be genuinely his own private affair. No pressure of expediency or social necessity suggested the relevance of the doctrine that private business was clothed with a public interest. The older business attitudes persisted into the changed situation created by the revolution in the organization of business. Early corporate leaders held to the old doctrines and cared little what the public thought of them or of their industries. Moreover, the men who built up the great corporate concerns were often ruthless. The erection of great enterprises required men sturdy enough to suppress competition and skillful enough to build combinations, men who in another day might have been the barons, chieftains, and war lords. Then, too, they were engagingly frank. Witness the testimony of Henry Havemeyer, sugar refiner, in the nineties:

> *Senator Allen.* . . . If you fix the price at 4 cents for granulated throughout the United States the others obtain it, don't they? And in that way the price is controlled.
> *Mr. Havemeyer.* We undertake to control the price of refined sugar in the United States. That must be distinctly understood.
> *Senator Allen.* And the price of refined sugar in the United States

is higher to the American people in consequence of the existence of the American Sugar Refining Company than it would be if the different companies in your organization were distinct and independent companies?

Mr. Havemeyer. For a short time it is.

Senator Allen. And what difference does it make for the consumers in this country in a year, in your judgment?

Mr. Havemeyer. It has been in three years past three-eighths of a cent more on every pound they ate, as against doing business at a loss.

Senator Allen. And that would be about how much in round numbers?

Mr. Havemeyer. It is a large sum in the aggregate.

Senator Allen. How many millions?

Mr. Havemeyer. I should say it was close to $25,000,000 in three years.

Senator Allen. And you intend to keep your hold upon the American people as long as you can?

Mr. Havemeyer. As long as the McKinley bill is there we will exact the profit.

Senator Allen. Is that the result of the McKinley bill?

Mr. Havemeyer. We should not have achieved it without the McKinley bill; but a great deal of the profit is due to these men in consequence of combining the different interests and the skill and labor attending it.[24]

Mr. Havemeyer's candid views were not exceptional: they represented a widespread attitude among business leaders who took the position that the public be damned. In some formulations they advocated almost a doctrine of divine right. Thus, an executive of the anthracite mining industry in 1902 asserted that the rights of the laboring man would be protected, not by labor agitators, "but by the Christian men to whom God in his infinite wisdom has given control of the property interests of the country."

TOWARD THE CULTIVATION OF PUBLIC FAVOR   After 1900 the political difficulties of the expanding corporate enterprise multiplied. Prosecutions of the trusts, investigations of the practices of big business, and the public resentment of bigness brought a gradual recognition by private business that it was no longer really private; that public favor had to be cultivated; that a concern for the general good, whether genuine or not, had to be manifested. Ivy Lee, the first of the great public-relations counselors, opened shop in 1903. He and his imitators found clients aware of the new trend of events, and eventually every corporate executive had at hand an advisor on public relations.

[24] Senate Report No. 606, 53d Cong., 2d sess. (1894), pp. 337–38.

The public utility executives were among the first to set about systematically educating public opinion. Their industry had an exceptional political sensitivity and operated under the necessity of attempting to mollify those sectors of the public whose discontent might quickly be converted into demands for tighter regulation. President Vail of the Bell System in 1913 expressed the new viewpoint:

> All industrials, particularly utilities, are face to face with problems, the solution of which will largely determine the future of the business; they are, in the last resort, subject to a control and regulation far stronger than that exercised by commissions or by legislators, that influence and power that makes and unmakes legislator and judges; the influence and power of public desire and public selfishness, which if not regulated or controlled will lead to chaos and disaster. The only regulation or control for this is that common sense which, directed by education and observation, and rightfully administered and regulated, will conserve the interests of all.[25]

The American Telephone and Telegraph Company's devotion of careful attention to its public relations paid off handsomely in the long run. It became our largest nonfinancial corporation, a natural target for political attack, and virtually a national monopoly. Yet it weathered the New Deal without ill results; its store of public goodwill made it an unlikely object for attack by crusaders.[26] Lest the marvels of public relations be overestimated, it ought to be remembered that good service contributed to the goodwill enjoyed by the Bell System.

The public-relations specialist did not come into his own until after World War I, during which governmental propaganda agencies impressively showed the power of propaganda over the people. With this demonstration before them, industrialists more generally undertook to create a favorable context of public attitudes, and business associations planned and executed large-scale programs of public education. One of the greatest efforts was by the National Electric Light Association, a group that later dissolved when the magnitude of its propaganda program became generally known. The rationale of its program, and indeed of most organized efforts to mold public opinion, was stated in 1925 by B. J. Mullaney, a utility leader:

> I am fairly familiar with legislative practice and procedure and have not many illusions in that quarter. Sometimes the political road has to be traveled. When a destructive bill is pending in a legislature it has to be dealt with in a way to get results. I am not debating that. But to

[25] N. E. Long, "Public Relations of the Bell System," *Public Opinion Quarterly,* October, 1937, p. 18.

[26] See Richardson Wood, "The Corporation Goes into Politics," *Harvard Business Review,* 21 (1942–43), 60–70.

depend, year after year, upon the usual political expedients for stopping hostile legislation is shortsightedness. . . . In the long run isn't it better to lay a groundwork with the people back home who have the votes, so that proposals of this character are not popular with them, rather than to depend upon stopping such proposals when they get up to the legislature or commission? [27]

Business associations and individual corporations pursue their own objectives in public relations; yet it appears that beginning during World War II business interests more and more utilized their public-relations resources for the dissemination of political ideology. Particular objectives, particular legislative proposals, and short-term campaigns for this or that objective became overshadowed by an almost overwhelming propaganda of doctrine. With their unfortunate experiences with the New Deal behind them, with no goods to sell, with high tax rates which made advertising relatively inexpensive, corporations began to advertise ideology on a large scale. The popular periodicals carried advertisements pointing to the merits of the "American way" and to the virtues of free enterprise as well as now and then to the iniquities of socialism. The exploits of business under free enterprise were praised, and the great achievements of American business in production and technology were publicized. The services of this or that corporation to scores of communities and the bounty that flowed from the corporation to its suppliers over the country were chronicled.[28] In this advertising a common ideological theme dominated: a theme of free enterprise, of "the American way," of the essential goodness of business. It was made to appear not only impertinent but unpatriotic to suggest that American business might have its blemishes.

While the gross impression from the propaganda programs of business may have been one of salience of political philosophy, campaigns to mold public opinion on particular policies probably gained strength from the saturation of the media with advertising calculated to sell ideas rather than merchandise. Thus the National Association of Electric Companies and associated groups took up the burden of selling the cause of the private utilities after the utility industry reached its nadir in public favor with the passage of the Public Utility Holding Company Act of 1935, the initiation of the TVA, and the construction of government-owned generating plants. All these

[27] Federal Trade Commission, *Summary Report . . . on Efforts by Associations and Agencies of Electric and Gas Utilities to Influence Public Opinion*, Sen. Doc. No. 92, Pt. 71A, 70th Cong., 1st sess. (1934), p. 17.

[28] F. X. Sutton, *et al.*, *The American Business Creed* (Cambridge: Harvard University Press, 1956) ; L. I. Pearlin and M. Rosenberg, "Propaganda Techniques in Institutional Advertising," *Public Opinion Quarterly*, 16 (1952), 5–26; M. H. Bernstein, "Political Ideas of Selected American Business Journals," *Public Opinion Quarterly*, 17 (1953), 258–67; J. H. Bunzel, *The American Small Businessman* (New York: Knopf, 1962) ; H. Zeigler, *The Politics of Small Business* (Washington: Public Affairs Press, 1961).

measures were predicated on the need for regulation of an industry that enjoyed a monopolistic position that could be, and was, abused. Over a period of 15 or 20 years the propaganda campaigns of the association implanted a new image of the utilities in the public mind. Eventually proposals to limit federal hydroelectric power, criticisms of the Rural Electrification Administration, or advocacy of a higher return to the utilities were regarded as respectable doctrine rather than as favoritism toward utility magnates.

Although no careful analyses have been made of the effects of business campaigns to mold public attitudes, the utility campaign may suggest some clues. Sustained campaigns over long periods of time, through the power of repetition and through the shortness of public memory, may have a marked effect on public attitudes. Further, the political importance of campaigns may rest primarily in the fact that they may create a climate of opinion in which the propagandizer's political friends can act in his behalf without putting themselves in an indefensible position. Thus, in 1935, say, proponents of government "partnership" with private utilities would have brought down on their heads outraged cries of a sellout. In the 1950's, after over a decade of propaganda and after other factors had also had their effects, public reaction to advocacy of the utility cause by politicians seemed to be far less hostile.

No simple measure can readily be devised of the effects on public attitudes of the heavy expenditures of business associations and corporations to shape the public view on political issues and ideologies. Obviously large sums are completely wasted. Yet the chances are that the cumulative impact over the years is imposing. The great political triumph of large-scale enterprise has been the manufacture of a public opinion favorably disposed toward, or at least tolerant of, gigantic corporations, in contrast with an earlier dominant sentiment savagely hostile to monopolies and trusts. That fact is of fundamental importance in the workings of the American political system.

FEEDBACK FROM PUBLIC OPINION   The relations of business and public do not amount simply to a one-way transmission of propaganda in which business and its public-relations specialists mold an infinitely malleable public. Business attempts to manipulate public opinion; but business itself—especially big business—is, within limits, manipulated by a public opinion beyond its control. As industrial power grew and the conscious policy of managing public attitudes to retain that power came to be adopted, big businessmen underwent a curious metamorphosis. They came to act like politicians; or, as they termed it, they became "industrial statesmen." Similarly, they became sensitive to public criticism and planned their major policies and decisions with a sharp eye to the anticipated public reaction. And, like politicians, their decisions have come to be influenced by the anticipated public reaction. The doctrine that corporate office is a public trust was promulgated; and to it, at least at times, more than lip service was paid.

The late Eugene Holman, president of Standard Oil of New Jersey, put the matter in this way:

> There is another powerful influence on the policies of large-scale operations. Companies today are very largely influenced—and necessarily so—by public opinion. I believe the controlling force of public opinion is not always realized by some of us in this country. But the fact is that no management today—especially no big company management—can successfully develop its policies and practices without a keen awareness at all times of the public interest.[29]

The skeptic who insists that Mr. Holman's observations amount to nothing more than pious window dressing errs. Businessmen adopted his view as they learned the consequences of ignoring public reactions and as they saw the limits on the management of public opinion. The public-relations experts soon discovered that their artistry could not make a business managed by scoundrels smell sweet; a clean-up job had to be done before they could do their work. It is apparent that many types of business behavior are influenced by public opinion. Even pricing decisions, in the short run at least, may be so influenced. In some lines large concerns manifest solicitude for their small competitors; they serve as insurance against antitrust prosecutions. And, on occasion, the monopolist prudently seeks out another firm to share the market for the same purpose. Policies on labor matters and on production practices likewise bear the imprint of public reaction. Beyond such matters of internal management, the efforts of individual concerns and of business associations to mold public attitudes on broad political questions quite often are affected by judgments of existing public predilections. The occasional internal commotions leading to shifts in the leadership of business associations have at times been battles over policy toward a public that had shown itself unmoved by the older policies of the association.

It would be absurd, of course, to make too much of the sensitivity of business to public opinion. Moreover, "industrial statesmanship" seems to be most notable among those firms, monopolistic or semimonopolistic, that both need to cultivate public favor and can afford to do so. In a truly competitive industry of many small firms, the industry has no mechanism by which it can act as a unit to remedy the "abuses" of the industry or to take positions in response to public criticism. Nevertheless, in some types of industry the hovering spook of public opinion may be on hand at the directors' meetings to cast the deciding vote.

[29] Eugene Holman, *The Public Responsibilities of Big Companies* (Standard Oil of New Jersey, 1948), p. 4. See, though, Robert Engler, *The Politics of Oil* (New York: Macmillan, 1961).

Accountability of Centers of Private Power

The substance of the preceding chapter suggested general observations about the existence of private governments within the social system. There the contention was that the governing process, if adequately defined, includes the workings of many centers of group power not ordinarily regarded as political. These power nuclei guide human behavior on a variety of matters and at times apply sanctions which may be harsh indeed. Professional societies promulgate standards of conduct and on occasion penalize nonconformers by deprivation of the right to practice. Labor unions may determine whether a man can get a job, as well as the manner in which he shall work; they may also in some circumstances exert almost a power of life and death over employers. And all private associations, from the Farm Bureau Federation to the American Legion, affect the attitudes of their members on questions of public policy and, to varying degrees, restrain the expression of dissent.

The materials of this chapter identify additional centers of private power: business associations and giant corporations. At times business associations, especially when they restrain trade, exercise potent sanctions to hold the members in line, and they may also affect the community as a whole for good or ill. While in the field of political and legislative action it is the business association that is most visible, it is probably comparatively insignificant in its social power alongside the 100 to 150 giant corporations that dominate American business. Corporations are, of course, far more tightly knit institutional entities than, say, the American Farm Bureau Federation or the Chamber of Commerce of the United States. They differ from associations or pressure groups, but their achievements in the organization of human effort endow them with power in relation to persons within the organization, with respect to their suppliers, their distributors, their customers, the communities within which they operate, and to the workings of the economy generally. Not only do they exercise power; they perform in a sense a public function. They are run, to be sure, to make money. Yet so essential to the public welfare is the proper management of their affairs that they tend to be clothed with a public purpose. Their shortcomings cannot be left, as in the fabled economy of atomistic competition, to be cured by the beneficent workings of the bankruptcy statutes. The bankruptcy of General Motors, if so improbable an event could be imagined, would be a public disaster. Nor can it be assumed, as the classical economist would have us believe, that the great corporation is kept sterile of power by a subordination to the forces of the market. Although the workings of these structures erected by the organizational genius are only dimly understood, it is clear that corporate decisions have effects far beyond the factory gate.

These observations, which constitute the merest suggestion of the variety of types of private centers of power, provide a backdrop for comment about another broad question of politics, namely, the problem of accountability of private centers of power. The American political tradition abhors irresponsible power, be it in private or governmental hands. Our political processes provide procedures for enforcing an accountability of those who hold public authority; they also provide, willynilly, ways and means, often tortuous and nearly always sluggish and cumbersome, for bringing to a reckoning those who abuse private power.

The freedom to build up private power complexes—be they huge corporations, business associations, labor organizations or what not—has, as its reciprocal, accountability. Hierarchies of private authority are a great convenience in the management of the affairs of mankind, but they can be tolerated only so long as there is an ultimate accountability. Autonomous, private exercise of authority over matters of general concern becomes a dispensable luxury unless the assigned social purpose is fulfilled, an adequate observance of "due process" occurs, and only a few toes are stepped on. In a way, the drive for freedom in the exercise of private power on grounds that this promotes the public weal concedes an ultimate accountability. Businessmen probably have not thought this one through, for their exuberant estimates of what business can do if unrestrained may well intensify the severity of the enforcement of accountability when business performance sags below promise.

Under many circumstances the holders of private power may operate only in accord with statutory standards, but the phenomenon that excites attention at the moment is the enforcement of accountability outside the formal governmental processes. That phenomenon, often inchoate in form, rarely patterned in recurring sequences, highly variable in its efficacy, and erratic in its incidence, cannot be described in simple terms. Yet the informal enforcement of responsibility of private centers of power may well be one of the fundamental differentiating characteristics of a free society. Lest the entire idea of such accountability be dismissed as an imaginary construct, it is proper to raise such questions as: Accountability to whom? Accountability for what? Accountability by what means?

Nominally the holders of authority in private governments are accountable to their respective groups: the corporate management to the stockholders, the labor union hierarchy to the members, the pressure group leadership to its dues-paying constituency. Yet nothing seems clearer than the proposition that the internal political processes of organizations tend to be inadequate even to protect the rights of members of the groups themselves much less to take into account the interests of the larger public in the operations of governing centers of private groups. Corporate stockholders can go to court to obtain redress against abuses of power by corporate officers, but probably more significant in the protection of their immediate interests are operations

of informal controls developed outside government in the reporting requirements of the stock exchanges, in the probings of the security analysts, and
in the pressures from institutional investors—all of which thrust corporate
management into a gold-fish bowl. From time to time arbitrary and corrupt
union leaderships oppress and exploit union members, a state of affairs
which is beyond prevention by internal political processes of the union.
External controls must come into play to restrain abuses internal to the
group.

The processes by which private centers of power are held accountable
to their own immediate constituency scarcely touch the broader question of
accountability for group actions with effects beyond the boundaries of the
organization itself. The mechanisms by which this responsibility to the
"public" is enforced, short of explicit governmental intervention, are diverse
in form and effectiveness. It has long been evident that in the narrowly
political sphere the power of some groups may be neutralized or held in
check by the opposing power of other groups. Professor Galbraith has noted
the workings of the same "countervailing power," as he christens it, in the
economic sphere. The public may be protected from monopolistic or quasi-
monopolistic control over prices by the rise of competing centers of power
with capacity to bargain in the market place. Chain stores, for example,
have a power to cope with the manufacturer; their ultimate sanction is to
develop their own source of supply. Labor organizations rise to combat, in
the labor market as well as in politics, the power of large employers. All
the relations of conflict between great groups outside the government may,
of course, seep over into political conflict. The efficacy of countervailing
power, as Professor Galbraith points out, differs in different sets of circumstances and at different times. Yet in some situations a system of checks
operates totally outside the public government to restrain the powers of
private government.[30]

The broad conception of countervailing power is that the giants pit
their strength against each other and the public incidentally benefits from
the resulting balance or stalemate. Another more nebulous but pervasive
mode of enforcing accountability of the holders of private power is by the
vague but nevertheless real force of public opinion. Those who make decisions
of public import tend to take into account the squawks their actions may
evoke.[31] Adolph Berle, an exceptionally well-informed observer, concludes:
"Hardly any present-day board of directors or corporation management

[30] See J. K. Galbraith, *American Capitalism* (Boston: Houghton Mifflin, 1952).

[31] Thus, Joseph L. Block, president of Inland Steel, in a 1957 speech to the Iron and
Steel Institute, recalled President Truman's proposal to build federal steel mills if the
industry failed to provide needed capacity: ". . . we dare not wait until action is advocated by governmental leaders or others in the public eye. We must be alert and ever
vigilant to prevent the development of conditions which are conducive to such ideas." In
1961, in the midst of a hue and cry about blood and thunder on television, W. S. Paley,
president of CBS, spoke to CBS affiliates of the industry's freedom, a freedom that "presupposes, in us as broadcasters, a clear sense of responsibility. If we fail to see the dimen-

would take the position that it could afford to disregard public opinion—or would last very long if it did." [32] Moreover, corporation managements hire survey specialists to discover the state of public opinion.

What goes on in the minds of corporate directors as diverse factors struggle for primacy in decision is rarely a matter of public record. Though the weight of public opinion in the process can only be conjectured, it is doubtless not uniform. The impact of public opinion is far more visible, though not necessarily more effective, in the actions of business associations, labor organizations, and other such groups. The reflections that occur to the leaders of such groups are suggested by the remarks of the chief of the Brotherhood of Locomotive Engineers about the AFL-CIO merger, which he viewed with disfavor: "If there is one thing this country will not tolerate it is dictation to it by any power which seriously threatens the sovereignty of the nation itself." The greater the power, he said, "the smaller the area of unrestricted activity. The United States Bank learned this to its sorrow in the Nineteenth Century. The railroads still are learning it." Similar estimates of the price of a hostile public opinion doubtless have moved national labor leaders to attempt to clean up malodorous situations in some unions. A common sort of visible deference to public opinion consists in the trimming of legislative demands toward forms that are less likely to be generally regarded as outrageous. Even such brass-riveted outfits as the NAM and the AMA eventually modify their positions in the light of public reaction.

The inner guides of norms and conscience may be of greater significance in steering the behavior of the controllers of centers of private power than are sanctions of public opinion or the fear of hostile counteraction from other groups. Leaders of private groups are, after all, of the culture and sharers in its broad values. "It seems to me almost axiomatic," says Crawford H. Greenewalt, a former president of Du Pont, "that, over the long stretch of corporate life, no business can prosper unless it serves the public interest in all of its many facets." Nor does he view the growth of the size of business units with alarm, "for the pressures of society will inevitably produce their own controls and stabilizers. These pressures for the preservation of a particular moral code are great indeed, particularly in the area that has been called 'obedience to the unenforceable'—the things we do, not because they are required, but because they are right. This strength is much more potent and compelling than the law." [33]

Leaders of great business enterprises have their own ideas of the public interest, just as the rest of us do, but the important point is that they have a notion of public interest. Moreover, a comparison of Mr. Greenewalt's com-

---

sions of that responsibility and to measure up to them, we are in for constant threats of restrictions and policing."

[32] *The 20th Century Capitalist Revolution*, p. 56.

[33] In a speech before the Bureau of Advertising of the American Newspaper Publishers Association, April 26, 1956. For a thoughtful statement of the new type of business outlook, see J. C. Worthy, *Big Business and Free Men* (New York: Harper, 1959).

ments with Mr. Havemeyer's, quoted earlier in the chapter, suggests the radical change that has occurred in the viewpoint of business leaders over the past half-century. While the world cannot be governed by relying on everyone to follow his own rules of fair play, the existence of private aggregates of power within the realm is more likely to be tolerable when a disposition toward "obedience to the unenforceable" prevails.

More tangible than these factors in its influence on the holders of private power is the threat of state intervention which could deprive them of their authority or regulate the manner of its exercise. The policies of private power centers are not infrequently modified to ward off new legislation. On occasion, so great is the sensitivity to the threat of public action, that a speech on the Senate floor may have about the same effect as would the enactment of a statute. Modifications of private practice to avert state intervention are perhaps most noticeable in great corporations which have within themselves the power to act to that end. Looser types of organizations, such as trade associations, professional societies, and labor federations, are deficient in the capacity to bind their members to action in avoidance, although the threat of state intervention may induce efforts to do so.[34]

The broad point of these few pages has been that, within limits, private centers of power have an accountability, beyond that to their immediate membership, for the exercise of their authority. A few illustrations of the nature and mode of enforcement of this accountability have been set out. The identification of this type of behavior, which clearly exists, should not be confused with an estimate of the frequency of its occurrence or with its importance in the entire process of governance. Often private power seems to know no restraints of its own. At some times these informal modes of accountability are more potent than at others. Nevertheless, the operation of a society that permits the accumulation of great aggregates of power in private hands requires the existence of informal modes of control and of enforcement of accountability. When those informal methods of holding to account fail, government must move in and exercise its formal power of coercion.[35] The price of freedom of centers of private power is their own behavior in the general interest.

[34] Thus, after it had initiated a campaign of self-policing, the Advertising Federation of America in its 1961 convention resolved "that in view of the earnest and effective campaign of self-regulation which the advertising industry has voluntarily undertaken and has so successfully advanced no additional governmental controls or restrictions are warranted at this time." Or, in 1961, after bills had been introduced to require auto makers to install "blowby" devices to burn crankcase fumes, the board of directors of the Automobile Manufacturers Association recommended that all manufacturers make these devices standard equipment beginning with the 1963 models. Legislators dropped their campaign, and the auto makers congratulated themselves on their fine sense of public responsibility.

[35] See A. T. Mason, "Business Organized as Power: The New Imperium in Imperio," *American Political Science Review*, 44 (1950), 323–42.

5.

OTHER INTEREST

GROUPS

FROM THE DISCUSSION of organizations resting on economic foundations it might be deduced that a group theory of politics is essentially a theory of economic determinism. Under that theory it might be reasoned: A steel industry exists; therefore an American Iron and Steel Institute will exist, and it will have predictable views on public policy. If there is a steel industry, the chances are good that there will be something on the order of the Institute, but what its views will be is not so predictable. Group views are not cleanly cast from the matrix of economic circumstance: they are hammered out by internal group debate and conflict. Moreover, to equate a group theory with a theory of economic interest is to ignore the many groups whose endeavors have only the most tenuous economic basis. The Anti-Defamation League, the Americans for Democratic Action, the National Catholic Welfare Conference, the League of Women Voters, the Daughters of the American Revolution, the American Correctional Association, the American Friends Service Committee, and the John Birch Society can all raise quite a commotion and, under propitious circumstances, influence public policy.

Obviously all sorts of groups that affect public policy have fundamental similarities; one common denominator is that the members of each group possess shared attitudes. These attitudes may or may not be related to the economic interest of the members of the group. Even if they are, they are not extruded in a predetermined form from a given set of circumstances.

They develop somewhat unpredictably in the processes of interaction—the give-and-take—among the members of the group. Thus, many years ago the American Medical Association took a benign attitude toward health insurance proposals. Then gradually it swung around to the most spirited opposition in response to the shifting balance of power in its own internal politics.

In his group theory David B. Truman holds that shared attitudes, not property, income, or other material concern, constitute group "interests." [1] Under this conception of interest, the Izaak Walton League is as much an interest group as is the Gray Iron Founders Society. The members of each group share attitudes that underly its offensive excursions and defensive maneuvers in relation to government and to other private groups. Under this theory, too, an interest group need not possess the apparatus of formal organization to carry weight in the political process. Even though no group machinery exists, politicians will take into account and seek to exploit the common attitudes of the home owners, the suburbanites, the good people of eastern Oregon, or the fine citizens of downstate Illinois. More commonly, of course, organization exists, and an executive secretary and a board of directors see that group attitudes are translated into resolutions and communicated to the points of decision.

The conception of group interest as shared attitudes also permits one to take into account other aspects of politics that escape us if the notion of group is limited to organized group. Among the population are many categories of people with like attitudes, but they are quiescent politically and do not technically constitute groups. Once interactions develop among these people —communications, discussions, reactions, responses—an operative, although not necessarily organized, group comes into being and affects the balance of strength among existing groups. These groups, called to life by events that activate the latent attitudes of their members, Professor Truman calls "potential" groups. A new highway, say, is to be routed through a residential district. The citizenry concerned are activated, the potential group quickly becomes a reality, and its executive committee builds a fire under the state highway commission. Or a bill that appears to be a big steal seems about to be passed by the legislature. Mass meetings are called, indignant editorials appear, delegations call on the governor; a quiescent or potential group, based on a shared attitude of hostility toward thievery, becomes a reality for the duration of the crisis and then may lapse back into mere potential.

The idea of interest group that has been set out has sufficient breadth to include all the organizations dealt with earlier. It also covers others that have less of an economic base. Thousands of groups make themselves heard in the affairs of local, state, and national government. To catalogue all pressure

[1] For a statement of the essentials of his theory, see David B. Truman, *The Governmental Process* (New York: Knopf, 1951), ch. 2.

organizations would be a task of censuslike proportions, but their variety may be suggested by brief mention of several classes of groups.

One category consists of those groups concerned with the scope and nature of public activities. Commonly a pressure group moves the government to act (or not to act), though at times organized groups come into being after the government has acted. The beneficiaries of governing activities are likely to be alert and insistent in presenting their recommendations on appropriations and legislation. Examples are the National Rivers and Harbors Congress, the National Reclamation Association, the National Rehabilitation Association, the Mail Order Association of America, and the National Rural Electric Cooperative Association. Similarly, groups may be concerned chiefly with the character of specific regulatory or tax measures. Organizations of public employees at times wield a powerful influence.

Women are banded together in diverse groups with a concern about public policy. The National Federation of Business and Professional Women's Clubs has fought, with some success, for the elimination of economic discrimination against women. The League of Women Voters has a long record of lobbying in support of governmental measures ordinarily in the general interest, and the American Association of University Women has been active on some issues. The General Federation of Women's Clubs has stood for such proposals as the elimination of roadside billboards. Women, as women, have few common political interests, and, hence, women's organizations often have difficulty in finding issues in which their members have a joint concern and in avoiding issues that generate schisms. Women's groups with a multiclass membership maintain unity on only the most innocuous matters. Women's groups with a class membership, however, can push for sharply defined objectives without threatening their unity.

Another differentiation among groups may be noted. Some groups— most of those discussed in earlier chapters—are permanent organizations that act from time to time as public issues of concern to their members arise. Another sort consists of organizations created, *ad hoc*, to agitate for or against specific proposals; they are usually fairly short-lived. They often serve to mobilize or to coordinate the efforts of several permanent associations with a common concern about legislation. Illustrative are the National St. Lawrence Project Conference, the National Committee for Repeal of Wartime Excise Taxes, and the National Committee to Defeat the Mundt Bill.

Pressure organizations are also clustered about state and local governments. Each state capital has its own complement of representatives of organized groups within the state. Often the division of functions between national and state government is paralleled by a division of spheres within a federated national private organization. The American Medical Association takes care of matters in Washington, while the state medical societies handle problems of state legislation and politics. State manufacturers' associations, state labor federations, state chambers of commerce, and other organizations are further examples.

A few of this miscellany of groups may profitably be subjected to analysis. Their prominence on the national scene justifies attention to veterans' organizations, religious groups, associations concerned with foreign policy, and professional associations. Consideration of their operations will also permit reference to some patterns of behavior that are characteristic of many other groups.

Veterans' Organizations

"The American idea of war," said Thomas B. Reed, Speaker of the House, in 1897, "is to take the farmer from his plow, and return him to his plow— with a pension!" Every war has been followed by the establishment of a society of veterans to bring pressure for the creation of conduits from the Federal Treasury to the pockets of the veterans. Yet it may be a fair question whether the pension objective is the basic cohesive element in veterans' organizations. Deeply etched recollections of shared experiences that set the soldier apart from the civilian undoubtedly cement such groups together, though their preoccupation with bonuses, pensions, and like matters is their most conspicuous characteristic.

GRAND ARMY OF THE REPUBLIC   Of organizations of old soldiers, the greatest, until the American Legion, was the Grand Army of the Republic, which consisted of Union veterans of the Civil War. The GAR played a peculiar role in American politics. About 3,000,000 persons served in the Union armies in the Civil War. Normally they would be expected to be adherents of the Union, later known as the Republican, party. The political affiliations of the GAR membership and its sectional concentration gave the pension issue an especial appeal to Republican politicians. Pension appropriations would in most instances reach Republican hands and, in turn, would cement the Civil War veteran more thoroughly to the Republican party. The loyalties of northwestern war veterans, assured by pension legislation as well as by the Republican homestead policy, must be given a place among the factors that for many years held together the divergent interests of eastern finance and western agriculture within the Republican party.[2]

In form the GAR followed a policy of nonpartisanship, but its relations, clandestine and not so clandestine, with the Republican party were both intimate and numerous. The nonpolitical façade of the organization permitted it to attract those of Democratic inclination. Once they are in the ranks, an

[2] The Confederate veterans looked to their state governments for pensions, and consequently southern Democrats viewed coolly proposals for federal pension legislation.

Indiana GAR leader observed, we must quicken within "them a lively sense that those who fought and saved this country by force of arms are the same men who now try to uphold it by peaceful means with the same sentiment." In all gatherings of the old soldiers, he concluded, "the Republican party is indirectly benefited." Republican politicians had a hand in the formation of the GAR and, in turn, GAR politicians became Republican politicians. On occasion, Republican party committees subsidized the good works of GAR leaders among the old soldiers.[3]

AMERICAN LEGION   The success of the GAR in extracting money from the Federal Treasury has been greatly overshadowed in magnitude by the operations of the American Legion. Formed after World War I, the Legion soon achieved a membership of around 1,000,000, or about one-third of those eligible for membership. It gave promise of eventually disappearing with the death of its generation of veterans, but a new crop of veterans came with World War II. The Legion's vigorous campaign to recruit younger veterans enabled it to claim a membership of over 2.7 million in 1961.

The Legion is organized in local posts, which are grouped in state legions, all capped by the national organization led by the National Commander. Legion policies are formulated at annual conventions, colorful gatherings that became somewhat more sedate during the interwar years with the advancing age of World War I veterans. During the interim between conventions the National Commander and the executive committee, with the aid of a staff of over 200 at national headquarters, carry out Legion policies. The Legion constitution provides:

> The American Legion shall be absolutely non-political and shall not be used for the dissemination of partisan principles nor for the promotion of the candidacy of any persons seeking public office or preferment. No candidate for or incumbent of a salaried elective public office shall hold any office in the American Legion or in any Department or Post thereof.

This clause places no limitation on the Legion in the promotion of public policy. Like the Farm Bureau Federation or the National Association of Manufacturers, the Legion does not nominate or endorse candidates for public office; nevertheless, it brings its strength to bear on legislative bodies on questions of public policy. The nonpartisan policy serves the same function in the Legion that it does in other pressure groups, that is, it prevents division on questions of candidates for public office and at the same time permits the maintenance of unity on those issues on which Legion members possess a common interest.

[3] For a discerning study of the GAR, see Mary R. Dearing, *Veterans in Politics* (Baton Rouge: Louisiana State University Press, 1952).

While the Legion has taken an interest in a wide range of public issues, one of its central concerns has been the hope for additional compensation, perhaps ultimately a general pension, from the Federal Treasury. In 1920 the Legion succeeded in persuading Congress to raise the monthly pension for disabled veterans from $30 to $100 a month. In 1924 came its first great success when it induced Congress to grant adjusted service compensation, or the "bonus," which was, in effect, a bonus to be paid with accrued interest in 1945. In 1931 the Legion was back again asking, successfully, that veterans be permitted to borrow on their bonus certificates. In 1936 legislation providing for immediate payment of the bonus was passed. In its bonus campaigns the Legion was able to drive bills through Congress over the vetoes of Presidents Coolidge, Hoover, and Roosevelt. In 1955, probably in an attempt to head off general pension legislation, the President appointed a commission, under the chairmanship of General Omar N. Bradley, to inquire into the matter and to make recommendations. The commission recommended a coordination of veterans' benefits with the general system of old-age insurance, a proposal quickly followed by sharp and effective dissent from the Legion.[4]

In the public mind the Legion is identified chiefly with the bonus and pensions, yet it has been interested in a wide range of legislation. At a recent session of Congress the Legion legislative committee pressed for action on 124 pieces of legislation. It ordinarily takes a nationalistic position on foreign policy questions and favors strong defense measures.[5] A matter of major interest has been the question of hospital facilities for veterans. This service was originally limited to veterans disabled in the course of military duty, but under Legion pressure eligibility for public hospital and medical care has been broadened toward public medical care for all who have served in the armed forces regardless of whether the need arises from service-connected causes.[6] Another important point in the Legion program has been veterans' preference in public employment, a demand that veterans be given preference with little regard to their ability in comparison with other applicants. Over one-half of all federal civilian employees are veterans.

A handful of Legion politicians controls its national policies and defines its legislative strategy. When necessary, though it rarely is, the Legion leadership can squelch discussion and ram a resolution through its national convention along with the best of the high-handed. In 1955, for example, in the face of a recommendation to the contrary by a committee that had conducted

[4] President's Commission on Veterans' Pensions, *Veterans' Benefits in the United States* (Washington, 1956).

[5] Roscoe Baker, *The American Legion and American Foreign Policy* (New York: Bookman Associates, 1954).

[6] About two-thirds of Veterans' Administration hospital patients are nonservice-connected cases. The service-connected case load consists to an unknown degree of cases with a most improbable linkage of illness to military service. The connection is defined by statute rather than by medical science.

a thorough investigation, the Legion convention in 30 seconds adopted a resolution denouncing UNESCO. *Life* observed that the convention did not represent the Legionnaires over the country but "only the handful of king-makers who run the national Legion as their private dictatorship." [7] The pronouncements of the national leadership certainly do not flow up from the local Legion posts, whose meetings are more likely to be dedicated to conviviality than to heavy thought about the global problems that agitate the national leadership. On the other hand, probably a selective process occurs in which those veterans attracted to activity in Legion posts are not unhappy with the line promulgated from Legion headquarters in Indianapolis. In any case a dissenting Legion post would probably soon be in trouble.[8]

The Legion is not exceptional in its control by a small oligarchy. In his theory of groups, Professor Truman has christened the leadership cliques of private groups as the "active minority." [9] In all kinds of groups a comparatively small and energetic crowd grasps control of the group machinery and proceeds to manage it and to speak in the name of the group. In labor unions, in farm organizations, in churches, and in chambers of commerce, leadership and management are concentrated in a few hands. It does not necessarily follow that the leadership is out of line with sentiment within the group or that the group processes are "undemocratic." Yet it is a fact of group life that leadership tends to fall into specialized, even professionalized, hands.

Within a comparatively narrow range of public policy the Legion exerts a formidable, if not invariably controlling, influence. How is this power of the Legion, a comparatively small group of activists, to be explained? Undoubtedly war veterans, especially those disabled in battle, have a special claim on their country. The general sentiment supporting that claim creates a favorable atmosphere for the pressure activities of the Legion.[10] Moreover, from a political standpoint, a matter of no small importance is the fact that the Legion has no compact and determined counter-pressure group against which it has to work. If the AFL, for example, strikes out for legislation, its lobbyists will likely collide with those of the National Association of Manufacturers. The Legion, however, in its main endeavors encounters less determined op-

---

[7] October 24, 1955.

[8] In 1946 the National Commander of the Legion opposed a veterans' emergency-housing bill; a New York Legion post held a rally to support the bill. Shortly afterward the local post was suspended. See Justin Gray, "The Legion Under Control," *New Republic*, May 10, 1948.

[9] *The Governmental Process* (New York: Knopf, 1951), pp. 139–55.

[10] The Legion can direct a stream of telegrams and letters to Capitol Hill, but it remains problematic whether to vote against the Legion increases a Congressman's chance of defeat at the next election. In opposing a 1956 veterans' measure, Representative W. H. Ayres, of Ohio, a veteran himself, opined: "You would be amazed at the pressure they can employ through various individuals, but I honestly do not believe that the commander of any post, whether it be the American Legion, DAV, AMVETS, or Veterans of Foreign Wars, controls any vote other than his own. Sometimes I think he has difficulty in telling his wife what to do." *Congressional Record* (daily ed.), June 26, 1956, p. 9960.

position, although it has had brushes with the American Medical Association.[11] The big guns of big business do not go into action against Legion forays on the Treasury, a circumstance that gives plausibility to the hypothesis that a tacit alliance prevails between business and Legion leadership. For business the quid pro quo is the generally conservative position of the Legion. On labor matters in particular, the Legion, not so much by its public pronouncements as by the activities of its local posts, has earned the reputation of being aligned with business.[12]

OTHER VETERANS' GROUPS   Although the Legion has been the largest veterans' organization, other groups have maintained a separate existence. The Veterans of Foreign Wars, formed after the Spanish-American War, limits its membership to veterans who have had overseas service and thereby excludes the home-front soldier. The program of the VFW is a "bread-and-butter" program much like that of the Legion. One of its recent legislative programs, for example, included 91 items, a large proportion of which related to veterans' perquisites. The Disabled American Veterans, a relatively small group, consists of persons with disability incurred in military service, a condition of affiliation that gives its legislative demands a special moral force.

After World War II the older veterans' organizations campaigned vigorously to enlist the generation of ex-soldiers. In its past record the Legion had both an asset and a handicap in its membership campaigns. The Legion had consisted mainly of the more prosperous veterans of World War I. As a consequence its program on issues apart from narrow "bread-and-butter" questions had been conservative, if not reactionary. This record stimulated those of contrary political inclinations to attempt to form new organizations to attract the veterans of World War II.

The two principal new groups formed were the American Veterans of World War II (known as Amvets) and the American Veterans Committee (commonly called the AVC). Neither organization made much headway in recruiting members against the competition of the entrenched groups, which did their utmost to discredit and freeze out the upstart societies. Yet the existence of even small dissenting groups serves to remind legislators that not all veterans agree with the Legion's top brass. The AVC stands for "Citizens First, Veterans Second." An organization espousing so novel a doctrine could scarcely be 100 per cent American in the view of the older veterans' groups. Both the AVC and Amvets urge restraint in the dispensation of largesse from the Treasury to veterans; they also urge more adequate com-

---

[11] The AMA has urged a narrowing of eligibility for Veterans' Administration hospital care. The Legion's response is that "only a selfish interest" gives rise to such a view.

[12] Justin Gray, *The Inside Story of the Legion* (New York: Boni & Gaer, 1948); R. S. Jones, *A History of the American Legion* (Indianapolis: Bobbs-Merrill, 1946).

pensation to those seriously disabled, a group that seems to be outdistanced in the lobbying rush by the able-bodied. The AVC proclaims that the "millions" receiving unjustified benefits should abandon the "role of postwar mercenary." On the other hand, the Legion has been outdone in its zeal for veterans by the Veterans of World War I of the United States of America, Inc., an organization chartered by Congress in 1958. The "Wonnies," as the group is called, at first advocated a flat $100 monthly pension for all veterans of World War I but later scaled down its demands. In 1960 the "Wonnies" spent $200,000 in lobbying, a larger sum than was reported by any other registered lobbying group. In 1962 they almost succeeded in forcing a House vote on their pension proposal, a measure that Representatives would have felt it unfortunate to be recorded against in an election year.

Nonparty Groups and Foreign Policy

Interest groups, as was argued earlier, rest on the shared attitudes of their members which may or may not be associated with a common economic interest. In either case the basis of the group is the shared attitude and not the objective economic interest. People may have different attitudes about the same economic concern, and those attitudes may change from time to time. An association, for example, comes into existence because its members share attitudes and not because, say, they all happen to be retail merchants. This differentiation between attitude and material interest as the basis of group may be regarded, from observation of pressure groups in domestic politics, as a semantic trick rather than as a perceptive insight. A look at the activities of pressure groups designed to influence American foreign policy, however, makes much more apparent the fact that shared attitudes are the building blocks of groups. Those attitudes may, to be sure, be about some objective economic concern, but they may also rest on beliefs, aspirations, memories, prejudices, generosities, and hatreds.

GROUPS WITH EXTERNAL INTERESTS   A feature of peculiar significance in the formation of American foreign policy is the role of groups of citizens who, in a sense, also belong to groups abroad that may be affected by American policy. The pursuit of national interest externally is at times profoundly conditioned by the necessities of maintaining political support at home. Support at home for policy abroad is always a necessity; the American circumstances merely complicate and enlarge the problem of contriving foreign policy that will not arouse domestic dissent.

Groups of particular national origin are often most sensitive about American policies affecting the homeland. These groups perhaps make themselves felt more effectively through the electoral process than by the activities of their pressure organizations. A Congressman from an Irish district can be counted upon to twist the lion's tail occasionally without being prodded by the Ancient Order of Hibernians in America.[13] The land abounds with Irish, German, Italian, Scandinavian, and Polish societies. Such groups do some lobbying, but the volatility of their members' electoral preferences assures a respectful consideration of their sentiments by politicians without a reminder from the lobby.

Religious groups on occasion seek to bend foreign policy to the cause of their coreligionists abroad. In recent years the Zionist Organization of America and related groups have worked energetically to influence policy toward Israel, to the extent, it is charged, of opposing attempts to permit oppressed Jews to migrate to the United States because that would discourage them from going to Israel. That and other Zionist positions, such as claims on the fealty of Jews wherever they are which may make suspect the national allegiance of American Jews, stimulate dissent from some Jews. The principal anti-Zionist spokesman, the American Council for Judaism, deplores the tendency "to relate American Jews indiscriminately, to Israeli national policies, problems, and Israel's international conflicts." The Council claims to be neither pro-Israel nor pro-Arab but pro-American.[14] On some issues Catholic groups have sought to mold foreign policy in the interest of the Church abroad. Thus, during the civil disorders in Mexico in Wilson's Administration, Catholic lay societies and some lesser clerics took a critical line toward the Administration's refusal to intervene to protect the Catholic interest.[15] Later Catholic groups concerned themselves about policies toward Franco's Spain. Protestant churches on occasion seek State Department intervention to obtain toleration for their missionaries in Catholic countries.

NATIONALISTS AND INTERNATIONALISTS   While most of the great interest groups—agrarian, labor, and business—make pronouncements on foreign policy, other groups give it a prominent place in their program, and still others exist solely to influence it. One broad class includes

---

[13] Thomas R. Marshall recorded that as governor of Indiana he had cheerfully approved a bill to require that The Star Spangled Banner be sung in its entirety in the public schools. He later learned that the bill had been put through the legislature by the Clan na Gael; the Celts wished the anthem to be sung in full because one stanza gave the lion's tail "a vicious and nerve-racking twist." *Recollections of Thomas R. Marshall* (Indianapolis: Bobbs-Merrill, 1925), pp. 126–27.

[14] The forthright pronouncements of the Council appear in its periodical, *Issues*. See also Samuel Halperin, *The Political World of American Zionism* (Detroit: Wayne State University Press, 1961).

[15] J. M. Blum, *Joe Tumulty and the Wilson Era* (Boston: Houghton Mifflin, 1951), pp. 91–106. For an analysis of attitudes on foreign policy of a wide range of private groups, see Gabriel Almond, *The American People and Foreign Policy* (New York: Harcourt, Brace, 1950), ch. 8–9. See also L. H. Fuchs, "Minority Groups and Foreign Policy," *Political Science Quarterly*, 74 (1959), 161–75.

organizations whose programs have a strongly nationalistic tone, such as the patriotic societies and the major veterans' associations. The American Legion, thus, has consistently supported the maintenance of a powerful military establishment as a foundation for American foreign policy. It supported universal military training, for example, from 1922 to 1940 when that cause had little popularity. While the Legion favored American adherence to the United Nations, it generally views international involvement with a cautious reserve and urges that the United States operate and negotiate from impregnable military strength. The Legion expresses a "vigorous opposition to the participation of the United States in any form of world government or federation." Among the patriotic societies the Daughters of the American Revolution is conspicuous in the bellicosity of its nationalism. Less formidable, but no less forthright, are the Sons of the American Revolution.[16]

Radically different in outlook are organizations with an internationalist orientation. The nationalist groups regard themselves as hard-headed judges of the iniquities of the world that dictate that foreign policy should be at heart the wielding of a big stick from a position of strength. The internationalist groups, on the other hand, have a greater faith that by negotiation, by organization, by striving in one way or another a degree of peace and order can be introduced into the world. When their efforts verge on utopianism, these groups attract their quota of crackpots, though it must be said that it requires a fine discrimination to differentiate between those in the crackpot fringe of internationalism and their opposite numbers among the isolationists.[17]

In the years between World Wars I and II, before the ascent of Soviet Russia to great power and before the atom bomb, the peace movement developed considerable momentum under the leadership of internationalist and pacifist organizations. Disarmament plans, the World Court, the outlawry of war, neutrality, imperialism, and the elimination of the profits of war were some of the questions debated. On all these matters the internationalist organizations conducted an influential propaganda, and their efforts affected some lines of governmental policy. One of the largest and most effective organizations was the National Council for the Prevention of War, established in 1921 as a clearinghouse for 17 national organizations. The Women's International League for Peace and Freedom, a small organization but ably represented on the Hill, won major credit for the initiation of the Nye investigation of munitions, whose findings contributed not only to the adoption of the Neutrality Act of 1935 but also to the wide dissemination of the conception

---

[16] For the background of these and other similar groups, see W. E. Davies, *Patriotism on Parade: The Story of Veterans' and Hereditary Organizations in America, 1783–1900* (Cambridge: Harvard University Press, 1955).

[17] These remarks make it relevant to observe that in the explanation of political behavior psychiatry is at times more useful than economics.

of munitions makers as merchants of death.[18] The League of Nations Association, later reincarnated as the United Nations Association, advocated collaboration with the League of Nations before its demise.

These and like organizations were paralleled by groups dedicated to the study of problems of international relations and to the dissemination of information. By and large, however, these groups contributed to the stream of agitation hopefully looking for some way toward a peace which was not to come.[19] In an odd way the internationalists and isolationists complemented each other. One could capitalize on the hatred of war to keep military strength weak; the other, by contending that noninvolvement in international affairs was both feasible and wise, made military readiness seem superfluous. The net result was American paralysis as the world moved toward war in the thirties.[20]

THE BATTLE OF THE COMMITTEES, 1940–1941   The activities of pressure organizations in the formation of American policy in the period immediately preceding our involvement in World War II constitute a notable example of how the leadership of public opinion even on great issues may move from the political parties into the hands of nonparty groups. The making of foreign policy in a democratic state presents problems of special delicacy since government, if it is to be popularly responsive, cannot diverge markedly from public sentiment. On the other hand, the public needs to be informed and presented with the alternatives if it is to form a judgment. Commonly these functions are regarded as duties of the party system. Yet at moments when great choices have to be made, the parties may be impotent. They may be neutralized by their own inner conflicts over the issues that confront the nation. Or initiative may be foreclosed to them for the reason that an exceptionally high degree of public agreement may be requisite for action on some questions.

The circumstances of the late 1930's conspired to transfer the burden of leadership and debate in the foreign policy field in considerable measure to two nonparty groups, the Committee to Defend America by Aiding the Allies and the America First Committee. The Committee to Defend America grew out of the Non-Partisan Committee for Peace through the Revision of the Neutrality Law. Under the legislation in force the hands of the government were virtually tied. To embargo the shipment of arms to China and Japan,

---

[18] See Dorothy Detzer, *Appointment on the Hill* (New York: Holt, 1948).

[19] For a review of the period 1918–1936, see Merle Curti, *Peace or War: The American Struggle, 1636–1936* (New York: Norton, 1936), ch. 9.

[20] The student of 1964 may not easily comprehend the beliefs prevalent in 1940 about the feasibility of isolation. A few weeks before Pearl Harbor, the *Chicago Tribune*, representative of a widespread and doubtless sincere opinion, said: "What vital interest of the U.S. can Japan threaten? She cannot attack us. That is a military impossibility. Even our base at Hawaii is beyond the effective striking power of her fleet."

for example, would have weakened China and done little damage to Japan, a result not believed at the time to be in accord with the national interest. In September, 1939, President Roosevelt asked Congress to repeal the legislation forbidding the sale of arms to warring nations and to permit cash-and-carry sales. To drum up support for this recommendation, persons associated with the League of Nations Association took the initiative in setting up the Non-Partisan Committee for Peace under the chairmanship of William Allen White. This committee of several hundred persons—Republicans, Democrats, businessmen, and religious leaders—put in motion a propaganda campaign, and its members set to work on Republicans in Congress.

After the Nazi movement into Norway and Denmark, White and his associates took the lead in forming the Committee to Defend America by Aiding the Allies. As the crisis developed, local chapters of the committee sprang up over the country—300 by July 1, 1940, three months after the establishment of the national committee. As events marched the committee maintained close liaison with the Administration. Although it advocated no measure opposed by the Administration, it could hardly be called an instrument of the Administration. It pushed for speedy action; its leaders fretted about the inertia of the government. As legislative issues arose, it laid down a barrage of telegrams on Congress. It carried on an extensive propaganda to build up support for such measures as the transfer of destroyers to Britain. It sought to bring the 1940 platforms of both parties into line with its program.[21] Apparently the Administration moved more slowly than majority opinion. Events in Europe were more influential than the Committee's propaganda in shaping public opinion, though the Committee doubtless brought into sharp focus public sentiment in support of a series of concrete actions.

The America First Committee led the isolationist or noninterventionist cause. Formed in September, 1940, it became the spearhead for the diverse strains of opposition to involvement in the European war and was headed by General Robert E. Wood, chairman of the board of Sears Roebuck and Company. The national committee consisted of prominent persons from over the country, but its strength appeared to center in Chicago. It ran a newspaper advertising campaign, sponsored radio broadcasts, and encouraged the establishment of local chapters to further its cause. America First took the line that Britain's war was not America's war. It opposed the passage of the Lend-Lease bill, the Chicago chapter obtaining 628,000 names on petitions against this legislation. It proposed a national advisory referendum on the question of war. Although its leadership drew heavily from the ranks of conservative midwestern Republicans, the America First Committee was plagued by allies it did not seek. It excluded pacifists from its membership, but it had their support as well as that of Socialists. Nazis and Fascists, too,

[21] For an account of the work of the committee, see Walter Johnson, *The Battle against Isolation* (Chicago: University of Chicago Press, 1944).

infiltrated the organization; mushrooming organizations are especially vulnerable to infiltration. The America First Committee defeated no major Administration foreign policy proposal in Congress, but its mobilization of noninterventionist opinion affected the course of government action. Its efforts, Professor Cole concludes, "undoubtedly helped to discourage" the President "from moving further and faster to help Britain defeat Hitler." [22] Certainly the strident debate made governmental action in any direction difficult. The resolution of the issue came not from internal political processes but from the attack on Pearl Harbor. Shortly afterward the America First Committee's final statement asserted: "Our principles were right. Had they been followed war could have been avoided."

Whether the battle of the committees exudes any clear moral may be doubted; nevertheless, it points to a special characteristic of the American party system as well as to the special problems of a foreign policy responsive to public opinion. Commentators on the American system often make the point that some types of great public questions are avoided by the parties and are settled, if they are settled at all, by the mobilization of sentiment by nonparty processes. When the parties fail, the political system spawns other institutions to occupy the vacuum and to carry on the battle over the issue. Something on this order happened in the fight between the Committee to Defend America and the America First Committee. While perhaps a preponderance of Democratic national leaders leaned toward intervention and the weight of sentiment in the Republican leadership was isolationist, the parties as parties feared to take the initiative in what, either way, was a most perilous undertaking. In effect, the country found itself realigned under the leadership of the committees along a battle line different from that between the parties. The Committee to Defend America managed to form the more powerful following in this new alignment.

Clergymen in the Lobby

Organized religion seeks, both through action by the church itself and by lay groups, to influence governmental action. The prominence of these groups on the political scene creates an obligation to mention them. Yet the fulfillment of that obligation is a hazardous enterprise. The most innocent comment about religious groups can arouse the sharpest reaction. Critical comment easily becomes bigotry or even an irreverent challenge to the work of the Lord. All of which suggests that the currents of religion run so deeply in our politics that people prefer not to talk about the topic lest discussion

[22] W. S. Cole, *America First* (Madison: University of Wisconsin Press, 1953), p. 198. See also R. A. Divine, *The Illusion of Neutrality* (Chicago: University of Chicago Press, 1962).

set off debates over questions irreconcilable because they present, at least potentially, conflicts of divergent absolutes.

RELIGIOUS ORGANIZATIONS Protestants, Roman Catholics, and Jews are represented by a variety of organizations that have at least an incidental concern about questions of public policy.[23] These organizations differ radically in the scale of their activities, in their methods, and in the range of their objectives. Some maintain staffs in Washington; others may dispatch a man to Washington occasionally. Some eschew lobbying and limit themselves to public education; others make the strongest representations to Congress. Some concentrate on a single issue; others express themselves on a broad range of questions.

Among Protestant agencies perhaps the most conspicuous is the National Council of the Churches of Christ in the U.S. of A., which was formed in 1950 by a merger of the Federal Council of the Churches of Christ in America and other organizations. The Federal Council had been formed in 1908 as a loose federation of Protestant denominations and had had as one of its broad objectives to "secure a larger combined influence for the churches of Christ in all matters affecting the moral and social condition of the people." The Board of Temperance of the Methodist Church maintains its headquarters across the street from the Capitol. While it is noted chiefly for its earlier campaigns in support of prohibition, its interests range more widely in the promotion of "the public morals" chiefly by educational means.[24] The Women's Christian Temperance Union, founded in 1874, continues as an organization for agitation by Protestant women on the liquor question. The Friends are represented in Washington through the Friends Committee on National Legislation.

The National Catholic Welfare Conference, formed in 1919 by the bishops of the United States, has its headquarters in Washington. Most of its activities have no direct bearing on public policy, but its Social Action Department has a continuing interest in welfare legislation. The National Conference of Catholic Charities, established in 1910, gained respect from Congress in part because of its able representation by Monsignor John O'Grady. The National Catholic Rural Life Conference keeps in touch with legislation on rural matters and makes the Catholic view known to Congress.[25]

---

[23] In 1957 sample surveys indicated that the civilian population was about two-thirds Protestant, one-fourth Roman Catholic, and 3 per cent Jewish. Of the Roman Catholics, 72 per cent said they attended church "regularly"; of the Protestants, 39 per cent.

[24] The Anti-Saloon League was, of course, far more important in the prohibition movement. On the techniques of this organization, see the pioneer study by Peter H. Odegard, *Pressure Politics: The Story of the Anti-Saloon League* (New York: Columbia University Press, 1928).

[25] See L. E. Ebersole, *Church Lobbying in the Nation's Capital* (New York: Macmillan, 1951), chs. 2–4; Dayton D. McKean, "The State, the Church, and the Lobby," in J. W. Smith and J. L. Jamison (eds.), *Religious Perspectives in American Culture* (Princeton: Princeton University Press, 1961).

CHURCHES AND SOCIAL WELFARE   In the terrain of legislation for social betterment, the major religious organizations, Protestant, Catholic, and Jewish, appear—at least to an eye untutored in the niceties of ecclesiastical differentiations—to push generally in the same direction. The clergymen seem to be men of goodwill disposed to advocate reforms, both by private action and by legislation, to improve the lot of mankind. The Social Action Department of the National Catholic Welfare Conference has favored such propositions as stable employment, the availability of employment "at not less than a family living income," limitations of hours of labor, collective bargaining "as a basic right of labor," legal minimum wage standards, security in old age, decent housing for all people, and other such matters.[26] Compulsory health insurance has had both Catholic and Protestant backing. On the Protestant side the Federal Council of Churches of Christ contended for the right of labor to organize long before it was popular to do so and has set out such goals as "the provision of decent housing and assured medical care, equal access to employment and other benefits of our society regardless of race and creed, the wider distribution of income and power."

In the advocacy of these broad social goals Catholic organizations seem to proceed with considerably less dissension in their ranks than do the Protestants. This may not be entirely a matter of differing ecclesiastical organization. The much stronger representation of upper-income business elements in Protestant denominations accounts for some dissent from the social gospel program of the National Council of Churches of Christ. Some laymen of means contend that the clerics ought to limit themselves to preaching the gospel and should make no pronouncements, especially liberal pronouncements, on social and economic issues. That criticism edges over into allegations of communist infiltration of the National Council, a charge made most shrilly by small, fundamentalist Protestant groups which also have their theological axes to grind against the Council.[27]

FRICTION AMONG CHURCHES   While the churches push in the same general direction over wide ranges of public policy, on other questions they differ among themselves. Some of their less incendiary differences, but nevertheless differences posing vexing problems for politicians, are about questions of the law and moral policy. The prohibition movement and subsequent efforts to restrain the liquor industry by such methods as restriction on advertising have been primarily Protestant movements. Catholics, no less devoted to temperance, doubted that prohibition was an effective means to

[26] See the statement of principles made in 1938 by Bishop Edwin V. O'Hara, chairman of the Social Action Department, quoted in full by Anson Phelps Stokes, *Church and State in the United States* (New York: Harper, 1950), III, 13–14.
[27] See P. A. Carter, *The Decline and Revival of the Social Gospel: Social and Political Liberalism in American Protestant Churches, 1920–1940* (Ithaca: Cornell University Press, 1954).

the end. On public policy toward lotteries and other forms of gambling, the National Council of Churches urges a strong stand against an evil that not only demoralizes character but visits its losses mainly "upon the poor." The Catholic position is one of condemnation of lotteries if carried to excess, but under certain conditions a lottery is not to be condemned as immoral. In practice Catholic policy seems to vary from place to place; in some localities Catholic clergymen have raised a powerful voice against the legalization of lotteries and against other forms of gambling. In other localities the issue of legalization of bingo when conducted for the benefit of churches has divided Protestant and Catholic. Thus, in New York in 1955 the Protestant Council of the City of New York fought a proposal to permit bingo for the benefit of churches. The New York Board of Rabbis resolved that the raising of funds through bingo would not be "in consonance with the high standards of morality and dignity which the synagogue sets for the general community."

On these questions of public morals, religious issues may become quite warm, but far deeper cleavages develop on aspects of public policy that may concern a high-priority church policy or that may affect a church as an institution. Legislation bearing on the dissemination of information about birth control stirs up the sharpest controversy between Catholic and Protestant. Statutes and court actions on the weight to be given religious factors in adoptions excite acrimonious debate.[28] Even more heated differences have developed on questions of education. The formal Catholic position is one of nonparticipation in the public schools,[29] an institution traditionally enjoying a place of basic importance in the American civic scheme. Catholic demands for financial support in one form or another for parochial education have been a prime factor in delaying the initiation of federal aid for elementary and secondary schools. Protestant opponents regard aid for private education as a breach in the wall between church and state and see it as a step toward the political separatism and fragmentation to which they regard the Catholic hierarchy as committed.

ISSUES OF THE PLACE OF GROUPS WITHIN THE STATE
When pushed to their ultimate such issues raise broad questions of the relationship of church and state. Some observers forecast that with the growth of Roman Catholicism in a nation historically predominantly Protestant great political ingenuity will be required to contrive formulas to fix satisfactorily

[28] See Leo Pfeffer, *Church, State, and Freedom* (Boston: Beacon Press, 1953).

[29] The encyclical on the Christian education of youth states that "the frequenting of non-Catholic schools, whether neutral or mixed, those namely which are open to Catholics and non-Catholics alike, is forbidden for Catholic children, and can at most be tolerated, on the approval" of the bishop "and under determined circumstances of place and time, and with special precautions." In fact, of course, in the United States, if for no other reason than the limited capacity of parochial schools, large numbers of Catholic children attend public schools.

to all the division of functions between church and state. Profound anxieties and suspicions based on estimates of developments possible in the long run color the debate on lesser current problems and tend to put them beyond the realm of rational political solution.[30] A growing Catholicism, with its philosophical foundations so sharply in contrast with those of Protestantism, tends to be regarded as a threat to basic elements of the political and social order.

In some ways the question of the relation of church and state is, in form at least, essentially the same question that arises in defining the relation of other kinds of groups to the state. Issues develop about the range of freedom of private groups and the degree of authority they shall be permitted to exercise. The rub comes when ecclesiastical claims conflict with the claims of the state or when the clergy insists that the authority of the state be brought to its service by the conversion of church policy into the law of the land. Other groups, too, on occasion make claims that conflict with the claims of the state, and they insist that the authority of the state be brought to their service. The clergy would be quick to assert that their claims rest on a differ-ent foundation from those of a trade union, a business association, or the American Medical Association.

In the normal course of politics such conflicting claims between private groups and the state are compromised case by case in the give-and-take of the governmental process. The critical moment comes when neither side is disposed to give; the authority of both is brought into play, and some public officials may be placed in a most uncomfortable position. Thus, in 1956 *Catholic Action of the South,* official organ of the Archdiocese of New Orleans, indicated that excommunication would be incurred by those who worked for a pending legislative proposal to force segregation in private schools, a measure supported by several Catholic legislators.[31] Such conflicts of loyalty are commonplace, although other private groups may rest their claims to loyalty on something less authoritative than a canon of the church. A union functionary who happens to be a member of a legislature may be

---

[30] For a temperate and informed review, see Leo Pfeffer, *Creeds in Competition* (New York: Harper, 1958). See also a series of discussions by Catholic laymen, *Catholicism in America: A Series of Articles from the Commonweal* (New York: Harcourt, Brace, 1954); Will Herberg, *Protestant-Catholic-Jew* (Garden City: Doubleday, 1955); John J. Kane, *Catholic-Protestant Conflict in America* (Chicago: Regnery, 1955); R. A. Billington, *The Protestant Crusade, 1800–1860* (New York: Macmillan, 1938); R. D. Cross, *The Emergence of Liberal Catholicism in America* (Cambridge: Harvard University Press, 1958); Paul Blanshard, *God and Man in Washington* (Boston: Beacon Press, 1960); John Tracy Ellis, *American Catholicism* (Chicago: University of Chicago Press, 1956). Bits of evidence suggest that religious belief may affect broad political outlook quite apart from its bearing on questions of explicit concern to the religious group. See G. Lenski, *The Religious Factor* (New York: Doubleday, 1961); B. Johnson, "Ascetic Protestantism and Political Preference," *Public Opinion Quarterly,* 26 (1962), 35–46.

[31] *New York Times,* February 25, 1956.

bound by ties of loyalty to his union. Or a businessman is subject to sanctions of trade groups with which he is associated. One of the conditions requisite to the maintenance of a viable pluralistic order—with wide ranges of freedom of action accorded to private groups—is the minimization of the number of questions not readily compromisable and the avoidance of circumstances that assure collision of determined forces in diametric opposition. Another condition may be that groups possess sufficient ideological flexibility to enter into the give-and-take essential for the mitigation of conflict, seldom a characteristic of the zealot who firmly believes that the Lord is on his side.

The Professions

Although it is commonly said that all public questions are matters of general concern, many legislative decisions and administrative acts have immediate effect upon only a few people. In such situations the affected group can often determine what public policy shall be; the lack of challenge to its recommendations may be interpreted as unanimous consent. Its position of informal authority may be enhanced if the matter appears to require judgments on questions on which members of the group are expert. Such considerations bear on the fact that within certain restricted spheres the professions are quite as powerful as the Farm Bureau or the American Federation of Labor. Yet when professional associations venture beyond these areas their influence may wane. When their demands run counter to those of other well-organized groups, the conflict may end in compromise or defeat.

CONTROL OF ENTRY TO PROFESSIONS   Of great concern to professional associations is the control of entrance to the professions. Since the licensure of trades and professions is within the jurisdiction of the states, the chief political activities on this matter have been by state associations, but the national professional associations have provided leadership. State medical societies and state bar associations have consistently fought for the establishment by law of higher qualifications for the right to practice these professions. In the continuous drive to raise the standards of admission, the medical societies and bar associations have been animated by mixed motives. The medical men have sought to drive out the incompetent and the quack in the name of the public interest. The lawyers have attempted to prevent the licensing of persons who would be unable competently to serve their clients. Further, both professions have been motivated by a desire to restrict competition.

One method of controlling entrance to a profession is by permitting its numbers to grow until professional fees are forced down by competition to the point at which economic considerations make entrance into the profession unattractive. Another is to raise the educational requirements and make more difficult the entrance examinations. Lawyers and doctors have adhered to the latter doctrine—a sort of "planned economy" for the professions. But it cannot be said that their attempts to ration the supply of lawyers and doctors have been based on any thoroughgoing analysis of public need for these services.

Encouraged by the success of the lawyers and doctors, other groups have requested the intervention of the state in the matter of licensure. These groups, with more or less plausibility, justify their demands with the claim that they occupy a position analogous to that of the professions. Plumbers, accountants, engineers, electrical contractors, barbers, cosmetologists, pharmacists, architects, chiropractors, dentists, osteopaths, movie-projector operators, optometrists, real-estate salesmen, insurance agents, morticians, nurses, naturopaths, and others have persuaded legislatures to create licensing boards. In the building trades the power to license is notably abused; its control by the leaders of local unions, acting in combination with builders' associations, is often used to restrain competition.

TENDENCY TOWARD A SYSTEM OF GUILDS   A characteristic of the politics of the professional associations is their tendency to seek the reality, if not invariably the form, of a guild system. That is, in form the state may control the profession, but in fact the profession itself generally succeeds in fixing the requirements for entrance to the profession and in establishing the standards of professional conduct. In practice, a sort of pluralism has arisen in which the profession controls itself in the name of the state. When legislative action is needed, the well-established professional societies can usually obtain it. "Within its field," says Dayton McKean, "the New Jersey Medical Society is very influential. It can usually block such bills as it does not like, and it can secure passage of the measures it approves." [32] In the administration of licensing laws the organized profession usually has a strong voice. The governor will give heed to its recommendations in the appointment of members of the examining board. Not infrequently the statutes require the governor to appoint from the nominees of the professional society, and sometimes the law even delegates the power of appointment to the association. The trend toward the guild system has gone to the logical extreme in the establishment in some states of an "integrated" or "self-governing" bar to which all licensed lawyers must belong and which exercises, by delegation from the state, the power to admit to the profession and to discipline for unprofessional conduct. Some state licensing and regulatory authorities can act only with the consent of the regulated group. Regulations

[32] *Pressures on the Legislature of New Jersey* (New York: Columbia University Press, 1938), p. 71.

of the South Dakota state optometry board, for example, do not become effective until approved by the state association of optometrists.[33]

The profession attempts to protect its sphere from encroachments by new and competing groups. Orthodox medical practitioners have resisted efforts of chiropractors, osteopaths, and "drugless" healers to establish themselves. The first line of resistance has been on the question of licensure. Chiropractors, for example, have usually had to obtain positive legislation to permit them to practice before they could follow their calling without violating the state medical-practice acts. The medical men have usually been able to do no more than delay the chiropractors in their effort to obtain legislation. Then the battle shifts to other fronts. The unorthodox healers seek to obtain the right to practice in publicly supported hospitals and to serve the beneficiaries of workmen's compensation laws. The orthodox medical men fight in the name of the protection of the public against quacks; the newer groups demand the protection of the individual's right to choose his own physician. Similarly, bar associations resist the practice of law by laymen. The encroachments of banks and trust companies in the field of estates and trusts have been fought by the lawyers, but large areas formerly exclusively in the province of the lawyer have been lost.[34]

Most lobbying by professional associations does not make the front pages. It concerns mainly questions related to the arcane lore of a professional group whose spokesmen enjoy a deference arising from their supposed expertness. When the professional association ventures beyond the narrow realm in which it is virtually accorded the right to make law, its influence may be tempered by opposition from other interested groups. On a matter of legal ethics the American Bar Association may be subject to less challenge than when it endorses the Bricker Amendment, a proposal about which the judgment of the lawyers may be no better than that of almost anyone else.

EXTERNAL RELATIONS OF PROFESSIONS: THE AMA AND HEALTH INSURANCE   The professional societies and many other private groups as well exercise a relatively autonomous authority over a wide range of matters. The governance of mankind would not be so vexing a task if each private group could be self-governing; then politicians would not have so much to worry about. Unfortunately, in the exercise of its own authority the private group sooner or later affects adversely other interests.

[33] For a survey of legislative and judicial tendencies, see J. A. C. Grant, "The Guild Returns to America," *Journal of Politics*, 4 (1942), 303–36, 458–77. Also the note, "The State Courts and Delegation of Authority to Private Groups," *Harvard Law Review*, 67 (1954), 1398–1408. For a broad philosophical treatment, see H. S. Kariel, *The Decline of American Pluralism* (Stanford: Stanford University Press, 1961).

[34] See M. L. Rutherford, *The Influence of the American Bar Association on Public Opinion and Legislation* (Chicago: Foundation Press, 1937), pp. 93–99.

These conflicts require the interposition of government lest chaos or gross injustice prevail.[35]

A striking illustration of these broad remarks may be found in the reactions of the American Medical Association to proposals for the establishment of systems of health insurance, systems that could have altered practices long governed by the customs and codes of the profession. The AMA campaign against health insurance also incidentally exemplifies the capacity of an extremely small group—less than a quarter of a million persons—to exert a most impressive resistance to political change. The AMA consistently opposed suggestions for health insurance in the 1930's and 1940's, but it mounted a major drive against the idea in the years 1948–1952. In early 1948 President Truman proposed a system of compulsory health insurance, and shortly after the November election the AMA assessed its members $25 each for a nationwide plan of "education." In the next three and one-half years the AMA spent over $4.5 million in "educating" the American people about the hazards of "socialized medicine." A public-relations firm managed the campaign which, on the whole, allied organized medicine with the Republican party.[36] To inform the people about the dangers of "this un-American excursion into State Socialism," the AMA found it convenient to schedule $1,100,000 worth of advertising in the weeks immediately preceding the 1950 congressional elections, a step not calculated to aid the Democratic ticket. In the presidential campaign of 1952 the firm managing the AMA propaganda campaign moved over to handle the work of the National Professional Committee for Eisenhower-Nixon, whose chairman had also been chairman of the committee in charge of the AMA educational program. The Republican platform had declared against compulsory health insurance. To fend off a proposal to finance medical care for the aged through the social security system, in 1960 the AMA backed President Eisenhower's plan for medical care for the indigent aged by federal grants to state welfare programs, which was enacted. In 1961 and 1962 the AMA again rallied its rather formidable forces in opposition to the Democratic plan for medical care for the aged through the social security system. In 1962 it formed the American Medical Political Action Committee, after the model of the AFL-CIO-COPE. AMPAC, technically separate from the AMA, could support financially friendly congressional candidates, an action precluded to the AMA if it wished to maintain its status as a tax-exempt, nonprofit organization.

[35] Private groups may also do grievous wrong to those of their own number who happen to violate the group norms, a matter that may also require public intervention. Consider the restraints on medical practitioners associated with the Health Insurance Plan of Greater New York as reported by E. T. Chase, "The Politics of Medicine," *Harper's Magazine*, October, 1960, pp. 125–31.

[36] For an account of the campaign, see Stanley Kelley, Jr., *Professional Public Relations and Political Power* (Baltimore: Johns Hopkins Press, 1956), ch. 3; see also W. A. Glaser, "Doctors and Politics," *American Journal of Sociology*, 66 (1960), 230–45.

While the activities of the AMA could be interpreted as nothing more than a concerted effort by a group of upper-income professionals driven by a fierce determination to retain that status, the chances are that the episode can partly be explained by other characteristics of behavior. Through the medical argumentation there runs a consistent thread of anxiety that health insurance would alter the medical craftsman's control of the manner of his work—of his relations with other practitioners and with his patients. Bureaucratic controls might be substituted for individualism in the fixing of terms and conditions of work. The mores, customs, and habits that develop around work—jobways, so to speak—acquire a tenacity and a sanctity, whether the job be that of surgeon, lathe operator, or pedagogue.

The AMA campaign also bears on the origins of group attitudes. With a little administrative and political ingenuity, doctors could have built compulsory health insurance into a system that would have made it unnecessary for them to worry about collecting bills or about the ability of a patient to pay, all without disturbing their ways of work. Yet medical men opposed the scheme with awesome vigor. The attitudes of groups are molded and not innate. The attitude of the medical profession had been shaped by long and persistent indoctrination by the central bureaucracy of the AMA. The indoctrination of a high-status, high-income, literate class of persons and their political management, oddly enough, seem to be far more feasible than is the mobilization of lesser peoples who are supposedly easy to manipulate. The profession's leaders over a period of years did a thorough job of educating the rank and file; such dissent as remained was drowned out by the sheer volume of official AMA propaganda.[37]

GROUP CAPACITY IN RESISTANCE OF POLITICAL CHANGE   The health insurance campaign strikingly illustrates what seems to be a general capacity of even small groups to resist successfully proposals for political change. Unless their position can be made to appear completely untenable morally or equitably, those defending the status quo enjoy great advantage, a circumstance that may cause no end of fretting but which doubtless contributes to the stability of a social order. The early social reformers usually did not foresee the power that could be brought to bear against their proposals by comparatively small numbers of interested upper-class persons. Through their infiltration of other organizations, through their individual capacity as opinion leaders, through their leverage over the drug industries,

[37] Charles A. Wolverton, chairman of a House committee, felt it expedient not to identify in the record the AMA member whose letter expressed support of legislation mild enough to be sponsored by the Eisenhower Administration: "It is my impression that a fair number of physicians share these sentiments. I honestly believe the central organization [of the AMA] in Chicago has no idea what the average physician wants his patients to have." House Committee on Interstate and Foreign Commerce, 83d Cong., 2d sess., *Health Inquiry*, Pt. 7 (1954), p. 2230.

and through other such connections, the medical men delayed, if they did not permanently kill, health insurance.[38]

Common Elements in the Miscellany

This chapter, which has ranged over the most disparate sorts of pressure societies, has served to bring to attention characteristics of behavior common to many groups. Those points, which are of utility in understanding groups generally, may be summarized.

A leading theory of the nature of interest groups suggests that such groups rest on shared attitudes rather than on material "interest." Those attitudes may or may not be related to a material concern. So defined, both the American Peace Society and the National Association of Manufacturers fall within the conception of interest group. This idea of group is useful in the interpretation of the political role of groups, for it permits an avoidance of the side issue of determinism.

The policies and programs of groups—and the shared attitudes on which they are based—are shaped by the interactions within the group, the experiences of its members, the environmental circumstances affecting the group, and other factors. Interest group activity is not, thus, to be regarded as a simple reflex action. Rather, group objectives take shape from the deliberations, the debates, the strivings, and all the internal processes leading to group action. The outcome of that process may be conditioned, but not necessarily determined, by objective external circumstances.

In the formation of the views of interest groups the controlling oligarchy, the "active minority," usually plays an influential, if not a determinative, role. The leadership may indoctrinate the membership, speak in the name of the group without much guidance from group sentiment. The character of these internal group relations becomes a matter of public concern as the organs of the group seek to influence the course of public policy.

As private groups gain authority over their members the point may be reached when the power of the group conflicts with that of the state or, to

---

[38] All the debate may have had some effect. Earlier medical societies opposed privately operated group practice and insurance plans and backed up the opposition with punishment of offending doctors by expulsion and deprivation of privileges. As the clamor for some sort of prepaid medical service rose in volume, the AMA and the state societies moved over to acceptance and sponsorship of voluntary medical insurance (under medical control), which they urge as an alternative to government insurance. State societies have obtained state legislation to control and restrict group practice and prepayment plans. See J. H. Means, *Doctors, People, and Government* (Boston: Little, Brown, 1953), ch. 9. Also Oliver Garceau, *The Political Life of the American Medical Association* (Cambridge: Harvard University Press, 1941) and the note, "The American Medical Association: Power, Purpose, and Politics in Organized Medicine," *Yale Law Journal*, 63 (1954), 938–1022.

put it in another way, when the individual is torn by a conflict between his loyalty to the private group and his loyalty to the state. A multiplicity of loyalties is commonplace in a complex social order; the maintenance of the social order requires both a minimization in the conflicts of those loyalties and suitable methods for the resolution of unavoidable conflict.

6.

ROLE AND TECHNIQUES

OF PRESSURE GROUPS

THE TREATMENT of individual pressure groups and
the analysis of selected aspects of their behavior leave untouched the question of their place in the political system as a whole. This matter may be
approached by an examination of the methods employed by groups in their
relations with government. An understanding of their interactions in the
political process will lay a foundation for characterization of their collective
role in the political order.

Interest groups have existed since the founding of the Republic, yet the
great proliferation of organized groups came in the twentieth century. Our
complex array of private organizations sprang from changes in the social
order that created political needs met only inadequately by older political
institutions and procedures. Chief among these changes were the diversities
introduced by specialization in the production and distribution of goods and
services. This multiplication of specialized segments of society threw upon
government an enormous new burden. Specialization has as its corollary interdependence; interdependence has as its consequence friction. New frictions
put to government new problems in the mediation of conflicts born of the
new relations among interests within society. The growing work load alone
strained the capacity of representative and administrative institutions designed for a simpler day, but the old institutions were also ill-adapted to many
of the newer problems brought to government for settlement. New types of
interests needed new mechanisms to formulate and state their needs—instru-

ments better suited to the purpose than the older type of geographical representation of interests.

Increased specialization almost inevitably means increased governmental intervention to control relations among groups. In turn, governmental intervention, or its threat, stimulates the formation of organized groups by those who sense a shared concern. This chain reaction may be set in motion not so much by government itself as by the formation of one organization to press its claims, through the government, upon other groups which in turn organize in self-defense. Almost every proposed law represents the effort of one group to do something to another. When a law or a proposed law impinges upon a class of individuals, they are likely to be drawn together by their common interest in political offense or defense. Organization begets counterorganization.[1]

The upshot of these processes has been the erection of an impressive system of agencies for the influencing of public attitudes and for the representation of group interests before Congress and other governmental agencies.[2] Perhaps 500 organizations have a continuing interest in national policy and legislation. While the major groups may not number over two or three score, hundreds of others have an occasional interest in legislation. A complete picture of the system of group representation would also take into account the great corporations which often deal directly with Congressmen rather than through trade organizations. The views of individual corporations tend to be made known with less fanfare than are the demands of organized groups. Often single firms constitute substantial proportions of their industries, and they have a stake in public policy warranting advocacy by the individual firm. A corporation such as Pan American Airways, with its dependence on public policy, could scarcely rely solely on an association of air transport companies to look out for its interests.[3] On the other hand, in an industry

---

[1] For example, according to A. H. Kelly the "precipitating factor in the organization of a state manufacturers' association in Illinois came in 1893. The General Assembly, inspired by pressure from the State Federation of Labor, Jane Addams and Florence Kelly of Hull House, and various Chicago trade union groups, in June enacted a statute limiting the hours of labor for women to eight per day. The response was immediate." Leading industrialists "organized the Illinois Manufacturers' Association, for the specific purpose of destroying the law." *A History of the Illinois Manufacturers' Association* (Chicago: University of Chicago Libraries, 1940), pp. 3–4. The National Association of Broadcasters had its roots in collaboration by station owners to resist collection of royalties by the American Society of Composers, Authors, and Publishers for the performance of copyrighted music over radio.

[2] The same tendency is manifest in other countries. See H. W. Ehrmann, *Interest Groups on Four Continents* (Pittsburgh: University of Pittsburgh Press, 1958); Jean Meynaud, *Les groupes de pression en France* (Paris: Librairie Armand Colin, 1958); J. D. Stewart, *British Pressure Groups: Their Role in Relation to the House of Commons* (New York: Oxford University Press, 1958).

[3] A notion of the scale of lobbying activities can be had from the fact that under the Federal Regulation of Lobbying Act reports of expenditures total over $4,000,000 per year. That figure is, however, no exact measure, for the reports include sums spent

made up of many small units the association commonly plays a larger role.

As he speculates about the significance of pressure groups the student may well keep in mind a warning about the popular stereotypes of these organizations. The term "pressure" itself can be misleading, for much of the work of these groups does not involve turning the heat on Congress. Nor is the notion correct that groups invariably seek indefensible privilege; their objectives spread over as wide a spectrum of good and evil as do the motives of mankind generally. The view that pressure groups are pathological growths in the body politic is likewise more picturesque than accurate. A safer assumption is that groups developed to fill gaps in the political system.

Techniques in Group Offense and Defense

The organized group exists in an environment of other groups and other institutions. With some groups it has conflicts of interest; with others it shares objectives. Governmental institutions, legislative and administrative, constitute elements of its environment as does that vague entity the general public. The group must either adapt its objectives to the limits fixed by this environment or seek to mold the environment toward acceptance of its objectives. This process is not necessarily one of constant struggle. An equilibrium—or a fairly stable pattern with something of a gyroscopic quality —tends to develop in the relations between a group and its surroundings. Yet at times the relationship becomes one of flux, with bursts of effort either by a particular group or by elements in its environment to alter the position of a particular interest in society. The focus here rests on the techniques utilized by groups in this interaction with their environment. These methods, touched on incidentally in earlier chapters, may be summarized here in an analysis that arranges them according to the targets toward which group strength is directed.

MANIPULATING PUBLIC OPINION   Cultivation of public opinion occupies an important place only in the programs of organizations able to finance the costly task of manipulating mass attitudes. Public-relations efforts are essentially of two sorts. An intensive, short-term campaign may be designed to whip up public opposition to or support of a particular legislative measure. In contrast is the long-term effort to manage basic public

---

for purposes that are scarcely lobbying, and no reports are filed on large expenditures to influence public opinion on legislation. The *Congressional Quarterly Weekly Report* periodically carries analyses of lobbyists' reports. On direct corporate representation, see P. W. Cherington and R. L. Gillen, *The Business Representative in Washington* (Washington: Brookings Institution, 1962).

attitudes toward support of a broad viewpoint or to create a favorable sentiment toward a particular corporation or industry.

Although labor and farm organizations seek public favor, the peculiar position of business creates for it a special reliance on programs to influence basic public attitudes. The public utilities have perhaps been the most consistent large-scale operators in opinion management; they seek to implant in the public mind the notion that there is something essentially good about electric power produced by "investor-owned" utilities, an endeavor that costs them hundreds of thousands of dollars annually. The American Petroleum Institute tells of the accomplishments of the oil industry in advertisements scented with ideological overtones: ". . . this will continue only as long as we maintain our American system of private free enterprise—the greatest force for scientific and industrial development the world has ever known." Individual corporations, through their institutional advertising, help carry the burden of long-term opinion-molding.

The assumption of these campaigns is that the creation of favorable public attitudes generally will make for smoother sailing when particular questions of public policy arise. The technique is that of the so-called "new lobby." In their origins these public-relations programs were thought to be a way of avoiding the malodorous practices of the "old lobby," which relied mainly on direct contacts with legislators, sometimes on a pecuniary basis. Thus, in 1956 a spokesman for the Natural Gas and Oil Resources Committee explained why his committee had spent about $1,750,000 for the education of the public on natural gas but had done no legislative lobbying: ". . . if the consumer understood he couldn't get supplies in a free economy unless the producer had an incentive, the problem was two-thirds solved." His committee left the other one-third of the job to others.

Though public-relations campaigns may build a status for a group in the public mind, a group's deeds may have more effect on the public's impression of the group. Its record may put it in the doghouse beyond easy reprieve by ransom paid to the public-relations specialist. Or its record may command for it a public deference. The status of the group supposedly bears importantly on its political effectiveness. The group may be accepted, respected, feared, heeded, or it may be regarded as ridiculous, inconsequential, irresponsible, suspect, even contemptible. The spokesmen for one group may be heard with respect; those of another may even have little opportunity to state its case. The views of one group may carry great weight; those of another may be deemed unworthy of much consideration.

In contrast with long-term campaigns are efforts to mobilize popular views on a specific legislative proposal. These campaigns range in magnitude from a few newspaper advertisements to those that involve outlays of millions of dollars. Illustrative of the large-scale programs was the 1950 AMA campaign against health insurance. At its beginning congressional mail—in the offices of the 100 Representatives studied—was running 2½ to 1 in favor of health insurance; nine months later it ran 4 to 1 against it.

Both in their long-term campaigns and in their efforts to obtain passage of particular legislation, private associations give attention to the communications media, which are, within limits, independent centers of power in the political system. Organized interests "lobby" the press and television-radio, just as they do the government, and in so doing use means running from artifice to economic pressure. Professor Casey finds that newspaper editors regard religious and nationalistic groups as the most importunate in their demands. People seem to be extraordinarily sensitive about their religion and their national origin; communications media must tread lightly on these subjects or suffer the consequences.[4] Some newspapers have even accepted clerical censorship of religious stories in order to stave off a boycott. With respect to economic and social policy, the fact that publishing is a business of considerable scale itself contributes to the differentials among groups in their access to the press. Some readily obtain newspaper support; others cannot hope even to make their views known through the press.[5]

PERSUADING LEGISLATORS   Pressure groups are most conspicuous in their activities in support of and in opposition to legislative proposals. They have developed this work into a fine art; whether applied in Washington or in state capitals, their methods are much alike. An association's staff is ordinarily in immediate charge of its legislative activities. The larger associations maintain permanent offices in Washington; whereas the more common practice in the states is to assign men to the capital during legislative sessions. These men—lobbyists, legislative counsel—have often served in Congress or in the state legislatures. If they lack that experience, they are usually well informed on legislative procedure and tactics. Their tenure is likely to be longer than that of many legislators; and in the course of their service they may gain the confidence and respect of the legislators.[6]

The use of the term "pressure" conjures up a picture of a wicked lobbyist attempting to coerce a righteous legislator to deviate from his disposition to follow the public interest. By and large, the relations between organized interests and legislators must be described in other terms, though on occasion

[4] R. D. Casey, "Pressure Groups and the Press," in N. C. Meier and H. W. Saunders, *The Polls and Public Opinion* (New York: Holt, 1949).

[5] Few interests enjoy the ease of access that comes with ownership, but Anaconda Copper owned eight daily papers in Montana until 1959. See R. T. Ruetten, "Anaconda Journalism: The End of an Era," *Journalism Quarterly*, 37 (1960), 3–12.

[6] In some functional areas government may be so inadequately staffed and the lobbyist so well backstopped by technicians that he comes to exert an influence based on a not disinterested competence. On the Pennsylvania Economy League, see E. F. Cooke, "Research: An Instrument of Political Power," *Political Science Quarterly*, 76 (1961), 69–87.

the crudest pressures are invoked for indefensible purposes. Each group has its friends and allies in Congress, men whose constituency and party connections dispose them generally favorably toward the group. Often these men are ahead of the pressure groups in the advocacy of a cause and may even enlist the support of pressure organizations on specific matters.[7] From the farming states come Senators and Representatives who will aid the American Farm Bureau Federation. The National Association of Manufacturers and the AFL-CIO have their legislative allies from the industrial states. Lobbyists and friendly legislators labor together in common cause.[8]

A major point of contact between Congress and the interest group is the committee hearing. On legislative proposals of importance, when the appropriate committee of Congress holds public hearings, representatives of organized groups appear to present their case. At times their presentation may rest on substantial factual research and provide genuine help to the committee in estimating the effects of a proposal; the hearings, incidentally, give committee members an opportunity to push as deeply as they wish into the motivations and interests of the group. The committee members may indulge in a bit of heckling and push the group representatives hard for justifications of their position. More and more the professional secretaries of pressure groups depend on the officials of their organizations to appear before committees: the full-time lobbyist is merely a "hired man"; he brings in the president and vice presidents of the organization, coaches them on the bill, and they appear before committees.

While committee hearings are designed primarily to enlighten the committee members, they may also be an element of a broader propaganda strategy to advance or defeat a measure. The purpose may not be so much to inform the committee as to gain publicity in the press. The management of hearings may, indeed, be designed to give one set of organizations the opportunity to build an impressive case and to handicap the opposition by drastic limitations on its hearing time.[9] Moreover, though hearings may not always change legislators' minds, they produce a record to support a position —in either direction—and make it appear that the legislator is responding to some widely held view in society.

Given the controlling influence of the committee on many legislative

---

[7] Representatives, for example, try to persuade the National Rivers and Harbors Congress to include their local projects in the list which the Rivers and Harbors group recommends to Congress for adoption. See A. A. Maass, "Congress and Water Resources," *American Political Science Review*, 44 (1950), 576–93.

[8] See D. R. Matthews, *U.S. Senators and Their World* (Chapel Hill: University of North Carolina Press, 1960), ch. 8.

[9] See Bertram Gross, *The Legislative Struggle* (New York: McGraw-Hill, 1953), ch. 15. The hearings on the Employment Act of 1946 provide an instructive example of collaboration between congressional sponsors and interest groups in the conduct of hearings. See Stephen K. Bailey, *Congress Makes a Law* (New York: Columbia University Press, 1950).

questions, often an interest group contents itself with an appearance before the committee, and perhaps with interviews with committee members, to make certain that the group's views are understood. The lobbyist then philosophically hopes for the best possible outcome on the assumption that he has presented his case on a complicated question with which the committee members have to wrestle.[10] Problems of tactics arise, however, when it seems expedient to acquaint as many legislators as possible with the views of the group.

Of the measures considered by a session of Congress relatively few involve extensive mobilization of pressure. Of the bills of interest to even a large lobbying organization, on only a few will there be any effort to stir up pressure on Congress. Some lobbyists regard the barrage of telegrams on Congress as "death bed" politics to be resorted to only under dire circumstances. Others regard such techniques as ineffective. Indicative of the strategy of a seasoned lobbyist is the remark of an AFL legislative representative that his organization appealed to the general membership to write to their Congressmen only "infrequently" and then only "in an acute situation." [11]

When pressure organizations attempt to direct upon a legislator influence from his constituency, they have a choice of two broad sorts of pressure: the "rifle" type and the "shot-gun" type. The first consists in enlisting the support of a few persons thought to have great influence with an individual legislator. Obviously its utility differs with the type of bill and the circumstances of the individual legislator. Some legislators, given the character of their constituency and their policy commitments, are strongly resistant to persuasion on some types of bills, and efforts to pressure them are a waste of time.[12] Yet on other measures the same member may have only doubt about what he should do, and a word from an influential constituent may sway his vote.[13]

[10] L. W. Milbrath, "Lobbying as a Communication Process," *Public Opinion Quarterly*, 24 (1960), 32–53; "The Political Party Activity of Washington Lobbyists," *Journal of Politics*, 20 (1958), 339–52.

[11] W. C. Hushing in J. B. S. Hardman and M. F. Neufeld (eds.), *The House of Labor* (New York: Prentice-Hall, 1951), pp. 143–44. On occasion a heavy flow of letters to Congress is almost self-starting. Congressmen have commented on the large volume of mail they have received on bills such as one to require humane slaughter of meat animals while their correspondents were saying little about pending major legislative issues.

[12] Thus, a lobbyist against a bill to eliminate federal control of natural gas prices had on his list of Senators one group he considered "there was no sense in approaching." They came "from the producing states," and he thought "it would be a waste of time" to see them.

[13] The superior access of constituents to legislators is suggested by a comment by Senator John L. McClellan of Arkansas: "If anybody wants to talk to me about legislation, if they are from my State, they certainly get to see me if they will be patient. If they are from some group or organization of people out of my State, then it depends upon the mood I am in at the time."

To bring to bear upon a Senator or a Representative pressures from persons influential with him requires an elaborate intelligence service. Some associations designate "contact" men who are thought to be known favorably to their Representatives. The National Association of Retail Druggists developed such a system in its fight for fair-trade legislation. The journal of the association described the system:

One of the outstanding achievements of the association through its Washington Office was the organization of the congressional contact committees. Under this plan, in 1935 and 1936, there were organized in each congressional district committees of pharmacists who were known to be friends of or intimately acquainted with Senators and Congressmen. These committeemen were the "minute men" upon whom the association relied to act, quickly and decisively, whenever the association's legislative program needed special attention. . . .

This year the congressional contact committees were reorganized on a county basis, nearly every county in the entire United States being represented on the contact committee lists in the Washington Office. These organizations, kept alive and enthused by the regular messages from the Capital, proved their effectiveness time and again this spring. Now, these committees are busy among the pharmacists and other independent businessmen of their counties, keeping a steady barrage of letters and telegrams directed upon the White House, in an effort to convince the President that he should reconsider his action in delaying the passage of the Tydings-Miller bill.

Other associations have built up such systems of contact men; still others attempt on a smaller scale to bring to their support men thought to be influential with individual Congressmen. Such tactics may elicit resentment as well as support, but the nudge from a large campaign contributor, a powerful supporter, the man who holds the mortgage, or some other such individual may be decisive.

The "shot-gun" type of pressure campaign encourages all and sundry to wire their Congressmen. Often this sort of effort is but an incident in a short-term campaign designed to build up public favor for or against a particular piece of legislation. The object may be to panic Congress into action by promoting the appearance of a universal and insistent public demand. The opposing strategy will be to delay until the dust settles in order that considerations other than the volume of artificially induced clamor may govern. The pressure organization may, indeed, in some of these campaigns on particular pieces of legislation succeed in activating a latent public sentiment to the service of its cause.

Letters and telegrams have some effect on some legislators on some bills, but most of these missives fall on fallow ground. Legislators speak with disdain of communications obviously stimulated by an interested party.[14] Even if a legislator is disposed to be guided by these instructions, he soon finds that advice is offered often in ignorance of the parliamentary situation, at an untimely moment, or without an understanding of the details of the bill. Legislators, however, speak with tears in their voices of the influence of the letter written in pencil on a low-grade paper without complete mastery of the rules of English composition.[15] Yet on rare occasions a mass mail campaign may have its effects. That may have been the case in the 1962 campaign against the Administration proposal for withholding at the source income taxes on dividends and interest. One Senator reported that within a few weeks he received 50,000 letters, most of them from persons who did not understand the legislation but nearly all of them from persons doggedly opposed to it. By a campaign of misrepresentation, savings and loan associations, which constitute an interest not notable for its public morality, moved their depositors to express opposition. Never have so many persons been brought so effectively to the aid of tax evasion.

Pressure-group lobbyists may play a role in shepherding a bill through the legislative mill. The processes of legislation are intricate and the channels can become clogged at many points. Lobbyists may give a push at one point and another to keep their bill in motion and may serve both as gadflies and strategic advisers to their legislative friends. If the purpose is to defeat a bill, their skill and attention may be even more effective. The procedure of legislatures gives advantage to those who seek to prevent action. At many stages, from committee consideration to executive approval, a bill can be killed, and an alert legislative counsel may perhaps carry the day at one step if not at another.

Implicit in the importunities of a lobbyist may be the threat that his organization will at the next primary or election throw its strength against the legislator who does not vote right. Historically the most impressive example of this type of persuasion has been the Anti-Saloon League which had enough of a following to determine the results of many elections. Most groups that have a numerically large membership analyze the voting records of

[14] For example, in 1949 the National Tax Equality Association, a group seeking to tax cooperatives, sent to its members a half-dozen sample telegrams and urged that wires be sent to legislators. In four days one Senator received 44 telegrams reading: "Urge your support of excise tax reduction, replacing revenue loss by taxing the untaxed." Eleven of his constituents followed a second form, 17 a third, 38 a fourth, 14 a fifth, and 21 elected to use the sixth form. In 1959 one Senator received 789 telegrams opposing the Landrum-Griffin bill; 427 followed one form and 362 another. Of his replies, about 100 were returned by the postal service with such notations as "no such street" and "unknown."

[15] See L. A. Dexter, "What Do Congressmen Hear: The Mail," *Public Opinion Quarterly*, 20 (1956), 16–27; Frank Bonilla, "When Is Petition 'Pressure'?" *Public Opinion Quarterly*, 20 (1956), 39–48.

legislators and inform the membership of the candidates' stands on issues of concern to them. Such operations may affect some votes, but it is doubtful that most legislators need have much fear of such activity. The number of voters who know both the name of their Congressman and how he voted on any measure is quite small, and, of those, the candidate may gain as much by his vote on one measure as he loses on another. Moreover, often the admonitions of a pressure group only re-enforce other pressures on a legislator. A Representative from a working-class district may have his back stiffened by a word from the AFL-CIO but he need not fear a candidate backed, say, by the state manufacturers' association. On the other hand, a Representative from a suburban Republican district who consistently supports labor measures has no right to be astonished if he faces primary opposition financed by those interests against whose wishes he has voted. In any case, it is not so much the rank-and-file legislator who receives the dedicated attention of pressure groups in campaigns as it is the conspicuous advocate or opponent of measures. The legislator who spearheads a movement that touches some interest in the pocketbook should give close attention to his political fences.

Any catalogue of methods of dealing with legislators would be incomplete without mention of the methods of corruption. That such techniques are employed is undeniable; the extent of their use is another matter. The prevailing supposition is that their use has declined over the past half-century and that they survive chiefly in sporadic applications in state legislatures.[16] Instances of bribery—and near-bribery—seem to be associated with the maneuvers of relatively small groups interested in legislation that involves the grant or denial of privileges of great, immediate, monetary value. In such general category could be placed revelations during the 1930's and 1940's of the activities of small-loan companies, public utilities, race-track promoters, highway transport groups, gambling syndicates, and the like. Pecuniary ties between lobbyist and legislator may take forms other than

---

[16] There is a lurid folklore of the old-fashioned lobby and its techniques. How accurate the stories were, or remain, is a matter of conjecture. One of the approaches "was to furnish sumptuous free meals without number, and great quantities of assorted intoxicating liquors to legislators." Another was to "let the persons to be influenced actually win large sums of money" in poker games. Still another was "to debase them morally by procuring for their entertainment lascivious women who were on the payroll of the lobbyist and who were willing to run the whole gamut, so to speak, of immorality." The author of the quoted remarks, Eugene D. O'Sullivan, former Representative from Nebraska, understood that the "practice of having legislators and others embraced in the toils of the harlots is still in vogue at the seat of many state governments but has been practically abandoned in Washington, D.C." See *Congressional Record* (daily ed.), June 29, 1950, p. A5076. Reflective of the traditional view is a 1957 Wisconsin statute providing penalties for registered lobbyists for "Directly or indirectly furnishing or being concerned in another's furnishing to the governor, any legislator, or to any officer or employee of the State, to any candidate for State office or for the legislature, any food, meal, lodging, beverage, transportation, money, campaign contributions, or any other thing of pecuniary value."

an outright bribe. Thus, in the skirmishes over the 1956 natural gas bill an attorney for the Superior Oil Company spread about gifts of $2,500 which were later described as contributions to senatorial campaign funds made with no understanding about any Senator's vote on the bill. Human credulity has its limits, but the distinction between a campaign contribution and a bribe cannot always be made with certainty.[17]

What estimate is to be made of the significance of pressure-group representations in the determination of a legislator's votes? The unsatisfactory answer is that it "all depends." It depends in part on the strength of other factors bearing on legislative behavior; those factors vary from bill to bill, from time to time, and from legislator to legislator. The strength of party leadership may at times offset group pressures; the insistent but inarticulate demands of constituency may outweigh group representations. Another variable is the nature of the group itself. One group may be able to guide some legislators along the desired direction and another may be completely powerless. Still another variable may be the type of bill. All these factors and others are mixed in proportions that vary from legislator to legislator as well as from roll call to roll call. Such complexities warn against the easy generalization that Congressmen are usually pushed around by lobbyists.

RELATIONS WITH ADMINISTRATORS   Pressure groups are at their most spectacular in their support of and opposition to legislation, but equally important are their continuous relationships with the administrative agencies of government. A group may be instrumental in obtaining the passage of legislation; it may follow through with pressure, aid, and encouragement to the agency charged with responsibility for enforcing the act. Legislation may be applied vigorously or otherwise, and the choice may not be unrelated to the concern of various groups about the matter. With the growing complexity of government, legislative bodies have had to delegate authority to administrative agencies to make rules and regulations. Administrators become legislators, and pressure groups inevitably direct their activities to the point at which authority to make decisions is lodged. Where power rests, there influence will be brought to bear.

Within the federal administration, procedures have evolved that regularize the role of private associations in the rule-making process. The Federal Administrative Procedure Act of 1946 requires most federal agencies to give public notice of proposed rules, to permit interested persons to present arguments, and to receive petitions for the issuance, amendment, or repeal of a rule. Pressure-group staffs keep track of such notices and when their organizations are affected prepare statements of the group position on the proposal.

[17] If the data could be turned up, the conclusion probably would be that money is used (in any of a variety of ways) far more frequently to sustain friends than to convert opponents.

Such practices, to a degree at least, put the rule-making process into a gold-fish bowl and recognize a right of all concerned to be informed of proposed action and to be given an opportunity to make their views known.[18]

In contrast, when rules are issued without such procedures a premium exists on access to administrators through the back door, and the administratoɪ may act without being confronted by the claims of all those to be affected. In 1955 a congressional investigation brought to light the easy access to the Department of Interior enjoyed by western utilities. Changes in regulations, to the advantage of the utilities, were issued in substantially the form recommended by the lobbyist whose advice had been requested by the Under Secretary of Interior. The action fell outside the terms of the Administrative Procedure Act, and the reversal of a policy of the Truman Administration was accomplished quietly and without fanfare. Advocates of regularized procedures, in effect, assume that if the opponents of an action have an opportunity to stir up a commotion, the decision will be different. Thus, the American Public Power Association, after it saw that private utilities had an inside track to the Interior Department, urged Congress in 1956 to extend the Administrative Procedure Act to decisions on the marketing of electricity.

Pressure groups on occasion mount a propaganda campaign against administrative agencies, a campaign calculated to discredit an agency and to influence its decision. This may even extend to attempts to influence a quasi-judicial agency which is obligated to act somewhat as a court. In 1952 the Federal Trade Commission initiated a proceeding that involved a disputed interpretation of fair-trade legislation. The Bureau of Education on Fair Trade, a lobbying outfit, proclaimed the action to be an effort to obstruct the will of Congress; it urged all concerned to "Tell your Congressmen and Senators about this Threat Now." The bureau declined an invitation to appear before the commision as *amicus curiae* to present its views; it sought rather to affect the legal decision by pressure on the commission to drop the proceedings.

A well-worn channel by which private groups attempt to influence administrative agencies about both general rules and decisions in individual matters is through Representatives and Senators. Congressmen, so the reasoning goes, control appropriations and legislation, and their word may approach intimidation in its effect on administrators. Legislative intervention may also jog a timid administrator to fulfill a plain duty or to moderate arbitrary practices. The administrative-legislative-lobby triangle at times includes group influence calculated to emasculate legislation by influencing Congress to make inadequate appropriations. Contrariwise, those groups desirous of adequate programs may re-enforce the requests of administrators for appropriations.

---

[18] On procedures for administrative consultation of private groups in Wisconsin, see W. W. Boyer, "Policy Making by Government Agencies," *Midwest Journal of Political Science*, 4 (1960), 267–88.

Appointments to administrative posts are by no means a matter of indifference to the association whose members are affected by the agencies in question. Organized labor is deeply interested in who is Secretary of Labor; organized business hopes that the Secretary of Commerce is a man acceptable to it. Other groups with specialized interests may cherish the wish that a friendly bureau chief will be appointed. Private groups seldom have publicly proclaimed "candidates" for these appointments; by less formal means they make their wishes known to appointing authorities. Often groups with conflicting interests have an interest in the same appointment; their differences may be aired in the process of senatorial confirmation if the equities are grossly violated by the designation of a person likely not to be impartial.

The notion should not prevail that the administrator and the organizations of those affected by his agency engage in endless strife. Apparently in the course of time a customary balance develops in their relations. The administrator of a new piece of legislation may be in fairly steady conflict with the regulated groups until the administration shakes down, the bugs are ironed out of the legislation, and those subject to the law become reconciled to it. The resulting equilibrium may well draw the fangs of the legislation; it may also reflect a condition of willingness to live and let live. The happy state of affairs reflected in a pattern of peaceful co-existence may be disturbed by changes in the political situation. The election of 1952, for example, gave many groups hope that they might alter the administrative environment and stimulated them to propaganda and lobbying efforts against administrative relations to which they had adjusted with reluctance.

PRESSURE GROUPS AND THE COURTS   The role of the American courts in the determination of public policy brings them within the range of agencies with which, under some circumstances, pressure organizations must concern themselves. The records of presidential appointees to the Supreme Court undergo a searching scrutiny by pressure organizations, which are quick to oppose the confirmation of individuals thought to be biased against group interests. Given the customs of judicial action it is not good form to attempt to pressure judges.[19] Yet interest groups often play an active role in litigation to test the constitutionality of legislation; the existence of an organization incidentally permits a sharing of the costs of such cases. Beyond the realm of constitutional questions, in some areas the reality of law is fixed not so much by the initiative of public authority as by the vigor of private litigation to maintain rights. The activities of the National Association for the Advancement of Colored People present perhaps the most con-

[19] Indecorous approaches to judges may also subject one to a penalty for contempt. In 1959 Congress also made it a criminal offense to picket or parade with the object of impeding or influencing the administration of justice in United States Courts. 164 Stat. L. 1018.

spicuous instance of group endeavor over a long period to mold the law in its effects on a group of citizens. Other organizations, too, appear as friends of the court in Supreme Court cases. Their participation has, as Professor Vose says, "often given litigation the distinct flavor of group combat." [20]

INTERGROUP LOBBYING   Officials are not the sole recipients of the attentions of lobbyists. Lobbyists also lobby each other. Any proponent of action, or inaction, must take into account private as well as public centers of power able to obstruct or to help the cause. With potential friends and potential foes, a group's relations naturally differ. In many instances a group's objectives will run diametrically counter to those of some other group or constellation of groups. Such groups can only fight it out to a stalemate or to a compromise imposed by public authority.[21] At times, however, opposition may be foreseen and coped with in advance. Modifications of a legislative proposal may remove its sting for groups with only a tangential interest in it or a concern about some incidental feature.[22]

Group spokesmen lobby among potential friends for support. They often attempt to obtain endorsements from other groups with a secondary interest in a proposal. For example, in 1951 the marine committee of the Veterans of Foreign Wars adopted a resolution criticizing the State Department for directing its personnel to fly rather than travel by sea and thereby be bound by a statute requiring them to travel by American-flag vessels. It turned out that a member of the VFW marine committee was also the vice president of a shippers' association. All of which suggests parenthetical mention of the general practice of interests sharply affected by public policy of "boring from within" all opinion-forming groups to which they can obtain access. Intergroup lobbying sometimes verges on coercion.[23] Some associations re-

[20] Clement E. Vose, "Litigation as a Form of Presure Group Activity," *Annals*, 319 (1958), 20–31. See also his *Caucasians Only: The Supreme Court, the NAACP, and the Restrictive Covenant Cases* (Berkeley: University of California Press, 1959). In some types of litigation community influences may play without pity upon the judiciary. Consider the problem of southern federal judges and desegregation cases treated by J. W. Peltason, *Fifty-eight Lonely Men* (New York: Harcourt, Brace, 1961).

[21] Or they may try to convert their opponents. Thus, American Nursing Association spokesmen reported in 1961 that doctors had pressed the nurses to reverse their stand in support of Social Security health care for the aged. The good ladies stood their ground. Nor did the AMA succeed in bringing completely to its service the American Hospital Association or the American Public Health Association.

[22] The neutralization or avoidance of opposition is of basic tactical significance. On a recent agricultural appropriation bill 61 groups sought changes. In 52 instances the subcommittee moved in the desired direction, but in the few instances in which the request would have "hurt" some other group it was invariably refused.

[23] The executive of a chain store group in reporting on the enlistment of support of the head of a cooperative creamery organization in opposition to a chain tax said: "It appears that considerable 'persuasion' may be necessary in order to induce Mr. Brandt to 'go to bat' for the chain stores in Minnesota, although it seems to be obvious that chains are among the best customers of farmer cooperatives in that state." Quoted by J. C. Palamountain, Jr., *The Politics of Distribution* (Cambridge: Harvard University Press, 1955), p. 172.

gard it as sound strategy not to prejudice their main cause by involving themselves in side issues.[24]

Intergroup lobbying may be not a matter of winning reluctant allies but of bringing together groups with similar interests in a piece of legislation. The promotion of important legislative proposals often involves the formation of a committee to lead the efforts of a large number of groups with a common concern. Dr. Riggs points to the importance of such "catalytic groups," as he labels them, which exist either on an *ad hoc* or permanent basis. His study of the Citizens Committee to Repeal Chinese Exclusion indicates that this committee pulled together the efforts of a large number of organizations and that most of the witnesses who appeared before the congressional committee in support of repeal did so at the request of the Citizens Committee, which itself went unmentioned in the committee hearings.[25] Similarly, the Association of American Railroads, the National Coal Association, the United Mine Workers, and other groups formed the National St. Lawrence Project Conference to unify the efforts of those opposed to the St. Lawrence Seaway.

Interest Groups and the Governing Process

The student may inquire what all these activities of organized groups have to do with politics. Campaigns and elections, it may be repeated, are not the totality of politics. Our conception of the political process is broad enough to cover all sorts of efforts to guide, influence, or affect governmental action. The striving for power, for status, for privilege is never-ending and not restricted to campaigns and elections. Administrators take action every day. Legislators make laws. Organized groups incessantly seek to influence these decisions which are, in a sense, the pay off of the process of politics in which elections are but episodes, albeit significant episodes. The decisions taken between elections constitute the basic stuff of politics, the pelf and glory for which men and groups battle. And the stakes of between-elections politics are great. A conservative estimate, say, of the costs imposed on consumers by the public policies borne of the efforts of the sugar lobby would be $100,000,000 annually.[26]

A working conception of the political *process* must take into account the

---

[24] The executive vice president of the National Association of Real Estate Boards wrote in 1949: "I went to the offices of the American Medical Association and talked to them about our working together. There was nothing doing. They felt very decidedly that they could fight against socialized medicine most effectively and they did not want to mix up their issues with public housing and the like." *Hearings*, House Select Committee on Lobbying Activities, 81st Cong., 2d sess., Pt. 2 (1950), p. 49.

[25] F. W. Riggs, *Pressures on Congress: A Study of the Repeal of Chinese Exclusion* (New York: King's Crown Press, 1950).

[26] A figure probably nearer to the reality is $666,000,000, an estimate made by Senator Paul Douglas. See *Congressional Record* (daily ed.), March 29, 1961, p. 4826.

interactions among groups, interests, and governmental institutions that produce such decisions. Moreover, a working conception of the political *system* must make a place for organized interest groups: they not only seek to exert influence; they are a part of the political system—elements quite as integral to the system as are political parties.

REPRESENTATIVE FUNCTION OF PRIVATE GROUPS
Obviously, organized groups, for good or ill, perform a function of representation in the political system. The characterization of the lobby as the "third house" puts the point vividly if somewhat exuberantly. The explanation of the development of this system of spokesmen for specialized segments of society probably rests in part on the shortcomings of geographical representation in a highly differentiated society. Legislators could speak authoritatively for the more or less homogeneous interests of their districts in a less complex society. The relative simplicity of legislative questions permitted easy accommodation of geographical representation to such necessity as existed for functional representation. The growth of the number of specialized interests in society and the increasing complexity of legislative questions created tasks beyond ready performance by spokesmen for geographical areas. No legislator could regularly be relied upon to look out for interests that spread across many districts. Organized groups supplement the system of geographical representation.

Representation does not consist solely in serving as a conduit for sentiments already in existence among the members of a group. Antecedent to the expression of group views is a process of creation of those views. Associations —or their committees—engage in extensive study and discussion in reaching decisions on their program for legislation. By this process differences are ironed out and the association can approach the public and the government with a united front. Reconciliation of differences within interest groups facilitates the work of legislatures and of Congress by reducing the number of conflicts with which they have to deal, as well as by giving the government an authoritative statement of the group position. Government is then left with the task of ironing out conflicts between opposing groups.

The hammering out within private groups of consensus on public policy often produces legislative proposals that both reflect the views of the group and take into account the angularities of the situation with which legislation deals. Legislators, to be sure, could work out the details of policy proposals. On major issues they may do so, but countless lesser legislative schemes evolve within the groups to be concerned, greatly to the relief of legislators and often by no means to the detriment of the public interest.[27] In fact, the most

---

[27] Illustrative of the legislative attitude is the observation of a publication of the National Lumber Manufacturers' Association that public officials prefer to have "the view of an industry, rather than to listen *ad infinitum* to the variant views of countless

efficacious statutes may well be those enacted at the behest of private groups which advocate measures to protect the group as a whole from the actions of its unethical fringe—or from its competitors.

Representation includes more than advocacy; it extends to the maintenance of close watch on the legislative process to spot threats to the interest of the constituency represented. The staffs of pressure groups perform this intelligence function, an operation that requires skill, for often hidden away in bills are clauses with the most untoward effects, at times not intended by anyone concerned. An alert lobbyist may prevent foolish or uninformed action. Whatever the portent of a bill may be, the group staff sounds the alarm to arouse the membership. One sometimes suspects that the staffs thrive on attempts to panic the members by horrendous accounts of what is in prospect in the way of public regulation. The group bureaucracy prospers as it succeeds in arousing fears, but individuals are likely to be much less well informed on what the legislative trend holds in store for them than are their lobbyists.[28]

To say that pressure groups perform a representative function is not to assert that public officials should not be wary of them. Most groups do not include nearly all persons of the class they purport to represent. The National Association of Manufacturers includes only a small proportion of the manufacturers of the nation. Probably two-thirds of the farmers are not affiliated with any farm organization. Members of pressure groups tend to be the more aggressive, often the more prosperous, or the larger units of the potential membership. Thus, the larger farmers affiliate with farm groups in a higher degree than do others. This greater frequency of affiliation from the upper brackets appears to be common to nearly all organized groups.[29] Even among the aged pensioners, it seems that those who are "slightly privileged" are the more active.[30]

---

individuals." Quoted by Donald Blaisdell, *Economic Power and Political Pressures* (Monograph No. 26, Temporary National Economic Committee, 1941), p. 3. Members of industries, too, prefer to iron out their differences in private. Consider the comment of the president of a life insurance company: "The writer was aghast at the way certain parts of the life insurance business viciously attacked other parts in front of the Senate Finance Committee. All of this bickering should have been conducted on the floor of some meeting room in a hotel, before any representations of any kind were made to Congress." *Congressional Record* (daily ed.), May 1, 1959, p. A3649.

[28] Closely akin to legislative intelligence is the function performed by many groups of keeping their members posted on laws and regulations affecting them. Large corporations may keep track of these things themselves, but trade associations perform this service for smaller concerns. The process at times shades over into the explanation of the factors underlying public policies which aids to a degree in obtaining acceptance and consent.

[29] See C. R. Wright and H. H. Hyman, "Voluntary Association Memberships of American Adults: Evidence from National Sample Surveys," *American Sociological Review*, 23 (1958), 284–94.

[30] See F. A. Pinner, *et al., Old Age and Political Behavior* (Berkeley: University of California Press, 1959).

Resolutions, programs, and platforms may reflect the views of its leaders and bureaucracy rather than those of the association's membership. At times the controlling oligarchy may, of course, express sentiments widely held within the membership. On other occasions the leadership of a nonparty group may be unfaithful to its trust or may misrepresent the views of the association.[31] Still other situations may by no means be what they seem. An organization with an impressive letterhead and name purports to speak for thousands or hundreds of thousands of persons when it consists of nothing more than an energetic promoter financed by some interest not eager to make its identity known. Or the promoter may simply have seen an opportunity to make a killing by collecting contributions from the gullible. Or perfectly respectable organizations may be used as fronts. A recurring situation is illustrated by the remark of an official of the Association of American Railroads about a bill sponsored in the New Jersey Legislature by the Chamber of Commerce of the State of New Jersey: "Mr. Russell thinks it inadvisable to let it be known . . . that this bill was prepared by railroad counsel or is in any sense sponsored by a committee of the Association." Or false-front organizations may be established for short-term tactical advantage.[32]

These observations make clear that groups differ in their performance of the representative function. The spokesmen of some groups may be relied upon to present a case that has been preceded by extensive group deliberation. Others speak only for a small but active minority within the group. Some lobbyists gain reputations as men who will provide legislators with trustworthy information and advice; others follow hit-and-run tactics.

LEGISLATION AS INTERGROUP NEGOTIATION   Another dimension of the role of organized groups in the political process may be seen in the phenomenon of legislation by negotiation. An act of a legislature may be in reality only the ratification of an agreement negotiated by the representatives of those private groups with an interest in a specific question. The legislative body, far from being pressured into conversion of private understandings into the law of the land, may act with an alacrity that comes from the pleasure of avoiding the agony of deciding a dispute between groups.

[31] Perhaps, too, it is in the nature of organization for the leadership echelon to adhere in special degree to the pure and undefiled group doctrine. We expect the clergy to be more pious than the laity; perhaps we should expect a pattern no different in other organizations.

[32] Such hoaxes can become fairly subtle. Thus, in 1958 the "Association of First Class Mailers" ran large ads in the *Washington Post* against a proposed increase in first class mail rates. It turned out that the Association's president was a printer and mailer for big users of third class mail and that some of the financial support came from the Mail Advertising Service Association. The supposition was that if first class rates were increased, the low rates enjoyed by "junk" mailers would become less defensible. See *Congressional Record* (daily ed.), March 27, 1958, p. 4930.

An illustration of this pattern, drawn from the work of the Vermont legislature, has been recorded in detail by Oliver Garceau and Corinne Silverman.[33] In 1951 the Associated Industries of Vermont found itself faced by a CIO-sponsored proposal to bring silicosis under the Workman's Compensation Act. The Associated Industries, on the other hand, wished to tighten the eligibility requirements for unemployment benefits, while the CIO favored an increase in both the duration and the level of benefits. In the negotiations the CIO, bargaining from a relatively weak position, agreed not to push its bills for more liberal unemployment benefits; the AIV agreed to drop its plea for tightened qualifications for benefits. The AIV conceded an occupational disease bill to deal with the silicosis question in a manner far less unacceptable to it than was the CIO proposal. All these negotiations took place in a situation that limited the demands each group could make. Enactment by the legislature came automatically when sponsors of the legislation announced that both industry and labor thought the bill should pass. The operation involved no buttonholing or pressuring of legislators, only a few of whom knew of the negotiations leading to the agreement.

In Illinois the process of legislation by negotiation has at times been formalized, according to studies by Gilbert Y. Steiner. Early in the century agreements between Illinois miners and operators "stipulated that neither party should introduce bills affecting the industry without previously consulting with the other." Under these arrangements the terms of a good many legislative proposals were fixed by collective bargaining. Labor might yield a point here and the operators concede a point there. An "agreed" bill would then be supported before the legislature by both the union and the operators, a set of circumstances likely to produce legislative results. Negotiation apparently became feasible in part because either group could block within the legislature proposals by the other.[34]

These examples of lawmaking by negotiation among private groups followed by formal legislative ratification raise the question of how frequently this pattern occurs. Does a large proportion of legislation find its way to the statute books by this means? The answer is that nobody knows, but many acts are preceded by negotiation and agreement among private groups. Often, predictable opposition from other groups moves the interest sponsoring legislation to yield a point in advance with or without negotiation. The pattern shades over into one in which members of the legislative committee mediate among affected groups and bring them to agreement.[35] Legis-

---

[33] "A Pressure Group and the Pressured: A Case Report," *American Political Science Review*, 48 (1954), 672–91.

[34] For Professor Steiner's insightful analysis, see his *Legislation by Collective Bargaining* (Urbana: University of Illinois, 1951).

[35] The following interchange between Representatives illustrates the point:

"*Mr. Gavin.* I am tremendously interested in the bill also and I wanted to state that the bill as amended has been approved by the Izaak Walton League, the Outdoor

lators, rather than undertake the onerous task of negotiating a compromise or the painful responsibility of deciding between conflicting interests, may even postpone action until the groups concerned narrow their differences. Administrative agencies at times take the lead in the negotiation of agreement among groups interested in legislation.

GROUP INVOLVEMENT IN ADMINISTRATION   Organized groups, as was noted earlier, may play a role of representation in relationships with administrative agencies. They advocate the cause of their members, provide information, encourage, and, on occasion, intimidate. In another range of relationships they attempt to bring under their dominion administrative agencies of concern to them. One can only speak of recurring tendencies, for the realities differ from time to time and from situation to situation. Moreover, though the relationships often elude precise description because of their subtlety, they range from friendly collaboration, through virtual subjection of the administrative agency to the will of the organized group, to formal assumption of governmental powers by the private group.

Interest groups tend to share and advocate a similar fundamental philosophy about administrative role and organization. The doctrine recurs that the role of administrative agencies should be to function as advocates within the government of the interests within society with which they are concerned: the Department of Commerce should look out for business; Agriculture, for the farmer; the Bureau of Wildlife Management, for the sportsmen. Adherence to this doctrine by public officials, as often occurs, paves the way for harmonious relations between organized groups and their opposite numbers within administration.[36]

The philosophy of administrative representation of private interest carries with it the doctrine that administrative structure should be arranged to facilitate the exertion of group influences over administration, though rarely does a group make the contention so baldly. Thus, groups often advocate administrative arrangements that segregate into compact units governmental activities of concern to them. Such an arrangement facilitates the development of relations of mutual interdependence. For example, the teamsters union and truck transport associations urge that road transport regulation be handled by an independent agency and not by the Interstate Commerce

Writers Association, the National Parks Association, the Wilderness Society, and the Wildlife Management Association.

"*Mr. Bonner.* The gentleman is correct; and I wish to advise him and the other Members of the House that we, and the committee, have had a difficult time working this bill out so that it would receive unanimous support of both the commercial fishing interests and the sportsmen of the Nation, which the amendment I have added to the Senate bill does." *Congressional Record* (daily ed.), July 7, 1956, p. 10911.

[36] Consider the 1954 statement by Secretary of Commerce Sinclair Weeks: "I'm down in Washington pitching all the time for business." *Boston Herald*, October 5, 1954.

Commission, an agency that also deals with railroads. The commercial fishermen hope for a separate bureau dedicated to their problems.

These administrative arrangements may create a relationship between agency and clientele in which the clientele, in the reality of politics, comes to control agency policy or at least have a veto over it. In state governments, for example, it is often difficult to tell at what point the state banking department ends and the state bankers' association begins. Professor Fesler, after examining the situation in several states, concludes: "State banking departments are typically dominated by the bankers' association of the state." He finds that the control of state departments concerned with insurance and building and loan associations is "roughly analogous to that of banking departments." [37] Not often is the relation between the administrative agency and affected interest quite so intimate as is the case with the Kansas state board of agriculture which is elected by delegates from county farm organizations and certain other agricultural associations. Pieces of federal administrative machinery also at times come virtually under the control of private groups. In 1946 the Executive Committee of the American Legion had the effrontery virtually to summon General Omar Bradley, the Administrator of Veterans Affairs, to appear before it in Indianapolis to defend his policies. The General found it "impracticable" to attend and invited the committee to appear in his Washington office. The incident warrants attention only because it indicated that the usual plasticity of the Administrator at the hands of the Legion did not prevail in this instance.

Formalized advisory and consultative relations between government agencies and those affected by its action provide a linkage that may closely approach group management of the agency. During World War II, the War Production Board built up an extensive system of industry advisory committees to aid in the formulation of policies concerning particular industries. These committees consisted of businessmen chosen by the board in a manner to be representative of all segments of industry: large and small, trade association and nontrade association.[38] The Business and Defense Services Administration of the Department of Commerce has maintained an extensive system of industry advisory committees. During the early years of the Eisenhower Administration the BDSA even followed a policy of appointing as directors of its industry branches industrialists who served for short periods and without compensation. That policy brought such practices as the rotation

---

[37] "Independence of State Regulatory Agencies," *American Political Science Review*, 34 (1940), 943. For another case of the power of interest groups in controlling administration, see P. O. Foss, *Politics and Grass* (Seattle: University of Washington Press, 1960).

[38] For a treatment of the practical and theoretical aspects of representation of interest, see Avery Leiserson, *Administrative Regulation: A Study in Representation of Interests* (Chicago: University of Chicago Press, 1942).

of the directorship of the aluminum branch among men from the three major aluminum producers—Alcoa, Reynolds, and Kaiser.[39]

Authority is both elusive and mercurial, and in these and other relations the determination of who is the boss at a particular time—government agency or private group—is often not easy. Private associations at times virtually take over an administrative agency by their control of the appointment of its chief. The capacity to exert this control varies, but a private group almost invariably desires the chief of an agency of concern to them to be one of their own kind, a person who "understands" their problems.

All these relationships between administration and private group produce varying results. The situation recurs in which the private group tends to convert public administration to group purpose. At the extreme, the power of the state is formally delegated to private organization, and the line between public and private realms, often hazy at best, is erased. Even when that point is not reached, private organizations, interwoven as they tend to be with the state's administrative apparatus, constitute to a degree an element of the machinery of government. Observation of the tendency of private groups to become assimilated into the apparatus of the state has led some political philosophers to advocate a formal incorporation of private groups into the governmental machinery. While such theories of pluralism once enjoyed considerable vogue, the prevailing American view is that such aggrandizement of centers of private power would mightily complicate the problem of governing in the general interest.

Restraints on Particularism

We have seen that nonparty groups perform significant roles as virtual elements of the political system. Much public policy emerges from the deliberations and experiences within private groups, as well as from friction, attrition, and agreement among groups. Private codes may be transmuted into statutes. Governance may be with the consent of the governed; it may also be at the initiative of the governed. The stuff of politics consists of these intricate and variegated group processes, as well as the great weighing of strength in a presidential election.

Probably the political role of the nonparty group flows inevitably from social specialization and differentiation. If the system of organized groups did not exist, it would have to be contrived. Yet the operations of groups may endanger the general welfare—or more certainly the liberties and rights of members of other groups. While group objectives run from the selfless ambi-

---

[39] See Michael D. Reagan, "The Business and Defense Services Administration, 1953–57," *Western Political Quarterly,* 14 (1961), 569–86.

'ion to promote an unexceptionable cause to the most indefensible advancement of human greed, groups almost inevitably promote particularistic causes and partial interests. That endeavor need arouse no great concern until one partial interest collides with another or threatens a general interest. A major preoccupation of government is the policing of conflicts of interest.

BALANCING OF INTEREST   To some extent, the outrageous demands of pressure groups are checked by the demands of other groups that may be equally outrageous. In situation after situation legislators and administrators are confronted by groups pushing in opposite directions, a state of affairs that permits government to balance one off against the other and to arrive more easily at a solution thought to represent the general interest.

Though the restraint of mutual antagonism is built into the group system, that check does not operate in many situations. Groups well disciplined and amply supplied with the matériel of political warfare often are countered by no organization of equal strength. The opposing interest may, in fact, be completely unorganized. The lobbyists for electrical utilities, for example, are eternally on the job; the lobbyists for the consumers of this monopolistic service are ordinarily conspicuous by their absence. The representation of these unorganized sectors of society becomes the task of politicians who, bedeviled by the group spokesmen on the ground, may succumb to the immediate and tangible pressures. In short, while group pressures often cancel each other out, this process restrains particularism erratically and uncertainly. On occasion conflicting groups even combine to gain their cumulated demands against the interest of the rest of the public.

OVERLAPPING GROUP MEMBERSHIP   Another restraint built into the group system lies in the limitations on group action arising from overlapping or multiple membership. Private groups rarely encompass all the interests or command the complete loyalty of their members. An upstanding citizen may be a member of both a parent-teachers association and a taxpayers' association. He seeks both better schools and lower taxes. The leadership cliques of both groups may be limited by the risk that their members, or at least some of them, will not follow if they go too far.[40] The sensitivity of the leaders of private organizations to such conflicting claims often is heightened by the fact that a goodly portion of their energies are consumed merely by the effort to keep the organization alive.

Overlapping membership may do more than dull the sharpness of group demands; it may immobilize a group on some issues. Thus, in a recent

---

[40] Withdrawal is the ultimate sanction of the member unhappy about the policy line of an association. Thus, in 1959 the Savings Bank Association of the State of New York resigned from the American Bankers Association in protest against the ABA position on taxation of savings banks.

Massachusetts campaign on a proposal to modify legislation prohibiting the dissemination of birth-control information, the state medical society refrained from taking a position in deference to its minority Roman Catholic membership. In the same campaign the state federation of women's clubs took a stand in favor of liberalization and, when the rumblings began, hastily backed off. "We do have," an officer told the press, "people of many faiths and it's difficult when something controversial comes up. It's caused a lot of difficulty." Similarly, national labor organizations have adopted policies favorable to desegregation, though not without considerable anxiety about its effects on organizational unity. Many southern unionists belong also to white citizens' councils. On some questions members of business organizations have been torn between their loyalties to their trade association and their loyalties to the Republican party, a conflict that developed as the Eisenhower Administration asked business groups to turn off the heat on some questions in view of the exigencies it faced.

REGULATION OF LOBBYING   An old maxim of American political reform is that publicity is a powerful corrective of wrong-doing. If lobbyists work openly, the reasoning goes, their animus will be known to all and both legislator and public will be protected. Congress and over half the states require lobbyists to file financial reports which are available for public inspection. So mild a requirement may be of more significance than might be supposed, if one judges from the dodges employed to evade it.

The Federal Regulation of Lobbying Act of 1946 requires individuals, associations, corporations, and others seeking to influence legislation to register and file quarterly reports. These reports include an indication of specific bills in which the reporter is interested, a listing of publications issued in connection with legislative interests, receipts (including names of contributors of $500 or more during the quarter), and expenditures (including the names of recipients of expenditures of $10 or more). The reports, filed with officials of the House and the Senate, are assembled and printed quarterly in the *Congressional Record*. Although the Lobbying Act is ambiguous with respect to coverage and the facts to be reported, its operation has produced more comprehensive data than have hitherto been available on groups and individuals seeking to influence Congress.[41]

[41] For an analysis of the act, see Belle Zeller, "The Federal Regulation of Lobbying Act," *American Political Science Review*, 42 (1948), 239–71. See the McClellan Committee's proposed revision of the act, S. Rept. 395, 85th Cong., 1st sess. (1957), pp. 83–105. Whatever regulation of lobbying occurs must not, to meet constitutional challenge, restrict the right of petition or abridge freedom of speech. In United States *v.* Harriss, 347 U.S. 612 (1954), the Supreme Court held that the federal act did not limit these rights, but in so holding the Court interpreted rather narrowly the definition of persons to whom it applied. For a discussion of litigation under the act, see Senate Report No. 395, 85th Cong., 1st sess. (1957), pp. 66–68. Presumably the same constitutional protections do not extend to public-relations men employed by foreign governments

The requirement of periodic reports from lobbying organizations is supplemented by congressional investigations of pressure activities.[42] Such an inquiry may be instituted as an incident to a battle over a particular piece of legislation. Thus, in the 1935 debate over the Public Utility Holding Company Act, inquiry brought out that utility people working to arouse opposition to the bill had let their enthusiasm run away with them. Wearied in their solicitation of telegrams to Congressmen, they began to sign to messages names selected at random from city directories. The timely revelation of such hijinks on the front pages presumably saps the potency of pressure. In 1956, even if it affected few votes in the Senate, a special inquiry into the gentle rain of $2,500 contributions to senatorial campaign funds at least made clear what sort of campaign was being waged on natural gas legislation.

To be contrasted with such investigations in connection with individual bills are the occasional broad inquiries into the lobbying process generally. In 1949–1950 a House select committee, under the chairmanship of the late Frank Buchanan, a Representative from Pennsylvania, conducted a broad investigation that produced 10 volumes of hearings, an invaluable source of information on lobbying activities. In 1956 the Senate set up a committee, under the chairmanship of Senator McClellan, to inquire generally into lobbying activities.[43]

Registration and financial reports do not furnish information on the manner in which a group arrives at its legislative program, the representative

---

to influence American opinion. They are required to register under the Foreign Agents Registration Act. See Douglass Cater and Walter Pincus, "The Foreign Legion of U.S. Public Relations," *The Reporter*, December 22, 1960. Registered foreign agents at times function primarily as lobbyists. Thus, in 1962 efforts to influence congressional action on quotas under the Sugar Act yielded aggregate fees of around $500,000 to lobbyists, mostly Americans. In some instances the fees were contingent, that is, the size of the fee depended on the size of the quota the lobbyist wheedled from Congress for his client nation. It is an odd, if not outrageous, state of affairs when a commonwealth permits its citizens to sell their influence over their own government to foreign powers.

[42] For a guide to such congressional inquiries and other related material, see D. C. Tompkins, *Congressional Investigation of Lobbying* (Berkeley: University of California Bureau of Public Administration, 1956).

[43] The power of Congress to inquire into the activities of those seeking to influence legislation has been challenged. In 1950 Edward A. Rumely, of the Committee for Constitutional Government, claimed that the guarantee of freedom of speech and press protected him from the demand of a congressional committee that he disclose the names of purchasers of publications of his committee. Instead of accepting "contributions" (which are required to be reported by the lobbying act), Dr. Rumely's committee accepted "orders" for books and other literature which were then distributed by the committee. The investigating committee's chairman called this a "phony sales dodge." Dr. Rumley wanted, he said, to avoid exposing the purchasers to "the pressure of the labor bosses or the smear of left-wingers." In 1951 Dr. Rumely was convicted for contempt of Congress because of his refusal to answer the committee's questions. The Supreme Court upheld a reversal of the conviction by the circuit court, but avoided the constitutional question by resting its decision on a finding that the investigating committee had exceeded the authority granted to it by the House. See U.S. v. Rumely, 345 U.S. 41 (1953).

or nonrepresentative character of the group, or other data useful to the legislator in appraising the statements of group spokesmen. In the routine course of committee hearings, legislators often seek such information from those who appear before them as legislative counsel.[44]

Statutory regulation of the activities of private associations presents questions both of constitutional power and of policy. Such control as is exercised must not abridge freedom of speech or restrict the exercise of the right of petition. Prohibition of lobbying would infringe the liberty of the citizen.[45] Special difficulties, both of constitutional power and of policy, attend the problem of controlling those group activities designed to "educate" the public rather than to deal directly with Congress. The question arises of the sorts of disclosures of contributions and expenditures that may be required of private groups without limiting freedom of speech and press.[46] Business groups even complained that their liberties were infringed by the tax rule that denied deduction from gross business income of expenditures for influencing legislation and for propagandizing the public. In 1962 Congress, at the behest of both business groups and Washington lobbyists and lawyers, amended the long-standing rule to allow as a business expense in income tax calculation expenditures in connection with appearances before, or communication to, committees and members of Congress or other legislative bodies with respect to legislation or proposed legislation of "direct interest" to the taxpayer. That part of the dues paid to any organization used for like purposes also became deductible. Thus, a small loan company could, at the then current rates, charge to the Federal Treasury 52 per cent of its costs in blocking, say, a truth-in-lending bill, whereas individuals, weary of being defrauded by small loan companies and disposed to push for the passage

[44] Organization to influence public opinion and legislation has been held not to be a conspiracy within the terms of the Sherman Antitrust Act. Pennsylvania truckers in 1953 sued the Eastern Railroad Presidents Conference under that act for damages claimed to have been incurred as a result of a campaign to obtain and retain legislation restrictive of truckers. To the astonishment of all concerned, the lower courts held against the railroads, which had done nothing more heinous than exercise the ancient right of the citizen to try to flimflam the public and the legislature. The Supreme Court reversed that holding in Eastern Railroad Presidents Conference *v.* Noerr Motor Freight, 81 S. Ct. 523 (1961). See Andrew Hacker, "Pressure Politics in Pennsylvania: The Truckers vs. the Railroads," in A. F. Westin, *The Uses of Power* (New York: Harcourt, Brace & World, 1962).

[45] The possibilities in repression are suggested by the parallel actions of several southern states in 1956 and 1957 in harassment of the NAACP. Included were prosecutions for barratry, for activities tending "to create a breach of the peace," for doing business in the state without a permit, and investigations designed to make public membership lists to allow private coercion, economic and otherwise, of the members. The Supreme Court rebuffed most of these endeavors. See NAACP *v.* Alabama, 357 U.S. 449 (1958); NAACP *v.* Alabama *ex rel.* Patterson, 360 U.S. 240 (1959); Harrison *v.* NAACP, 360 U.S. 167 (1959); Bates *v.* City of Little Rock, 361 U.S. 516 (1960); Louisiana *ex rel.* Gremillion *v.* NAACP, 81 S. Ct. 1333 (1961).

[46] See the discussion of the matter in "Registration of Groups Tending to Influence Public Opinion," *Columbia Law Review*, 48 (1948), 589–605.

of such legislation, would have to bear all the costs they incurred in doing so. Congress, however, declined to permit businesses to treat as deductible costs campaign contributions or expenditures to influence the general public or segments thereof with respect to legislation.[47]

Pressure Groups and Political Parties

Organized interests constitute elements in the total political system and play significant roles in the political process as a whole. To account for the directions and content of public policy, these groups, as well as political parties and the formal apparatus of government, must be brought into the picture. Earlier this chapter set out the major types of relations between pressure groups and such elements of the formal institutional system as the legislative body and administrative agencies. In the description of the place of groups in the political system a question remains about the relations between pressure groups and political parties. Both types of organization are informal and extraconstitutional agencies that provide a good deal of the propulsion for the formal constitutional system. Unless some idea of the pattern of their relationships can be constructed, the mistaken notion may be left that they are independent and unrelated.

One broad proposition descriptive of the place of organized interests seems to fit, or to arrange in orderly fashion, a great many of the facts about their role in and linkage to the political system. At one extreme, along a scale of differentiation, the organized group pursues its objective in dealing with governmental functionaries—legislative and administrative—more or less independently of political parties. Its characteristics and the circumstances of its operation permit it to function more or less autonomously as a mechanism of communication between its membership and government. At the opposite extreme are organized groups that tend to operate in the closest communication with one or the other of the political parties. Their relationship may be one not only of parallelism of objective but of active collaboration.

[47] In 1959 the Supreme Court upheld the validity of the long-standing rule of non-deductibility of political expenditures as it was applied to outlays by beer wholesalers to resist initiative measures restrictive of their enterprises. Cammarano v. U.S., 358 U.S. 498 (1959). The Internal Revenue Service then issued a clarification of its rule which specified as nondeductible "expenditures for lobbying purposes, for political campaign purposes (including the support of or opposition to any candidate for public office), or for carrying on propaganda (including advertising) related to any of the foregoing purposes. . . . " *Federal Register*, 24 (1959), p. 10,901. The regulation also provided that dues to trade associations or labor organizations would be deductible unless a "substantial part" of the organization's activity was devoted to the specified purposes. This rule and the underlying statutory provision were modified by the Revenue Act of 1962. Elements of the press and the advertising world were left unhappy by their failure to induce Congress to make the costs of propagandizing the public on legislative proposals a deductible business expense.

Between these two extremes are groups approaching in degree one or the other of the poles of the continuum. In one of its dimensions, such a con- ception amounts to the idea that a division of labor prevails between political parties and pressure groups; in another, it takes into account the collabora- tion that sometimes prevails between parties and pressure groups. The broad idea also implicitly recognizes that there are groups and groups; their size, composition, and objectives differ; so do their role and function in the politi- cal system.

DIVISION OF LABOR BETWEEN PRESSURE GROUPS AND PARTIES   In the workings of the political system a division of labor occurs between political parties and pressure groups. This is not necessarily a clean-cut separation of functions. Parties perform some functions almost never undertaken by pressure groups; and some of the activities of groups— and perhaps most of the activities of many groups—concern matters that parties seldom take a position on. On the other hand, on some matters parties and at least some groups work either in collaboration or in opposition.

Among those functions assigned to parties is the nomination of candidates and the assumption of responsibility for the conduct of the government once an election is won. To be sure, a party may be, even in this activity, only a mask for a pressure group. On occasion a party within a state or a smaller jurisdiction may be the creature of a manufacturers' association, a farm group, or a labor organization. Yet by and large, the party does nominate candidates and does assume responsibility for running the government (al- though it is not to be denied that individual groups may run small pieces of the government).

Parties, too, make commitments on broad questions of public policy. So do some pressure groups, but parties do not, and need not, take positions on wide ranges of public policy and administration. To private organizations falls the task of formulation of recommendations and their advocacy in this sphere of government action that includes matters important to limited num- bers of persons, quite technical matters, and the minutiae of government policy and operation as they affect particular interests.[48] To cite an instance: The American Glassware Association urges the Census Bureau to tabulate imports of small shipments of glassware, a question that scarcely needs to be a matter of party policy. Or the American Beekeeping Federation opposes the

[48] Perhaps a line should be explicitly drawn between group action and individual action vis-à-vis government. Even in legislation, government continues to deal, more often than is commonly recognized, with the individual case rather than with the rights and duties of categories of persons. Thus, a bill to rehabilitate coastwise shipping turns out to be a bill to rehabilitate the finances of an individual shipping concern. Tax legis- lation is shot through with clauses designed for the advantage of a particular indi- vidual or firm, although they may be cast in general language. See S. S. Surrey, "The Congress and the Tax Lobbyist—How Special Tax Provisions Get Enacted," *Harvard Law Review*, 70 (1957), 1145–82.

"discriminatory part of the proposed prune juice order which prevents honey from being used as an added ingredient." Neither party need be regarded as derelict if it fails to become exercised about the question.

Furthermore, pressure-group staffs may perform a significant function of communication linking together government and the membership of their group. They may needle administrators into action—the functional equivalent of the action of the ward boss in taking care of a citizen's complaint about rubbish collection. They may advise; they may provide information; they may disseminate and explain rulings and regulations to their membership. Collectively this humdrum labor mightily relieves the party and the legislative representative. Congressmen must, of course, run an appalling number of errands and seek out the answers to a steady bombardment of inquiries. Their tasks would be even more formidable if the staffs of organized groups did not do a great deal of this work.

PARTISAN CLUSTERS OF INTEREST GROUPS   Though a division of labor exists between political parties and pressure groups, it seems clear also that many pressure groups—perhaps most of the more important ones—have a partisan orientation. That proposition, which will be elaborated shortly, needs to be set against the traditional conception of pressure groups as nonpartisan organizations that pursue their objectives by building fires quite impartially under legislators of both parties. Since, so the reasoning went, major policy questions cut across both parties, their settlement required the construction of bipartisan legislative coalitions.

The old stereotype of pressure-group operation has been extended far more generally to group activity than the facts seem to warrant. It described quite well some of the great pressure-group campaigns. The Anti-Saloon League in its prohibition agitation built up a following that cut across party lines and pushed its measures through legislative bodies by building bipartisan coalitions. Organizations spearheading the movement for woman suffrage similarly recruited support wherever they could find it. While an occasional large-scale movement develops that cuts across party lines, more often a group—at least a major group economically based—finds most of its friends in one party and only a few in the other. All pressure groups avoid formal affiliation with a political party and nurture their friends whatever party label they bear; nevertheless, most of a major group's friends are likely to have the same party label.

On the national scene certain major pressure groups cluster about each party. The policy orientations of the parties plow a furrow through the group system, and most of the major groups—and some of the lesser groups —find one party far more congenial to their tastes than the other. There should scarcely be dissent from the proposition that the leadership of certain peak organizations rests far more easily when the Republican party controls the national government. Included would be such groups as the Chamber of Commerce of the United States, the National Association of Manufacturers, the American Iron and Steel Institute, the National Association of Electric Companies, and the American Farm Bureau Federation. This is not to say that all members of these organizations are Republicans or that the organizations get everything they seek from a Republican Administration. Yet they enjoy easier access to points of authority, and their own policies tend to converge with those of the Republican party. Nor is this to say that such organizations cannot do business under a Democratic Administration; they only believe that they do business with the government under those circumstances under less favorable terms. A contrasting but less-imposing array of organizations runs with the Democrats. Perhaps most important is the AFL-CIO, which, like other groups, flies nonpartisan colors but seems to flourish most under Democratic rule. The Farmers' Union feels out in the cold when Republicans hold office. Importers' associations generally regard Democrats warmly as do the American Public Power Association and the National Association of Rural Electric Co-operatives.

The contention is not that either party commits itself unreservedly to its camp followers among the pressure groups. Yet, given the drift of policy of either party, it attracts some groups and repels others. Democratic policy, for example, created no bond of affection between the party and the National Association of Manufacturers.[49] On the other hand, the AFL-CIO, while not enamored of all Democrats, began to encounter rough sledding when Republicans won Congress in 1946, and its leaders after 1952 were consulted by the White House far less frequently than before. Similar differences in relations occur in the administrative departments; a change of administration tends to change the faces of the most influential lobbyists around a Secretary's office.

The partisan orientation of large groups with a varied membership becomes more noticeable as these groups move from the advocacy of the narrow interests of their membership toward an attempt to represent the views of their members on almost the whole range of public questions. The resolutions of such organizations as the Chamber of Commerce, the AFL-CIO, and the American Farm Bureau Federation are not limited to matters of business, labor, and farming. All these organizations resolve on everything from atomic energy to public education. When groups expand their range of concern over the affairs of mankind they are bereft of cues to action in their immediate self-interest and grasp hold of whatever ideological rudder seems to suit their taste. Thus, in 1956 the board of directors of the American Farm Bureau Federation adopted a resolution supporting the position of the Eisenhower Administration on the development of hydroelectric power of Hells Canyon in Idaho. Farmers as farmers had no clearly defined concern about the matter,

[49] See R. W. Gable, "NAM: Influential Lobby or Kiss of Death?" *Journal of Politics,* 15 (1953), 254–73.

and the directors simply followed the ideological line of an organization generally as one with the Republican party and not indisposed to adopt a resolution at a strategic moment to aid their partisan allies.[50] Or when in 1955 the president of the CIO appeared before the House Committee on Agriculture to urge support of the Democratic-sponsored farm bill, he was performing a role different from that of the old-fashioned lobbyist who stuck to his own knitting.

Partisan and ideological differences may strain the unity of organizations based on common vocation or economic pursuit. Such differences may, indeed, provide the basis for groups of similar economic concern but of differing ideologies. For example, the policy differences between the Farmers' Union and the Farm Bureau Federation are probably much wider than are the economic circumstances of their membership. Farm Bureau control has been grasped in the main by persons with a long-standing conservative and Republican orientation. Evidently the Farmers' Union, perhaps by the accidents of history, attracts a membership tinged with old Populist rambunctiousness. These ideological orientations guide the organizations as they wander over the expanse of public questions and adopt resolutions purportedly reflecting membership preferences. Given the program or ideological choices organized groups face, they wind up generally on one side of the fence between the national parties. The result is not necessarily party adoption of the group program; it may be modified in the light of the broader objectives of the party as a whole.[51]

INTERWEAVING OF PARTY AND GROUP ACTIVITIES
Alliances of opinion and attitude between party and pressure group are supplemented by relations of mutual defense and offense in the legislative and electoral field. These relations invariably fall short of formal affiliation with the party; groups maintain a façade of nonpartisanism.

In the workings of legislative bodies, lobbying is often said to be destructive of party discipline and subversive of party leadership. At intervals, the legislative allies of an interest group do form a coalition cutting across party lines and wrest leadership from the parties. With the major econom-

[50] The Farmers' Union which also spoke for farmers but from a different ideological base regarded the Eisenhower power policy as "a total surrender to the electric company lobby."

[51] For general statements on the place of groups, see G. A. Almond, "A Comparative Study of Interest Groups and the Political Process," *American Political Science Review*, 52 (1958), 270–82; Joseph LaPalombara, "The Utility and Limitations of Interest Group Theory in Non-American Field Situations," *Journal of Politics*, 22 (1960), 29–49; R. C. Macridis, "Interest Groups in Comparative Analysis," *Journal of Politics*, 23 (1961), 25–45; D. B. Truman, "Organized Interest Groups in American National Politics," in A. J. Junz, *Present Trends in American National Government* (New York: Praeger, 1961); Oliver Garçeau, "Interest Group Theory in Political Research," *Annals*, 319 (1958), 104–12.

ically based pressure groups clustered around the Republican and Democratic parties, the broad tendency is that lobbying on many issues re-enforces the leadership of the party with which the group is allied. When Democratic leadership and the AFL-CIO are allied, the effects of pressure and party leadership operate in the same direction. The labor lobby may aid in holding in line a few wavering legislators. On the other hand, a lobbying organization, insofar as it exerts influence, may pull from the party generally opposed to it a few representatives whose circumstances are such that they can be weaned from their party leadership. Pressure groups cannot well assume the function of general legislative leadership. Yet they may be extremely influential in the prevention of action especially when party or presidential leadership is weak. The power to obstruct is for many special interests the power to prevail, for their goal is the prevention of action in the general interest.

The influence of private groups may be felt in the drafting of party platforms, in the making of nominations, and in the election itself. Here again a differentiation must be made between those private groups that maintain a fairly genuine freedom from involvement with political parties and those that approach the reality of alliance with Republicans or Democrats.

In the drafting of national platforms, resolutions committees, or their subcommittees, hear representations of the larger organized interests. The nature of the reception of the spokesmen for private interests depends largely on the broad relationship of their organization with the party. Labor leaders observe that they are received more cordially by Democratic committees and that Democratic platforms tend to lean more to the labor viewpoint. Similarly, business spokesmen have easier sledding with Republican resolutions committees. These differentials in access to the parties flow in part from the fact that the membership of private groups overlaps that of the party hierarchies. Labor leaders often sit in Democratic conventions as delegates and also occupy posts in the party hierarchy. While businessmen are not absent from Democratic conventions, they occupy a position of considerably greater prestige in Republican gatherings.

Even in the making of presidential nominations private groups may exercise something of a veto, though it may be expressed by means far less formal than a resolution. An aspirant for a Democratic presidential or vice-presidential nomination is likely to have only gloomy prospects if he is opposed by the leaders of organized labor. Nor is a Republican a good prospect if he has earned the disfavor of the business community, though that disfavor is not likely to be expressed through formal actions by business organizations.

In the campaign itself organized groups vary from aloofness to complete involvement. What stance to assume involves a strategy question of considerable import for the group. A comparatively weak group whose objectives stir no great partisan issues may be far better advised to remain completely quiet during campaigns. They are strong enough to offend people who may win and with whom they will have to deal; they are too weak to create strong friends among those who win. On the other hand, the interests of some groups are so completely identified with those of a party that they might as well join in the fray and risk the consequences.

Private groups may engage in several types of campaign activity. Circulation of the voting records of legislators is a frequent practice. Labor organizations ordinarily indicate that most of the legislators with "good" voting records are Democrats, while business sees statesmanlike qualities more frequently among Republicans.[52] The compilation of records may or may not be accompanied by a public endorsement of candidates. Public identification of a candidate with a particular group may be of negative value; group endorsement may drive away more votes than it attracts. A group leadership sensitive to the proprieties consults a candidate before announcement of its support.

Endorsement may be backed up with active support. Labor organizations, working through their political subsidiaries, often help to get out the vote and to man the polls. In a few states, especially those in which the Democratic party had long been moribund, the labor movement in the 1930's virtually took over the Democratic organization. Manpower for the performance of party chores may also be supplemented by contributions to campaign funds. The role of labor organizations in party finance has been more or less open and aboveboard. Most of their political money goes to support Democratic candidates; and, in at least one union, the official who does the lobbying also doles out campaign contributions. If other national organizations, as organizations, contribute to campaign funds, it is not a matter of public record. In all sorts of organizations with a leaning toward this party or that, a handful of ringleaders in the group often turns up under another guise as members of party finance committees or as fund solicitors. The association in form may not contribute, but the relationships built up within the group can easily be converted to fund-raising purposes.[53] Short of actual campaign contributions,

[52] This relationship may or may not hold with respect to state legislators, depending upon whether party lines mean anything in the state. The 1955 legislative report of the Associated Industries of Massachusetts listed 76 legislators with a zero record on measures of interest to industry during that year. All 76 happened to be Democrat. Another 82 legislators, all Republicans, scored 100 per cent in their votes on measures of interest to industry.

[53] Doubtless some pressure groups channel organization funds to candidates, but not much of this activity is a matter of record, though union support of friendly candidates is well known. Arthur H. Samish, once a noted California lobbyist, represented among other clients the California State Brewers Institute. In his appearance before Senator Kefauver's committee in 1951 Mr. Samish was somewhat evasive, but the general drift of his story was that each campaign year he and his clients looked over the situation from the Oregon line to the Mexican border and decided which candidates to support from city councilman up. An undetermined proportion of the institute's annual fund of around $150,000 for public relations went for political purposes. Evidently in California certain types of pressure groups regularly make campaign contributions to a

the general propaganda campaign of a pressure organization may incidentally promote the candidates of the party most in tune with its cause. During the 1950 congressional campaigns "not a single comment was made regarding the congressional campaigns" in the *Nation's Business,* the official organ of the Chamber of Commerce. In August, however, the magazine "began a series of articles entitled 'Seed Beds of Socialism' in which it characterized the Federal Security Administration as a blueprint for a totalitarian state, and the Department of Agriculture and Interior as more evidence of the destruction of American freedom." [54]

---

goodly number of legislative candidates. See Leonard Rowe and William Buchanan, "Campaign Funds in California: What the Records Reveal," *California Historical Society Quarterly,* 41 (1962), 195 210.

[54] Joseph G. LaPalombara, "Pressure, Propaganda, and Political Action in the Elections of 1950," *Journal of Politics,* 14 (1952), 300–25.

II

THE PARTY SYSTEM

In some respects a pressure group is a fairly simply entity. Brewers, for example, are threatened by a prohibition movement. They sense danger, recognize their common concern, and form an association to defend their shared interest. The group possesses a sharply defined membership, a concrete purpose with which all the members are psychologically identified, and the unity essential for concerted action. Not all pressure groups, to be sure, fit this simple pattern. As their membership increases, as they become less homogenous, as the common interest dwindles, they become aggregates, many of whose "members" identify themselves with the group only vaguely or intermittently.

A political party, at least on the American scene, tends to be a "group" of a peculiar sort. Perhaps only by courtesy may a party be designated as a group. Among many of its members the sense of belonging, the awareness of shared concern, and the impulse to action in the same direction may be scarcely discernible.

A fundamental difficulty about the term "political party" is that it is applied without discrimination to many types of groups and near-groups. Discussion may be facilitated by some preliminary differentiations of the usages of the word "party." Within the body of voters as a whole, groups are formed of persons who regard themselves as party members. The Democratic group and the Republican group are mobilized only on election day, but in the intervals between elections the members of each group—or many of them— react in characteristic ways to public issues. Party in this sense of the "party-in-the-electorate" [1] is an amorphous group, yet it has a social reality.

In another sense the term "party" may refer to the group of more or less professional political workers. The Republican national committeemen, the Republican state central committees, the Republican county chairmen, and all the men and women who do the work of the political organization constitute a "group" more or less separate and apart from the party-in-the-electorate, but not necessarily independent of it.

At times party denotes groups within the government. Thus, all Democratic Representatives form a group within the House that acts with high solidarity on many matters. Similarly, Republican Senators form a party group. At times there may be a "party-in-the-government" including the President, groups of his party in both House and Senate, and the heads of executive departments. We tend always to speak as if there were such a group which could be held accountable for the conduct of the government.

There are other senses in which the term "party" is used. Often it refers to an entity which rolls into one the party-in-the-electorate, the professional political group, the party-in-the-legislature, and the party-in-the-government. "The Democrats (or the Republicans) are to blame for the parlous state of the country." In truth, this all-encompassing usage has its legitimate application, for all the types of groups called "party" interact more or less closely and at

[1] The phrase is Ralph M. Goldman's. See his "Party Chairmen and Party Factions, 1789–1900." Unpublished Ph.D. dissertation, University of Chicago, 1951, ch. 17.

*times may be as one. Yet both analytically and operation-
ally the term "party" most of the time must refer to several
types of group; and it is useful to keep relatively clear the
meaning in which the term is used.*

*No attempt has been to organize the entire book along
the distinctions of the foregoing paragraphs. Though the
chapters that make up Part Two include a great deal of
data on the party-in-the-electorate, their principal objective
is to explain the function of the party system in the American governing process.*

7.

THE PARTY BATTLE,

1896-1960

A SKETCH of recent party history may serve as a bridge from our survey of the great interests within society to a detailed analysis of the party system. Political history is often sterile stuff, a collection of names, titles, and events beaded on a chronological string. Yet a time perspective can yield an awareness of dimensions of the political system that otherwise escape detection. The wars of domestic politics, like those between nations, are not events of a moment but extend through the years.[1]

Modern political systems seem to be in a state of ceaseless unease. Social changes threaten their stability; external dangers jeopardize their existence. Groups within the political system respond, defensively or offensively, to changes in their circumstances that develop with the march of history. Similarly, the party system undergoes profound modification in its movement from the past into the future. The problems it meets are radically different from those of pressure groups. Political institutions must provide for the legitimate aspirations of group interests, a function partially met by toleration of organized groups. Yet a society built only of pressure groups would be

---

[1] The only comprehensive party history is by W. E. Binkley, *American Political Parties*, 4th ed. (New York: Knopf, 1963). See the excellent historical summary by James M. Burns, *The Deadlock of Democracy* (Englewood Cliffs: Prentice-Hall, 1963), chs. 1–8. On the formative period, see W. N. Chambers, *Political Parties in a New Nation: The American Experience, 1776–1809* (New York: Oxford, 1963). See also F. R. Kent, *History of the Democratic Party* (New York: Century, 1928); Malcolm Moos, *The Republicans* (New York: Random House, 1956).

a regime of incessant turmoil. Order must be imposed upon clashing particularisms; a semblance of national unity of purpose must be achieved.

To the political parties falls the task of keeping the peace among group interests. Political parties both comprehend and transcend the special interests of society: they must take into account the demands of interest groups; they must also consider aspirations not represented by organized groups; they must seek to speak for the nation as a whole—or at least for a substantial majority—and not merely for a small part of it. Their energies actuate the machinery of government, which is a powerful engine for the allocation of this world's goods among classes and groups. Yet parties must do more than combine interests for the satisfaction of mutually compatible greed: they must, at least in their American incarnation, implant a widespread belief that their policies promote the common weal.

Alterations in the party system from decade to decade result in part from changes in relative size, number, and relations of the underlying social interests. The rise of new groups and the disappearance of old compel readjustments in the coalitions formed by party leadership. Yet party leadership is more than a pawn of social forces. Party leaders seek to maximize their power by experimentation with formulas to bring together winning coalitions. Their cleverest schemes for the cumulation of strength may be offset by a more skillful opposition leadership. Particular combinations of personality, political doctrine, and economic interest may gain great popular deference for a time. External danger, economic disaster, or a competing idea may tear the combination asunder and set off frantic efforts to put humpty-dumpty together again.

In this process of maneuver to create combinations powerful enough to govern—in a manner to win the plaudits of the multitude—both parties have had to preoccupy themselves with the same problems. A major thread that runs through recent party history is a concern with problems born of industrialization. The decline of agriculture, the rise of manufacturing, the growth of a laboring class, urbanization, and the concentration of economic power created both the salient issues of political debate and the social groupings that were the building blocks of party coalitions. Amidst the confusion of new interests growing in importance and of old interests declining, party leaders strove to construct governing coalitions, as well as to contrive philosophies to justify their operations.

Though the problems associated with industrialization have dominated the tasks of party management, a second major strand of concern, that of foreign policy, has emerged which sharply modifies the problem of party leadership. World War I marked the arrival of the United States to a new status in world affairs, a role that the country sought for two decades to reject. World War II and the events afterward compelled the United States to meet its responsibilities as a world power. That necessity posed new

problems for party leaders in the construction of coalitions to support a government both stable enough and vigorous enough to cope with the exigencies
of our external politics. The new cleavages introduced by competing views
about foreign policy sometimes paralleled and sometimes cut across the old
divisions created by the frictions of industrialization; always they posed perplexing tasks for party leadership as it attempted to maintain political support
at home for what it had to do abroad.

Conservative Dominance Tempered
by Insurgency, 1896–1912

With only a bit of poetic license, it may be said that the coalition constructed under Republican leadership after the Civil War controlled the country until 1932. The Democrats attacked the dominant Republican combination
and from time to time gained control of the government for short periods, a
control never firm enough to permit the establishment of policies diverging
markedly from the prevailing pattern. The long period of Republican rule
was based on the successful conduct of a domestic war, which identified
the Republican party with the Union, with patriotism, and with humanitarian-
ism. Yet the inner strength of Republicanism did not rest on sentiment alone.
Sentiment clothed bonds of substance. To the old soldiers—old Union soldiers—went pensions. To the manufacturers of the Northeast went tariffs. To
the farmers of the Northwest went free land under the Homestead Act. To
railroad promoters went land grants for the construction of railroads that tied
together the West and the North—and assured that the flow of commerce
would bypass the South.[2] The synthesis of self-interest and glory formed a
cohesive combination. The GOP represented a wonderfully effective contrivance not only for preserving the Union but for holding together East
and West, magnate and factory worker, homesteader and banker, in the great
enterprise of continental unification, development, and exploitation.

The postwar Democratic party, too, had its elements of strength, minority
though it was. The political scars of war project themselves powerfully,
through the generations, into peacetime antipathies toward old enemies and
loyalties to old comrades in arms. National policies toward the South mightily
re-enforced its Democratic predilections. Conquest and occupation by even
a fraternal army place a durable imprint on political attitudes. By its defeat
in war, the South also lost the old, old debate on the tariff, and had to reconcile itself to the status of a producer of raw materials exploited by manufacturing interests sheltered by a tariff wall. Yet its addiction to free trade
gave it allies among those northern businessmen with a parallel outlook.

---

[2] The above follows generally W. P. Webb, "How the Republican Party Lost Its
Future," *Southwest Review*, 34 (1949), 329–39.

To a degree, Republicans and Democrats in national campaigns refought the Civil War for two decades. Republican orators waved the bloody shirt, and Democrats struggled to overcome the handicaps from their identification with the cause of the South. The lines of cleavage seared into the electorate by the war and its aftermath persisted. Meanwhile industrialization proceeded apace and created the great political problems that were to put new strains on the party system. The rate and magnitude of economic changes wrought by industrialization from 1850 to 1900 can be set out in statistical tables, but their impact on people can only be suggested. From 1850 to 1870, railroad mileage grew from 8,700 to 54,000 and by 1900 to 193,000. The transportation network sucked the life out of little businesses in villages and hamlets over the land; it made farmers far less self-sufficient and far more vulnerable to the implacable fluctuations of the market; it created both an incentive for and the possibility of combination among manufacturing businesses. By 1890 farmers were outnumbered by workers in manufacturing, transportation, and related pursuits. And with the growth of large-scale factory employment, problems new in scale, if not in kind, emerged in the relations of employers and workers.

In short, in a brief period as time goes, the country underwent an economic revolution that posed radically new problems for the political system. The travail of adjustment set off political disturbances and discontents which on the whole found expression outside the major political parties. In the 1870's and 1880's exotic new parties and movements appeared on the American scene, symptomatic of the growing pains of the economy. Among farmers the Grangers, the Greenbackers, the Farmers' Alliance, and eventually the People's party arose to protest the subjection of the agrarians to industry and finance. The Knights of Labor held their first national convention in 1878 and by 1886 had over 700,000 members. The grand master workman of the Knights, Terrence V. Powderly, had advised the wage earner to join together with other men "in an effort to overturn existing conditions in the industrial world which made of him a serf in a land of liberty and sunshine." In the same era trade unions, by a series of steps, merged into the American Federation of Labor. Socialist groups arose to advance the cause of the working classes. Workingmen's parties put forward candidates here and there. The anarchists urged the superiority of dynamite over ballots as a weapon against the oppressors of labor. The single-taxers, inspired by Henry George's *Progress and Poverty*, advocated their formula for social justice.

Of panaceas there was no end; and now and then workingmen rioted. Nor were anxiety and bewilderment restricted to farmers and workers. Businessmen, threatened by the rapid growth of combinations and trusts, feared the depredations of the industrial and financial buccaneers. Latter-day revisionists regard them as constructive pirates, but pirates they were, nevertheless. Upstanding citizens read Edward Bellamy, and middle-class humanitarians and reformers pondered what might be done to cushion the impact of the new industrialism.[3]

1896: REFERENDUM ON SILVER AND A NEW ALIGN-MENT   No little time was to be required for the political system to digest the new industrial order. All the ferments and discontents of the 1870's and 1880's came to a head in the election of 1896 and led to a realignment of the old political cleavages by which the Republican combination gained new strength.

The election of 1892 had given the Democratic party simultaneous control of the Presidency and Congress for the first time since the Civil War. Its leadership had neither the capacity nor the disposition to annex to the party the smoldering elements of discontent.[4] President Grover Cleveland, by his use of troops in the Pullman strike of 1894, earned the animosity of labor. By his support of the gold standard he alienated the western silver faction of his party, mainly western debtor agrarians hard pressed by deflation.

Along with its other consequences industrialization brought the possibility of disastrous depressions. Financial panics were not new, but in the new industrialism contractions of economic activity struck both more sharply and more pervasively. Cleveland had the misfortune to be President when the depression of 1893 came along. Banking and commercial failures, urban unemployment, industrial stagnation, and low farm prices led to heavy Democratic losses in the 1894 congressional elections. Cleveland had pushed through Congress a revision of the tariff, which fact probably had no bearing on the panic but enabled Republicans to claim that low tariffs did not assure prosperity.

The forces of economic protest gained control of the Democratic convention of 1896, disavowed the policies of Cleveland, and set forth to unite all varieties of opposition to the established order. The Democratic platform declared for the free and unlimited coinage of both silver and gold at the ratio of sixteen to one. In debating this plank William Jennings Bryan stirred the delegates to a frenzy by his speech containing the famous passage:

> We shall answer their demand for the gold standard by saying to them: "You shall not press down upon the brow of labor this crown of thorns. You shall not crucify mankind upon a cross of gold."

By their stand on silver and their nomination of Bryan, the Democrats appropriated the chief issue of the People's party, which had polled over a mil-

---

[3] For an account of the ideas of the leaders of protest, see C. A. Madison, *Critics and Crusaders* (New York: Holt, 1947).

[4] In 1892, division among the Republicans assured Democratic victory. Of Cleveland, A. W. Dunn says, "Big Business was behind him and there was no end of campaign money furnished to the national committee." *From Harrison to Harding* (New York: Putnam's, 1922), I, 97.

lion votes in 1892. After some debate on the dangers of fusion, the Populists also nominated Byran.

By its strategy in 1896 the Republican party not only turned back the first serious threat to the governing coalition it had built; it also added elements of enduring strength to the combination. That strategy involved, first, advocacy of the gold standard; thus, they wrote off the silver-producing states and the advocates of the free coinage of silver. On its positive side, the strategy looked to the retention of the support of manufacturing interests, the solidification of the loyalties of financial groups, and the recruitment of a substantial vote from industrial labor. The nomination of McKinley, who had become in Congress the leading exponent of protective tariff, assured the loyalty of the traditional hard core of Republicanism—the manufacturing interests. Banking and finance were terrified by the threat of inflation and contributed generously to the party committed to the maintenance of the gold standard.

Democrats sought to unite industrial labor and western farmers by making free silver the symbol of their joint protest against the depredations of the plutocracy. Republicans countered, successfully, with several appeals. The panic of 1893 enabled them to make the Democrats the party of depression, a label that stuck for a generation. The protective tariff became, under the ministrations of Republican campaigners, an assurance of employment to the factory worker as well as a boon to his employer. McKinley, pictured on the billboards as the "Advance Agent of Prosperity," promised a full dinner pail. Even the gold standard had its appeal for factory workers, who were educated about the effects of inflation on real wages, a process of instruction that included warnings by employers that factories would be shut down if the Democrats won. Both McKinley and his manager, Mark Hanna, also had a personal attractivenes to the industrial worker. Earlier in his career McKinley had, when it took courage, defended striking workingmen against prosecution, and Hanna had earned the respect and affection of workers in his own enterprises.

The cumulative effect of the planks shaped for specific sectors of the population was a broad appeal to all those of conservative instinct. The crusading Bryan was pictured as the leader of a ragtag band of radicals that would upset the foundations of the Republic. The gold standard itself became a symbol of financial rectitude which titillated the moral sensibilities of men, especially of mortgagees. The oblique reference by the Democratic platform to the action that should follow a reversal by a reconstituted Supreme Court of a recent decision holding the income tax unconstitutional spurred the Republicans to greater effort and fed the anxieties of men of substance.

The usual interpretation of the election of 1896 is that the manufacturers and financiers of the East succeeded in persuading industrial workers to help them beat off the threat of the embattled agrarian debtors and radicals of

Table 7.1   Presidential votes, 1896–1960

Year	Candidate	Electoral Vote	Popular Vote (in millions)	Per Cent of Two-Party Vote
1896	William McKinley (R)	271	7.1	52.2
	William J. Bryan (D)	176	6.5	47.8
1900	William McKinley (R)	292	7.2	53.1
	William J. Bryan (D)	155	6.4	46.9
1904	Theodore Roosevelt (R)	336	7.6	60.0
	Alton B. Parker (D)	140	5.1	40.0
1908	William H. Taft (R)	321	7.7	54.5
	William J. Bryan (D)	162	6.4	45.5
1912	William H. Taft (R)	8	3.5	35.6
	Woodrow Wilson (D)	435	6.3	64.4 [a]
	Theodore Roosevelt (Prog.)	88	4.1	
1916	Charles Evans Hughes (R)	254	8.5	48.3
	Woodrow Wilson (D)	277	9.1	51.7
1920	Warren G. Harding (R)	404	16.2	63.8
	James M. Cox (D)	127	9.1	36.2
1924	Calvin Coolidge (R)	382	15.7	65.2
	John W. Davis (D)	136	8.4	34.8 [b]
	Robert M. La Follette (Prog.)	13	4.8	
1928	Herbert Hoover (R)	444	21.4	58.7
	Alfred E. Smith (D)	87	15.0	41.3

the West. The reality seems to have been more complicated. The old Republican electoral following, inherited from the Civil War, was modified in several respects. Losses in the West were more than offset by gains in the manufacturing states of the East. Republicans enlisted in their cause large numbers of industrial workers. They carried the 10 largest cities of the country. Within the cities all types of neighborhoods—working class, middle class, and upper class—shifted from their 1892 vote toward the Republicans. Here and there wards returned Democratic majorities but such wards were fewer and were Democratic by smaller margins than in 1892. Moreover, in New England a marked rural shift to the Republicans occurred, rural Yankee Democrats moving over to the Republican ranks more or less permanently. Such gains as the Democrats made were in the silver-mining states; both

Year	Candidate	Electoral Vote	Popular Vote (in millions)	Per Cent of Two-Party Vote
1932	Herbert Hoover (R)	59	15.8	40.9
	Franklin D. Roosevelt (D)	472	22.8	59.1
1936	Alfred M. Landon (R)	8	16.7	37.5
	Franklin D. Roosevelt (D)	523	27.8	62.5
1940	Wendell L. Willkie (R)	82	22.3	45.0
	Franklin D. Roosevelt (D)	449	27.3	55.0
1944	Thomas E. Dewey (R)	99	22.0	46.2
	Franklin D. Roosevelt (D)	432	25.6	53.8
1948	Thomas E. Dewey (R)	189	22.0	47.7
	Harry S. Truman (D)	303	24.1	52.3
	Henry A. Wallace (Prog.)	0	1.2	
	J. Strom Thurmond (States' Rights)	39	1.2	
1952	Dwight D. Eisenhower (R)	442	33.8	55.4
	Adlai E. Stevenson (D)	89	27.3	44.6
1956	Dwight D. Eisenhower (R)	457	35.6	57.8
	Adlai E. Stevenson (D)	73	26.0	42.2
	Walter Jones	1		
1960	John F. Kennedy (D)	303	34.2	50.1
	Richard M. Nixon (R)	219	34.1	49.9
	Harry F. Byrd	15	.3	

[a] Percentage division of three-party vote: Taft, 25.1; Wilson, 45.3; Roosevelt, 29.6.
[b] Percentage division of three-party vote: Coolidge, 54.3; Davis, 29.0; La Follette, 16.7.

mine owners and mine workers plumped for free silver with the same enthusiasm as the western farmer but for a different reason.[5]

1900: IMPERIALISM   The Republican coalition, forged in the 1896 campaign, was to prevail in national affairs until 1912. That election, in effect, determined who was to govern for the next 16 years. It did not settle

[5] Marcus Daly, the Montana silver miner, backed the Bryan campaign by contributing more than $300,000, or so his son-in-law reports. See J. W. Gerard, *My First Eighty-three Years in America* (Garden City: Doubleday, 1951), pp. 91–92.

much else. The social strains and frictions emerging from industrialization remained to plague the Republican leadership as it sought to hold together a dominant coalition.

The McKinley Administration redeemed its tariff pledge by the Dingley bill of 1897, which tied the manufacturing interests of the nation even more closely to the Republican party. Before the campaign of 1900 the Spanish-American War intervened and furnished the new issue of imperialism. The upsurge of national fervor induced by war redounded to the advantage of the party in power, which also had the good fortune to have the currency problem eased through no effort of its own—new gold strikes increased the money supply. An upward movement of industrial production contributed to Republican popularity. McKinley had no difficulty in obtaining renomination by the 1900 Republican convention. The principal event of the convention, as it later turned out, was the nomination of Theodore Roosevelt, a person cordially distrusted by Hanna, for the Vice Presidency. Matt Quay, Pennsylvania boss, who had a grudge against Hanna, joined with Boss Platt of New York, who wanted to be rid of Roosevelt as governor of New York, to bring about the nomination.[6] Western Republicans, still restive under control of the party by financial and manufacturing interests, welcomed the Roosevelt nomination.

The Democrats again nominated Bryan, who contended that the campaign was only another episode in the battle of "Democracy against Plutocracy." The contestants were the same; only the issues were new, he argued. He viewed imperialism as merely another manifestation of plutocratic influence. The party platform asserted "that no nation can long endure half republic and half empire." Imperialism "abroad will lead quickly and inevitably to despotism at home." The Democracy declared monopolies to be "indefensible and intolerable." The charge was that "trusts are the legitimate product of Republican policies, that they are fostered by Republican laws, and that they are protected by the Republican administration, in return for campaign subscriptions and political support." The Democrats denounced the Dingley tariff as a "trust breeding measure," and reaffirmed the 1896 declaration in favor of the free coinage of silver. They opposed "government by injunction" and proposed the creation of a Department of Labor.

The Democrats were unable to crack the Republican coalition by these appeals. The Democratic percentage of the total popular vote fell only slightly, but the electoral vote was more favorable to McKinley than in 1896. Kansas, Nebraska, South Dakota, Utah, and Washington returned to the Republican fold, while Kentucky atoned for its apostasy of 1896 by going for Bryan.

---

[6] McKinley refused to permit Hanna to use the power of the Administration to control the vice-presidential nomination. Hanna is supposed to have remarked: "Don't any of you realize that there's only one life between that madman and the Presidency? Platt and Quay are no better than idiots!" Dunn, *op. cit.*, I, 335.

R O O S E V E L T   T H E   F I R S T   After McKinley's assassination Theodore Roosevelt succeeded to the Presidency as well as to the task of holding together the Republican coalition. He saw the potential rifts in Republican ranks and took steps to cut into the Democratic monopoly of championship of the underdog. He sought to shift Republican policies in the same direction that the Democrats had been moving, only not so far.

The party's conservative wing, under the leadership of Senator Nelson W. Aldrich, held firm control of Congress, and Roosevelt recognized the strength of these formidable opponents. For the duration of McKinley's incomplete term, Roosevelt did not challenge the conservative wing in Congress but acted in areas in which he did not need congressional collaboration. In 1902 Roosevelt's Attorney General instituted antitrust proceedings against the Northern Securities combination, a scheme to restrict competition between railroad titans for Chicago-Seattle traffic, and thereby lifted the spirits of those western Republicans who regarded trusts and railroads as the villains grinding down the poor and honest. In the same year the anthracite miners struck, and the operators stood on the God-given rights of property and refused to negotiate. Roosevelt intimated that federal troops might be used to take control of the mines, which would be operated by the government unless the mine owners arbitrated the dispute.

1 9 0 4 :   D E M O C R A T S   A S   R E A C T I O N A R I E S   Roosevelt's tactics helped hold to the party those recruited to its support in 1896, but they disturbed the manufacturing and financial interests. To them, Roosevelt was "unsafe," an estimate based on his actions in the coal strike, in the Northern Securities case, and on the muscular tone of his oratory critical of abuses in high places. Yet they had no alternative candidate, and Roosevelt won the 1904 nomination.

As 1904 approached, Bryan argued that the Democrats, to retain their position as the party of protest, should take even more advanced positions, but the conservative wing triumphed in the nomination of Judge Alton B. Parker of the New York Court of Appeals. Southern Democrats, hopeful of victory and patronage, joined with the northeastern conservatives in a nomination that squeezed the meaning from the platform's ringing denunciations of the trusts.

Roosevelt's gestures to the West, to the progressives, and to labor held their support, and to the conservatives his bark, impressively ferocious though it was, seemed worse than his bite. The Democratic party's turn to conservatism pushed its percentage of the total popular vote down to 37.6, the lowest point it was to reach until 1924.

After he became President in his own right in 1904, Roosevelt took a somewhat stronger line in the fraternal differences among Republican factions. On some, but by no means all, issues he threw his strength to the progressive wing of the party. The battle was joined in the congressional dispute over railroad regulation; Aldrich led the eastern wing of the party against granting power to the Interstate Commerce Commission to control rates more effectively. The western radical wing of the party, supported by shippers, recruited support from the Democrats to pass the Hepburn bill. Roosevelt stirred up popular enthusism for other measures that the conservative branch of his party viewed with alarm. The Pure Food and Drug Act thus became law, as did legislation providing for the inspection of meat-packing houses.

1908: TAFT AND THE PROGRESSIVES   As 1908 approached, the coalition constructed by McKinley and Hanna and perfected by Roosevelt was subjected to growing internal strains. The business wing of the party became more reluctant to pay the price of power, that is, acquiescence in Roosevelt's leanings toward progressivism. Yet it was evident that the Democrats, disillusioned by the results of their conservative turn of 1904, would make capital of a resurgence of standpattism among the Republicans. Roosevelt exerted himself to unite the Republican party on William Howard Taft, an heir to carry on the Roosevelt tradition. In this endeavor he had to conciliate the party's conservative branch, which feared a continuation of his policies. He also had to persuade the progressive element of the party that Taft subscribed to the articles of progressive faith. The conservatives, oddly enough, swallowed Taft with bitter protest; the progressives took Roosevelt's word that Taft was one of the anointed.

Taft, victorious over the luckless Bryan, soon departed from the Roosevelt policies—and the fat was in the fire. Taft lacked Roosevelt's capacity to ride horses determined to veer off in different directions, but by Taft's time the elements of the Republican combination were becoming more difficult to manage. The progressive wing of the party had become stronger and the spirit of revolt within the party flourished. Into the progressive movement most of the old streams of protest had merged. That movement, whose temper is difficult to reconstruct, was a mixture of economic discontent, of middle-class protest against plutocratic influences, and of moral and religious fervor, as well as of more than a trace of sectionalism. It denounced special privilege and bossism and fought for popular rule. It supported the direct primary, which was coming into use. Direct election of Senators was urged, and in some western states was becoming a reality although the constitutional forms were preserved. The Senate, the "millionaires' club" and a bulwark of property, was thus threatened. Conservatives became panicky as the initiative and referendum spread. The muckrakers uncovered graft and corruption in high places; the new cheap magazines disseminated their writings widely. State after state elected progressive governors, who drove through their legislatures tax and regulatory measures unpleasant for corporation executives to contemplate. Courageous men challenged the pillaging of municipalities by combinations of corrupt political organizations and special interests. City after city elected reform administrations, and municipal ownership of street railways became a favorite cause among reformers. Gambling houses were raided and houses of joy closed. Business enterprise of every kind quaked; the day of judgment apparently had come. The ordained institutions were said to be threatened, and right-thinking men bemoaned the decay of our society, the rise of the proletariat, and the wickedness of demagogues, like Roosevelt, who catered to the masses.[7]

The progressive movement had, in addition to its moral overtones, some substantial economic foundations. Midwestern Republican farmers, as well as the Democrats, demanded a reconsideration of tariff policy. Agitation to that end had been noisy as early as 1903, when Mark Hanna took the position that, as things were, the Republican party should stand pat on the existing tariff law. He knew, said Herbert Croly, that "the tariff was the keystone of the whole Republican system. He knew that any revision upward would not be tolerated by public opinion, and any revision downward would tear the party to pieces."[8] From another quarter, the Republican coalition was threatened by labor. In 1906 the AFL, in its Bill of Grievances, asserted that the Congress had "been entirely preoccupied looking after the interests of vast corporations and predatory wealth." In the campaign of 1908 the Federation threw its weight, such as it was, to the Democrats, who had adopted platform planks favorable to labor.

Fate dropped the amiable and obese Taft into this situation. As he was at heart no crusader, his sympathies lay with the conservative wing of the party. Desirous of maintaining party unity, he lacked the adroitness to manage its warring factions. He had in his following Republicans like Aldrich of Rhode Island, high priest of protectionism, and equally genuine Republicans like La Follette of Wisconsin, hero of the progressives. Under Taft's heavy touch the Republican alliance began to disintegrate. His Administration got off to an inauspicious start in a battle over tariff revision. The 1908 platform, to placate Republicans of the corn- and wheat-producing areas, had declared "unequivocally for a revision of the tariff by a special session of Congress immediately following the inauguration of the next President."

[7] The spirit of the progressive movement can be sensed from the *The Autobiography of William Allen White* (New York: Macmillan, 1946). See also J. M. Blum, *The Republican Roosevelt* (New York: Atheneum, 1962).

[8] *Marcus Alonzo Hanna* (New York: Macmillan, 1912), p. 418. Tariff legislation with specific rates on specific commodities—in contrast with a uniform *ad valorem* rate on all imports—constituted a wonderfully effective means for creating a lively sense of party obligation. Never could there be doubt about who received what benefits from whom. By the same token the making of tariffs required a skilled political hand to maximize the cumulation of obligation, for each specific action antagonized some people as it gratified others.

Taft called the special session and Aldrich led the high-tariff forces in Congress. Chided about his deviation from party promises, Aldrich responded that the promise was for "revision," not necessarily downward. Midwestern Senators—La Follette of Wisconsin, Dolliver of Iowa, Beveridge of Indiana, Cummins of Iowa, Bristow of Kansas, Clapp of Minnesota—opposed the Aldrich leadership, but the right wing of the party triumphed and passed a bill distinctly to the advantage of eastern interests. Taft's inept leadership on the tariff question brought disfavor which was compounded by his departures from the Rooseveltian conservation policies. He bobbled again in negotiating a reciprocity treaty with Canada which, had it gone into effect, would have subjected the western farmer to competition from Canadian farm products and would have aided the eastern manufacturer. Finally, perhaps in an attempt to retrieve the favor of the progressives, the Administration initiated antitrust prosecutions which made enemies of some prominent Republicans of the industrial world.

The Republican coalition fell apart. In 1910 progressive Republicans joined with Democrats to cut down the powers of the Speaker of the House, a post that had become under "Uncle Joe" Cannon a symbol of standpat dominance of the Republican party. Taft failed in the primaries of 1910 to purge the Republican party of those of progressive bent, and the country returned a Democratic majority to the House. The remainder of his term was marked by further division within the Republican party and by the formation of the battle lines for 1912.

Democratic Interlude and the New Freedom

If a party is to govern, it must bring into mutually advantageous alliance an aggregate of interests powerful enough to win a presidential election. If it is to govern for long, it must see that the loaves and fishes are divided in a manner to command popular approbation. The alliance contrived by McKinley and Hanna and continued by Theodore Roosevelt amassed power to govern for a substantial period, but it could not solve the problem of the loaves and fishes. Roosevelt's gestures toward reform were in the main heroic verbalisms with a political function rather than an operational effect. Few indeed were the actions from 1896 to 1912 directed toward basic resolution of the dislocations associated with industrialization already apparent in 1896. Yet such problems do not take care of themselves and the campaign of 1912 set off a notable debate on their solution. Both shades of Republicanism had champions in the debate. The Democrats, under the leadership of Woodrow Wilson, put forward their program as they attempted to annex to their rock-bottom strength in the South and in the northern urban centers those elements of the people resentful of Republican policies.

CAMPAIGN OF 1912   The campaign of 1912 stands out as one
of the fabulous chapters of American politics. Roosevelt campaigned energetically to win the Republican nomination and to regain control of the party,
but the Taft Administration controlled a majority of the delegates. Roosevelt
was undoubtedly the choice of the mass of the party insofar as its wishes were
expressed in those states choosing convention delegates by the direct primary. Taft, however, had early signed up the delegates of the southern states
and was able to control a convention marked by controversy. The progressives, asserting that they had been robbed,[9] proceeded to bolt the Republican
party and to found the Progressive party, with Roosevelt as its standard-
bearer. It was a personal party, a party permeated with intense moral flavor,
a crusade for righteousness or at least a movement rationalized in terms of
righteousness. Progressive conclaves were wont to sing the "Battle Hymn
of the Republic," and Roosevelt's speech to the Progressive convention was
billed as a "Confession of Faith."

Roosevelt, with his doctrine of "New Nationalism," lifted political discussion to a new plane of sophistication. He attacked the virtues of weak
government and expounded the idea that a government, as strong as it need
be, should use its powers to promote the liberties of the weak against the
greed of those in high places. For the traditional antitrust demonology that
proposed to cure economic ills by jailing a few rascals, he substituted the
idea of public control of more or less inevitable industrial combines. This
idea was not unacceptable to Progressive men of wealth, who regarded some
type of governmental control as in the cards.[10] Roosevelt espoused all the
progressive panaceas calculated to make government more responsive to the
people: direct primaries, a nationwide preference primary for candidates
for the Presidency, popular election of Senators, the initiative, referendum,
and recall. The Progressives also pledged themselves to a long list of specific
reforms: prohibition of child labor, minimum wages for women, the eight-
hour day, regulation of security sales, social insurance, the establishment of
a Department of Labor, and others.

The Democrats, still mindful of the electoral catastrophe that followed
their conservative turn in 1904, determined to set a progressive tone for their
own campaign, but this determination came after no little dispute in their
national convention. Bryan, still the oustanding figure of the party, put the
convention into an uproar—and the Democratic conservatives into a corner
—by proposing the following resolution:

> *Resolved,* That in this crisis in our party's career and in our coun-
> try's history this convention sends greetings to the people of the United

[9] Victor Rosewater, Republican national chairman in 1912, rebuts the charge of
thievery in *Back Stage in 1912* (Philadelphia: Dorrance, 1932).

[10] On divisions among businessmen, see R. H. Wiebe, *Businessmen and Reform*
(Cambridge: Harvard University Press, 1962).

States, and assures them that the party of Jefferson and of Jackson is still the champion of popular government and equality before the law. As proof of our fidelity to the people, we hereby declare ourselves opposed to the nomination of any candidate for President who is representative of or under obligation to J. Pierpont Morgan, Thomas F. Ryan, August Belmont, or any other member of the privilege-hunting and favor-seeking class.

Be It Further Resolved, That we demand the withdrawal from this convention of any delegate or delegates constituting or representing the above-named class.

The conservative wing of the party fumed, but to have voted down the resolution would have been bad politics indeed. To accept it would make difficult the nomination of a conservative candidate. The second clause of the resolution would have compelled some eminent gentlemen to retire from the convention. After Mr. Bryan withdrew that clause, the conservatives manfully voted for the resolution. And the cartoonists pictured Bryan burning the progressive brand into the hide of the Democratic donkey.[11]

Woodrow Wilson won the nomination, after Champ Clark of Missouri had attained a majority but not the two-thirds then necessary to nominate. Wilson, a recent convert to progressivism, had been president of Princeton University and governor of New Jersey. His doctrines belonged to an older tradition than those of Roosevelt; his "New Freedom" stemmed from Jefferson. He sought to free men from restraints, monopolistic or otherwise, which restricted their liberties and prevented the full use of their talents. He regarded Roosevelt's "New Nationalism" with its powerful state as a threat to liberty. The Wilsonian doctrine, Roosevelt retorted, was "rural toryism," which would, if applied, lead to the repeal of all legislation for the protection of the social and industrial rights of man.

Taft could not compete in the campaign with men of the histrionic talents of Roosevelt and Wilson. He was a poor third in the running, polling 3,486,000 votes to 4,118,000 for Roosevelt and 6,296,000 for Wilson. The Republican split gave Wilson the victory. The electoral vote was: Wilson, 435; Roosevelt, 88; Taft, 8. The split within the Republican party was not sectional, although Roosevelt's popular vote was highest generally in the Middle and Far West. He won the electoral vote of Michigan, Minnesota, Pennsylvania, South Dakota, and Washington, and 11 of the 13 votes of California.

WILSON AND THE PRESIDENCY   Wilson brought to the Presidency both a program and a conception of presidential responsibility for leadership in the enactment of a party's legislative program. Supported by

[11] For Bryan's account of the convention, see W. J. Bryan, and M. B. Bryan, *The Memoirs of William Jennings Bryan* (Philadelphia: United Publishers, 1925), Pt. I, ch. 10.

the spirit of progressivism abroad in the land, he pushed through Congress a remarkable program of legislation to cope with long-standing problems of the new industrial order.

The tariff had been debated for over a decade, but the Wilson Administration actually reduced the tariff—an action especially pleasing to the southern wing of the party. The tariff bill included an income tax; the Democrats came to power just as the income-tax amendment, proposed in 1909 by a coalition of Democrats and Republican insurgents, had finally been ratified. The currency problem—reflected in the agitation of the Grangers, the Greenbackers, the Populists, and the free silverites of 1896—was dealt with by the establishment of the Federal Reserve System. The solution differed from the panaceas proposed earlier, but the Reserve Act rectified shortcomings of the banking system that had plagued the country for decades. The Federal Trade Commission was created to attack the problem of restraints on competition in a manner different from the traditional antitrust procedures. The Clayton Act, in addition to its provisions regarding monopolies, exempted labor unions from the antitrust laws and contained other provisions that enabled Samuel Gompers, over-optimistically, to hail it as the "Magna Carta of Labor." Wilson approved an act of safeguarding the rights of seamen. The Adamson Act fixed an eight-hour day for railroad workers.

After reversing his earlier views, Wilson urged the adoption of a statute prohibiting child labor, a law later to be held void. The Democrats also had something for the farmer: the Federal Farm Loan Act created banks to make long-term loans at low rates of interest. Governmental intervention on so many fronts amounted in its day to a bold assault on the problems of the time. Mild though it seems in retrospect, it aroused acrimonious opposition from those—mainly the business brass of the Republican party—who regarded themselves as injured thereby. By the same token the program strengthened the Democratic loyalties of those who had put Wilson into office.[12]

1916: "HE KEPT US OUT OF WAR" The thinness of the Democratic margin of victory in 1916 indicated that Wilson had not yet constructed a new coalition capable of assuming a dominant role for long. While his early legislative successes welded new support to the Democratic party, perhaps the fact that war intervened prevented the completion of the task of weaving together a new coalition with lasting cohesiveness. At any rate war checked the tide of reform, and in the 1916 campaign the conservative-progressive issue loomed less large than that of foreign policy. The Republicans, chastened by the experience of 1912, went beyond the ranks of the dedicated standpatters and nominated Charles Evans Hughes, who had gained renown for his work in the Armstrong investigation of life insurance and

---

[12] For a discussion of Wilson's ideas, see Richard Hofstadter, *The American Political Tradition* (New York: Vintage Books, 1954), ch. 10.

for his moderately progressive record as governor of New York. The regular Republican organization attempted in other ways to bring back into the fold those who had followed the Progressives out of the party in 1912. Roosevelt refused to accept the Progressive nomination again, and Hughes and Wilson fought a two-party battle in which Hughes' austerity evoked little enthusiasm; the Democratic record, with the aid of some ineptness in Republican campaign management, brought victory.

The Democratic organization emphasized the slogan, "He Kept Us Out of War," but the candidate refused to commit himself to a position that might later restrict his freedom of action. On foreign policy the issue was not clearly drawn; both parties were for American rights and adequate preparedness. They differed on who should be responsible for executing the policy. The polling resulted in an electoral vote of 277 to 254. Wilson carried the states of the Solid South and the West and broke into Republican territory to capture Ohio and New Hampshire. Professor Binkley attributes Wilson's victory in Ohio and California to the support of organized labor; railway workers were especially fearful that Republicans would repeal the Adamson Act, an inference from Hughes' attacks on the eight-hour day.[13]

Soon war came; though domestic politics was not adjourned, the issues became different. Wilson's handling of foreign affairs aroused the animosity of Republican senatorial leaders. The senatorial cabal that defeated the League of Nations won control of the Republican party and removed from it the last taint of the progressive spirit of 1912. In the campaign of 1918 Wilson appealed to the country to return Democratic Congressmen who would support him in his policies; but it returned a Republican majority to the House—the period of normalcy had begun.

Normalcy and Its Aftermath, 1920–1932

When alarums and diversions distract the people, those with a steady eye on the main chance can make hay. In their energetic and unremitting pursuit of short-term gains, they may build up their accountability for a day of reckoning which, blindly, they believe will never come. Of alarums and diversions there was no lack in 1920. Disillusionment displaced the wartime spirit of idealism. Appeals for a return to isolation struck a responsive chord; the American people acted like an ostrich hell-bent for a sandpile. Voters of Irish and German extraction, in revenge for Democratic alliance with the British, were notably susceptible to isolationist oratory. Amidst this confusion, the business elements gained unchallenged control of the Republican party. The progressives by and large were dead and gone. The war had given a tremendous fillip to business expansion, and a new generation of

[13] Binkley, op. cit., pp. 368–69.

corporate leaders had come to power. The interests that had been dominant within the party before 1912 climbed back into the saddle. Yet this generation had neither the sagacity nor the restraint of McKinley and Hanna who took the elementary precaution of carefully tending their political fences outside the business community.

HARDING AND COOLIDGE   In the preliminaries to the Republican convention of 1920, the Republican senatorial leadership controlled the Republican organization. It was clear that the nominee would be a safe and sane man unlikely to challenge the primacy of the elder statesmen of the Senate. The mantle fell on Warren G. Harding, undistinguished in his record as a Senator and unmarked by any characteristic of greatness as an Ohio newspaper editor and publisher. In the convention maneuvers leading to his nomination, the principal leaders, William Allen White said, "wore unwittingly the collar of some commodity unit: steel, coal, oil, textile, banking, copper." The Republican platform reflected the views of the old guard, but made some genuflection to progressive principles. On the question of the League of Nations, the party stood for an "international association" to be based upon "international justice." The platform promised international agreements to "meet the full duty of America to civilization and humanity," but "without surrendering the right of the American people to exercise its judgment and its power in favor of justice and peace." In this language there could be found no germ of a strong international organization to promote peace.

Probably the Democrats had lost the election before the campaign began. The party chose James M. Cox, former governor of Ohio and another newspaper editor, as its presidential candidate. Franklin D. Roosevelt, who had been Assistant Secretary of the Navy, accepted the vice-presidential nomination. The Democratic party stood on Wilson's record, advocated entrance of the United States into the League of Nations, condemned the Republican party generally, and went down to defeat. Harding's promise of "normalcy" voiced the feelings of a nation weary of war, eager to restore things as they had been. Harding swept the nation with an electoral vote of 404 to 127. The western states moved back into the Republican column, and Cox carried only 11 southern states.

In the Harding and Coolidge Administrations, finance and industry became dominant. No measure enacted by the Democrats for the control of business was repealed, but such laws were made harmless by tempered administration. Government by injunction prevailed, and labor was put in its place, a tactic that would have drawn corrosive comment from Mark Hanna. Andrew Mellon, Secretary of the Treasury, preached the reduction of taxation of the rich in order that they might invest their money in employment-producing enterprise. Much of it, however, went into stock-market speculation. The Republican Administration, under the prodding of midwestern insurgents, expanded the farm-credit system, but this step was not enough to quiet the grain-growers, another anchor point in the old Republican combination. Even in Coolidge's first Administration the midwestern farmer was on a rampage, asserting that prosperity did not trickle down to him. Advocates of farm relief, in forms ancestral to the Agricultural Adjustment Act, began to make themselves heard.

1924: MEDIOCRITY VS. MEDIOCRITY   The New England rectitude of Calvin Coolidge and mounting prosperity carried the Republicans triumphantly through the election of 1924; so weak was the spirit of protest that the country paid little heed to the Teapot Dome scandals. The Democratic party, rent by internecine struggle, did little to encourage the public in the belief that it had the capacity to govern. Its 1924 national convention was a savage bout beautiful to behold. The points of internal weakness in the coalition that is the Democratic party made themselves manifest; when urban Irish Catholics disagree with rural Protestants bitterness is bound to ensue. The New York convention fought over what, if anything, should be said in condemnation of the Ku Klux Klan, but most of all it fought over whether Alfred E. Smith or William G. McAdoo would be the party nominee. Behind Smith were arrayed the urban, Catholic, and "liberal"—by now some people were beginning to suspect that prohibition did not come up to forecast— elements of the party. McAdoo had the support of the southern, rural, dry, Protestant sectors. A hundred ballots could not break the deadlock, and on the one hundred and third ballot the convention compromised on John W. Davis.

The Democracy, in its platform flayed the Republicans with might and main, but the conservative, though eminent, John W. Davis had neither the beliefs nor the manners of a leader of protest. He could give no punch to the platform charge that the Republican party believed "that prosperity must originate with the special interests and seep down through the channels of trade to the less favored industries, to the wage earners and small salaried employees." The resolutions' writers proclaimed: "A vote for Coolidge is a vote for chaos." They charged that the Mellon tax plan was "a device to relieve multimillionaires at the expense of other taxpayers"; they denounced the Fordney-McCumber tariff as "class legislation which defrauds the people for the benefit of a few." They announced that the "predatory interests" had, "by supplying Republican campaign funds, systematically purchased legislative favors and administrative immunity."

The oratory had little effect on the electorate. The Republican affirmation of "its devotion to orderly government under the guarantees embodied in the constitution" probably had no more effect. The Republicans pointed to prosperity, to the reduction of taxation, to the wise tariff provision that had been enacted, and to measures for the benefit of agriculture.

The Republican landslide gave Coolidge 382 electoral votes to 136 for Davis. The Democratic proportion of the total popular vote fell to an all-time low. Wise men predicted that the day of the Democratic party was done; but all was not well within the Republican party. Its midwestern wing was restive; limited secession occurred in 1924 in support of the Farmer-Labor candidates of Robert M. La Follette and Burton K. Wheeler, who polled about one out of every eight popular votes in the nation. The Farmer-Labor platform proclaimed the great issue as "the control of government and industry by private monopoly."

After the election of 1924 the Coolidge Administration yielded no great legislative achievement. The midwestern agrarians of the Republican party became more vocal and succeeded in passing the McNary-Haugen bill, which Coolidge vetoed. The plaints of the farmer were drowned by the unprecedented prosperity of the speculators. Whether Coolidge was wise enough or whether he could have done anything to check the coming crash is problematic. William Allen White concluded that Coolidge perfectly expressed the dominant forces of the day.[14] However that may be, Coolidge rode the tide; but, apparently sensing what was coming, in 1927 he chose not to run in 1928. Mrs. Coolidge, at a family gathering, was reported to have explained: "Poppa says there's a depression coming." [15]

HOOVER AND THE CRASH   With Coolidge's renunciation of the 1928 nomination, Herbert Hoover, his Secretary of Commerce, was soon in pursuit of the nomination. Tagged by friend as the "Great Engineer" and by enemy as the "Wonder Boy," Hoover easily outdistanced other aspirants for the Republican nomination. He had to convince the Republican organizations that he could win; he did not belong to the inner circle of Republicanism as had Harding and Coolidge. By the nomination of Hoover, the Republicans yielded somewhat to the discontent within the party, for Hoover had accomplishments to his credit that placed him in a different category from the old-fashioned standpatter.

Northeastern elements of the party dominated the convention and easily overrode the demands of midwestern farm leaders for more positive promises to farmers. The prohibition issue aroused debate, but the party pledged itself to the vigorous enforcement of prohibition. The old Republican standby, the protective tariff, was acclaimed as the source of all prosperity and as a boon to every section and to every class, though it was conceded that some revision of existing arrangements might be required in the light of the world situation.

The Democrats again essayed their role as the party of protest; they again demonstrated the incohesiveness of the elements that must make up such a party in comparison with the ties that bind a party whose ranks include the solid industrial and financial interests. The conditions were not

[14] *A Puritan in Babylon* (New York: Macmillan, 1938).   [15] *Ibid.,* p. 366.

ripe for a party of protest to win, but in making their nomination, the Democrats conspired with the forces working for their defeat. They chose Alfred E. Smith of New York as their nominee. A dripping wet, he renounced the party's dry platform plank. A child of the streets of New York, he could not induce the midwestern farmers to believe that the Democratic farm-relief plank meant what it said. A Catholic, he could not persuade many Protestants that the Pope would not make of the White House a branch Vatican.

Hoover later remarked that "the growing left-wing movement, embracing many of the 'intelligentsia,' flocked to Governor Smith's support," while Hoover committed himself to "the American system, as opposed to all forms of collectivism." [16] Such matters were pushed to the background by the tempest over religion and prohibition which operated to Republican advantage. In the South, Smith's religion and his wetness were too much for dry, native-white Protestants. Hoover broke into the Solid South, and carried Florida, Kentucky, North Carolina, Oklahoma, Tennessee, and Texas. The electoral vote was 444 to 87. Had they studied the election returns more closely, the Democrats could have found cheer. Their proportion of the total popular vote jumped to 40.8 per cent from the 1924 figure of 28.8. They won the electoral vote of Rhode Island and Massachusetts, an omen of further growth of Democratic support in urban, Catholic, industrial centers. In every state north of the Ohio and east of the Mississippi their proportion of the total popular vote increased over the 1924 level. Hoover ran powerfully in the northern and eastern rural precincts, but Smith boosted Democratic strength in the metropolitan and manufacturing centers.

In the cruelty of the polemics of politics Mr. Hoover became the symbol of the failures of an era, an attribution of responsibility far beyond the capacities of any individual, even though he may be President of the United States. Yet the governing coalition of which he had been a part had, it seemed almost as by an urge toward self-destruction, pursued policies that could only sap its own foundations. Nor did the crowd running the country have the will or the ingenuity to tackle any of the great problems of management of the new industrial order which were, by now, becoming more and more acute. That incapacity to act had its background in the long dedication of the Republican party to the belief that the economic system, if left alone, would take care of itself. "The abdication of responsibility revealed in 1929," says Professor Stromberg, "grew from the whole tradition of negativism ripening for upwards of fifty years. No group of men could have achieved such magnificent ineptitude spontaneously." [17] Whatever the explanation, the policies of the 1920's paved the way for national disaster and for a sweeping reconsideration of governmental policy.

[16] *Memoirs of Herbert Hoover 1920–1933* (New York: Macmillan, 1952), p. 202.
[17] Roland N. Stromberg, *Republicanism Reappraised* (Washington: Public Affairs Press, 1952), p. 40.

The Democratic Era

The presidential election of 1932 marked a turning point in American party history. Under the impact of the Great Depression, the Republican following disintegrated and the circumstances were created for the formation of a new Democratic party. The new Democratic party built on its old foundations and enlisted much larger proportions of the economically less-favored groups. Under its leadership occurred the broadest governmental intervention in economic affairs that the nation had seen in times of peace, and far-reaching measures of reform were enacted to cope with problems of the industrial order.

1 9 3 2   A N D   T H E   N E W   D E A L   The campaign of 1932 presented no great uncertainties for the political forecaster. The Republican delegates who convened at Chicago to renominate Mr. Hoover exuded a synthetic enthusiasm in public but were privately appalled by the prospects. The Democrats, sure of victory, vied among themselves for the nomination and after a warm dispute agreed upon Franklin D. Roosevelt as their nominee.

The most clear-cut alternative of policy presented in the campaign was on prohibition: the Democrats were against it. Mr. Roosevelt appealed to all classes; he proposed a farm program, a labor program, a banking program, a business program, and stood for the theory of working in concert with all groups rather than of relying chiefly on industrial and financial leadership to lift the country out of the depression. Mr. Hoover was saddled with his record and with the impact of events and could scarcely obtain a respectful hearing in the campaign.

It is doubtful that the appeals of either candidate had much to do with the election results. All types of people had suffered deprivation; all were eager for a change. Poor men, rich men, middle-class men, farmers, workers, all moved over into the Democratic ranks in sufficient number to give Roosevelt a resounding victory. All could identify themselves with the "forgotten man," and they could equally feel themselves deserving of a "new deal" without insisting on exact definition of what the "new deal" was to be. The electoral vote was 472 to 59; Hoover carried only Connecticut, Delaware, Maine, Pennsylvania, and Vermont.[18]

Washington was soon treated to a spectacle the like of which it had never seen. The Democrats who assembled to take control of the government were a motley crew indeed. Southern statesmen of the old school mixed with Bull Moosers, with suave and tough labor bosses, with intellectuals, with the

---

[18] See Roy V. Peel and T. C. Donnelly, *The 1932 Campaign* (New York: Farrar & Rinehart, 1935).

Democratic contingent from big business, with bright young men from the Harvard Law School. Ghosts of the past were resurrected as former lieutenants of Bryan and Wilson emerged to take high places, and now and then an old Socialist who had been converted to the Democracy made a place for himself. Presiding over this assemblage was a man who, to the astonishment of all concerned, turned out to be a genius at the art of political leadership.

The country cried for action, and Roosevelt gave it action. After dealing with the immediate problem of restoring the nation's banks to operation, he proceeded to drive through Congress a series of measures for recovery and reform without parallel. Yet most of the measures stemmed from the American stream of reform agitation. The Democrats redeemed planks in their platforms of 1908 and later years; they put into law proposals in the Progressive platform of 1912; they breathed life into other long-past campaign promises.

The farmers were taken care of by the passage of the Agricultural Adjustment Act, which embodied means to control production, a step that Mr. Hoover's Farm Board had concluded to be necessary. Farm-mortgage moratoria were authorized to check foreclosures. Banks received aid and were subjected to restraints. A major reform was the separation of banks from their security affiliates. The bank deposit insurance plan became law, albeit without Mr. Roosevelt's support. The Democrats in 1908 had plumped for a "guarantee fund" to pay off "depositors of any insolvent national bank." The dollar was devalued; thereby commodity prices were given a boost and the burdens of debtors eased. Horrendous results were predicted by spokesmen of the gold-standard cult. The Home Owners' Loan Corporation was created and given $3,000,000,000 to stave off foreclosures of distressed homeowners, and relief funds were voted in huge sums.

A reciprocal tariff act, whose concept had earlier been vigorously opposed by the Republicans, was adopted. Also, a securities act became law, the objectives of which recalled the Progressive platform of 1912, which had pointed out that people were "swindled" out of millions every year by investing in stocks offered by "highly colored prospectuses" and that it was the duty of the government "to protect its people from this kind of piracy." The Tennessee Valley Authority Act settled the long dispute over the utilization of the Muscle Shoals Dam and the development of the water-power resources of the Tennessee Valley. Business leaders met in the annual session of the Chamber of Commerce of the United States and advocated a larger measure of governmental compulsion to aid business in its attempts at self-regulation. The National Industrial Recovery Act, one of the less well-advised New Deal measures, became law and was put into operation with great fanfare.

All these measures, and others, too, left Congress a bit groggy; Congressmen who were inclined to balk heard from their constituents, and in 1934 the

Democratic party gained congressional strength in the midterm elections, the first time a party in power had done so since the Civil War. There was more to come. The Social Security Act of 1935 provided, to meet immediate needs, a system of old-age assistance based on a means test and like arrangements for assistance to the blind and to dependent children. The same act, to meet the problem of the aged over the long pull, established a system of old-age insurance to be financed by compulsory contributions by employers and employees. The act also provided for unemployment insurance and for enlarged public health services. The National Labor Relations Act guaranteed to labor the right to organize and to bargain collectively.

Although the New Deal had its roots in earlier political discussion, it marked a sharp deviation from the policies of the preceding years, which had been dominated by the notion that the public good was promoted best by a government that restricted the sphere of its activities. One scholar concluded that "the New Deal represents the most zestful and thorough attack yet seen on those Whig principles which, with relatively minor exception, have dominated public policy since the days of the Federalists." [19]

1936: REFERENDUM ON THE NEW DEAL   In the election of 1932 all sorts and classes of people deserted the Republican party. In 1936 a reshuffling and sharpening of the lines of party battle occurred. As the New Deal took shape it attracted to the Democratic party, even more completely than in 1932, voters of those classes that were its most immediate beneficiaries. On the other hand, the unfolding of the New Deal drove back to the GOP many Republicans who had left their party in 1932.

As the campaign of 1936 approached—there was no doubt that the Democrats would renominate Roosevelt—the Republicans gave thought to the strategy of attack. They resolved upon a frontal assault upon the New Deal whose principal planks ran diametrically counter to the doctrine of nonintervention in the economy. The big-business elements of the party reacted with especial vigor to governmental restraint. Finding the Republican party an inadequate vehicle for the expression of their indignation, they formed the Liberty League to save the country, and it conducted a vigorous campaign of protest. The Republicans nominated Alfred M. Landon, governor of Kansas, and promulgated a platform dedicating themselves to "the preservation of . . . political liberty." They invited men of all parties to join them in defense of American institutions and pledged themselves to maintain the Constitution and to preserve free enterprise. They condemned unemployment insurance and old-age annuities as "unworkable." They proposed that labor have a right to bargain through representatives "of its own choosing without

[19] T. P. Jenkin, *Reactions of Major Groups to Positive Government in the United States, 1930–1940* (Berkeley: University of California Press, 1945), p. 396.

interference from any source," a qualification reflective of the delusion of businessmen that union members are held in bondage by their leaders.[20]

The country failed to be disturbed by Republican forecasts of disaster; Roosevelt was returned by a larger majority than in 1932, carrying every state save Maine and Vermont. By now the public opinion polls had come into operation, and it was easier to discern the kind of coalition that Roosevelt had built up. He had brought together the votes of traditional Democratic territory and the northern urban laboring vote. The population dependent upon public relief supported him overwhelmingly, as did the Negroes, who had been wooed away from Republicanism. Businessmen in the main remained Republican, but each successively lower-income group voted Democratic in larger proportions.

The problem of holding this diverse coalition together grew more difficult after the President's 1937 proposal for the "rejuvenation" of the Supreme Court. The Court had long been regarded as the great bulwark of property rights. Supported by conservatives generally, it had often been attacked by labor and protest groups. In 1936 the Democrats proposed, if necessary, a "clarifying amendment" to the Constitution to permit the enactment of laws necessary "to regulate commerce, protect public health and safety, and safeguard economic security." This declaration followed Supreme Court decisions invalidating the Agricultural Adjustment Act and the National Industrial Recovery Act. Roosevelt went beyond the platform and proposed to "pack" the court and thereby set off a battle that solidified the conservative interests of the country and opened wider the split between his party's conservative and liberal factions. Defeated in his court proposal, Roosevelt won his primary objective. The Court itself soon altered the direction of its decisions, and retirements permitted him to name judges of a more acceptable political philosophy.

1940: THIRD TERM AND WORLD WAR II   By 1940 the New Deal had run its course. The outbreak of the war in Europe and its potential effect on the United States commanded the attention of the public and of political leadership.

The coalition of interests cemented together by the New Deal held its main outlines in 1940, though the question of the United States' role in the emerging crisis caused some erosion as well as some accretions. Italo-Americans and German-Americans moved to the Republican ranks in large numbers. On the other hand, gains accrued to the Democrats among pro-British sectors of the population. Substantial, but not noisy, new Democratic

[20] For a sympathetic and informed account of the role of Landon in the campaign, see D. R. McCoy, "Alfred M. Landon and the Presidential Campaign of 1936," *Mid-America: An Historical Review*, 42 (1960), 195–218. On the Liberty League, see George Wolfekill, *The Revolt of the Conservatives* (Boston: Houghton Mifflin, 1962).

support came from those elements of eastern finance and industry deeply concerned about foreign policy questions.

Wendell Willkie, the Republican nominee, agreed in general with Democratic pronouncements on foreign affairs, and it appeared that the foreign policy issue would be taken out of the campaign. Minor Republican orators, though, tried to pin the "war party" label on the Democrats, and toward the end of the campaign Willkie, under the urging of the Republican professionals, began predicting war in a short time if the Democrats should win. "Don't Change Horses in the Middle of the Stream" became the Democratic slogan; Republicans attempted to raise the specter of dictatorship, attacked Democratic domestic policies, and appealed to the hallowed two-term tradition—but to no avail. Roosevelt won by 449 to 82 electoral votes. Willkie captured the loyalty of the mass of Republicans but was viewed coolly by the Republican machines as an amateur and a renegade Democrat. He carried only 10 states.[21]

Of the politics of World War II it needs only to be noted that Roosevelt managed to hold together the antithetic elements composing the Democratic party. The party's internal strains made themselves more apparent in the events leading to the campaign of 1944. At the Democratic convention southern state organizations, conservative Democrats elsewhere, and the AFL succeeded in preventing the nomination of Henry Wallace, strongly backed by the CIO, for the Vice Presidency. But the party closed ranks for the campaign and again defeated the Republican nominee, this time Governor Thomas E. Dewey of New York. The Democratic proportion of the total popular vote again declined, but between 1940 and 1944 Roosevelt acquired additional support from business and professional groups, reflective perhaps of the Administration's swing toward the right and of the sense of responsibility of these groups in foreign affairs. Farmers, however, continued their movement toward the Republicans, resentful of Democratic policy toward labor and of Democratic policy calculated to keep food prices down.

TRUMAN AND THE FAIR DEAL   With the death of Roosevelt, Harry S. Truman inherited both the Presidency and the task of holding together the pieces of the Democratic party. Beset by adversity on every side, he confounded both his critics and his friends by winning the election of 1948. For the most part he followed policies initiated by Roosevelt and attempted to carry some of them somewhat further.

In forming their forces the Republicans had their own internal difficulties. The right wing of the party had by no means yet become reconciled to the New Deal. While the national conventions in 1944 and 1948 fell under the control of the Republican faction disposed to retain the New Deal—and to

[21] See D. B. Johnson, *The Republican Party and Wendell Willkie* (Urbana: University of Illinois Press, 1960).

manage it better—the tenor of the pronouncements of the right wing of the party created a popular suspicion that the Republican party, given authority, would liquidate the New Deal. That belief had some foundation in the actions of the Republican Congress, elected in 1946, in whittling down the position of labor by the Taft-Hartley Act. Dewey, the 1948 nominee, was called a "me-too" candidate, but Republicans of all hues rallied to his support.

Truman seemed to be defeated before the campaign began. Southern resentment over national civil rights policies ignited a revolt by the Dixiecrats, while Henry Wallace led another splinter into the so-called Progressive party. Yet these losses were more than offset by gains elsewhere, and Truman's campaign tactics—and circumstances—stirred the main elements of the Roosevelt alliance to his support. Labor, in gratitude for Truman's opposition to the Taft-Hartley Act, exerted itself on his behalf. Rapidly falling farm prices—coupled with the failure of the Republican Congress to authorize actions to facilitate price support—renewed the Democratic attachments of midwestern farmers.[22] In the grain-growing areas of the Midwest, Truman's vote exceeded that of Roosevelt in 1944, a rise probably accounted for in part by a return to the Democratic party of those who had voted Republican in 1940 and 1944 on foreign policy grounds. Negroes turned out in record numbers to support Truman, a response to his civil rights position.

Roosevelt's New Deal and Truman's Fair Deal left a thick residue of legislation but they also introduced a new sharpness into American political debate. While the Democratic program merely executed in many instances projects long considered in American politics, the total effect was to present in new form the broad issue of individualism versus collectivism. The New Deal emerged from the tradition of American progressivism, but it operated with a superior political leadership and applied its measures with a more sophisticated administrative technique. Instead of relying on moral castigation and the penalization of a few rascals to promote the public weal, it spent money, set up commissions and agencies, issued orders and rules and regulations, and generally used the powers of government. All these measures sharpened political conflict and raised broadly the question of the role of government in promoting the interests of its citizens. The overwhelming support of labor gave strength to the government, but it also solidified upper-class sentiment in opposition. Spokesmen for the more prosperous contended that the American way was threatened, that dictatorship was coming, that individual liberties were being bartered for a mess of pottage. This sort of discussion was not new: Theodore Roosevelt and Woodrow Wilson had been cursed with almost the same abandon as Franklin Roosevelt. Yet the New Deal strained the capacity of the upper classes to accede to change, and right-wing predictions of leftist dictatorship were matched by leftist assertions

[22] Corn dropped from $2.86 a bushel in January, 1948, and to $1.37 in November.

that men of property and wealth had too little belief in democracy to stand idly by and allow the fulfillment of the logic of rule by the majority.

General Eisenhower, the New Republicanism, and Afterward

The sequence of elections before 1952 had, by their cumulative impact, made it plain that the Republican party could not win the Presidency if it seemed clearly to threaten the gains of the principal beneficiaries of the New Deal. The New Deal had to be accepted or victory had to be won by diversionary tactics, by indirection, or by the rise of new circumstances that could be turned to Republican advantage.

The candidate and circumstances necessary to dislodge the Democratic coalition converged in 1952. The candidate, General Dwight D. Eisenhower, brought to the party a great personal popularity and no offsetting liabilities in commitments to political beliefs likely to antagonize any major voting group. From his defeat of Robert A. Taft in the contest for the Republican nomination, the image emerged of a candidate who diverged from the prevalent popular stereotype of Republican leaders as isolationists and economic reactionaries. Mr. Taft had come to personify standpat Republicanism. Precisely what sort of Republican General Eisenhower was, nobody knew, but he was presumably different from Taft, an impression enormously helpful in the presentation of the General as a new Republican.

Eisenhower held the support of the upper-income classes which had to an extraordinary degree coalesced under the Republican banner, but even unanimity among these classes is not enough to win presidential elections. New support had to be recruited from those attached to the Democratic cause. That end was accomplished, but whether by the potency of Republican campaign appeals or by the circumstances creating discontent with the Democratic Administration one cannot say. The weariness of the nation with the Korean War and its concern about our position in world politics were exploited skillfully by Republican campaigners. Their candidate's experience, it could be contended, would assure competent management of military matters. Republican strategy blended an exploitation of anxiety about the Soviets abroad with the party's line on domestic policy. The party had been hammering for several years on the theme of "liberty against socialism," a propaganda tactic thought to be more promising than attack upon specific Democratic policies. In 1952 these themes became intertwined. In the more irresponsible Republican characterizations the Democratic Administration became a Communist-Socialist clique not to be trusted to defend American rights abroad and bent on the destruction of private enterprise at home.

The Democrats nominated Adlai Stevenson, a candidate who lacked Eisenhower's personal appeal. To no small degree Democratic campaigners in 1952 were still running against Herbert Hoover as they recalled the days of depression and the benefits from Democratic actions. But memories are short and perhaps the new circumstances made the old appeals to important blocks of voters no longer effective. Workers feared that further inflation would reduce still more the worth of their wages. Farmers perhaps concluded that there was nothing more that Democratic agricultural policy could do for them. Further, the upward trend of family incomes had moved millions of people into those economic strata to which the traditional Republican orientation is most congenial.

Whatever weight may be assigned to particular factors influencing voters in 1952, the total effect of the campaign was a movement toward the Republican party among people of all economic classes, all occupations, all geographic sections, and most religious and ethnic groups. Even in the South Eisenhower drew heavy support, especially in the middle- and upper-income brackets of the cities. The General polled slightly more than 55 per cent of the vote, enough to yield a landslide in the electoral college. To an unusual extent his was a personal victory rather than a party triumph; so thin were Republican margins in the House and Senate that a normal midterm sag in 1954 gave control of Congress to the Democrats.

The election of 1956 left no doubt that the country still liked Ike; whether it liked the Republican party was another question. The return of Democratic congressional majorities simultaneously with the overwhelming re-election of a Republican President was an extraordinary event. To a degree, the election reflected a recurrence of an old Republican ailment, western trouble. Its losses in House and Senate came in the farming areas west of the Mississippi and in the states of the Pacific Coast, perhaps reflective of discontent with Republican farm and conservation policies. On the other hand, Eisenhower gained over his 1952 vote in metropolitan areas and among industrial workers, indicative of a weakening of the Democratic ties of these groups. The retention of southern support in 1956 made it clear that 1952 had marked a durable increase of Republican strength in the South.[23]

The Eisenhower victory inaugurated a Republican interlude; it evidently did not create a durable new Republican coalition. Eisenhower failed to draw together the long existent factions of the Republican party into a new amalgam, yet he probably increased the proportions of "new Republicans" in the party. His espousal of policies to fulfill the simple necessities in international affairs brought a wider acceptance of involvement in foreign politics among Republicans. In domestic policy he was no great innovator, yet he gave little encouragement to the genuinely reactionary wing of the party. The Republican

[23] See C. A. H. Thomson and F. M. Shattuck, *The 1956 Presidential Campaign* (Washington: Brookings Institution, 1960).

party at the end of his Administration enjoyed a greater popular strength and a more favorable public image than it had had when he assumed its leadership, though the changes fell short of Eisenhower's hopes.[24]

DEMOCRATIC REINSTATEMENT   The 1960 victory of the Democratic nominee, John F. Kennedy, has been termed "a reinstating election." [25] This conception rests on the assumption that the balance of electoral strength may be "normally" Democratic or Republican over considerable periods. The "normal" majority may be displaced by the impact of chance events, such as were manifested in the election of Eisenhower, but the "normal" majority in due course reasserts itself in a reinstating election. The strategy of the candidates in 1960 made it appear that they accepted this theory. Mr. Kennedy lost no opportunity to emphasize that he was a Democrat and often pointed with pride to the record of his party, a tactic calculated to stir the partisan loyalties of Democrats. Mr. Nixon, on the other hand, did not parade his Republicanism but made appeals in larger measure on nonparty grounds, appeals that hopefully might attract rather than repel Democratic identifiers.[26] The pattern of voting seemed to vindicate the assumptions underlying the strategies. The vote marked generally a return toward the pattern of the earlier Democratic coalition but modified by the cross-current of the religious issue. Among the Protestant voters of some areas Mr. Nixon showed more than "normal" Republican strength, while Mr. Kennedy was especially successful in some Catholic areas in drawing back to the fold the "normal" Democratic vote—and more.[27]

Morals of Party History

This sketchy account may activate enough of the student's knowledge of recent history to provide a chronological framework within which subsequent discussion of the party system may proceed. Apart from this mundane utility, even so condensed a tale points to a few observations about characteristics of the party system.

PARTY LEADERSHIP AND COALITION FORMATION The great function of party leadership in the formation of governing coalitions obtrudes from the recital of the chain of major events. From the vantage

[24] See Sherman Adams, *Firsthand Report* (New York: Harper, 1961).
[25] Philip E. Converse *et al.*, "Stability and Change in 1960: A Reinstating Election," *American Political Science Review*, 55 (1961), 269–80.
[26] See T. H. White, *The Making of the President, 1960* (New York: Atheneum, 1961).
[27] See Paul T. David (ed.), *The Presidential Election and Transition, 1960–1961* (Washington: Brookings Institution, 1961), ch. 6.

point of time, no doubt should remain that persistent contrasts prevail in the sorts of aggregates formed by the two major American parties. Since 1896, at any rate, the Republican party has, by and large, commanded the loyalties of the great manufacturing, financial, and transportation interests, and its leadership has endeavored, with varying success, to enlist in its support other blocks of the population sufficient to govern. On the other hand, the Democratic party has had, most of the time, a relatively small following within the economic elite. Usually stronger in the northern cities than in the northern rural sections, it has, from its southern base, competed with the Republican party for the margin of victory among northern workers, midwestern farmers, and the people of the mountain and coastal regions of the West.

The process of coalition, though described in the orthodox manner in the preceding pages, is not so simple as it might have seemed. The story may read as if farmers, businessmen, industrial workers, and other such categories were solid blocks to be won or lost to this party or that. That condition of solidarity is approached in some groups at some times, but more commonly the reality differs. In the 1930's, for example, well over a majority of industrial workers were Democrats but certainly not all such workers. In 1900 a larger proportion—how large nobody knows—of factory labor was Republican than in 1936. In 1944 more than a majority, but not all, midwestern farmers were Republican. In 1928 urban northern Catholics were predominantly, but not unanimously, Democratic; in 1952 a smaller proportion was Democratic.

FLUIDITY OF ELECTORAL ALIGNMENTS   A look backward suggests something of the nature of the process of construction of partisan coalitions powerful enough to govern. It also makes clear that a fairly high degree of fluidity has existed in the partisan loyalties of the electorate. Over the short term, partisan attachments may seem to be rigid but over the long run, if a half-century qualifies as the long run, wide swings in the division of party strength have occurred.

This quality of electoral inconstancy reflects, if it does not account for, significant characteristics of the American party system. The party battle might be a recurring test of strength between cohesive groups of voters, each seeking to recruit the narrow margin of support necessary to enable it to govern; but it is not usually so on the American scene. Wide shifts in party support occur over the long pull. The breadth of the great fluctuations assures authoritative popular action at crucial moments rather than a decision on points, so to speak, which might carry no aura of authority.

Perhaps of greater importance than the amplitude of the fluctuations in party strength is the fact that voters of all classes, sections, and income levels participate in the great shifts from party to party. This enables each party to assert that its mandate to govern rests on the consent of all the people. Even

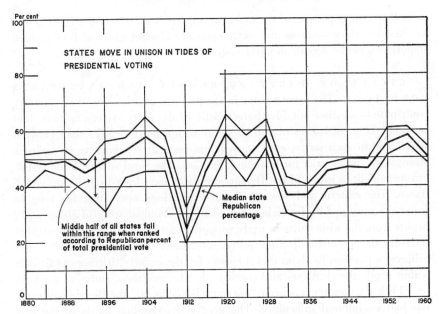

Figure 7.1   Middle half of states according to Republican percentage of total state presidential vote, 1888–1960

though that fiction contains a variable admixture of fact, the possibility of its propagation has a significance in the process of governance. That significance may be divined if one considers the possibilities of a prolonged and bitter conflict for control of the government between highly disciplined groups of people defined along class, religious, or sectional lines. The fluidity of electoral attachments in a way limits the ferocity of political conflict; and there are limits to the extent and intensity of conflict a political system can endure.

These comments about the nature of the swings from party to party do not rest on so solid a body of fact as might be desired. Had Mr. Gallup's polls been in operation over this entire period, our knowledge of the political shifts of occupational, income, religious, national-origin, and other demographic categories would be more precise than it is. The suggestion that the wide swings are participated in by most elements of the electorate gains some support from the fact that voters in all sorts of states seem to move in the same directions as the great cycles rise and fall. In Figure 7.1, data appear to show the manner in which the broad fluctuations in party strength in the states occur in unison. Half of the states, as the figure indicates, cluster in a quite narrow range in their Republican percentage of the presidential vote and move up and down together through time. The country as a whole, not just a part of it, tends to move toward this party and then toward that. The figure suggests that among persons of the most varying kinds there is a similar response to changing circumstances and party appeal, a characteristic of fundamental importance in the American party system.[28]

CYCLES OF PARTY SUPREMACY AND INTRAPARTY CONFLICT   The great swings in the partisan attachments of the country contribute to another notable characteristic of the party system, namely, that many of the great battles of politics occur within parties rather than between them. Within each party, even when it has been driven back to its bedrock strongholds, bases exist for intraparty friction. The rural southern and northern metropolitan wings of the Democratic party have long lived in uneasy alliance. The eastern and western Republican wings never live for long in fraternity untinged by fratricide. Yet when the standpat wing of either party profits from the wide shifts in party support, it attaches to itself elements that intensify the discord within the party. As a party enlarges its following and achieves a position to claim that it speaks for the country, it comes to include within itself the cleavages and conflicts that bedevil the country as a whole.

When the country has been "normally Republican," the Republican party has had its internal difficulties. The progressive-standpat battle of the first decade of the century became an outright party split; in the 1920's the western agrarians and progressives gave the Republican national leadership more difficulty than did the Democrats. In the era of Roosevelt and Truman conflict within the Democratic party took the center of the stage. When Eisenhower brought new adherents to the Republican party, he brought together a following far less homogeneous than had been the Republican minority.

[28] The student should be warned that the data on this proposition also indicate that minor movements by sharply defined groups with the most specific interests occur in both directions at each election.

8.

NATURE AND

FUNCTION

OF PARTY

G OVERNMENT derives its strength from the support, active or passive, of a coalition of elements of society. That support may be rooted in interest, consent, fear, tradition, or a combination of these and other factors in proportions that vary from society to society. In one instance a comparatively small group with control of instruments of violence may cow the populace into submission. In other instances authority may stem in far greater degree from the consent of the governed. In some states those in power may claim the right to retain their places without challenge; in others, provision may be made for periodic changes in the personnel of government by orderly processes.

In times past, the right to rule was assumed—or grasped—by small groups who based their claim to authority on the rights of religion, birth, family, class, force, or wealth. In modern times such narrowly based power has been challenged, if not swept away, by the demand that an ever-larger proportion of the people share in the process of governance. The party politician, rather than the prince, becomes the characteristic contestant for power. The political party becomes the instrument for the organization of support in societies founded on the doctrine of the consent of the governed.[1] Inherent in that

[1] See H. M. Clokie, "The Modern Party State," *Canadian Journal of Economics and Political Science*, 14 (1949), 139–57; Avery Leiserson, *Political Parties* (New York:

doctrine is the idea of popular displacement of governments and the substitution of other rulers preferred by the people. The only way so far contrived by which such popular decisions may be made is through competition among political parties.

Within all sorts of human associations "political parties" exist, though they may not ordinarily be so designated. Affairs of a group—be it a nation, a church, a union, or a chamber of commerce—do not and cannot take care of themselves; small factions of men offer to assume responsibility for handling them. "Ringleaders" propose ways of dealing with group problems and vie for place; they exercise leadership. While the germ of party may be observed in private clubs and associations, the party system in the nation possesses special characteristics. The party system of a fraternity may be organizationally no more intricate than a back-room caucus. A party system for a nation includes means for the conduct of competition for control of the government in contrast with the more common existence in private groups of oligarchies infrequently challenged in their position. Moreover, a party system for the nation (or a state or a large city) must create organization to extend its leadership over considerable areas or over large numbers of people.

Party in the Governing Process

According to literary convention a discussion should be introduced by a definition of its subject. Pat definitions may simplify discussion but they do not necessarily promote understanding. A search for the fundamental nature of party is complicated by the fact that "party" is a word of many meanings. Indeed, the genus party comprehends many species. To define sharply one party may be to exclude another, for the role of party may differ from country to country. Moreover, even within the same political order the term "party" may be applied to different elements of the governing system. An approach more indirect than the proposal of a two-sentence definition may lead toward a comprehension of the basic nature of party in the American system: the nature of parties must be sought through an appreciation of their role in the process of governance.

GENESIS OF PARTY IN DEMOCRATIZATION   Governments operated, of course, long before political parties in the modern sense came into existence. Men grasped power over their fellow men, maintained their position by a variety of techniques, and justified their authority by a variety of philosophies. Yet the regimes antecedent to modern democratic

Knopf, 1958); R. A. Dahl, *A Preface to Democratic Theory* (Chicago: University of Chicago Press, 1956); N. A. McDonald, *The Study of Political Parties* (Garden City: Doubleday, 1955); A. Ranney and W. Kendall, *Democracy and the American Party System* (New York: Harcourt, Brace, 1956).

orders had in common the monopolization of power and authority by comparatively narrow social classes. Whether the mechanism of governance was a monarchy or a monarchy tempered by consultation with the aristocracy, authority rested in the hands of a few people who claimed to rule their subjects by right. Government might be ruthless or benevolent, but in neither circumstances did it concede to its subjects a share in the governing process; their duty was to obey their betters.

Political parties developed as these ancient practices were modified by democratic ideas, which undermined the foundations of the old order. The challenges to the privileged classes carried with them assertions, revolutionary in their day, of the right of the "people," or at least of some of them, to be consulted, to give or to withhold their consent to the exercise of authority, or to participate in the governing process in other ways. Such doctrines, now commonplace, were subversive of the ordained institutions.

The proclamation of the right of men to have a hand in their own governing did not create institutions by which they might exercise that right. Nor did the machinery of popular government come into existence overnight. By a tortuous process party systems came into being to implement democratic ideas. As democratic ideas corroded the old foundations of authority, members of the old governing elite reached out to legitimize their positions under the new notions by appealing for popular support. That appeal compelled deference to popular views, but it also required the development of organization to communicate with and to manage the electorate. Thus, members of a parliamentary body, who earlier occupied their seats as an incident to the ownership of property or as a perquisite of class position, had to defer to the people—or to those who had the suffrage—and to create electoral organizations to rally voters to their support. In a sense, government, left suspended in mid-air by the erosion of the old justifications for its authority, had to build new foundations in the new environment of a democratic ideology. In short, it had to have machinery to win votes. While the exact events of institutional development rarely fit precisely any such neat pattern, such a theory of the genesis of political parties is suggestive of their basic function.

A variant of this broad explanation refines the theory to find the birth of political parties in virtual revolution. As democratic ideas spread, those dissatisfied with the old order rallied the masses, or at least many of those who had had no hand in government, against the established holders of authority. In effect, the outs played demagogue, lined up the unwashed in their support, and, at the elections, by superiority of numbers and organization they bested those dominant in government. Those who suffered such indignities were compelled in self-defense to defer to the people, no matter how distasteful it was, and to form organizations to solicit electoral support.

RISE OF AMERICAN PARTIES   Early events in the development of American parties accord to some extent with these general patterns.

Until after the adoption of the Constitution the gentry by and large ruled. They held office, not so much from their skill in swaying the multitude, but as a matter of generally recognized right associated with their status. The essence of the political system appears in the early processes of nomination. Members of the dominant political classes became nominees by individual announcement of their availability; or a friend of the candidate put him in nomination by an address published in the press. Leading personages, at least in the areas where aristocratic influence prevailed most strongly, needed no party organization to nominate them or to campaign for them; gentlemen ordinarily regarded electioneering as bad form.

The Jeffersonian Republicans, who sought to oust the old order, developed party organization both to nominate candidates and to enlist voter support. A step was taken on the way to party organization in the formation of the Democratic societies, which flourished in 1793 and 1794. They provided channels for the expression of hostility toward the Federalists, friendship toward France, and antipathy toward "monarchical aristocratical" principles. Some of them did a bit of electioneering for candidates. The controversy they aroused indicated a significant transformation of attitude that had to occur before party government could exist. The notion that assaults on the government by the outs should be expected and could be tolerated had scarcely become established. In his message of 1794, Washington spoke of the commotions "fomented by combinations of men" who were "careless of consequences" and disregarded "the unerring truth that those who rouse cannot always appease a civil convulsion." The differentiation between criticism by the outs and the threat of revolution had not become understood by the ins —and perhaps not by the outs either.

The Democratic societies died out and the Jeffersonians took basic steps in the formation of a party system as they contrived a new political organization to throw the Federalists out of office. In Pennsylvania, New Jersey, New York, and Delaware they developed the delegate convention to nominate candidates upon whom their strength might be concerted. The convention— in sharp contrast with the individual modes of nomination congenial to the gentry—provided a means for centering popular strength on candidates. Moreover, the convention permitted a combination of strength over large areas. Delegates from precincts gathered at the county seats, and those from the counties met at the state capital. To assemble delegates at the county seat —given the means of travel of the day—was an operation quite as great as gathering a state convention today. The political activists who shared in the nominating process in turn worked in their own territories to round up the vote for their candidates.

This new organization of political activity marked a profound change in the political system. Earlier, gentlemen of status offered themselves to the voters as candidates. The new system produced candidates whose nomination proceeded, in appearance at least, from the voters. It also provided an organ-izational apparatus reaching out into the electorate to rouse the voters. Often, as the system developed, the number of voters increased remarkably as political workers stirred the electorate to action. A party mechanism purporting to represent the generality drove the unorganized Federalists from power.[2]

Federalists saw the source of their woes, but, outside of Delaware, they tended to bemoan rather than to imitate the new modes of political action. In 1806, for example, a Federalist journal in New Jersey spoke of the "combina-tions of men" who had "governed the elections of New Jersey." These com-binations, or conventions of Republicans, had, in effect, decided "who should and who should not be voted" for by the people. "It is time to discountenance such proceedings. These combinations disgrace the state by appointing igno-rant, weak and crazy men to go to Congress." Most Federalists of the old school were unable to bring themselves to adopt the low tactics of their op-position. Hamilton, however, defeated by Aaron Burr's concerted cultivation of the electorate, concluded that the Federalists "erred in relying so much on the rectitude and utility of their measures as to have neglected the cultivation of popular favor by fair and justifiable expedients."

In a broad sense party organization to nominate candidates, to rally elec-toral support, and to link officialdom to voters evolved as a means for con-solidating the outs to capture control of the government. The technique amounted to a functional equivalent of revolution. When, in his Farewell Message, Washington warned against the spirit of party he was expressing the fears of the upper orders against those who would rouse the rabble.[3] He was also speaking for an era that had not yet seen the possibility of routinely conducting government in an environment of continuous partisan attack by a minority seeking to gain power.[4]

After his review of these events Henry Jones Ford concluded that Jeffer-

---

[2] These remarks lean heavily on G. D. Luetscher, *Early Political Machinery in the United States* (Philadelphia, 1903). See also D. R. Fox, *The Decline of Aristocracy in the Politics of New York* (New York: Columbia University Press, 1919), and J. Charles, *The Origins of the American Party System* (Williamsburg, Va.: Institute of Early Ameri-can History and Culture, 1956).

[3] "The very idea of the power and the right of the people to establish government presupposes the duty of every individual to obey the established government. All ob-structions to the execution of the laws, all combinations and associations under whatever plausible character, with the real design to direct, control, counteract, or awe the regu-lar deliberations of the constituted authorities, are destructive of this fundamental prin-ciple and of fatal tendency."

[4] A recognition of the legitimacy of the role of the minority is an essential in the acceptance of party government itself. Though an opposition existed earlier, it was not until 1826 that the term "His Majesty's Opposition" was applied to the British parlia-mentary minority. A better phrase could not have been invented, a member of the minor-ity asserted in the debate in which it occurred, "for we are certainly to all intents and purposes a branch of His Majesty's Government." See Caroline Robbins, " 'Discordant Parties': A Study of the Acceptance of Party by Englishmen," *Political Science Quar-terly*, 73 (1958), 505–29.

son's "great unconscious achievement" was "to open constitutional channels of political agitation." Into his Republican party flowed all the discontents that might otherwise have found expression in revolutionary strife or insurrection. By the channeling and the organization of these forces into a political party, change "became possible without destruction." [5]

These interpretations boil down to the argument that party organization and the associated practices of electioneering and deference to mass sentiments evolved to provide popular support for government as the old rationalizations of governmental authority were destroyed by democratic ideology. Party organization developed first among the outs who sought to replace the established holders of authority. Though the party process has an ancestral relation to revolution, in the descent a new means evolved for the displacement of governments from power.[6] The strivings of the outs for office become, by this reasoning, a sublimation of revolutionary movements.

These general ideas are further refined in the interpretation of party conflict as a competition by factions of the "governing classes" for the favor of the masses. Whether that conception has much validity today, it did have in the formative era of American parties. Jefferson and his associates, at odds with the Federalists, were equally of the gentry. In the view of the day, because "of party spirit gentlemen betrayed the interests of their order and menaced the peace of society by demagogic appeals to the common people." [7]

The extension of party organization over the country in the formative period also contributed to national unification. Party lines emerged earliest in the deliberations of Congress as men of like views from the several states combined to advance their common cause. Members of Congress in turn gave encouragement to the creation of party organizations in the states, which were linked together by their interest in national politics. Until the demise of the congressional caucus, the party members in Congress served as the capstone of the party organization.

INSTITUTIONALIZATION OF PARTY CONFLICT   The party system gradually achieved what we now regard as its characteristic form, a process that occurred more rapidly in some states than in others. A major second phase in its growth was the establishment of organization among the opponents of the Republicans, the group that had first capitalized upon the

[5] See *The Rise and Growth of American Politics* (New York: Macmillan, 1898), chs. 7 and 8.

[6] One of the difficulties in detail of this sort of argument is that the caucus existed in cities such as Boston long before conventional party organization came into being. Luetscher emphasizes the difference between the delegate convention as the Republicans developed it and the old-time caucus. The delegate convention permitted a combination to develop over a state or other considerable area while the caucus was commonly restricted to a smaller unit.

[7] Ford, *op. cit.*, p. 90. See Noble E. Cunningham, Jr., *The Jeffersonian Republicans* (Chapel Hill: University of North Carolina Press, 1957).

possibilities of organized effort. As party practices took root, party conflict became institutionalized: that is, generally expected and accepted patterns of organization, of behavior, and of action developed. By the groping and halting processes by which human organization evolves, new habitual ways of governing came into being. Those new methods implemented the ideas of popular government; they provided a means for obtaining popular consent in keeping with democratic ideologies. But party did more. Party operations provided a substitute for revolt and insurrection and a new means for determining succession to authority. As the party process took form, the workability of organized nonviolent conflict for control of government became established. Organized criticism and concerted efforts to replace those in power came to be regarded as routine. Once authority becomes subject to such challenges, and once sequences of elections occur, party government is extending its roots. The institutionalization of party warfare marked a major innovation—or invention—in the art of government. Rituals, ceremonies, and rules of the game developed to guide the conduct of domestic hostilities which in an earlier day might have been fought out at the barricades.[8]

The Two-Party Pattern

A salient characteristic of the American party system is its dual form. During most of our history power has alternated between two major parties. While minor parties have arisen from time to time and exerted influence on governmental policy, the two major parties have been the only serious contenders for the Presidency. On occasion a major party has disintegrated, but in due course the biparty division has reasserted itself. For relatively long periods, single parties have dominated the national scene, yet even during these eras the opposition has retained the loyalty of a substantial proportion of the electorate. Most voters consistently place their faith in one or the other of two parties; and neither party has been able to wipe out the other's following.

CONCEPT OF PARTY SYSTEM   Since many of the peculiarities of American politics are associated with the duality of the party system, the significant features of that system need to be set out concretely. An identification of its main operating characteristics will supplement the insights gained

[8] Children of the twentieth century may perceive only dimly the profound change involved in the subjection of government to partisan criticism and to the threat of partisan overthrow. Consider the assumptions about the place of government implicit in the fine of $100 assessed under the Alien and Sedition Acts against a Jerseyman named Baldwin "for expressing a wish that the wad of a cannon discharged as a salute to President Adams had hit the broadest part of the President's breeches." Ford, *op. cit.*, p. 112.

about the role of party in the governing process from our excursion into the genesis of party. To speak of a party *system* is to imply a patterned relationship among elements of a larger whole. A pattern or system of relationships exists between, for example, two football teams. Each team has a role to play in the game, a role that changes from time to time. Within each team a subsystem of relationships ties together the roles of each player. Or, if one prefers mechanical figures, the components of an internal combustion engine combine and perform in specified relation to each other to produce the total engine, or system.

Similarly, a party system consists of interrelated components, each of which has an assigned role. The American party system consists of two major elements, each of which performs in specified ways or follows customary behavior patterns in the total system. To remove or alter the role of one element would destroy the system or create a new one. If one ignores for the moment the internal complexities of parties, the broad features of the system as a whole are simple. The major parties compete for electoral favor by presenting alternate slates of candidates and differing programs of projected action. It is a basic characteristic of the system that each party campaigns with hope of victory, if not in this election perhaps at the next.

In their relations to the electorate, another element of the system, the parties confront the voters with an either-or choice. Commonly the electoral decision either continues a party in power or replaces the executive and a legislative majority by the slate of the outs. The system, thus, differs fundamentally from a multiparty system which ordinarily presents the electorate with no such clear-cut choice; an election may be followed by only a mild modification of the majority coalition. The dual arrangement assigns to its parties a radically different role from that played by parties of a multiparty system. The voters may throw the old crowd out of power and install a completely new management even if they do not set an entirely new policy orientation. The differences in the roles that their respective systems assign to them make a party of a multiparty system by no means the equivalent of a party of a two-party system. A party that may expect to gain complete control of the government must act far differently from one that may expect, at most, to become a component of a parliamentary coalition.

To be distinguished from the roles of parties in electoral competition are the functions of party in the operation of government. The candidates of the victorious party assume public office. As public officers they may become more than partisans: they are cast in public rather than party roles. Yet the party role remains, for the government is operated under the expectation that the party may be held accountable at the next election for its stewardship. To the minority falls the role of criticism, of opposition, and of preparation for the day when it may become the government itself. These functions belong mainly to the minority members in the representative body, but they may also be shared by the party organization outside the government. The minority role constitutes a critical element of the system. The minority may assail governmental ineptitude, serve as a point for the coalescence of discontent, propose alternative governmental policies, and influence the behavior of the majority as well as lay plans to throw it out of power.

In addition to the elements described, the party system includes customary rules which prescribe, often imprecisely, the manner in which the elements of the system shall interact. Of these, the most basic rule is that the government that loses the election shall surrender office to the candidates of the victorious party, a commonplace expectation which becomes significant only by contemplation of the relative infrequency of adherence to such a custom in the history of the government of man. Other rules and customs place limits on the conduct of party warfare. For example, the niceties of the etiquette of parliamentary conflict compel the attribution of good faith, patriotism, and even intelligence to the most despised enemy. Similar limitations, more poorly defined and less effectively sanctioned, apply to party warfare outside the legislative chambers. Multiparty systems are able to accommodate parties opposed to the fundamental principles of the political order. The maintenance of a two-party competition—a winner-take-all system—must, over the long run, rest on a mutual recognition of equal loyalty to the political order.

Such are the rough outlines of the American two-party system described in terms similar to those employed by social theorists in their conception of social systems generally. Real party life does not precisely fit any such pattern of relations among sets of actors. Yet the conception of system alerts the observer to the interrelations of the elements of party institutions.

WHY TWO PARTIES? Foreign observers manifest the utmost bewilderment as they contemplate the American two-party system, and native scholars are not overwhelmingly persuasive in their explanations of it. The pervasive effects on American political life of the dual form make the quest for the causes of this arrangement a favorite topic of speculation. Given the diversity of interests in American society one might expect numerous parties to be formed to represent groups with conflicting aims and objectives. Yet that does not occur. In the less sophisticated explanations of why, the system is attributed to a single "cause." A more tenable assumption would be that several factors drive toward dualism on the American scene.

PERSISTENCE OF INITIAL FORM Human institutions have an impressive capacity to perpetuate themselves or at least to preserve their form. The circumstances that happened to mold the American party system into a dual form at its inception must bear a degree of responsibility for its present existence. They included the confrontation of the country with a great issue that could divide it only into the ayes and the nays: the debate over the adoption of the Constitution. As party life began to emerge under the Constitution, again the issues split the country into two camps.

The initial lines of cleavage built also on a dualism of interest in a nation with a far less intricate economic and social structure than that of today. Arthur Macmahon concludes that, in addition to other influences, the two-party division was "induced by the existence of two major complexes of interest in the country." [9] A cleavage between agriculture and the interests of the mercantile and financial community antedated even the adoption of the Constitution. This conflict, with a growing industry allying itself with trade and finance, was fundamental in the debate on the adoption of the Constitution and remained an issue in national politics afterward. The great issues changed from time to time but each party managed to renew itself as it found new followers to replace those it lost. The Civil War, thus, brought a realignment in national politics, yet it re-enforced the dual division. For decades southern Democrats recalled the heroes of the Confederacy and the Republicans waved the "bloody shirt" to rally their followers. As memories of the war faded new alignments gradually took shape within the matrix of the pre-existing structure, with each party hierarchy struggling to maintain its position in the system.

INSTITUTIONAL FACTORS   A recurring question in political analysis is whether formal institutional structure and procedure influence the nature of party groupings. Though it is doubtful that formal governmental structures cause dualism, certain features of American institutions are congenial to two-partyism and certainly over the short run obstruct the growth of splinter parties.

Some commentators, in seeking the influences that lead to two-partyism, attribute great weight to the practice of choosing representatives from single-member districts by a plurality vote in contrast with systems of proportional representation which are based on multimember districts. In a single-member district only two parties can contend for electoral victory with any hope of success; a third party is doomed to perpetual defeat unless it can manage to absorb the following of one of the major parties and thereby become one of them. Parties do not thrive on the certainty of defeat. That prospect tends to drive adherents of minor parties to one or the other of the two major parties. The single-member district thus re-enforces the bipartisan pattern. Each of the contending groups in such a district must formulate its appeals with an eye to attracting a majority of the electors to its banner.[10]

An essential element of the theory is its plurality-election feature. If, so

[9] *Encyclopedia of the Social Sciences*, XI, 595–601.

[10] The single-member-district interpretation is presented in a comparative study by F. A. Hermens, *Democracy or Anarchy?* (Notre Dame: The Review of Politics, 1941). See also E. E. Schattschneider, *Party Government* (New York: Farrar & Rinehart, 1942), ch. 5; Maurice Duverger, *Les partis politiques* (Paris: Armand Colin, 1951) ; J. G. Grumm, "Theories of Electoral Systems," *Midwest Journal of Political Science*, 2 (1958), 357–76.

the hypothesis goes, a plurality—be it only 25 per cent of the total vote— is sufficient for victory in a single-member district, the leaders of a group consisting of, say, 15 per cent of the electorate, will join with other such groups before the voting to maximize their chance of being on the winning side. They assume that if they do not form such coalitions, others will. Moreover, concessions will be made to attract the support of smaller groups. If a majority, instead of a plurality, is required to elect, a second election to choose between the two high candidates in the first polling becomes necessary. Such a situation may encourage several parties to enter candidates at the first election, each on the chance that its candidate may be one of the two leaders. Of course, under systems of proportional representation the incentive to form two coalitions, each approaching a majority, is destroyed by the opportunity to elect candidates in proportion to popular strength whatever the number of parties.

The validity of the single-member-district theory has not been adequately tested against the evidence.[11] Obviously, in those states of the United States in which third parties have developed fairly durable strength, the institutional situation has stimulated moves toward coalitions and mergers with one or another of the major parties. Yet the single-member-district and plurality election can at most encourage a dual division—or discourage a multiparty division—only within each representative district. Other influences must account for the federation of the district units of the principal party groups into two competing national organizations.

The popular election of the Chief Executive is commonly said to exert a centripetal influence upon party organization and to encourage a dualism. The supposed effect of the mode of choice of the President resembles that of the single-member constituency. The winner takes all. The Presidency, unlike a multiparty cabinet, cannot be parceled out among minuscule parties. The circumstances stimulate coalition within the electorate before the election rather than within the parliament after the popular vote. Since no more than two parties can for long compete effectively for the Presidency, two contending groups tend to develop, each built on its constituent units in each of the 50 states. The President is, in effect, chosen by the voters in 50 single-member constituencies which designate their electors by a plurality vote. The necessity of uniting to have a chance of sharing in a victory in a presidential campaign pulls the state party organizations together.

SYSTEMS OF BELIEFS AND ATTITUDES   Certain patterns of popular political beliefs and attitudes mightily facilitate the existence of

[11] Maurice Klain has pointed out that almost half of the American state legislators are chosen from multimembered districts, a practice of long standing in many states. See his "A New Look at the Constituencies: The Need for a Recount and a Reappraisal," *American Political Science Review*, 49 (1955), 1105–19. Given the associated voting procedures, these multimembered districts should not be expected to have the divisive effects attributed to proportional representation.

a dualism of parties. These patterns of political faith consist in part simply of the absence of groups irreconcilably attached to divisive or parochial beliefs that in other countries provide bases for multiparty systems. Although there are racial minorities in the United States, either they have been politically repressed, as has the Negro, or they have been, as in most instances, able to earn a niche for themselves in the nation's social system. Nor do national minorities form irredentist parties. For example, the Germans of Milwaukee do not form a separatist party to return Milwaukee to the Fatherland. Nor has any church had memories of earlier secular power and the habit of political action that would lead to the formation of religious political parties. Class consciousness among workers has been weak in comparison with that in European countries, and labor parties have made little headway. When one group places the restoration of the monarchy above all other values, another regards the prerogatives of its church as the highest good, still another places its faith in the trade unions, and perhaps a fourth group ranks the allocation of estates among the peasants as the greatest good, then the foundations exist for a multiparty politics.

The attitudes underlying a political dualism do not consist solely in the absence of blocks of people with irreconcilable parochial faiths. A pattern of attitudes exists that favors, or at least permits, a political dualism. Its precise nature must remain elusive, but it is often described as a popular consensus on fundamentals. Powerful mechanisms of education and indoctrination, along with the accidents of history, maintain broad agreement, if not a universal conformity, upon political essentials. At times, it can be said, with a color of truth, that we are all liberals; at another time, it may be equally true that we are all conservatives. Given this tendency for most people to cluster fairly closely together in their attitudes, a dual division becomes possible on the issue of just how conservative or how liberal we are at the moment. Extremists exist, to be sure, who stand far removed from the central mode of opinion, but they never seem to be numerous enough or intransigent enough to form the bases for durable minor parties.

Explanations of the factors determinative of so complex a social structure as a party system must remain unsatisfactory.[12] The safest explanation is that several factors conspired toward the development of the American dual party pattern. These included the accidents of history that produced dual divisions on great issues at critical points in our history, the consequences of our institutional forms, the clustering of popular opinions around a point of central consensus rather than their bipolarization, and perhaps others. The assignment of weights to each of these is an enterprise too uncertain to be hazarded.[13]

[12] On the problem of causation, see Leslie Lipson, "The Two-Party System in British Politics," *American Political Science Review*, 47 (1953), 337–58. See also A. Downs, *An Economic Theory of Democracy* (New York: Harper, 1957).

[13] The discussion can be turned on its head and the question put why a single party does not achieve a monopoly. Or how it is that a minority manages to survive. Some

Structure and Impact of Dualism

Whether an adequate explanation can be contrived why a people organizes its politics into a two-party pattern, the fact that it happens to do so has the most pervasive effects on the political system. The pattern of organization, once established and endowed with momentum, profoundly conditions the out-look and orientation of the top leadership of each party. It affects as well the role of party leadership in the molding of mass opinion. It influences the nature of the conflict that occurs between parties and thereby the role of the parties in the political system. A foundation may be laid for some observations about these consequences by an examination of a few of the more general features of the internal structure and composition of the major parties.

INNER STRUCTURE OF PARTY   The inner structure of party represents a special case of the more general pattern of relationships between leaders and led. Those relationships involve an interaction between the inner core of leadership and the group membership. Leaders may carry along their followers, who also may mold both the tactics and objectives of the leaders. The echelons of leadership in both Democratic and Republican parties man-age, within limits, the attitudes of their respective followers, but, in turn, the attitudes of the loyal rank and file within each party may, again within limits, fix the orientation of the leadership. The broad outlooks peculiar to Demo-cratic and Republican leadership structures tend to be associated with the characteristics of their respective followings.

The distinction between the inner core of party activists and the mass of membership leads some commentators to see the reality of party as the inner circle of party leaders and workers. Professor E. E. Robinson asserts that to

---

observers see forces in the system that push toward an "equilibrium" between the parties near the 50-50 point. The party division fluctuates over time around this point somewhat like an agitated set of balances that moves its pointer to and fro across the zero mark on the scale. The equilibrium concept probably describes better than it explains. It may be simply too costly for the majority, given the social composition of the population, to attempt to swallow the minority. Enlargement of a majority introduces elements anti-thetical to its core of basic support. The Democrats might, for example, adopt a program designed to attract the business community but it would thereby outrage standpat Democrats. Minorities, too, have means for self-defense. See D. V. Smiley, "The Two-Party System and One-Party Dominance in the Liberal Democratic State," *Canadian Journal of Economics and Political Science*, 24 (1958), 312–22. Great surges of strength to one party seem to have a way of being gradually offset by inroads on its following by the minority. The gains of one party tend to generate antagonisms that are exploited by the minority leadership as it seeks to maintain itself. In a general sense, forces seem to prevail that push the balance back toward the 50-50 level after wide swings occur. See D. E. Stokes and G. R. Iverson, "On the Existence of Forces Restoring Party Com-petition," *Public Opinion Quarterly*, 26 (1962), 159–71; a forthcoming study by C. G. Sellers, Jr., "The Equilibrium Cycle in American Two-Party Politics."

comprehend the nature of a political party we must concentrate attention on the party's inner core or organization which comes

> into being for the purpose of fighting and governing. It is not concerned with matters of fact, or doctrine, or even of principle, except as they bear upon the great cause for existence: success at the polls. Such organizations not only contain men of divergent views; they must also appeal to voters of differing opinions, prejudices, and loyalties. It is folly to talk of finding an actual basis [for political parties] in any set of principles relating to public welfare.

He sees party as a "comparatively small and compact body of men. Real power rests with them. They formulate appeals, direct campaigns, discuss in advance, and decide the nature of programs to be submitted to the voters." [14]

Emphasis on the inner group of leaders and workers centers attention on the main sources of party action, but the inner circle would amount to nothing without its following of faithful partisans. This is not to say that a more meaningful definition of party comes from defining it as a group consisting of those persons voting or registered as Democrats or as Republicans. In many states membership in either major party is gained simply by a person's indicating the party with which he wishes to affiliate when he registers as a voter; affiliation is even less formal in other states. The process of gaining membership in the party is unlike that of affiliation with more tightly organized groups. The party member does not go through a ritual of induction into the group; in most instances he is neither acquainted with nor knows the name of the ward or county chairman of his party; he probably never supports his party in any way financially; the privileges and responsibilities of party membership rest lightly on his shoulders.

Despite the informality of acquisition of legal membership in a party, the psychological attachment of the great mass of partisans to their party possesses remarkable durability. Even if the party member is an unfaithful attendant at party functions and an infrequent contributor to its finances, he is likely to have a strong attachment to the party heroes, to its principles as he interprets them, and to its candidates on election day. These loyalties, moreover, tend to persist. Even when he deserts his party's candidates, the voter may still regard himself as a good Republican or Democrat. The fairly stable party membership conditions the attitudes of party leaders, who must act in a manner to retain its loyalty.

The psychological attachment of voters to their party varies in intensity from the most unquestioning loyalty to the most casual sense of affiliation. The inner core and the mass of a party may be pictured as a set of concentric circles. A small hard core of leaders and workers, mostly the professionals,

[14] E. E. Robinson, "The Place of Party in the Political History of the United States," *Annual Reports of the American Historical Association for the Years 1927 and 1928* (1929), 202.

is surrounded by party members of intense devotion. As one moves from the center, successive circles may be taken to represent categories of persons with declining degrees of attachment to the party. This sense of belonging has been called party identification by Angus Campbell. A person regards himself as a Democrat or a Republican; he has a sense of identification with the party group and tends to regard its cause as his cause.

Campbell's studies establish the existence of these concentric circles of party adherents of varying party loyalty. At various times from 1952 to 1961 the respondents in national samples of the electorate rated the strength of their party identification in the proportions indicated in Table 8.1. The interviewees

Table 8.1   Distribution of respondents in five national samples, 1952–1961, according to strength of party identification [a]

Party Identification	October 1952	October 1954	October 1956	October 1960	October 1961
Strong Democrat	22%	22%	21%	21%	26%
Weak Democrat	25	25	23	25	21
Independent Democrat	10	9	6	8	9
Independent	5	7	9	8	10
Independent Republican	7	6	8	7	5
Weak Republican	14	14	14	13	13
Strong Republican	13	13	15	14	11
Apolitical, don't know	4	4	4	4	5
	100%	100%	100%	100%	100%

[a] Angus Campbell and H. C. Cooper, *Group Differences in Attitudes and Votes* (Ann Arbor: Survey Research Center, 1956), p. 17, and data from Survey Research Center.

classified themselves in response to the question, "Generally speaking, in politics, do you usually think of yourself as a Republican, a Democrat, an Independent, or what?" If the answer was "Republican" or "Democrat," this question followed: "Would you call yourself a strong (Republican or Democrat) or a not very strong (Republican or Democrat)?" Independents were asked whether they regarded themselves as "closer to the Republican or Democratic party" and were classified accordingly as independent Republicans or Democrats. These measures of party identification have a validity in that those who called themselves "strong Democrats" (or Republicans) differ in their voting behavior and in other ways from those who regard themselves as weak or "not very strong" Democrats (or Republicans).[15]

[15] The flavor of the attitudes of the strong identifiers is illustrated by the observations of a pair of the respondents: "I was just raised to believe in the Democrats and they have been good for the working man—that's good enough for me. The Republicans

The processes by which party identification is established and maintained are not well understood, but it is clear that the family is influential in building a sense of party identification. Commonly, 75 per cent or more persons vote as their parents did, and those whose parents were independents tend to be independents in high degree. The family and other primary groups also help to maintain party loyalties once they are formed.[16] However party identification may be created, it is, to a degree, independent of factors often thought to be determinative of partisan loyalty. Voters to some extent act as they do, not because they are workers or proprietors or farmers, but because they are Republicans or Democrats.[17]

SIMILARITIES AND DISSIMILARITIES IN PARTY COM-POSITION   Party leaders must seek to retain the loyalties of those who identify with the party. In so doing they tend to reflect as well as to shape the outlooks of their followers. Some clues toward an understanding of the nature of the two-party system can be found by an examination of the characteristics of Democrats and Republicans in the mass: their social attributes and their political attitudes. Broadly, the two sets of partisans differ, on the average, in their social characteristics and political opinions. These differences are as-

---

are a cheap outfit all the way around. I just don't like Republicans, my past experience with them has been all bad." "I'm a borned Republican, sister. We're Republicans from start to finish, clear back on the family tree. Hot Republicans all along. I'm not so much in favor of Eisenhower as the party he is on. I won't weaken my party by voting for a Democrat." See the other similar quotations in Angus Campbell, *et al., The Voter Decides* (Evanston: Row, Peterson, 1954), pp. 91–92, and their discussion of party identification in ch. 7. Such inherited party attachments weaken when the second generation happens to carry them into an unfriendly or inconsistent social environment. See R. W. Dodge and E. S. Uyeki, "Political Affiliation and Imagery Across Two Related Generations," *Midwest Journal of Political Science,* 6 (1962), 266–76.

[16] See Herbert McClosky and H. E. Dahlgren, "Primary Group Influence on Party Loyalty," *Amercan Political Science Review,* 53 (1959), 757–76; V. O. Key, Jr., *Public Opinion and American Democracy* (New York: Knopf, 1961), ch. 12; M. L. Levin, "Social Climates and Political Socialization," *Public Opinion Quarterly,* 25 (1961), 596–606. The widespread existence of a sense of identification wth party may be a stabilizing influence of fundamental significance. It may obstruct the disturbing quick rise and fall of transient groupings born of circumstances of the moment. Contrast the French situation where the sense of party identification is weak, as reported by Philip E. Converse and Georges Dupeux, "Politicization of the Electorate in France and the United States," *Public Opinion Quarterly,* 26 (1962), 1–23.

[17] The maintenance of a party attachment in conflict with other pressures often sets off psychological gymnastics within individuals. Thus, partisans whose policy beliefs diverge from that of the presidential candidate of their party may not see the conflict or may even perceive the candidate as in agreement with themselves. Or partisans may invent intricate rationalizations for a party attachment in conflict with their apparent objective interest. Even when he deserts his party the partisan may deceive himself. Of a sample of New Orleans voters who voted for Eisenhower in 1952, almost half either thought of him as an independent or declined to say whether they thought of him as a Republican or Democrat. K. N. Vines, "Republicanism in New Orleans," *Tulane Studies in Political Science,* 2 (1955), 119–20.

sociated with divergent orientations of the two party leaderships. Paradoxically, though, Republicans and Democrats in the mass are also often similar.
The average differences conceal the overlaps of Democratic and Republican
identifiers with like policy views, and on some issues not even the averages
differ. These similarities also find reflection in leadership outlooks that blur
the differences between parties.

The data support Charles Beard's conclusion that "the center of gravity
of wealth is on the Republican side while the center of gravity of poverty is
on the Democratic side." [18] The Democratic following consists in larger proportion of the lower-income groups, of the less well educated, of the lower-
status occupations, and of unionized workers than does the Republican following. The composition of party voters in the 1948 election, in which factors of
party identification evidently played an especially significant role, reveals these
differences in a marked form. In that year more than twice as large a proportion of Truman voters as of Dewey supporters had had only a grade school
education. Five times as many Dewey supporters as Democrats, relatively,
were college trained. The proportion of the Republican ranks composed of
professional and managerial persons was about four times as great as for the
Democrats. These details appear in Table 8.2. In addition, Protestants bulk
much larger among Republicans than among Democrats, while the Democratic
party, especially in the North, relies more heavily upon support from the
newer strains of immigration than does the Republican party.

The national leaderships of the Republican and Democratic parties see
different pictures when they look over their shoulders at their followings. Yet
the composition of the party supporters varies from election to election and
the supporters of each party always include substantial representations from
all sorts of people. The survey data on recent presidential elections are presented in Table 8.3 to show the partisan division of voters within occupational
and other groups. In the elections of 1952 and 1956 Eisenhower drew far
higher proportions of the votes of workers than Dewey drew in 1948. In 1960
Kennedy attracted the support of a much larger proportion of Catholics than
this group ordinarily gives to Democratic candidates, though it has usually
leaned Democratic.[19]

The data of Table 8.3 make clear that such differences as exist between
the party supporters are matters of degree, or of averages, and that these
differences are far more marked at some times than at others. Yet the facts,

[18] *National Municipal Review*, 6 (1917), 204. See Seymour E. Harris, *The Economics
of the Political Parties* (New York: Macmillan, 1962).

[19] For an analysis of the partisan inclinations of religious groups, see Wesley and
Beverly Allinsmith, "Religious and Politico-Economic Attitude: A Study of Eight Major
U.S. Religious Groups," *Public Opinion Quarterly*, 12 (1948), 377–89. See also D. B.
Walker, "The Presidential Politics of the Franco-Americans," *Canadian Journal of Eco-
nomics and Political Science*, 28 (1962), 353–63. On the capacity of economic issues to
split religious groups, see Oscar Glantz, "Protestant and Catholic Voting Behavior in a
Metropolitan Area," *Public Opinion Quarterly*, 23 (1959), 73–82.

Table 8.2   Demographic characteristics of Republicans and Democrats, November, 1948 [a]

Characteristic	Truman Voters	Dewey Voters
Education		
Grade school	48%	27%
High school	43	30
College	8	43
Not ascertained	1	
	100%	100%
Occupation		
Professional and managerial persons	9%	37%
White-collar workers	14	17
Skilled and semiskilled workers	40	14
Unskilled workers	13	7
Farmers	12	8
Others and not ascertained	12	17
	100%	100%
Trade-union affiliation		
Member	39%	11%
Nonmember	58	89
Not ascertained	3	
	100%	100%

[a] Source: Survey Research Center, University of Michigan.

Table 8.3   Democratic percentage of two-party presidential vote within demographic categories [a]

Category	1948	1952	1956	1960
Professional and business	20%	31%	32%	46%
White-collar	50	35	38	44
Skilled and semiskilled	78	56	45	59
Unskilled	74	69	55	59
Farm operators	65	37	46	32
Negro		80	64	70
Protestant	47	36	35	37
Catholic	65	51	45	81

[a] Source: Survey Research Center, University of Michigan. Data on Negro vote not available for 1948.

such as they are, suggest that each party has had a fairly durable bedrock following that contrasts with that of the other party. On the Republican side, the financial and manufacturing interests have been consistent sources of strength as have the upper-income groups generally. The Democrats, on the contrary, have—apart from their southern strength—tended to find their most marked support among industrial, urban, lower-income classes. This is not to say that Democrats invariably hold the support of a preponderance of the groups. The point is rather that even in their days of little hope, Democrats generally attracted larger proportions of such voters than they did of the typically Republican sectors of society. To a degree the party struggle could be described as a competition between the party leaderships for the support of workers. In their triumphs the Republicans may win popular majorities in working-class wards, as they often did in 1956, but even at such times the Democrats draw their highest vote percentages, low though they may be, in such areas.

Parallel to the differences and similarities in demographic makeup are differences in outlook on questions of public policy. Few public issues attract the opposition of most Democrats and the support of most Republicans, or vice versa. Some issues divide the parties scarcely at all; the issue cuts across party lines and splits both parties in about the same manner. Yet on contentious matters a common pattern is that the "center of gravity" of the opposition is to be found among the adherents of one party, whereas the larger proportion of the proponents will be found among the followers of the other party. In 1948, for example, seven of eight favoring the repeal of the Taft-Hartley Act voted Democratic; six of every seven persons opposing repeal voted Republi-

Table 8.4   Relation of party identification to opinions on scope of social legislation [a]

Opinion	SD	WD	ID	I	IR	WR	SR
Should do more	41%	20%	23%	35%	38%	22%	11%
Doing about right	38	55	55	34	35	45	50
Should do less	4	8	4	7	12	15	22
Other responses	17	17	18	24	15	18	17
	100%	100%	100%	100%	100%	100%	100%
N	248	288	97	82	68	159	146

[a] The question was: "Some people think the national government should do more in trying to deal with such problems as unemployment, education, housing, and so on. Others think that the government is already doing too much. On the whole would you say that what the government is doing is about right, too much, or not enough?"

Source: A telescoping of table from Angus Campbell and Homer C. Cooper, *Group Differences in Attitudes and Votes* (Ann Arbor: Survey Research Center, 1956), p. 91.

can. Policy cleavages infrequently follow party lines so closely. On many issues, though, the numbers of Republicans and Democrats with contrasting views outnumber those with similar outlooks. Consider the 1954 data of Table 8.4. Among strong Democrats, those who thought the government should "do more" in the field of social welfare were proportionately almost four times as numerous as among strong Republicans. Those who thought the government should "do less" were far more numerous among strong Republicans than among strong Democrats. On the other hand, party differences were muted by the large numbers of both Democrats and Republicans who thought the government was doing "about right." [20]

INTERACTION OF PARTY ELITE AND MASS   The contrasts and similarities between the partisans of the two major parties are, thus, paralleled by similar distributions of individual attitudes on issues between the parties. Do these characteristics of the followers help to account for the nature of the role of each party? The characteristics of the mass of a party result to a degree from the nature of the party leadership; every great presidential candidate leaves a heritage of devoted partisans. Yet, given a system in momentum, the mass of each party also conditions the behavior of its leadership and its role in the system.

If the broad record of this century may be taken as an index, the conclusion appears clear that the leadership of each party has been anchored to its most reliable following. The record of party promise and performance contains a divergence parallel to the differences in party composition. The Democratic party in this century has elected Woodrow Wilson, Franklin D. Roosevelt, Harry S. Truman, and John F. Kennedy. Their administrations were characterized by programs and proposals for economic reform and by an inclination to limit the power of business. Under the leadership of these Presidents, policies calculated to improve the lot of labor made far more notable headway than in Republican administrations. Democratic administrations promoted the cause of the farmer, especially the southern farmer, more vigorously than did Republican. Of the Democratic leaders who did not achieve the Presidency during this period, Bryan belonged to the same tradition as Wilson and Roosevelt, but Parker and Davis would have felt at home in the Republican party.

Over this period, the Republican party has had a fundamental policy orientation also in accord with the inclinations of its most faithful supporters. The campaign of 1896 cemented the bulk of the financial and manufacturing

[20] Limited evidence suggests that there may also be psychological differences between adherents to the two parties. For example, higher proportions of Republicans than Democrats are "very much interested" in elections and more Republicans feel themselves to be politically effective. See Angus Campbell, "The Case of the Missing Democrats," *New Republic*, July 2, 1956, pp. 12–15. See also Herbert McClosky, "Conservatism and Personality," *American Political Science Review*, 52 (1958), 27–45.

community to the Republican party, and in 1962 Eisenhower could remark in a speech: "They call ours a party of business and I'm proud of the label." In the affairs of the party, solvent citizens who feel that they can take care of themselves without government intervention, unless it is on a matter such as the tariff, have exerted great influence. Hence, the Republican party has been less disposed to advance the cause of labor by governmental action; it has felt that what is good for business is good for the country. In this century the Republicans have no great reform for the regulation of business to their credit, yet at times they have proceeded with vigor against business abuses, as under Theodore Roosevelt and Taft in the prosecution of combinations in restraint of trade. Many of the contrasts in orientation express themselves in the common denominator of fiscal policy. Republicans regard Democrats as soft touches for mendicants, and Democrats make remarks about their opponents' hearts of flint. Insofar as we have a "conservative" and "liberal" cleavage, that cleavage is along Republican-Democratic lines. Even this distinction fails in many times and situations. Yet after discounting the statement to allow for campaign exaggerations, a residue of fact remains in Wilson's assertion that "the chief difference between the Democratic and Republican parties is that in the Republican party the reactionaries are in the majority, whereas in the Democratic party they are in the minority." [21] The troubled voter cannot use this as an infallible guide, for in each party sometimes the minority gains the upper hand, and always broad areas of agreement exist between the parties.

The tug of the durable foundation of strong support within each party tends to fix the fundamental policy orientation of each party. Yet the makeup of each party also restrains the zeal of the leadership in the advocacy of the cause of any single element within the party. Leaders in congressional districts may be extremists in the cause of organized labor, of suburban upper classes, of the Negro, of the Jew, of the wheat farmer, of the cotton farmer, of the manufacturers, or of some other element within each party; nevertheless, that segment of the party leadership with a national outlook—fundamentally those concerned with victory in presidential elections—must keep in view all elements within the party.

The diversity of the composition of a party operates thus to moderate the outlook of its national leadership. Those who make their way to positions of national leadership tend to be fundamentally sound on matters of concern to the party's inner core but they temper their devotion by an allowance for other interests within the party. Those with serious aspirations for a Democratic presidential nomination need to be sound on labor but they also must not unnecessarily frighten Democratic businessmen. No serious aspirant for a Republican presidential nomination can afford to be known as one who

---

[21] Quoted by Josephus Daniels, *The Wilson Era: Years of Peace, 1910–1917* (Chapel Hill: University of North Carolina Press, 1944), p. 11.

would put business in its place, yet he must have a somewhat benevolent re-gard for labor. On many other matters the national leadership is driven toward ambiguous stands by the conflicting elements within the party. The spectacle of a Democratic leader attempting to retain the support of both southern whites and northern Negroes exemplifies the matter as do the cross-pressures the Republican leadership undergoes as it is ground between the party's isolationist and internationalist wings. The top party leadership must try to restrain the extremists within the party ranks, search out areas of agree-ment and capitalize upon them, and, in general, attempt to hold together an unstable compound that often seems on the verge of disintegration.

In short, the diversity of pressures from within the party upon the leader-ship drives it toward moderation. While lower-level leaders may flourish by the fanning of extremists and particularist emotions, the top echelons must seek to hold together divergent and often conflicting elements. The situation generates a radically different sort of imperative for the leadership than does the context in which party leaders of a multiparty system operate: they may be driven to accentuate the separatism of their electoral following.[22]

COMMON INFLUENCES ON COMPETING PARTY LEAD-ERSHIPS   Still another aspect of the situation within which party leader-ship operates helps to account for additional characteristics of party behavior. Each party leadership must maintain the loyalty of its own standpatters; it must also concern itself with the great blocks of voters uncommitted to either party as well as with those who may be weaned away from the opposition. These influences tend to pull the party leaderships from their contrasting an-chorages toward the center. In that process, perhaps most visible in presi-dential campaigns, the party appeals often sound much alike and thereby contribute to the bewilderment of observers of American politics.

The compulsions that pull the leaderships of both parties toward the center result in part from the simple arithmetic of presidential pluralities. To win a presidential election a party must both retain its traditional support and make gains among all sorts of people—farmers, laborers, white-collar workers, and the business and professional classes. While the competing appeals may stress differences in proposed modes of action, in competence to act, or in the timing of action, to antagonize any considerable class or group of voters is folly. The hearts of both Democratic and Republican orators may bleed, for example, with equal profuseness for the farmers, although what they propose to do for, or to, the farmers may differ in substantial detail. The practical necessity of appealing to all sorts of people and to all shades of opinion was emphasized by Thomas E. Dewey in his 1950 Princeton lectures. He spoke of impractical theorists who

---

[22] See the comparative analysis by Seymour Lipset, "Party Systems and the Repre-sentation of Social Groups," *Arch. Europ. Sociol.*, 1 (1960), 50–85.

want to drive all moderates and liberals out of the Republican party and then have the remainder join forces with the conservative groups of the South. Then they would have everything neatly arranged, indeed. The Democratic party would be the liberal-to-radical party. The Republican party would be the conservative-to-reactionary party.

The results would be neatly arranged, too. The Republicans would lose every election and the Democrats would win every election.

Calculations of what is necessary for victory doubtless contribute to the tendency of both parties to make multiclass and multigroup appeals. Yet it seems evident that subtle characteristics of American political culture also contribute to an explanation of the nature of the party battle. An expectation of that culture seems to be that the object of government should be the maintenance of a concert of interests rather than the intensification of conflict or the establishment of the dominance of a particular interest. No matter how devoted a party leadership may be to its bedrock elements, it attempts to picture itself as a gifted synthesizer of concord among the elements of society. A party must act as if it were all the people rather than some of them; it must fiercely deny that it speaks for a single interest. Selections from the campaign oratory of Franklin D. Roosevelt and Dwight D. Eisenhower have a remarkably similar ring. Both on occasion placed emphasis on the interrelations of the interests of farmers, workers, businessmen, bankers, all of whom had common cause in the achievement of great national purposes. And to a degree party victory represents the victory of a conception of national purpose, not the undiluted triumph of a particular interest.

All such partisan oratory contains, to be sure, an ingredient of campaign buncombe; it does not necessarily reveal the groups to which a party will be beholden if it wins. Yet the oratory doubtless also represents an obeisance to widely shared beliefs in the population. Generations of civic education have implanted an antipathy to "special" interests, a concern for the general interest. Each party must develop a conception of the general interest to mask its association with relatively narrow sectors of society. While that necessity has consequences of profound significance, one of the lesser results is that parties are made to appear more alike than they actually are.

The total pattern of party structure appears to be one in which the top echelons in each party are much more widely separated in their policy attitudes than are the mass of party identifiers. The principal evidence on this point comes from studies by Herbert McClosky. He compared opinions of party leaders (as exemplified by delegates to the national conventions of 1956) and of party followers as estimated from a sample survey. On a series of issues the average scores of Republican and Democratic leaders differed considerably more than did the average scores of the two sets of followers.[23]

[23] Herbert McClosky, *et al.*, "Issue Conflict and Consensus among Party Leaders and Followers," *American Political Science Review*, 54 (1960), 406–27. See also D.

The assumption may be made that the necessities of winning office compel the leadership groups to move nearer together in their public appeals for votes than they would like, could they be governed only by their private preferences. Some evidence also indicates that those persons highly concerned about politics more often adopt the views popularly thought to be typical of their party than do those persons with little interest in politics.[24]

Dualism in a Moving Consensus

Although each party leadership tends to be anchored to the fundamental interest of the party, the total electoral situation and ideological climate pull both parties toward a point between the extremes. So flat a statement—and it is the essence of the argument to this point—may help to discern some of the order underlying the confusion of the American party system. Yet the proposition states only part of the reality. The process by which the parties move toward a point between the extremes is erratic, jerky, disorderly, and accompanied by no little friction. Moreover, the point of consensus or policy equilibrium toward which the parties move is itself not fixed: it moves as the parties approach it. In short, a conception of the party system must take into account its dimension of time. It may be useful to think of the party system as an historical process rather than as patterned and static institutional behavior.

FOUNDATIONS IN CONSENSUS   If the time dimension is ignored, emphasis on consensus in the interpretation of American politics may convey a conception of a static politics and lead to the inference that the party battle is meaningless. If a differentiation is made between levels or types of consensus and if the party process is viewed through time, additional aspects of the workings of party dualism may be identified. Any competitive party system must rest on an agreement among all concerned about certain fundamental principles. In the United States, as in other working democratic regimes, such a consensus on fundamentals prevails, though no precise understanding may exist about what the fundamentals are. Obviously a significant area of agreement concerns the constitutional structure and procedure; no powerful element of society advocates the destruction of the constitutional order and the substitution of another. Beyond agreement on methods of government a vague area of substantive consensus concerns the acceptance in broad terms of the capitalistic system. Perhaps the more basic element of

---

Marvick and C. R. Nixon, "Recruitment Contrasts in Rival Campaign Groups," in Marvick (ed.), *Political Decision-Makers* (New York: Free Press of Glencoe, 1961), pp. 193–217; R. S. Hirschfield, *et al.*, "A Profile of Political Activists in Manhattan," *Western Political Quarterly*, 15 (1962), 489–506.
[24] Key, *op. cit.*, ch. 17.

the consensus consists in the understandings and customs about how authority shall be exercised and in what manner changes shall be made rather than in agreement that certain matters shall not be changed.[25]

Without some such acceptance of the regime party politics could scarcely exist. A party system cannot be built in a society of irreconcilable sects, each of which proposes to install its own brand of political system. Those bent on mortal combat cannot practice a party politics. To affirm the necessity of a framework of shared beliefs as a basis for party politics is not to deny the possibility of the sharpest party conflict that does not strike at the foundations of the political order. The line between fundamentals, not to be questioned, and nonfundamentals, open to debate, may be illusory. That is, modification of the modifiable may, by insensible steps, alter the basic nature of a political order. Nevertheless, in practice a range of debatable issues exists whose limits define the terrain over which the party battle rages.

CUMULATIVE ZONES OF CONSENSUS   It is within the limits of the arguable that the party battle occurs. In the adjustments to the settlements made within this range it may be said that parties, in the long run, tend to move toward the same point between the two extremes. Innovation often meets the bitterest challenge; it is resisted; it may be accepted grudgingly; it may finally become conventional. In this process another aspect of the nature of the party system becomes manifest.

Triumphant parties that advocate great causes or that come into power at moments of great stress must contrive and enact measures that may be thought, even widely, to be destructive of the principles of the Republic. Yet unless gradual acceptance of such innovation comes about, the cleavage between the parties could grow into a chasm unbridgeable by the compromises of party politics. Or alternations in party control, with the accompanying changes of policy, would jolt the social and economic system beyond the bounds of toleration.

In the interactions between the parties—which are spread over considerable time periods—what seems to occur is that to one party falls the lot of innovation. Its creative measures stir dissension and embitter the minority, though their more extreme aspects may be toned down in the process of enactment through the checks and restraints built into the governmental machinery. To the extent that new measures are both technically successful and evocative

[25] John Fischer has argued that among the unwritten rules is that each of the many groups of society "tacitly binds itself to tolerate the interests and opinions of every other group. It must not try to impose its views on others, nor can it press its own special interests to the point where they seriously endanger the interests of other groups or of the nation as a whole." By the arrangements of the party and governmental system each group can exercise an implied veto, but in its exercise the group must "make every conceivable effort to compromise, relying on its veto only as a last resort." "Unwritten Rules of American Politics," *Harper's Magazine*, November, 1948, pp. 27–36.

of popular support, they become embedded in the consensus by the impact of popular ratification in successive elections. The minority party eventually recognizes the inevitable and accepts the new order. Matters once contentious are relegated to the body of settled questions, and the growing edge of the political system moves on to new fields where new problems await solution and invite conflict.[26]

In this century the Democratic party has, perhaps both by chance and by the dynamics inherent in its makeup, been thrust into the role of innovator. The Wilson Administration put on the statute books a mass of new legislation, but its product became relatively slight alongside the statutory accretion of the New Deal. Both by conviction and by its attraction for all those antagonized by the Rooseveltian program, the Republican party became a vehicle of resistance to the New Deal. In the 1936 campaign Alfred Landon, the Republican standard bearer, attacked even the Social Security Act. The bulk of the Republican leadership viewed the National Labor Relations Act with revulsion, and most of those who regarded themselves as affected adversely by each major Democratic measure found themselves in the Republican ranks.

Gradually the Republican party moved toward acceptance of the principal New Deal policies. This movement was accompanied by warm disputes among Republicans, and Republican candidates were long unsuccessful in persuading the electorate that their "me-tooism" was genuine. Perhaps the elections of 1946 and 1948 clinched the New Deal. The Republican Congress elected in 1946 made sounds as if it wished to dismantle the New Deal. The response of the country in 1948 persuaded even the most hard-shelled standpatters that the New Deal was here to stay.

The events of the 1952 campaign and of succeeding years brought more general Republican accord with the changes that had been wrought in both domestic and foreign policy. Eisenhower's convention victory over Taft represented a defeat of the isolationist and economically reactionary wing of the party. His election turned in considerable measure on his capacity to gain the confidence of erstwhile Democratic voters who continued to subscribe to Democratic views on public policy. Once in office a goodly proportion of the crowd brought to power with the General seemed to interpret the election as a mandate to repeal the New Deal. Tentative steps in those directions with respect to farm policy, to housing, to the TVA, to the REA, and in other fields brought sharp public reactions. The congressional elections of 1954 reminded the Administration of the terms on which it could enjoy public confidence. Perforce, the Republican leadership became reconciled to the statutory precipitate of the New Deal. It could chip away at New Deal measures by inconspicuous administrative action; it could refuse to carry those policies further; but it could not re-open settled questions.

---

[26] Such remarks are suggested by analysis by Arthur W. Macmahon, "Conflict, Consensus, Confirmed Trends, and Open Choices," *American Political Science Review*, 42 (1948), 1–15.

In the field of foreign policy a similar transformation occurred. Though Eisenhower had to contend with a determined rear-guard action by the isolationist wing of his party, the Republican leadership accepted a larger role in world affairs than Republicans had traditionally contemplated with comfort. The new orientation by a Republican President brought a shift in the attitudes of rank and file Republicans.[27] Long in a state of disenchantment, they were brought to espouse policies that they had regarded as Democratic heresies.

INNOVATION, RESISTANCE, RECONCILIATION   Although reservations may be made about the thoroughness of Eisenhower's renovation of the Republican party, the process described diluted the Republican nostalgia for the good old days and brought a semblance of reconciliation to the new order. Not all American party history can be neatly fitted into this pattern of innovation, resistance to innovation, and reconcilation. While some such process has recurred, each instance of a broad shift in the point of consensus had had its peculiarities. In each of the great episodes of our party history the political system gradually digested—or absorbed into the consensus—the consequences of far-reaching innovations.

If the parties are viewed in this temporal framework, one may better appraise the old saw that the parties offer the electorate only a choice between tweedledum and tweedledee. In fact, the differences between the parties vary from stage to stage in the conversion of controversy into new consensus as does the significance of the outcome of national elections. A Republican victory in 1936, for example, would have braked the New Deal to a halt and probably resulted in the repeal of its major measures. A series of Democratic victories demonstrated majority acceptance of the Rooseveltian reforms and time brought Republican recognition of that fact. By 1952 the policy differences between the parties had become far narrower, and the practical consequences of a Republican victory in 1952 differed radically from those of 1936. An election may abruptly check the growth of a new line of policy as did the 1918 and 1920 Republican victories in foreign affairs. It took another world war to set in motion again the drive toward reorientation of foreign policy vetoed by the elections of 1918 and 1920. By 1956 the spread between the parties on foreign policy had narrowed, and the choice faced by the electorate more nearly approached one of tweedledum or tweedledee than it had been in the elections of 1920 and of 1940. And in the 1960 campaign Mr. Nixon could assert that his party differed with the Democrats on a series of domestic questions only with respect to the choice of means.

For well over a half-century, perhaps since the Civil War and certainly

---

[27] While some persons become identified with a party because its leaders advocate policies pleasing to them, others adopt policy attitudes because they are identified with a party. The evidence seems to indicate that many Republicans, once the party leadership became perceptibly nonisolationist after 1952, changed their attitudes to accord with the new party line. See Angus Campbell and Homer C. Cooper, *Group Differences in Attitudes and Votes* (Ann Arbor: Survey Research Center, 1956), pp. 102–4.

since 1896, the party orientations fixed by the upper echelons of each party have determined the fundamental role that each might play in the evolving consensus. With the liquidation of its progressive wing in 1912, the Republican party became so bound to its corporate constituency that it could take no major initiative in social and economic reform; perhaps the accidents of history that placed it in the minority in times of international crisis also induced within it a paralysis in the reconstruction of foreign policy. Its internal dynamics and its place in the total system cast the Democratic party into a contrasting role. The correct generalization may be that neither party can well take drastic steps that may affect adversely its hard core of support.

ROLE OF THE MINORITY   To observe the party system through the sweep of time suggests an elaboration of the earlier analysis of the opposition party's role in the dual system. The minority leadership, beyond the continuing function of reminding the majority that it is not really all the people and of assailing governments for their ineptitude, arbitrariness, and crookedness, has the task of promoting within its ranks an acceptance of modifications of the old order and of bringing its followers into accord with the dominant norms of the political community. Without the accomplishment over the long run of this sort of reconciliation, the two partisan camps could become so estranged as to paralyze the orderly processes of government.

This function falls by and large to the minority that has felt outraged by innovation and not to the minority that has lost a routine election followed by no abrupt changes in public policy. Such a minority function, moreover, becomes perceptible only from a long-term view of the party process. Similarly, the minority from the same sort of time view has another major role in the system: that of consolidating sufficient strength to oust the government and to carry through the occasional thoroughgoing reorientation of the political order that circumstances and national conscience demand. The long look at the party system makes perceptible the significance of the availability of a minority force capable of making drastic adjustments of the political order when the occasion demands.

This is not, of course, to deny the importance for the dual system of the role of the opposition in more routine times. Without an opposition party there can be no dual system. The opposition makes possible the periodic presentation to the electorate of choices between governing cliques and of policy alternatives of a sort. The minority also must play a role in the conduct of government by maintaining a running fire of responsible criticism.[28] The

[28] In the field of foreign policy a special role falls to the minority leadership or at least to that sector of its leadership most sympathetic with Administration policies. The term "bipartisan foreign policy" is something of a misnomer; yet at times the achievement of foreign policy objectives absolutely requires the concurrence of a substantial part of the minority senatorial group, and appropriate interparty consultative relations have developed. The etiquette is suggested by the fact that in the midst of the

American party system is singularly ill-adapted to the performance of this latter function, for the minority tends to be poorly organized for that purpose. Its titular leader, the defeated presidential candidate, may be without influence over his partisan colleagues in Congress to whom fall the day-to-day determination of party position. Given the fact that the congressional minority tends to speak only for one shade of the spectrum of party belief, odd sorts of minority views often predominate. For long the country shuddered at the image of the Republican party that emerged from the operations of its standpat leadership in Congress, and a minority Democratic party has its similar problems.

LIMITS OF PARTISAN CONFLICT   The breadth of the American political consensus keeps the party conflict within tolerable limits. "We cannot have," Pendleton Herring long ago observed, "a radical party standing for revolutionary change and a conservative standpat party. Such parties may exist only on the plane of discussion. Revolutionary communism can be tolerated by democracy as long as it remains an academic question." [29] On the other hand, the political system must have within it the means for substantial policy alterations from time to time. Such reorientations need to be managed so that over the long pull practically the entire society is carried along. Otherwise, the gradual accretions to the ranks of the irreconcilables would ultimately produce a bipolarization of antipathies hardly congenial to the existence of party government. Fundamental to the avoidance of the development of that sort of dual confrontation is the prevalence of a pragmatic outlook—as well as some self-restraint among the innovators. Yet the dual organization of politics, by the necessities it imposes upon those who would gain power, may contribute to the political adjustment of the community to change through time.[30]

---

presidential campaign of 1948 President Truman asked Arthur Vandenberg, Republican leader on foreign policy, to "slip in the back door" of the White House for a "private chat," in the course of which the President expressed his appreciation of the "judicial" tone of a campaign speech by Vandenberg and observed that the retention of the bipartisan foreign policy was more important than "who was elected President." A. H. Vandenberg, Jr. (ed.), *The Private Papers of Senator Vandenberg* (Boston: Houghton Mifflin, 1952), p. 452.

[29] "Political Parties and the Public Interest," *Essays in Political Science in Honor of W. W. Willoughby* (Baltimore: Johns Hopkins Press, 1937), p. 102.

[30] In 1955 midwestern, standpat, isolationist Republicans convened in Chicago on Lincoln Day for oratorical festivities devoted to belligerent criticism of Eisenhower, Dewey, and the eastern wing of the party generally. They regarded Eisenhower as a dangerous leftist, they despised Dewey, they were unhappy about American involvement in the United Nations. Even so the idea of bolting the party had little attractiveness. "While a lot of us get irritated with Eisenhower out here," concluded General Robert E. Wood, "we still figure he's a lot better than anybody the Democrats can put in there." *New York Times*, February 14, 1955. At the other end of the political spectrum, the extreme liberal may be observed in ingenious rationalization as he accepts the Democratic policy and ticket,

9.

SECTIONALISM,

URBANISM,

AND PARTY

A N E X T R A O R D I N A R Y characteristic of the American party system has been its continuity despite the most far-reaching changes in the underlying social and economic circumstances of the nation. From 1860 to 1960 the population grew from about 31.4 million to 179 million. Over the same period vast areas of the West were settled and the great movement of people from farm to city took place. In more recent decades a restless mobility has carried people from section to section. Tens of millions of immigrants, most of them different in language and religion from the earlier settlers, found places for themselves in American life during the past century. In the same period industrialization proceeded apace. Withal a dynamic and changing social system has existed, one quite unlike the systems of those nations whose modern politics is restricted to the interstices of an ancient and rigid structure of status and class and rests on an economy of stagnation rather than of growth.

Through all these changes the major parties have maintained a continuous existence, at least since the Civil War, and the dual system has prevailed in its essence almost since the founding of the Republic. For a century, it may seem, the major parties have remained the same. In fact, only the system has remained more or less the same: the parties have changed. New wine has been poured into old bottles and old wine has been transferred from bottle to bottle. Old parties moved with the population into the newly settled territories. The parties managed to attract and to make places within their ranks for new Americans. They reached out to accommodate themselves to the consequences of industrialization.

The ceaseless alteration in the composition and orientation of the major parties and in the character of the conflict between them makes problems for the political analyst. One era's classic treatment of parties obviously does not fit the facts of a later period though its clichés and generalizations may outlast the phenomena they describe. A full treatment of the process by which the parties have been molded by the changing social system and by which the parties themselves have perhaps molded the evolving society would be a formidable task. Yet some of the major elements of continuity and change in the parties may be identified in broad terms.

Sectional interests have constituted important building blocks for the American parties. Each party has had its roots deep in sectional interest and each has sought to build intersectional combinations powerful enough to govern. While the sectional foundations of American parties have contributed mightily to the appearance of immortality of the parties, those foundations have for a half-century been undergoing a steady erosion. Urbanization can serve as a shorthand term inclusive of a variety of tendencies destructive of sectionalism, such as industrialization, a sharpening of class consciousness, and immigration.

Sectionalism and Continuity of the Party System

For its two-party form and for the persistence of that form, American politics probably owes a considerable debt to an underlying dual sectionalism, which, for well over a century, contributed to a partisan dualism; and undoubtedly in the earlier decades of the Republic mightily aided in molding enduring political habits. The Federalists vied with the Jeffersonian Republicans; the Whigs and the Jacksonian Democrats competed for supremacy; the Democrats and the new Republicans fought a war, and they continued the battle later on the hustings.

Originally sectional dualism was associated with the advancing frontier. Among great nations of modern times the United States has been unique in possessing a sectional conflict growing out of the gradual spread of population over a continent. Long-established nations have their sectional issues, but the American westward movement caused a special type of political conflict. The areas settled first along the Atlantic seaboard furnished capital for the development of the western wilderness and thereby created a relationship of creditor and debtor between geographically differentiated groups; and, as

James Madison observed, the clashes of interest between debtor and creditor have always been a "durable" source of faction. In other ways the interests of the East and of the advancing frontier were in conflict. A thinly populated agricultural West had interests that often ran counter to those of the more densely populated financial and industrial East. And the dominance of the East in all matters was threatened by the development of the West. Though the particular area constituting "the West" changed as the frontier advanced, there was always a West.

SECTIONALISM AND THE FORMATION OF THE CONSTITUTION   Even the debate over the adoption of the Constitution took the form of a dual sectional conflict, a dispute between the frontier and the seaboard. Then, as is generally true, sectionalism masked underlying differences between territorially segregated interests. In his classic study, *An Economic Interpretation of the Constitution of the United States,* Charles A. Beard showed the importance of economic interests at stake in the adoption of the Constitution. In identifying the groups involved in the formulation and ratification of the document, Beard noted the existence of an important class of small farmers located mainly back from the seacoast, on the fringe of westward settlement, from New Hampshire to Georgia. This western inland section had interests antagonistic to those of the people of the seaboard. The small farmer was frequently in debt, often to a seaboard speculator, for his land; and he had to rely on the capital of the seaboard to develop the newly opened country. In consequence of the difference of interests between the West and the East, there germinated from time to time legislative proposals disquieting to the East, such as easy-money schemes to alleviate the lot of the debtor and laws postponing the collection of debts.

Opposition to the adoption of the Constitution came principally from "the agricultural regions, and from the areas in which debtors had been formulating paper money and other depreciatory schemes." [1] On the other hand, support for the new system of government came chiefly from the "regions in which mercantile, manufacturing, security, and personality interests generally had their greatest strength."

The cleavages in the battle over the adoption of the Constitution projected into politics under the new government. Time was on the side of the growing West, which found its first great spokesman in Jefferson. The power of the Federalists depended primarily on the

. . . support of the wealthier classes of people and rested particularly on a combination of the commercial interests of the North Atlantic coast region, the tobacco planters of Virginia, and the rice planters of South

[1] *An Economic Interpretation of the Constitution of the United States* (New York: Macmillan, 1913), p. 291. But, see Forrest McDonald, *We the People: The Economic Origins of the Constitution* (Chicago: University of Chicago Press, 1958).

Carolina. In 1801 Jefferson at the head of the Democratic-Republican party broke the power of this combination and obtained control of the federal government. There has been much discussion in recent years of the economic basis of Jeffersonian Republicanism. Out of the dust of controversy emerges the simple proposition that Jefferson succeeded in organizing the greater portion of the back country grain growers from Maine to Georgia into a coherent "bloc," which formed the strongest element in his victorious combination.[2]

JACKSONIAN DEMOCRACY   Under the vigorous leadership of Jackson the western forces were again united against those of the East, or at least against the moneyed parts of the eastern population. Jefferson and Jackson built their fences on the solid soil of unity of the sectional interest of the then West. Says Professor Woodburn:

> For fifty years after Jefferson's triumph the democracy which he promulgated found its support not only in the western parts of the original thirteen states but in all the oncoming new states of the West. Omit the South and think only of the states of the Northwest, Ohio, Indiana, Michigan, Iowa, Wisconsin. The party of Jefferson and of Jackson was able to carry these states, as also Pennsylvania, until close to the days of the Civil War, until the restriction of slavery had become the dominant issue in American history and the Democratic party had come largely under the control of southern slaveholders.[3]

The conflict between the seaboard and the frontier never arrayed all westerners against all easterners. The West had its allies in the East and the East by no means lacked support in the West. As people moved to the West they carried their partisan loyalties with them. Settlers from Federalist and Whig areas retained their old attachments in their new surroundings, while Virginians, Kentuckians, Tennesseeans, and North Carolinians clustered in settlements that turned up as Democratic patches on the maps of election returns.[4] Even in the Pacific Northwest the settlers "were steeped in the Jeffersonian-Jacksonian tradition. Those from the slaveholding states of the upper and deep South may not have brought their slaves with them, but they did bring the principles of the Democratic party."[5]

As the slavery issue grew in intensity and salience, the old cleavage be-

[2] A. N. Holcombe, *The Political Parties of To-day* (New York: Harper, 1924), p. 83.

[3] J. A. Woodburn, "Western Radicalism in American Politics," *Mississippi Valley Historical Review*, 13 (1926), 143–68.

[4] Thus the politics of Indiana and to a lesser extent Ohio retained the marks of southern settlement in rural areas even in the middle of the twentieth century. Most of these rural areas of special Democratic strength were settled by southerners.

[5] R. W. Johannsen, *Frontier Politics and Sectional Conflict* (Seattle: University of Washington Press, 1955), p. 14.

tween East and West was replaced by a new sectionalism. The pattern of sectional politics became one of conflict between North and South. As the "solid West" disintegrated, "rival societies, free and slave, were marching side by side into the unoccupied lands of the West, each attempting to dominate the back country." [6] The outcome was the Civil War, which imprinted on American politics a new and lasting pattern of sectionalism.

Politics of Sectionalism after the War

The Civil War made the Democratic party the party of the South and the Republican party, the party of the North. That grand sectional division, which manifested a remarkable persistence, rested in part on a regional economic differentiation and the associated conflict in political objectives. Cotton growing and related agricultural pursuits dominated the South and contributed to a homogeneity of political outlook. A different, and more variegated, sectional interest generated the driving forces of the Republican party. So long as employing groups retained the confidence and loyalty of substantial numbers of factory workers the Grand Old Party had both votes and campaign funds. Yet the clashes of interest founded on economic geography did not alone provide the basis for the Democratic-Republican split. In the assessment of the strength of the sinews tying men of all classes of the North and South to the Republican and Democratic banners, heavy weight must be assigned to the regional patriotisms forged by war. Those loyalties were long sustained by the bloody shirt and the rebel yell. Of course, underneath the froth of sentiment substantial sectional economic interests prevailed after, as before, the war.

NATURE OF SECTIONALISM   A more precise statement of the character of sectionalism ought to be interpolated lest the emphasis on its importance in American politics convey an erroneous impression. In an extreme form sectionalism might be taken to refer to a condition of absolute sectional solidarity in which the people of the South, say, were united on all issues against the people of the North, who were equally united in opposition to the South. To be sure, such a high degree of sectional cohesion and intersectional antagonism rarely occurs within a working polity. Nevertheless, a sectional politics commonly involves a sharing of interests and attitudes by people of all sorts in a major geographical region against a similar clustering of interests and attitudes of the people of another region. Over long periods most people in each section may make common cause against the other over a single great issue or grouping of issues. Yet friction along lines of geographic

[6] F. Turner, *The Significance of Sections in American History* (New York: Holt, 1932), p. 27.

cleavage is commonly mitigated by a sharing of interests across sectional lines by at least some classes of people. Bankers, farmers, laborers of a wheat-producing section may unite against all outsiders on policies affecting wheat. On other matters, bankers of wheat-growing areas may join with bankers of other regions in common cause.[7]

Sectionalism tends to mask territorially separated interests. Sectional and regional loyalties—to the South, to the West, to New England—are not without strength. Differences in dialect, in social customs, and in history set off the people in one area from those of another.[8] While such differences furnish some basis for regional rivalries, the concentration of cotton growing in the South and of manufacturing in the Northeast more persuasively explains decades of sectional political competition than does the fact that some people called themselves southerners and others regarded themselves as northerners. Perhaps the more homogeneous in interest the sections are, or the more complete the dominance of a single interest in each section, the sharper intersectional tension may become. On the other hand, the destruction of sectional homogeneity paves the way for political divisions along nongeographical lines.

Sectionalism, or conflict along territorial lines, may threaten national unity as sectional cohesion tightens and the lines of cleavage between sections deepen. The way of life of a region may lead its citizens to look upon the "outsider" as an "alien"—a feeling not unlike that of the people of one nation toward those of another. Territorial differentiation and conflict in extreme form may pose for the politician the problem of manufacturing a formula for the maintenance of national unity. Only once did the American politicians fail in this endeavor, but we came to have, as the late Professor Turner said, "unlike such countries as France and Germany, . . . the problem of the clash of economic interests closely associated with regional geography on a huge scale. Over areas equal to all France or to all Germany, either the agricultural or manufacturing types are here in decided ascendancy." [9] He likened the deliberations of party conventions and Congress and their results "to treaties between sections, suggestive of treaties between nations in diplomatic congresses."

MESHING OF SECTIONALISM AND THE PARTY SYSTEM   The sectional clusters of interest, founded on economics, hardened by the Civil War, and re-enforced by subsequent events, formed the hard cores

[7] Sectionalism is a matter of the degree of unity within sections. Many issues take a transient sectional form. The poultry raisers of New England, buyers of grain, may fulminate against midwestern grain growers over price-support policies. Yet most people of both sections have neither concern nor knowledge of the conflict. True sectionalism involves a greater salience of interregional conflict and a more widespread sense of mutual antagonism.

[8] See Merrill Jensen (ed.), *Regionalism in America* (Madison: University of Wisconsin Press, 1952).

[9] Turner, *op. cit.*, p. 36.

of the major parties. According to the more extravagant sectional interpretations, the South and the North competed for the support of the West in their battle for control of the national government. While so forthright a view glosses over the confusing detail, it fitted for many decades the broad contours of our politics.

Neither the hard core of the Democratic party, the South, nor the sectional bedrock of the Republican party, the North of 1861, consisted of peoples nicely homogeneous in attitude and interest as might be supposed from a simple sectional theory of politics. Rather within each of these sections, those interests associated with the leaderships of the Republican and Democratic parties managed to establish a position of sufficient dominance to maintain regional control over comparatively long periods.

Each great section inherited, to be sure, a durable sense of unity from the Civil War, but that unity had to be renewed and maintained by a composition of internal differences and by an exploitation of areas of common interest among different elements of each section. In the North the hegemony of the Republican party rested on the skillful maintenance of a combination of manufacturers, industrial workers, and farmers. The protective tariff, opposed by the South, provided a common bond for manufacturers and workers in protected industries. The same policy created difficulties in holding the grain growers of the Midwest in the Republican ranks. They could see the merit of a high tariff on cereals, but felt no enthusiasm for protective levies on farm implements and supplies. The frequent nomination by Republicans of presidential candidates from Ohio, Indiana, and Illinois served, in Professor Holcombe's interpretation, to make the most "effective appeal to the farmers of the corn-growing regions." [10]

The Democratic party similarly, but with less difficulty, maintained its dominance in its southern hard core. Southern solidarity rested on the common memories of military defeat, on the common interests of an agrarian region vulnerable to the fluctuations of the world market, and on the problems of race. Latent cleavages between commercial interests and poor farmers, manifest in such disturbances as the agrarian unrest of the 1890's, were suppressed by the stimulation of anxieties about the threat of black rule. The combination of circumstances enabled the Democratic party to establish far more thorough control in the South than did the Republican party in the North.

Within each party the sectional interests, which form the reliable and faithful core, gain a disproportionate influence in the party and thus assure that these interests will be amply represented in party councils. Democratic Senators and Representatives from the Solid South, re-elected term after term, gain positions of power in congressional committees under the seniority rules. Similarly, in national conventions and in the informal party councils these

[10] Holcombe, *op. cit.*, p. 352.

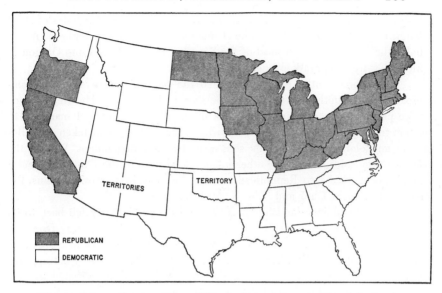

Figure 9.1   Sectionalism: Electoral vote in presidential election of 1896, by states

persons, through long service in party affairs, gain positions of vantage from which to defend and promote the interests of their region. Likewise, Republican leaders from the Northeast climb, through seniority, to positions of power in their party.

Neither the Old South nor the "Old" North, that is, the North of 1861, could alone control the nation. The party of each section had to seek support from outside to elect the President and a majority of Congress. In the process intersectional combinations were formed of South and West and of North and West. Their formation required either the existence of common or non-conflicting objectives or the compromise of differences within the dominant multisectional alliance.

The nature of the patterns of competition and combination between sections may be made graphic by a few maps showing the division of electoral votes between the major parties in selected presidential elections. The election of 1896, the results of which appear in Figure 9.1, involved a sharp sectional conflict. The Democrats sought to join the agrarian South with the discontented debtor farmers of the West against finance and manufacturing of the Northeast. In the West silver-mining interests, hopeful of disposing of their product at a high price, allied themselves with the Democrats. In the Northeast the Republicans succeeded in uniting the manufacturing classes and a substantial proportion of factory workers against the threat of lower tariffs and inflation. As Figure 9.1 indicates, the Republican strategy held together their bedrock support in the Old North and annexed to it the border states of West Virginia, Kentucky, Maryland. The Democrats added to their southern strong-holds the electoral vote of most of the West but lost California and Oregon to McKinley by comparatively narrow margins.

In the presidential election of 1916 the pattern of intersectional com-bination took another form, as may be seen in Figure 9.2. The Republicans were pushed back to their strongholds in the "Old" North, but managed to retain the support of Oregon, a state which, incidentally, had taken on a Re-publican coloration through its settlement by New Englanders. Wilson, the Democratic candidate, on the other hand, added most of the West to the Solid South and moved into Republican territory to take, by narrow margins, the electoral votes of Ohio and New Hampshire.

In the Republican landslide of 1920 the Democratic party fell back to its southern redoubt while the Republicans again extended their sway from the North over the entire West. Harding even managed to take the electoral vote of one state of the South, Tennessee.[11] The sectional pattern of 1920 appears in Figure 9.3. This map, as well as the others, gives an exaggerated impres-sion of the sectional quality of the electoral decision. Each party polled a sub-stantial minority vote in those states whose electoral vote went to the opposi-tion.

GEOGRAPHY AND POLITICAL BEHAVIOR   These sectional disputes in politics arose largely from the divergent economic interests of dif-ferent regions, which, in turn, rested fundamentally on differences in the na-ture of regional economic resources. This relation between geography and political attitude suggests parenthetical allusion to theories of the geographical conditioning of political behavior. The association of types of geographical environment with varying political attitudes has stimulated speculation about the geographical basis of politics.

The writings of Montesquieu provide an early example of a geographical interpretation of politics. He placed emphasis on the influence of climate on human character and, in turn, on the nature of government. He believed, for example, that the colder climates produced a more restless and irritable people and a greater degree of political liberty; that warmer climates produced an indifferent and lethargic people readily susceptible to subjugation and des-potism. Similarly, plains people, without natural defensive barriers, were

[11] The movement of the West away from the Democratic coalition began in the congressional elections of 1918. S. W. Livermore contends that an influential issue in the 1918 voting arose from Wilson's veto of a measure to increase the government pur-chase price of wheat. Cotton prices, not under regulation, climbed upward. Charges of favoritism to the South colored the Republican campaign of 1918 in the West. "The Sectional Issue in the 1918 Congressional Elections," *Mississippi Valley Historical Re-view*, 35 (1948), 29–60.

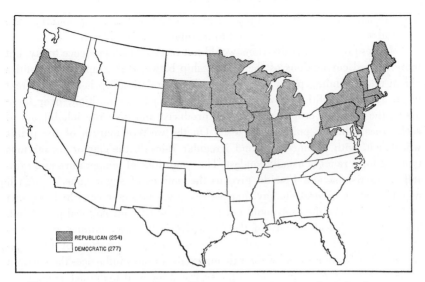

*Figure 9.2   Sectionalism: Electoral vote in presidential election
of 1916, by states*

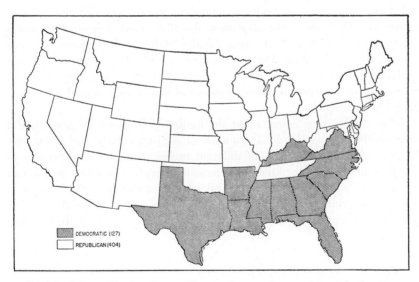

*Figure 9.3   Sectionalism: Electoral vote in presidential election
of 1920, by states*

likely to live under a despot; those of broken and mountainous country were better able to defend themselves and to maintain political liberty.

Montesquieu's generalizations would not receive much credence today, but more refined correlations of the relationship between geography and politics aid in understanding political behavior. Such a relationship is most apparent in an agrarian politics in which geographical factors condition, over large areas, the types of crops that may be produced and give the inhabitants of such areas common political interests. On the western margin of the plains wheat belt, with its uncertain and irregular rainfall, the clamor for various types of farm relief is usually loudest. The conditions of temperature and rainfall in Louisiana and Florida give us the politics of sugar cane, though it might be more accurate to say that politics gives us sugar cane in Louisiana and Florida, since the crop could not be produced without political protection. The seat of political activity of the extractive industries—mining and petroleum production—is determined by the geographical location of those resources. The juxtaposition of the raw materials for steel influences the location of the metal industries and, hence, the sectional locus of manufacturing.

At times the notion of geographical influence has been pushed to the form of an extreme geographical determinism; more recently students have pointed out that man may affect geography as well as geography, man. The geography of the South did not predestine it to cotton culture and slavery; a complex of cultural factors—a demand for cotton, the availability of slaves, the existence of attitudes condoning slavery—brought about the utilization of southern soil by a slavocracy. Likewise, both the cotton and wheat belts have been pushed farther west by the breeding of plant strains that require less moisture and a shorter growing season; land geographically "destined" for grazing has been brought under cultivation. The textile industry, formerly concentrated in New England partially because of factors of climate and the availability of power, has moved southward with the development of new sources of power and new industrial techniques.

Man can to some extent offset the limitations imposed by geographical environment. Yet within the framework of a given culture and technology the geographical endowments of different regions undoubtedly determine to a considerable extent the kinds of economic enterprise in which people can engage and thereby color their political interests and ambitions. When technology, industrial or agricultural, overcomes geographical factors influencing the kinds of occupations people follow, geography ceases to "condition" political behavior.

The South, the War, the Negro

Since the South has been our most cohesive section, the factors underlying its solidarity deserve special mention. For many decades it formed the bedrock of the Democratic party. It stood for the party and the party spoke for it. For 50 years changes in both the North and the South have been gradually undermining southern solidarity. Those tendencies came to a head in 1948 when several southern states declined to follow the northern Democratic leadership and bolted the party in the presidential election. In 1952 and 1956 the underlying developments predisposing some southerners toward Republicanism found expression in the vote for Eisenhower. Yet the intensity of southern reaction in the 1950's against school integration made it plain that southern solidarity of a sort would remain for some time.

BACKGROUND OF SOUTHERN SOLIDARITY   The historic solidarity of the South arose from a combination of economics, of race friction, and the events of history. Although the region long possessed an antipathy toward the tariff policies fostered in the North, that basis of unity did not alone suffice to solidify the South. An element of southern leadership succeeded in establishing a regional hegemony despite the existence of considerable economic heterogeneity. Even prior to the Civil War, marked cleavages of interest existed within the South, and they found expression in competing parties. "The economic and political interests of the southern Whigs were the 'special interests' of the slavocracy. During the early forties the Whig party was frequently denounced as the aristocratic party of the slaveholders." The Democratic party drew on the "opposite side of the social scale—especially upon the small farmer of the back hill-country who could always be reached by the party's appeal to the agrarian spirit." [12] The South became a cohesive section when the slavocracy established its dominance in the region. In 1860 about 11,000 southern planters (about three-fourths of 1 per cent of the total free population) owned 50 or more slaves each. About 100,000 smaller planters owned from 10 to 50 slaves each. The slaveholding segment of the population, which had almost a monopoly of wealth, talent, and leadership, was able to impose its will on the South.

Great crises often mold political behavior into a durable pattern. Southern sectionalism bears the imprint of the trauma of history. The experiences of a war, an unsuccessful war, produced a regional cohesion with impressive qualities of persistence. A military occupation—known as Reconstruction—further solidified attitudes of hostility toward the outsider. Common resistance to the carpetbagger and Negro governments, no matter how much their misdeeds may have been exaggerated, further sharpened the sense of regional cause and further crystallized the determination to keep in his "place" the Negro, the innocent cause of all the trouble.

The liquidation of the Reconstruction governments restored the Negro to his role of political subordination in the South, but the interracial equilib-

---

[12] A. C. Cole, *The Whig Party in the South* (Washington: American Historical Association, 1914), pp. 69–72.

rium was threatened by the agrarian radical movement of the 1880's and 1890's. That movement promised a restoration of two-party politics in the South. The Populists and the Republicans of the southern highlands appeared as more or less lineal descendants of the pre-Civil War Democrats, while the Democrats functioned as successors of the pre-Civil War Whigs. The farmers' uprising in the South, unlike the Populist revolt in the Northwest, was slowed down, if not snuffed out, by the race question. Populists and bourbon Democrats bid against each other for support of the Negro. The danger that white disunity might restore carpetbagger or Negro government was harped upon, perhaps deliberately to frighten the discontented agrarians. Although the pattern differed in detail from state to state, the upshot of the agrarian crusade in the South was that the agrarians were quelled, the state constitutions were amended to record the fait accompli of the exclusion of the Negro from the vote, and the proposition was established that southerners should stand together in national politics.[13]

INDICES OF SOUTHERN UNITY   The unity of the South is generally exaggerated, yet on one set of issues—those relating to the status of the Negro—a high degree of political cohesion prevails. Concern about the Negro may, in fact, be about all there is to southern solidarity, a proposition that may be illustrated by a few simple sets of data. Anthropologists tell us that in primitive cultures the cohesion of social groups is mightily promoted by the proximity of unlike groups. If that phenomenon occurs generally, it would be expected that the strongest roots of southern unity would be found in those parts of the South in which Negroes constituted a large part of the population. On the other hand, it might be supposed that the bonds of southern unity would be weakest in those areas with fewest Negroes. The evidence supports the proposition that the whites of the black belt make up the backbone of southern solidarity.[14] In 1928 the nomination of Alfred E. Smith, a Catholic and a wet, strained the Democratic loyalties of the South. Several southern states went Republican. Though there were exceptions, the areas with the highest proportions of Negro population tended to remain loyal to the Democratic party. Of 191 southern counties over 50 per cent Negro in population, 184 returned majorities for Smith. Of 266 counties less than 5 per cent Negro, only 79 gave him a majority. A map of North Carolina illustrative of the relation between the distribution of the Negro population and the 1928 Democratic vote appears in Figure 9.4.[15]

[13] See Vincent P. De Santis, *Republicans Face the Southern Question: The New Departure Years, 1877–1897* (Baltimore: Johns Hopkins Press, 1959).

[14] The fact that the migration of Negroes from black-belt counties is reducing their Negro population proportions should not lead to predictions of a rapid softening of white attitudes toward blacks in these areas. H. D. Price demonstrates that white attitudes in such areas remain hostile long after a decline in Negro population proportions. See his *The Negro and Southern Politics* (New York: New York University Press, 1957), pp. 41–44.

[15] It may be advisable to note that it is in the areas of high Negro-population concentrations that relatively fewest Negroes vote.

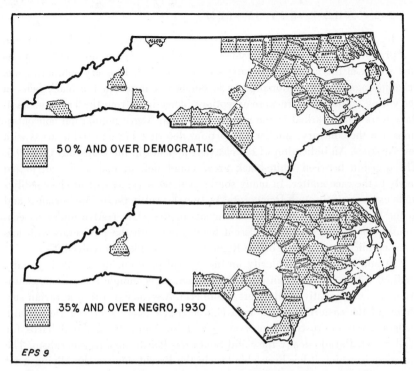

Figure 9.4   The black belt and the die-hard Democratic vote:
North Carolina counties over 50 per cent Democratic in 1928 presidential election and counties with 35 per cent or more Negro population, 1930

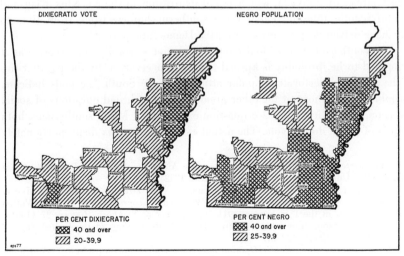

Figure 9.5   The black belt and the Thurmond vote in 1948: The
case of Arkansas

In 1948 the Democratic party espoused, through both its platform and the pronouncements of its presidential candidate, views on race relations that struck at the heart of the party's southern wing. In every southern state, rebellion against the national party leadership centered in the black belt. In the voting, although there were exceptions, defections from the Truman candidacy were most marked in the regions with high Negro population concentrations. On the contrary, smaller proportions deserted Truman in the areas with few Negroes. An indication of the cleavage appears in the maps in Figure 9.5. The division between white-black areas could not, of course, be attributed solely to the race matter. In many southern states a vague sort of class politics finds expression through Democratic factions based in the fertile lowlands and in the less productive highlands. Elements of the party restive under its economic policies could express dissent by joining with the Dixiecrats with less inner conflict than support of the Republicans would have involved.[16]

In addition to its solidarity on the Negro question, the South is usually credited with a uniform conservatism. In fact, on economic issues some southerners are conservative and others are liberal. A strong strain of agrarian suspicion of the eastern interests long characterized many southern Democratic leaders. Even so crusty a conservative as John Nance Garner had barbs for Wall Street. Paradoxically the Solid South has had to nurture liberalism. The only way in which it has been able to win the Presidency was by allying itself with the West or with the laboring masses of the North. At propitious times the Democrats emerged from their southern hibernation with a Woodrow Wilson or a Franklin D. Roosevelt to challenge Republican dominance. Yet the South has not wished to compromise on some issues to maintain Democratic unity. On the question of race relations it has stood adamant. It has had a dark streak of nativism, which found expression in the Ku Klux Klan and in anti-Semitic utterances. All these southern characteristics from time to time have driven deep fissures within the Democratic party.[17]

The southern congressional bloc, though not so solidly conservative as it is reputed to be, probably is pushed toward conservatism by the peculiarities of the southern electorate. Popular attitudes in the South, the polls indicate, resemble closely those of the other great regions on broad questions of social and economic policy (the race question excluded).[18] Many southerners, both white and black, do not vote. The actual electorate consists disproportionately

---

[16] For a treatment of the 1948 campaign, see Alexander Heard, *A Two-Party South* (Chapel Hill: University of North Carolina Press, 1952).

[17] For data on the range of southern congressional attitudes on liberal and conservative scales, see Chapter 24. See also H. W. Allen, "Geography and Politics: Voting on Reform Issues in the U.S. Senate, 1911–16," *Journal of Southern History*, 27 (1961), 216–28; J. H. Fenton, "Liberal-Conservative Divisions by Sections of the United States," *The Annals*, 344 (1962), 122–27.

[18] See V. O. Key, Jr., *Public Opinion and American Democracy* (New York, Knopf, 1961), ch. 5.

of persons from the more conservative strata, a factor that may affect the outlook of southern Representatives. As the sectional peculiarities of the South project themselves into Congress, they, of course, contribute significantly to the special characteristics of the national party system.

IMPACT OF SECTIONALISM ON THE PARTY SYSTEM
The broad patterns of intersectional rivalry and combination are obvious enough, but the strong sectional tinge in our politics also accounts for some other characteristics of our politics that puzzle native and foreign observers alike.

The notable element of traditionalism in our partisan attachments may hinge in considerable degree on sectionalism. In the South—and in the rural areas of the North—entire communities have remained overwhelmingly committed to the same party for generations. Both sectionalism and stability of party loyalty may rest on a continuing interest of a region. Yet beyond such conditioning factors, social and psychological features of sectionalism may contribute to persistence of party attachments. Economically based sectionalism in its more extreme form tends to be agrarian and rural. When a single interest dominates a huge area both economically and politically, the probabilities are that social pressures for political conformity result in a structure of partisan attitude with special powers of self-preservation. Even when sectional interests begin to change, the heritage of political faith may lag in its adjustment to the new state of affairs. The new technologies of transport and communication doubtless are reducing the durability of rural party attachments, but perhaps even yet rural communities retain a greater capacity to transmit and maintain party loyalties than do metropolitan communities.

A striking example of the phenomenon under discussion appears in Figure 9.6, which consists of a series of maps of Tennessee. At the time of the Civil War this state divided mainly between its western and eastern halves. In East Tennessee farmers of the highlands owned few slaves, whereas in Middle and West Tennessee the climate and topography favored the use of slaves. These regions differed over whether to secede from the Union. The people of East Tennessee who opposed secession later became Republicans. Those of Middle and West Tennessee became Democrats. This pattern of party division within the state remained relatively stable from 1860 to 1948, as the maps in the figure impressively show.

Sectionalism also contributes to the multiclass composition of each of the major parties, a characteristic bewildering to those who regard only a class politics as "natural." A politics that arrays the people of one section against those of another pulls into one party men of all social strata. A common interest bound the southern banker, merchant, cotton farmer, and wage earner together against the northern combination of finance, manufacturing, and

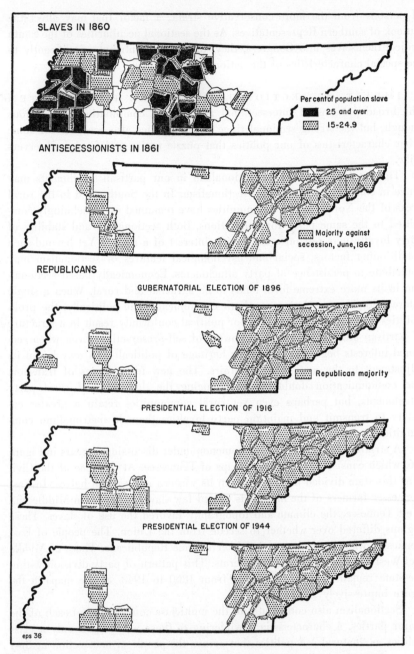

Figure 9.6   The Civil War, traditionalism, and Tennessee party
lines: Distribution of Republican popular strength, 1861–1944

segments of industrial labor.[19] That latter coalition across class lines rested also on a presumed common concern about national policy.

Beyond the effect of common interest in uniting different classes of voters, the circumstances of rural and small-town sectionalism apparently facilitated the imposition on an entire society of the values of the dominant groups. Existence of all types of people in relatively close communion, in contrast with the class segregation inherent in the patterns of metropolitan residence, evidently tends to restrain the expression or development of latent cleavages. The structure of rural and small-town society thus apparently made for a higher degree of community unity across class lines than might be expected from the diversity in the objective characteristics of people of the small towns and the countryside.[20]

Urbanization and the Growth of Class Politics

Sectionalism in American politics has always been to some degree a cartographic illusion. Representation on maps of regional voting blocs conceals the fact that within each region a minority exists which remains unmoved by appeals to the predominant sectional interest. Nevertheless, when a high degree of regional homogeneity prevails, political cleavages are likely to follow geographical lines. On the other hand, when sectional homogeneity declines—when a variety of interests exists in each region—and the differences between the various sections of the nation decline, political conflict is not so likely to be between geographically defined groups. So long as we were predominantly an agrarian nation it could be assumed that the great crop regions, founded on climate and geography, would act as sectional units. But when the dominance of cotton in the cotton belt and of corn in the corn belt is challenged, the economic basis for sectional unity becomes weaker.

DILUTION OF SECTIONALISM   Diversification of interest dilutes sectionalism. The fading of the memories of the Civil War bears on the

[19] Even in 1952, by which time the old sectional solidarity had been strained, 46 per cent of the professional and managerial voters in the South were Democratic as against 28 per cent outside the South. Of other white-collar workers in the South, 58 per cent were Democratic in contrast with 32 per cent outside the South. These percentages were derived from data provided by the Survey Research Center from its 1952 election study.

[20] The data on these points are limited but suggestive. See Duncan MacRae, Jr., "Occupations and the Congressional Vote, 1940–1950," *American Sociological Review*, 20 (1955), 332–40; Leon Epstein, "Size of Place and the Division of the Two-Party Vote in Wisconsin," *Western Political Quarterly*, 9 (1956), 138–50; W. E. Miller, "One Party Politics and the Voter," *American Political Science Review*, 50 (1956), 707–25; N. A. Masters and D. S. Wright, "Trends and Variations in the Two-Party Vote: The Case of Michigan," *American Political Science Review*, 52 (1958), 1078–90.

decline of sectional sentiment, but the weakening of sectional blocs comes fundamentally from the multiplication of interests within regions. Most of the alterations in the basic interests of agrarian sections are associated in one way or another with urbanization. Manufacturing, distribution, finance, and most other nonagricultural pursuits center in the cities. Moreover, most of the new ethnic groups disturbing to the old patterns of sectional unity have settled in the cities. Urbanization thus serves as an index of a complex of social and economic changes with political repercussions.

A simple set of figures portrays the moderation of sectional cleavages. Under a sectional politics the states of one section may be expected to give an overwhelming vote to one party; the states of the opposing section, a heavy vote to the other party. The net effect of the weakening of sectional solidarity has been a long-run tendency for the states to divide more nearly alike in their popular vote in presidential elections. As each party gains support in the ancient strongholds of the other, the dissimilarities among states dim. A rough measure of these tendencies appears in the graph in Figure 9.7. The presidential election of 1896 marked a high tide of sectional solidarity in mutual antagonism as the South and West opposed the North. When the states were ranked according to the Republican percentages of their popular votes in that year, the middle half of the states ranged from 56 per cent in North Dakota to 30.3 per cent in Texas. That wide difference among the states produced the

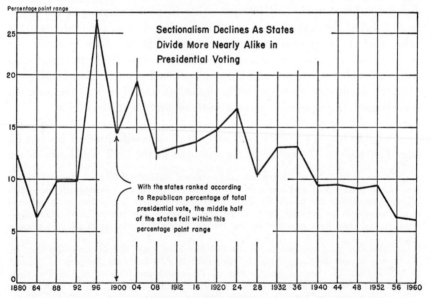

Figure 9.7   *Interquartile range of states when ranked according to Republican percentage of total presidential popular vote, 1896–1960*

1896 peak in the graph. Gradually, and somewhat erratically as the graph reveals, the middle half of the states came to divide more and more alike and to be compressed into a narrower and narrower range. In 1952 the middle half of the states clustered between Oregon's 60.6 per cent Republican and Delaware's 51.7 per cent. This decline in the dispersion of the states crudely measures one dimension of the consequences of the erosion of sectional solidarity.

The processes of modification of sectionalism are most visible in the South, a region that long seemed monolithic. In its rapid urbanization of the past few decades, the South has undergone metamorphoses that occurred decades earlier in the North. These changes built within the southern cities neighborhoods of upper-income proprietors and managers with an economic base largely independent of the region's old agrarian interests. The new business classes, like the old business classes of the North, had little enthusiasm for the New Deal and Fair Deal. During Democratic eras a southern bloc often made common cause with Republicans in Congress to delay or to modify Administration proposals. After 1936 the Republican presidential vote began to increase in those neighborhoods of southern cities inhabited by the growing business groups. In 1952 Eisenhower's most marked strength fell in the upper-income residential areas of the major southern cities, while Stevenson drew his heaviest support in wards and precincts at the opposite end of the scale, a pattern that recurred in 1956.[21] In short, as the pulls of sectionalism have worn down, southerners come to divide politically more like the people of the remainder of the country.[22] The slackening of sectional cohesiveness seems to be most notable in urban communities which are both most drastically affected by industrialization and somewhat less bound by anxieties about race.[23] Thus, desegregation of schools encounters less stubborn resistance in the cities than in the country.[24] Moreover, the stance of the national parties, either of which

---

[21] The high Republican presidential vote in southern cities may be explained in part by the fact that southern urban labor is becoming politically activated at a much slower rate than southern upper classes. In 1952, 51 per cent of southern skilled and semiskilled labor voted, in contrast with 80 per cent voting outside the South. For the unskilled, the contrasting participation rates were 28 and 78.

[22] See J. W. Prothro, *et al.*, "Two-Party Voting in the South: Class vs. Party Identification," *American Political Science Review*, 52 (1958), 131–39. The economic trends have also affected the unity of the South in support of free trade. The South now has its protectionists who seek to restrict the import of textiles and other products competitive with its industry. See M. E. Jewell, "Evaluating the Decline of Southern Internationalism through Senatorial Roll Call Votes," *Journal of Politics*, 21 (1959), 624–46; C. O. Lerche, Jr., "Southern Congressmen and the 'New Isolationism,'" *Political Science Quarterly*, 75 (1960), 321–37.

[23] See the careful analysis by D. S. Strong, *Urban Republicanism in the South* (University, Ala.: Bureau of Public Administration, University of Alabama, 1960). See also Bernard Cosman, "Presidential Republicanism in the South, 1960," *Journal of Politics*, 24 (1962), 303–22; Russell Middleton, "The Civil Rights Issue and Presidential Voting among Southern Negroes and Whites," *Social Forces*, 40 (1962), 209–15.

[24] See T. F. Pettigrew and M. R. Cramer, "The Demography of Desegregation," *Journal of Social Issues*, XIV, 4 (1959), 61–71. Also T. F. Pettigrew and E. Q. Campbell,

in the southern view is as bad as the other on race policy, now encourages southern voters to make choices between presidential candidates on other grounds.

EXTENT AND RATE OF URBANIZATION   As the southern trends suggest, the changes associated with urbanization undermine the structure of historic agrarian sectionalism. A great area producing a major crop may be expected to carry along with it in national politics its small cities and villages that forage on the countryside. But a great industrial city has a political character of its own: it contains a variety of economic, racial, and social interests, often with little unity of purpose. It is possible to speak of wheat, say, as the dominant concern of several million people scattered over several states, but an equal number of people concentrated in the small area of a single city are not likely to be characterized by a like unity of interest.

It is commonplace that American cities have grown rapidly, yet it is difficult to grasp the magnitude of the change and its almost cataclysmic political consequences. In a period of less than a century a radical alteration in the way of life of a large proportion of the people has occurred. In 1870 only one out of four persons resided in an incorporated place of 2,500 or over; by 1940 almost three out of every five persons were urban dwellers. In 1870 only every tenth person lived in a city of 100,000 or more; by 1960 the proportion was about three out of ten. Or, to look at the matter from the obverse view, in 1870 three out of four Americans were rural dwellers; by 1950 only about two out of five persons were thus classified and over half of them were grouped by the census as "rural non-farm."

Of special significance has been the growth of the great urban agglomerations of population, for it is in the larger cities that the political consequences of urbanization manifest themselves most sharply. By 1960, 212 standard metropolitan areas (cities of 50,000 and their surrounding urban fringe) accounted for almost two-thirds, 62.9 per cent, of the entire population. The trend may be illustrated in another way. In 1900 we had 78 cities of over 50,000 population; in 1960, 333. More graphically, in 1960 the three largest metropolitan regions—those of New York, Chicago, and Los Angeles—contained a larger total population than did the six states of New England plus Kentucky, Tennessee, Alabama, Mississippi, Nevada, and Wyoming.

CITY, CLASS, AND PARTY   Urbanization affects every aspect of the governmental process. It creates a host of new problems to be met by governmental agencies. It places on government the burden of the mediation of a vast number of new relationships associated with the interdependence of the components of an urban society. In its bearing specifically on the party

"Faubus and Segregation: An Analysis of Arkansas Voting," *Public Opinion Quarterly*, 24 (1960), 436–47.

system urbanization also has had a variety of consequences. It profoundly modified the sectional base of the party system which gradually adapted itself to the new state of affairs. Evidently as population changes took place in the North the Democratic party became gradually more and more a party of the great cities. Democratic dependence on the urban vote began to increase long before the party became dominant in the cities in the 1930's. Simultaneously the Republican party became more dependent on rural and small-town support.

The growth of northern metropolitan influence in the Democratic party came to be symbolized by the conspicuous roles in national Democratic affairs of leaders of such centers as Chicago, Pittsburgh, New York, Providence, and Boston. The party was caricatured as a distrustful alliance of northern urban bosses and southern planters. From 1932 to 1948 the metropolitan centers contributed significantly to Democratic presidential victories, as has been demonstrated by Samuel J. Eldersveld, who analyzed in detail the bearing of metropolitan pluralities on the statewide plurality of the winning presidential candidate in 10 of the most urban states containing in all 12 cities, each with a population of over 500,000.[25] The Democratic metropolitan pluralities in these 10 states accounted for the following numbers of electoral votes for the Democratic candidates in the elections of 1932–1948: 1932, 168; 1936, 142; 1940, 212; 1944, 193; 1948, 106. In the elections of 1920 and 1924, metropolitan pluralities favored the Republicans, but they won only eight electoral votes through such pluralities in 1920 and 39 in 1924. "In 1940, 1944, and 1948," Eldersveld calculates, "the Democrats would have lost the presidential election" without the urban pluralities they received from these 12 major cities. He opines that the "metropolitan vote may well have become the balance-wheel in our political system." [26]

The significance of urbanization for the party system does not come solely from the fact that the Democratic party developed urban bastions. Rather, the processes of urbanization created the raw materials for party cleavages more nearly along class lines than was the politics of sectionalism. Urbanization created new kinds of Republicans and Democrats. Those at the upper end of the income scale became more nearly united in their attachment to the Republican party as a similar loyalty to the Democratic party developed in the lower-income brackets. Under American circumstances class attachments may not fix rigid partisan orientations, but the existence of an industrial society assures cleavages along class lines when class-relevant issues become salient. Evidently what has happened is that a sense of class politics and of class solidarity remains stable at a high level among the upper-income groups while middle- and lower-income groups vary from time to time in the degree

[25] The states are New York, Massachusetts, Pennsylvania, Maryland, Missouri, Illinois, Michigan, Ohio, Wisconsin, and California.
[26] "The Influence of Metropolitan Party Pluralities in Presidential Elections Since 1920," *American Political Science Review*, 43 (1949), 1189–1206.

to which class and politics are associated. Perhaps in the election of 1936 the party division most nearly coincided with differences of income and occupation. That coincidence declined as class-relevant questions faded from the forefront, and in 1952 and 1956 Republicans won substantial support in the lower-income groups.[27]

Urbanization may have introduced a new element of volatility into electoral behavior rather than a stable and continuing class cleavage. That is not to say that the electorate will over the short term—say, from election to election—necessarily swing erratically, but that over a longer period an urban electorate may be susceptible to wider shifts in partisan attachment than would have been expected of the rural electorate of an earlier day.[28]

Urbanization has not completely dissolved sectionalism, and the blending of sectional and class interests in the party system helps to account for some of its peculiar characteristics. In the metropolitan areas party cleavages tend to follow class lines, though class and party vary in the degree to which they approach congruency. Each party, however, contains sectional interests which in a measure cut across economic class lines. The class and sectional composition of the Republican party makes for a higher degree of coherence than does the sectional and class makeup of the Democratic party. Rural interests—at least under certain conditions—have a general outlook that can be reconciled with the upper-class orientation of the urban wing of the Republican party. On the other hand, the rural wing of the Democratic party often finds itself at loggerheads with the urban, laboring-class element. Rural Democrats often make common cause with the Republicans, some of whose leaders occasionally fondly contemplate a coalition with the Dixiecrats. Yet, when Republicans annex sufficient support to win the Presidency, they bring into their fold enough urban workers to temper the position the party had taken as a minority.

SUBURBANIZATION   After World War II, suburbanization replaced urbanization as the most conspicuous type of population redistribution. The great central cities settled down to a fairly stable, or even declining, population as their suburbs mushroomed. Political observers saw in this demographic phenomenon the foundations for political changes of basic signifi-

[27] See Angus Campbell, *et al.*, *The American Voter* (New York: Wiley, 1960), ch 13. A special feature of American urban "class" structure has been its association with differences in national origin. The most recent immigrants have tended to move into lower occupations, though over time ethnic aggregates rise in the status scale. See C. B. Nam, "Nationality Groups and Social Stratification in America," *Social Forces*, 37 (1959), 328–33.

[28] It has been suggested that the middle classes, an imprecisely defined category, constitute the balance wheel in the new politics of urbanism. Those most imbued with middle-class values may play a special role in the long-term alternations in party position, but the evidence indicates that persons of all income and occupational classes participate in these movements from party to party. See A. N. Holcombe, *The Middle Classes in American Politics* (Cambridge: Harvard University Press, 1940).

cance which were said to have made an initial appearance in the presidential voting of 1952. The interpretation was that people, moving up the occupational and income scales, were making their way to the suburbs. There, surrounded by neighbors of unimpeachable respectability and Republicanism, the new suburbanites would gradually be absorbed into the GOP. This process of expansion of the middle classes would, sooner or later, mightily weaken the Democratic party.

The evidence is mixed on whether such a long-run tendency actually prevails. Eisenhower increased the Republican proportion of the vote in the suburbs in 1952 (as the suburban proportion of the total vote was increasing), but he also made inroads on Democratic strength in the central cities. Detailed studies of the political transformations associated with suburbanization yield differing findings.[29] To a considerable degree new suburbanites bring their partisanship with them, though in some instances conversion may occur. There are suburbs and suburbs: working-class suburbs, middle-class suburbs, and doubtless a few of the old-fashioned, upper-class suburbs dedicated to gracious living. Some growing suburbs are becoming more Democratic; in others, Republicans are holding their own or gaining.

Fundamental changes of political import are undoubtedly occurring in American society, and though they may have been associated in the popular eye with suburbanization, they are also occuring elsewhere. Suburbanization may not be the best index of those changes which include changes in income level, alterations in occupational distribution, and the acculturation of the most recent waves of immigrants. Trends in the income level are almost startling in their rate and magnitude. The trends from 1939 to 1958 appear in Table 9.1.

Table 9.1   Percentage distribution of income units, families and unrelated individuals, by income levels, 1939–1958

Income Level	1939	1945	1949	1954	1955	1958
$1–999	41.2	18.3	12.7	14.9	14.0	11.0
$1,000–2,999	49.3	46.6	38.1	24.4	23.3	21.3
$3,000–4,999	7.2	26.3	32.3	28.5	27.7	23.7
$5,000 and over	2.3	8.8	16.8	32.0	34.9	44.0
Median Income	$1,231	$2,390	$2,959	$3,730	$3,909	$4,500

Source: *Statistical Abstract of the United States*, 1951, p. 269; 1956, p. 308.

[29] See Samuel Lubell, *The Future of American Politics* (New York: Harper, 1952); G. Edward Janosik, "The New Suburbia," *Current History*, August, 1956, 91–95; J. G. Manis and L. C. Stine, "Suburban Residence and Political Behavior," *Public Opinion Quarterly*, 22 (1958–59), 483–89; F. I. Greenstein and R. E. Wolfinger, "The Suburbs and Shifting Party Loyalties," *Public Opinion Quarterly*, 22 (1958–59), 473–82; Angus Campbell, *et al.*, *The American Voter* (New York: Wiley, 1960), pp. 453–72; Bernard Lazerwitz, "Suburban Voting Trends: 1948 to 1956," *Social Forces*, 39 (1960), 29–36.

In 1939, only 2.3 per cent of the income units (families and individuals living unattached to families) had annual incomes of $5,000 or more; that percentage had grown to 44.0 in 1958. Over the same period the percentages of income units with incomes of under $1,000 declined from 41.2 to 11.00. Though these changes in part reflect inflation, they are substantial. The data of the table should not be taken to mean that poverty has been abolished. One out of three income units in 1958 had less than $3,000 income annually. Yet at the other end of the scale a many-fold increase had occurred in the proportions of families with incomes of more than $5,000, a sum sufficient to make them, at least in the 1950's, far more responsive to Republican doctrine than they had been in their less palmy days.[30]

Along with these income changes, gradual alterations in the occupational distribution are occurring. Perhaps most marked is the growth in the proportions of white-collar workers and other salaried workers. Such persons tend to develop identifications with upper-class norms and with the Republican party more frequently than do blue-collar workers at comparable income levels. For several decades the proportion of blue-collar workers has remained fairly constant, but it is probable that the statistical categories of skilled and semiskilled conceal changes in skill and outlook of some significance for political behavior.

In the great cities a notable process of acculturation has affected the more recent immigrants. A generation or so of education, indoctrination, and adaptation reduces the differential between these groups and the older citizenry. These processes come to be associated with a residential dispersion which destroys the concentrations of persons both dependent upon and manageable by the old-fashioned city machine. To some extent the immigrants of yesterday are replaced by the Negroes and Puerto Ricans of today, but the numbers available for ready mobilization by old-style methods have declined.

SOCIAL CHANGE, NEW ISSUES, AND THE PARTY SYSTEM   The capacity of the American two-party system to adapt itself to social change has been one of its remarkable features. Major alterations in the composition and orientation of the parties develop gradually in delayed response to the glacial alterations in the underlying social structure. That process of change has been pictured as one in which an approach toward a class cleavage gradually displaced a tendency to divide along sectional lines.

[30] These changes in income distribution did not impoverish the upper-income levels. In 1953 the top 5 per cent of families in income drew 20.7 per cent of all family income before taxes, 18.2 per cent after taxes. Yet from 1939 to 1950 an extremely sharp decline occurred in the proportion of all income going to those in the upper 5 per cent. That decline resulted in large measure from increases in income of groups lower in the rank order rather than from absolute declines for the upper 5 per cent. It is not improbable that these losses of relative status (along with federal tax policy) stimulated political cohesiveness in the top-income levels.

While that correctly describes the trend, it also greatly oversimplifies the complex process by which the party system maintains itself in the face of ceaseless modification of the social matrix within which it operates. The party system exists in a state of continual flux.

Changes in population characteristics (or the addition of new population elements) create problems of adaptation for the party system. A party tends to recruit or to attract those new population groups that can be most readily accommodated within its existing complex of interests. Thus, the Republican party seeks to annex the new managerial and financial elements of the South. A dominant party may avoid appeals to new population elements with concerns antithetical to those of the inner core of the party. A minority may attract those who are rejected by the majority, a tendency that helped to account for the early movement into the Democratic party of immigrants along the eastern seaboard. It also accounts for the later movement into the dwindling Republican ranks in that region of many Italo-Americans who regarded the Democratic party as a private preserve of the Irish. Fundamental or far-reaching socioeconomic changes may induce modification of party appeals. Thus, the upgrading of income levels makes the Democratic party more solicitous of the middle-income groups. A system of production and distribution that increased sharply the goods and services available to lower-income groups would probably have an astonishing impact on the political system. The best guess though, is that the differences between the haves and have-nots will not soon disappear. In all these adjustments of the party system some sort of compensatory process seems to operate. When one party gains the support of one group it may drive another to the opposition. Whatever the process, as party maneuver occurs each party manages, at least nationally, to maintain itself. In the process each party may be altered both in its composition and in its policy outlooks, a result that would be unlikely if the parties had an ideological rigidity.

Parties are built, or grow into, groups of considerable stability despite the movement to and fro across party lines. These formations, though, may be seriously disturbed by the impact of great new issues that cut across the old party lines, issues that are not made by party leaders but are imposed by internal conditions or external circumstances. Historically the salient issues of domestic politics have fundamentally fixed party lines. The new issues of foreign policy may well affect the party system in the most unpredictable ways. Unlike the issues of domestic politics, the common concerns of class or section provide no imperative cue for the citizen in the determination of political preference. For that reason, conceivably problems of foreign policy, if they remain salient, could introduce an instability into the party system.

10.

THE PLACE OF

MINOR PARTIES

THE MAJOR PARTIES make up a system that in a sense, amounts to more than the sum of its parts. The system consists not simply of the Democratic party *and* the Republican party: rather, each party plays a role in a pattern of relationships involving both parties, the electorate, and the government. Moreover, through time the role of the individual party is transformed as it shifts from majority to minority, from governance to criticism. Neither party exists in isolation; each, whatever its role at the moment, is essential for the operation of the system, and, in turn, the system gives meaning to the activity of the individual party. Hence, a party can best be comprehended in the light of its place in the total political structure.

The earlier exposition conveniently ignored the fact that the two-party system never exists in pure form. Minor parties also appeal to the electorate in every presidential campaign. Some of them have a long history; others spring to life, attract a heavy vote at one presidential election, and then disappear. The question now arises of the place of minor parties in the system. Do they play a role, in their interactions with the major parties, in making the system as a whole what it is? Or are minor parties merely fifth wheels that contribute nothing to the system as a whole?

The political scientist seeks uniformities of action to be able to describe political phenomena in general terms. When he follows that bent in an attack on the minor parties, he quickly finds that "minor party" is not a useful analytical concept, for such parties are diverse. A meticulous student might well conclude that each minor party should be differentiated from all others.

Each certainly has its unique qualities, but if it has nothing in common with others the analyst is hard put to discover any recurring role of minor parties in the system. One way out of the difficulty is to proceed on the supposition that different classes of minor parties exist. Those parties within each category may possess broad similarities of function, though each minor party may also possess unique characteristics.

A cursory look at the array of minor parties suggests a classification that is useful for analytical purposes. One group of minor parties consists of those formed to propagate a particular doctrine; most of them have nominated presidential candidates at election after election over fairly long periods. Their duration may be more significant than is their doctrinal coloration in their differentiation from other minor parties. The Prohibition party and the Socialist party are illustrative of such parties that have been kept alive over long periods by little bands of dedicated souls. To be contrasted with such standing minor parties are transient third-party movements. American party history is marked by turbulences generated by the rapid rise, and equally rapid decline, of minor parties. Though they may move onto the political stage as a prairie fire running ahead of a strong wind, they die out after an election or so and are remembered principally by historians.

Minor parties of these two broad types would be expected to play different roles in the party system. The continuing, doctrinal parties are in a sense outside the system. The recurring, short-lived, minor-party eruptions, on the other hand, are intimately connected with it. A sketchy examination of a few of the principal episodes of minor-party activity may help in our quest for a theory about third parties. For convenience, the short-lived third parties may be divided into parties of economic protest and secessionist parties, though the line is not always sharp between a party formed by secession from a major party and one that rises up more or less outside the major parties. That discussion will be followed by brief treatments of the doctrinal parties.[1]

Parties of Economic Protest

A minor party can expect to win the Presidency only if the party system is undergoing a radical transformation, with one of the major parties in process of dissolution. So drastic a reconstruction of the party alignment occurred most recently when the Republicans achieved major-party status. Since the Civil War, leaders of minor parties have from time to time nourished a belief that they had a chance to win, but that belief soon waned.

[1] See H. P. Nash, Jr., *Third Parties in American Politics* (Washington: Public Affairs Press, 1959) ; W. B. Hesseltine, *The Rise and Fall of Third Parties* (Washington: Public Affairs Press, 1948) ; T. H. Greer, *American Social Reform Movements* (New York: Prentice-Hall, 1949) ; M. S. Stedman, Jr., and S. W. Stedman, *Discontent at the Polls* (New York: Columbia University Press, 1950).

Since the minor parties on the national scene do not win elections and do not campaign with any hope of success, they cannot be regarded as miniatures of a major party. They share the name "party" with the major parties but there the resemblance ends. If they play a role in the party system, it differs from that of the major parties. In our search for the function of minor parties, a plausible inquiry would be to determine whether their place in the system may not consist in their effects upon the major parties. Do third parties, and we have in mind the transient and sporadic upthrusts of minor-party dissent, contribute to the nature of the system by influencing the roles and positions of the major parties? The question is much broader than the usual speculation whether this or that 3 per cent of the vote polled by a minor party constituted a balance of power and swung the election in this or that state. The inquiry must go more broadly to the question where these aperiodic departures from the two-party pattern affect significantly the orientations of the major parties and their roles in the system.

THE POPULIST PARTY   Several of the principal episodes of third-party activity have welled from serious economic discontent. In most of them agrarian distress has loomed large, though these parties have also often attempted to bring industrial labor into alliance with the farmer. The more spectacular farmer-labor movements have had their main strength in "the West." [2] The sequence of events leading to the fusion of the Populist party, a party of western agrarian protest, with the Democrats in 1896 may be examined profitably for evidence on the role of minor parties.

After the Civil War a long-term deflation punctuated by occasional sharp, short-term dips in farm income generated a series of agrarian political movements. The Granger movement exerted enormous influence but did not take the form of a political party. As the Grange began to wane in the 1870's, the Greenbackers arose to attempt direct political action. Western farmers, a debtor class, responded with enthusiasm to monetary panaceas. Their ills, they believed, could be cured by a generous dose of inflation. The Greenback presidential candidate in 1876 polled only a small vote, but in 1878 the voters sent 14 Greenbackers to Congress, including General James B. Weaver of Iowa who became the party's presidential candidate in 1880.

After 1878 the Greenback vote fell off and later agrarian discontent found expression through other channels. In the campaign of 1890, independent and "People's" candidates for state and local office, backed by the Farmers' Alliance and allied groups, met with considerable success in southern and northwestern states. The leaders of these scattered movements gathered in Cincinnati early in 1892 and agreed to form a political party to fight for reforms on a

---

[2] Given the character of the system for the election of the President, a minor-party movement with a sectional concentration of its strength is a factor much more to be reckoned with in national politics than is a movement with like total popular strength distributed evenly over the country.

nationwide basis. Later in the year the new party, the People's, or Populist, party, nominated General James B. Weaver, the former Greenbacker, for the Presidency.

Weaver's strong showing in the election of 1892 severely jarred the old party alignments. His party won a handful of seats in the lower house of Congress, placed its candidates in the governor's chair in three states, and elected hundreds of local officials. One of every 12 popular votes went to the Populist candidate who won 22 electoral votes. His strength was greatest in the western and southern states. In the western states the Populists often fused with the Democrats and at times in reality took over the Democratic party. The distribution of the Populist presidential strength by states appears in Figure 10.1. In the East the Populist party made little headway, though it caused shudders there. An impressive vote had been drawn by a party advocating unlimited coinage of silver at a ratio of 16 to 1, a graduated income tax, public ownership of the railroads, and other measures thought in the East to be destructive of the ordered course of things.

What impact did the Populist show of strength have on the party system? It seems evident that the Populist uprising contributed significantly to the marked realignment between the parties that jelled in the election of 1896. That realignment brought a sharper contrast in the policy orientations of the major parties, a contrast that was to persist long after the faithful few Populists last convened in 1908 to nominate a presidential candidate.

The strong Populist showing in 1892 set off a struggle within the Demo-

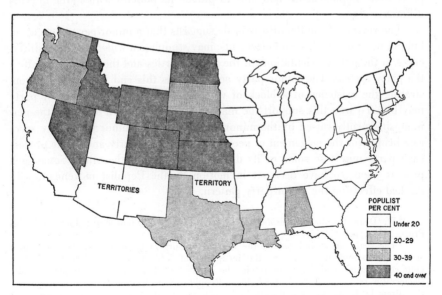

Figure 10.1   Populist strength in presidential election of 1892, by states

cratic party over the silver issue. The differences among Democrats were intensified by the policies of Cleveland, the President and leader of the conservative and sound-money wing of the party. William Jennings Bryan, who stood for about everything that Cleveland abominated, won the Democratic nomination in 1896. The fact that the insurgent wing of a party in power could control its national convention gives a measure of the extent of the Populist infection among Democrats. In its candidate and in its platform the Democratic party "swallowed the Populist party almost entirely (or vice versa!) and quite possibly saved itself from extinction in so doing." [3] Or as an old Populist leader remarked of Bryan: "We put him to school and he stole the schoolbooks."

The strong infusion of Populism within the Democratic party was accompanied by desertion by conservative Democrats, and the party acquired a different policy orientation from the party of Cleveland. The new policy—broadly one of opposition to "the interests"—persisted after 1896, save for the experiment of 1904 which demonstrated that the Democrats could not win by outbidding the Republicans for conservative support. Bryan himself later turned up in Wilson's cabinet, and the strain of Populism persisted, may even still persist, in the Democratic party. On the other hand, the redrawing of party lines in 1896 drove from the Republican party many who were attracted by Populist doctrines and by the same token drew to it additional strength, especially in the East, from those groups fearful of the unorthodox doctrines proclaimed by the wild men from the West. The exchange left the Republican party more homogeneous and able to pursue its policies with fewer internal differences.[4]

The review of the Populist episode suggests that a minor-party movement, but not necessarily all such movements, may stimulate a widening of the differences in the policy orientations of the major parties and thereby deeply affect the party system. The minor party accomplishes this end in part by demonstrating the existence of a block of voters for whose support a major party may bid. To woo this support the major party must take a stand on the new issues insistently raised by the minor party. Thus the minor party may serve as a bridge for the movement of people from party to party and in the process each party may lose some of its dissident elements to the other. Some such process seems to have been set in motion by the Populist movement, with marked effects on the major-party pattern.

[3] W. Dean Burnham, *Presidential Ballots, 1836–1892* (Baltimore: Johns Hopkins Press, 1955), pp. 154–55.
[4] The realignment induced by the Populist upsurge was limited in the states west of the Mississippi apparently by the incapacity of local Democratic leadership, often both conservative and inept, to retain the support of Populists who surged into the Democratic ranks in 1896. Instead, local Republican leadership often turned progressive, drew back into the Republican fold the deserters of 1892 and 1896, and remained for decades a thorn in the side of the national Republican leadership.

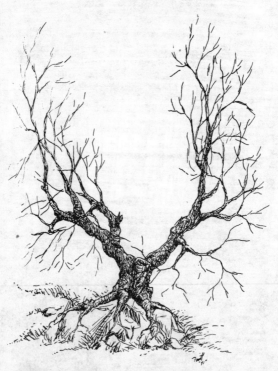

𝔚hitaker 𝔏ibrary

CHOWAN COLLEGE
MURFREESBORO, NORTH CAROLINA

The Populists also had an influence that extended beyond Democratic acceptance of their doctrines. Their energetic agitation in support of their cause gave currency to ideas that eventually gained wide support and became law. They preached the doctrine of popular government and demanded the direct election of United States Senators, the direct primary nominating system, the initiative and referendum, and woman suffrage. They agitated, too, for the adoption of new substantive policies. They criticized the inelasticity of the currency; the Federal Reserve Act coped with this problem by means different from that urged by the Populists. The germ of the idea of the present system of federally sponsored credit agencies for farmers was to be found in the Populist platform. The Populists were not solely responsible for the eventual adoption of these and other policies, but they did agitate for many policies later put into law.[5]

PROGRESSIVE CAMPAIGN OF 1924   Measured by electoral strength, the Progressive candidacy of Robert M. La Follette for the Presidency in 1924 was more impressive as a manifestation of economic discontent than the Populist crusade of 1892. One out of every six voters supported La Follette. While Progressive agitation in 1924 was in part an intensification of the historic western insurgency, it constituted more largely a response to the particular conditions of the early 1920's. Western agriculture, which had prospered during World War I, fell upon evil days with the sharp drop in farm prices in 1921. Labor had flourished under the Wilson Administration. The Republicans under Harding leaned toward the agricultural policy of eastern finance and set about to return business to its rightful place of pre-eminence. The restoration of normalcy struck railroad labor with special destructiveness. The Administration helped the railroads break the strike of 1922 by injunction proceedings and by encouraging the formation of company unions and the employment of strikebreakers. The eastern, industrial wing of the party, symbolized by Andrew Mellon, the Secretary of the Treasury, held sway in the Republican party, a party, William Allen White observed, "with no liberal flaw, spot, or blemish in its creed," which completely represented the "yearnings of a benevolent plutocracy." The Democratic party, rent by internal struggle over the Klan-Catholic issue, did not offer a promising vehicle for the expression of the unrest in the land.

From among those disadvantaged by the events of 1921 and 1922 came the movement that led to La Follette's 1924 candidacy. In 1922, on the call of the railroad brotherhoods, the Conference for Progressive Political Action convened in Chicago. Its purpose was to "discuss and adopt a fundamental economic program designed to restore to the people the sovereignty that is rightly theirs, to make effective the purpose for which our government is

---

[5] The chief work on the Populists is John D. Hicks, *The Populist Revolt* (Minneapolis: University of Minnesota Press, 1931).

established, to secure to all men the enjoyment of the gain which their industry produces." Important among the groups affiliated with the conference were the railroad unions, the Nonpartisan League and other agrarian groups, the Socialist party, and sundry reform leaders.

In 1924 the conference called a convention which, on July 4, endorsed La Follette for President. La Follette had long been a progressive Republican leader in Wisconsin and in the Senate, and his views expressed the demands of the forces of discontent. The convention delegated the selection of a running mate to a committee which later named Burton Wheeler, a Senator from Montana, who had a record as a Democrat opposed to the "interests." [6] La Follette's crisp platform was prophetic of the New Deal. It reiterated the old cry against monopoly and privilege. It proposed to guarantee to labor the right to organize and bargain and to abolish injunctions in labor disputes. It asked that Congress be empowered to overrule decisions of the Supreme Court. It urged immediate tariff reductions and ultimate public ownership of railroads and water power. It supported measures to assure "fair prices" to farmers.

In its day the La Follette program was regarded as radical, and the campaign of 1924 was marked by bitter and demagogic charges by those who felt their interests to be threatened by his candidacy. Those who felt themselves most endangered were Republicans. It was "Coolidge or Chaos," and La Follette was pictured, in unrestrained terms, as a danger to the established order. The Progressives attempted to make monopoly and special privilege the great issue; the Republican orators wrapped themselves in the flag and propagated a caricature of the Progressives as advance agents for the proletarian revolution. Certainly, La Follette and his followers challenged the policies of those dominant at the time. Farmers felt themselves discriminated against by the eastern wing of the Republican party. Labor felt its status to be endangered and the executive committee of the American Federation of Labor endorsed La Follette. The railroad brotherhoods were out for revenge for what they regarded as acts of repression. The Socialists thought the time opportune to make no nomination of their own and to line up with the Progressives.

The Progressive campaign of 1924 continued the tradition of western dissent, and the geography of the 1924 vote resembled that of the 1892 Populist vote. La Follette carried only Wisconsin, his home state, but in 10 other western states he ran ahead of Davis, the Democratic candidate. In California the Democratic percentage of the total popular vote fell to 8.2; in Minnesota, to 6.8; in North Dakota, to 7.0; in Washington, to 10.2; in Iowa, to 16.5. From such figures it is usually deduced that La Follette drew

---

[6] The convention did not "nominate" but "endorsed" La Follette's independent candidacy. For some of the groups concerned this gambit was important as a means of avoiding the issue of affiliation with a political party.

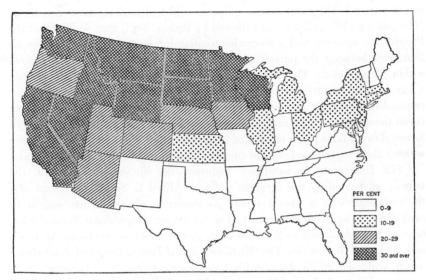

Figure 10.2   Popular vote for La Follette and Wheeler, presidential election of 1924, by states

most of his votes from the Democrats. It seems evident, however, that in the western states in which he was strong, many of his supporters also came from the Republican ranks. In most of these states the Republican percentage of the total vote dropped markedly from 1920 to 1924. In Idaho, to cite an extreme instance, the Republican percentage fell from 66 to 47 per cent. Although no detailed investigation has been made of the sources of La Follette's western strength, it is probable that he had a special attraction for farmers who had been touched by Nonpartisan League activities. Such was certainly true in North Dakota. And the chances are that many old Populists were to be found in the Progressive ranks.

In two respects La Follette's strength differed from the 1892 Populist pattern. He drew little support in the South but he picked up strength in scattered industrial localities in the Northeast. In Cleveland, Ohio, he ran ahead of both major-party candidates and demonstrated strength in the industrial belt along the shore of Lake Erie. In Pittsburgh and the surrounding industrial counties he did well. Rochester, New York, and Passaic, New Jersey, were other centers of notable strength. La Follette drew support, not in industrial areas generally, but in places in which local leaders had been active in progressive agitation and had prepared the way for their support of La Follette. In these localities his vote came by and large at the expense of the Democrats whose share of the vote declined sharply from 1920.

La Follette's candidacy was a lost cause from the outset, but what can be said of the effects of the 1924 upheaval on the subsequent behavior of the major parties? The exact course of events differed in form from the 1892–1896 pattern of Populist revolt followed by fusion. Yet it may well be that the Progressive uprising had a somewhat similar influence in sharpening the alternatives between the parties and in preparing the way for a realignment within the electorate. The heavy La Follette vote in the West constituted both a warning and an invitation to Democrats and Republicans alike. In 1928 they responded differently and on the crucial issues of 1924 widened the gap between themselves in their campaign pronouncements. The Republicans in 1928 turned down a farm plank calculated to appeal to the West; they had won once without the Progressive vote and presumably thought they could do so again.

The Democrats in substance endorsed the McNary-Haugen bill, the remedy advocated by the agrarian radicals. Alfred E. Smith, who went into the campaign with a liberal record as governor of New York, sought to capitalize on agrarian discontent. The prominent Republican farm leader, George N. Peek, bolted to the Democrats as did Senators Norris of Nebraska and Blaine of Wisconsin. The *Madison Capital-Times*, the chief La Follette organ, endorsed Smith. Despite his best efforts, Al Smith, a Tammany Hall man in a brown derby, could not make himself plausible as the spearhead of a farmers' uprising.[7]

More compelling issues arose to divert attention from the discontents of 1924 and to postpone the consequences, if any, of that campaign on partisan alignment among the voters. In 1928 the questions of prohibition, of religion, of Tammany Hall outweighed whatever disposition existed among western voters to take the step from their Republican apostasy of 1924 to Democratic conversion in 1928. If support of La Follette was a way station for voters moving from the Republican to the Democratic party, they did not shift in large numbers until 1932. Nye says the Democratic party in 1932 "seemed to be the common rallying point for all the shreds of earlier progressive movements, for the 1912, 1924, insurgent, Wilsonian, and La Follette liberals."[8] Clearly many of the leaders who clustered about La Follette became supporters of Franklin D. Roosevelt in 1932. Doubtless most of those Democratic voters who turned to La Follette in 1924 returned to the party in 1932. It is a fair guess, though the data are scant, that Republicans who followed La Follette in 1924 were especially prone to vote for Roosevelt in 1932.

Secessionist Parties

Several of the principal third-party movements have emerged by secession from one of the major parties. The 1912 Progressive candidacy of Theodore

---

[7] The above treatment leans on the excellent study by K. C. MacKay, *The Progressive Movement of 1924* (New York: Columbia University Press, 1947).

[8] R. B. Nye, *Midwestern Progressive Politics* (East Lansing: Michigan State College Press, 1951), p. 354.

Roosevelt sprang from a fatal cleavage in the ranks of Republican leadership. Similarly, in 1948 the States' Rights or Dixiecratic movement originated in rebellion against the dominant Democratic faction, and other instances of party fission have occurred on a smaller scale. Such secessionist parties can be differentiated only formally from those grouped earlier as parties of economic protest. In their role in the party system as a whole the two sorts of parties appear to be fundamentally similar.

PROGRESSIVE MOVEMENT OF 1912   The Progressive party, formed in 1912, was born of the ferment that agitated the country in the years before World War I. The progressive movement included a strident populistic strain which manifested itself in agitation for the adoption of instruments of direct democracy such as the intiative, referendum, and recall. It also gave voice to a revulsion against abuses, in both business and government, brought to light by the muckrakers. It probably reflected middle-class reaction against the growth in power of big business. Settlement-house reformers as well as millionaire reformers found places in the movement, which was characterized more by a hopeful but nebulous idealism than by a nicely wrought consistent creed.

Theodore Roosevelt, unhappy with the conservative leanings of William Howard Taft, his own choice to succeed himself in 1908, sought the Republican presidential nomination in 1912. In that endeavor he had support from his personal admirers and also from party organization men who feared that Taft could not ferry their state and local tickets into office. Some industrial leaders thought it inevitable that a progressive would be elected in 1912 and that Roosevelt was the safest of an undesirable lot. Others were attracted by his philosophy which might legitimize monopoly under a degree of public control.[9] The Old Guard managed to hold firm control of the national convention, and Roosevelt's followers marched out to form the Progressive party, a coalition of discordant elements bound together by his personality.

Wilson, another progressive, with the aid of William Jennings Bryan, captured the Democratic nomination. From the outset of the campaign Taft's cause was doomed, and the canvass turned out to be a battle between Wilson and the picturesque Teddy. Roosevelt polled a larger popular vote than did Taft (27.4 per cent of the total against 23.2 per cent), and Wilson won the Presidency. Whether Roosevelt's candidacy threw the election to Wilson, as is often supposed, is questionable. The chances are that had Roosevelt not been in the race, many Republican voters of progressive inclination would have supported Wilson or, immobilized by the conflict between their Republican loyalty and their distaste for Taft, simply stayed at home on election day. Such a surmise gains some support, as Louis Bean has pointed out, from the

[9] See Amos Pinchot, *History of the Progressive Party, 1912–1916* (New York: New York University Press, 1958).

fact that the voting in the 1912 congressional elections seemed to show that Wilson's party had enough popular support to win the Presidency without benefit of the Republican split.[10]

The effects of the Progressive bolt on the party system persisted long after election day of 1912. The more conservative, or at least less ebullient, Republicans had won unchallenged control of the Republican party machinery. The progressive Democrats were in the saddle in their party. The Progressive party organization was kept alive in the hope that the threat of another candidacy in 1916 would wrest platform concessions and an acceptable candidate from the regular Republicans. William Allen White, a leader in the move to exert this leverage, thought Charles Evans Hughes, associate justice of the Supreme Court, who had made a reputation as a progressive when governor of New York, would be acceptable. Meanwhile, Taft worked behind the scenes to checkmate the Roosevelt crowd; he, too, promoted Hughes. Taft calculated that the Progressives could "easily regard Hughes as a Progressive," but he also believed that Hughes had "learned a great deal since he was governor." In short, Taft thought Hughes had become a sound man with "more sense and a greater breadth of view." [11]

Taft's judgment seemed to be vindicated by Hughes' campaign. William Allen White wrote that Hughes gave the impression in the West that he was "one of those good men in politics—a kind of business man's candidate . . . always hovering around the status quo like a sick kitten around a hot brick!" [12] Although Roosevelt campaigned vigorously for Hughes, many of his Progressive followers dragged their feet in the 1916 campaign. The bulk of the 1912 Progressives returned to the Republican ranks in 1916, but it is evident that many also turned Democratic in 1916.[13] Wilson also doubtless gained through the new issues arising out of the European war which set off movements across party lines unlike those of 1912.

Of the effect of 1912 on the party leadership, George Mowry concludes that Roosevelt "contributed much to the conservatizing of the Republican party." [14] Many prominent progressive Republicans bolted to support Roosevelt in 1912. Of those in elective office, some lost out in the subsequent feuds

[10] *How to Predict Elections* (New York: Knopf, 1948), ch. 7.

[11] H. F. Pringle, *The Life and Times of William Howard Taft* (New York: Farrar & Rinehart, 1939), II, 885–91.

[12] Walter Johnson, *William Allen White's America* (New York: Holt, 1947), p. 267.

[13] In California Hiram Johnson, undoubtedly a genuine Progressive, was on the ballot as the senatorial candidate in 1916. He polled 67 per cent of the vote against a Democratic candidate as Hughes lost by a narrow margin. In San Francisco Johnson drew 77 per cent of the vote; Hughes, 45 per cent. Hughes' loss of California (and the Presidency) has been attributed to his unintentional snub of Johnson during a swing through California, but the size of the margin between Hughes and Johnson makes plausible the supposition that Hughes simply had less appeal to the old Progressives of 1912 than did Wilson.

[14] *Theodore Roosevelt and the Progressive Movement* (Madison: University of Wisconsin Press, 1946), p. 378.

between Republican progressives and standpatters. Others made their way back into the party but, Mowry says, "did not return to the powerful places" they had held in 1912.[15] By the same token, the episode bred within the Democratic party a generation of Wilsonians who, fired by the eloquence of their idol, long claimed for their party a monopoly of the tradition of progressivism.

DIXIECRATIC MOVEMENT OF 1948   The most significant recent secessionist party, the States' Rights or Dixiecratic movement of 1948, had as its hard core the controlling elements of the Democratic organizations of several southern states. Leaders of the movement, notably Gessner T. McCorvey, then chairman of the Alabama State Democratic Committee, developed a theory of the nature of party organization to support their refusal to be bound by the decisions of the party's national convention on nominees and platforms. Their theory grew from the strivings of the conservative wing of the southern branch of the Democratic party to restrain the policies of the party as a whole. A first, but abortive, step was taken in Texas in 1944 when the Texas "Regulars" attempted to carry the state for a Democratic slate of electors committed to vote against Roosevelt but not instructed to vote for any specific individual. The assumption was that uninstructed electors, given a close electoral vote, could bargain with the leading contenders for the Presidency. A similar tactic also failed in Mississippi in 1944.[16]

By 1948 dissident southerners thought the time was ripe for a southern veto of Democratic national policies, particularly on the race question. The problem was how to revolt without seeming to bolt, how to support the Democratic party without supporting its presidential candidate. The theory now evolved that the national party was a confederation and that each state party could follow whatever course it might choose: it could, therefore, nominate on its Democratic ticket a slate of presidential electors pledged to support a candidate other than Harry Truman, and the loyal Democrat could vote for these electors without committing the sin of bolting.

Unsuccessful in blocking the nomination of Harry Truman and in obtaining a satisfactory platform plank on the civil rights issue, a few southern Democrats walked out of the national convention. With other States' Rights Democrats, they met at Birmingham to consider lines of action. The Dixiecrats in 1948 rejected the idea of running uninstructed presidential electors;

[15] No systematic analysis has been made of the reshufflings of political leadership associated with such cataclysms as 1912. Probably older leaders have special difficulties in moving from one major party to another. The major figures in 1912 Progressivism did not have much alternative but to return to Republicanism. On the other hand, an event such as 1912 may have a marked effect on younger men with leadership potential. For example, Dean Acheson records that, stirred by the bugle calls of T.R. and disillusioned by the triumph of the Old Guard, he eventually found himself to be a Democrat. See *A Democrat Looks at His Party* (New York: Harper, 1955), pp. 13–15.

[16] Alexander Heard, *A Two-Party South?* (Chapel Hill: University of North Carolina Press, 1952), p. 159.

they preferred to name a candidate to "symbolize the cause." They recommended to the state Democratic organizations J. Strom Thurmond of South Carolina and Fielding Wright of Mississippi as nominees for the Presidency and Vice Presidency. A struggle ensued within the southern states between the "loyalists" affiliated with the national leadership and the Dixiecrats for control of the state parties and for the authority to designate presidential electors to run on the Democratic ticket. Dixiecrats placed electors pledged to Thurmond and Wright on the ballot as Democrats in South Carolina, Alabama, Mississippi, and Louisiana. In these states where they were the "official" Democratic nominees, Thurmond and Wright won the electoral vote. Truman's name did not appear on the ballot in Alabama, but in the other three of the four states electors pledged to Truman were on the ballot, though not in the Democratic column. On the other hand, the Dixiecratic candidates did not win in a single state in which they had to run under a label other than that of the Democratic party.[17]

The Dixiecratic movement clearly illustrates some of the effects of minor parties on the party system. Some of those effects may be short-term; others may be felt only over a longer period. In the 1948 election itself the southern revolt was by no means a complete loss to the Democrats nationally. Truman chose to make a hard-hitting campaign on the issues of civil rights and economic policy. In effect, he wrote off the South in advance, and in the process he picked up much support in the North that would have been lost had he attempted to appease the southern rebels. Samuel Lubell has argued that no third party "is ever a complete liability. If it diverts votes, it also adds votes in counterattraction." [18] Northern Negroes went overwhelmingly for Truman.

The longer-term repercussions of the Dixiecratic movement included the stimulation of prayerful thought by the northern Democratic leadership on how to keep the South in the party. The national convention of 1952 gave extended, if somewhat inept, attention to the matter. While some southern Democratic leaders bolted the party in the presidential campaign, a southern third-party candidacy did not recur. In the prelude to the 1956 convention national Democratic leaders busily contrived lines of compromise and incessantly negotiated with their southern brethren on the terms of party unity. In short, the movement compelled in 1956 a weightier consideration of southern sensibilities in the deliberations of the national councils of the party.[19]

---

[17] The total Dixiecratic popular vote was 1,169,000; the electoral vote, 39. One Tennessee elector, chosen on both the regular Democratic and States' Rights tickets, cast his electoral vote for Thurmond.

[18] *The Future of American Politics* (New York: Harper, 1952), p. 203.

[19] An earlier party secession which probably contributed to a redirection of major-party policy was the 1872 Liberal Republican nomination of Horace Greeley, who also received the Democratic nomination. The Liberal Republican movement had originated in Missouri and had there as a major objective the mitigation of the harshness of policies toward southern sympathizers and supporters in the Civil War. In its national aspect it also favored a more lenient policy toward the South, along with various reforms,

The extent to which the Dixiecratic movement set up a conduit by which southern Democratic voters could make their way to the Republican party is problematic. The evidence seems to indicate that in some places the 1948 Dixiecrats became 1952 Republicans; in others, 1948 Dixiecrats returned to the Democratic fold. The 1952 movement to the Republican party in the South continued a longer-term trend for the conversion of upper-class, urban southerners to Republicanism, a process perhaps accelerated by the Dixiecratic revolt but largely independent of it.[20]

An assumption has crept into these observations that ought now to be made explicit: it is that each minor-party episode should not be treated as an isolated event unconnected with what followed or preceded. Commonly the analysis of a minor party is restricted to the moment of its climax, with little inspection of its bearing on the stream of party life. The party system exists through time. Judgments of the place of minor parties in the system must be made in the setting of the temporal flow of the system.[21] Before formulation of such an appraisal, however, it is necessary to examine other, quite different, minor parties.

Marxist Parties

To be sharply differentiated from the aperiodic upsurges of nonrecurring minor-party activity are the doctrinal parties with a long-continued existence. These groups can scarcely be regarded as political parties in an operative sense. Nor are they leading actors in domestic political crises as the one-shot parties have been. Rather, they resemble sects only tenuously connected with

and its actions in 1872 probably contributed to the eventual reconciliation of North and South. See E. D. Ross, *The Liberal Republican Movement* (New York: Holt, 1919).

[20] See the analysis by D. S. Strong, "The Presidential Election in the South, 1952," *Journal of Politics*, 17 (1955), 343–89. In 1960 southern white supremacists nominated no presidential candidate but in several states backed unpledged presidential electors. The unpledged slate of "independent Democrats" won in Mississippi, and six of the 11 Alabama electors were also uninstructed. In a sense, the movement for unpledged electors is a minor-party movement with a doctrine but no candidate. Its views could not be accommodated within either major party, a circumstance that, by indirection, helps explain the dualism of the party system. If we had more such blocs of irreconcilable opinion, we would have more minor parties.

[21] Samuel Lubell, in somewhat different terms, makes this point in his analysis of the Union party of 1936. Its candidate was William Lemke, who polled 880,000 votes, and one of its principal leaders was Father Coughlin. The party made a powerful appeal to Roman Catholics, with an anticommunist line including an attack on the Democratic Administration for its diplomatic recognition of Soviet Russia. Lemke drew especially heavy votes in some metropolitan Catholic precincts. Lubell's interviews persuaded him that in 1948 the Lemke voters of 1936 returned to the Democratic fold on one side as Wallace and the left-wingers went out on the other. Truman attracted an especially heavy Catholic vote, a feat made possible partially by the absence of the Wallaceites. See Lubell, *op. cit.*, pp. 203–14. See also E. C. Blackorby, "William Lemke: Agrarian Radical and Union Party Presidential Candidate," *Mississippi Valley Historical Review*, 49 (1962), 67–84.

the political system. Yet their members evidently derive profound satisfaction from participation in activities that have only the gentlest impact upon the course of events.

Most of these parties exist to agitate for one or the other of the many varieties of socialism. Although such American thinkers as Edward Bellamy exerted great influence in the early propagation of socialist ideas, American socialism is largely a transplanted growth that has failed to take political root in new soil. The great thinkers and philosophers of socialism have been Europeans; their ideas of objectives and of political strategy have been formulated from observation of European conditions. Almost all movements in European socialist thought have been paralleled by the formation of movements and organizations in the United States. The history of the fissions and internal battles of the socialist movement makes a complex story that is recounted with great solemnity by participants in the movement. Spokesmen for each faction and splinter acclaim themselves as the true apostles of Marx and denounce each other as traitors to the master, all with little effect on the American political scene.[22] Of the influence of socialist ideas there can be no denial,[23] but that the socialist parties have had much of a hand in this influence is dubious.

SOCIALIST LABOR PARTY   The oldest Marxist party in the United States is the Socialist Labor party. Though the party can be traced to the 1870's, it fixes 1890 as the beginning of its "real history." [24] That year marked the entry into its affairs of Daniel DeLeon, who became its chief philosopher, its revered leader, and, after his death, its saint. The Socialist Labor party program provides "for the taking over, by the mass of the people collectively (the working class), the means of production, to administer these in the interests of the useful producers (which include all who labor, whether so-called manual or mental labor), through democratically elected representatives from the industries, chosen democratically by the mass of the people themselves who work in the industries." It regards itself as a revolutionary party which can by some way or another liquidate the capitalist system peacefully.

[22] See, for example, J. P. Cannon, *The Struggle for a Proletarian Party* (New York: Pioneer, 1943); H. Kuhn and O. M. Johnson, *The Socialist Labor Party during Four Decades, 1890–1930* (New York: New York Labor News Co., 1931). Socialists are quite articulate and have produced an appalling quantity of literature on the cause. One volume of the two-volume work, *Socialism and American Life*, edited by D. D. Egbert and Stow Persons (Princeton: Princeton University Press, 1952), consists of a selective and critical bibliography.

[23] For example, see Murray Seidler, "The Socialist Party and American Unionism," *Midwest Journal of Political Science*, 5 (1961), 207–37.

[24] For an account of the complexities of American socialism from 1870 through 1901, see H. H. Quint, *The Forging of American Socialism: Origins of the Modern Movement* (Columbia: University of South Carolina Press, 1953).

In its battle to promote working-class consciousness the SLP denounces the AFL and CIO as "preeminently capitalist weapons to bridle the working class," as "pro-capitalist" in philosophy, and as under the leadership of "labor-fakers." As for Stalinism, it is not true Marxism: "The only difference is that instead of being exploited by a capitalist class (as American workers are), the Russian workers are exploited by the State, and for the benefit of a privileged, bureaucratic caste." Norman Thomas' Socialist party is dismissed as a bourgeois party with no "program for dispossessing the capitalist class." Moreover, the SLP charges that the Socialist party "is a fraud, a swindle perpetrated on the American workers, an organization that is up to its ears in capitalist politics." In rounding out the list of its antagonists, the Socialist Labor party includes the "international Vatican organization . . . a universal political machine, bent on world power, and less and less concerned about concealing its ends or disguising its means." [25]

The SLP makes strong medicine in its propaganda but polls few votes. In 1952 its presidential candidate, Eric Hass, drew 30,267 votes. In 1956 Mr. Hass was again nominated and proclaimed himself to be the only true socialist candidate in the race.[26] Again in 1960 he was the candidate, was on the ballot in 18 states, and polled 47,000 votes.

SOCIALIST PARTY   The complex process of fission, mutual antagonism, and combination in the socialist movement yielded up in 1901 the Socialist party, the best known of the American socialist factions. As a right-wing socialist group, it has urged the achievement of public ownership of the means of production by parliamentary tactics. Along the road to the socialist state, the Socialist party advocates the ordinary liberal-democratic ameliorative measures, flavored perhaps with a dash of Christian socialism. All in all, the social democracy of the Socialist party has been characterized by a mildness that lent it a certain respectability in contrast with the doctrines of the more belligerent socialist sects.

First Eugene V. Debs, then Norman Thomas, led the Socialist group from 1904 to 1948. With two exceptions, one or the other of them was the Socialist candidate at the presidential elections during that period. In 1916 A. L. Benson headed the ticket, and in 1924 the party supported La Follette. In 1904 and 1908 Debs polled almost 3 per cent of the total presidential vote, and in 1912, in the high tide of progressivism and reformism, his vote climbed

---

[25] Quotations are from leaflets issued by the party and from its official organ, *The Weekly People.*

[26] Not to be confused with the SLP is the Socialist Workers' party, a group of Trotskyites expelled from the Communist party in 1928. The SWP first nominated a presidential candidate in 1948, Farrell Dobbs, who denounced the Stalinists, the Norman Thomas Socialists, the Democrats, the Republicans, and the Wallaceites, as he portrayed his party as the "hope of the American working class." Mr. Dobbs was again the nominee in 1952, 1956, and 1960. In 1960 he was in the ballot in 12 states and polled about 40,000 votes.

to 900,000 or about 6 per cent of the total. In 1916 and 1920 the vote sagged back to the normal 3 per cent and in 1928 dropped to less than 1 per cent. The depression-fed protest boosted Thomas' vote in 1932 to 881,000, a bit over 2 per cent of the total; afterward the party's support again declined to well under 1 per cent.

The geographical distribution of the Socialist vote indicates a curious characteristic of the American socialist movement. With a program tailored for the industrial proletariat, the party achieved its greatest strength in presidential voting in the western agricultural and mining states, areas in which the Populists had earlier made their best showing. In 1912, when the party polled its peak percentage of the total vote, the highest Socialist vote was in Oklahoma, where 16.6 per cent of the voters indicated a Socialist preference. States with more than 10 per cent of their vote Socialist were Oklahoma, Nevada, Montana, Arizona, Washington, California, and Idaho.

From 1928 to 1948 Norman Thomas carried the Socialist banner in presidential campaigns. His best vote came in 1932, but even under the conditions of 1932 the Democrats apparently got most of the votes of the downtrodden proletariat. In 1948 he attracted the suffrage of not much more than 100,000 voters. Perhaps wearied by his exertions in six futile presidential campaigns, Thomas proposed to the 1950 Socialist convention that the party conduct campaigns "only where circumstances make campaigns specifically and practically advantageous." He advocated that Socialists be encouraged to work within other groups and to support candidates of other parties when the Socialists had none. This policy, Thomas argued, would "release Socialist energy and funds for a more intensive campaign of organization and education for Socialism." The convention decisively voted down Thomas' proposal and decided to continue Socialist candidacies and to shun coalition with other parties. The members were adjured, even when the party had no candidate for an office, to avoid supporting candidates of "capitalist parties." The convention's rejection of Thomas' proposal was regarded as marking the end of his leadership of the party. Again in the 1956 convention he urged that energies be devoted to agitation rather than to the circulation of petitions to get presidential candidates on the ballot. Again his proposal was voted down as the convention nominated Darlington Hoopes, of Reading, Pennsylvania, but in 1960 Thomas brought the convention to his view and the party did not place a presidential candidate on the ballot in that year.[27] To put a national ticket in the field is thought to help Socialist candidates for local office. Persistent patches of local Socialist strength exist in such places as Milwaukee,

[27] For a single-volume treatment of the Socialist party, see David A. Shannon, *The Socialist Party of America* (New York: Macmillan, 1955). See also Ira Kipnis, *The American Socialist Movement, 1897–1912* (New York: Columbia University Press, 1952) ; M. B. Seidler, *Norman Thomas: Respectable Rebel* (Syracuse: Syracuse University Press, 1961) ; H. W. Morgan, *Eugene V. Debs: Socialist for President* (Syracuse: Syracuse University Press, 1962).

Wisconsin, Bridgeport, Connecticut, and Reading, Pennsylvania, where candidates who are regarded as essentially bourgeois reformers on occasion win office.

COMMUNIST PARTY   The intricate steps leading to the establishment of the American Communist party would require a book to relate.[28] The main events began in 1919 when the left wing split off from the Socialist party. The left itself splintered into numerous Marxist groups, which paralleled the currents of schism within communist activity abroad and perhaps in some instances reflected only the ambitions of American leaders. In 1921, after a visitor from Moscow attempted to iron out differences among communist groups, the Workers' (Communist) party emerged as the American group with recognition from Moscow. In 1929 the name was formally changed to Communist party. The shifts in policy and strategy of the Communist party from 1921 on appear to have been governed either by the policy of Moscow or, when communications were imperfect, by what the local leaders thought to be the wish of Moscow. The party, thus, differed markedly from other parties on the American scene. It functioned by and large as an instrument of Soviet policy, and it more or less consistently regarded itself as an instrument of ultimate revolution, though its expressions of policy ranged from gradualism to violence. None of these characteristics is compatible with existence as a party within the American constitutional framework.

The exigencies of Soviet foreign policy and the restrictions of federal legislation since 1940 further reduced the resemblance of the Communists to a conventional third party. In 1940 Congress, by the Voorhis Act, required organizations affiliated with foreign governments to register with the Attorney General and to file with him certain information about the organization. The Communist party, on paper, abandoned its affiliations with Moscow. The Smith Act of 1940 attempted virtually to outlaw the Communist party. That legislation made it a criminal act to "advocate, abet, advise, or teach the duty, necessity, desirability or propriety of overthrowing or destroying any government in the United States by force or violence." It also made it a crime to form a society to advocate such doctrines or "to be a member of, or affiliate with, any such society." [29] In 1951 the Supreme Court upheld the act as applied in a charge of conspiracy against 11 members of the national executive committee of the Communist party.[30] The Department of Justice proceeded then to obtain indictments and convictions of second-string party leaders. In

[28] See James Oneal and G. A. Werner, *American Communism* (New York: Dutton, 1947) ; Theodore Draper, *The Roots of American Communism* (New York: Viking, 1957) ; Irving Howe and Lewis Coser, *The American Communist Party* (Boston: Beacon, 1957) ; David Shannon, *The Decline of American Communism* (New York: Harcourt, Brace, 1959) ; Nathan Glazer, *The Social Basis of American Communism* (New York: Harcourt, Brace, 1961).

[29] 54 Stat. 671.   [30] Dennis *v.* United States, 71 S. Ct. 857 (1951).

1957 the Supreme Court reversed convictions of West Coast Communists on the ground that the Smith Act did not prohibit advocacy of overthrow of government "divorced from any effort to instigate action to that end." [31] The same decision made it doubtful that persons could be punished on the sole charge of party membership unaccompanied by evidence of acts of incitement to revolution.

The constitutionally troublesome penalty for membership was upheld in 1961, but only as applied to "active" (and not "nominal") members who had knowledge of the party's aim to overthrow the government illegally and a "specific intent" to bring about that overthrow.[32] At the same time the Supreme Court affirmed an order by the Subversive Activities Control Board that the American Communist party register as an organization dominated by the foreign Communist movement as required by the Internal Security Act of 1950. Registration under that act included the submission of the names of officers and members who would thereby become subject to certain penalties. The court declined to consider, as prematurely raised, the contention that registration would constitute self-incrimination, in effect, a confession of guilt under the Smith Act.[33] The Communist party refused to obey the Board's order that it register, for which it was convicted late in 1962, an action which opened the way for ultimate determination by the Supreme Court of the constitutional question of self-incrimination and other issues left open by the 1961 decision.

In keeping with its character as something other than a political party in the ordinary sense, the Communist group placed little emphasis on electioneering. It ran candidates from time to time, and in 1932 its presidential nominee polled slightly over 100,000 votes. Yet its major efforts were in other directions. By infiltration of disciplined cliques into other organizations, such as local parties, trade unions, and "nonpartisan" groups, it succeeded in using those groups to further its purpose of the moment.[34] That purpose might be all-out support of national policy, as during the period of Soviet–United States alliance, or it might be simply the stimulation of confusion, division, and dissension.

Although the details are disputed, it is evident that Communists exerted considerable organizational influence in Henry Wallace's Progressive party of 1948. The Communist national committee took credit, probably too much credit, for "the forging of the new alignment and people's coalition." Apparently, once Wallace had decided to make the presidential race, the Com-

[31] Yates v. United States, 77 S. Ct. 1064 (1957).

[32] Scales v. United States, 81 S. Ct. 1469 (1961).

[33] Communist Party of the United States v. Subversive Activities Control Board, 81 S. Ct. 1357 (1961).

[34] See David J. Saposs, Communism in American Politics (Washington: Public Affairs Press, 1960). Electoral activity also came to be discouraged by state statutes that excluded from the ballot parties dedicated to the overthrow of government by force.

munists joined up in force and, for lack of a surge of noncommunist liberal leaders to Wallace, gained position in the organization. After the 1948 campaign a battle continued between the Communist and noncommunist wings for control of the shell of the party. In 1950 Wallace resigned from the party in protest against its pro-Soviet position on the Korean war. In 1952 the Progressive candidate, Vincent Hallinan, who happened at the time of his nomination to be in jail for contempt of court, drew 140,000 votes in contrast to Wallace's 1,150,000 in 1948.[35]

The entire American experience with the Communist party in the 1930's and 1940's strained the capacity of a democratic order to cope with a group not committed to the constitutional principles of that order without abandonment of those principles. Although their loyalties were committed to the Soviet state, the Communists scarcely came under the proscriptions of treason or other conventional methods of self-defense of a national order. Unable to invent a satisfactory formula to cope cleanly with communism, the democratic order struck more or less blindly with crude instruments. In the process, native radicals, untinged by communism, suffered no little damage. And, indeed, those wielding anti-Communist weapons often aimed to discredit all political liberalism and radicalism, whatever its origin or hue. It requires a fine discrimination to repress one type of dissent and to refrain from repressing others.

ROLE OF DOCTRINAL PARTIES   From these comments, it is evident that a doctrinal party is not the equivalent of the occasional outburst of short-term and relatively large-scale minor-party activity intimately connected with the conflicts of the major parties of the time. The doctrinal parties pursue their courses fairly independently of the major parties and can scarcely be said to affect the results of elections or to deflect the policy orientations of the major parties.[36]

Minor Parties in States

The conspicuous minor parties have been national parties with little substructure of state and local organization. In a few cities the Socialist party contests municipal elections with success. A few of the powerful but transient

[35] See K. M. Schmidt, *Henry A. Wallace: Quixotic Crusade 1948* (Syracuse: Syracuse University Press, 1960).

[36] Perhaps for analytical purposes the Prohibition party could be classified with the ideological parties. It, too, lives a life largely apart from the determinative battles of politics. It has had presidential candidates at each election since 1872. Its 1956 vote was 41,937. In 1956 the party's nominee was Enoch A. Holtwick and in 1960, Rutherford Decker. See D. L. Colvin, *Prohibition in the United States* (New York: Doubleday, Doran, 1926) and Roger W. Babson, *Our Campaign for the Presidency in 1940* (Chicago: National Prohibitionist, 1941).

third-party movements have been accompanied by considerable activity in state politics, as in 1892 and 1912. Yet the handful of minor parties of much consequence in state politics have existed independently on their local foundations rather than as branches or offshoots of one of the minor parties on the national scene.

Given the federal character of the American system, many state and local parties might be expected to develop from the special circumstances and needs of each state and locality. By and large the major parties nationally have demonstrated a capacity to accommodate themselves to considerable variety among their state and local affiliates as well as a capacity both to absorb and to discourage deviant groups. On occasion, coalitions, formal or informal, of Republicans and Democrats have crushed minor groups in state and local elections. Further, by their control of national patronage the major parties can create a special obstacle to independent state parties. Only in exceptional circumstances is a national administration disposed to nourish a minor state party with patronage and policy, in competition with the "regular" state organization. Thus, the Farmer-Labor party of Minnesota elected governors, but the Democratic national committeeman distributed federal patronage within the state.[37] In due course, the state party joined with the Democrats to form the Democratic-Farmer-Labor party. The factors entering into the merger were numerous, but the maintenance of a state party unconnected with one of the major national parties encounters no little difficulty.

When a state or local minor party has no hope of becoming a majority, its leaders are under temptation to fuse with one of the major parties in return for whatever concessions may be wrested from the major party. Usually the minor party finds itself swallowed up and digested in the process of fusion. The ordinary electoral procedures give no measure of the contribution of the minor party to the outcome of an election. The leaders of, say, the Pro-Solvency party, may strain their diaphragms and stretch their vocal cords in support of the Republican candidate endorsed by their group; but, after the votes are in, only a seer can determine the number of Pro-Solvency votes, if any, delivered to the Republican candidate. And the Republican leaders, if they win, need not pay much heed to the importunities of the Pro-Solvency leaders, for it is a fairly safe bet that by the next election the Pro-Solvents will be dissolved.

Electoral procedures employed in New York have enabled minor parties to demonstrate precisely how many votes they contributed to a candidate. Under the laws of that state it has been permissible for a single individual to be the nominee of two or more parties. The candidate is listed on the ballot

[37] See J. R. Starr, "Labor and Farmer Groups and the Three-Party System," *Southwestern Social Science Quarterly*, 17 (1936), 7–9; G. H. Mayer, *The Political Career of Floyd B. Olson* (Minneapolis: University of Minnesota Press, 1951); D. R. McCoy, "The Formation of the Wisconsin Progressive Party in 1934," *The Historian*, 14 (1951), 70–90.

or the voting machine under the emblems of the several parties that have nominated him. Votes for him as the minor-party nominee are tallied separately. Minor-party leaders can thus point to their contribution to the vote of the victorious candidate. And they may also demonstrate that if their party had named its own candidate or endorsed the opposing candidate, the outcome would probably have been different. They may also hold out promises of what they propose to do or not to do when the next election rolls around.

The principal minor parties of New York have been the American Labor party and the Liberal party. In 1936 labor leaders, at the instance of President Roosevelt, formed the ALP to garner labor and independent support for him in his campaign for re-election. David Dubinsky of the International Ladies Garment Workers, Sidney Hillman of the Amalgamated Clothing Workers, and other union leaders associated with them in the ALP had long wished to see a labor party and had been unhappy with Samuel Gompers' "nonpartisan" policy for labor. They responded to Roosevelt's suggestion with alacrity and, after the 1936 campaign, were not disposed to regard the party, which had been supported by union funds and votes, as a one-campaign affair to be allowed to die.

Roosevelt's professional Democratic advisers in New York viewed the whole ALP venture with coolness; an ally today might become an enemy tomorrow. Events justified their fears. In 1937 the ALP virtually compelled the Republicans to renominate LaGuardia for mayor, and with ALP aid he handily defeated the Democratic candidate. In 1942 the ALP, unwilling to accept the Democratic nominee for governor, ran its own candidate and thereby helped Dewey to win.

As time wore on Communists filtered into the ALP and won control of local units of the organization. Hillman and Dubinsky, with the aid of upstate ALP units, only barely managed to induce the 1940 state convention to endorse Roosevelt for re-election. A battle for control of the ALP ensued that resulted in the withdrawal from the party of David Dubinsky and his anti-Communist union to form the Liberal party. The Liberals in 1944 supported Roosevelt for the Presidency, as did the ALP, but they declined to support state and local candidates with ALP endorsement. After Hillman's death his union also withdrew from the ALP.

It gradually became apparent that in officiating at the accouchement of the ALP, Democratic leaders had helped to life something more than a mechanism by which labor could support the New Deal. When Democratic candidates received ALP endorsement, they were charged with being allies of communism. When the ALP or the Liberal party ran its own candidates, the election often went to the Republicans. Both the ALP and the Liberal party from time to time found Republican candidates for local and legislative office to be in accord with their principles and nominated them. Although such nominations attracted votes that would otherwise have gone mainly to the Democratic party, even the Republican professionals had no love for the labor interlopers in the great game of politics.

Old-line party leaders sought a way to free themselves from the gadfly splinter parties. They proposed to prohibit all dual nominations, but the legislature in 1947 compromised the matter by forbidding a person enrolled in one party to seek the primary nomination of another without the consent of the appropriate committee of the party whose primary he was invading.[38] Thus, Vito Marcantonio, ALP leader who had won Democratic nominations, could no longer run for a Democratic primary nomination without the consent of the Democratic county committee. The legislation also required that members of one party who were nominated by another should accept the nomination in writing.

Prohibition of dual nominations would probably sooner or later kill off third parties, but the 1947 New York law left open the possibility of their continuance and left to candidates and party authorities the question of coalition. Regular party leaders expressed general condemnation of coalitions but in practice the situation rather than principle seemed to govern. In 1948, Edward J. Flynn, Democratic leader of the Bronx, rejected ALP and Liberal alliance propositions in his own locality but conceded that outside his own county circumstances might be different. In negotiations participated in by the White House, coalition occurred on presidential electors. Dewey was highly critical of splinter alliances, yet many Republican legislative candidates accepted ALP endorsements.

The dissolution of the ALP in 1956 left the Liberal party as the principal minor party in New York. In most statewide campaigns it makes the Democratic nominee its own and sometimes contributes the margin necessary for victory. In the 1949 senatorial race the percentage division of the total vote was:

Dulles, Republican		48.0
Lehman, Liberal	8.6	
Lehman, Democrat	43.4	
Lehman, Total		52.0

In the 1954 gubernatorial election Harriman's victory depended on his vote on the Liberal line. The percentage division of the three-party vote was:

[38] In some states antifusion statutes prohibit the appearance of a candidate's name on the ballot in more than one place. In other states party-raiding statutes require that the candidate be a member of the party that nominates him. In the absence of either sort of act, a candidate may appear on the ballot several times as the nominee of several parties. For a survey of the legislation, see "The Constitutionality of Anti-Fusion and Party-Raiding Statutes," Columbia Law Review, 47 (1947), 1207–14.

Ives, Republican		49.9
Harriman, Liberal	5.2	
Harriman, Democrat	44.9	
Harriman, Total		50.1

In the 1960 presidential election Kennedy's majority in the state hinged on the Liberal contribution to his vote. The percentage division of the total vote was:

Nixon, Republican		47.3
Kennedy, Liberal	5.6	
Kennedy, Democrat	47.0	
Kennedy, Total		52.5
Dobbs, Socialist Worker		.2

Such election results regularly move the Republican legislature to attempt to modify the election laws to obstruct Democratic-Liberal coalitions. Measures that would have handicapped joint nominations were vetoed in both 1956 and 1957 by Governor Harriman.[39]

New York minor parties have contrived, perhaps inadvertently, an electoral procedure favorable to the operation of minor parties, but it should not be supposed that New York's electoral laws alone produced these parties. Other conditions contributed to their vitality over a life longer than average for such parties. Of pivotal importance is the comparative indifference of their leaders to public office. With a leadership fairly solidly based in the trade-union bureaucracy, the principal party leaders can subsist quite well if they never win office themselves. They can afford to guide themselves by consideration of "principle" unlike the so-called "professional" politician who makes a living from his work. Moreover, the New York procedure circumvents the ancient dilemma of third parties—that if they nominate a candidate of their own, they might thereby contribute to the defeat of the major-party candidate most nearly agreeing with their principles.[40]

---

[39] In 1960 the Republican legislature permitted the Liberal party to function in upstate counties in which its committees did not have a full membership in return for an agreement not to endorse the Democratic opponents of 16 of the 17 incumbent Republican members of the legislature from New York City.

[40] For a survey of New York minor parties, see Warren Moscow, *Politics in the Empire State* (New York: Knopf, 1948), ch. 7. In 1962 right-wing New York Republicans formed the Conservative party which, they hoped, would eventually be able to influence Republican nominations for state office after the manner of the Liberal party's operations in Democratic affairs. The new group wished, its executive committee said, "to make it possible for the Republican party to shake loose the tyranny of liberal interlopers." The party regarded the 1962 Republican nominees, Rockefeller and Javits, as no better than Democrats and put forward its own slate. Its gubernatorial nominee, David Jaquith, polled about 120,000 votes, probably largely at the expense of Rockefeller.

NONPARTISAN LEAGUE   The Nonpartisan League provides another illustration of the problem more or less deviant groups face within the states in surviving in the face of the absorptive capacities of the major parties. The League remains influential only in North Dakota, but in the years 1916–1922 it was a force to be reckoned with in the triangle from Wisconsin to Oklahoma to Washington. It demanded state ownership and operation of services thought to be controlled by exploiters of the farmer: grain elevators, flour mills, packing plants, mortgage banks, hail insurance. This was socialism for the other fellow. The League did not propose public ownership of farms and ranches.

The League chose to operate not as a political party but as a faction within the established parties. It early gained control of the government of North Dakota by supporting its candidates in the Republican primaries. In the states in which it operated from 1916 to 1922 it elected over 950 candidates to state and national office, usually by nominating its men in one of the major-party primaries. By "boring from within" it could side-step the problem of weaning voters from their old party attachments; and by controlling the outcome of the primary of the dominant party in a state it could compound its own strength by the addition of the diehard party voters who would stomach the League program rather than bolt the party.[41] After 1921 the League rapidly declined in strength outside North Dakota, but there it remained as a highly disciplined faction within the dominant party of a one-party state. In essence the League became a political party equipped with organization and with procedures for nomination of slates of candidates to be backed for nomination in the Republican primaries. The League's long persistence in North Dakota was remarkable, though eventually the national party system's magnetism began to make itself felt. In 1956 the League began an attempt to move into the Democratic party and to leave the local Republican party to its conservative rivals in state politics.

Minor-Party Functions

The plainest moral of this tale of minor-party activity is that the language of politics is not a language of precision. The term "minor party" covers the most diverse sorts of political phenomena.[42] A recognition of that diversity

[41] For a discerning analysis of League tactics, see S. P. Huntington, "The Election Tactics of the Nonpartisan League," *Mississippi Valley Historical Review*, 36 (1950), 613–32. For an able general review, see R. L. Morlan, *Political Prairie Fire: The Nonpartisan League, 1915–1922* (Minneapolis: University of Minnesota Press, 1955).

[42] At every election minor parties, in addition to the continuing ones mentioned in the text, appear on the ballot in one or more states. In 1960 they included National States Rights, Independent Afro-American Unity, Tax Cut, Independent American, Conservative, and Constitution parties.

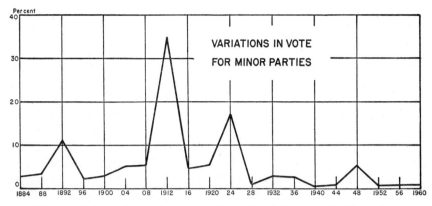

Figure 10.3   Percentage of total presidential vote polled by minor-party candidates, 1884–1960

must be a first step in any effort to cope with the broad problem posed at the outset of the chapter, namely, what is the place of the minor party in the two-party sysem?

The doctrinal parties can best be disposed of first. Their principal differentiating characteristics have been their long duration and their relatively exotic doctrinal positions. The position has been that they are not really operating elements of the party system. Rivulets alongside the main streams of party life, they maintain on the whole an isolated existence. Many an old Socialist might dissent from the application of this observation to his party, but it is difficult to see that even this party, both the most successful and the mildest of the doctrinaire parties, has had influences of perceptible significance on the workings of the party system.

On the other hand, the evidence seems to indicate that the rather large-scale, episodic, nonrecurring minor-party movements must be regarded, somewhat paradoxically, as integral elements of the so-called two-party system. They spring from the center of the political melee, and in turn they affect the nature of the major parties and the relationships between them as they cumbersomely make their way from election to election. The remaining comments about minor-party functions will be limited to this type of third-party movement.

Commonly the significance of these minor parties is assessed in terms of the arithmetic of a single presidential polling. Hicks says, for example, that "in possibly half a dozen instances the third party vote has snatched victory from one major party ticket to give it to the other." [43] Perhaps so; perhaps not. Such calculations rest on assumptions not readily testable. At times, minor parties may, indeed, wield a balance of power and affect the outcome

[43] John D. Hicks, "The Third Party Tradition in American Politics," *Mississippi Valley Historical Review*, 20 (1933), 26.

of an election.[44] Nevertheless, their larger role in the party system must be sought elsewhere.

The general role of the minor party can be discerned only with difficulty, for each of the principal third-party aberrations has had its peculiar characteristics. Yet each of these episodes appears to have had an impact, not only at the moment of the election, but subsequently on the character of the major parties of the system. That impact is uniform neither in degree nor in nature from episode to episode.

With respect to the policy orientations of the major parties, the minor-party eruptions in some instances nudge the major parties differentially and widen the policy gap between them. The years 1892, 1912, and 1924 appear to have been instances of this sort. In other instances, the policy impact of the minor party may bear chiefly on a single major party, as perhaps with the Dixiecratic movement.

As for the composition of the major parties, minor-party candidacies at times are but a step in the reshuffling of voters between the major parties. In the process each major party may gain by losing its most discordant elements to the other. The demonstration of the bearing of minor-party candidacies on the flow of voters from party to party is difficult because often the movement is concealed and confused by other types of movements of voters that occur from election to election. Hence, the effects of third-party candidacies on voter alignments are at times postponed or offset by other factors.

When we attempt in this manner to specify the role of minor-party movements in the system as a whole, their integral connection with the system becomes apparent. In considerable measure, the minor parties develop because the major parties are as they are, and in turn the major parties take the shape they do in part because of the operations of the minor parties. Minor-party activity tends to be a continuation of processes that are always occurring within, and between, the major parties. Factions within major parties continually strive to win the party to more complete commitment to their views. The opposing party, sensing discord in the enemy's camp, may put out bait to attract the wavering. Even in days of surface serenity, latent discord renders uneasy the life of a major party. That so few of these internal dissensions explode into minor-party candidacies is cause for astonishment.[45]

---

[44] Such assumptions are often made by practical politicians. A major party may even surreptitiously foster a minor-party candidacy in the belief that it will weaken the opposition. In 1948 in Indiana the States' Rights Democrats were denied a place on the ballot because of irregularities in the petition. In litigation on the matter it was revealed that the States' Rights petitions were printed in the Republican state headquarters without, the Republican state chairman blandly announced, his knowledge.

[45] The price that must be paid by secessionist leaders may be a great deterrent to major-party fission. They have little future if they try to cross to the opposition; they are regarded as suspect if they return to the fold. Hence, leaders of party rebellions often tend to be strongly entrenched in their own bailiwicks or otherwise in a position to assume the risks of a politics of retribution.

If these observations are correct, it follows that in its bearing on the major parties, the minor-party movement may be the functional equivalent of various inter- and intraparty processes. For reasons that are by no means self-evident, on some occasions an outburst of third-party activity occurs to realign the parties, to reorient their policies, or perhaps to redirect only one of the major parties. On other occasions, these consequences occur without the facilitation of third-party endeavor.

Students of the topic seem to agree that the day of the third party, at least in presidential elections, is done. Several justifications are advanced for this view. One of the less compelling, but nevertheless important, is that the procedural hurdles that must be negotiated by third-party candidates to get on the ballot have been made higher and higher.[46] Another is that the general adoption of the direct primary has made it possible for dissident groups within the major parties, particularly when their membership is geographically concentrated, to nominate and elect their leaders as Senators and Representatives under the banner of a major party. Deviant opinion thus can ensconce itself within the duly accredited congressional ranks of a major party. Under these circumstances, to advance the cause there is, so the argument goes, no need to resort to the quixotic tactic of forming a third party.

A marked upthrust of minor-party strength is symptomatic of an incapacity of one or the other of the major parties to cope with the issues of the moment in a manner to maintain party unity. Third parties, Lubell argues, shed "penetrating light on the inner torments of the major party." [47] Those inner torments work themselves out sometimes through third parties, sometimes through other means. The major parties, after a century of trial and error, may have learned how to solve their "inner torments" without fission. The party system as a whole is better able to accommodate economic discontent than it was in, say, 1890, for the reason that the major parties have a greater contrast in orientation toward economic policy. The John Birch Society may quarrel with the Republican party, but it will have nothing to do with a third party. The ADA may be unhappy about Democratic policy, but its members remain Democrats nonetheless. The occurrence of great episodes of third-party activity depends on the rise of movements or bursts of sentiment which cannot work themselves out through a major party. Whether the day of the third party is done depends on whether such circumstances will again develop. If and when they do, we may expect the next surge of minor-party activity.

[46] For concrete examples of the vicissitudes of new parties, see Schmidt, *op. cit.*, ch. 6. The national interest might be fostered if it were made easier rather than more difficult for minor candidates to be placed on the ballot. A relatively few crackpots can generate a frightening clamor in political debate. If they could readily place a candidate on the ballot, the automatic census of their numbers that would ensue in the election would deflate their pretensions.

[47] *Op. cit.*, p. 205.

11.

STATE PARTIES

M ANUALS on American politics commonly focus on the epic battles of Republicans and Democrats for control of the national government, on the interests clustered around the national party banners, and on the grand policy issues that preoccupy Congress. Scholars, like most citizens, pay less heed to the problem of political organization and leadership for the conduct of state governments. Yet state governments perform functions of no mean significance and determine policies of great concern to powerful social groups. The problem of party organization and function in the governments of the American states is of corresponding import.

If the operations of state governments were not overshadowed by national affairs, the problem of state politics would appear of a magnitude to warrant the closest attention. Many American states could rank as substantial members of the family of nations. New York's population exceeds that of the Dominion of Canada, and California's is larger than that of Australia. The government of New Jersey serves slightly more people than does that of Switzerland, and Portugal is only a little more populous than Ohio. The Irish Free State and Minnesota have approximately the same population. Illinois' politicians must cope with as many people as do those of Belgium, and there are about as many North Carolinians as there are Finns. Colorado almost equals Paraguay in population. The people of Pennsylvania outnumber those of the Netherlands, and the Virginia state machine should be able to man the government of Norway if the ratio of politicians to people is fairly uniform from culture to culture. Only enough Swedes remain in Sweden to give it a population not much larger than that of Michigan, and the citizenry of Massachusetts slightly exceeds that of Denmark.

Population provides no exact measure of governmental problems, but these comparisons suggest that the American states are political entities of respectable stature. Unlike independent states, they have no responsibilities in the field of foreign affairs, international trade, or the management of major defense forces. The Constitution assigns authority over such matters to the national government, yet there remains within the jurisdiction of the state governments a wide range of basic public functions. The construction of great public works, such as highways, the conduct of the mammoth American system of public education, the management of hospitals and other similar institutions, the adjudication of the bulk of private litigation, the creation and tutelage of institutions of local government, the regulation of public utilities, the levying of taxes to support state activities—all these and other public functions are the business of the states.

Around the government of each state a party system—or a factional system—develops to propel the machinery of government. Groups of men contend for control of state government. Although state parties are intertwined with national parties and politics, in varying degrees the skirmishes for control of state governments are fought out on different issues and to some extent by different cliques of leaders than those involved in the federal battle. Political structures and practices differ widely from state to state, and it is feasible here only to set out a few major characteristics that suggest the variety in state party systems.

Varieties of State Political Systems

Political parties perform functions essential to the operation of a democratic order. They seek to build majority coalitions powerful enough to control the government. They advocate broad views on public policy; they designate candidates; and, once in power, they attempt to run the government in a manner to hold together the coalition that put them into office. The minority party maintains a critical vigil against the day when circumstances will permit it to oust the majority.

The institutions developed to perform these functions in each state often differ markedly in form from the national parties. It is an error to assume that the political parties of each state are but miniatures of the national party system. In a few states that condition is approached; more often, though, practices in the conduct of political competition only remotely resemble the national system. Each state has its own pattern of action which often deviates markedly from the forms of organization commonly thought of as constituting party systems. It may fit neither the biparty nor the multiparty pattern. Moreover, the patterns of political action and organization differ widely among the states.

The obvious contrast between the national and state party arrangements consists in the degree to which parties, as parties, compete for control of government. Within the national arena, Democratic and Republican parties vie for power on fairly even terms, at least over the long run, and present to the electorate a choice between broadly differing policy tendencies. In a few states that condition is approximated, but more commonly a single party dominates the government of the state. It may be ousted from control only infrequently. Under these conditions political competition takes place within the dominant party of the state and departs drastically, at least in form, from the pattern of struggle for control of the national government.

Each state has, to be sure, its Republican party and its Democratic party. The organizing forces of national politics imprint their form and their names on state political systems. The state parties operate as affiliates of the national political parties in national politics. Even in that role, they possess a high degree of independence, but in their roles with respect to the state governments, state parties are autonomous in keeping with the constitutional theory of the federal system. That is, national party authorities do not make it their business to instruct a state affiliate to nominate a particular individual for governor or to take a particular line on policy.[1]

DEVIATIONS FROM THE TWO-PARTY PATTERN   Since a salient characteristic of most state party systems is their deviation from the two-party competitive pattern, states are commonly characterized as solidly Democratic, as strongly Republican, as leaning this way or that, or as competitive. None of these classifications describes state political systems with precision. One measure of the degree of attachment of states to the Republican or the Democratic party will group the states in one way; another, in another. At one time a particular measure will yield one result and at another time, another. Nevertheless, a few crude indices will indicate the range among the states in their balance of Republican and Democratic strength.

The office of the chief executive in the states, as in the nation, is a focus of party conflict. The extent to which a single party dominates this office provides a rough measure of the extent to which a state approaches or deviates from the pattern of bipartisan competition. An arrangement of states according to the number of years of Democratic control of the governorship in the years 1929–1962 appears in Table 11.1. The states of the Solid South had an unbroken series of Democratic governors during these years as did Oklahoma. At the other extreme, only New Hampshire and Vermont had a continuous chain of Republican governors. In six other states grouped in the table Democratic gubernatorial victories were most infrequent. Among these strongly Republican states were Kansas and South Dakota. In Oregon and

---

[1] If state parties were subject to national direction, a political unitarism would, of course, be superimposed over the formal federalism of the Constitution.

Table 11.1   *Variations in partisan control of state governorships, 1929–1962*

Years Governor Democratic	State Groups
34	Alabama, Arkansas, Florida, Georgia, Louisiana, Mississippi, North Carolina, Oklahoma, South Carolina, Tennessee, Texas, Virginia
22–27	Arizona, Colorado, Connecticut, Kentucky, Maryland, Missouri, New Mexico, Ohio, Rhode Island, West Virginia
18–20	Idaho, Indiana, Massachusetts, Michigan, Nevada, New Jersey, New York, Utah, Washington, Wyoming
10–16	Delaware, Illinois, Iowa, Maine, Montana, Nebraska, North Dakota, Pennsylvania
0–8	California, Kansas, Minnesota, New Hampshire, Oregon, South Dakota, Vermont, Wisconsin

California also, Republicans managed to control the governorship most of the time despite the existence of goodly numbers of Democratic voters.

About a dozen states drop into a slot in the middle of the table reflective of the fact that Democrats and Republicans either alternated in power or held the governorship close to half the time during the period. Among these fairly competitive states were the Rocky Mountain states of Idaho and Utah and the older industrial states of Indiana, Michigan, New York, and Ohio. The table also identifies two other groups of states, one in which Democrats held the governor's office well over half the period and another in which the advantage rested with the Republicans.[2]

Another measure of party strength groups the states somewhat differently. Figure 11.1 shows the average Democratic percentage of the membership of the lower houses of the state legislatures in four groups of states

[2] The proportion of a period in which a single party held the governorship has its drawbacks as a measure of interparty competitiveness among different states. For example, in one state the Republicans might win a series of elections against a moribund Democratic party and then be replaced by an enlivened Democratic party for another series of elections. In another situation the parties might battle close elections and alternate in power so as to fall in the same pigeonhole as the first state. For an attempt to take both these factors into account in a comparison of the states, see J. A. Schlesinger, "A Two-Dimensional Scheme for Classifying States According to Degree of Inter-Party Competition," *American Political Science Review,* 49 (1955), 1120–28. Schlesinger considers all statewide elective offices as he compares the states in "The Structure of Competition for Office in the American States," *Behavioral Science,* 5 (1960), 197–210.

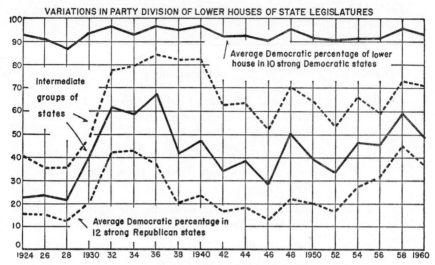

Figure 11.1   Average Democratic percentage of membership of lower house of legislatures in four groups of states, 1924–1960

over the period 1924 through 1960. In one group, as may be seen from the upper graph of the figure, the Democratic percentage of legislators averaged around 90 per cent over the entire period, indicative of the practical non-existence of the Republican party in these states.[3] At the other extreme are those strong Republican states in which the Democratic legislative representation is weak. In these states, whose averages appear in the bottom graph in the figure, Democrats win substantial legislative representation only under the most exceptional circumstances.[4]

The two groups of states represented by the graphs between the strong Republican and strong Democratic groups in Figure 11.1 show considerably more variation from election to election in the party division of legislative membership. One of these groups leans toward Republican control of the lower house of the legislature, though on occasion Democrats may control.[5] The average of the other group leans toward the Democratic side of the fence, but Republicans can win the lower house in most of these states with varying degrees of frequency.[6]

[3] The strong Democratic states averaged in the top graph of the figure were Alabama, Arkansas, Florida, Georgia, Louisiana, Maryland, North Carolina, Oklahoma, Tennessee, Texas, and South Carolina.

[4] The states grouped as strong Republican, by the measure of strength in the lower house of the state legislature, were Connecticut, Iowa, Kansas, Maine, Michigan, New Hampshire, New Jersey, North Dakota, Oregon, South Dakota, Vermont, and Wisconsin.

[5] The states included in this group were California, Colorado, Delaware, Idaho, Illinois, Indiana, Massachusetts, Montana, New York, Ohio, Pennsylvania, and Wyoming.

[6] The states classified as leaning Democratic were Arizona, Missouri, Nevada, New Mexico, Rhode Island, Utah, Washington, and West Virginia. Obviously wide differences

The graphs in Figure 11.1 oversimplify the realities; they suggest that four clearly differentiated types of states exist. One could draw across the chart a graph for each state, an operation that would produce a complete but confusing picture. While the averages conceal some of the confusion, they serve to make plain the variation in the balance of party strength among the states. The figure also draws to attention characteristics of the state party systems not revealed by our inspection of control of the governorships. The legislative figures often rank the states differently than do the gubernatorial data, a consequence in part of gerrymandering of state legislatures. The upper and lower graphs reflect the high degree of stability of legislative strength of the dominant party in the states at both the Republican and Democratic ends of the political spectrum. Even in the more competitive states, as the figure indicates, a most drastic set of conditions—namely, the Great Depression—must develop to bring about wide swings generally in the division of party strength, though the averages conceal a few individual states with frequent shifts of considerable amplitude.

SECULAR SHIFTS IN PARTY BALANCE   One of the technical problems of classifying or describing state party systems comes from the fact that over fairly long periods some states undergo marked realignments in their partisan loyalties. The classification according to periods of control of the governorship in Table 11.1 conceals such a secular shift in the party balance. Some of the changes, however, that have occurred in some states during the past three or four decades are reflected in Figure 11.1 on the division of legislative strength. Note there the curve of Democratic strength in the states that lean Democratic. In these states in the 1920's Republicans dominated the legislatures, but after the upthrust in Democratic strength in the 1930's these states, as a group, settled down to a new plateau of much higher Democratic strength. A similar but less-marked shift occurred, as may be seen from the figure, in those states grouped as leaning Republican.

It is not entirely wrong to say that parties win elections in some states, not by the excellence of their candidates or the intensity of their campaign exertions, but by the slow cumulation of the effects of economic and demographic changes that make a state normally Democratic rather than normally Republican or vice versa. This process of realignment finds illustration in the conversion of Rhode Island from a stronghold of New England Republicanism to a normally Democratic state. The change is shown in the graphs in Figure 11.2. Before 1932 Democrats could win the governorship and the lower house of the state legislature under such exceptional conditions as the little depression of 1921–1922. After 1932 the balance of power was reversed and the Republicans became able to win the state only at rare intervals.

In recent decades similar secular shifts have taken place in other states.

exist among these states, and some of them, such as Rhode Island and West Virginia, have, during the period covered by the graph, undergone a political realignment.

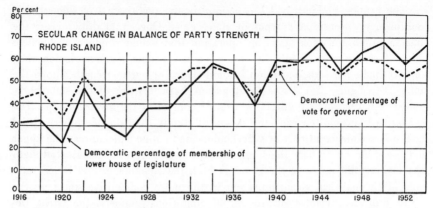

Figure 11.2   Democratic percentage of two-party vote for governor and of membership of lower house of state legislature, Rhode Island, 1916–1954

The long-term growth of the Democratic party in Michigan has given it frequent control of the governorship, but the legislative apportionment enables Republicans ordinarily to hold control of at least one house of the legislature.[7] Secular Democratic gains have occurred in Pennsylvania. In Maryland the drift seems to have been toward the Republicans. In some southern states, notably Florida, a long-term Republican growth has been far more evident in the presidential vote than in state politics.

NATIONAL SECTIONALISM AND STATE ONE-PARTYISM
Our measures indicate that the states range from those overwhelmingly Democratic in local affairs to those not quite so overwhelmingly Republican and that few states may be said to be equipped with party systems that are miniatures of the national party pattern. To a degree, state departures from the national pattern result from the fact that the states are segments of the nation. If state party systems were small-scale replicas of the national parties, the national system would differ radically from its present form.

Among one group of states apparently those factors that make them solidly one-party in national politics rebound, so to speak, upon state politics and mold it into a one-party form. This phenomenon has been most notable, of course, in the South. The Civil War gave impulse to unity in national politics to defend the peculiar regional practices against the North. To support Republicans in national affairs was to support the sectional enemy. The maintenance of partisan unity in national affairs destroyed, or at least pre-

[7] See J. K. Pollock and S. J. Eldersveld, *Michigan Politics in Transition* (Ann Arbor: University of Michigan Press, 1942), and Stephen and Vera Sarasohn, *Political Party Patterns in Michigan* (Detroit: Wayne State University Press, 1957).

vented the development of, Republican parties for the purposes of state politics. The necessities of unity against an external threat compelled a degree of unity at home. In time a technique developed by which external unity could be maintained and the conflicts of state politics could be fought out within the Democratic parties of the states. In the states of the North the war had a similar impact whose effects, though felt for decades, have by now largely worn way.

Another sort of interconnection between national and state politics may also push a state toward one-partyism. A state's social and economic characteristics may drive it toward one-partyism in both national and state affairs. To take an extreme hypothetical instance, a state dominated by industries organized by the CIO would have been in recent decades strongly Democratic nationally. It would also have probably been overwhelmingly Democratic in state affairs. Given the potency of the issues of national politics in shaping popular attitudes, the circumstances fixing the cleavages in national politics may incidentally form the divisions within state politics. Not often is a state so homogeneous in composition or attitude that it is driven to an extreme of one-partyism, although to some degree the predominant orientation on national politics operates in many states toward one-party dominance locally.

Nature of State Parties and Factions

The upshot of the foregoing analysis is that in about only a third of the states do the two major parties compete on a fairly even basis. The remainder of the states diverge in varying degrees from the two-party pattern. The net effect of the overwhelming attachment of many states to one or the other of the national parties means that, in reality, no party system exists within such states for state purposes. The great functions of parties—the construction of coalitions, the designation of candidates, the engineering of consent, the conduct of the government, and so forth—must be performed in these states in one way or another. But they are carried out by more or less amorphous institutions that are hardly the equivalent of party systems in the ordinary usage of the term. The general balance of power within the state—pro-Republican or pro-Democratic—fixes a framework within which factions, in a most bewildering variety of forms, struggle for supremacy. A description of the ins and outs of all state political systems would fill a shelf of books, but the variation among them may be indicated briefly.

VARIATIONS IN PATTERNS OF POLITICAL COMPETI- TION   For purposes of analysis—and not necessarily for purposes of precise description—the state political systems may be regarded as occupying positions on a scale. At the center of the scale the Democratic and Republican parties compete for control of the state government more or less after the fashion of the national parties. As one moves from this central point in one direction, the Democratic party becomes stronger and stronger and the functions of political parties are more and more performed by factions within that party. As one moves in the opposite direction toward the Republican end of the scale, the business of state politics comes to be carried on by factions within the Republican party. Toward the two extremes on the scale parties simply do not function in the sense of providing choices to the electorate between groups of men and sets of policies. In these states elections determine nothing; the essential decisions are made in the nominating processes of the dominant party. Yet, it should be remembered, there are more states at the Democratic than at the Republican end of the scale.

The predominance of a single party pushes back into the direct primary of that party the controlling electoral decisions of a state. In the party's primary battles, leadership may be assumed by well-defined factions, by newspapers, by groups formed around the issues of a particular primary, or by other instrumentalities that develop to carry on the business of politics when the party system is estopped from doing so. The degree to which the conflicts of state politics become intraparty battles rather than interparty struggles differs from state to state. At the extremes of Democratic strength no candidate of the lesser party has won a general election victory within the memory of any man now living. In states less thoroughly committed to a single party, the decisions of politics are commonly intraparty determinations, though occasionally the lesser party wins a general election.

These variations between the extremes of biparty competition and intraparty conflict are roughly reflected in the frequency of spirited contests within the party primaries for nominations.[8] In a general way in strongly Democratic states, the primaries for nomination of Democratic candidates for the governorship are the occasion for warmly fought contests. In the same states the Republicans, if they nominate a candidate, ordinarily must draft some soul willing to make the sacrifice rather than choose from among eager aspirants. In contrast, in strong Republican states the Democrats must exert themselves to dredge up a respectable candidate while the fireworks explode in the contest for the Republican nomination.

These differences may be shown by data on the proportion of Democratic primaries warmly fought in different groups of states. If the leader in the primary draws less than half of the primary vote, a sharp contest for the nomination has usually occurred. Here are the percentages of Democratic gubernatorial nominations (in primaries not involving incumbent governors) made over most of the life of the primary system by less than 50 per cent of the primary vote:

[8] Primary procedures and practices are treated in detail in Chapter 14.

Strong Republican states	6%
Competitive states	17
Strong Democratic states	61

In a state such as Vermont the Democratic nomination for governor goes by default. In the competitive states presumably the impulse is for party leaders to attempt to negotiate agreement on nominations and to maintain the maximum possible unity for the war against Republicans. In that group of states, as the figures show, close primary contests are infrequent. In the one-party Democratic states nearly all primaries (not involving incumbents) set off rivalry between contending candidates and factions, which is reflected in the large proportion of the primaries with less than half the primary vote to the leading aspirant for the nomination.

For the same groups of states the proportions of Democratic gubernatorial nominations made by 90–100 per cent of the primary vote present a reverse relationship. Those proportions were:

Strong Republican states	56%
Competitive states	37
Strong Democratic states	0

To be matched up with these figures are the proportions of governors Democratic in these groups of states during the period covered by the primary data:

Strong Republican states	15%
Competitive states	49
Strong Democratic states	98

Republican gubernatorial primaries show a somewhat similar variation in the incidence of competition among different groups of states.[9] In states such as Vermont, Maine, South Dakota, Iowa, and Nebraska, Republican primaries commonly are marked by sharp rivalry for the nomination which ordinarily determines who will become governor. In the southern states, on the other hand, competition for the Republican nomination, whether made by primary or by convention, is seldom spirited.

TYPES OF ONE-PARTY FACTIONALISM The foregoing analysis shows that as states deviate from the two-party pattern intraparty competition intensifies. Yet it tells us nothing about the factions that compete within the dominant party for the control of state affairs. The form and nature of those factions change from time to time within individual states and at

[9] For the states included in the groupings in the text and for the measures used in defining the groups, see V. O. Key, Jr., *American State Politics: An Introduction* (New York: Knopf, 1956), p. 109.

a particular moment differ enormously among the states. The data do not suffice for a systematic classification of state political structures; nevertheless, a few examples will illustrate differing types of situations.

The factional systems of a few one-party states in reality seem to be party systems within the dominant party. That is to say, two groups develop, each with a recognizable policy orientation and each with an organizational hierarchy, which fight it out in the direct primaries much after the fashion of the parties in a two-party system. Moreover, in a few instances this informal party-system-within-a-party has maintained an existence over a considerable period of time.

Louisiana has had such a bifactional system. The battles between Huey Long and the conservative elements of the state precipitated the formation of the Long and anti-Long Democratic factions which have lived long after the circumstances of their origin. A major factor in their longevity seems to be that they rest on durable differences of interest and attitude which might, in other places and circumstances, find expression through groups organized as parties rather than as intraparty factions. Huey Long, though treated in the national press as a buffoon and an ordinary southern demagogue, made an effective appeal to the less-favored classes and rewarded their loyalties with programs of concrete action. His successors continued that broad policy orientation, while the conservative interests of the state rallied around whoever happened to be the anti-Long leader of the moment. The two sets of factional leaders constructed popular followings with a relatively high degree of continuity from primary to primary. The popular cleavage resembled that between Republicans and Democrats in two-party states, and in presidential politics Republican support came predominantly from the conservative anti-Long faction.[10]

A factional system such as has existed within the Louisiana Democratic party presents to the electorate about as clear a choice between policy alternatives as does a two-party system. In effect, for purposes of state politics, a bifactional instead of a biparty system operates. Not often do intraparty factional groupings of one-party states have an equivalent degree of stability and differentiation. In North Carolina over a period of several decades, organization and anti-organization factions competed for control of the state, each developing its strongest and most cohesive following in specific sections of the state. These followings had a fairly high degree of persistence and continuity through time as may be inferred from the maps in Figure 11.3, which indicate the areas of highest support for organization candidates in primaries from 1912 to 1948. The structure of the North Carolina organization following was probably fixed to a degree by the strength in county elections of Republicans in the western part of the state. Democrats in a minority locally or seriously

[10] See A. P. Sindler, *Huey Long's Louisiana* (Baltimore: Johns Hopkins Press, 1956).

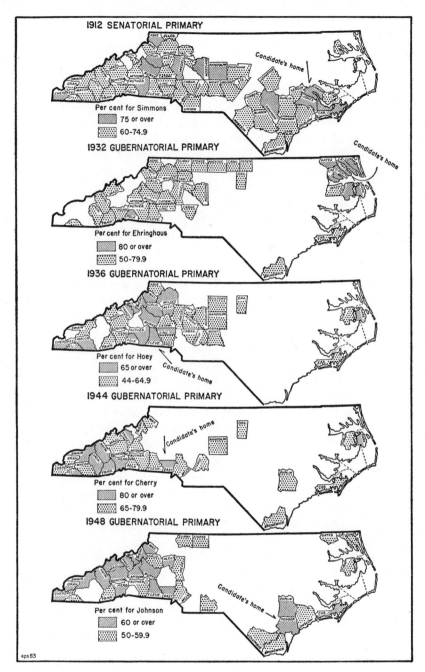

Figure 11.3   Persistence of factions within a one-party state: Points of highest strength of "organization" candidates in North Carolina Democratic primaries, 1912–1948

threatened by the Republicans have an incentive to unite under central leadership in the intraparty struggles for control of the Democratic party and of the state.

North Dakota for many years had a clear-cut bifactional system within the Republican party. The Nonpartisan League and the Republican Organizing Committee regularly held conventions, framed platforms, and designated slates of candidates to be supported in the primaries for the Republican nomination. The Nonpartisan League drew its heaviest popular support in the southern and western sections of the state, areas, on the whole, of a less prosperous agriculture than the strongholds of the Republican Organizing Committee in the eastern section of the state. The ROC had urban commercial support and appealed to conservative people generally. The NPL-ROC cleavage also to some extent paralleled ethnic differences in the state with those of Germanic origin preponderantly aligned with the NPL, while Scandinavians tended more toward the ROC. Their economic outlook pulled many NPL followers toward the Democratic party nationally while their noninterventionist foreign policy views attracted them to the isolationist wing of the Republican party. In 1956 the NPL convention decided to enter its candidates for state office in the Democratic party, a move resisted by the older generation of the League. That step may, or may not, turn out to have marked the beginning of the development of a dual party competition in state affairs.

A state may be overwhelmingly attached to one party or another and yet lack well-organized, stable, and continuing factions. In such states the lines that divide the voters in one primary election may differ radically from the dividing lines in the next primary. The electorate appears to be fluid and amorphous and the leadership cliques poorly defined and certainly not perceived by the electorate as differentiated and competing groups. At widely separated moments of tension similar cleavages may recur in a mapping of the division of the primary vote, but these clusters of voters soon dissolve and are replaced by other groupings around the candidates of the day.[11] In such states it can scarcely be said that factions that are the equivalent of political parties exist within parties.

Still another type of factionalism tends to develop in the dominant parties of states that have a substantial minority-party vote.[12] These states are characterized by a pseudo-dualism; while the parties compete on fairly even terms in the popular vote, only rarely does the minority party win. Kentucky could be regarded as a state with a pseudo-dualism, but without a minority suffi-

[11] See H. J. Doherty, Jr., "Liberal and Conservative Voting Patterns in Florida," *Journal of Politics*, 14 (1952), 403–17; M. B. Parsons, "Quasi-Partisan Conflict in a One-Party Legislative System: The Florida Senate, 1947–1961," *American Political Science Review*, 56 (1962), 605–14.

[12] See John H. Fenton, *Politics in the Border States* (New Orleans: Hauser, 1956). On Republican factionalism in Wisconsin, see Leon D. Epstein, *Politics in Wisconsin* (Madison: University of Wisconsin Press, 1958).

ciently strong to compel unity within the dominant party. Republican capture of the governorship is rare. The major battles of state politics take place between Democratic factions. Now and then, though, Democrats are unable to bridge their differences and a Republican slips into office at the general election. Fenton has described this type of pattern as a three-party system. Until the Democratic party gained strength in the 1950's, Pennsylvania was a state with a pseudo-dualism in which Republicans usually won the governorship and the determinative battles were fought out between Republican factions.

All these illustrations do not add up to a comprehensive classification of types of one-party systems; rather, they suffice to underpin the proposition that the term "one-party state" covers diverse types of organization of political power and leadership. Further investigation would identify other types of subparty groups and would make the general impression far more complex than the preceding paragraphs show it to be.

BASES OF BIPARTY STRUCTURES   The party systems of well under half the states resemble the national party system. In these states the outcome of the general election is frequently unpredictable and the vital electoral choices are made between parties rather than between rival leaders of factions of a single party. The internal struggles within the parties of such states may be bitter, but their outcome does not settle the question of who is to control the state government.

Although some one-party states (in state affairs) tend to be competitive in presidential voting, by and large those factors that make a state competitive nationally also push toward the development of a dual pattern in state politics. The fundamental prerequisite is the existence of two complexes of interest with sufficiently divergent objectives to permit them to serve as the foundations for competing parties. Those "interests" need not be solely economic but may have an ethnic or religious tinge. The impulse to political division between such complexes within a state may, of course, be repressed by the heritages of history which happen to deter the formation of party cleavages paralleling those of the nation.

One of the most common foundations for two-party competition within individual states is that of the metropolis against the countryside. This is only a convenient shorthand description of a complex political pattern. Metropolis and country do not align solidly against each other. Ramparts are not erected where country meets city to divide the state sharply into two political groups. Rather, the typical pattern is that more than half the metropolitan electorate leans in one direction, whereas more than half the rural population leans in the other. Moreover, the urban-rural cleavage approaches in reality a group cleavage with urban-industrial wage earners opposing propertied groups both urban and rural. Often factors of religion and of ethnic origin also underlie

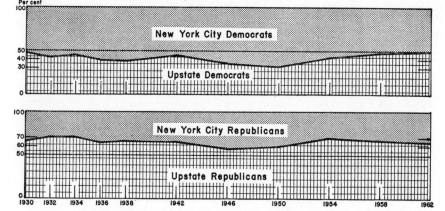

Figure 11.4   Metropolitan base of Democratic party and upstate base of Republican party in New York: Percentage division of vote polled by gubernatorial candidates of each party between New York City and upstate, 1930–1962

the rural-urban differences. Yet the chances are that, independently of such factors, metropolitan and nonmetropolitan ways of life generate political differences.[13]

New York State represents a party system built on metropolitan and non-metropolitan bases, as well as one that manifests in state affairs no small degree of independence from national political trends. In New York State campaigns the Democratic metropolitan stronghold yields over half the vote for Democratic gubernatorial candidates. On the other hand the Republican gubernatorial vote is similarly weighted by reliance on the faithful Republican vote of upstate towns, villages, and rural areas. The division of Democratic and Republican vote between New York City and upstate in gubernatorial elections during the period 1930–1962 is shown in Figure 11.4. The chart does not indicate the full extent to which the party cleavage approaches the rural-urban grouping, since both urban and rural upstate are lumped together.

New York's party structure illustrates some of the moderating influences built into the two-party system. Neither party can hope to succeed by advocat-

[13] For an attempt to identify the factors associated with varying degrees of party competitiveness, see R. T. Golembiewski, "A Taxonomic Approach to State Political Party Strength," *Western Political Quarterly*, 11 (1958), 494–513. Also R. H. Salisbury, "Missouri Politics and State Political Systems," Missouri Political Science Association, *Research, Papers 1958*; Heinz Eulau, "The Ecological Basis of Party Systems: The Case of Ohio," *Midwest Journal of Political Science*, 1 (1957), 125–35; R. S. Friedman, "The Urban-Rural Conflict Revisited," *Western Political Quarterly*, 14 (1961), 481–95; T. A. Flinn, "Continuity and Change in Ohio Politics," *Journal of Politics*, 24 (1962), 521–44; T. W. Casstevens and C. Press, "The Context of Democratic Competition in American State Politics," *American Journal of Sociology*, 68 (1963), 536–43.

ing without restraint the cause of its own hard core. During a long period of Democratic control of the governorship by Alfred E. Smith, Franklin D. Roosevelt, and Herbert H. Lehman, the interests of New York City were not neglected. Yet to win the state these leaders had to dissociate themselves from Tammany Hall sufficiently to allay upstate suspicion. To win they had to hold their own in the City and at the same time recruit upstate support. In the process the Democratic program became considerably more than a City program. In turn, Thomas E. Dewey had the strong upstate Republican vote to build on, but he also needed to wean City voters from their Democratic predilections. In the process of playing both ends against the middle, Dewey became a governor scarcely fitting the caricature of a reactionary Republican. In 1950 Dewey could boast of his program of rent control, public housing, fair employment practices, public health services, and other measures that Washington Democrats might claim as their own. Moreover, he interpreted his election that year as a mandate for state development of St. Lawrence power.[14] Similarly, Governor Rockefeller took positions that enabled him to attract sufficient metropolitan support to win.

In several other states the metropolitan-rural cleavage underlies a two-party competition for state control. In Illinois, Chicago and Cook County Democratic strength contributes disproportionately to the Democratic state vote, while the Republican vote has been more predominantly a downstate vote. In Massachusetts the Democrats of metropolitan Boston are pitted against the Yankee Republicans of the remainder of the state. In Michigan bipartisan competition has its Democratic bastion in Detroit, while the Republicans draw more heavily on the outstate.

In some states the metropolitan-rural pattern is confused by the existence of two or more metropolitan centers, a factor that probably operates to make more difficult the management of the Democratic forces. In Missouri the Democrats have had strong support in St. Louis and Kansas City, a metropolitan base diluted within the party by rural Democratic enclaves including "Little Dixie," a transplantation from the states further to the south. Connecticut represents an instance of a two-party state with no dominant metropolis but with a Democratic party that relies heavily on several major urban centers, as the rural and village areas remain preponderantly Republican.

Emphasis on the urban-rural foundations of party competition obscures a complex reality. Often, especially in the Northeast, the urban-rural confrontation merely masks a system of rivalries among the ethnic subdivisions of polyglot populations. These ethnic differences tend to be associated with socioeconomic status as well as with residence. Typically the party battle is pictured as conflict between Yankee Protestant and immigrant Catholic. Yet Republicans in Massachusetts and Rhode Island, for example, make strenuous, and

[14] See Warren Moscow, *Politics in the Empire State* (New York: Knopf, 1948), chs. 5–6.

sometimes successful, efforts to capitalize on Italo-American restiveness with Irish domination of the Democratic party. Both states have had Republican governors of Italian origin. On the other hand, Republicans manage to control New Hampshire without much genuflection to the Irish or the French-Canadians, groups whose squabbles within the Democratic party keep it impotent.[15]

SIGNIFICANCE OF FORMS OF POLITICAL STRUCTURE

What are the consequences of these variations among the states in the organization of political activity? The question cannot be answered with much confidence; estimation of the effects of institutional arrangements belongs to the realm of art rather than precise measurement. Moreover, given the extreme variety in types of situations, generalization is most difficult. Yet a few more or less educated guesses may be made.

Exceptions exist and the situation may differ from time to time even within the same state, yet as states deviate from the two-party pattern certain circumstances may tend to develop. First, the electorate may be presented with confusing and unclear alternatives as it is compelled to make the controlling decisions by choosing among individual leaders within the dominant party. A choice between party labels, each with a tradition and record behind it, may differ radically from a choice between aspirants for nomination identified with no policy tendency and running with no identifiable crowd of politicians.

The process of decision in the primaries of the dominant party also may introduce an element of pure chance into the electoral process. When three or more candidates seek a nomination, the peculiarities of their individual followings, the consequences of low electoral turnout, and the interactions among their candidacies may make the decision quite like a lottery. Election by lot may or may not be damaging in particular situations.

Another set of consequences may flow from the depressed condition of the minority party. So certain is it to be defeated that it attracts an inadequate leadership, a circumstance that redounds to the general disadvantage when a landslide happens to throw it into office. By the same token, the second party becomes unable to perform effectively the vital function of criticism of the government. That activity may be carried on through internal squabbles within the majority, but greater effectiveness may be expected from an ably manned, institutionalized second party with a vested interest in exposing the weaknesses and abuses of the majority.

Differing patterns of competition, whether they be interparty or intraparty, also have differing consequences for the substance of public policy. The difficulty comes in establishing what those varying consequences are. The ex-

---

[15] See Duane Lockard, *New England State Politics* (Princeton: Princeton University Press, 1959). See also Frank H. Jonas (ed.), *Western Politics* (Salt Lake City: University of Utah Press, 1961).

pectation from general democratic theory would be that competition between leadership cliques for mass support would tend to result in the adoption of policies for mass benefit. Over the long run such results may accrue, yet the conditions necessary for such results in the short run do not always exist. Imperfections in the flow of information, frailties in political leadership, the unremitting efforts of special interests to protect or advance their causes, the capacity of side issues to divert the electorate, and other factors may affect the character and results of competition. Political competition may be a condition precedent to government in the popular interest; it does not invariably produce that result.

Legislative Apportionment and Party Government

State parties differ radically in the degree to which they approximate the two-party pattern. State political systems also diverge sharply from the national model in another respect. The institutional apparatus into which the state parties are fitted obstructs party government. Often Democrats win the governorship of a state, but one house or both houses of the legislature may be beyond their reach. In fewer states the Republicans can on occasion place their gubernatorial candidate into office but are unable to capture majorities of both houses of the state legislature. This assurance of divided partisan control of state government flows in part from institutional factors such as the manner of distribution of legislative seats and, perhaps to a degree, from the nature of the party systems themselves. Whatever the cause, the consequence is that party government cannot operate in accord with the conventional conceptions in many states much of the time. The mechanism of government does not permit party government but, in effect, puts teeth into the doctrine of checks and balances by assigning different branches of the government to different parties.

DIVISION OF PARTISAN CONTROL OF STATE GOVERN- MENT The hornbook theory of American parties runs to the effect that the party system overcomes the obstacles to governance in the separation of powers. A single party captures the executive and majorities in the legislative houses, and extraconstitutional collaboration of fellow partisans directs the legislative and executive powers along the same path.

In the practice of state government this theory seldom nicely fits the facts. In one-party states the minority party is so weakly represented that the function of legislative organization and leadership falls to whatever factions develop a majority within the dominant party. In states with two-party competition the governmental machinery is so contrived that opposing parties often control the executive and the legislature. Or the party in opposition to the governor controls one house of the legislature. Legislation becomes a process of interparty negotiation or perhaps interparty warfare rather than one of the execution of a party program.

The tendency toward partisan division of control of the executive and legislature seems to be most marked in those states that most nearly approximate the two-party pattern in the organization of their politics.[16] In New York, for example, Republicans are virtually assured of legislative majorities by constitutional law. In Connecticut the overrepresentation of the small towns makes it probable that a Democratic governor will have to deal with a Republican lower house, even though his party may control the senate.

The extent of division of partisan control in state governments varies in the different stages of the political cycle. The imperfect meshing of party and constitutional system becomes most marked in eras when Democrats enjoy popular favor. Their gubernatorial candidates may attract sufficient popular support to go into office at such times, but the simultaneous elections of state legislatures yield Republican majorities. On the other hand, as popular sentiment shifts toward the Republican party its gubernatorial candidates are more likely to carry into office with themselves legislative majorities of their own party.

The extent of divided partisan control of state governments and the differentials in legislative opposition faced by Democratic and Republican governors are shown for a group of 17 fairly competitive states in the panels in Figure 11.5. The curves in the lower panel reflect the marked spread between the numbers of states electing Democratic governors and the numbers simultaneously placing Democratic majorities into control of the legislature over the period 1928–1960.[17] The upper panel indicates the relative infrequency with which Republican governors in the same group of states have to cope with whatever problems arise from opposition majorities in the legislatures. Probably the sound general rule is that the lesser party, be it Democratic or Republican, may expect to be more successful in electing governors than in winning legislative majorities. Occasionally Kentucky and Maryland elect a Republican governor but he commonly has to deal with a Democratic legislature. In a greater number of states Democrats find themselves in the relative power position of the Republicans in the states mentioned.

[16] In one-party states control of the governorship and of the legislature rests nominally in the hands of the same party, but often there may be a situation equivalent to partisan division in two-party states. One party faction may control the governorship and another may be strong in the legislature. In many state legislatures the lesser party is too weakly represented to be much of a factor in the legislative process. After the 1960 elections, in 19 states the minority had no more than 30 per cent of the seats in either legislative house.

[17] The states analyzed in the figure were Colorado, Connecticut, Illinois, Indiana, Maryland, Massachusetts, Michigan, Missouri, Montana, New Jersey, New York, Nevada, Ohio, Rhode Island, Utah, Washington, and Wyoming.

Number

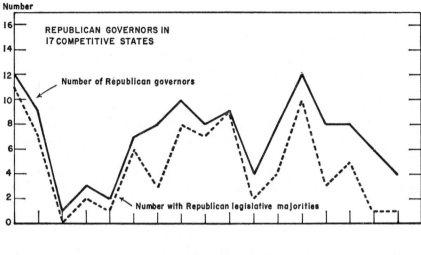

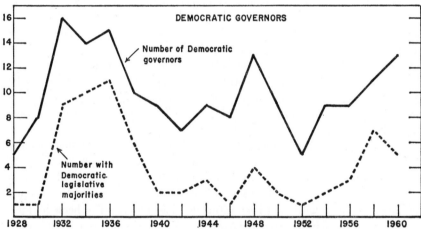

*Figure 11.5   Division of governorship and legislative control be-
tween parties in seventeen "competitive" states, 1928–1960*

FACTORS CONDUCIVE TO DIVIDED CONTROL   While
the gerrymander accounts in large degree for split party control of state governments, other factors share responsibility for this condition. On rare occasions the electorate for good and sufficient reason deliberately chooses
divided control. The general trend may be toward the Republican ticket, say,
but the voters, or enough of them to control the decision, reject the Republican
gubernatorial candidate. Over a long period of time in Ohio, Democratic
gubernatorial candidates have succeeded in winning against Republican presidential and legislative tides. In the 1920's Vic Donahey and in the 1940's and

1950's Frank J. Lausche won majorities time and again as the rest of the Democratic ticket went down to defeat. It may be assumed that the voters knew what they were doing in these elections.

More commonly, divided control rests on a distribution of legislative seats that makes it impossible for a Democratic popular majority to elect a Democratic legislative majority. To some extent this consequence results from the concentration of Democratic voters in the metropolitan centers. There they may carry legislative seats by top-heavy majorities. Were their strength more widely distributed, the same number of popular votes would yield a larger number of seats by smaller margins.

More significant than the incidental consequences of geographic concentration of Democratic voters is discrimination against cities in the allocation of legislative seats. Insofar as Democratic-Republican lines parallel urban-rural lines, discrimination against cities in legislative representation falls on the Democratic party. Underrepresentation of cities comes about through several methods, all of which are loosely described as gerrymanders. Narrowly defined, the term "gerrymander" refers to the deliberate formation of legislative districts in such a way as to gain partisan advantage in the composition of the legislative body. If district boundaries are drawn in the appropriate manner, one Republican (or Democrat) can be made to grow where two flourished before, and at the same time district equality in population may be maintained. Such ingenious exercises in political geography are not so significant as are applications of general rules of representation that give advantage to rural areas.

Some state constitutions explicitly recognize territory rather than population as the basis for representation. In New Jersey, for example, each county elects one senator, and a majority of the senate may be made up of senators from counties including only 15 per cent of the state's population. Equal representation of counties has been rationalized as a "federal" scheme by false analogy with the national Senate. A number of states employ a modification of the system of equal representation of territorial units; the constitution declares that representation shall be allocated among counties in accordance with population but hastens to provide that each county shall be entitled to at least one of a fixed number of representatives. In North Carolina, to illustrate, the 120 members of the lower house are apportioned among the counties according to population, except that each county is entitled to at least one representative, a proviso that gives the populous counties less than a proportionate share of the legislative seats. Some state constitutions specifically limit the representation of the metropolis of the state. In Pennsylvania no city or county is permitted to elect more than one-sixth of the senators, a provision adopted to limit the influence of Philadelphia. However discrimination in representation is accomplished, the result is a restriction of the strength of the larger cities in the legislatures and, in most states outside the South, an artificial limitation of Democratic legislative representation.[18]

DISCRIMINATION IN REPRESENTATION AND POPULAR GOVERNMENT   A consequence of the institutional systems that have been described is that in many states much of the time the political party cannot perform its supposed function of casting a net of unity over the separated organs of government. With one party in control of the legislature and the nominee of another in the governor's chair, the legislative process may become stalemated; [19] partisan bickering may be the rule; and action may be the result of negotiation between opposing party leaders, a condition that may or may not be conducive to the general good.

Yet the effects of institutional depressants of party government cannot be estimated solely from observation of the workings of state governments in which parties share control. The effects must to a high degree be surmised from guesses about what does not come about because of that condition. The course of politics in many states involves fairly regular victory for a single party. At intervals an exasperated public withdraws its favor from the dominant party, but its discontent finds only partial expression, for at least one house of the legislature remains beyond the reach of such movements of sentiment. In effect, the electorate cannot completely dislodge one crowd from control of the state government and replace it by another. Hence the occasional powerful movements for reform or for change tend to be frustrated by institutional blockades. Those interests committed to negativism gain advantage by the institutional rules of the game.[20] The phenomenon gains in significance when it is recalled that these obstructions to action are characteristic of most of the more populous states.

The high incidence of divided party control of state governments makes it essential that techniques be developed for the conduct of public business across party lines; otherwise states would be completely paralyzed. A wide range of state questions arouses no sharp partisan divisions, and the degree of

[18] For a comprehensive analysis of the extent of malapportionment in the states, see Paul T. David and Ralph Eisenberg, *Devaluation of the Urban and Suburban Vote* (Charlottesville: Bureau of Public Administration, University of Virginia, 1961). In 1962, in Baker *v.* Carr, a case originating in Tennessee, the Supreme Court opened the door to federal judicial challenge against state legislative gerrymanders. If the case should lead to widespread reapportionment, the long-run consequences for state politics would be most significant. See M. E. Jewell (ed.), *The Politics of Reapportionment* (New York: Atherton, 1962).

[19] See N. S. Thomas, *et al.*, *Parties and Politics in Michigan* (Ann Arbor: Michigan Citizenship Clearing House, 1961).

[20] Alfred E. Smith, in the New York Constitutional Convention, charged that upstate Republicans, overrepresented in the legislature, had "opposed every progressive piece of legislation proposed in this State in the last generation." New York State Constitutional Convention, 1938, *Revised Record*, IV, 2881–84.

cohesion within party groups also differs greatly from state legislature to state legislature. Yet it is clear that the systems of representation and the divisions of party control dictate the nature of state action or inaction on a goodly number of basic issues. The constitutional or statutory apportionment of the legislative membership settles, or at least fundamentally conditions, the decision on those questions that divide the parties.[21]

States and the Tides of National Politics

Another broad factor powerfully conditions the operations of political systems within the states. The great tides of presidential politics tend to engulf the affairs of states and often to determine the results of state elections. The Democratic party may win control of a state as it rides into office on the coattails of a popular presidential candidate and through no merit of its program or its candidate. So may the Republican party gain state victory. Either party may be unceremoniously booted from office by the sweeps of national politics. Obviously the intrusion of extraneous factors obstructs the maintenance of a state politics with a focus on state affairs.

CYCLES IN PARTY CONTROL OF GOVERNORSHIPS The interlocking of state and national politics is by no means tight. The one-party Democratic states of the South have a capacity in their local affairs to resist Republican landslides. In these states no Republican governors rode into office with General Eisenhower in 1952; nor did Herbert Hoover's coattails in 1928 have sufficient pulling power to upset Democratic governors in these states. At the Republican end of the spectrum only Vermont has shown an equivalent capacity to resist national Democratic tides.

With these major exceptions, a striking interlocking of state and national voting occurs, a relationship that appears most clearly from the behavior of state politics over a long period. When a region shifts its political preferences from Democratic to Republican, the presidential results, the elections to the House of Representatives, and the choices of governors tend to move in the same direction. Republicans replace Democrats, or vice versa, in about the same proportions. While both state and national voting may, in these great swings, be responsive to common causes, to some extent voting on state and local offices represents a more or less automatic extension of strong preferences or dislikes in national politics. The pervasive effect of national politics

[21] See W. Duane Lockard, "Legislative Politics in Connecticut," *American Political Science Review*, 48 (1954), 166–73; W. J. Keefe, "Party Government and Law-making in the Illinois General Assembly," *Northwestern University Law Review*, 47 (1952), 55–71; W. J. Keefe, "Parties, Partisanship, and Public Policy in the Pennsylvania Legislature," *American Political Science Review*, 48 (1954), 450–64; M. E. Jewell, "Party Voting in American State Legislatures," *American Political Science Review*, 49 (1955), 773–91.

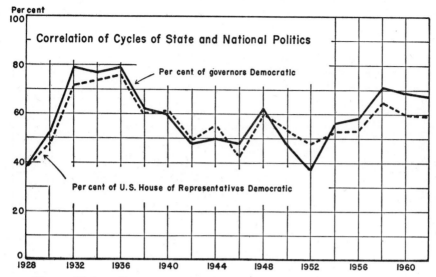

Figure 11.6   Percentage of U.S. House of Representatives and of governors Democratic, 1928–1962

becomes patent when inconspicuous state and local candidates, hidden away far down the ballot, ride into—or are ousted from—office with the movement of the national pendulum.

The graphs in Figure 11.6 picture the interrelation over one great swing of the political cycle between the results of elections to state governorships and to the national House of Representatives. The proportionate division of these posts between the two maor parties varies with the ebb and flow of popular preferences. The actual shifts between parties of both House seats and governorships, of course, tend to be concentrated geographically in the areas of relatively close party competition. Given the division of states extreme in their partisan attachments, Democratic peaks in the cycle leave the Republicans in control of fewer governorships than the Democrats hold when Republican strength nationally is at its highest point.

CORRELATION   IN   STATE   AND   NATIONAL   VOTING
The common subjection of state and national politics to the great fluctuations in the fortunes of the parties is made clear by the comparison of the results of state and national elections over long periods of time as was done in Figure 11.6. The interlocking of voting for candidates at the two levels of government may also be seen from an analysis of the voting at a single election.

A sample election chosen to indicate the character of this interrelationship is analyzed in the scatter-diagram in Figure 11.7, which shows the

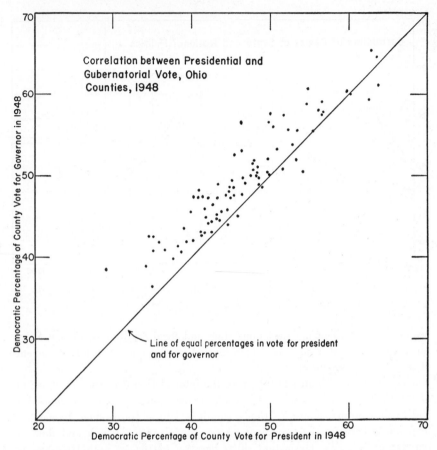

Figure 11.7   Relation of Democratic percentage of presidential vote and Democratic percentage of gubernatorial vote in Ohio counties, 1948

relationship between the proportions of the vote in each Ohio county polled by Harry Truman and by the Democratic candidate for governor, Frank Lausche, in 1948. A fairly close relationship prevailed from county to county in the strength of the two candidates. In those counties in which Truman showed his greatest pulling power his gubernatorial running mate also drew his heaviest vote. On the other hand, as Truman's strength declined, so did Mr. Lausche's. The diagram also indicates that in most counties Mr. Lausche ran somewhat ahead of Mr. Truman, a fact probably reflective of Mr. Lausche's peculiar strength in the state rather than of Mr. Truman's weakness.

A diagram such as that in Figure 11.7 gives a minimum impression of the degree of ticket-splitting. It reflects only the net splitting in each county. That is, some Democratic presidential voters doubtless supported the Republican candidate for governor but they were exceeded by the Dewey voters who either did not mark their ballot for governor or supported the Democratic candidate. From the examination of many such diagrams, the impression builds up that presidential voting preferences are more volatile than are those in state and local elections. A presidential candidate may run ahead of his state ticket or he may fall behind, depending on the trend of his party's fortunes nationally. Great movements of voters from one party to the other in national elections do not in the same degree dislodge people from their customary predilections in state politics.[22]

SEPARATION OF STATE AND NATIONAL POLITICS   Designers of state governmental systems have on the whole held that some way ought to be devised to separate state from national politics. Their assumption has been that the settlement of the debates of national politics should not also fix more or less automatically the outcomes of state elections. Often the argument runs to the effect that there is no Republican or Democratic way to run a state government; the questions are mainly those of honesty and efficiency. It seems more accurate to say that, at least in domestic matters, people tend to divide in roughly the same way on the broad issues of state and national politics. Straight-ticket voting in principle may make sense, although from time to time a worthy citizen may be well advised to vote against an incompetent or a crook who happens to win his party's nomination for governor.

Despite the interlocking in the movements of party strength on both the state and national levels, the electorate often manages to make an effective separation of its choices of presidential and state candidates. The Democrats, under the leadership of Alfred E. Smith and Franklin D. Roosevelt, controlled the governorship of the state of New York during an era when Republican presidential candidates were rolling up big majorities in the state. Thomas E. Dewey and his Republican followers managed to control the state government during a period when the Democratic presidential candidates usually carried the state.

In the strongly one-party states the outcome of the gubernatorial election almost certainly will be the same as in the presidential elections, but in states with a semblance of a two-party system, split results are by no means uncommon. The narrower the popular margin by which a presidential candidate carries, a state, the greater is the probability that enough votes will be split to give the gubernatorial victory to the opposing party. An analysis of gu-

[22] From the inspection of these relationships in many elections, the impression also develops that the interconnection between presidential and gubernatorial voting has been declining over the past half-century.

bernatorial elections over the period 1932–1950, presented in Table 11.2, demonstrates the point. In those states carried by Democratic presidential candidates by less than a 5 per cent margin, about one-half of the governors elected simultaneously were Republicans.

Table 11.2   Two-year governors outside the South, chosen in presidential years and in off years, 1932–1950, related to Democratic percentage of state presidential vote [a]

Democratic Presidential Percentage	Number of State Elections	Per Cent of Governors Democratic	
		Presidential Years	Following Off Years
Under 45	10	20.0 [b]	20.0
45–49	17	29.4	17.6
50–54	20	55.0	25.0
55–59	21	90.5	57.1
60 or more	15	93.3 [c]	80.0

[a] States and elections analyzed: Arizona, Colorado, Connecticut, Idaho (through 1946), Iowa, Kansas, Maine, Massachusetts, Michigan, Minnesota, Nebraska, New Mexico, New York (through 1938), North Dakota (except 1936–1938), Ohio, Rhode Island, South Dakota, Wisconsin (except 1932–1942), and Wyoming (1932–1934).

[b] The deviant states in this cell were Maine in 1932 and North Dakota in 1940.

[c] The deviant state in this cell was North Dakota, which elected Wm. Langer as its Republican governor in 1932.

In the close states presidentially, the circumstances thus permit the electorate to discriminate between presidential and gubernatorial candidates, or so it would seem from the relationships that appear in Table 11.2. In fact, probably what happens in the main is that the party entrenched in power in a state has, by virtue of the organization built up over a long period, a capacity to resist the effects of national tides. The more forceful the swing against it nationally, the less are the chances that the dominant party locally will survive the impact. Republican state organizations, while they might not have been able to deliver the state against Roosevelt or Truman, often managed to hold power themselves. Similarly, some Democratic organizations held state control in 1952 and 1956 although Eisenhower rode to an easy presidential victory in their bailiwicks. The capacity of the prevailing state organization to survive is suggested by the right-hand column of Table 11.2. The data there show that in the period covered by the table Republican candidates recaptured gubernatorial posts in the off years when there was no presidential campaign and when the national sweep was not running against them.

The greater separability of state and national questions in the off years has led some states to schedule their gubernatorial elections in those years. The justification of this arrangement is that it permits the affairs of state politics to proceed unembarrassed by the considerations of national campaigns. In fact, the arrangement seems to give advantage in state elections to the candidates of the party that does not control the national government, as may be seen from the data in Table 11.3. That table compares, in relation-

Table 11.3   Four-year governors outside the South, chosen in presidential years and in off years, 1932–1950, related to Democratic percentage of state presidential vote [a]

Democratic Presidential Percentage	Presidential Years		Off Years [b]	
	Governors Elected	Per Cent Democratic	Governors Elected	Per Cent Democratic
45–49	5	40.0	6	33.3
50–54	10	40.0	13	23.1
55–59	15	80.0	4	50.0
60 and over	10	100.0	11	63.6

[a] The states electing governors in presidential years covered by the table were Delaware, Illinois, Indiana, Missouri, Montana, Utah, Washington, and West Virginia. The off-year states were California, Idaho, Maryland, Nevada, New York, Oregon, Pennsylvania, and Wyoming. Some of these states elected in the off years only for a part of the period 1932–1950.

[b] The off-year states are grouped according to their presidential vote in the preceding presidential election. The two groups of gubernatorial elections compared are thus, of course, elections in different states with similar Democratic presidential margins. Apart from the fact that few cases are involved, it should be kept in mind that factors in addition to the presidential division affect the results of the gubernatorial elections.

ship to the margin in the presidential voting, the results of gubernatorial elections in states choosing governors for four-year terms in presidential years and in another group of states electing governors for four years in nonpresidential years. In a Democratic era nationally, off-year scheduling of state elections gave advantage to Republican gubernatorial candidates.

On the other hand, Democrats gain advantage from off-year election scheduling in the days of Republican triumph nationally. Constitution makers have not invariably realized that off-year scheduling may have one effect at one time and another at a later time. During the years of Democratic dominance, Republicans in several states initiated movements for constitutional reform and managed to time gubernatorial elections so that their candidates were relieved, in effect, of the inconvenience of running against Franklin D. Roosevelt. Among the converts to the four-year term were Connecticut and New York. In the off year of 1954, Mr. Harriman in New York and Mr. Ribicoff in Connecticut eked out Democratic victories which would have doubtless been beyond their reach had they been running against a ticket with General Eisenhower at its head. In 1954 also, the Democrats carried Pennsylvania, another four-year state, a feat that would have been most difficult to accomplish had the General been on the ticket.

While it seems evident that different results in the presidential and gubernatorial voting within states flow in part from the capacity of state party organizations to withstand the impact of the presidential swing, it should not be supposed that this is an automatic braking effect. On occasion the people of a state may have ample provocation to rise up and indignantly and deliberately throw a governor out of office even though his party ticket as a whole rides to an overwhelming victory. For example, in Ohio, Mr. Lausche survived the Eisenhower tide, but he was a rather dilute Democrat, in many respects not unlike the General in the style and orientation of his politics.

EFFECTS OF ISOLATION OF STATE POLITICS   Governmental gadgets designed to shield state politics from the blasts of the national political conflict have a superficial appeal. On its face, the theory that the electorates of states should be encouraged to focus their attention on state questions when voting in state elections is eminently reasonable. Yet to the extent that states can be isolated from national affairs, one-party dominance of states is probably facilitated. The minor party, deprived of the pulling power of its victorious national ticket, remains a minor party. The long-run strengthening of the lesser party would probably be aided by an occasional victory in a national landslide. Whether a strong second party in a state is desirable may be another matter. Yet in most states the lesser party sooner or later does win in a national landslide, and the better equipped it is with competent leadership the less disturbing may be the consequences of coattail victories.

Political Paralysis and the Role of the States

The analyses of the organization of state political systems cumulate into the conclusion that the states tend toward a structure of political leadership that is hamstrung if not paralyzed. The overwhelming commitment of many states to one or the other of the national parties is associated with a one-partyism within the states, a form of organization that confuses popular decision and handicaps political initiative. Many state elections seem to be decided by the more or less fortuitous impact of the external forces of national politics. When the foundations and impulses toward an effective party system exist, they are likely to be obstructed by institutional devices contrived to make energetic government impractical.

One broad consequence of the ineffectiveness of state political leadership appears to be an encouragement of federal centralization. Even though a matter may be within both the constitutional competence and the fiscal capacity of the states, unless adequate political initiative exists within the states no action may be taken. The fact that some groups are virtually blocked from winning control of a state government, even though they may command a popular majority, moves them to take their case to Congress. Those groups tend to be associated with the Democratic parties of the states, against which the institutional depressants operate with special rigor. To be sure, the characteristics of political organization within the states are by no means solely responsible for the march of authority to Washington. Given the national character of the organization of the economy, a broad range of matters is beyond the capacity of the states. Yet within that area in which state action remains feasible, political organization prone to inaction prevents a realization of the potentialities of state action and encourages movements for federal action.

A federal system may have inherent difficulties for the practice of popular government within its constituent units. At least when national questions overshadow those in the competence of the states, one consequence may be, as has been argued, the warping of state political systems into forms not so well adapted as they might be to the necessities of popular government. Even beyond that infirmity, in the competition of two levels of popular government for popular attention and interest, that concerned with the more dramatic issues would be expected to be salient in public awareness. Questions within the national jurisdiction have come more and more over the decades to monopolize popular attention, a circumstance that probably affects the quality of state government and administration.

The consequences for state government of the types of organization of state politics that have been described may be most grave at moments of crisis. Most of the time, state governments manage to perform their tasks more or less satisfactorily. Most of the time, too, no burning issues agitate the people. It is when crisis does develop, when serious questions demand attention, that the incapacity of the state political systems to act decisively and boldly has its most marked consequences for popular government. Those moments, fortunately, arise infrequently.

III

PARTY STRUCTURE
AND PROCEDURE

*Attention now shifts to another broad aspect of political
parties. In the preceding chapters the major focus was upon
their place in the process of governance, with emphasis on
the American party system. In the development of the argument the broad, special characteristics of that system were
set forth, as well as the policy orientations and composition
of its individual parties. The picture needs to be rounded
out by an examination of the machinery and procedures
parties use in the fulfillment of their roles in the governing
process. The chapters that follow will deal with the organizational apparatus of parties and with the procedures and
rituals by which they designate candidates and formulate
programs. The discussion, therefore, will be concerned more
with the work of the party professionals than with the mass
of party membership, with the apparatus for making party
decisions rather than with voters. Such organizational apparatus, sometimes called "party-outside-the-government," is
common to parties of all democratic orders, but the machinery of American parties includes features peculiar to
this country—such as direct nominating procedures—to
which special attention will be devoted.*

12.

PARTY ORGANIZATION

Organization exists to facilitate collective activity. To understand party organization one must keep in mind the functions of party. A prime function is the nomination of candidates for office. When a crowd of people first foregathered and agreed to center their support on specified candidates in an election, "party" was born. As a corollary to nomination, party has the function of mobilizing electoral support. It may formulate policy proposals, or at least put into words the policy predilections of the group. Party may serve as a link between electorate and candidates and between people and government. It is a mechanism for the attainment of power; as such it may determine who gets power, and it may influence the exercise of authority as well. These attributions of function imply that party is considered, for the moment at least, to be the comparatively small group of political activists—the "pros," the "politicians," the amateur politicians—those who devote time and effort to the business of politics. How many such persons there are can only be guessed; they surely do not number more than three or four million in an electorate of over 100,000,000.[1]

How are the political activists, however large or small their number, to perform functions of the party? This is in essence the problem of party organization. What assignments of duties are to be made? What are the relations of authority, responsibility, and leadership among the persons concerned? What are the rewards and punishments? Who makes what decisions?

---

[1] George Gallup estimates that 5,180,000 persons claimed to have "worked" in the 1954 congressional elections: 3,020,000 for the Democrats; 2,160,000 for the Republicans. Projection of survey findings indicates that in the neighborhood of 8,000,000 persons gave money or bought tickets to help the 1956 campaigns.

What procedures shall be followed in arriving at decisions for the party? In short, how are the activists to collaborate in carrying on the business of the party?

To cope in detail with such questions would require a treatment of encyclopedic dimensions. Yet broad aspects of party organization may be set out. Mechanisms for nomination are a basic element of the party apparatus. The national convention serves as the instrument for the designation of presidential and vice-presidential candidates. Through it the activists of each party select the candidates. The saying that the professionals choose the presidential candidates and the voters choose between them retains some validity. For other offices, both state and national, the prevailing mode of nomination is the direct primary, a procedure that compels the professionals, to a greater or lesser extent, to share with the rank and file in the nomination of candidates. The national convention and the direct primary will be treated in detail in succeeding chapters.

Beyond the nominating mechanisms are the party hierarchies—the "machine"—the organizations whose principal function is to mobilize voter support; they may also exert a controlling influence in the designation of candidates, whatever the formal procedure may be. The "party machine" is often described as if a military discipline prevailed from the national chairman at the peak of the hierarchy to the precinct captain at the base. That is by no means the reality. An outstanding characteristic of American party organization, viewed from the national aspect, is its decentralized nature. In a sense, no nationwide party organization exists, though each party, to be sure, has its national organs. Rather, each party consists of a working coalition of state and local organizations. The units allied together differ widely among themselves in the form and manner of their organization and operation. Yet, without becoming bogged down in the variety of state and local organizations, the general contours of the national party structure as a whole may be delineated.

Formal Party Organization

The formal organization of the party is prescribed by the rules of the national convention, by state laws, and by rules adopted by state and local party authorities. The paper organization so prescribed is rarely identical with the informal or working organization. The man with the title of chieftain may not actually be the boss and the formal structure may be moribund. Nevertheless, formal organization has its functions and informal organization is usually intertwined with it.

Party organization, like other organizations, is structured by the task to be accomplished. The major objective of party organization is the winning of elections. Hence party organization is built around the geographic divisions of the country for electoral purposes. The unit cell of the party is the precinct executive. The precinct is the basic unit of electoral administration and includes within its boundaries, on the average, several hundred voters. In the larger cities the next higher level of party organization is formed about the ward or district presided over by a leader whose jurisdiction comprises several precincts. From the wards or districts, councilmen or legislators are elected. More commonly the next higher level of party organization above the precinct is the county committee, which may consist of precinct executives or of persons chosen by them. The county is an electoral unit for a variety of purposes: the choice of county officials, often the election of state legislators, and it may even be a congressional district. The party has a state committee or state central committee whose chairman is ordinarily a party figure of some importance. The next layer of party organization is the national committee, which includes representation from each state and whose chairman ranks high among the professional politicians of his party.

The party organization is sometimes regarded as a hierarchy based on the precinct executive and capped by the national committee, but it may be more accurately described as a system of layers of organization. Each successive layer—county or city, state, national—has an independent concern about elections in its geographical jurisdiction. Yet each higher level of organization, to accomplish its ends, must obtain the collaboration of the lower layer or layers of organization. That collaboration comes about, to the extent that it does come about, through a sense of common cause rather than by the exercise of command.

NATIONAL COMMITTEES   The capstone of the formal party organization is the national committee. The Democratic national committee consists of one man and one woman from each state (plus members from territories and dependencies). The same principle governed the composition of the Republican national committee until the 1952 convention gave certain states a third member, the state party chairman. The state chairmen entitled to membership were those whose states (a) had cast their electoral votes for the Republican presidential candidate at the preceding election, (b) had a Republican majority in the state's congressional representation, that is, Senators plus Representatives, or (c) had a Republican governor. The enlargement of the committee encountered opposition from southern states, which expected to qualify less regularly for the third member on the committee than would the Republican strongholds, and from women, who lost their equality of representation on the committee with the addition of the state chairmen.[2]

In form the national convention elects the national committee to serve for four years from the adjournment of the convention. In practice the delega-

[2] 1952 Republican National Convention, *Proceedings*, pp. 278–89.

tion from each state proposes to the convention the national committee members from that state.[3] In some instances a state's convention delegation has the actual power of nomination of the national committee members. In others, the decision is made by a direct primary in the state, by a state convention, or by the state committee of the party. Often the selection of national committeemen becomes entangled with the rivalries of aspirants for the presidential nomination since they are usually designated at the same time and often by the same authority that chooses convention delegates. Thus, in the events leading to the 1952 Republican national convention, a goodly number of pro-Eisenhower men replaced pro-Taft committeemen.

Since membership on the national committee entails cost in both time and money, national committeemen tend to be men of both substance and political stature in their states. Most of them are either lawyers or businessmen; many mix law, business, and politics. The lawyer's shingle is often a cloak for a full-time dedication to politics, while some of the businessmen devote themselves to businesses peculiarly political, such as insurance. The national committeeman may be the real chief of his state party organization or his national power may be rooted in the leadership of a metropolitan center. He may be a lieutenant of the real leader of his state party, or his membership on the national committee may be a recognition by the state organization for financial support or an accolade for an elder statesman.

The duties of the national committee include direction of the presidential campaign, filling vacancies on the party ticket caused by death, maintenance and supervision of the national party headquarters, conduct of public-relations programs, raising funds, and making arrangements for the national convention. The committee fulfills many of its responsibilities either through committees or through the national chairman and his staff. Its decisions that attract most public attention are those on convention arrangements, for these actions often affect the interests of aspirants for the presidential nomination. The committee selects the convention city, issues the call for the convention, prepares a temporary roll of delegates, and recommends a slate of temporary officers. In addition, it has assumed the power to recommend permanent officers to the convention.

The meetings of the national committees bring together party chieftains from over the country and furnish opportunity for consultation, combination, and maneuver concerning the party's next nominee. If the party is in power and the President is in line for another nomination, the committee may commend his record and demand that he accept renomination. In January, 1944, for example, the Democratic national committee expressed its confidence in

[3] On rare occasions the fact that the formal power of appointment rests in the national convention rather than the state party authorities becomes of practical importance. In 1958 the Louisiana State Democratic Committee attempted to replace Camille F. Gravelle as national committeeman on the charge that he was "moderate" on the race question. The national committee refused to recognize the action.

Roosevelt and "earnestly" solicited "him to continue as the great world leader." If the party is out of power, the managers of contenders for the nomination will be on hand negotiating for support from the leaders assembled, but in such situations the national committee itself makes no formal endorsement.

Since the national conventions meet only once every four years, significant issues of national policy arise between conventions on which an expression of party policy may be desirable. The national committee derives its authority from the national convention which gives it no mandate to function as a policymaker between conventions. Nevertheless, on rare occasions the national committee issues pronouncements of party policy roughly analagous to platform planks. Committee debates on policy may be mingled with the maneuvers of aspirants for the nomination or with the rivalries of factional leaders. The Republican national committee, for example, in its April, 1942, meeting became embroiled in a battle between the isolationists, led by Robert A. Taft, and the international collaborationists, led by Wendell Willkie. The committee adopted a resolution to serve in effect as a platform for the 1942 congressional campaigns, and in this resolution attempted to cleanse the party of its isolationism by recognizing an "obligation to assist in the bringing about of understanding, comity, and cooperation among the nations of the world." More commonly the national committee deliberations on policy matters result only in recommendations to the national convention. For example, the Democratic committee, after a series of regional meetings and extensive consultations with party leaders, recommended to the 1956 convention that the loyalty pledge be abrogated and replaced by a milder formula acceptable to all concerned.

A move toward a wider policy role for the Democratic national committee between conventions occurred after the 1956 defeat when its chairman, Paul Butler, set up an advisory council to issue policy pronouncements as occasion required. The national committee, in approving the creation of the advisory group, resolved: "The Democratic National Committee understands its function to be, during the interim between national conventions, the application of the party's platform to fast-moving events and the interpretation of party policies in the light of changing conditions." Within the "framework of the party's platform," the advisory committee would aid the national committee. The advisory council of about 25 members included prominent Democrats not on the national committee, such as Harry S. Truman, Adlai Stevenson, and Mrs. Franklin D. Roosevelt. Democratic House and Senate leaders declined to serve on the advisory council. Connection with a body outside the chambers that made pronouncements on legislation could have embarrassed them in their parliamentary leadership, a consideration that probably coincided with a disinclination to accept leadership from the clique around the national committee. As the campaign of 1960 approached, the advisory council issued frequent pronouncements, either critical of the Republican Administration or in advocacy of new policy lines. Its steady barrage of propaganda planted in the media an image of the Democratic party different from that which would have appeared had the congressional leadership dominated the public prints. After the Kennedy victory the committee dissolved the council on the theory that party policy leadership should then come from the White House.[4]

NATIONAL CHAIRMAN: GENERAL POSITION The national committee, from its very size, cannot function as the working executive of the party. The kingpin of the national organization is not the national committee but its chairman. His most onerous responsibility is the management of the presidential campaign, but other duties occupy him between elections. At the party's national headquarters in Washington he has under his supervision a staff of from 50 to 150 persons. During campaigns the national staff mushrooms as special units are created to care for phases of the campaign. After the campaign the electioneering machinery is dismantled and the national chairman is left with the direction of the party's day-to-day business. Not the least of his tasks is that of raising funds to support the normal activities of the national committee—and perhaps to pay off the deficit incurred in the last campaign.[5]

[4] After 1960 Republicans were disadvantaged by a party image fixed by the congressional leadership. In February, 1962, the Republican national committee authorized the creation of an "All-Republican Conference," a broadly representative advisory group. National chairman William E. Miller said that the Conference would "help develop a positive image which some Republicans think we are deficient in." Announcement of the formation of the Conference, which included prominent former members of the Eisenhower Administration, Republican governors, and others outside the Republican congressional leadership, set off grumblings among Republican congressional leaders who claimed the right to speak for the party. The exchange of views had its ideological overtones; notable among the critics of the Conference was Senator Barry Goldwater who regarded it as a manifestation of Republican liberalism. Nevertheless, the unhappiness over the Conference (as over the Democratic Advisory Committee) reflects in part a basic difference between the "party-in-the-government" and the "party-outside-the-government," which in Britain takes a clearer form in the friction between the parliamentary party and the extraparliamentary party. (The same problem turns up in Canada. See David Hoffman, "Intra-Party Democracy: A Case Study," *Canadian Journal of Economics and Political Science,* 27 [1961], 223–35.) Elected officials tend to be ambivalent toward party organization. They want to control it or, sometimes it seems, to destroy it. The organization sooner or later tries to tell them what to do or to displace them. The basic problem found recognition at another level in remarks by Mayor Robert Wagner, of New York, in 1961 after he had bested the Democratic organization in a primary battle. He argued that party leadership should rest in elected public officials rather than in the formal party leaders. "Those in charge of the technical components of the party mechanism . . . must never again determine the directions in which the party goes and to choose, on their own motion, those individuals who are to be offered to the people as the leaders of government."

[5] Cabell Phillips, "Party Chairman: Study in Feuds and Funds," *New York Times Magazine,* July 1, 1956.

In form the national committee elects the national chairman; in fact he is designated, ordinarily immediately after the national convention, by the party's presidential nominee. If a vacancy occurs between campaigns in the chairmanship of the party in power, the President customarily fills the vacancy.[6] If the chairmanship of the party out of power becomes vacant between campaigns, the national committee elects a new chairman. These elections may be a test of strength between leaders or factions of the party and sometimes they reflect a dispute over policy. Thus, in August, 1949, the Republican national committee elected Guy Gabrielson as its chairman. He had the support of forces friendly to Senator Taft. Or the chairmanship may go to a man not in bad odor with any faction. Joseph Martin records that he remained Republican chairman after the 1940 campaign because "no successor could be found who was acceptable to all factions." [7]

The broad position of the chairman may be inferred from the customs governing his designation. He is a personal agent of the candidate or of the President if his party is in power; he may achieve a degree of independence if his party is out of power—a set of circumstances in which, however, he has little scope for action. Despite the limits of the office a few national chairmen have invested it with prestige and power; those who are credited with doing so happen to have been chairmen in palmy days of party victory. Mark Hanna, Will Hays, and James A. Farley are ranked among the great chairmen.[8] Farley's role as leader of the organization Democrats throughout the country has become legendary. The mass of professional party workers had a deep affection for him, a valuable asset to help keep the wheels of the organization turning. Yet the national chairman remains in a sense a hired man subject to the party's leader, the presidential candidate, though it should be said that this understanding of his role gained clarity only in this century.

The custom of designating the personal agent of the presidential nominee as national chairman has its disadvantages for the work of the national committee. The disruption of the committee's work is magnified by the fact that a new chairman often replaces most of the principal staff members with persons of his own choosing. In 1952 Clarence Budington Kelland, Arizona Republican national committeemen, attacked the custom of permitting the presidential nominee "to destroy a going organization on the eve of the campaign"; his

[6] The nominee or the President may assure himself that his candidate for the chairmanship is not unacceptable to the leaders of important party factions. In 1953 both Taft and Dewey approved Leonard W. Hall for the Republican chairmanship before he was endorsed by Eisenhower. The committee, after Hall assured it that he would strive to give committeemen more of a hand in the distribution of patronage, elected him unanimously.

[7] Joseph Martin, *My First Fifty Years in Politics* (New York: McGraw-Hill, 1960), p. 126.

[8] See James A. Farley, *Behind the Ballots* (New York: Harcourt, Brace, 1938); *The Memoirs of Will H. Hays* (Garden City: Doubleday, 1955); Herbert Croly, *Marcus Alonzo Hanna* (New York: Macmillan, 1912).

pronouncements seem to have had no perceptible effect on practice. The parties would benefit from a well-managed headquarters staff with continuity of top personnel, but they have not developed a "permanent undersecretary" for the national party staff.

NATIONAL CHAIRMAN: ACTIVITIES BETWEEN CAM-PAIGNS   Between campaigns both chairmen are beset by the problem of raising money; otherwise the role of the chairman of the victorious party differs materially from that of the chairman of the losers. The custom used to be that the chairman of the victors became Postmaster General, a post that once controlled the largest single repository of federal patronage. The national chairmanship has become a full-time job, post-office patronage has become relatively less important than it once was, and the positions have been separated.

The post of national chairman of the ins takes on special importance either when a new President has been elected or when party control of the government has just changed. In either event a considerable reshuffling of top governmental personnel is in store. Applicants for patronage jobs must usually "clear" through the office of the national chairman, who must dispense patronage and favors in a manner to keep peace and harmony in the organization as well as to reward the truly deserving. Furthermore, he has to satisfy, insofar as practicable, those who hold liens on party action by virtue of their campaign contributions. By judicious intervention at troublesome points in the party organization over the country, he seeks to strengthen the support of the Administration, to iron out local disputes, and to encourage state and congressional candidacies that may strengthen the party.

The President may call on his national chairman for aid in holding party lines in Congress on important votes. On occasion Jim Farley quietly aided Roosevelt in lining up congressional support. Under President Truman the Democratic national chairman's function with respect to policy expanded, or at least became more visible. His staff came to engage in more extensive propaganda in support of Administration policy, and at times he attempted to stir up grass-roots pressure to bring recalcitrant Democratic Senators and Representatives into line. In the unsuccessful endeavor in 1949 to obtain Senate confirmation of the reappointment of Leland Olds as a member of the Federal Power Commission, the national chairman, William M. Boyle, Jr., wired national committeemen and state chairmen for support in convincing the reluctant Democratic Senators that the rank and file of the party was with the President. Rejection of the nomination would be, he said, "a defeat for the millions of Americans who are entitled to fair power rates and a victory for the power lobbyists and the Republican party." The action was taken at the instruction of the President, who regarded the appointment as in execution of party pledges on utility policy. Senators and Representatives, especially those in disagreement with the President, do not take kindly to his use of the machinery of the national committee to attempt to maintain party discipline in Congress. Nor do they relish the propaganda activities of the national committee on controversial issues, even though it may be merely supporting platform planks duly approved by the national convention.

When the President seeks re-election, the chairman of the ins usually dedicates no little effort to the management of the renomination and re-election. The limitation of neutrality among aspirants for the Presidency which holds for the chairman of the outs does not apply in this situation. Thus, Robert Hannegan, Democratic chairman under Truman, laid down the rule to his publicity staff: "Don't do anything unless it advances the cause of President Truman's election. We do not want publicity for the sake of publicity. So on every proposal you make, first try it against this rule." [9]

The national chairman of the party out of power is beset by different, if not fewer, worries than the chairman whose party holds the Presidency. Not long since, the national organization of the minority party was practically nonexistent between campaigns. In the 1920's Franklin Roosevelt observed that the Democratic national headquarters consisted of "two ladies occupying one room in a Washington office building." Over the past 30 years the national organizations of the minority have become far more active in the periods between presidential campaigns. After his defeat in 1928, Al Smith suggested that the minority party carry on a positive educational program rather "than sit by and adopt a policy of inaction with the hope of profiting solely by the mistakes or failures of the opposition." In 1929, with the appointment of Charles Michelson as director of publicity for the Democratic national committee, the minority party took the offensive. The publicity division prepared statements to be released mainly under the name of Democratic Senators and Representatives in criticism of majority policies. The minority obtained a wide hearing for its attacks, irritated Republican leaders, and seldom failed to take advantage of an error by the majority. The barrage of publicity helped lay the basis for Democratic victory in 1932.[10] The Republican party, after the disastrous election of 1936, set about under the leadership of Chairman John Hamilton to build a permanent headquarters to function year round, election or no election.[11]

The national chairman of the outs has an opportunity to move into the vacuum created by the lack of a dominant party leader and to function as

[9] Jack Redding, *Inside the Democratic Party* (Indianapolis: Bobbs-Merrill, 1958), p. 44.

[10] See T. S. Barclay, "The Publicity Division of the Democratic Party, 1929–30," *American Political Science Review*, 25 (1931), 68–72; Charles Michelson, *The Ghost Talks* (New York: Putnam's, 1944), ch. 2.

[11] Karl A. Lamb, "John Hamilton and the Revitalization of the Republican Party, 1936–40," *Papers of the Michigan Academy of Science, Arts and Letters*, 45 (1960), 233–50.

party spokesman. Yet the antagonisms between the congressional wing of the party and the presidential wing make it necessary that he tread warily. The congressional wing, even though it may reflect a special shade of opinion in the party, regards itself as authorized to make the record and the issues for the party. That sector of the party leadership with a national outlook points to the necessity of a program that will appeal to those areas in which the party congressional representation is weak. The situation places the national chairman of the outs between conflicting forces. Perhaps his problems are more acute if he is a Democrat. In 1959 Paul Butler, the highly articulate Democratic chairman, came into conflict with the southern congressional leadership of his party when he took a strong position on civil rights. Butler, in his own activities and by his sponsorship of the Democratic advisory council, set a new pattern of activity in policy leadership by the national chairman of the outs.

One of the incidental worries of the minority chairman is how to keep his job. As the designee of a defeated presidential candidate he may lack prestige in the party; then, too, he is likely to become the victim of maneuver for control of the party machinery by factions interested either in party policy or in the next nomination. During the long Republican minority era after 1932, that party's national chairmanship frequently became a bone of contention among party factions. Herbert Brownell, chairman designated by Dewey in 1944, for example, found it expedient to resign in 1946. One factor was the fear by some that Mr. Brownell might use his post to promote the renomination of Mr. Dewey in 1948. Considerations, personal and political, often conspire to make the tenure of a national chairman quite brief. Each party must from time to time get along with a volunteer or a stop-gap chairman who is willing to make only a limited commitment to what is at best an insecure job.

The chairmen of the ins and of the outs have certain duties in common. They direct the continuing publicity efforts of the committees, which usually include some form of periodical distributed to a relatively few of the party faithful.[12] They supervise the committee research program, usually a small undertaking. They organize regional conferences of party officials and conduct training sessions for party officials.[13] They must be concerned with the off-year congressional campaign. Thus, William E. Miller, shortly after his designation as Republican chairman in 1961, announced that his major effort would be put into electing Republican Senators, Representatives, and governors in 1962.

[12] These periodicals change in title and format from time to time and occasionally cease publication for a while. The Democrats published the *Democratic Digest*, a monthly, from 1953 through 1960. It was succeeded by *Democrat*, a biweekly leaflet. The Republicans in 1960 replaced *Straight from the Shoulder* with *Battle Line*.

[13] Philip S. Wilder, Jr., *Meade Alcorn and the 1958 Election* (New York: Holt, 1959).

SENATORIAL AND CONGRESSIONAL CAMPAIGN COM-
MITTEES   The party groups in both House and Senate maintain campaign committees. The National Republican congressional committee, the
Democratic senatorial campaign committee, and the National Republican
senatorial committee exist independently of the national committees and are
accountable to their respective legislative groups. The Democratic congressional committee, for example, according to the party rules "has no organic
connection with either the Democratic National Convention or the Democratic National Committee." It cooperates with the national committee and
with the senatorial committee but "it has no official connection or fiscal relation with either." Though the autonomous position of these committees
parallels the separation of powers, the notion of an independent congressional
campaign committee is said to have originated at a time of strained relations
between President Johnson and the Republican majority of Congress in 1866.
Lest the President use the national committee against it, the party in Congress
formed an independent committee to campaign for the election of Republican
Representatives in 1866. Later the Democrats created such a committee. With
the adoption of popular election of Senators a need for senatorial committees
arose.

The Republican congressional committee consists of one Representative
designated by the Republican delegation from each state with Republican
representation in the House. The Democratic national congressional committee
likewise consists of a Representative similarly chosen from each state with
Democratic representation, though the Democratic committee chairman may
also appoint a woman member from each state on recommendation of the
state's regular committee member, an option not often exercised. Thus each
committee consists of from 35 to 40 members and each is equipped with a
staff and several subcommittees. The large size of these committees has led to
the designation of a small executive committee for each of them.

In recent years the activities of the Republican congressional committee
have been far more extensive than those of the Democratic committee. The
staff of the Republican committee collects data about close districts, analyzes
the records of incumbent Democrats, conducts general publicity, provides
publicity and other campaign services for Republican incumbents and to a
lesser extent to nonincumbent Republican candidates, and attempts to stimulate local organizations to put forward promising candidates. In 1954 a staff
of about 30 persons dedicated its efforts to these activities. The Democratic
committee has had a far smaller staff, not more than a half-dozen, and has
provided its candidates with fewer services. In addition to staff services,
both committees make contributions, usually fairly small, to the campaigns
of at least some of their House candidates.

The Democratic senatorial campaign committee exists independently of
the congressional and national committees. An organ of the Democratic group

within the Senate, it usually consists of from seven to nine members appointed by the Democratic Senate leader. Members are chosen biennially from among those Senators not facing campaigns for re-election. Nor is a Senator with a senatorial colleague of his own party up for re-election in his own state eligible for membership. The Republican senatorial campaign committee, named by a chairman designated by the Republican Senate conference, varies in size from four to ten members.

Both senatorial committees maintain headquarters in the Senate Office Building in Washington and have small staffs—usually not more than five. The staffs engage in publicity work, dig up data for their party's candidates, provide campaign speakers, and generally make themselves useful. The committees allocate funds to candidates, again on a relatively small scale—insofar as the record goes.

The existence of the three national authorities—the national committee, the senatorial committee, and the congressional committee—for each party creates its administrative difficulties.[14] Relationships among the committees vary from time to time and range from hostility to friendly collaboration. Special problems arise in raising money, since contributors become unhappy when approached by several solicitors from the same party. The Republicans attempt to maintain a combined financing operation, put the bee on contributors only once, and divide the proceeds among the committees. Democrats are in this respect, as in many others, less systematic and more variable in their practices. Nor does the division of concern about national elections among the three committees simplify the conduct of campaigns, yet the existence of the independent senatorial and congressional committees enables the congressional wing of a party to protect itself, or so it believes, against neglect by the national committee.[15]

STATE COMMITTEES   The next layer below the national party organs, though by no means subordinate to them, consists of the state committees of the parties. Variety characterizes their composition, method of selection, duties, and even formal titles. They range in size from a handful to a group that can meet only in a convention hall. Their authority at one extreme amounts to that of a constituent body for the party in the state; at the other, it amounts to little more than the ministerial performance of duties minutely prescribed by statute.

Whereas the national committee exists as an extralegal creation of the national convention, state committees ordinarily are based on legislative act.

---

[14] In the preliminaries to the 1958 congressional campaign Richard Simpson, chairman of the Republican congressional committee, advised Republican candidates to confine their campaigns to "local issues" and to endorse "only those policies of the President which meet the demands of the candidate's constituents."

[15] These paragraphs lean heavily on Hugh A. Bone, *Party Committees and National Politics* (Seattle: University of Washington Press, 1958), ch. 5.

State committees—sometimes called state central committees or state executive committees—are built on electoral subdivisions of the state. The Kansas state committee, for example, consists of the chairman and vice-chairman of each of the county committees, a total of 210 members. The voters of each of Alabama's congressional districts choose at the party primary eight members of the 72-member state committee. In some instances state legislative districts constitute the geographical base of the committee. The delegates to Texas state conventions from each of the state's 31 senatorial districts designate one man and one woman to membership on the state committee. The state chairman often occupies a position vis-à-vis the gubernatorial candidate similar to that of the national chairman in relation to the presidential candidate.

The method of selection, as these instances indicate, differs from state to state. Some state executive committee members hold their posts ex officio by virtue of their position in county units of the party. Others may be selected by county conventions, as in South Carolina where each county convention elects a member of the state committee. The direct primary is a common method of selection. In Illinois and in Ohio the party voters in the primaries elect state committee members in congressional districts; in Massachusetts the state senatorial districts are areas for the selection of state committee members. In some states the delegates to the state convention from the county or other representative district select a member of the state committee. In other instances a single committee may have members chosen in different ways. California's state central committee of over 600 members consists of delegates to the state convention, all county chairmen, and three appointees of each convention delegation. Such an institution provides a means for bestowing minor honors on the party faithful but can hardly be an agency for the conduct of party business which has to be handled through an executive committee.

The chief function of state committees is the conduct of campaigns through their officers and agents; they also perform other duties in connection with the government of the party. The range of these functions and the degree of discretion vested in the committee are widest in the southern states and in a few other states in which the party has been subjected to little detailed statutory regulation. Included in the powers of state committees (but not necessarily within the powers of any single committee) are such matters as the following, when not otherwise regulated by law or party rule: issuance of the call for the state convention, selection of temporary officers for the convention, preparation of a temporary list of delegates, fixing the time of the primary, prescribing standards for party membership for participation in primaries, making nominations to fill vacancies created by death or disqualification in the party slate of nominees, canvassing and certifying results of primaries, deciding primary contests, and generally supervising the party's primaries.[16]

The state committee may also exert a determining influence in the choice of delegates to the national convention, a factor that on occasion underlies struggles for committee control. The committee itself selects them in some states. In states that choose their delegates by convention the factional leader who has allied with himself most of the members of the state committee may enjoy great advantage. Even when the delegates are chosen by direct primary, control of the committee may be worth a battle. Thus, in California in 1954 a coalition including Senator William F. Knowland and Governor Goodwin J. Knight captured the Republican state central committee against forces allied with Vice President Richard M. Nixon. The maneuver was not unconnected with the possibility that General Eisenhower would not run in 1956 and that Mr. Knowland might seek the nomination. Again, in Texas in 1956 Senator Lyndon Johnson and Representative Sam Rayburn fought successfully for control of the Texas state Democratic organization for objectives of national rather than state politics.

COUNTY COMMITTEES   The county committee constitutes a unit of major significance in the party machinery, and its chairman may be a local political potentate of considerable importance. Most commonly the county committee is an assemblage of the party's precinct committeemen, township committeemen, or party functionaries from other subdivisions of the county. The county committee concerns itself with campaigns for county offices; it is ordinarily tied into the state organization, formally or informally, through the county chairman. The 3,000 or so county chairmen of each party are the second lieutenants, or perhaps the non-coms, of the political army and have under their immediate direction and leadership the troops—the party workers who get out the vote.

The lowest and basic layer of the party organization consists of the precinct captains or committeemen, sometimes elected by the members of the party in the precinct through the direct primary, sometimes selected by precinct conventions or caucuses, and in some instances appointed by higher authority. The precincts or election districts number more than 100,000.

Usually the statutes or rules also provide for party committees for dis-

[16] In some southern states the party organization could be called "nonpartisan" in state and local matters. The party organization does not need to conduct a general election campaign. It tends to be obligated to neutrality among candidates in the primary. Often it administers the primary, a role which also imposes an obligation of impartiality toward candidates and factions within the party. Control of the state committee is important in such states for its uses in the choice of delegates to presidential nominating conventions and in other phases of presidential politics. In some nonsouthern states also, party organizations are limited, by tradition or statute, to a role of neutrality in contests for primary nominations.

tricts not coterminous with counties from which officials are elected. The county chairmen of the counties included within a congressional district may, for example, constitute a district committee. Similarly, committees may be provided for state legislative and judicial districts. Ordinarily these district committees play no significant role in party affairs and often remain dormant unless they are called upon to perform some statutory duty, such as filling a vacancy on the ticket. Especially notable for purposes of the national party is the dearth of strong and active committees based on congressional districts.[17]

INTERRELATIONSHIPS OF ORGANIZATIONAL STRATA
The foregoing description suggests the bare contours of the formal party organization which has its roots in the electorate at the precinct level and reaches an apex in the office of national chairman. The entire structure is often likened to a military hierarchy, yet that conception is erroneous. County, state, and national party organs are each to a degree autonomous. So far as the formal authority goes the national chairman cannot issue directions to the state chairmen or the state chairman to the county chairmen. Though the levels of party organization are intimately interrelated, the linkage is from the bottom up rather than from the top down. This type of relationship appears strikingly in those instances in which precinct executives come together as a county committee which elects the county chairman; the county chairmen foregather as the state committee which chooses the state chairman; and now, on the Republican side, a great many state chairmen happen to be members of the national committee. Even when the formal procedures do not provide such a pattern of interconnections, similar sorts of interrelationships often develop.[18] Members of party committees, no matter what the committee's level, usually have a base of power in some geographical area smaller than the jurisdiction of the committee on which they sit. An influential county committeeman is apt to be a power in his precinct, township, or election district. A member of the state committee to be reckoned with is usually a leader of note in his county. And those national committeemen whose word is paid much heed are men who have achieved prominence in their state organizations. Advancement in the political organization tends to be an expansion of influence from a geographical base rather than an ascent up a ladder.[19]

[17] The organizational apparatus of both parties includes various auxiliary groups such as the Young Republican National Federation and the Young Democratic Clubs of America. The National Federation of Republican Women, an autonomous organization, maintains its headquarters with those of the national committee.

[18] Thus, in New York, though the state committeemen are elected by the voters they are regarded as agents of the county chairmen. See R. A. Straetz and F. J. Munger, New York Politics (New York: New York University Press, 1960).

[19] The interconnection of levels of organization is illustrated by the multiple roles in 1956 of the Hon. W. L. Dawson, Democratic Representative from Illinois. He was a precinct captain, a ward committeeman, vice-chairman of the Cook County Democratic committee, secretary of the Democratic congressional campaign committee, and vice-

Unity and Disunity: National Party

Such are the broad outlines of the manner in which the party activists organize themselves to do the party's work. Viewed over the entire nation, the party organization constitutes no disciplined army. It consists rather of many state and local points of power, each with its own local following and each comparatively independent of external control. Each of the dispersed clusters of party professionals has its own concerns with state and local nominations and elections. Each has a base for existence independent of national politics. Each in fact enjoys such independence that more than a tinge of truth colors the observation that there are no national parties, only state and local parties.[20] Yet in one way or another the cumbersome decentralized party apparatus is brought to life as a national party organization. At the call of the national committee the state committees set into motion the processes for the choice of delegates to the national conventions (unless that function has been preempted by public authority), and the state party organizations bestir themselves to play a part in the choice of a presidential candidate. Once the nomination is made the party apparatus becomes a mechanism for nationwide electioneering.

NATIONAL ORGANIZATION A COMBINATION OR COALITION What holds the elements of the national party organization together? What gives it such unity as it has? What are the counterforces that create centers of autonomy within the party? If the organization is not hierarchical, what is its character? These questions of the degree of unity and disunity within the national party organization usually arouse extensive comment about the lack of discipline rather than awe that at least a modicum of unity is achieved among political activists spread across a continent.

To explain the unity that develops within the national party organization one must look beyond the apparatus of party machinery itself and examine the social matrix within which the organization exists. The groups, classes, and sorts of people that attach themselves to each of the major parties were

---

chairman of the Democratic national committee. John M. Bailey, who became Democratic national chairman in 1961, served simultaneously as Connecticut state chairman.

[20] President Eisenhower, when questioned in a press conference in October, 1956, about the somewhat doubtful "new Republicanism" of several Old Guard Senators, responded: "Now, let's remember, there are no national parties in the United States. There are 48 state parties, then they are the ones that determine the people that belong to those parties. There is nothing I can do to say that no one is not a Republican. The most I can say is that in many things they do not agree with me. . . . We have got to remember that these are state organizations, and there is nothing I can do to say so-and-so is a Republican and so-and-so is not a Republican." Press conference of October 11, 1956.

identified in Chapter 8. The geographically dispersed clusters of activists who make up the party organization are anchored in those sectors of the community loyal to their party. These social interests, though scattered, may have parallel or common objectives. When Republican leaders gather in national conclave, they tend to share an outlook springing from their association with the business elements of their home communities. When the Democratic professionals convene, many of them, by virtue of their positions at home, will be oriented favorably toward organized labor; others will be bound together by a concern over the peculiar problems of the South. The social context of national party organization contributes to its internal cleavages as well as to its unity.[21]

All the factors that contribute to the grouping of sectors of the electorate into each of the party followings assure a degree of cohesiveness within the national party machinery. When it is said that national party is a coalition, the reference may be to the coalition or combination of social interests for which the party speaks. That combination induces unity within the political machinery, narrowly defined, and the combination may, of course, be to a degree a product of the workings of the party machinery.

It is well to emphasize the fundamental importance to national party organization of the underlying coalition of social blocs and interests. Yet it remains for the politicians to work out the details and terms of the coalition. That process starkly reveals the nonhierarchical structure of national party organization. The party nationally tends to be an alliance of state and city leaders who work together most faithfully during a presidential campaign. The national committee is a gathering of sovereigns (or their emissaries) to negotiate and treat with each other rather than a staff conclave of subordinates of the national chairman. The basic coalition-forming process occurs in the national convention which nominates the candidate who succeeds in lining up a commanding block of state organizations. The nominee symbolizes the terms of the coalition at the moment; the platform may make them explicit. Or, on occasion, the decisions of the convention may leave gaping cleavages indicative of the inability of the politicians to bridge the differences among the elements of the party.

PARTY   DISCIPLINE   IN   PRESIDENTIAL   CAMPAIGNS
Within the broad limits set by the composition of the party coalition, the national organization may be unified in greater or lesser degree by skillful

---

[21] From reflections such as these some observers leap to the conclusion that party organization is simply derivative of some more inclusive power structure of society. That argument should be taken with reserve. Certainly at times a party machine acts clearly as an agent for other interests in society. On the other hand, it always enjoys a sphere of independence and not infrequently becomes master of its own supposed principal. For empirical data on the question in a local situation, see R. A. Dahl, *Who Governs?* (New Haven: Yale University Press, 1962), Book III.

leadership. During a national campaign the tethers linking the state organizations to the national chairman tend to be less slack than at other times. The hope for victory induces a willingness to accept leadership. The stronger that hope, the more cohesive is the national organization. If the presidential candidate seems to be a sure loser, the national chairman is likely to be as a sovereign without subjects.

In earlier times the national organization doled out sums from its war chest to state and local organizations and gained some authority over the general conduct of the campaign. Although subventions from the national party to state parties have declined since the Hatch Act limited national committee expenditures to $3,000,000 in any one year, the national leaders are in contact with the sources of funds and can aid a local organization by steering contributions to it.

Some of the difficulties of whipping the state organizations together in a national campaign come from the administrative frailties of a huge organization, manned largely by volunteers and often at critical points by incompetents.[22] In the campaigns of 1932 and 1936 James A. Farley, Democratic national chairman, undertook to cut through the administrative layers to tie the local party committeemen more closely to the national committee. The national headquarters sent campaign literature in small quantities to each precinct committeeman in contrast with the previous practice of hopefully sending literature in bulk to state committees for redistribution to local workers. Mr. Farley observed that the

. . . fellow out in Kokomo, Indiana, who is pulling doorbells night after night and respectfully asking his neighbors to vote the straight Democratic ticket gets a thrill if he receives a letter on campaigning postmarked Washington or New York, and we made sure that this pleasure was not denied him.[23]

If the presidential candidate lends strength to the ticket, the state and local organizations can be expected ordinarily to work in harmony with the national leaders during campaigns. Without much urging from national headquarters, the state organization will agitate for Eisenhower and Stratton, or Kennedy and Elmer Smith, or whoever the local candidate is. When the presidential nominee is thought to handicap the party's candidate for state and local office, the state and local organizations often keep quiet about the national ticket, endorse it in muted tones, or even quietly cut the head of the ticket. Though the national chairman lacks effective sanctions against such

[22] A goodly sprinkling of inactives and incompetents grace party organization from the precinct level even to national committeeman. They cling to their honorific posts almost unto death. Party leaders often seek to beef up the party by steering new and zealous workers into the women's auxiliaries, the Young Republicans, the Young Democrats, and the citizens' organizations that spring up during campaigns.

[23] J. A. Farley, *Behind the Ballots* (New York: Harcourt, Brace, 1938), pp. 159–60.

tactics of noncooperation, a presidential candidate, unexpectedly elected, can even out old scores as he allocates patronage.

State leaders who bolt the party to support the presidential candidate of the opposition or of a third party place the ultimate strain on the national organization. Certain sorts of penalties, if not preventives, are available to the national committees. The Republican national committee may declare vacant the seat of any member who refuses to support the presidential nominee. The Democratic committee has exercised the same power, though its authority to do so did not become explicit until 1952. The Democratic committee in 1949 struck from its membership rolls the names of six Dixiecrats from four southern states—Mississippi, South Carolina, Alabama, and Louisiana. After the Texas national committeeman supported Eisenhower in 1952, the committee refused to recognize him as a member. In 1956, as a part of the compromise over the loyalty pledge for convention delegates, the Democrats adopted a requirement that every member of the national committee "declare affirmatively for the nominees of the convention." Failure to do so would be cause for expulsion by the committee. The same compromise expressed the "understanding" that by sending delegates to the convention each state Democratic party undertook to see that the voters of their state had an opportunity to vote for electors pledged to the convention nominees.

Such aggravated situations as the difficulties of the Democratic national organization with some of its southern state subsidiaries cannot be coped with by administrative sanctions. They are symptomatic of the existence in the party of an irreconcilable element rather than of defects of organizational arrangements. To maintain party unity the incompatible element must be driven from the party or ousted from control of the state organization. When in 1956 in several southern states Democratic leaders dedicated to Republicanism lost control of the party organizations to leaders committed to the support of the national party nominees, the problem of discipline disappeared.

PATRONAGE: A COHESIVE FACTOR?   The party in power nationally has much greater opportunity and much greater resources than the party out of power to construct a truly national party organization. The patronage in the hands of the national leaders is great enough to weld the state machines into a semblance of national unity. The power of patronage, among a great many other things, is reflected in the fact that a President can usually gain a renomination at the end of his first term. Patronage ties state organizations to the national leadership most effectively in those states in which the national majority is a weak minority locally. Southern Republican organizations historically have been beholden to the national leadership for favors received. Democratic organizations in Republican strongholds occupy, when Democrats control the national government, a similar relationship of dependency.

Serious limitations restrict the utility of patronage in the binding of state and local centers of power to the national leadership. In a measure, patronage distribution may be guided by commitments, tacit or explicit, made in the formation of the combination that won the nomination for the President. State organizations, moreover, demand their share as a matter of right and attempt to reduce the President's discretion in using patronage to strengthen his personal following. Furthermore, in the distribution of patronage, Senators and Representatives have an important voice, and they are not interested in building an organization with power centered in the hands of the national leaders. Instead, they wish to strengthen their own organizations or those state or district organizations with which they are affiliated. And when patronage appointments are made on the recommendations of Senators and Congressmen, the appointments will be such as to strengthen allegiances to the state and local organization.[24]

Senatorial courtesy may give state leaders quite as much control of some appointments as the President has. In 1950, for example, President Truman appointed Martin A. Hutchinson of Virginia to a post on the Federal Trade Commission, which required senatorial confirmation. Hutchinson had long been a prominent leader of the anti-Byrd faction in the Virginia Democratic party and had also led the 1948 campaign in the state for Truman while the regular Democratic organization remained neutral. At the urging of Senator Byrd the Senate refused to confirm the nomination. Thus the President was blocked in an attempt to recognize a Democratic faction loyal to the party nationally. In any event, patronage is of doubtful efficacy in the construction of an organization loyal to the national leadership against the opposition of a hostile state machine. The Indiana Republican state chairman, who did not much like Ike, remarked in 1957 to reporters: "I've told Alcorn [the Republican national chairman] that he better not hand out any patronage in this state without going through us. . . . I said that if there is anything like that, the national committee will not get a cent from Indiana."

NATIONAL PARTY ROLE IN LEGISLATIVE ELECTIONS
The centripetal influences of the presidential campaign induce a degree of unity in the party organization over the entire nation during a campaign. Yet that unity is the consequence of a coalition, a convergence of interest, rather than of the power of national party headquarters. The role of the national leadership in the election of Senators and Representatives reflects the underlying nature of national party structure. A truly national party would have some influence over the designation of candidates for the Senate and the House; a slate of candidates consisting of persons with views generally in accord with national party policies would be supported for nomination. Instead, state and

---

[24] See J. P. Harris, *The Advice and Consent of the Senate* (Berkeley: University of California Press, 1953).

local leaders insist that the choice of party candidates for the Senate and House is a local matter.[25] They resent and generally defeat efforts by national leaders to participate in such nominations. In turn, the national party leadership usually considers itself bound to support for election the local nominees bearing the party label whatever their views on party policy may be. One of the prices of unity in support of the presidential nominee is a tolerance by the national leadership of the diverse shades of opinion within the party coalition. If politics did not make strange bedfellows, there could be no national party.[26]

POLITICAL BASES OF ORGANIZATIONAL DECENTRALI-ZATION   Both unity and disunity within the national organization have their roots in the diverse social, economic, and political interests in the party following. Yet another foundation of deconcentration of party leadership is the federal form of government. State and local party organizations are built up around the patronage of state and local government; and these organizations, particularly in cities and states dominated by one party, have a continuous life, regardless of whether the party is in or out of power nationally. State and local patronage makes the local machine financially independent of the national headquarters. Federalism in our formal governmental machinery includes a national element independent of the states, but in our party organization the independent national element is missing. Party structure is more nearly confederative than federal in nature. The state and local machines, built on state patronage, are allied with or paralleled by machines built around the patronage controlled by Senators and Representatives; and owing to the method of dispensation of this patronage, the resultant machines are almost as independent of central control as are the purely local organizations. Federalism in government tends to encourage confederation in the party's government.

Informal Organization: State and Local

The discussion of the confederative character of national party organization has proceeded as if tightly organized party machines would be found

[25] Congressional nominations are treated in Chapter 16.

[26] National headquarters may support senatorial and congressional nominees with varying degrees of enthusiasm. In 1950 Howard Latourette, Democratic opponent of Wayne Morse in the Oregon senatorial campaign, submitted to national headquarters a campaign budget of $64,000. He received a check for $2,000 which he returned, with the charge that the national leadership preferred Morse, who often voted with Senate Democrats, over a genuine believer in "Democratic principles free from socialistic influence." In 1954 Democratic national chairman Stephen A. Mitchell refused to support, financially or otherwise, the House campaigns of James Roosevelt and Robert Condon in California. Mr. Condon had been labeled a "security risk" by the Atomic Energy Commission and Mr. Roosevelt had had his marital troubles.

in the states and cities. In fact, behind the façade of the formal party organization the widest variety characterizes the actual organization of the political activists in the states and cities. The manner in which they manage to join forces to carry on the business of the party—the selection of candidates and the conduct of campaigns—varies greatly from place to place and from time to time in the same state or locality. Moreover, the extent to which the formal party organization—the formal mechanism prescribed by rule or statute—is the real organization differs from place to place. In some states it coincides with the working party organization; in other localities, manned by hacks, it is moribund, and groups of political workers completely outside the formal organization stir up candidates and advance their cause.

TYPES OF ORGANIZATIONAL PATTERNS   So few are the systematic analyses of the informal organization of parties that an attempt toward a typology of party structures would be hazardous. To suggest the range of variety, however, it may be useful to picture state and city organization as distributed along a scale from the highest degree of unity to thorough fractionalization. The manner of the conduct of campaigns serves as a fairly reliable index of the position of an organization along this scale of unification-atomization. A tightly knit clique of political activists ordinarily exists when campaign efforts are designed to promote the cause of the entire ticket, when the individual candidate usually says a good word for his running mates, and when the canvassers work for the party cause rather than for individual candidates. Contrast with this the pulverization of the activists when it can scarcely be said that party organization exists. The gubernatorial candidate may have his own headquarters and his own campaign organization. Each other candidate on the ticket will have a staff to prepare press releases, to mail literature, or to canvass the voters. Each candidate may carefully avoid involvement with other persons on the ticket and may even dissociate himself from his party label. Each may attempt to maximize his support from that sector of the electorate to which he presumably has the greatest appeal. This multiplicity of campaigns ordinarily reflects the existence, not of a cohesive stratum of political workers, but of a system of loosely allied clusters of professionals, each attached to the fortunes of an individual candidate.

The manner of nomination of candidates constitutes another index of the character of party organization. If a state or city committee endorses a slate of candidates for nomination in the primary and usually manages to bring about their nomination, often without even token primary opposition, a relatively cohesive organization probably exists.[27] If, on the other hand, the

[27] For example, in New Jersey in 1961, Democratic county leaders met with Governor Robert B. Meyner and agreed upon a candidate for governor who won the primary with only token opposition. The Republicans, on the other hand, were unable to agree and fought out their differences in the primary in which James P. Mitchell, former Secretary of Labor, won with the support of Senator Clifford Case and Republican Congressmen from the state.

route to the primary nomination seems to be wide open and individual aspirants build their own organizations to fight for the nomination, a more fractionalized informal organization usually exists. Instead of a party organization, the actuality may be a congeries of personal and factional cliques.

Only the most impressionistic estimates can be made about the distribution of organizations along our scale. The common belief, whether right or wrong, is that party organizations east of the Mississippi and north of the Mason-Dixon line tend to be more cohesive than those of the West, though conspicuous exceptions may be found on both sides of the River. Frequently a differentiation prevails between state and federal cliques: a cluster or clusters of activitists devote their efforts mainly to senatorial, congressional, and presidential politics; other clusters associate their fortunes with those of candidates for state and local office. Party structures are probably more tightly articulated in jurisdictions that nominate through the convention than in states with a custom of wide-open primary races.[28]

State organizations differ along other dimensions, too. One differentiation consists in the simple fact whether they maintain a staff and a headquarters to work steadily at the business of the party. The Michigan state Democratic central committee, under the chairmanship of Neil Staebler, built a skilled central staff to conduct organization work, to recruit candidates, and to handle publicity.[29] At the opposite extreme is the type of state organization that is inert between campaigns and may be even without a permanent office.[30] Along another dimension, state organizations differ in the degree to which local organizations are geared into state party activity. In some instances state headquarters can rely on local organizations to do their part in campaigns; in others, they cannot. In Connecticut town committees obligingly deny renomination to legislators not in good standing with the state leadership. In New York the Republican county chairmen help to maintain the party lines in Albany. More usually the relation of state and local organization is tenuous.

The variations in unity of state and local organizations tend to spring from the composition of the party following. As has been indicated in Chapter 11, state parties are highly variable in their makeup and are often split along

[28] Many professional politicans are quite happy with a disintegrated party structure. They have a vested interest in the power they gain as feudal chieftains by virtue of the atomization of party structure; the more secure they are in their little organizational bailiwicks, the less concern they need feel for the fortunes of the party as a whole.

[29] See the analysis by R. L. Sawyer, Jr., *The Democratic State Central Committee in Michigan, 1949–1959* (Ann Arbor: Institute of Public Administration, University of Michigan, 1960). See also J. W. Lederle and R. F. Aid, "Michigan State Party Chairmen: 1882–1956," *Michigan History*, September, 1957. The rarity of state chairmen with a reputation for being good at their jobs may be an indicator of the nature of state party organization.

[30] Alexander Heard reports that in 1956 and 1957 only 37 Republican and 26 Democratic committees employed one or more full-time professional staff persons. *The Costs of Democracy* (Garden City: Anchor Books, 1962), p. 364.

ethnic lines, rent by religious rivalries, and torn by other divisive factors. Of special significance in some states are the differences between the metropolis and the countryside. Party organizations founded on heterogeneous followings achieve unity themselves only with the greatest difficulty.

PARTY ORGANIZATION, OLD-STYLE   Variety is the reality of party organization, but the stereotype of old-fashioned machine organization persists and is often regarded as more generally approximated than it actually is. Yet from place to place highly disciplined organizations continue to exist, chiefly with domains limited to counties and cities, much as they did in the past century.

The classic machine took a clearly hierarchical form, with a boss at the head of an organization of workers held together by the spoils of politics and capable of determining the party's nominations and of exerting a mighty influence in elections as well. In its most fully developed form the urban machine became the government in that many major decisions, as well as minor matters, were decided by the party functionaries who managed their puppets in public office.

Patronage is an important factor in building up lines of command and in establishing internal cohesion and discipline in the machine. Leaders who hire can also fire. In a machine-governed jurisdiction a large proportion of the officials of the party organization also hold public office, appointive or elective, and others may enjoy other perquisites or may be ambitious for public place. In a 1935 study of party committeemen in selected upstate New York cities, Professor Mosher found that 19 per cent of 3,618 committeemen had places on the public payroll. In Albany, 35 per cent of the Democratic committeemen were also public officials, and in Syracuse and Auburn the figure was 28.[31] In Chicago in 1928, 59.2 per cent of the precinct captains had public jobs.[32] In Pittsburgh, 73 per cent of male Democratic committeemen are reported as holding public jobs; 24 per cent of the male Republican committeemen.[33] Hugh Bone, in a 1952 study of a sample of Republican precinct committeemen in Seattle, found 13.8 per cent to be public employees; the figure rose to 20 per cent when precinct committeewomen were classified according to their husbands' occupations.[34] How representative these cases are cannot be known. Certainly in many states and cities large proportions

[31] W. E. Mosher, "Party and Government Control at the Grass Roots," *National Municipal Review*, 24 (1953), 15–18.

[32] H. F. Gosnell, *Machine Politics: Chicago Model* (Chicago: University of Chicago Press, 1937), p. 54.

[33] W. J. Keefe and W. C. Seyler, "Precinct Politicians in Pittsburgh," *Social Science*, 35 (1960), 26–32.

[34] Hugh A. Bone, *Grass Roots Party Leadership* (Bureau of Government Research, University of Washington, 1952). Precinct committeemen in their ethnic and occupational characteristics tend to resemble the voters of their areas. See E. E. Cornwell, Jr., "Some Occupational Patterns in Party Committee Membership," *Rhode Island History*, 20

of party functionaries labor for the love of the game, for the recognition party posts bring them, and, frequently, because they are drafted by their fellow partisans to do a job they regard as a civic duty.

Patronage enables the organization leadership to weld together a cohesive group of workers animated by an appreciation of past favors and, even more, by an expectation of future rewards. The relationship is nicely illustrated by a noted statement by a Chicago ward leader to his precinct captains just before a 1926 primary:

> "I don't want applause; what I want first is pledge cards, but, more than that, votes. This is a real fight, and every man must do his share. Look at that chart—some of the precincts show no pledge cards at all. Who is the man from this precinct?"
>
> "That's mine, Mr. ————. I have thirty cards at home and am just waiting to copy them before turning them in."
>
> "You're expecting a raise in salary in your job, aren't you?"
>
> "Yes, sir."
>
> "Carry your precinct or you not only won't get it, but you'll lose your job altogether.
>
> "I don't want to scold, but I believe I've been as good to this ward as it has to me. . . . I want to say that if any man does not carry his precinct on the thirteenth of April, he'll be fired on the fourteenth. If a man means anything in his precinct, he can carry it. If he doesn't mean anything in his precinct, he has no business in politics and holding a job. The reason that ———— is on the ticket for municipal judge in spite of the fact that he is a new man in the ward is that he had the banner precinct. . . . I promise that whoever turns out the biggest vote in his precinct will be on the next county ticket, if I sit on the state committee, and I think I will.
>
> "What is more, any of you that don't get out the vote and have jobs will lose them, and they'll go to those who do work and have no job. I'm looking at one right now that has no job, and he'll have one that someone else now has unless you get out the vote. Don't think I don't mean this. I've fired the ward committeeman and I've fired the president of this ward club, although he had a $6,000 job." [35]

Loyalty to the party machine depends by no means solely on the pecuniary tie. "In a few cases," Gosnell says in his study of Chicago precinct captains, "precinct captains were bound to their ward committeemen by personal ties of loyalty which grew out of crisis situations. When a ward boss could dra-

---

(1961), 87–96; "Party Absorption of Ethnic Groups: The Case of Providence, Rhode Island," *Social Forces*, 38 (1960), 205–10.

[35] C. H. Wooddy, *The Chicago Primary of 1926* (Chicago: University of Chicago Press, 1926), pp. 7–8.

matically come to the rescue of some man who was in trouble with the police, he could count on that man for steady precinct work from that time on." [36] No less an authority than James A. Farley states that "those people who are inclined to imagine that patronage and patronage alone, is the only thing that keeps a political party knit together are off on a tangent that is about as far wrong as anything humanly could be. I am convinced," he says, "that with the help of a few simple ingredients like time, patience, and hard work, I could construct a major political party in the United States without the aid of a single job to hand out to deserving partisans." [37]

The ties of party loyalty, the obligations of individual to individual, the leverage of patronage, and the harnessed ambitions of men may create a compact and manageable group of party workers. Under ordinary circumstances, when the organization is not rent by dissension, it is almost futile to challenge it in the primaries. And if one controls the primary, he has gone a long way toward controlling all.

The organization is often pictured as a dictatorship, a description that fits in some localities at some times. More often the organization assumes the form of clusters of personal loyalties about nuclear individuals. The latter, in turn, are bound to persons higher up the hierarchy, often by materialistic ties, eventuating in a more or less effective control of the whole by a few individuals at the apex. Within this structure the more lowly offer a continuous challenge to those higher up in the machine. Precinct captains fight their way up the ladder. Ward leaders may look to the day when they may become city leader or, as a lesser achievement, extend their dominion over neighboring wards. In turn, the upper leadership occupies itself with purging the disloyal or rebellious by the withdrawal of patronage, by supporting a rival against the troublesome subordinate. By the continuing struggle within the organization those most fit for party warfare survive and a few men manage to establish themselves as upper-level leaders.

In the orthodox accounts of organization potency prominence is given to the role of the precinct captain in rallying voters to the organization. The precinct executive "is the actual connecting link between the people and the organization, and he is the only connecting link—the only man in the machine who has any point of direct contact with the voters, who knows anything about them, who has any real influence with them." [38] In building a following the precinct executive can begin with his family, relatives, and friends. He can add the votes of those whose support can be recruited with election-day perquisites. He can usually designate two or three precinct election officials and thereby annex their votes and those of their families and

---

[36] Gosnell, *op. cit.*, p. 67.
[37] *Behind the Ballots* (New York: Harcourt, Brace, 1938), p. 237.
[38] Frank R. Kent, *The Great Game of Politics* (New York: Doubleday, Doran, 1923), p. 1.

friends.[39] On primary and election days he has at his disposal funds allocated to him for election-day expenses. He may have from $25 to $100 to hire watchers, runners, and other persons to get out the vote. With each accession to his payroll a vote or two or more is added to his little bloc.

The precinct captain, however, works throughout the year and adds to his strength by continuous service to the voters of his precinct. Especially in the poorer neighborhoods he is likely to become a sort of social agency. W. S. Vare, Philadelphia Republican boss, boasted:

> In every precinct of the city there are two representatives of the Organization, elected directly at the Republican primaries and who are known as committeemen. They maintain contacts with the voters and are at their beck and call for 24 hours of each day of the year. In time of stress the poor or other unfortunates always turn to these Organization representatives to assist them. It is they that see that the sick are cared for and that the poor are provided for, and then even in death aid may be rendered. The Philadelphia Organization gives a real social service and one without red tape, and without class, religious, or color distinction.[40]

In addition to his social service work, the precinct executive serves as a buffer between governmental agencies and the voters of his precinct. He steers the alien through the naturalization procedure. He aids in obtaining private as well as governmental employment for the people of his precinct. He aids in contacts with public social agencies. He may see the judge and attempt to mix mercy with justice. In all these relationships he may obtain treatment for his friends that amounts to favoritism, but in a substantial proportion of these services he is primarily a guide. Governmental agencies are so numerous and complex that the average citizen is bewildered and does not know to whom to apply for any given service. The precinct executive "knows the ropes" and can be of service even when no question of favoritism is involved. Yet when he can have the traffic ticket "fixed" he can create a great obligation to himself.[41] By these means the working precinct executive can build a bloc of votes to be swung to the support of the organization slate in the primaries and mobilized for the party in the general election.[42]

[39] The attractiveness of election-day jobs declines in periods of full employment. In St. Louis County in 1954, the county election board, to man the polls, had to summon about 75 persons to duty under its power to compel citizens to serve as precinct election officials. *St. Louis Post-Dispatch*, August 3, 1954.

[40] Quoted by D. H. Kurtzman, *Methods of Controlling Votes in Philadelphia*. Privately published thesis, University of Pennsylvania, 1935, p. 29.

[41] See H. F. Gosnell, *Machine Politics: Chicago Model* (Chicago: University of Chicago Press, 1937), chs. 3 and 4; Roy V. Peel, *The Political Clubs of New York City* (New York: Putnam's, 1935); Sonya Forthal, *Cogwheels of Democracy: A Study of the Precinct Captain* (New York: The William-Frederick Press, 1946).

[42] Many are the tales of prodigious feats of precinct leaders in swinging the voters

Credulous students and Europeans subscribe to the view that the United States is blanketed by boss-led party organizations that subsist at the public trough and command a following of voters attached to the party by a mixture of charity and chicanery. In some localities that sort of organization does exist. In others remnants of old-time organization remain. In still others the organization is most attenuated. The executive director of the Republican national committee reported that in 1948, 357 counties had no Republican chairman or vice-chairman and that 28,000 or almost one-fourth of all precincts had no Republican leadership. In the same year in Oregon the Democrats had operating organizations in only 13 of 36 counties. Nor are all of even the largest cities thoroughly organized. R. L. Morlan reported in 1949 that in no Minneapolis ward "is there a party organization adequately covering every precinct the year round." He says that "except in the weeks just preceding an important election, roughly 100 of the 634 possible precinct captaincies will be unfilled and not over half the remainder are filled by active party workers who can be depended upon all the time." [43]

TRENDS AFFECTING PARTY ORGANIZATION   Although we have no precise measures of the change, clearly over the past 50 years American party organizations have undergone radical alterations. Tightly managed statewide party organization has become exceptional and has been largely replaced by a fractionalized system of personal and factional cliques of professionals within each party. Within cities and counties the same process of atomization has occurred, even though a few old-style machines remain. Along with these changes the capacity of the party organization to control nominations has declined markedly, and primary routs of famed old machines by upstarts recur. Politicians are not disappearing, to be sure, but the manner of their organization and of their operation is changing. Machines always have had their ups and downs, but the American party machines have been undergoing secular changes rather than simply suffering periodic reverses. Moreover, the situations with which organizations must work have also undergone alteration, which, in turn, affects both the nature and effectiveness of the organization. All these trends, their exact nature and the magnitudes of their consequences, have not been carefully studied, but they may be taken into account here.

---

as they wish. Kurtzman, for example, tells of two Philadelphia committeemen who had been pardoned through the efforts of a man who subsequently became a candidate for a judgeship. Out of gratitude to this man they delivered to him 450 of the 460 votes cast in their division. For accounts of other like incidents, see Kurtzman, *op. cit.*, pp. 33–34.

[43] "City Politics: Free Style," *National Municipal Review*, 38 (1949), 485–90. In 1962 the Republican national committee, disposed to attribute its 1960 losses to organizational weaknesses, urged party leaders to see that the precincts were manned in the big cities. See *Report of the Committee on Big City Politics* (Washington: Republican National Committee, 1962).

On the whole, the supply of public jobs to support organization workers has probably declined in the face of the rise of the merit system and the professionalization of the public service. The spoils system has not been eradicated and state and local services on occasion are shot through with patronage abuses, but for the country as a whole, organizational cohesion born of a shared anxiety about job security is probably not what it was a half-century ago.

Public welfare services now dwarf the old-time social services of the precinct captain and the ward boss. Some local machines have captured and converted the public welfare agencies to their purposes, but others have lost the battle to the professionals who man these new services. The voter now may not look to the district leader for a bucket of coal but may be concerned about how his Congressman votes on an amendment to the Social Security Act.

Dependent populations that once constituted bulwarks of organization strength have become far less numerous over the decades. After a generation or so, education, cultural adaptation, and economic advance create a new sort of population far less in need of the welfare services of the party and of its function of cushioning the relations of the group with a strange society. Pockets of manageable populations remain; Negroes in northern cities, for example.[44] Yet the characteristics of the population on which urban machines supposedly most depended have been substantially altered.

The people are different; so are the modes of communication with them. And the newer communications media gain in importance as sources of political intelligence and as means of political manipulation in part because the people are different. Hence, to an extent startling in its degree in some jurisdictions, the doorbell ringers have lost their function of mobilizing the vote to the public-relations experts, to the specialists in radio and television, and to others who deal in mass communications.

The adoption of the direct primary opened the road for disruptive forces that gradually fractionalized the party organization. By permitting more effective direct appeals by individual politicians to the party membership, the primary system freed forces driving toward the disintegration of party organizations and facilitated the construction of factions and cliques attached to the ambitions of individual leaders. The convention system compelled leaders to treat, to deal, to allocate nominations; the primary permits individual aspirants by one means or another to build a wider following within the party. In some jurisdictions the revolt against the party organization associated with the introduction of the direct primary was so thoroughgoing that the party organs were forbidden to support candidates for nomination in the primary.

COUNTERTRENDS IN ORGANIZATION   The recital of the long-term trends in party organization should not be taken to mean that

[44] See James Q. Wilson, *Negro Politics* (Glencoe: Free Press, 1960).

professional politicians are disappearing or that they will disappear. Rather, the manner in which they organize to do their job is changing, the image they seek to present to the public is changing, their mode of operation is changing, and the sorts of people who function as professionals are also undergoing modification.

Of the changes in the manner of organization, perhaps the most striking has been the fractionalization of integrated organization in the states and localities and the substitution of complexes of cliques of professionals grouped about individual leaders, a process which has proceeded in differing localities. Where organizations retain a semblance of unity, greater attention is devoted to the promotion of programs of public action. The organization undergoes a face lifting; good government is espoused as good politics, a transformation at times more than skin deep.

Beyond such changes, in a few states new-style organizations have developed based more on common policy outlook and less on a common ambition for patronage. These organizations seem to have a way of growing up outside the formal party organization, whose form and manner of operation are closely regulated by law. They also have in common an attempt to regain for the organized activists a determining voice in nominations, a reaction from experience with the direct primary, whose results often seem most erratic.

In Wisconsin the "Republican voluntary committee" arose to champion the business outlook within the Republican party against the La Follette leadership. It developed an apparatus, including a convention, outside the formal, legally regulated organization which it controls. It controlled most major direct primary nominations. Presently a similar informal organizational structure developed among Democrats. Frank J. Sorauf comments on these organizations:

> Rising above all of the decentralizing forces in both voluntary committees is a great unifier—the common ideology. Party leaders in both parties share a common ideological allegiance that makes of them a homogeneous leadership group within each party. And it is this unity that the voluntary committees provide so much better than the statutory organization could. Motivated by a loyalty to principles, the party leaders are commonly serving without anticipation of personal gain from patronage or election to office. The common ideology, therefore, provides a common goal, binds the various levels of the party together, and makes for a certain degree of centralization. To the extent that this unified party outlook fosters like-thinking party candidates, the ideology works toward a party responsibility.[45]

[45] "Extra-Legal Parties in Wisconsin," *American Political Science Review*, 48 (1954), 692–704, at p. 703. See also Leon Epstein, "Party Activism in Wisconsin," *Midwest Journal of Political Science*, 1 (1957), 291–312.

In California informal party organizations have developed outside the formal organization somewhat on the order of the Wisconsin pattern. Again, a concern with nominations and a fairly high degree of policy homogeneity characterize the new organizations.[46] Whether these instances portend the shape of party reconstruction, they reflect experimentation among politicians in a quest for a mode of action appropriate to the new circumstances.

Popular Control of Party Organization

Party organization, as was suggested, may usefully be conceived as the problem of arranging collaboration among the political activists, those who carry on the business of the party—recruiting and designating candidates and promoting their election. Party organization does not encompass all activists nor are all holders of posts in the organization activists. Business leaders, labor-union officials, editors, advertising men, suburban housewives, and all types of persons may actually be included in the thin rank of activists within each party. Nor are the activists limited to any particular social class; they tend to be distributed over the spectrum of income and status. Yet among the activists the professional politicians, those holding office, and those holding positions in the formal and informal party organization are most conspicuous.[47]

It may be more or less inevitable that relatively small numbers of persons will make up the active elements of the party system. In a democratic order, as in other orders, power and influence gravitate into few hands. The fact that professional politicians, or a larger circle of activists, work together to put forward candidates, to proclaim their merits, and, often, to drag people to the polls to vote for them creates alternatives between which the electorate can choose. Paradoxically the operation of a democratic order depends on having some oligarchies about the premises seeking to grasp public office for one of their number.

LEGAL REGULATION OF PARTY ORGANIZATIONS   The cliques of people who make up party organizations from time to time gained almost unlimited power in some states and cities. Such closely held power ran counter to the notions of popular democracy, and legislators set about to remedy the matter by bringing the party organization under popular control. By the adoption of the direct primary, the organization was stripped of its most important function, that of nomination. The party organization itself, consisting largely of self-appointed individuals, was made in varying ways

[46] For additional comment on these organizations, see Chapter 14.
[47] See the study of organization in Elmira, New York, by Berelson, *et al., Voting* (Chicago: University of Chicago Press, 1956), ch. 8.

popularly elective, on the supposition that this mode of choice would make the organization responsive to the rank and file.

With the conception that the Republican organization should act for all Republicans in the electorate or that the Democratic organization should serve as the agent for all Democrats, it perhaps followed that party officers should be chosen by the rank and file. That such a supposition represents the behavioral realities may be doubted, for no matter how the party functionaries are formally chosen they tend to be more or less self-appointed. Most people have no concern about the party organization. When party committeemen are chosen by popular vote few people bother to express a choice. Ordinarily no contest develops for the posts, and when it does develop, cliques of professionals test their strength with only limited involvement of the rank and file. Not atypical were the elections of 301 state committeemen in Massachusetts in 1944 and 1948. In 73 per cent of the elections only one name was on the ballot. In only two races were over 3,000 votes cast; in each district, judging by the general election vote, the potential partisan vote ranged to over 30,000. In two-thirds of the elections of committeemen less than a thousand votes were polled.

On the whole, the introduction of procedures for the popular control of party organization has scarcely made the organization more of an agent of the rank and file. That does not mean that party organizations are not responsive to the rank and file. Many means exist, apart from popular election of ward committeemen, to bring party organization and mass sentiment into a rough harmony. It is the business of the party activists to estimate the intensities and directions of popular sentiment. Even though the organization may be internally dictatorial, it must win elections to remain alive. The problem may be one not so much of popular control of party organization as it is of so arranging party structure that the activists can perform those functions essential for a well-ordered party government.

DEMOCRACY BETWEEN RATHER THAN WITHIN PARTIES   Against the viewpoint that parties must be governed internally in a "democratic" fashion is to be set the notion that "democracy" is achieved by popular choice between parties. The internal affairs may be, and perhaps have to be, oligarchical in their management. To a degree this kind of situation prevails at the level of presidential politics. That there are presidential primaries must be conceded, but by and large the designation of candidates falls within the purview of the professionals and associated activists of each party. The electorate chooses between party candidates rather than among aspirants within each party, although the electorate is not without influence on the professionals even though its direct participation in nominations is limited.

One of the difficulties of the doctrine of interparty, as against intraparty, democracy is that its application requires the existence of two parties. That condition is not met in many states and localities. Unless intraparty democracy prevails the electorate has no choice. Yet it may well be that intraparty democracy tends to encourage the development of one-partyism and to make the politics of many states and cities, not a party politics, but a politics of factions, cliques, and individuals with amorphous popular followings.

13.

PARTY MACHINE AS

INTEREST GROUP

I N E A R L I E R chapters the idea was put forward that organized interests—business, labor, agriculture, religion, reform—are concerned with the acquisition of political power and influence in order that they may promote public policy favorable to their ends. Political parties are differentiated from pressure groups; they, unlike pressure groups, nominate candidates who seek formal control of the government. In doing so, parties must appeal to the entire community rather than to a single interest. Yet in one respect the inner core of the party—the machine or the party organization—may be considered to be in the same category as a pressure group: like the Chamber of Commerce of the United States, the party machine wants to bring about certain types of governmental action and to prevent others on questions of immediate concern to it. Though the party machine seeks many things from government, the end that excites the largest number of its members is public employment. The organization may be considered, in effect, as a pressure group that desires to control the selection of as many public employees as possible and to control the distribution of other favors and perquisites in which members of the party hierarchy have an interest. The object of this chapter is to set out the principal matters with which the party machine is concerned as an interest group.

The Patronage System

The patronage system may be viewed in several ways. From one angle it may be considered as the response of government to the demands of an interest group—the party machine—that desires a particular policy in the distribution of public jobs. That policy is phrased by the more moderate party men in some such terms as these: "Other things being equal, a party worker should be appointed to public office." The more extreme adherent of the spoils doctrine would omit the phrase "other things being equal."

The patronage system may be considered, too, as a method of financing party activity. The operation of a party organization requires the services of many men and women. Its social and friendly functions go on the year round; during campaigns, when literature must be distributed, electors canvassed, meetings organized, voters brought to the polls, and other campaign chores done, the work reaches its peak. Though much of this work is performed by unpaid volunteers, their efforts are not adequate. Indirectly, a considerable part of party expense is met by the public treasury, and the chief means of channeling public funds to party support is through the appointment of party workers to public office.

From still another viewpoint the patronage system, with its rotation in office, has been considered as a means of filling offices that is peculiarly in keeping with democratic theory. Andrew Jackson was the great proponent of this conception of the system. He argued:

> There are, perhaps, few men who can for any great length of time enjoy office and power without being more or less under the influence of feelings unfavorable to the faithful discharge of their public duties. Their integrity may be proof against improper considerations immediately addressed to themselves, but they are apt to acquire a habit of looking with indifference upon the public interests and of tolerating conduct from which an unpracticed man would revolt. Office is considered as a species of property, and government rather as a means of promoting individual interests than as an instrument created solely for the service of the people. Corruption in some and in others a perversion of correct feelings and principles divert government from its legitimate ends, and make it an engine for the support of the few at the expense of the many. The duties of all public officers are, or at least admit of being made, so plain and simple that men of intelligence may readily qualify themselves for their performance; and I cannot but believe that more is lost by the long continuance of men in office than is generally to be gained by their experience. I submit, therefore, to your consideration whether the efficiency

of the government would not be promoted, and official industry and integrity better secured, by a general extension of the law which limits appointments to four years.

Because of his expression of this doctrine, Jackson is generally given more credit than he deserves for the introduction of the spoils system, whose roots antedated Jackson. "It is admitted now that President Jefferson removed about the same proportion of officeholders as did Jackson, and further that the principles governing his removals were essentially the same as Jackson's," says E. M. Ericksson. He concludes: "If one would be just in his estimate he must admit that the development of the spoils system was a gradual process for which no one man or administration can be blamed." [1]

PRESSURE ON EXECUTIVES FOR APPOINTMENTS However ever the system started, it has been the source of continued pressure on Presidents, department heads, governors, and others in executive positions. President Polk, for example, in January, 1847, recorded in his diary that many persons had called to see him on "the contemptible business of seeking office for themselves or their friends." He felt that in making appointments he was unable to rely on the recommendations of Congressmen and others of "high station" who imposed on him and induced him "to make bad appointments." Succeeding Presidents were subjected to the same demands. In Cleveland's first Administration the demand on his time by office-seekers was so great that he announced he would no longer "grant interviews to those seeking public positions or their advocates." A large part of his time during the first eight months of his term had been devoted to the consideration of applications for office. The public welfare, he thought, required that "the time of the President should be differently occupied."

In the present century the pressure on the President for appointments has been reduced by civil service legislation but it has by no means been eliminated. James A. Farley described the movement of would-be office-holders on Washington following the Democratic victory in 1932:

> I had anticipated quite a rush of deserving patriots who were willing to help F.D.R. carry the burden. But, to be frank, I had never had the slightest conception of what was about to happen. They swarmed in and flocked in by the hundreds and thousands until it seemed as though they must have been arriving by special trainloads. . . . For two or three months I was compelled to hand over the running of the Post Office Department to my worthy assistants.[2]

[1] "The Federal Civil Service under President Jackson," *Mississippi Valley Historical Review*, 13 (1927), 517–40. See also L. D. White, *The Jacksonians* (New York: Macmillan, 1954), ch. 16.

[2] *Behind the Ballots* (New York: Harcourt, Brace, 1938), pp. 226–27.

CUSTOMS IN PATRONAGE DISTRIBUTION   Though the
party seeks to control appointments to public place, party organization consists of dispersed and loosely linked centers of power. That internal skeleton
of party becomes starkly apparent as one observes the distribution of jobs.
Nice calculations of strength and status must be made in the allocation of
patronage among claimants for recognition, and precautions must be taken
to assure clearance with those whose status in the party suffices to command
that they be consulted about appointments.

The statutes vest authority to make appointments in the President and
heads of departments and agencies. The management of patronage requires
that arrangements be established for consultation with party functionaries in
the exercise of this authority. The problems of patronage administration
revolve around the determination of whom to consult and around the allocation of patronage among those whose recommendations are entitled to be given
weight. In a measure the problem of allocation distills down to one of division
of the spoils among the party's Senators and Representatives.

Ordinarily the chairman of the national committee of the President's party
serves as a center for the distribution of patronage.[3] In Eisenhower's first
Administration, for example, the White House directed the Republican national chairman to receive applications sponsored by Republican Senators,
Representatives, and state leaders and to transmit them to the appointing
agencies. The departments and agencies were instructed to report to the committee each month on vacancies and to give it weekly reports on positions
filled.[4] The existence of such a patronage channel incidentally permits the
maintenance of central records of appointments "charged" against individual
Senators and Representatives, information useful in dealing with those who
complain of their treatment in the distribution of patronage.

By custom certain classes of patronage posts are assigned to Senators and
Representatives of the President's party. Senators have asserted, under the
prerogative of senatorial courtesy, control of appointments requiring sen-

---

[3] National chairmen become annoyed when the President makes appointments without clearance through organization channels. Ed Flynn, Democratic national chairman
in 1940, found that Roosevelt had made appointments of persons neither cleared with
nor acceptable to state organizations. This, Flynn told the President, "caused great unhappiness and animosity throughout the party." The President did not always keep his
promise to clear appointments with Flynn, who was thus caused "a great deal of
distress." *You're the Boss* (New York: Viking, 1947), p. 162. With great regularity
complaints about the handling of patronage occupy the majority's national committee
at its sessions early in the term of a new President.

[4] The White House memorandum to the agency heads observed: "A government
position for a loyal Republican of proven ability to do a better job of government will
thus earn votes of confidence next November and in 1956." The memo, issued in 1954,
also stated that "Personal patronage resulting from highly personalized recruiting by
certain uncooperative personnel people who are not in sympathy with this Administration
has resulted in a terrific loss of opportunity to recruit qualified loyal Republicans."
Quoted by H. Hollander, *Crisis in the Civil Service* (Washington: Current Issues, 1955),
p. 87.

atorial confirmation to posts in their states, with certain concessions to Representatives. The Senators of the President's party, more usually the senior Senator if there are two, exercise a controlling voice in patronage appointments to other federal posts with responsibilities over the entire state. On the other hand, Representatives of the President's party may expect to be recognized in appointments to patronage posts within their own districts. Thus, both Senators and Representatives seek to control those posts most closely connected with their own political fortunes, those in their own states and districts which they wish to be filled, if not by friends, at least not by enemies. When the allocations have been made to Senators and Representatives of the President's party, there remain positions in offices located in states and districts represented in Congress by the minority party. For such places, the national committeeman or state chairman of the President's party most often make recommendations, though for such positions the President enjoys some discretion in the recognition of a patronage referee.[5]

In his recommendations the Senator or Representative may exercise his own discretion or he may be merely the terminal point of a chain of endorsement that reaches down the party hierarchy. An action of the latter type would be a recommendation for an appointment that originated with a county chairman, cleared the office of state chairman and that of the national committeeman, and eventually reached the state's Senator who processed it through the national committee. When this kind of procedure operates in its pure form, the power of appointment, for at least certain types of posts, in fact rests in the lower levels of the organization.

To a degree the distribution of patronage becomes bureaucratized with fairly clear understandings about who is entitled to what; yet vexing problems always remain for the President, the national chairman, and other national leaders. Save for a few renegades, the party's Senators and Representatives have to be taken care of, but in states and districts with no party representation in Congress decisions must often be made on which party factions or leaders are to control patronage. The Eisenhower Administration had to decide which Republican organizations in southern states to recognize and what to do for the Eisenhower Democrats. When the state chairman and the national committeeman became embroiled in disputes over who gets what, the problem reaches the doorstep of the national chairman.[6] Or the national leadership

---

[5] See Harvey C. Mansfield, "Political Parties, Patronage, and the Federal Government Service" in *The Federal Government Service* (New York: The American Assembly, 1954).

[6] For example, in 1949 the New Jersey state chairman and his faction of the state party importuned Democratic national chairman W. M. Boyle, Jr., to give "due recognition" to recommendations made through the state chairman and thereby to break the patronage monopoly of Frank Hague, the national committeeman. On a similar patronage dispute in Michigan, see R. L. Sawyer, Jr., *The Democratic State Central Committee in Michigan* (Ann Arbor: University of Michigan, Institute of Public Administration, 1960), p. 125.

must make a choice between battling state factions, one of which may claim to be the true ally of the national Administration. In 1961, in an endeavor to induce a reorganization of the strife-torn New York organization, the Kennedy Administration paid no heed to patronage recommendations flowing up through the state chairman, Michael Prendergast, or the national committee-man, Carmine De Sapio. It dealt directly with county chairmen or made appointments of New Yorkers without clearance with any New York party authority. After the triumph of Mayor Robert Wagner in the 1961 mayoralty primary, the Administration recognized him as the patronage referee.

Patronage problems press most heavily upon the Administration of a party that has been out of power, and the management of patronage has wide ramifications both for the conduct of the government and for the nature of the party. Arrangements with Senators and Representatives may bear on the success of the legislative program.[7] Then, too, the system of clearances within the party organization over the country may be employed, within limits, to give aid and comfort to adherents to the President's faction of the party.

PRESSURE GROUPS AND PATRONAGE   In their strivings to control appointments to higher posts, Senators, Representatives, and party functionaries may serve as fronts for pressure groups with which their political fortunes are associated. The objective may be not so much to reward service to the party as to control future policy to the benefit of groups allied with the party. The airlines have an interest in the members of the Civil Aeronautics Board; the natural gas and power corporations are not indifferent to the membership of the Federal Power Commission; the railroads have a concern about the Interstate Commerce Commission. Organizations with a varied membership, such as the NAM, may maneuver informally to influence even cabinet appointments. Organizations with a narrower and homogeneous membership have a direct interest in lesser posts. "So the mine workers concentrate on the chief of the Bureau of Mines, the real estate people on the FHA, the commercial banks on the Comptroller of the Currency and the Federal Reserve Board, the savings and loan league on the Home Loan Bank Board, the airlines on the Civil Aeronautics Board, and so on."[8]

STATE AND CITY PATRONAGE PROCEDURES   Procedures for the allocation of patronage by city and state organizations vary, but, as with federal patronage, the pattern of operation tends to be influenced by the character of the organization and in turn affects the character of the organiza-

---

[7] A recurrent practice is for a new Administration to withhold patronage until the legislative program is well under way, a technique calculated to enlist legislators in the Administration's cause. In the first six months of the Kennedy Administration only seven federal judicial posts were filled. New judgeships and vacancies through retirement totaled about 100.

[8] Mansfield, *op. cit.,* p. 106.

tion. In a state or city with an atomized party the patronage of each department or agency is likely to be used to strengthen the personal following of the
head of the agency concerned. As the organization becomes more unified, the
tendency seems to be to bring all patronage into a single pool and to develop
a systematic procedure for its allocation among the principal party functionaries. In Chicago, for example, patronage appears to be largely in the hands
of the ward committeemen, the number of jobs under the control of each varying with the population of the ward, with the ramifications of the committeeman's power beyond his ward, and with the esteem in which he is held by the
higher party leaders.[9]

COST OF PATRONAGE   The stake of party machines in the game
of politics through their control over patronage appointments has not been
estimated in any accurate way, but certainly the annual cost runs into the
millions. In 1932 Raymond Moley estimated that "roughly half" the cost of
support of the magistrates' courts of New York City at that time went "either
to political work or to utter waste and inefficiency."[10] In May, 1933, the New
York Civil Service Reform Association found that the annual pay for positions
exempt from civil service requirements in New York City "was only $7,000,-
000, but about half of this sum [represented] sheer waste of public funds."
Most of the exempt positions were "passed around to the district leaders and
their henchmen." In 1937 Professor Pollock found that in Michigan the annual
turnover of public employees, owing in the main to the patronage system, was
25 per cent. He estimated the annual cost of breaking in new employees at
around a half-million dollars.[11]

The cost of the patronage system is not to be measured only by the salaries
of inefficient employees. Their errors may be extremely costly. For example,
a Chicago building inspector, appointed through party channels, inspected a
water tank atop a building. The 40,000-gallon tank later collapsed and fell
through six floors of the building, killing five men and injuring six others
enroute. The inspector's testimony before the coroner's jury follows:[12]

Q. How long have you been a building inspector? *A.* Nine months.
Q. What were you before that? *A.* I was a malt salesman.

[9] Patrick Nash, chairman of the Cook County Democratic committee, made the following statement after the election of Edward J. Kelly as mayor of Chicago by the city
council in 1933: "Before Mr. Kelly was definitely selected he promised that all jobs
would be filled through the ward committeemen. We all want jobs. But I know that no
ward committeeman wants a job at the expense of another ward committeeman or of
the taxpayers. For that reason there will be no one chasing Mr. Kelly around. All applications will come through the ward committeemen."
[10] Raymond Moley, *Tribunes of the People* (New Haven: Yale University Press,
1932), p. 263.
[11] J. K. Pollock, "The Cost of the Patronage System," *The Annals*, 189 (1937),
29–34.
[12] *Chicago Tribune*, June 2, 1934.

Q. When you were made a building inspector did you know anything about the work? *A.* No. I didn't know anything about it.

Q. When did you inspect the building and the tank? *A.* It was in January.

Q. Did you find anything wrong with the tank?

A. No. It looked all right to me.

Q. Are you in a position to know whether it was all right or not? *A.* No, I'm just the same as you or anybody else who might inspect it.

Q. Did you inspect the anchor plates? *A.* Well, I looked at them.

It is not to be concluded that all appointees who owe their jobs to the party organization are unfitted for office. Many persons of ability, industry, and loyalty to the public weal become public servants through party channels and remain permanently, to serve whatever party comes to power. They are overshadowed in public attention by such individuals as the building inspector whose disarming testimony has been quoted and by such rollicking cases as the minority registrar of the Baltimore Board of Supervisors of Elections. A patronage-starved Republican organization in 1941 and 1942 was so hard pressed for jobs that this $3,000 place was filled by a series of Republican ward executives. One would serve for a month, resign, and be replaced by another. Republican leaders defended the arrangement as a means of avoiding the evils of long continuance in office.

Political Neutralization of the Civil Service

The existence of a large body of civil employees of federal, state, and local governments active in support of the party in power supposedly tips the scales in favor of the party that controls the electioneering activities of these employees. Often the party in power is tempted to improve on this advantage by increasing the number of patronage employees. Although the party out of power cannot support its workers from the public treasury,[13] it commands the services of workers eager to obtain office as a result of future victory. And the hungry sometimes work harder than the well fed.

Whichever party wins, the public pays the cost of the patronage system. For this and other reasons there has been a persistent effort, to a degree successful, to remove the public employee from partisan activity. By political neutralization of the government service, technical merit may be established as the basis for the selection of public employees. The forces contending for political power will no longer need to form alliances with machines consisting primarily of public employees; and the control of government may be shifted from party to party without the disruption of the public service attendant upon large-scale turnover in subordinate administrative positions.

[13] In some localities at some times, though, a modest quantity of patronage fed to the minority restrains its ferocity.

The neutralization of the civil service requires that the civil servant serve with equal loyalty whatever party is in power. Permanence of tenure of office is in one respect a condition, in another, a consequence, of political neutrality. Political neutrality is a condition precedent to permanence of tenure, since no party can be expected to retain in the public employ individuals who have actively campaigned against it. On the other hand, when civil servants refrain from active participation in electoral campaigns, the government of the day may be stronger in its efforts to resist the demands of party workers that a clean sweep be made of the administrative services to provide places for those who have loyally served the party.

PENDLETON ACT OF 1883   The principal type of public policy to neutralize politically the great mass of administrative employees of government has been so-called "civil service" or "merit system" laws. The Pendleton Act of 1883 created the Federal Civil Service Commission and provided for recruitment of persons to fill positions in the "classified service" by competitive examination. By classified service was meant the aggregate of positions covered by the legislation; those positions outside the classified service remain subject to the patronage system. In the excluded class of positions were such offices as United States marshal, collector of internal revenue, federal district attorney, and (with modifications from time to time) postmasters. Since 1883 the scope of the classified service has gradually been increased, with the defenders of the patronage system fighting a slowly losing battle.[14]

A corollary of appointment through competitive examination and tenure during good behavior is neutrality in political campaigns. In practice political neutrality has been difficult to enforce, but the tendency in the federal service has been to make more stringent the rules against partisan activity by employees in the classified service. The original rule of the Civil Service Commission provided: "No person in the said service shall use his official authority or influence either to coerce the political action of any person or body or to interfere with any election." Apparently this rule did not adequately cover the situation, for President Cleveland in 1886 issued an executive order exhorting federal officeholders to refrain from "obtrusive partisanship." When Theodore Roosevelt was a member of the United States Civil Service Commission, he observed excessive partisanship among federal employees and was moved to write for the 1894 annual report of the commission:

A man in the classified service has an entire right to vote as he pleases, and to express privately his opinions on all political subjects; but he

[14] For an account of the civil service reform movement, see F. M. Stewart, *The National Civil Service Reform League* (Austin: University of Texas Press, 1929). See also Ari Hoogenboom, *Outlawing the Spoils* (Urbana: University of Illinois Press, 1962), and Dorothy G. Fowler, "Precursors of the Hatch Act," *Mississippi Valley Historical Review*, 47 (1960–61), 247–62.

should not take any active part in political management or in political campaigns, for precisely the same reasons that a judge, an army officer, a regular soldier, or a policeman is debarred from taking such an active part. It is no hardship to a man to require this. It leaves him free to vote, think and speak privately as he chooses, but it prevents him while in the service of the whole public, from turning his official position to the benefit of one of the parties in which the whole public is divided; and in no other way can this be prevented.

Almost the same language was used in 1907 when the rules under the Civil Service Act were amended to provide: "Persons who by the provisions of these rules are in the competitive classified service, while retaining the right to vote as they please and to express their opinions on all political subjects, shall take no active part in political management or in political campaigns." In the application of the rule against taking "active part in political management or in political campaigns," fine distinctions have to be made between what is and what is not permissible behavior by a civil servant. He may express his views "privately" but not in public places or by the publication of a letter or article in favor of any party or candidate. He may make political contributions but only to persons not in the service of the United States and to them only "voluntarily." He may be a member of a political club but not one of its officers; he may not be a candidate for elective office; he may attend a political convention as a spectator but not as a member; he must not wear campaign badges or buttons.[15]

HATCH ACT   In 1939 Congress, in the Hatch Act, broadened the application of the rule of political neutrality. The rules under the Civil Service Act affected only the classified service and left a substantial number of unclassified employees free to engage in political activities. The Hatch Act declared it

. . . unlawful for any person employed in the executive branch of the Federal Government, or any agency or department thereof, to use his official authority or influence for the purpose of interfering with an election or affecting the result thereof. No officer or employee in the executive branch of the Federal Government, or any agency or department thereof, shall take any active part in political management or in political campaigns. All such persons shall retain the right to vote as they may choose and to express their opinions on all political subjects and candidates.

Specified policy-forming officials, such as the President, the Vice President, the heads and assistant heads of departments, and other high officials whose business it is to make and defend governmental decisions are excluded from

---

[15] Political activity is permissible in purely nonpartisan local campaigns and in local campaigns in certain communities heavily populated by federal employees.

the prohibition of political activity. The effect of the Hatch Act was to extend to most employees outside the classified service the rules that had long governed those in the classified service.[16]

Quite apart from legislative taboos on patronage, the assumption by the government of technical functions requiring the services of professional classes has made it "bad" politics for the party to apply the patronage system to many departments and agencies. Congressmen, for example, often bring pressure on administrative officers to appoint loyal party workers as clerks, stenographers, messengers, or other routine workers, yet they will keep hands off the professional and expert groups. Such a rule is not universally followed, but the extent of its observance indicates a recognition by political leaders that it is not to their interest to use a certain class of positions to reward party workers.

FEDERAL PATRONAGE AFTER 1952   When the Republican Administration came into power after the election of 1952, it faced a demand from the party ranks for patronage and was confronted by a public service that had been largely blanketed under the civil service laws by preceding Democratic Presidents. A favorite topic of discussion at sessions of the Republican national committee was the shortage of patronage, and the Republican Senate policy committee grumbled about appointments without consultation with the Senate and the imposition of requirements by the Administration that made deserving Republicans ineligible.[17] President Eisenhower met the situation by removing from the classified service about 134,000 positions. By no means were all the holders of these positions replaced by Republicans, but the list was combed for positions that might be transferred to Schedule C, a category of positions to be filled without regard to formal merit procedures.[18] The contention was that certain types of appointments should be made at the discretion of the heads of administrative agencies in order that they might fulfill their responsibilities. That view had, to be sure, a degree of validity, but it could also be used to justify the replacement of competent and loyal career personnel by deserving Republicans. And, later, the same contention could be made on behalf of deserving Democrats.

[16] For detailed interpretations and an impression of the types of violations proceeded against under the Hatch Act, see U.S. Civil Service Commission, *Hatch Act Decisions* (Washington: Government Printing Office, 1949). For a summary of laws and rules, see *Political Activity of Federal Officers and Employees* (U.S. Civil Service Commission, Pamphlet 20, 1961). And see D. H. Nelson, "Political Expression under the Hatch Act and the Problem of Statutory Ambiguity," *Midwest Journal of Political Science*, 2 (1958), 76–88; Henry Rose, "A Critical Look at the Hatch Act," *Harvard Law Review*, 75 (1962), 510–26. On state and local practices, see *Regulating Political Activities of Public Employees* (Civil Service Assembly, Personnel Report No. 543, 1954).

[17] Senator Aiken of Vermont remarked that he was getting "sick of" the Administration's "setting up qualifications" for appointees "that only Democrats can meet."

[18] Nearly 70,000 jobs had been processed through the White House patronage machinery by the end of 1955. R. J. Donovan, *Eisenhower: The Inside Story* (New York: Harper, 1956), p. 101.

LIMITATIONS ON STATE AND LOCAL EMPLOYEES
Parallel to the federal enactments has been a trend toward adoption of the competitive method for recruitment to state and municipal offices, along with accompanying limitations on partisan activity. State and local rules against the participation of civil servants in political campaigns have been less effective than the federal regulations. In some states and municipalities stringent rules of neutrality in politics are consistently ignored. Only about a score of states have civil service commissions or like agencies that conduct competitive examinations for the selection of most state employees. Much less movement toward the substitution of merit for patronage has occurred in the counties, while about 40 per cent of the cities of from 10,000 to 100,000 population have no civil service system.[19]

In all states and localities a large group of employees has been brought under the merit system by conditions attached to federal grants. The most significant group affected by such requirements consists of state and local employees in charge of state programs of public assistance and employment security. A 1939 amendment to the Social Security Act provided that after January 1, 1940, all state agencies in these fields should, as a condition of receiving federal grants, make provision for "the establishment and maintenance of personnel standards on a merit basis."

Congress has also, by its leverage through federal subsidies, extended the limitations on political activity of the Hatch Act to a substantial number of state and local employees. The relevant 1940 statutory provision reads as follows:

> No officer or employee of any State or local agency whose principal employment is in connection with any activity which is financed in whole or in part by loans or grants made by the United States or by any Federal agency shall (1) use his official authority or influence for the purpose of interfering with an election or a nomination for office, or affecting the result thereof, or (2) directly or indirectly coerce, attempt to coerce, command, or advise any other such officer or employee to pay, lend, or contribute any part of his salary or compensation or anything else of value to any party, commmittee, organization, agency, or person for political purposes. No such officer or employee shall take any active part in political management or in political campaigns. All such persons shall retain the right to vote as they may choose and to express their opinions on all political subjects and candidates.

If the state authorities fail to remove from office a person found by the United States Civil Service Commission to have violated the act, a sum equivalent to two years' compensation of the violator is deducted from grants to

[19] In 1960 for each federal civilian employee there were about 2.6 state and local employees.

the state concerned. The Civil Service Commission has made findings and is-sued orders in a few such cases to the accompaniment of strident protests about states' rights and the constitutional privilege of the individual to participate in politics. Following the pattern of the federal legislation a goodly number of states and cities adopted laws and ordinances popularly known as "little Hatch Acts." [20]

There is some doubt about the efficacy of a limitation on political activity that is not accompanied by permanence of tenure and opportunity for a career in the administrative service. The affected state and local employees, Senator Thomas pointed out in the debate on the extension of the Hatch Act, "remain patronage employees. . . . Their tenure of office depends upon the success of their party at successive elections." Others may campaign, he said, "for the sole purpose of succeeding the Hatch mutes in office." When an employee knows that if his party loses the election he will lose his job, the temptation to engage in political activity in violation of the law is great.

LONG-RUN TRENDS IN PATRONAGE   During the past half-century the proportion of the public service selected by patronage and the proportion of public employees active in party work have declined. The impact of merit system laws, the rise of professionalism in the public service, and the increasing reliance on technical personnel have all taken their toll. Furthermore, the era of full employment after World War II and the changing conditions of private employment greatly reduced the appeal of public employment. Often the problem of the public administrator became one of attracting sufficient personnel to man the public service rather than one of warding off unqualified applicants carrying party endorsement.

Yet the patronage system remains, as it must, but to what extent is another question. A marked shrinkage of the patronage pool has occurred in the federal service. President Truman even succeeded, after a warm fight with the Senate, in transferring the collectors of internal revenue to the career service. Among states and localities the situation differs. In some cities almost the entire municipal service consists of persons who gained their positions through party channels and who devote a portion of their time to the work of the party machine. In a few cities, at the other extreme, the number of patronage employees is extremely small. Some states have developed civil services that serve loyally and impartially whatever party is in power and refrain from partisan activity; other states have an almost completely new set of employees, outside the federally protected departments, when a new party comes into power.

---

[20] The consequences of such legislation are illustrated by the following news story: "Mary Carrol . . . yesterday became the fourth municipal employee to resign from a post on the Republican Town Committee because of the 'little Hatch Act.' She has been vice chairman of the 27th Ward for 12 years. . . . She is matron in the women's comfort station in Church Street." *New Haven Courier-Journal*, May 31, 1951.

Diverse Party Spoils

A loyal organization man may find ample reward in a public job. Yet the organization seeks jobs for more than the sake of the job itself. Control of place may bring also to the organization control of powerful sanctions in the administration of law to reward its friends or to penalize its opponents. The party as a whole must concern itself with broad questions of public policy; the party machine is more likely to worry about the thousands of decisions that may affect an individual for better or worse. Officials from a police patrolman to cabinet member decide questions of most immediate concern to the individual. Party organization leaders often take a lively interest in these decisions; they may aid or injure members and friends of the organization.

To catalogue the types of decisions in which party organizations may interest themselves would require a listing of most activities of government. For the moment attention may be concentrated on types of public spoils that often serve about the same function as jobs in rewarding organization members and supporters. In the spending, managing, and controlling of public moneys and property many actions other than appointments to jobs may be converted to the purposes of the party organization.[21]

JUDICIAL SPOILS   In all political organizations lawyers are to be found in prominent positions, and in some localities those affiliated with the dominant party machine are favored in appointments by the courts of masters in chancery, receivers, trustees, and other judicial functionaries. The board of managers of the Chicago Bar Association reported in 1934: [22]

> Recently, in exercising their discretion in the appointment of masters, certain judges have deferred to the wishes of politicians. The appointment of a master in chancery as one of the political spoils belonging to a successful party, regardless of the qualifications of the master, is a subversion of the judicial powers of the court. As a result of this system, many masters in chancery have been nominated by politicians and appointed by the courts, who are wholly unfit to perform the functions required of them.

[21] H. F. Gosnell reports, for example, that in Chicago: "Of the seven Democratic ward committeemen who were not employed by some governmental agency in 1928, three were in occupations which enabled them to have many dealings with public authorities. One was in the sewer contracting business; the second was in a law firm which had many political ramifications; and the third was in the insurance business." *Machine Politics: Chicago Model* (Chicago: University of Chicago Press, 1937), p. 40.

[22] Report by the Board of Managers, Chicago Bar Association, February 1, 1934. Seven Democratic "reform" district leaders of New York created a stir in 1962 by their advocacy of the elimination of patronage practices in court appointments of lawyers to represent minors, incompetents, and unknown heirs. These appointments, often sinecures carrying generous fees, had long constituted a major patronage source.

Similar comments would be applicable to such appointments in many other localities; the federal district courts, too, have not been free from like practices. The large, sometimes exorbitant, fees drawn by receivers and similar officers acting in a fiduciary capacity under the supervision of courts make these appointments especially desirable to the legal lights of the party machine.[23]

POLITICAL CONTRACTS   Urban machines are likely to have several contractors occupying important posts in the organization; frequently the contractor may not be a district leader or a ward committeeman but a silent and inconspicuous member of the organization. Contracts for public works may flow to the organization contractors, often at unreasonable figures. In turn, the contractor may use a part of his profits to aid the party machine in financing its campaigns. The many jobs available on public works incidentally furnish an opportunity to allocate employment to the adherents of the machine. Supplies for public agencies may likewise be purchased from firms controlled by members of the organization. Firms providing services or materials on occasion pay a "commission" to an influential political leader, some of which may (or may not) benefit the party cause. Procurement officers may take special precautions lest contracts go to firms reputed to be associated with the opposition. Almost every major locality has its contracting firms that are commonly regarded, sometimes correctly, as "Democratic" or "Republican" concerns. Modern reform movements and the general improvement in the quality of public administration have reduced greatly the grossness of spoils in contracts and purchasing. The "organization" contractor often has advantage in obtaining awards, but he is more likely to do approximately what he is paid for than he was a few decades ago.

REAL ESTATE PURCHASE: ''HONEST GRAFT''   The purchase of real estate for public improvements has furnished opportunity for members of the upper strata of the party organization to enrich themselves. This practice, incidentally, contributed one of the classic phrases of the argot of politics, "honest graft." The late Senator Plunkitt, a godsend to the authors of textbooks, is reported to have said: [24]

> There's an honest graft, and I'm an example of how it works. I might sum up the whole thing by sayin': "I seen my opportunities and I took 'em."
> Just let me explain by examples. My party's in power in the city, and

---

[23] The prestige of the bench makes judgeships especially useful for granting recognition to minority groups. See W. S. Sayre and H. Kaufman, *Governing New York City* (New York: Russell Sage Foundation, 1960), pp. 538–48.

[24] Quoted in W. L. Riordan, *Plunkitt of Tammany Hall* (New York: McClure, Phillips, 1905), pp. 4–5.

it's goin' to undertake a lot of public improvements. Well, I'm tipped off, say, that they're going to lay out a new park at a certain place.

I see my opportunity and I take it. I go to that place and I buy up all the land I can in the neighborhood. Then the board of this or that makes its plan public, and there is a rush to get my land, which nobody cared particularly for before.

Ain't it perfectly honest to charge a good price and make a profit on my investment and foresight? Of course it is. Well, that's honest graft.

A somewhat different light was put on the matter by Leonard Wallstein in an investigation of real estate purchases by the Tammany administration in New York City during the twenties. He found that persons with inside information on the land needs of the city acquired land in the names of dummies with "no apparent financial means, but who produce substantial sums of cash from safe deposit boxes or office safes, buy up property and turn quick profits, which are again immediately converted into cash and vanish. Clearly these operators have been merely the dummies of puppets for influential undisclosed principals." In short periods tremendous profits were made on a relatively small cash investment.[25] Episodes of irregularity in the acquisition of rights-of-way for the federal interstate highway system suggest that "honest graft" is still with us.

OTHER PROPRIETARY OPERATIONS   The examples cited involved the utilization of discretion in the management of public expenditures for the purpose of rewarding, supporting, or financing the work of members of the party organization. The annals of American administration abound with instances of similar abuses in connection with other activities of government that might be classed as proprietary. The purchase of insurance by public authorities has been in many times and places notoriously for partisan benefit, and a goodly number of political leaders operate as insurance agents. Commonly they also provide bonds for contractors and others required to give surety for performance. The word gets around that it is advisable for contractors to be bonded through a particular agency. Services, such as hospital care, may be provided without charge in appropriate instances. The disposition of public property may be governed by partisan consideration.[26] Deposits of public funds may go to bankers supporting the organization.[27] All these and

---

[25] Leonard Wallstein, *Report on Law and Procedure in Condemnation Applicable to Proceedings Brought by the City of New York* (January, 1932).

[26] See M. R. Werner and John Starr, *Teapot Dome* (New York: Viking, 1959).

[27] A report by the New Jersey state treasurer in 1954 quoted a letter from a banker to his county Republican leader asking that his bank be given an additional state deposit: "As I can't scurry around for business from private sources I should at least get some public funds to fill in." The banker had been diverted from his business by his activities as county campaign manager. In due course, his bank received a deposit from the state treasurer. This incident was reported by a Democratic state treasurer as

other such uses of authority over funds and property occur, though they are often individual misdeeds rather than systematic utilization of authority for the benefit of the organization.

The Shady Side of the Law

The common American belief seems to be that politicians are engaged in a dirty business. While the belief usually caricatures the reality, it contains enough truth to warrant some attention. In the preceding pages emphasis rested on the expenditure of funds and the management of resources for the benefit of the party organization. At this point attention may be shifted to the application and misapplication of law to individual citizens in a way to reward party support, to recruit party support, or to penalize opposition. Such matters include anything from "fixing" a traffic ticket to an overly generous settlement of a disputed item of an income-tax return, from overlooking the violation of a minor municipal ordinance to expediting an export license covering millions of dollars worth of goods.

PATTERNS OF ACCESS TO GOVERNMENT   Democratic regimes possess no monopoly of favoritism and unevenness in the application of general rules of law to individual cases. Probably as long as man has governed man, fixers have sought to tamper with the scales of justice. The role of the political party in this process may be peculiar to democratic regimes, although one may well suspect that the parties—if they are parties—of dictatorial regimes are not above fixing a traffic ticket.

The pattern of relationships in which the party organization plays an intermediary role between citizen and government varies enormously. At one extreme might be placed the stereotype of the boss-ridden city in which the party boss and his aides in fact are the city government. To obtain almost any governmental action the citizen has to apply to the boss. So thorough an envelopment of the formal administrative apparatus by the party organization has become rare. In certain cities, to be sure, the situation approximates the old pattern. More often the ward committeeman or a similar party functionary is the person to see to obtain action on certain types of community services. At the other extreme one would place the role of the party organization as an "introducer" whose word insures a respectful hearing and a responsible consideration of the problem of the person who approaches government through party channels.

Between the extremes of complete control of government by the party apparatus and the party as a channel of access lie all sorts of irregular patterns

he prepared to switch into government bonds $23,000,000 deposited in banks by his Republican predecessors.

of relations between party and government. This district leader may have influence with a particular judge; that one may control the police department or parts of it. That ward committeeman may have an "in" with the prosecutor's office. This county committeeman may be the channel through which the tax assessor can be reached. The county chairman may have his lines into the governor's office. The state chairman or the national committeeman may be able to deal with the collector of internal revenue or the district attorney. Legislators frequently serve as channels to administrative agencies. Often the differentiation between party functionary and public official does not exist; a single individual may occupy both posts and may exercise his official authority to the advantage, or supposed advantage, of party in particular cases.

UNDERWORLD AND PARTY   Though a tortured interpretation of public policy may be served out for party advantage in any government activity, the most spectacular type of irregularity occurs in the relations between underworld and government, with party organization or some of its leaders often as an intermediary. The industries on the shady side of the law —gambling, narcotics, prostitution, liquor in dry areas—must arrange with government either directly or indirectly through party for the privilege of operating. This necessity for "protection" in order to exist often results in a close communion between at least elements of the party organization and underworld bosses and leaders.

What conception to apply to the relation between party, government, and underworld to produce a meaningful description presents a puzzling problem. The simple conception seems to be that the gambling-syndicate boss bribes the holder of authority, against his will, to permit illegal operation. That picture usually errs on the side of naïveté. Another view is that illegal enterprise attempts to mold its environment, just as does the legal enterprise, to permit the most convenient and profitable operation. The circumstances require that the illegal industry employ peculiar methods for shaping its environment; behavioristically, however, such a group interacts with other groups and with government in an attempt to develop a *modus vivendi* in much the same pattern as does a group tolerated by formal law. Yet this conception implies more regularity, more of a "pattern," than seems actually to prevail.

The privilege obtained by the underworld syndicate amounts to a monopolistic license. It is usually accompanied by a policy of restraining competition through enforcement of the law against those not affiliated with the protected group. These "franchises" form the basis for profitable undertakings. The New York State Crime Commission, for example, found that profits from slot machines in the rooms of fraternal clubs and in veteran's halls in a one-horse town in upstate New York amounted to $500,000 in five years. The profits from the operation of punchboards amount to fabulous sums. Estimates, necessarily with only sketchy bases, of the gross take of bookmakers for the nation as a whole run from three to ten billion dollars annually.[28]

The relation of the party organization to such enterprises is scarcely a matter of public record, and its description is fraught with difficulty. Often the party organization as such does not enter into the arrangement at all; even the patrolman on the beat may sell certain types of protection. Yet too often persons in the party hierarchy or their close associates have a hand in the fix. By no means all the enormous sums paid for protection go to party treasuries; yet, when campaigns have to be financed, underworld industries can be tapped for contributions. Moreover, in cities and parts of cities thoroughly organized by a gambling syndicate the runners, bookies, and other personnel can be converted into a formidable campaigning organization. The Chicago Crime Commission estimates that the handbook operators of that city can deliver 200,000 votes. Rather than pay party functionaries for protection, gambling and racketeering groups at times take over party organizations or segments of organizations. Warren Moscow reports, for example, that underworld leaders in the 1940's installed their own men as district leaders in the New York City Democratic organization: "The late Albert Marinelli was made leader of the old Second Assembly District on the lower East Side literally by the guns of Luciano's gorillas, the first leader to be installed by the underworld itself." [29]

Businesses that operate near the boundary between legality and illegality appear to be especially dependent on pecuniary leverage in their dealings with government, even when they are on the right side of the law. Legalized race tracks, for example, must have licenses—which may be revoked—to operate. Their stockholders seem to include an uncommonly large proportion of well-placed party leaders.[30] Such enterprises are also often vulnerable to demands that they hire their employees on the basis of party recommendations.[31] Similarly, the liquor business in all its phases from distilling to re-

---

[28] The extent and variety of underworld enterprises are suggested by the findings of the Kefauver committee. See *Hearings*, Special Committee to Investigate Organized Crime in Interstate Commerce, U.S. Senate, 81st Cong., 2d sess. (1950), and 82d Cong., 1st sess. (1951), pursuant to S. Res. 202. See also the committee's final report, Senate Report No. 725, 82d Cong., 1st sess. (1951).

[29] *New York Times*, November 26, 1950. For data on the associations between New York district leaders, Republican and Democratic, and entrepreneurs in illegal undertakings, see New York State Crime Commission, *Second Report to the Governor*, March 9, 1954 (Legislative Doc. No. 40, 1954).

[30] Illustrative are the revelations coincident with the resignation of J. Russel Sprague as Republican national committeeman from New York in 1953. A goodly number of important Republican leaders had made fortunate investments in race tracks in the neighborhood of New York City. One investment of $2,000 yielded a profit of $194,000, after taxes, when sold after being held 10 months. For a summary of the investigation into the matter, see *New York Times*, March 14, 1954.

[31] John Strohmeyer estimates that party leaders in Massachusetts, Rhode Island, and New Hampshire control jobs worth $1,000,000 a year at the tracks in their states. In

tailing puts large sums into politics. Not only must the legality of the industry generally be maintained; decisions must be assured on the rights of individual concerns to share in the business.

PENALITIES FOR OPPOSITION   Abuses of authority may penalize as well as reward. The powers of government may be utilized to bind individuals and groups to the support of the organization; they may also be used to penalize opposition and to intimidate those tempted to oppose. Corrupt party organizations over limited areas and for limited periods of time succeed in almost completely suppressing opposition. Those whose support cannot be obtained by fair means or foul may have life made miserable for them. Or the threat of reprisal may keep them mute. The annals of political irregularities contain endless examples, but the nature of the possibilities is suggested by the conclusion of Maurice Milligan concerning the Pendergast machine of Kansas City: "Make no mistake—this organization could do more than elect or defeat candidates for political office. It could make or break a business through tax levies, building permits, building condemnations by city inspectors, special favors, and in a hundred other ways." [32]

The Function of Spoils

The patronage system and various other types of spoils tend to be treated as an unfortunate manifestation of the innate perversity of man; and many specific instances of peculation, fraud, and nepotism in the public sphere are no different in motive or effect from departures from the code of proper conduct for persons in positions of trust in ecclesiastical, commercial, and labor associations. Yet the patronage system in the large is something more than a collection of unrelated cases of individual venality.

From one standpoint the patronage system and, to a certain extent, other types of spoils may be considered a means to aid in the financing of the elaborate party machinery that seems to be necessary under our form of government. With our innumerable offices filled by popular vote and our multiplicity of elections, it seems almost indispensable that many persons devote their time to party work. What men shall devote their time to this work? Only those who have adequate private means to permit them to dedicate themselves to the service of their party? That solution would hardly be in keeping with the spirit of American democracy. Carl Russell Fish argued that "the true cause for the introduction of the spoils system was the triumph of

---

1955, 44 New Hampshire legislators worked at the Rockingham track. See "Yankee Morals and the $2 Bet," *Harper's Magazine*, July, 1956.

   [32] M. M. Milligan, *The Inside Story of the Pendergast Machine by the Man Who Smashed It* (New York: Scribner's, 1948), p. 22.

democracy." The work of the party "requires the labor of many men: there must be captains of hundreds and captains of tens, district chiefs and ward heelers. . . . It is an essential idea of democracy that these leaders shall be of the people; they must not be gentlemen of wealth and leisure, but they must—the mass of them at any rate—belong to the class that makes its own living. If, then, they are to devote their time to politics, politics must be made to pay." [33] Fish contended that the spoils system served in the period of its establishment "a purpose that could probably have been performed in no other way, and that was fully worth the cost." Without the inducement of public jobs and other perquisites, the formation of party organizations becomes difficult. Nevertheless, in some places effective local machines of a middle-class character have been constructed without benefit of spoils.

From another viewpoint the entire spoils system serves to maintain discipline within the organization or, more precisely, within segments of it. The preceding chapter emphasized the loose articulation of the elements of the national organization as a whole. To some extent patronage helps hold together these elements, but the potency of patronage becomes more apparent in city organizations, state organizations, in the personal and factional following of Senators, Representatives, and other leaders. The adroit allocation of rewards aids a party leader in holding his organization together. The usefulness of jobs for this purpose is obvious, but other types of spoils may be employed in the same fashion. A rebellious district leader or ward committeeman may discover that his printing contract or his fire hose business has been cut off by the higher-ups in the organization. The spoils system may, thus, serve as a method consolidating into a cohesive group the persons constituting the machine. Yet one should by no means assume that the patronage system is invariably efficiently managed for party purposes. The fiction prevails that while party leaders may not always manage the public service well they are wizards in the conduct of party business. In actuality, patronage often goes to persons quite undeserving in terms of party service.[34] And the management of patronage may make enemies as well as friends. The saying is that a Senator, forced to endorse one of 10 applicants for a job, makes nine enemies and one ingrate.[35]

---

[33] *The Civil Service and the Patronage* (New York: Longmans, Green, 1905), p. 156.

[34] Consider the following announcement from the official organ of the Philadelphia Republican organization. Steps were to be taken "to comb out of city and county offices the social and fraternal and 'pull' appointees, so that places can be made for the men who pull doorbells and produce majorities. . . . This is Senator Vare's idea and comes direct. Men who can't produce are to 'walk the plank.' This will be good news to the men who deliver." D. H. Kurtzman, *Methods of Controlling Votes in Philadelphia.* Privately published thesis, University of Pennsylvania, 1935, p. 43. See also Frank J. Sorauf, "State Patronage in a Rural County," *American Political Science Review,* 50 (1956), 1046–56. See the reflective analysis by J. Q. Wilson, "The Economy of Patronage," *Journal of Political Economy,* 69 (1961), 369–80.

[35] In a speech of June 1, 1961, William Proxmire, Democratic Senator from Wisconsin, fixed the ratio at 20 enemies to one ingrate as he reported that he had received

The spoils of power are used to gain support of individuals and of groups under regimes in nondemocratic countries. Many commentators find the like use of spoils in the United States for this purpose to be monstrous and unparalleled, but the practice is as old as human government. Governors of all regimes use the perquisites at their disposal to command the support and loyalty of those susceptible to purchase in this fashion. The striking difference about American practice is the moral reprobation that accompanies it; conditions that elsewhere would be accepted as a matter of course are here considered not quite cricket.[36]

Nor can the spoils system be considered or understood in isolation. In a thoroughly machine-ridden city the observer, to comprehend the nature and function of the system, must look for the allies of the machine. "The major interests," says Odegard, "are content to leave minor spoils, such as jobs in the public service, to the party agents as long as these agents direct the affairs of state in a manner to promote the interests of the powerful oligarchies which control the economic and social destinies of the community."[37] If one examines a city corruptly governed at about the beginning of the century, he will observe a powerful political machine utilizing the spoils opportunities to the utmost. But allied with the machine probably would be found the telephone, traction, and power interests, which sought franchises and privileged treatment at the city's hands, underworld syndicates controlling gambling and prostitution, and perhaps other groups that required for their profitable existence a favorably disposed city administration. It was by the combination of the party machine, the utilities, and the underworld that control of the city could be gained, and by that control each segment of the power combination could obtain what it wanted.[38]

---

over 2,000 communications in behalf of candidates for postmaster appointments in Wisconsin.

[36] On the use of patronage to maintain party discipline, the following comment by Professor J. K. Pollock is relevant: "It has often been contended that patronage is a necessary aid to political leadership in this country. But it is interesting to note that many of our greatest governors—Grover Cleveland, Robert Marion La Follette, Judson Harmon, Hiram Johnson and Albert Ritchie, to name a few—men whose political leadership was undoubted and of a high order, were not merely advocates of civil service but were responsible for its establishment in their respective states." "The Cost of the Patronage System," *The Annals*, 189 (1937), 29–34.

[37] "Political Parties and Group Pressures," *The Annals*, 179 (1935), 69–81.

[38] The patronage-supported organization can, of course, become a unit of constellation of interests whose elements differ from those of the classic American urban machine. The power of patronage may be a counterpoise to business interests as well as an ally. Consider in this connection the remarks of Senator Paul H. Douglas in defense of senatorial patronage: "But I would like to have you consider just how long most liberals would be able to last in Congress if you stripped us of all patronage, as you desire. We who try to defend the interests of the people, the consumers and the taxpayers commonly face the powerful opposition of the special-interest groups which will spend enormous sums of money to defeat us. . . . If we are to survive we need some support rooted in gratitude for material favors which at the same time do not injure the general public." *New Republic*, July 14, 1952, p. 2.

Thus it came about that important interests outside the party machine itself were content to leave unlimited spoils to the party organization in order that their own interests might be advanced. When all the franchises had been awarded, when privileges sought had been legally granted, the important business interests associated with the party machine were likely to become converts to the doctrine of economy and efficiency in government. Consequently a sharp decline in the scope of the spoils system has occurred in many American jurisdictions. Where the spoils system still exists unchallenged and unashamed, usually the power combination controlling the jurisdiction contains important elements in addition to the party machine itself—elements that seek to gain, through toleration of their machine allies, governmental action or inaction that might not readily be obtainable in any other way.

The interest of the party in patronage and in other perquisites encounters opposition from other social groups. The party hierarchy is in this respect like any pressure group: the unlimited prosecution of group interests may meet a countermovement from people adversely affected. In this process the long-term trend has undoubtedly been to limit more and more the perquisites of the party hierarchy.[39] Merit system protection has been extended to most federal employees and to a substantial proportion of state and local employees. Many kinds of party spoils have been made illegal. Public services are manned to higher degree by a professionalized personnel animated by a higher professional ethic than prevailed in the past. Yet party machines resist encroachments on their ancient prerogatives, and movement toward weaning them away from their perquisites is slow and halting.

The truth is that we have contrived no system for the support of party that does not place considerable reliance on patronage. The party organization makes a democratic government work and charges a price for its services. Sometimes it becomes corrupt and levies an exorbitant charge. Fortunately not all political organizations are corrupt, and over the long run the spoils system has come to operate within narrower bounds. Yet until we invent some other system of political financing or new incentives for party service, the government, directly or indirectly, will contribute to the support of party activity.

[39] Frank J. Sorauf, "The Silent Revolution in Patronage," *Public Administration Review*, 20 (1960), 28–34.

14.

NOMINATIONS

IN THE STATES

A BASIC PARTY activity is the designation of candidates for public office. The American party system is characterized both by a variety of nominating customs and by modes of nomination peculiarly American. In most democratic countries the choice of candidates rests in the hands of a relatively few party leaders and activists. The group that Americans would call the "party machine" selects candidates entirely without legal regulation. Our presidential nominating conventions approximate that pattern. They are extralegal bodies that commonly include the party chieftains, who, of course, operate in a glare of publicity and are perhaps subject more and more to mass influence. On the other hand, nominations of most candidates for state and local office, as well as candidates for the national House and Senate, are made in accord with detailed regulations prescribed by state legislatures. Moreover, the choice rests, in form at least, not in a few party leaders but in the mass of the party membership, which is entitled to participate in nominating primaries.

The American practice of mass participation in party nominations points to a special characteristic of American parties, or at least to peculiarities of state and local parties. The classic conception of party assumes that a few individuals agree upon candidates who are advanced in the name of the party. That is the reality in some states and localities, but more often the party membership chooses the nominees after a campaign not unlike the election campaign. This procedure makes a party itself an entity different from the notion of a coherent leadership corps with a more or less identifiable popular following. Instead, the necessity for popular appeal to win nominations tends to splinter the leadership into cliques, factions, and even lone-wolf, individual aspirants for party power.

The bearing of nominating practices on the party systems of states and localities may be suggested by a brief survey of the evolution of nominating procedures, by an indication of the relation between nominating customs and variations in party structure, and by some attention to more technical aspects of the dominant form of nominations—the direct primary. Reserved for Chapter 16 is a consideration of special questions associated with the nomination of candidates for the House and Senate.

Evolution of Nominating Practices

Through the history of American nominating practices runs a persistent attempt to make feasible popular participation in nominations and thereby to limit or to destroy the power of party oligarchies. The legislative caucus fell before those who demanded that the people be given a voice in nominations. The new machinery, the nominating convention, itself became an instrument of party leadership and was largely replaced by the direct primary. These transformations of nominating procedures have not invariably taken control of nominations from the party leadership, but the fact that they have occurred points to the persistent belief that the mass of the people ought to have a hand in the management of party affairs. Attempts to associate the party membership with nominating decisions affects significantly not only state and local politics but also national politics.

LEGISLATIVE ASSUMPTION OF NOMINATING FUNC-
TION   Soon after the Revolution the legislative caucus became the means for nomination of candidates for state office. Legislators, however difficult travel might be, had to gather at the state capital. Obviously these men of influence in their respective constituencies made up a group that could conveniently offer party candidates to the voters. "This reflection occurred to the public, and in particular to the members of the state legislatures themselves, and they laid hands on the nominations of the candidates to the state offices." [1] The nominating caucus consisted of the party's members from both legislative houses meeting together. Its decisions were formulated as addresses by the participants as individuals and not in their capacities as legislators. By 1800 the legislative caucus was the prevailing mode of nomination in the states; it was also used in nominations for the Presidency from 1800 to 1828.

[1] M. Ostrogorski, "The Rise and Fall of the Nominating Caucus, Legislative and Congressional," *American Historical Review*, 5 (1900), 257.

The legislative caucus had hardly become established in the states when modifications began to be made to correct its shortcomings. It was unrepresentative in that those districts held by the opposition had no voice in the nomination. To remedy this defect, the "mixed caucus" came into use. In the mixed caucus special delegates sat to speak for the party members in those legislative districts represented in the legislature by the opposite party. In 1817 in New York, for example, a mixed caucus was held, "composed of the Republican members of the legislature, together with delegates chosen by the Republican voters in those counties represented in the legislature by Federalist members." [2] It was not devotion to the abstract notion of representation for all that led to the introduction of the mixed caucus; it was the practical fact that the pure legislative caucus might bring one result, the mixed caucus another.

JACKSON AND THE CONGRESSIONAL CAUCUS   The abandonment of the legislative caucus in the states was associated with the overthrow of the congressional caucus, which fell before the onslaughts of Andrew Jackson, the hero of New Orleans, the idol of the West, the symbol of a rising spirit of democracy and egalitarianism. As an aspirant for the presidential nomination in 1824, Jackson could not hope to gain nomination at the hands of an unsympathetic congressional caucus. His backers set out to discredit "King Caucus," an instrument of the anti-Jacksonians. His friends boycotted the 1824 Republican caucus, which was attended by only about one-fourth of the Republican members of Congress. The defeat of William H. Crawford, the caucus nominee, was interpreted as a verdict against the caucus itself. Before the election of 1832 the national convention came into use.

The destruction of the caucus represented more than a mere change in the method of nomination. Its replacement by the convention was regarded as the removal from power of self-appointed oligarchies that had usurped the right to nominate. The new system, the convention, gave, or so it was supposed, the mass of party members an opportunity to participate in nominations. These events occurred as the democratic winds blew in from the growing West, as the suffrage was being broadened, and as the last vestiges of the early aristocratic leadership were disappearing. Sharp alterations in the distribution of power were taking place and they were paralleled by these shifts in forms of nomination. The old order, as is usual, had its mourners. In 1843, for example, a Whig convention in Illinois offered a nomination to Governor Duncan of that state who rejected it with these words: [3]

---

[2] F. W. Dallinger, *Nominations for Elective Office in the United States* (New York: Longmans, Green, 1897), p. 28.

[3] Quoted by C. E. Merriam and L. Overacker, *Primary Elections* (Chicago: University of Chicago Press, 1928), p. 256.

This convention system, if adopted by both parties, will make our government a prize to be sought after by political gamblers. It throws the chains of slavery and degradation around its votaries, prostrates the fine feelings of nature, extinguishes every spark of patriotism, creates jealousies, distrusts, and angry divisions in society, and will ultimately make us an easy prey to some fiend, or despot, at the head of an army or church, whose followers, like themselves, love the spoils of power better than the liberty of their country. . . .

In fact, I look upon the convention system as designed by its authors to change the government from the free will of the people into the hands of designing politicians, and which must in a short time drive from public employment every honest man in the country. Is it not so to a great extent already?

SPIRIT OF THE CONVENTION SYSTEM   In spirit the convention system, which was gradually installed over the entire country, marked a break with the tradition represented by the legislative caucus. The convention mechanism constituted in form a means for transmitting, from local assemblies, the wishes and impulses of the mass of party membership to a central point, where the selection of nominees was made. The convention was a means for the expression of the "popular will" of the party; it was representative government for the party.

In practice the state convention consisted of delegates chosen either directly by the party membership in local units—towns, cities, or counties—or, more often, of delegates chosen by county conventions whose membership, in turn, had been selected by the party membership in smaller local units. These basic gatherings of party members to select delegates were called variously, "precinct conventions," "caucuses," or "primaries." In addition to state conventions, other conventions were held to nominate candidates for offices filled by voters of other areas: cities, counties, state legislative districts, congressional districts, and other electoral areas.

DISENCHANTMENT WITH THE CONVENTION   The convention remained the dominant mode of nomination of party candidates until about 1910; eventually it fell into disrepute, as had the legislative caucus, and for much the same reasons. The convention came to be regarded as an instrument of organization control, as a means of boss rule, as an institution at war with aspirations toward "democratic" government.

After the Civil War the rapid growth of industry and finance made control of state governments a valuable prize for the seekers of legislative privilege. The expansion of cities laid the foundations for fortunes for those who could extract from city councils franchises and other rights. Those who sought control of government worked through the convention because it happened at the time to be a critical link in the governing process. The convention itself was blamed for their abuses.

At the "precinct convention" or "caucus" stage unfair practices often occurred. "Snap" primaries, those called without adequate notice, could readily be controlled by the party machine. On occasion, strong-arm squads in the cities intimidated opposition in the precinct caucuses. High-handed presiding officers might recognize only the members of their own faction. In the state or city convention itself the controlling faction might refuse to seat duly elected delegates and, instead, recognize contesting delegations affiliated with the machine. On occasion, money was used to manage the delegates.

Perhaps more important than such abuses for the downfall of the convention was the fact that it often came under the clear and open domination of a boss, of a city machine, or of a state organization. Almost inevitably, such an assemblage—even though it be an ecclesiastical convention—will be managed by a small clique. Yet the rings controlling nominating conventions consisted often of unsavory characters allied with both the moneyed interests and the underworld. The convention was a spectacle dramatizing the dominance of such combinations in states and cities. The impression conveyed by the convention is suggested by Professor Charles E. Merriam's recollections of his experience as a delegate to a city convention:

I recall my last local convention under the old "deliberative" regime. The delegates had been chosen on the day before, and as soon as the returns began to come in the bosses gathered and began to appraise their strength in terms of the new battle. All night long the leaders counting their blocks of delegates had been sitting in high conclave, dividing the places on the ticket, trading back and forth, combining and recombining, bluffing and finessing. There were so many commissioners here and so many there, a county office here and another there, the patronage value of each carefully calculated in the bargain, sub-jobs, arrangements, understandings in regard to a wide variety of perquisites and privileges, all nicely calculated in determining the equitable balance. Over all hung the shadow of possible war in the convention, possible combination for control between some two or more of the trading powers.

We assemble at high noon, a restless multitude of delegates; half-past twelve comes and nothing happens; one o'clock and we become impatient; but we are told that "They" have not arrived. "They" have not finished the slate. "They" will soon be here. "They" are coming and finally "They" arrive, and the convention solemnly opens. A motion is made here and there. A vote is called for and there is a murmur of voices. Many voices, for they must all be named by roll-call and the incantation continues. Another and another. Who was named then? And finally we hasten out, buying copies of an evening extra, and learn the names of the nominees. The ritual is over. And this is sometimes called "deliberation." [4]

Attempts were made to prevent convention abuses by law. Originally the party was a private association; it was no more illegal to commit fraud in the party caucus or primary than it would be to do so in the election of officers of a drinking club. Beginning in California in 1886, regulation of caucuses and conventions by law, at first optional with the party and later compulsory for all parties, was attempted. By the time that regulation became fairly general, the convention system was on the way out. Popular revolt against control by the groups that managed the conventions was directed also against the convention itself, an instrument of domination by the "interests."

SPREAD OF THE DIRECT PRIMARY   Although the convention persists for the nomination of presidential candidates and in a few states for the designation of state candidates, the direct primary is now used for most nominations for state and local office. Under this system candidates are chosen through an election in which all members of the party, or in some instances any person qualified to vote, may participate. The voters act directly in contrast with their indirect choice through conventions made up of delegates one or two stages removed from the precinct caucuses or primaries.

The mechanism of the direct primary admirably suited the needs of the ideology of the progressive movement, which stirred American politics in the years following 1900. The leaders of that agitation demanded a restoration of government to the people and attacked the trusts, the interests, the seekers of special privilege, and the party machines. To them the direct primary constituted a means by which an enlightened people might cut through the mesh of organized and privileged power and grasp control of the government. They had a faith that the people, once equipped with the proper weapons, would throw from the office the rascals in possession of the city halls and state houses. While the primary had been experimented with elsewhere and had been used in the South, Wisconsin, under the leadership of Robert M. LaFollette, enacted the first statewide direct primary law in 1903. Other states, mainly in the West where the progressive movement was strongest, soon followed. "In 1907 Iowa, Nebraska, Missouri, North Dakota, South Dakota, and Washington passed such laws; in 1908 Illinois, Kansas, Oklahoma, and Ohio followed; and finally, in 1909, Arizona, Arkansas, California, Idaho, Michigan, Nevada, New Hampshire, and Tennessee were added to the list." [5] By 1917 the direct primary had been adopted for most nominations in all save a few states.

The spread of the direct primary is commonly attributed to its appeal as an instrument of popular rule, yet probably the nature of the party struc-

[4] *Ibid.*, pp. 259–60.   [5] *Ibid.*, p. 62.

ture in the areas of its origin stimulated its growth. In the 1890's the party system had broken down in the sense that a single party dominated many states and localities. The lesser party not infrequently was under the control of the same interests that owned the principal party. In the South the destruction of the Republican party in the aftermath of Reconstruction left the Democratic party unchallenged. If governors and other officials were to be popularly elected, they had to be elected, in effect, by a direct primary within the Democratic party.

The direct primary first achieved fairly complete development in South Carolina, by party action rather than by statute. There the overturn of the convention system was also associated with drives against the ruling orders. Ben Tillman, the advocate of the primary system, led the back-country farmers against the so-called Bourbons. The triumph of the Tillmanites in 1891 was followed by the installation of the direct primary. Concurrently in Georgia a movement for the direct primary led to its introduction for the nomination of candidates for local office and eventually to its use for statewide nominations. Similarly, in Wisconsin and surrounding states the Republicans ruled without serious challenge. The ties of party—given the recency of the Civil War—made it simpler to advance popular government by introducing the direct primary to permit intraparty competition than to proceed by a realignment of parties. The convention system in a one-party situation does not serve well to produce acceptable decisions on contests that stir the multitude.

In due course misgivings arose about the direct primary. It turned out that party organizations, party machines, and politicians had to manage the primary as they had always taken care of party affairs. Yet the direct primary created new conditions of work for party leaders, conditions that affected their manner of operation and influenced the nature of party itself.

Nominating Processes and Party Structure

The evolution of nominating procedure has left the direct primary as the dominant method of nominating candidates for the thousands of state, county, and city offices, as well as for places in the United States Senate and House of Representatives. Parties continue to nominate through the convention in only a few places. New York, Indiana, Connecticut,[6] and Delaware retain the convention for nominations for offices filled by the voters of the entire state.[7] Michigan parties nominate for the lesser statewide offices through

[6] For a vivid account of an unsuccessful candidacy at a Connecticut convention, see Joseph P. Lyford, *Candidate* (New York: Holt, 1959).

[7] On the Indiana convention system, see Frank Munger, *The Struggle for Republican Leadership in Indiana, 1954* (New York: McGraw-Hill, Eagleton Case 23, 1960). Delaware rotates the gubernatorial nomination among its three counties, and the nomination is, in fact, settled by a caucus of the convention delegates from the county

conventions. Other states retain the convention to choose delegates to the national presidential nominating convention or to adopt platforms and to settle other party questions. Yet direct primaries, held usually from April to September preceding the November elections, in most states settle the nominations of candidates.

CORRELATION BETWEEN NOMINATING FORMS AND NATURE OF PARTY   The convention system of nominations seems to be associated with a general type of party system, while the most bewildering variety of party structures exists behind the façade of the direct primary. In those jurisdictions employing the convention, "party" tends to approximate the old-time conception of it as a fairly cohesive crowd of activists—of professional politicians—who are able to settle their differences over candidates through the oligarchical processes of the convention. Aspirants for nomination at the hands of a convention must cultivate the goodwill of the comparatively small clique of persons who manage conventions. Agreement among a few leaders not uncommonly decides the nomination. Those leaders may have to choose among ambitious and powerful contenders or they may have to draft a promising prospect reluctant to make the race. However the party leadership operates, nominations are made with precious little popular participation, though the leadership may take its decisions with an acute awareness of the probable popularity of its candidates at the general election.

The remnants of the convention system are mainly in states that retain a fairly even and continuous competition between the major parties for control of the state government. These states are also older states in which party organizations have inherited and maintained a comparatively high degree of solidarity. The existence of two closely competitive parties probably made the propaganda of the enthusiasts for the direct primary less persuasive in these states; a "democratic" popular choice between parties existed even though the intraparty procedures for the designation of candidates were quite "undemocratic."

In contrast, the fact that a state uses the direct primary provides no indication of the underlying character of party organization. The direct primary procedure can accommodate itself to the most varied sorts of organization among the political activists. Then, too, existence of the primary itself may encourage variety in forms of political organization. In some one-party states a two-party system, in effect if not in form, exists within the major party. In two-party jurisdictions both party organizations may be so well disciplined that their informal selections of candidates are ratified routinely in the direct primary; or political leadership in a state or community may be so pulverized that a myriad of personal factions compete in the primaries for nominations.

whose turn it is. See Paul Dolan, *The Government and Administration of Delaware* (New York: Crowell, 1956), pp. 35–36.

In effect, party may not exist in the sense of organized leadership effort to capture the government by advancing candidates.

SITUATIONAL CONSEQUENCES OF THE DIRECT PRIMARY   A new institution or procedure may create a new situation in which candidates or officials must work. The new situation, because it involves new sorts of opportunities for action, may pave the way for, but not necessarily result in, new forms of behavior. The direct primary established a new set of circumstances within which political leaders concerned with nominations had to work. The character of these new circumstances encouraged the development of new forms of organization and disorganization of party leadership.

The fundamental alteration in the nominating situation brought by the direct primary was a broadening of popular participation in nominations. The mass of party members had had the privilege of participating indirectly in convention nominations by taking part in precinct caucuses or primaries, yet few took advantage of the opportunity. The convention process by and large involved either the ratification of the decisions of a handful of leaders or the settlement of conflicts among factions of the party leadership.

Adoption of the direct primary left the way open for all voters to share with the party leadership in the designation of candidates. In fact, the extent of popular participation in the primary differs widely from state to state and from time to time. In over two-thirds of the primaries to nominate gubernatorial candidates in a group of nonsouthern states from 1926 to 1952 less than 35 per cent of the potential voters participated in one or the other of the major party primaries. Though no data are available on popular participation in the choice of delegates to conventions, doubtless the primary brought a much wider participation in the nominating process.

Another measure of participation in nominating primaries appears in Table 14.1, which compares the total vote in party primaries to nominate gubernatorial candidates in all states with the vote cast in the general election for the primary nominee. Fewer than 60 per cent as many persons vote in most Republican primaries as vote for the Republican candidate in the general election. Outside the southern states the Democratic primary vote tends to be smaller in relation to the general election vote than is the Republican primary vote. In the southern states, however, the Democratic primary vote often exceeds the Democratic vote in the general election, a fact reflected in the distribution in the Democratic columns of the table.

Popular participation in nominations altered the situation confronted by the upper echelons of party leadership, by the party machine, and by aspirants for nominations. Rival factions and leaders now could fight out their differences in a campaign directed to the electorate—or a substantial segment of it—rather than be bound by the decisions of an assembly of delegates. Aspirants for nomination could likewise appeal directly to voters—or to those

Table 14.1   Contested Democratic and Republican gubernatorial primaries, 1940–1956, distributed according to percentage total primary vote was of general election vote for primary nominee

Primary Vote as Per Cent of General Election Vote	Republican Primaries		Democratic Primaries		Total Primaries	
	Number	Per Cent	Number	Per Cent	Number	Per Cent
10–19	6	4.8	6	4.1	12	4.4
20–39	17	13.6	41	28.1	58	21.4
40–59	55	44.0	18	12.3	73	26.9
60–79	28	22.4	20	13.7	48	17.7
80–99	8	6.4	13	8.9	21	7.8
100 and over	11	8.8	48	32.9	59	21.8
Total	125	100.0	146	100.0	271	100.0

who voted in the primary—rather than be limited largely to the cultivation of the professionals who controlled the convention and constituted the operating core of the party. By the same token new elements of power were introduced into the nominating process. Prominent among them were newspaper publishers and others in control of channels to reach the public.

As these rival forces seek to determine nominations, they must influence primary voters who differ from the party's general election supporters and the electorate as a whole as well. At least in two-party states it seems that those who vote in the primaries are a special breed. Strong partisans from those areas of the state in which a party is dominant tend to vote in primaries in especially high degree. Primary winners may, thus, reflect a particular strain of party outlook or type of party follower. The standpat conservatives may control; the metropolitan ethnics may prevail; or some other sector of the party may give the dominant tone to state primary results. Candidates capable of popular triumph in the primary under such circumstances may not be strong candidates before the larger electorate in the general election.[8]

COMPETITION FOR PRIMARY NOMINATIONS   Clues to the ways in which the party leadership echelons adapted themselves to the new situation created by the direct primary may be found in analyses of the incidence of competition among aspirants for primary nominations in different sorts of circumstances. The frequency of contests in the primaries differs with the balance of strength between the two major parties in the

[8] The bearing of differentials among types of people in primary participation on the kinds of candidates chosen has not been adequately studied, but see V. O. Key, Jr., *American State Politics* (New York: Knopf, 1956), pp. 145–65.

general election voting. If the Republicans usually attract a small vote in a jurisdiction, their primary nomination tends to go to an unopposed aspirant who has taken the trouble to get his name on the ballot. As the usual size of the Republican vote increases, primary contests occur more frequently. When the Republican vote becomes so high that the Republican nominee invariably wins the general election, the frequency of contests for Democratic nominations varies among classes of constituencies with differences in the customary strength of Democratic candidates at the general election.

These relationships in the division of strength between the parties and competition within parties for nomination were demonstrated by data on gubernatorial primaries at an earlier point.[9] Their existence in primaries to nominate candidates for the United States Senate and House of Representatives is shown in a later chapter.[10] Another illustration of the relationship appears in Table 14.2, which shows the incidence of competition in Republican

Table 14.2   Balance of party strength and competition for primary nominations: Contests for nominations for Missouri House of Representatives, 1948–1950 [a]

Democratic Percentage General Election	Seats	Per Cent of Nominations Contested in—			
		Both Primaries	Neither Primary	Democratic Only	Republican Only
Under 40	66	0.0	47.0	0.0	53.0
40–49	63	7.9	44.4	7.9	39.7
50–59	72	11.1	56.9	18.1	13.9
60 and over	107	6.5	44.9	43.9	4.7
Total	308	6.5	48.0	21.1	24.3

[a] A contested nomination is defined for this table as a primary involving two or more aspirants for the nomination.

and Democratic primaries for the nomination of candidates for the Missouri House of Representatives. As that table makes clear, simultaneous contests in both party primaries in a single legislative district are exceptional in Missouri; contests tend to take place in the primary of the stronger party in a district. Similar analyses in other states show variations in frequency of primary contests associated with differences in the balance of power between the parties.[11]

[9] Pp. 290–92.   [10] Pp. 438, 447.

[11] See Samuel K. Gove, "The 1960 County Primaries," *Illinois Government,* January, 1961; M. E. Jewell, "Party and Primary Competition in Kentucky State Legislative Races," *Kentucky Law Journal,* 48 (1960), 517–35; W. H. Standing and J. A.

VARIETIES IN LEADERSHIP STRUCTURE   As might be supposed, these variations in the incidence of primary contests reflect the existence of a variety of forms of organization of party leadership in states and in local electoral units. No satisfactory estimate can be made of the extent to which these different forms of organization prevail. Yet the nature of the major types may be roughly indicated.

In jurisdictions leaning strongly to one party or the other, as has been noted, contests for primary nominations in the primaries of the lesser party are relatively infrequent. Often a few leaders of the party agree upon a slate of candidates whose names are placed on the primary ballot. The problem usually is one, not of settling rivalries among would-be candidates, but of finding enough candidates to present a complete slate.[12] In other instances of uncontested nomination no concerted action to produce a slate occurs; scattered individuals, on their own initiative, circulate petitions or declare their candidacy and appear on the ballot. Under these circumstances often the party does not have candidates for all offices filled at the general election.

At times a radically different pattern of leadership stands behind an uncontested primary. The party organization, through its central committee or executive committee, endorses a slate of primary candidates. Such committee action may be customary, publicly known, and accepted. Thus, in Chicago campaign leaflets may be circulated at the time of the primary under the title, "Candidates Endorsed by the Democratic County Central Committee and the Democratic State Central Committee," or "Regular Republican Candidates Recommended by the Cook County Republican Central Committee." If the organization is united and well fortified with campaign resources, challenge of its slate may be futile in the primary.[13] The organization workers in each precinct marshal their following at the polls to win the nomination for the "regular" slate.[14] Either no challenge occurs or other candidates for

---

Robinson, "Inter-Party Competition and Primary Contesting: The Case of Indiana," *American Political Science Review,* 52 (1958), 1066–77; K. H. Porter, "The Deserted Primary in Iowa," *American Political Science Review,* 39 (1945), 732–40.

[12] Some state statutes give parties the option of nominating by convention or primary, and the lesser party often nominates by convention. The practice is especially notable among Republicans in southern states.

[13] For a study of a small city, see P. Cutright and P. H. Rossi, "Party Organization in Primary Elections," *American Journal of Sociology,* 64 (1958), 262–69.

[14] In some jurisdictions a large number of signatures is required to place a candidate on the primary ballot, a requisite readily met for the organization slate but an obstacle to other aspirants. A candidate may place his name on the primary ballot in some jurisdictions by a declaration of candidacy or by a petition signed by a nominal number of voters. The laws of over half the states require payment of a fee to obtain a place on the ballot; this requirement is often in addition to that of a petition. In southern states in which the party finances the primary the costs are assessed against the candidates; the individual fee may be several thousand dollars in a populous county. Michigan permits, as an alternative to a petition, a deposit of money, which is returnable if the candidate polls half as many votes as the nominee. For a summary of state primary laws as they relate to Senators, see Senate Document No. 86, 87th Cong., 2d sess. (1961).

nomination make only the most perfunctory race and draw only a few votes.[15] The absence of a primary contest may, of course, also mean that extensive bargaining has occurred within the leadership ranks to quell incipient rebellion.[16] Some state laws prohibit endorsement of primary slates by party committees. Under these circumstances the leadership core of the party may act informally or may even create extralegal political committees that assume the function of slate-making and leadership in the nominating process.

Serious contests within the primary may reflect a fractionalization of the leadership echelons of the party. Differences founded on rivalries of individual leaders, on ideological differences, or on other cleavages may be reflected in more or less continuing factional struggles within the party leadership. The primary opens the road for dissident elements of the leadership to carry their fight to the voters of the party, and that road is often traveled.[17] A recurring characteristic of these confused factional conflicts is that the voters often have no notion of the nature, composition, orientation, or objectives of the leadership factions that struggle for control of nominations. Instead of finding on the ballot a well-advertised "organization" slate and perhaps an "anti-organization" slate and a few volunteer candidates, the voter finds names of individual candidates backed by anonymous or the most nebulous groups or cliques. A handful of party officials, of associated interest-group leaders, and of other political activists may have agreed upon a man to back for governor, say, in the primary, but their deliberations may never be a matter of general public knowledge. Another clique of professionals and their associates with access to enough money to finance a primary campaign may place another man in the race. Or the moving force in forming leadership cliques may be the aspirants for the nomination. Or the battle may have ideological overtones, especially in one-party states.[18]

At times the direct primary operates without the help of more or less durable groupings of party leaders who advance persons for nomination. In-

[15] It may be that party organizations tend, other things being equal, to agree upon a slate and repress their internal differences, most often when the electorate customarily divides near the 50–50 mark. Groups, when threatened by a dangerous enemy, may tend to cohere more strongly.

[16] For example, the concession of patronage appointments by one party faction to another to ward off the threat of a primary challenge against an aspirant for, say, a senatorial nomination. Or a skillful allocation of places on the primary slate has satisfied all concerned. Or ambitious men have been promised that their turn will come next time.

[17] Bitter primary fights consume campaign resources and often leave scars that make it difficult to unite the leadership against the opposition in the general election campaign. The statutes often place obstacles in the way of the loser of a primary so unreconciled that he proposes to run as an independent in the general election. State laws at times prohibit an independent or third-party candidacy by a primary loser. Others achieve the same end by requiring that petitions for independent candidacy in the general election be filed before the party primaries.

[18] See R. A. Smith and C. J. Hein, *Republican Primary Fight: A Study in Factionalism* (New York: Holt, 1958).

stead a large number of individuals may attempt to build little followings to win the nomination for a particular office at a primary; the general rule of nomination by a plurality of the votes may enable the most unlikely aspirants for the nomination to win and may make the nomination a decision by chance. Or, given the large numbers of offices filled by election, little leadership clusters may be constructed at the time of each primary by the many individuals who seek to be candidates for the various offices. The professionals do not unite behind a slate; nor do they divide into a pair of groups. Rather, the process of struggle for primary nominations generates many small clusters of "pros" and "semi-pros" about aspirants for individual offices. And, in truth, at times it is utterly unreal to speak of the existence of any sort of party leadership group with any capacity to steer or influence the nominating process. Individuals, for example, with the "right" name may poll heavy votes without the aid of any support among the professionals, a circumstance that reflects the existence of an unbossed, unled, and often uninformed electorate.[19] Under these conditions the voters in the primary are often guided by religious or ethnic preferences, by the recommendations of newspapers, or by their recognition of a name that seems to them to be familiar and of good repute.[20]

PRIMARIES AS ELECTIONS   In many states and in many units of local government the winner of the primary almost invariably wins the election. In these one-party jurisdictions it can hardly be said that a "party" system exists. Nor can it be said that the primary is a method of nomination; it is the election. The real "parties" in these jurisdictions are the factional groupings that compete for electoral favor within the primary of the dominant party. The "party systems" in such jurisdictions take a variety of forms. In some southern states the competing factions within the Democratic party have a continuity, a solidarity, and an identity in the public eye that make them not unlike the major parties in a two-party state. In

[19] Thus, the nominee of the Wisconsin Democratic primary for attorney general in 1956 was one Robert La Follette Sucher, who was reported by the press to be "an unknown," but he had a name politically attractive in Wisconsin. In 1954 Massachusetts Democrats nominated for state treasurer one John Kennedy, another unknown who happened to have the name of Kennedy, a name made both popular and familiar by the then junior Senator from the state. Experimental evidence suggests that "name" candidates may enjoy greater advantage in primaries than in general elections where the voter has the offsetting cue of the party label on the ballot. See L. J. Kamin, "Ethnic and Party Affiliations of Candidates as Determinants of Voting," *Canadian Journal of Psychology*, 12 (1958), 205–13.

[20] The unbossed primary electorate which acts on a minimum of information permits some politicians to engage in a genteel form of extortion. In some districts an Irish name, or a Jewish name, or a Yankee name, or even any sort of name is good for a substantial number of primary votes. A name may be entered in the primary and used as leverage for the extraction of cash or other valuable consideration from the aspirant likely to be injured. On appropriate settlement, the name is withdrawn before the ballot is printed.

other states the factional groups in the dominant party may be amorphous, ill-defined, and kaleidoscopic. In counties, cities, towns, villages, and other one-party units the forms of intraparty factions are doubtless varied, but information about them is scarce. In these one-party jurisdictions, though the "nominations" are technically made by primary, the nominating process actually occurs at the stage when the "organization" puts candidates into the primary, when cliques rally behind an aspirant for the nomination, or when other preprimary maneuvers occur to sift out and designate the more formidable contenders for the formal nominations.

Many American state and local elections merely ratify the nominations of the primary of the dominant party. An analysis by Cortez A. M. Ewing suggests the degree of the finality of the primary. He finds that from 1896 to 1946 slightly more than half (53.5 per cent) of the elections to the national House of Representatives were by a 20 per cent popular plurality; that is, the winner had at least a 60–40 lead in the election. Thus, in half the contests the outcome was rarely much in doubt; the decision fell to the voters in the major-party primary. As would be supposed the states in which the largest proportions of congressional elections were won by pluralities of more than 20 per cent were in the South.[21]

In most states the party nomination goes to the candidate with the highest number of votes in the primary even though he may lack a majority of the votes. In two-party states minority nominations occur fairly frequently but create no widespread dissatisfaction. Most of the one-party states, however, have sought to assure majority nominations by requiring a second, or runoff, primary, if no candidate receives a majority at the first primary. At the second polling the contest is between the two persons polling the highest vote at the first primary. In Iowa the nomination goes to the person with the highest vote, provided that it amounts to at least 35 per cent of the vote cast. In the event that it does not, an infrequent occurrence, a state convention picks a nominee from among the primary aspirants.[22]

---

[21] "Primaries as Elections," *Southwestern Social Science Quarterly*, 29 (1948–49), 293–98. See also Professor Ewing's *Primary Elections in the South* (Norman: University of Oklahoma Press, 1953).

[22] The runoff primary for statewide offices exists in Alabama, Arkansas, Florida, Georgia, Louisiana, Mississippi, North Carolina, Oklahoma, South Carolina, Texas, and Virginia. Tennessee requires a runoff in the unlikely event of a tie vote. The systems in Arkansas, North Carolina, and Virginia diverge in detail from the pattern described in the text. Kentucky and Utah at one time or another have used the runoff. On Idaho, see note 35 of this chapter. In Georgia until 1962 the direct primary operated in conjunction with a convention. Convention delegates were bound, after the fashion of presidential electors, by the primary vote in their counties. Apportionment of convention delegates in the manner of state legislators made it possible for a candidate with a minority of the popular primary vote to win a majority of the convention vote. The Georgia system, the so-called county unit system, discriminated with special harshness against urban voters. In 1962, after a lower federal court had held the system void on the authority of Baker *v.* Carr, the state Democratic committee ordered the 1962

NONPARTISAN NOMINATIONS   The realities underlying the formal nominating process make it clear that in many areas and at many times party organizations as such have little to do with the designation of candidates. In many municipalities and other local jurisdictions, that reality is formalized in nonpartisan procedures for nomination and election, that is, the ballots carry no partisan identification of candidates and parties are not recognized in the relevant statutes or ordinances. One practice is to have two pollings. The two high candidates at the first are "nominated"; they vie in the second, which is the election. More commonly a single polling occurs, and the person with the high vote is the winner even though he does not draw a majority of the votes cast.

Nonpartisan procedures were introduced on the theory that partisanship in local government is positively injurious. "There is," the argument went, "no Republican or Democratic way to run a city." Nonpartisan elections are far more widespread than is commonly supposed. Most school boards are chosen in this manner as are city councils in about two-thirds of the cities of 5,000 population and over.[23] In several states, including California, all county officers are elected on a nonpartisan ballot and judicial posts are more generally nonpartisan. In Minnesota and Nebraska the party affiliations of state legislators are not indicated on the ballot.

Groups tend to develop behind the nonpartisan façade to perform the function of recruiting and backing candidates. Sometimes the party organizations themselves carry on this function, especially in larger cities. Groups as various as the merchants, the volunteer fire department, and the service clubs may play a role. These nonpartisan "political" groupings may be most transient and rudimentary. In many nonpartisan jurisdictions the issues generate a politics of quite low temperature. The problem is often to induce a reluctant citizen to serve as mayor or councilman rather than to settle the claims of rivals eager for office.[24] Probably on the whole the practice and or-

---

primaries to be held on a popular vote basis. In March, 1963, the Supreme Court, in *Gray v. Saunders,* upheld the lower court's invalidation of the Georgia scheme. Maryland's primary system has been the same in form as the Georgia county unit system, and must be regarded as unconstitutional under the doctrine of *Gray v. Saunders.* See R. S. Friedman, *The Maryland County Unit System and Urban-Rural Politics* (College Park: University of Maryland, 1958).

[23] *Municipal Yearbook,* 1961, p. 80.

[24] Systematic information is limited on the motivations that drive people to seek elective office. Since few people have a burning urge for office, parties, groups, or other centers of initiative that induce persons to run for office are of basic importance in a democracy. There may be no shortage of aspirants for major offices; for the scores of thousands of inconspicuous offices, though, the supply of suitable candidates must be maintained by social pressures. See C. B. Judah and D. P. Goldberg, *The Recruitment of Candidates from Bernalillo County to the New Mexico House of Representatives, 1956* (Albuquerque: Department of Government, University of New Mexico, 1959) ; L. G. Seligman, "Political Recruitment and Party Structure: A Case Study," *American Political Science Review,* 55 (1961), 77–86.

ganization of politics in nonpartisan jurisdictions do not differ so markedly from the customs that prevail in heavily one-party jurisdictions that operate through partisan forms.[25]

Primary and Party Responsibility

The direct primary procedure seems in general to make more difficult domination of the nominating process by the party organization and the interests affiliated with it. That result comes about in part because the primary encourages cleavages among the political professionals and careerists by permitting them to carry their differences to the primary voters for settlement. The selection of candidates may even become the fortuitous result of the interaction among many centers of influence. And at times the party leadership may seem to disappear as it disintegrates into picayune cliques. Indeed, the fact that aspirants for nomination must cultivate the rank and file makes it difficult to maintain an oranizational core dedicated to the party as such; instead, leadership energies operate to construct activist clusters devoted to the interests of particular individuals.

Such tendencies, it is often asserted, destroy party responsibility. The concept of party responsibility is ambiguous, but those who employ it in this context seem to mean that the weakening of the influence of party organization in the designation of candidates tends to produce ill-considered choices. The inner core may find its choice for nomination defeated in the primary by a banjo player, a demagogue who ought to be in the other party, or some other bizarre person whom the party wheelhorses cannot support with enthusiasm in the general election campaign.[26] From another angle the destruction of party responsibility may mean that discontented elements in the party may determine the nomination on issues that should have driven them to the opposite party. The complaint is made, for example, about the occasional nomination of Fair Deal Republicans in Republican primaries. From

[25] See Eugene C. Lee, *The Politics of Nonpartisanship: A Study of California City Elections* (Berkeley: University of California Press, 1960) ; C. R. Adrian, "A Typology for Nonpartisan Elections," *Western Political Quarterly*, 12 (1959), 449–58; O. P. Williams and C. R. Adrian, "The Insulation of Local Politics under the Nonpartisan Ballot," *American Political Science Review*, 53 (1959), 1052–63; Marvin A. Harder, *Nonpartisan Election: A Political Illusion?* (New York: Holt, 1958) ; C. E. Gilbert, "Some Aspects of Nonpartisan Elections in Large Cities," *Midwest Journal of Political Science*, 6 (1962), 345–62.

[26] The characterization by Boyd A. Martin of the situation in Idaho undoubtedly applies in some other states: "Many Republican politicians were afraid of insurgent groups within their own ranks, as well as of outside groups like the Non-Partisan League. The more conservative elements wanted a bottleneck at the top of the state party organization. This feature of control from the top was what the conservative leaders called *party responsibility." The Direct Primary in Idaho* (Stanford University: Stanford University Press, 1947), p. 76.

another aspect, the notion of weakening party responsibility may mean that most voters are attracted to the primary of one party and there fight out the issues that would otherwise be settled in the general election campaign, with the result that whatever consistency of attitude party candidates might otherwise have over a period of time is broken. In the process the minority party may be weakened or virtually destroyed.

PREPRIMARY CONVENTIONS   To offset some of the less-happy results of the primary nominating process and to permit an open and accepted role by the party organization in the choice of candidates, a few states have enacted legislation authorizing conventions to designate a slate of candidates before the direct primary. Ordinarily the primary ballot indicates that these candidates have the endorsement of the party convention. If the convention arrives at decisions acceptable to the major elements of the leadership, its choices may not even be challenged in the primary. Or if the convention leaders also have at their command an adequate electioneering organization, their slate can readily triumph over independent candidates. In effect, the preprimary convention procedure in some instances brings into the open and gives official blessing to the function of the party leadership in building organization slates for the primaries.

Some results attributable to the primary, as well as some considerations involved in the preprimary convention, are suggested by the Massachusetts preprimary convention. In that state the Republicans in 1948 and 1950 had slates for state offices composed entirely of Yankee Republicans. Some Republican leaders surmised that their misfortunes might have come from their failure to take into account in their slates the ethnic realities of Massachusetts. Yet to nominate in a free primary anybody other than a Yankee was difficult. Under Republican leadership, with some aid from Italo-American Democrats restive under Irish domination of their party, the 1951 legislature voted to authorize preprimary conventions. The Democratic governor vetoed the bill, but the Republicans proceeded to hold an extralegal convention to endorse a primary slate. A nicely balanced slate emerged from the convention deliberations: three Yankees, two Jewish-Americans, an Italo-American, and an Irish-American woman. The convention slate, which had the overwhelming support of the party leadership, won handily in the primary.

With the election of a Republican governor and legislature in 1952 the way was cleared for adoption of legislation on preprimary conventions, which occurred in 1953. Under the law, those endorsed are placed first on the ballot and are identified as holders of the convention endorsement. The Republicans adapted themselves readily to the convention and used it to produce "balanced" slates which won the primary nominations usually without opposition. The Democrats were restive under the preprimary convention law. The party consisted of many chieftains and no genuine warlords; it was unable

to negotiate through the convention slates of candidates that would be supported by all hands in the primary. A modicum of organizational unity is
necessary for the working of the preprimary convention.

Preprimary conventions are used, or have been used, in other states. For
a time New Mexico had a preprimary convention. In that state the Republican party is especially handicapped in operating through the direct primary
which tends to favor nominees from a handful of Republican counties, persons who often have a weak statewide appeal even though they may be popular
in their own party.[27] Nebraska also abandoned the preprimary convention.
Given the predominance of the Republican party in Nebraska at the time,
that state's action suggests that the conditions most favorable for the preprimary convention include the existence of a fairly even competition between
two parties. Peril probably moves the leadership of a party to seek party
unity through convention or negotiation. The dominance of one party almost
insures that the conflict for popular favor will be fought out in its primary;
the deliberations of a preprimary convention are not likely to produce agreement among all factions.

Usually the preprimary convention statute provides for the identification
of the convention slate on the primary ballot but also permits other aspirants
for nomination to gain a place on the ballot by petition. Under the Colorado
variant the name of any person receiving 20 per cent of the convention vote
goes on the ballot. If several persons so qualify, their names are placed on
the ballot in the order of the size of their convention vote. Other individuals
may be placed on the ballot by petition. Utah's preprimary convention designates two candidates for each nomination—if there are two convention aspirants—and no provision exists for other candidates to enter the primary
by petition.[28]

In several states the equivalent of the preprimary convention has grown
up in extralegal form in reflection of attempts to consolidate party leadership on nominations. California's development of informal preprimary assemblies is one of the more striking instances. The convention of the Republican Assembly endorses primary candidates, and when no suitable aspirant
turns up under his own power the Assembly may search out a prospect and
induce him to seek the primary nomination with its endorsement. The Democrats followed the precedent of the California Republicans and formed the
California Democratic Council in 1953 to make preprimary endorsements.
After the 1954 primaries, it could be said that "although the direct primary

[27] See Jack E. Holmes, *Problems Relating to Various Nominating Procedures in
New Mexico* (New Mexico Legislative Council Service, 1955) ; C. B. Judah, *Aspects of
the Nominating Systems in New Mexico* (Albuquerque: Department of Government,
University of New Mexico, 1957).

[28] Brief accounts of the preprimary convention systems may be found in *A Model
Direct Primary System* (New York, 1951), a report of the National Municipal League's
Committee on the Direct Primary, of which Joseph P. Harris was chairman. On the
Colorado and Utah systems, see F. H. Jonas (ed.), *Western Politics* (Salt Lake City:
University of Utah Press, 1961), pp. 117–21, 288–90.

election remained the formal method of nomination in both parties, the actual decision was made by extralegal groups, with few other aspirants entering the primary." [29] The Council gained authority because it was underpinned by a system of Democratic clubs of which it was the apex. The club membership of middle-class, policy-oriented party activists constituted an effective campaign apparatus.[30] In Wisconsin also, party associations have grown up outside the formal, or legally prescribed, party apparatus to hold conventions in order that the principal leaders of the party may agree upon programs and, in the case of the Republicans, endorse candidates to support in the direct primaries.

OTHER MODIFIED PRIMARY SYSTEMS   Another variation on the pure direct primary system is exemplified by the statute adopted in 1955 by the legislature of Connecticut, a state which had been steadfast in its adherence to convention procedures in nomination. The 1955 law provided for postconvention primaries by which candidates rejected by the convention might appeal to the party voters in a primary. Persons who received at least 20 per cent of the convention vote were permitted to challenge the convention nominee in a subsequent direct primary. The primary could be set in motion by filing a petition and making a deposit to be returned if the challenger polled at least 15 per cent of the primary vote. The Democratic state chairman opined at the time of the passage of the law that the new procedure would pose a problem for political leaders in that they would have to choose candidates who could overcome a primary challenge. A candidate with good prospects at the general election, he thought, might not necessarily do well in a primary. Conceivably the procedure for appeal from convention to primary will splinter the party leadership, although the full effects, if any, of the new situation on the cohesiveness of the party organization will materialize only gradually.[31]

OPEN AND CLOSED PRIMARIES   Another characteristic of direct primaries that bears upon the role and influence of party leadership in the nominating process concerns the question of what persons shall be en-

---

[29] Thomas S. Barclay, "The 1954 Election in California," *Western Political Quarterly*, 7 (1954), 597.

[30] Francis Carney, *The Rise of the Democratic Clubs in California* (New York: Holt, 1958); Dean R. Cresap, *Party Politics in the Golden State* (Los Angeles: The Haynes Foundation, 1954), ch. 7; J. P. Harris, *California Politics* (Stanford: Stanford University Press, 1955); Leonard Rowe, *Preprimary Endorsements in California Politics* (Berkeley: Bureau of Public Administration, University of California, 1961); James Q. Wilson, *The Amateur Democrats* (Chicago: University of Chicago Press, 1962), ch. 4.

[31] See Duane Lockard, *Connecticut's Challenge Primary: A Study in Legislative Politics* (New York: Holt, 1959). Also his "Connecticut Tries Its New Primary," *National Municipal Review*, 45 (1956), 494–96. Rhode Island's primary law, adopted in 1948, requires that candidates for nomination endorsed by the party committees be so identified on the primary ballot. Other aspirants may gain a place on the ballot by petition. In effect, the procedure permits an aspirant rejected by the party organization to appeal the decision to the party voters in the primary.

titled to vote in the primary. Participation in a "closed" primary is limited to party members. Under an "open" primary system the voter may decide when he goes to the polls whether he will vote in the Democratic or the Republican primary. The details of the administration of these systems, in reality, either obstruct or facilitate the movement of voters from the primary of one party to that of the other.

The most common mode of determination of party membership and, hence, of eligibility to vote in the closed primary of the party is by enrollment at the time of registration. At that time the voter "enrolls" as a member of the party of his choice or asserts an affiliation which is indicated on the registration record. On primary day he is given the ballot of the party shown on the registration record. In some jurisdictions the party preference for entry on the records is expressed on the occasion of the voter's first primary vote. Whatever the procedure for enrollment, the voter is put to some inconvenience if he wishes to change his enrollment from one party to another, a step which usually must be taken some time before the primary. Furthermore, registration lists commonly include names of persons who have chosen to affiliate with no party and thereby are ineligible to vote in the primaries.

Some versions of the closed primary system include no enrollment procedure. Rather, a test of party membership may be applied at the polls at the time of voting in the primary. Only infrequently is the right of persons to vote in such primaries challenged. The test of party membership is prescribed by law, by party rule, or by state action supplemented by party rule: it is usually in terms of past partisan allegiance, present affiliation, or future intention, or a combination of these. Past allegiance may be determined by the elector's assertion that he supported the party's nominees at a preceding election. Present affiliation consists ordinarily in the elector's assertion that he is a member of the party. Future intention consists in an intention to support nominees of the party in the general election. The Texas primary ballot, for example, contains the following pledge to meet the test of present affiliation and future intention: "I am a Democrat and pledge myself to support the nominees of this primary." Such "tests" become almost a matter between the individual voter and his conscience. Hence, the difference between the open primary and some forms of the closed primary at times becomes less than sharp. In a few states, including Missouri, Illinois, and Ohio, the closed primary approaches in form the open primary in that a person may switch his party on the day of the primary. If he is challenged at the polls, he must take an oath which indicates that the change is in good faith. Thus, in Missouri he must swear that he will support the party's candidates in the general election.

The essential idea of the open primary appears in the manner of conduct of primary elections. In some states the primary ballot contains several party columns. Each party column includes the names of aspirants for the party nomination, grouped by office, and the voter may make his choices for candidates for the several offices in whichever party column he chooses. If he votes in more than one party column, the ballot is invalidated at the count. Some states staple different party primary ballots together and permit the voter, in the polling booth, to detach and mark one which he deposits in the ballot box while he drops the unused ballot or ballots into a box for discards. Under either system, the voter's decision on which primary he is to participate in remains secret. Wisconsin, Montana, Michigan, and Utah have employed variations of the second form of open-primary ballot, while Minnesota, Idaho, and North Dakota have used the single ballot with separate party columns.[32]

Washington in 1935 carried the open-primary principle to its logical conclusion by adopting the "blanket" primary, under which a voter can split his vote by voting in different party primaries on different offices. The ballot is arranged in an office bloc form, with the party affiliation of each aspirant for a nomination indicated after his name. The voter may skip back and forth from party to party as he moves down the ballot from office to office.[33]

The ease with which voters may move from party to party under the open primary doubtless creates uncertainties for the party leadership in its efforts to control nominations as well as in tests of strength between leadership factions. The primary of one party may be raided by the voters of another in order to assure the nomination of a weak candidate who can be defeated in the general election. That maneuver requires, of course, a disciplined organization for its execution.[34] Or at times a battle between two strong candidates in the primary of one party may attract enough voters from the other party to govern the outcome. Thus, in 1956 Glenn R. Davis, who had the support of the Wisconsin regular Republicans, lost in the primary to Senator Alexander Wiley, an Eisenhower Republican. Whether rightly, the outcome was attributed in part to an invasion of the Republican primary by Democrats. In other states Republicans have at times moved into a Democratic primary to support a conservative Democratic aspirant for a nomination.[35]

---

[32] The most comprehensive treatment of the open-closed primary question is by C. A. Berdahl, "Party Membership in the United States," *American Political Science Review*, 36 (1942), 16–50, 241–62. See also Illinois Legislative Council, Research Department, *The Direct Primary Ballot* (Publication No. 25, July, 1940).

[33] See C. O. Johnson, "The Washington Blanket Primary," *Pacific Northwest Quarterly*, January, 1942, 27–39. See D. M. Ogden, Jr., "The Blanket Primary and Party Regularity in Washington," *Pacific Northwest Quarterly*, 39 (1948), 33–38.

[34] Even under the closed primary, occasionally an organization in a small area has such a surplus of voters that it can enroll enough persons as members of the minority to control its nominations.

[35] Idaho Democrats, regarding themselves as the victims of primary raids, adopted a runoff primary, first effective in 1960. The statute provided that if no candidate

While the consensus appears to be that party would be better able to perform its role in the advancement of candidates if the open primary were abandoned, it must be conceded that systematic knowledge of the practical consequences of the open primary is limited. Yet it seems fairly clear that the open primary at times makes difficult the maintenance of orientations differentiating the two parties and probably handicaps the lesser party in those jurisdictions in which one party holds a substantial advantage. The voters of the lesser party may find it more attractive to exercise a balance of power in the primary of the major party than to engage in the troublesome task of building up their own party.

CROSS FILING AND RELATED PRACTICES   Closely related to the question of what voters are to be permitted to participate in a primary is the question of what tests shall be met by persons who seek the party's nomination in the primary. In most states a person may run for nomination in only a single primary, and ordinarily he must meet a test of party membership to enter the primary. Eligibility is usually established routinely without controversy. Exceptions tend to arise at times of internal party crisis accompanied by desertion to the opposition. In some southern states, for example, the tests for primary candidates exclude individuals who campaigned against Democratic candidates at the preceding general election. Thus, some persons who bolted the Democratic party to support Herbert Hoover for President in 1928 found themselves ineligible to run for Democratic nominations in the primaries of 1930.[36]

The most notable exception to the rule that a person may seek the nomination of only one party has been California's cross-filing system. Until 1960 a person could run for the nomination for the same office in the primaries of both parties. If he won both primaries, he went on the general election ballot as both the Democratic and Republican nominee. California experience demonstrated that the party long dominant in an area gains advantage by the cross-filing system. Its leaders tend to be well known, and given the low level of information of the primary electorate, they can often capture the nomination of the lesser party as well as that of their own. Prominent Republicans

received more than 40 per cent of the primary vote, a second primary would be held in which only those who had participated in the party's first primary would be permitted to vote. That rule would presumably enable "real" Democrats to control the nomination. See B. A. Martin, "The 1960 Election in Idaho," *Western Political Quarterly*, 14 (1961), 339–42.

[36] The requirement of party loyalty for primary candidates had a strange consequence in Alabama in the 1948 election. In that state Democratic presidential electors are nominated in the party primary; persons voting in the primary pledge themselves to support the nominees in the general election. In 1948 presidential electors pledged to oppose Truman were chosen in the primary. Senators, Representatives, and other prominent officeholders favorable to Truman could not oppose Dixiecratic pledged electors without disqualifying themselves as candidates in future Democratic primaries.

in several instances even won both nominations for statewide office. More-over, as the Democratic registration in the state increased the proportions of dual nominations increased; Republicans more often found it useful to neutralize the drawing power of the Democratic label at the general election by seeking Democratic as well as Republican nominations. Democrats suc-ceeded first in obtaining a requirement that the party affiliation of aspirants be indicated on the primary ballot. This change in ballot form, which oc-curred as the Democratic organization itself was gaining strength, produced a marked change in primary results in 1954 and 1956. Democrats tended to win Democratic nominations. In 1959 cross filing was prohibited.

Probably the availability of a procedure for boring from within and capturing the nominations of the lesser party tends to obstruct or to delay a secular build-up of minority strength. The minority must be able to protect itself from capture by the majority if it is to fulfill its role in the system. Party leaders who can be routed in their own camp by the majority can scarcely be expected to lead a militant minority. The rule limiting entry to candidacy in the party primary is thus a rule of critical importance in the maintenance of party competition.[37]

In New York a variation of cross filing exists. It serves mainly to facili-tate coalition between the Democratic and Liberal parties. For those candi-dates nominated by convention in that state, parties may combine by nomi-nating the same candidate. For offices for which nominations are made by primary, candidates for nomination must be enrolled members of a party unless the appropriate party committee grants an exception to the rule. That arrangement, given the fact that New York party organizations usually con-trol the outcome of their primaries, permits negotiations between a third party and a major party for coalition by dual nomination.

REFORM OF NOMINATING PROCEDURES   Debate and contention over nominating procedures did not end when the direct primary generally superseded the convention system in the states. The direct primary came in on a wave of belief that here was a means by which the "people" might rule without much interposition by "politicians." Second thoughts have tended toward the view that ways and means should be found by which party organization might play a legitimate and effective role in nominations, a recognition of the elemental necessity for organized leadership in a demo-cratic politics. Indicative of this broad shift in emphasis is a report by the National Municipal League's Committee on the Direct Primary which recom-mends that the party organization, acting through committees or confer-

---

[37] See G. E. Baker and B. Teitelbaum, "An End to Cross-Filing," *National Civic Review*, 48 (1959), 286–91; J. C. Findley, "Cross-Filing and the Progressive Movement in California Politics," *Western Political Quarterly*, 12 (1959), 699–711; R. J. Pitchell, "The Electoral System and Voting Behavior: The Case of California's Cross-Filing," *Western Political Quarterly*, 12 (1959), 459–84.

ences, should be authorized to propose organization slates that would be so designated on the primary ballot.

The Committee on Political Parties of the American Political Science Association has taken a similar position on these points and goes further to express a preference for the closed over the open primary on the ground that the closed arrangement "tends to support the concept of the party as an association of like-minded people." [38] The general drift of such recommendations is toward a revitalization of party organization, a process most feasible in jurisdictions with a fairly evenly balanced two-party competition. The chances are that in the heavily one-party jurisdictions, state and local, the direct primary will long survive in a relatively pure form. The primary procedure provides the foundation for a brand of popular government in one-party areas that differs in form and structure from the two-party system but nevertheless is deeply rooted in the areas in which it exists.

Nominations and the Nature of Party

This survey of nominating procedures outlines the main features of a significant segment of political practice. The data, moreover, provide additional insight into the nature of party itself. Observation of the permutations of nominating procedures leads to the conclusion that whatever the form of the procedure, relatively small, more or less cohesive groups tend to take the lead in organizing support for candidates. Under the legislative caucus the party leaders in the legislative body took the initiative. Under the convention system the party organization, with its precinct, county, city, and state functionaries, constituted the group that guided and managed conventions. Under the direct primary the party organization remained and adapted its methods to the new machinery of nominations. Whatever the form of nominating procedure, its operation has required the collaboration of men working in concert toward common ends, and they are usually professional politicians, who perform a task that has to be accomplished to operate government. In speculation about the workings of the nominating process, the following comment by H. J. Ford is relevant:

> One continually hears the declaration that the direct primary will take power from the politicians and give it to the people. This is pure nonsense. Politics has been, is, and always will be carried on by politicians, just as art is carried on by artists, engineering by engineers, business by businessmen. All that the direct primary, or any other political reform, can do is to affect the character of the politicians by altering

[38] The committee's report, "Toward a More Responsible Two-Party System," was published as a supplement to the *American Political Science Review*, September, 1950.

the conditions that govern political activity, thus determining its extent and quality. The direct primary may take advantage and opportunity from one set of politicians and confer them upon another set, but politicians there will always be so long as there is politics.[39]

Although the tendency toward leadership and control by the closely knit inner core of the party may prevail, the conditions under which that core works may be seriously altered by changes in the nature of the nominating process. Adoption of the convention system marked a revolt against the "autocratic" character of the caucus system. The tendency toward democratization found expression in a new nominating form. Under the convention system there would be, it was thought, a means for the ready expression of the wishes of the mass of party membership. As it developed, the convention system itself was soon branded as "bossism." The direct primary was turned to as a means of obtaining a direct expression of choice of the party membership on nominations. Though the machine remained, in the formation of its slate for the primary it apparently has had to be more solicitous of the sentiment of party membership than it was under the convention system. Under this scheme the machine candidates have to run the gantlet of the primary, and this obstacle in the road to election may be serious. The conditions created by the primary may even pulverize the machine into little cliques or perhaps, under one-party conditions, stimulate the creation of two or three submachines or organizations within the major party.

Each major step in the development of the nominating process has marked a further obeisance to the doctrine that the will of the rank and file of party membership should prevail. While a change in the system of making nominations does not eliminate the function of the organized minority in leading party opinion, it may enable a different minority to prevail. "We are always pulling down bosses," Ford observed, "because transient combinations of would-be bosses and reformers may develop strength enough to overthrow a particular boss or a particular machine. But while bosses and machines come and go, the boss and the machine are always with us." [40]

[39] "The Direct Primary," *North American Review*, 190 (1909), 1–14.
[40] *Ibid.*, p. 4.

15.

NATIONAL

CONVENTIONS

T HE NATIONAL convention represents the solution by American parties of the problem of uniting scattered points of political leadership in support of candidates for the Presidency and Vice Presidency. Thus, it is the basic element of national party apparatus. The parties of other nations have their assemblies and conferences, none of which approximates in its role the American national party convention. The convention is unique among national party authorities because it nominates the candidates for the Presidency and Vice Presidency. In turn, the Presidency owes some of its fundamental characteristics to the fact that presidential nominations emerge, not from the deliberations of party groups in Congress, but from the national convention.[1]

The national convention did not come into being in a day: it evolved over a considerable period of time. Early presidential nominations were made by congressional caucuses, that is, gatherings of members of the party in Congress. When the Federalist representation in Congress was sharply re-

[1] The definitive work on national conventions is Paul T. David, Ralph M. Goldman, and Richard C. Bain, *The Politics of National Party Conventions* (Washington: Brookings Institution, 1960). Basic data on all conventions are assembled in a companion volume by Richard C. Bain, *Convention Decisions and Voting Records* (Washington: Brookings Institution, 1960). On the 1960 convention, see Paul T. David (ed.), *The Presidential Election and Transition, 1960–1961* (Washington: Brookings Institution, 1961); Paul Tillett (ed.), *Inside Politics: The National Conventions* (Dobbs Ferry, N.Y.: Oceana, 1962).

duced by Republican victories, the congressional caucus could not speak for the party as a whole. The Federalists had to devise other means for agreeing among themselves on a candidate whom the party would support. In 1808, at a secret meeting of Federalist leaders in New York, Thomas Pinckney and Rufus King were nominated for the Presidency and Vice Presidency. "This was," says S. E. Morison, "the original national nominating convention." [2] Again, in 1812 Federalist leaders met privately in New York to agree upon nominations.

These early cabals did not lead immediately to the full-fledged national convention. The congressional caucus fell before the onslaughts of Andrew Jackson. As an aspirant for the presidential nomination in 1824, Jackson could hardly hope to gain the nomination at the hands of an unsympathetic congressional caucus. His backers inaugurated a campaign to discredit the caucus itself. They boycotted the 1824 Republican caucus, which was attended by only about one-fourth of the Republican members of Congress. The caucus decision was accorded little respect by the party over the country. William H. Crawford, the caucus nominee, received fewer electoral votes than did Jackson. If the party was to act as a unit in presidential elections, an authoritative mode of presidential nomination had to be contrived.

By a series of steps the national convention evolved to nominate presidential candidates. The model of state nominating conventions was at hand, but its extension to national nominations required both time and the displacement of the congressional caucus. In 1828 state conventions, state legislatures, and state legislative caucuses made presidential nominations, that is, they nominated Andrew Jackson. [3] In 1831 the Anti-Masonic party held what is commonly regarded as the first national convention; later that year a Democratic convention assembled in Baltimore to nominate Martin Van Buren to run as vice-presidential candidate with Jackson in 1832.

The Democratic convention of 1831 amounted to little more than a body to ratify Jackson's choice of Van Buren as his running mate. Nor did the National Republican Convention held in the same year do more than execute a foregone conclusion, the nomination of Henry Clay. Only gradually did the convention become a body capable of reconciling factional differences and of commanding the acquiescence in its decisions of party leaders over the country. In 1832, for example, Pennsylvania's Democratic electors gave the state's electoral vote, not to Van Buren, the convention vice-presidential nominee, but to William Wilkins, one of that state's Senators. Similarly, in 1836 the Virginia electors bolted the party on the vice-presidential nominee,

[2] "The First National Nominating Convention, 1808," *American Historical Review*, 17 (1912), 744–63.

[3] The Jackson Convention at Harrisburg, Pennsylvania, in 1828, nominated a slate of presidential electors and required from each candidate for elector a written pledge to vote for Jackson. Florence Weston, *The Presidential Election of 1828* (Washington: Catholic University, 1938), p. 105.

and the choice of Vice President devolved upon the Senate in the absence of an electoral majority. In 1840 the Democratic convention renominated Van Buren but could not agree upon a vice-presidential nominee and resolved to "leave the decision to their Republican fellow-citizens in the several States." The Democratic electoral vote for Vice President went largely to Richard M. Johnson, though South Carolina, whose legislature continued to choose electors, cast its electoral vote for another candidate.

By its nomination of James K. Polk, the Democratic convention of 1844 was the first, says Goldman, to create "an original synthesis" that reconciled factional differences and produced unanticipated party unity.[4] Earlier conventions had in their presidential nominations chiefly proclaimed foreordained designations and had been unable most of the time to produce party unity on the vice-presidential candidate. In 1844 Polk was so dark a horse that he had no support on the first ballot. His nomination marked the coming of age of the convention as an institution capable of creating as well as of ratifying consensus within the party. Simultaneously with the development of the convention, presidential electors came to be chosen by popular vote, and the convention's supremacy in party affairs became evident as party candidates for presidential elector were brought under the discipline of the national convention. The rise of the convention represented a triumph for those politicians who wished to rest the position of the President on an appeal to the mass of the people rather than on the will of legislative politicians expressed through the congressional caucus.

Thus there developed a mechanism through which party leaders, dispersed over a nation of continental proportions, could negotiate sufficient agreement to maintain parties capable of governing through the presidential system. The creation of the convention as a route to the Presidency independent of Congress was congenial to the doctrine of separation of powers. Yet the establishment of the supremacy of the convention in the choice of presidential candidates had other consequences. The convention, diverse in its composition and unpatterned in its ways, remains free to choose presidential candidates from a range of alternatives. Had the congressional caucus prevailed, the chances are that the old war-horses of the party organization in Congress would have had the edge in the race for the Presidency. A Taft would have won over an Eisenhower, a Garner over a Roosevelt, a Johnson over a Kennedy. Those factors conducive to advancement in hierarchies would have governed in the successive screenings on the way to the Presidency. An institution so transient as a national convention can be unconventional in its choices, a circumstance that is sometimes frightening; yet it permits the occasional choice of leaders who probably could not have made their way up a tighter party hierarchy.

[4] Ralph M. Goldman, "Party Chairman and Party Factions, 1789–1900." Unpublished Ph.D dissertation, University of Chicago, 1951.

Preconvention Maneuvers

The process of nomination of a presidential candidate begins long before the convention, in campaigns to sell a potential candidate to the party and to obtain the selection of delegations instructed to support him at the convention. These preconvention maneuvers fit no set pattern and cannot easily be described in general terms. Yet they may be better understood if they are observed with an awareness that the task of the convention is to unite the party in support of a presidential candidate. That end may be accomplished by a compromise of the conflicts within the party or by a test of the strength of competing factions leading to a settlement on terms not beyond acceptance by the losers.

The character of the preconvention campaign to round up support for aspirants for the nomination thus becomes a function of the tensions and cleavages within the party. Durable bases for conflict exist within each party. Regional or sectional objectives diverge, as between southern and northern Democrats or between coastal and interior Republicans. Within each party, class and group ambitions may collide. Yet the latent internal differences are activated in varying degrees at different times. At one time a coalition of forces may have found a formula for unity that maintains relative calm within the party; at another, the most exacerbated relations may develop. These variations in the intensity of internal party conflict reflect themselves in the preconvention campaigns of would-be nominees.

CONTINUATION OF DOMINANT COALITIONS   In one type of situation the preconvention campaign tends to be relatively uncontroverted. A dominant coalition controls the party and proceeds in the preconvention period to the routine selection of delegates committed to a continuation of the existing leadership. Most commonly these circumstances exist when a sitting President seeks renomination. If the President wants a renomination, the preconvention campaign is likely to be a prosaic affair. By custom a President is "entitled" to a second nomination and he has the advantage of controlling the party machine in obtaining it. Though it is quixotic to challenge him, some small but noisy dissident faction occasionally attempts a revolt, proclaiming itself the true custodian of the party gospel.

In part, the President's capacity to win renomination comes from his control of the patronage and perquisities of government. More fundamentally his renomination reflects an expression of the power of the coalition he has constructed within the party. Thus, the 1956 Republican preconvention campaign generated no great suspense. While beset by anxieties about whether the President would be able to run again, the leaders of the Eisenhower coalition proceeded without much opposition to obtain the designation of delegates committed to him. The remnants of the old Taft wing of the party muttered but they were powerless against superior forces. The 1960 nomination of Richard Nixon, an heir apparent, amounted by and large to a new expression of the dominance of the Eisenhower coalition. On occasion the nomination by the party out of power may constitute a reassertion of the power of a coalition formed at the preceding convention, yet such a renomination is not ordinarily made without challenge. Dewey's renomination in 1948 represented a continuation of the leadership he had achieved in 1944, a reaffirmation won, however, against strong opposition.

FACTIONAL COMPETITION   When no coalition has working control of the party, factions within the party battle for delegates to the convention. Although the groups that struggle for ascendancy may be vaguely defined, at times sharply defined factions compete for favor in presidential primaries and vie for support from state conventions as they choose their delegations to the national convention.

The spirited competition between the Eisenhower forces and the Taft faction in the preliminaries to the 1952 Republican convention clearly reflected the major policy differences within the Republican leadership. At one extreme were those most critical of Democratic foreign policy, a group that coincided fairly closely with those Republican conservatives most critical of Democratic policy on economic issues. Senator Robert A. Taft and his associates attempted to bind these elements of the party to the support of his candidacy. In opposition were those Republican leaders more disposed to accept a role of American leadership in world affairs. The same group regarded itself as "progressive" on domestic policy.

These lines of party division in preconvention maneuvers differ from time to time in the same party. In his campaign for the 1932 Democratic nomination, for example, Franklin D. Roosevelt carefully cultivated the South and the West, regions whose leaders had a long-standing antagonism toward the conservative and so-called Wall Street crowd in the Democratic party of the time. Decades later, in 1952, another set of factions developed in the preliminaries to the Democratic convention. Averell Harriman sought the nomination as a gilt-edge and undiluted New Dealer, while Senator Richard Russell of Georgia rounded up delegates committed to the southern viewpoint on civil rights. Somewhere in between these positions was Senator Estes Kefauver. The nomination went to Adlai Stevenson, who had not campaigned for delegates, but whose characteristics were such that his supporters could align behind him the center and uncommitted elements of the party.[5]

The clarity with which factional lines are drawn in the preconvention

[5] See Walter Johnson, *How We Drafted Adlai Stevenson* (New York: Knopf, 1955).

maneuvers differs from time to time. Aspirants for the nomination often straddle issues and thereby muffle or avoid conflict. Often they also pull their punches in their encounters lest the basis for collaboration in the campaign be destroyed. At times the policy differences between competitors for the nomination may be negligible and the conflict becomes largely one of personalities.

FAVORITE SONS AND OTHER BARGAINERS   While some sort of factional cleavage is often perceptible prior to an open convention, many aspirants for the nomination scarcely fit into the factional pattern. Delegations from particular states may, for example, be instructed for a "favorite son" of the state: a man who usually has the support of his own delegation and no other. He is put forward to hold the delegation free for negotiations at the convention; bargains may be struck with a leading contender who needs the votes to win the nomination. The second place on the ticket may go to a favorite son, or there may be promises of other sorts of preferment if the party wins the election. Uninstructed and uncommitted delegations enjoy the same freedom of negotiation. The presence of delegations not irrevocably committed to any of the leading aspirants gives the convention flexibility as it strives toward consensus on a candidate.

TACTICS OF PRECONVENTION CAMPAIGNS   The tactics employed by aspirants and their supporters in building strength within the party before the convention are by no means stereotyped, though certain recurring problems have to be met. Ordinarily a small headquarters organization is established to handle publicity and to manage all the chores connected with building a bloc of delegates in advance of the convention. The manager of the campaign publicizes his candidate, negotiates with the party leaders in various states, arranges speeches at appropriate times on major issues, and attempts to make it appear that his man is the person who can win for the party. The preconvention campaign may be on a scale that makes it a rehearsal of the presidential campaign itself, and costs of well over a million dollars may be incurred.

A tactical problem confronted by all aspirants is the timing of the announcement of their candidacies. One maxim is that a candidacy announced too soon may be blighted like an early-blooming flower; too late an announcement may give an advantage to other contenders. In October, 1951, several Republican governors vowed a strong preference for Eisenhower as the 1952 nominee but expressed their fears that unless the General soon made his availability plain the nomination would go to Taft by default. Often candidates occupy a public office and make a great virtue of tending to their knitting as governor, say, as they await the most propitious moment to announce their candidacy. Their managers meanwhile busily engage themselves in recruiting support for their man whose eagerness for the nomination is hardly a well-kept secret. A candidate may even succeed in avoiding an announcement. In 1944 Tom Dewey, who had made a strong showing in the 1940 Republican convention, maintained the fiction that he was not a candidate although his managers were active in recruiting delegate support. In 1952 Adlai Stevenson made no campaign for delegates and consistently denied that he was a candidate. Nor did he agree to accept the nomination until after the first convention ballot. More generally, the problems of assembling organizations to fight primary campaigns dictate a declaration long in advance of the convention. Thus, early in January, 1960, Senator John F. Kennedy announced his candidacy for the Democratic nomination and a Nixon aide indicated that the Vice President was indeed an aspirant for the Republican nomination. Neither item, though, took anyone by surprise.

A major aspect of a preconvention campaign consists of enlisting the support of state and local leaders. Their influence may be decisive in the actions of state primaries and conventions in the selection of national convention delegates. The manager for the candidate early attempts to impress on these men that his candidate would make a strong head of the ticket; the candidate himself usually meets with small groups of these leaders in order that they may look him over. A candidate who has gained the leadership of one shade of opinion of the party is likely to obtain commitments from state and local leaders of like beliefs. Another candidate may mobilize the leaders of a different hue of party faith. When a party controls the state government, the governor ordinarily exerts great influence in the choice of the state delegation and managers of aspirants for his party's nomination pay court to him.[6]

While in a sense the preconvention campaign is both a campaign for the favor of a few thousand party leaders as well as perhaps a conflict among factions of those leaders, the preconvention rituals include appeals to the wider public. The leading candidates seek to build up a public image of themselves that accords with their judgment of the dictates of sound strategy. They usually make speeches on important current issues at widely separated points in the country to let themselves be seen and heard and to gain national attention. No little calculation enters into the decisions about what speeches to make and what to say. A forthright stand may make enemies as well as gain recruits. One speech may be enough to demonstrate that a man cannot capture popular favor, and his boom is deflated early.

A question of strategy that vexes managers of would-be nominees is

[6] Senator Taft, in his review of the 1952 nomination, recorded that a majority of Senators and Representatives favored him, while a majority of the Republican governors supported Eisenhower. "However," he said, "the Governors had far more political influence on delegates." In 1960 Lyndon Johnson, too, experienced the limits of the influence of congressional politicians in their home states.

whether to enter the presidential primaries that are held by about a third of the states from March to May to select convention delegates. An early victory in a pivotal state may win the delegation and impress the party in other states with the aspirant's vote-pulling power. On the other hand, a defeat may bring the boom to a premature end. Yet a refusal to enter the primary may be interpreted as a manifestation of lack of confidence. Since the primary choice may be governed by the wishes of the state organization, it would be rash to enter a primary unless the candidate has the support of the organization or of an important faction, or feels that he could defeat the state machine.

As the preconvention campaign unfolds, a few serious contenders emerge, and they are faced by the necessity of deciding what to do about "favorite son" candidates. Should a leading contender challenge a favorite son in his own state? To do so might antagonize men who will control delegates in the convention. One tactic is to ask for second-choice support after the favorite son. In 1939 this was the strategy of the McNutt managers, who said, "In no State that has a favorite son are we asking for more than second choice." By such an approach leading candidates hope to keep on good terms with the lesser contenders and perhaps gain their support in the convention. By the same strategy lesser contenders may avoid antagonizing a leading candidate. In 1952 Governor Earl Warren, of California, announced that he would not enter the Ohio primary: "Ohio is the home state of Senator Taft, and he is certainly entitled to the delegation of his home state if he wants it." The inviolability of the private preserve of the potential favorite son may be on the decline as front-runners succeed in undercutting favorite sons by building popular followings directly through the media. Thus, in 1960 Kennedy, by threats to enter state primaries, captured some delegate support that state leaders had wanted to control through the favorite-son stratagem.

The candidate who early develops significant strength is sometimes faced by a combination of other candidates who desire to prevent the settlement of the nomination prior to the convention. If a leading contender can be "killed off," the way is left open for a negotiated nomination in the convention, and other contenders will at least have a chance. One technique is not to oppose openly the prominent aspirant in his fights for delegates but to ask for the selection of uninstructed delegates. The state leaders then will also be in a better bargaining position in the convention. In 1932, to illustrate, the Smith forces desired to head off the Roosevelt movement, and Jouett Shouse, a Smith supporter, suggested that "it would be wiser not to instruct delegates to the Democratic convention in favor of any candidate save where such instructions are necessary under the law. The convention should be unfettered by instructions." By this means the Smith faction hoped to stop Roosevelt.

"AVAILABILITY" OF CANDIDATES   The lore of American politics includes suppositions about tests that would-be presidential nominees must meet in order to be "available." While the notion of "availability" is useful for feature stories every four years, its content lacks precision. Yet certain characteristics of the party system do operate negatively to make some eminent men "unavailable." A man with a record of antagonism toward an important sector of his party—as an antilabor Democrat—would probably be regarded as "unavailable." Or a person irrevocably committed to narrow ranges of policy—a Republican Asia-firster in 1952, for example —might not be expected to have a partywide appeal. On the positive side, to be available a man must be a well-known public figure, a person with no disqualifying blemishes on his record, and he must have about himself the aura of a potential chief executive. Residence, too, is a significant factor. A party leader from a state with a large electoral vote that might be thrown one way or the other in the election is in a much better position to fight for the presidential nomination than one from a state traditionally attached to one party. Moreover, with the large delegation from his own state he has the beginnings of a bloc of convention votes. A governor of New York, of Ohio, or of California may hope to be among the availables.

An aspirant should not be too closely affiliated with any particular interest or group, nor should he have committed himself on a great and contentious issue before the time is ripe. Yet he must stand for something or a complex of things—a general point of view—in public life. Until the election of 1960 it was supposed that a man had to be a Protestant of good "American stock" and name to be available. Persons of the most recent immigrant stock probably are not yet to be regarded as available. To go from the ranks of the availables to those of the nominees a man also needs a certain amount of luck. He must come on the scene at a moment when his combination of traits suits the temper of the times. In 1936, for example, an Eisenhower probably would have had rough sledding. Or, only a Roosevelt could have had the good fortune to strive for the Presidency at a moment when his qualities fitted the needs of his party and the spirit of the times so well.

PRECONVENTION SIFTING   The maneuvers that precede the convention narrow its range of choice. The candidate may be nominated in fact before the convention meets; the delegates may convene only to ratify an accomplished fact. A true "dark horse" nominee whose selection is a complete surprise is rare. Hence, in a consideration of the nominating process great emphasis must be placed on the events antecedent to the convention. These processes are not easily described in general terms. Each instance is likely to have its own peculiarities, and the most unpredictable developments may occur in the competition to get to the White House. That competition involves a complicated process of weighing, testing, rejecting, and admission into the circle of serious competitors. One boomlet may be killed by the demonstration that the aspirant simply has no vote-getting ability. Another would-be President may be vetoed by his failure to gain the confidence of an important bloc in the party. Another may be unable to attract enough financial support to make much of a preconvention showing. Others find their way at least partly through the maze of obstacles to the White House and go to the convention with substantial backing.

Apportionment and Selection of Delegates

The delegates whose support aspirants for the nomination seek are chosen within the states. The manner of their choice and the method of fixing the number of delegates to which each state is entitled are of basic importance in the determination of the character of the convention as an institution.

During most of the history of the national convention, votes have been apportioned among the states in accordance with their strength in the electoral college, a principle adopted by the Democratic convention in 1831. Each state was at first entitled to one vote for each of its two Senators and one vote for each member of the House of Representativess from the state; later the number of votes was doubled.[7] This rule remained in use in unmodified form by the Republicans until their convention of 1916 and by the Democrats through the convention of 1940.

APPORTIONMENT: SPECIAL PROBLEMS OF THE RE-PUBLICANS   The original rule of apportionment presupposed a more or less even spread of party strength over the entire country. As a matter of fact such a distribution did not exist, and solidly Democratic areas had relatively as great strength in Republican conventions as states with heavy Republican majorities. Application of the rule created no serious difficulties in the Democratic party, but its use led to party disaster for the Republicans and eventually to its modification by them. Until recent times the Republican vote was extremely light in the South; the rule of apportionment gave to the states of this region a far greater convention strength than their party vote warranted. In the southern "rotten boroughs" the Republican organization

---

[7] In the textual discussion "delegate" is used synonymously with "vote." The Republicans allow only one delegate for one vote and the rule is enforced. The Democrats have been troubled by the designation of delegates in excess of the number of votes, a way to "recognize" the party faithful and to assure them good seats in the convention. In 1940 one Mississippi district, entitled to two votes, sent 54 delegates to cast them. The 1940 convention attempted to cope with the problem by resolving that in future conventions no "fractional distribution" should be permitted that would give any delegate less than a half-vote.

existed to distribute patronage—when the party controlled the national government—and to deliver delegates in the national convention, a pair of operations not unrelated.

Although the equity of the apportionment system had long been questioned, it was not until 1912 that a combination of circumstances occurred to bring about an alteration of the rule. In that year the system, which was partly responsible for Taft's control of the convention, led to a split in the Republican party, with Taft as the regular nominee and Theodore Roosevelt as the standard-bearer of the rebellious Progressive faction. The split gave the election to the Democrats, and the Republican national committee in 1913 took steps to reduce the inequities in the apportionment of delegates by submitting a new plan of apportionment for approval by the state conventions. The rule, approved by them and first used in 1916, decreased the representation of the Solid South by 76 votes. The new rule left the weak Republican areas still overrepresented in relation to their Republican voting strength. A series of subsequent modifications, either by or under the authority of the national conventions of 1920, 1940, and 1952, made further adjustments designed to penalize those areas with relatively few Republican votes and to increase the relative strength of those states with heavier Republican popular strength.[8] The cumulation of these changes produced the following rule of apportionment under which the 1960 convention was chosen:

DELEGATES AT LARGE

1. Four delegates at large from each state.

2. Two additional delegates at large for each representative at large in Congress from each state.

3. Six additional delegates at large from each state casting its electoral vote of a majority thereof for the Republican nominee for President in the last preceding presidential election. If any state does not cast its electoral vote or a majority thereof for the Republican nominee in the last preceding election, but at that election or at a subsequent election held prior to the next Republican National Convention elects a Republican United States Senator or a Republican Governor then in such state shall be entitled to such additional delegates at large.[9]

DISTRICT DELEGATES

1. One district delegate from each congressional district casting two thousand votes or more for any Republican elector in the last preceding presidential election or for the Republican nominee for Congress in the last preceeding congressional election.

[8] The evolution of the rule is traced by David, Goldman, and Bain, *op. cit.*, pp. 165–68.

[9] In addition, the District of Columbia is entitled to eight delegates; Puerto Rico, three; and the Virgin Islands, one.

2. One additional district delegate from each congressional district casting 10,000 votes or more for any Republican elector in the last preceding presidential election or for the Republican nominee for Congress in the last preceding congressional election.

Under these rules the number of delegates fluctuates from convention to convention; in 1936, the total was 1,003; in 1940, 1,000; in 1944, 1,057; in 1948, 1,094; in 1952, 1,206; in 1956, 1,320; in 1960, 1,331.

APPORTIONMENT: DEMOCRATIC PRACTICE   The Democratic party has been more fortunate than the Republican party in the matter of apportionment. Until recently it has been able to follow the practice of allowing each state a delegation twice the size of its congressional representation without serious controversy because of the lack of a problem such as the Solid South presents to the Republicans. Yet the 1936 Democratic convention, to offset southern sentiment against the abrogation of the two-thirds rule, directed the national committee to submit to the next convention "a plan for improving the system by which delegates and alternates to Democratic National Conventions are apportioned." The committee was ordered, in formulating this plan, to "take into account the Democratic strength within each State, District of Columbia, and Territory, etc. . . ." The 1940 convention adopted a rule to grant to states that go Democratic in a presidential election an additional two votes in the next convention. The national committee in 1947 increased this bonus to four votes.

The simplicity of Democratic practice was marred in 1952 when the national committee, in keeping with precedents of 1912 and 1932, ruled that no state delegation should be reduced in size because of a loss of congressional representation under the reapportionment based on the 1950 census. Instead of reverting to standard practice in 1956, the national committee provided that each state should have all its 1952 vote (including even, if earned, the bonus votes for going Democratic in 1948) plus four votes if it had been Democratic in the presidential election of 1952 or had elected a Democratic governor or Senator then or later. In its call for the 1960 convention the national committee, to offset in part the inequities introduced by the cumulation of bonus votes, fixed state representation as follows: (1) 2½ votes for each United States Senator; (2) 2½ votes for each Representative, except that when the total so allotted resulted in a fractional vote, an additional ½ vote would be allotted; (3) ½ vote each for the national committeeman and the national committeewoman, who were given convention seats; (4) if these allotments (excluding the two ½ committee votes) did not equal the state's 1956 total, a number of votes to equal the deficiency would be added. These rules yielded in 1960 a convention of 1,521 votes in contrast with 1,372 in 1956.

METHODS OF CHOOSING DELEGATES   Two methods are employed in the selection of state delegations to the national conventions. About a third of the state governments conduct presidential primaries in which the voters may choose delegates directly and usually may also express a preference among the aspirants for the presidential nomination. In the remaining states the political parties designate delegates through conventions or committees. In a few instances district delegates are chosen by primary; the delegates at large, by the state convention.

CONVENTIONS AND COMMITTEES   A few states permit state committees of the parties to choose delegates to the national convention. More usually, in the absence of a presidential primary, the state parties act through conventions, which vary considerably in their form and mode of selection. Most commonly they are built on a system of indirect election beginning with precinct meetings of voters which choose delegates to county conventions from whence go delegates to the state convention. Yet in a few states the state conventions consist of delegates chosen by precinct committeemen and other party functionaries. The state convention may choose the entire delegation, or district conventions may choose district delegates and the state convention the delegates at large. The Republican rules express a preference for district conventions separate in time and place from the state convention. The equivalent result is at times obtained by district caucuses at state conventions; the convention chooses a slate of delegates built up of nominees of the district caucuses.

Ordinarily the convention procedure does not permit extensive participation by the rank and file of the party in the choice of delegates. Though the convention may not be bossed, selection of delegates becomes a matter handled almost exclusively by the party professionals. Yet, on the whole, the convention processes produce delegations representative of the general tenor of sentiment of the party in the state. The principal difficulties with selection by convention seem to occur when the convention members really have no constituents and are, perhaps for that reason, unable to produce a decision acceptable to all concerned. In several southern conventions in 1952 the old-guard professionals who had been managing party affairs for years dealt roughly with the influx of "new" Republicans who wished delegations instructed for Eisenhower. Under more normal conditions party managements seem to be generally able to guide the work of conventions toward decisions accepted as legitimate on all sides.

PRESIDENTIAL PRIMARIES   In 1960, 15 states and the District of Columbia conducted a presidential primary of one sort or another and in most of them all or nearly all of the national convention delegates were chosen by primary vote. The presidential primary came into existence at about the same time and for the same reasons that the direct primary was substituted for the convention method of nomination of candidates for state offices. Conventions were thought to be susceptible to manipulation by party leaders and a widespread faith existed that more popular participation would have a cleansing effect on politics.

Florida seems to have first used a presidential primary in 1904 when its Democratic convention delegates were chosen in a primary held under a general statute authorizing parties to conduct primary elections. Though Wisconsin in 1905 and Pennsylvania in 1906 adopted laws specifically providing for the direct election of delegates—all delegates in Wisconsin and district delegates in Pennsylvania—the birth of the full-blown presidential primary is usually traced to an Oregon law adopted by popular vote in 1910.[10] That law provided for a preference vote by the voters on presidential aspirants, as well as the direct election of all delegates to the convention. Between 1910 and 1916 the presidential primary spread so rapidly among the states that it was predicted that within a short period the national convention would become, like the electoral college, a mere mechanism for recording decisions already arrived at by the electorate. The drive for the presidential primary, however, was soon spent, and since its peak in 1916 several states have abandoned it.

T Y P E S   O F   P R E S I D E N T I A L   P R I M A R I E S   Early advocates of the presidential primary hoped to short-circuit the indirect convention procedures and give to the party voter an opportunity to express effectively a preference between aspirants for the presidential nomination. In fact, the extent to which the vote at the primary affects the votes of the delegates at the convention differs greatly from state to state with the form of the state primary, as well as with variations in local custom and tradition. The primary laws involve, in varying combinations: (1) presidential preference voting, as between Stevenson and Kefauver, the so-called "beauty contest," and (2) direct election of delegates to the convention. How these questions are presented to the voter on the ballot varies greatly and affects the clarity of the expression of voter sentiment, a proposition that may be made plain by mention of the principal forms of the primary.

1. *Presidential preference vote with election of national convention delegates by state convention.* The primary ballot permits an expression of preference between aspirants for the nomination, but the state convention continues to choose the delegates who may or may not turn out to be supporters of the candidate who wins the "popularity" contest. This arrangement has been on the books in Maryland for some time, and Indiana used it first in 1956.

2. *Combined expression of preference and vote for pledged convention*

[10] Louise Overacker, *The Presidential Primary* (New York: Macmillan, 1926).

delegates. By a single mark on the ballot the voter may express his preference for a presidential aspirant and vote for a slate of delegates pledged to support his preference. In South Dakota in 1952, for example, the Republican ballot included a column headed "Candidates Preferring Robert A. Taft for President." An X at the head of the column, in effect, combined an expression of a preference for Taft for the nomination with a vote for candidates committed to his support in the convention. California employs this form of primary with the election at large of the entire state delegation; the winner of the preference vote wins all the delegates. When delegates are elected by congressional districts, the winner of the statewide preference vote under the combined ballot form does not necessarily win all the state's delegates.

3. *Separation of preference vote and delegate election.* Another group of states complicates matters by requiring the voter to mark his ballot twice, once to indicate his choice among presidential aspirants and again to vote for convention delegates. In some states the ballot need not indicate the presidential preference of the delegate candidates, and the voter may even support delegates actually opposed to his presidential preference. The New Hampshire ballot in 1956, to illustrate, contained a presidential preference column headed: "I hereby declare my preference for candidate for office of President of the United States to be as follows." Other columns contained the names of candidates for delegates at large and for district delegates and alongside their names were indications of their presidential preference: "Favorable to the nomination of William Knowland for President," and so forth.

4. *Direct election of unpledged delegates, with no presidential preference vote.* In a few states delegates are chosen by direct primary, but the ballot permits no expression of preference for presidential aspirants nor does it indicate the intentions of the candidates for delegate. New York employs this arrangement and from time to time it has been used elsewhere. In other states that elect delegates with no ballot indication of their preference, this type of situation is approximated when no name happens to be entered in the presidential preference voting. In some campaigns slates committed to competing candidates may be in the field but the absence of ballot identification makes the expression of voter preference difficult. In New York the primary commonly attracts little interest since, by custom, about all it amounts to is a ratification of the slate of delegates chosen by the state organization, which operates very much as if the presidential primary did not exist.

The form of the presidential primary also varies in other respects. Delegates may in some instances appear on the ballot as pledged to a presidential aspirant without his consent; in other instances consent is required. The primary statutes also differ in the strength of the commitment demanded of the delegate to the candidate to whom he is pledged. In presidential preference primaries the consent of the candidate is usually required if his name is to appear, although an Oregon statute has permitted the secretary of state to place on the ballot the names of candidates "generally advocated or recognized in national news media," with the proviso that a person could keep his name off the ballot by filing an affidavit that he was not and did not intend to become a candidate. Presidential preference votes are also in some instances advisory to the delegates; in others, the statutes attempt to make the preference vote mandatory upon them.[11]

ROLE OF PRESIDENTIAL PRIMARY   The primary has introduced a considerably higher degree of popular participation in the choice of presidential nominees. That participation may not be determinative of the candidates, but those who would be nominees must ordinarily conduct campaigns directed to the voters to a greater degree than when the nominations were more exclusively in the hands of the party professionals. The primary probably makes some men presidential hopefuls who would not have been in an earlier day. Thus, Estes Kefauver, with a reputation developed through the televising of his crime investigations, became a far more serious contender for the nomination in 1952 and in 1956 than he would have been in the days before the presidential primary.

On occasion it seems as though the effect of the primaries is to kill off candidates rather than to determine which of the two or three aspirants who reach the convention with considerable blocs of delegates will be nominated. In 1944 Wendell Willkie withdrew from the race for the Republican nomination after an early defeat in the Wisconsin primary. He lost to a slate of delegates pledged to Dewey, who had disavowed the slate and not even bothered to campaign. Or in 1956, Stevenson's victory in the California primary was regarded as the death blow to the Kefauver candidacy. On the other hand, a spectacular performance in a primary may give a candidate a powerful boost and bring leaders to his bandwagon. In the 1952 "Minnesota miracle," when over 100,000 persons took the trouble to write in the name of Eisenhower in the primary, Republican leaders all over the land could see that a vote-getter had arrived on the scene. Similarly, in 1960, Kennedy, the front runner, strengthened his cause by his demonstration of vote-pulling power among Protestants in his West Virginia victory over Humphrey.

While the primary has modified nominating practices, it has not produced conventions of automata that mechanically record the preferences expressed by the voters at home. Party organizations in many states retain a fairly high degree of autonomy despite the primaries. Candidates for the presidency choose not to enter many primaries. State delegations often retain

[11] For full details on presidential primaries, see David, Goldman, and Bain, *op. cit.,* ch. 10 and pp. 528–55. On a noted primary, see H. W. Ernst, *The Primary That Made a President: West Virginia 1960* (New York: McGraw-Hill, Eagleton Case 26, 1962).

their freedom of choice by commitment to favorite sons through the primary as before; the voters may even vote for uncommitted delegations. Indeed, for the convention to be capable of achieving its broad objective of developing party consensus on a candidate, delegations must possess a range of discretion.

PROPOSALS FOR A NATIONWIDE PRIMARY   When the memory of the Republican convention of 1912 was fresh, numerous proposals were made for the establishment of a nationwide preference primary, which perhaps would have required a constitutional amendment. President Wilson, in his first message to Congress, urged a national system in these words: "I turn now to a subject which I hope can be handled promptly and without serious controversy of any kind. I mean the method of selecting nominees for the Presidency of the United States. I feel confident that I do not misinterpret the wishes or the expectations of the country when I urge prompt enactment of legislation which will provide for primary elections throughout the country at which the voters of the several parties may choose the nominees for the Presidency without the intervention of nominating conventions." Congress did not act on the recommendation. From time to time renewed flurries of interest in the matter develop. In 1952 a Senate committee even reported a bill to encourage the states, by financial assistance, to hold presidential preference primaries; the proposal died at that stage.

The invention of the straw poll has introduced a sort of nationwide preference primary. In recent conventions the nominations and the rankings of candidates for the nomination have followed fairly closely the sentiments of party members as revealed by the polls. It is doubtful that the polls control convention actions, though they may establish that convention actions do not deviate nearly so far from popular sentiment as some advocates of the presidential primary would have us believe. It has been contended that during the past half-century the convention has become, in fact, the captive of the forces of mass democracy. It is limited in its deliberations to consideration of those who have achieved, by one means or another, the status of a celebrity. When one person is clearly the national favorite the convention has, or so it is argued, no choice but to nominate him.[12]

Organization of the Convention

On the appointed day [13] the delegates convene to play their parts in our

[12] See W. G. Carleton, "The Revolution in the Presidential Nominating Convention," *Political Science Quarterly*, 72 (1957), 224–40.

[13] In 1960 the Democrats met in Los Angeles on July 11; the Republicans, in Chicago on July 25. The timing of the conventions assures a long campaign in comparison with other great democracies, and consideration is given from time to time to

great quadrennial political drama. The city fathers of the convention city [14] deck out the town in bunting and flags as if a huge county fair were in progress. Banners identify the headquarters of the presidential aspirants. Their managers issue optimistic predictions of their first-ballot strength and work frantically behind the scenes to try to approach in fact their predictions. By badges, arm bands, and buttons the delegates and visitors proclaim their allegiance. The convention gathers in a great auditorium—such as the Chicago International Amphitheater, the San Francisco Cow Palace, Madison Square Garden in New York—the main floor of which seats the delegates and their alternates, more than 2,000 in all; the galleries take care of the overflow of alternates from the main floor and of thousands of spectators. The scene presents a spectacle of confusion and disorder astonishing to foreign observers. The convention hall is equipped with amplifying apparatus so that the officials and delegates may make themselves heard. The radio and television chains have their equipment set up to report the happenings to tens of millions of people listening and looking throughout the nation, and hundreds of newspaper reporters are on hand to record their impressions of the proceedings.[15]

TEMPORARY ORGANIZATION   The convention is opened by the chairman of the national committee, who presides until the temporary officers are elected.[16] The national committee presents to the convention a slate of temporary officers, of which the temporary chairman is the most

---

proposals to schedule the conventions later. The Senate, in fact, in 1961 resolved that it was the "sense of the Senate" that conventions should not be held before Labor Day. The contrary view is that American parties, not continuously mobilized as are British parties, need time to create campaign organization. Moreover, when an unknown candidate is nominated, he needs time to make an impression on the electorate.

[14] The place of the convention is designated by the national committee. Esoteric considerations of party advantage are said to have a part in the selection. It is doubtful that the location of the convention affects the popular vote, but that possibility is urged by the advocates of specific cities. Aspirants for the nomination often attempt to influence the choice of location to avoid cities that would pack the galleries with hostile crowds and to seek the designation of cities where the gallery and newspaper atmosphere would be favorable or at least neutral. Prime considerations are that the convention city have adequate travel and hotel facilities and that it possess a suitable auditorium. Beyond these requirements the bonus—usually several hundred thousand dollars—offered by the local citizenry may be influential.

[15] The Iowa poll reported after the 1960 conventions that about 40 per cent of their sample had "paid no attention" to the television coverage of the conventions. The fact that 60 per cent of the nation pays some heed to the telecasts of the convention places the convention in a radically new context whose full effects have probably not yet been felt.

[16] Sessions of the convention are opened with prayer, by clergymen selected with an eye to representation of the leading faiths. Thus, at the 1940 Republican convention, prayers were offered by a rabbi, a Lutheran, a Christian Scientist, an Archbishop, an African Methodist bishop, a Presbyterian, the Chancellor of an Archdiocese, a Baptist, a Protestant Episcopal bishop, a Methodist, and the Chaplain of the Connecticut State Senate, a divine of unspecified denomination.

important.[17] The preconvention maneuvers of the aspirants for the nomination include efforts to gain sufficient votes in the national committee to assure a neutral, if not a friendly, temporary chairman. Usually the nominee of the national committee is approved by the convention, but at infrequent times the election of the temporary chairman becomes a test of the strength of contending factions within the party. In the Republican convention of 1912, for example, the national committee and the Taft forces successfully backed Elihu Root for the temporary chairmanship over the opposition of the Roosevelt delegates. In the same year Bryan and the Wilson delegates unsuccessfully opposed the national committee nominee for the Democratic chairmanship, Judge Alton B. Parker, who had the support of delegates pledged to Harmon and Underwood. In 1952 the Eisenhower forces made much propaganda about a rigged convention when the national committee proposed Walter S. Hallanan, a partisan of Taft, but they did not oppose his designation at the convention.

The temporary chairman presides until the permanent organization is effected. He may have opportunity to make rulings of critical significance for the results of the convention. He also has traditionally delivered the keynote speech, a custom from which the Republicans departed in 1952, 1956, and 1960. Their keynoters in those years, General Douglas MacArthur, Governor Arthur B. Langlie, and Representative Walter H. Judd were not incumbered with the duties of temporary chairman. The keynoter inveighs against the opposition, recites the great achievements of his party, evokes memories of the great party leaders of the past, and generally attempts to set a stirring theme for the convention.

An early step in the convention is the designation of its four great standing committees: (1) credentials, with the function of examining credentials, hearing challenges against the right of delegations to sit, and recommending a permanent roll of delegates to the convention; (2) permanent organization, which recommends a set of permanent officers for the convention; (3) rules, with the duty of reporting to the convention a set of rules to govern its procedure; and (4) resolutions, with the task of drafting and presenting a platform to the convention. In practice each state and territorial delegation names a person to sit on each of these committees, except that one man and one woman are designated by each delegation for membership on the resolutions committee. The Democrats adopted the innovation of female representation on the resolutions committee in 1940, and the Republicans followed in 1944.

---

[17] The other temporary officers—who are usually made permanent—include the secretary, sergeant-at-arms, parliamentarian, chief tally clerk, chief reading clerk, doorkeeper, and various other assistants and officials necessary for the operation of the convention.

PERMANENT ORGANIZATION: RIVALS MANEUVER FOR
ADVANTAGE   The first committee report disposed of by the convention
is usually that of the committee on credentials, but, for convenience, the
report of the committee on permanent organization may be mentioned first.
The item in the report of this committee that may give rise to controversy
is its recommendation for the post of permanent chairman. The factions
aligned behind each aspirant for the presidential nomination desire the selection of a permanent chairman who is at least not hostile to their candidates. A minority report from the committee on permanent organization may
furnish the occasion for a test of strength between candidates for the nomination. In 1932, for example, the majority of the committee on permanent
organization nominated Jouett Shouse, affiliated with the anti-Roosevelt bloc,
for the permanent chairmanship; the Roosevelt forces rallied a majority of
the convention to elect the late Senator Walsh of Montana as permanent
chairman. Usually, however, the suspense over who will be permanent chairman is not great. He has come to be ordinarily "chosen" long before he is
"elected" by the convention. The national chairman in consultation with
other party leaders or a subcommittee of the national committee acts on the
question usually several months before the convention which ratifies the
choice.[18] Each party has in recent conventions relied on its ranking member
of the House of Representatives. Joseph W. Martin, Jr., served as permanent chairman of the Republican conventions of 1944, 1948, 1952, and
1956 and Charles A. Halleck, as chairman of the convention of 1960. Sam
Rayburn chaired the Democratic conventions of 1948, 1952, and 1956, but
the task fell to Governor LeRoy Collins of Florida in 1960 when Rayburn
managed Johnson's campaign for the nomination.

The formal organization of the convention consists of the permanent
chairman, the standing committees, and the functionaries necessary for the
work of the assembly; in addition, as with congresses and parliaments, there
tends to be also an informal organization of the blocs and factions seeking
to steer the deliberations of the convention. Before the 1932 Democratic
convention, for example, the Roosevelt leaders held a caucus at Hyde Park
to agree on how to run the convention. It was decided that Walsh would be
permanent chairman, Arthur Mullen the floor manager for the Roosevelt
forces, Senator Hitchcock chairman of the committee on resolutions, and
that Judge Mack would nominate Roosevelt. At the 1952 Republican convention Thomas E. Coleman, of Wisconsin, served as floor manager for
Senator Taft; Senator Henry Cabot Lodge, for the Eisenhower forces.

[18] The preconvention arrangements under the authority of the national committee
also extend to the selection of the chairmen of the convention's standing committees
in order that they may begin work before the convention formally meets. State delegations
—or their leaders—also designate state representatives on the committees in advance
of the convention.

Lodge directed the strategy that struck with the "fair play" resolution relative to the seating of delegates, a move which, along with the accompanying propaganda, pictured the Taft forces to the country in the embarrassing position of opposing "fair play." [19]

On occasion the informal organization of the leading candidate plans the convention in great detail. When a convention meets to renominate a sitting President, his leaders may have the convention proceedings so thoroughly under control that practically every item of procedure is laid out in advance, even to the allocation of the honors of seconding motions for adjournment and of proposing resolutions of gratitude to the committee on local arrangements. When a stentorian voice echoes through the hall, "The chair recognizes delegate Jones from Wisconsin to offer a resolution," the script is merely being followed.

CREDENTIALS: CONTESTED DELEGATIONS   The national convention is the judge of the qualifications of its members. In the early history of the convention, the review of delegates' credentials was casual. When no formally elected delegates appeared to represent a state, chance visitors from the state might be allowed to cast its vote at the convention. With the regularization of convention procedure, practices developed for the determination of the right of delegations to convention membership. The question of the right of a delegation to sit commonly arises when a contesting delegation appears and claims to be the legitimate spokesman for the party in the state. Assertions may be made of irregularities in the choice of a delegation.[20]

Prior to the opening of the convention, the national committee of each party prepares a temporary roll of the delegates entitled to sit in the convention. To do so, it must make a preliminary decision on challenged delegations, if any, and to that end it hears the parties to such contests. The Republican national committee is required by party rule, however, to place on the temporary roll the names of those delegates certified by appropriate

[19] With the increasing size of conventions, maintenance of communications between the informal leadership and state delegations has become a problem. In 1960 the Kennedy high command had special telephone lines to friendly delegations and its floor workers carried walkie-talkies.

[20] In 1952 a contesting Louisiana delegation to the Republican convention (pledged to Eisenhower) asserted that the Taft delegation had been chosen by arbitrary management of parish mass meetings and the state convention. One parish mass meeting was said to have gone something like this: "Gentlemen, the purpose of the meeting is to elect delegates to the District and State Conventions. I nominate myself as Permanent Chairman, I second the nomination, I close the nominations, I declare myself the Permanent Chairman. I nominate myself as a delegate to the District and State Conventions, I second the nomination, I close the nominations, I declare myself the delegate to the District and State Conventions. Good evening, Gentlemen." *Original Brief on Behalf of Louisiana Delegates Representing New Republican Leadership in Louisiana* (by John Minor Wisdom and others as counsel), p. 49.

state officials as having been designated in accordance with state law. Some delegations, of course, go to the convention under certification of party officials rather than of public functionaries.

When the convention of each party meets, the documents used by the national committee in preparing the temporary roll are delivered to the committee on credentials.[21] It hears the claims of the contesting delegations anew and reports to the convention, which accepts or rejects the recommendation. The importance of the decision on contests arises from the fact that each delegation that claims to be duly authorized to represent a state may be pledged to a different candidate for the presidential nomination. In some circumstances the convention, in deciding which delegation to seat, may be deciding which candidate will be nominated. Hence the managers for each candidate take a keen interest in the contests and marshal their forces to assure a decision to their advantage, occasionally without much regard to the equities of the contest.

At almost every convention a contest or so develops, whose resolution often indicates which candidate for the nomination is in control of the convention. The most spectacular battles over credentials occurred in the Republican conventions of 1912 and of 1952. The national committee, in the preparation of the 1912 temporary roll, seated delegations pledged to William Howard Taft rather than the contesting delegations supporting Theodore Roosevelt. The committee on credentials and the convention itself followed in general the decisions of the national committee. The temporarily seated delegations, even though contested, were entitled to vote on all contests save their own; the action of the national committee and of the convention in seating Taft rather than Roosevelt delegates gave Taft the nomination.

The rule of 1912 to permit temporarily seated delegates to vote on the settlement of contests except the one affecting their own right to sit rose up to plague the Republicans in 1952. In their management of the regular Republican organizations in several southern states, the partisans of Senator Robert A. Taft had operated in a high-handed fashion to obtain control of the convention delegations against the protests of "new" Republicans, that is, mainly Democrats, who demanded the selection of delegates pledged to General Eisenhower. The Eisenhower managers advanced on the convention behind a smokescreen of outraged virtue; they had been robbed. The Texas state convention, Taft-controlled, had perpetrated a "steal." The offensive

---

[21] The 1952 Republican convention, as an aftermath of the battle over credentials in that year, adopted a rule directing the chairman of the national committee to appoint prior to each convention a "contest committee" to review the records and briefs submitted by contesting delegations and to report to the national committee the issues of law and fact raised by the contest. The national committee then proceeds to a hearing and decision on the issues posed by its contest committee. For the Republican rules on contests, see *Proceedings*, 1952, pp. 292–94.

led off with a convention motion, a so-called fair-play motion, to prohibit delegates on the temporary roll from Texas and Georgia and most of those from Louisiana from voting in the convention on any question until their right to sit had been finally settled. The Taft forces opposed changing the rules in the midst of the game and argued that by simply contesting enough delegations the convention could be made powerless to act. The Eisenhower forces won the adoption of their proposal.[22] They then induced the convention first to reject the southern delegations that had been given temporary seats by the Taft-controlled national committee and then to seat delegations favorable to the General.[23]

Democratic conventions in 1952 and 1956 had warm disputes on seating delegations from the South. In these instances the debate hinged, not on whether the delegations had been chosen in accord with regular procedures, but on their loyalty to the party and on their willingness to be bound by the action of the convention. The decision thus went beyond the technical validity of credentials and to the question of the authority of the convention in the party as a whole, a question to be explored later.

Platforms

The resolutions committee presents to the convention a recommended platform, which states broadly the party program. The platform of the party in power makes resounding and prideful references to its record of performance and to the magnificent qualities of its leaders. The out party usually includes in its resolutions caustic criticisms of the record of the ins. The adoption of the platform does not occur in isolation from the other activities of the convention but is ordinarily integrally related to the other major decisions by that body. Usually the group that controls the nomination also controls the resolutions committee. Commonly the questions of policy that are intertwined with the nomination will also vex the platform drafters.

PLATFORM SOURCES   A sitting President seeking renomination is likely to guide the deliberations of the resolutions committee of his party's convention. The sources of drafts and suggestions for the resolutions committee of an open convention or of a convention of the outs tend to be more

---

[22] Subsequently the convention amended its permanent rules to bring them into accord with the fair-play motion. The change prohibits voting in the convention by delegations under contest except those placed on the temporary roll by the vote of at least two-thirds of the members of the national committee. The latter proviso presumably limits the possibility of hamstringing the convention by frivolous contests.

[23] For a survey of the 1952 conflict over credentials, see Paul T. David, et al., *Presidential Nominating Politics in 1952* (Baltimore: Johns Hopkins Press, 1952), I, 68–88.

diverse. In 1932, although James Garfield was chairman of the Republican resolutions committee, "Secretary of the Treasury Ogden Mills brought the entire platform from Washington, with the exception of the plank on prohibition, which was written in Chicago by men who knew" Hoover's desires.[24] The Democratic platform of 1936 was written by Roosevelt and sent to the resolutions committee, which approved it after the alteration of one sentence.

The resolutions committee of a convention not controlled by an incumbent President receives from a variety of sources drafts of proposed planks or of entire platforms. A leading candidate for the nomination may have had a draft platform prepared by his associates in advance of the convention. A dominant personality in the party may exercise a controlling voice in the content of the platform. A recognized specialist of the party may draft the plank on his specialty. In the months before recent conventions Democrats have conducted regional conclaves of party leaders to discuss, among other things, platform questions. On occasion a study committee accumulates data and proposals for the resolutions committee.[25] In short, the resolutions committee suffers from no lack of advice about what ought to go into the platform.

COMMITTEE PROCEEDINGS   The resolutions committee ordinarily begins its work a week or more in advance of the opening of the convention. It holds hearings for the benefit of pressure-group representatives, party personages, and others who wish to expound and to publicize their proposals for the platform. This parade of pressure-group representatives is principally ritualistic, but the views of those interests most closely associated with each party tend to find their way into its platform.

While the actions of the resolutions committee may be determined in varying degrees by the wishes of the sitting President or by a dominant clique of convention leaders, its work is rarely mere formality. Commonly no controversy exists on the major part of the platform; yet, at least in a convention without clear centers of control, the committee itself must accomplish, through subcommittees and drafting committees, the considerable task of piecing together a platform. Its deliberations usually center on one or two

[24] R. V. Peel and T. C. Donnelly, *The 1932 Campaign* (New York: Farrar & Rinehart, 1935), p. 86.

[25] Study groups seem to develop most often when the party does not control the Presidency. Thus, the Democratic Advisory Committee fed materials to the platform drafters in 1960. Early in 1920 the Republicans created an Advisory Committee on Policies and Platform; in 1937, the Republican Program Committee, chaired by Glenn Frank; in 1943, the Republican Post-War Advisory Council; and in 1959, the Republican Committee on Program and Progress with Charles H. Percy as chairman. He became chairman of the resolutions committee of the 1960 convention. The work of these Republican committees has been analyzed by Karl A. Lamb, "Program Committees and the Nationalization of Republican Policy" (unpublished MS).

questions that are currently points of deep differences within the party. The accepted practice is to attempt to compromise these differences in order to arrive at a platform draft that will not provoke a debate on the floor of the convention.

Negotiations to bring about concurrence among the major factions of the party on contentious issues ordinarily involve the principal interested party figures even though they may not be members of the resolutions committee. In 1952, for example, the Democratic resolutions committee succeeded in negotiating agreement upon a civil rights plank, a perennial source of dissension among Democrats. In 1960 a notable platform conflict occurred among the Republicans when Governor Nelson Rockefeller demanded stronger planks on civil rights, national defense, education, and other matters. Agreement between Nixon and Rockefeller on the disputed points was followed by rebellious grumbling as the conservative resolutions committee was compelled to adjust its actions to the leadership accord.

APPEAL TO THE CONVENTION   When efforts to reconcile differences at the committee stage fail, the minority may submit a separate recommendation to the convention on the bitterly contested items in the platform. Convention leaders invariably attempt to avoid such a test of strength. In a sense, national party rests on coalition and compromise; when platform questions arise that are not susceptible of compromise, the limits of action by the national convention have been reached. A floor fight may deepen cleavages rather than settle controversy. Nevertheless, a minority of the resolutions committee may make a dissenting report to the convention. In the 1928 Republican convention, for example, a minority plank on agriculture, proposed by Earl C. Smith, a delegate from Illinois, was supported by 15 states in the committee on resolutions. The minority foresaw a defection of midwestern farmers from the Republican party: "We come to you within these four walls pleading with the delegates not to drive the farmers of the Republican States out of their party." [26] The minority plank was rejected, but it was not until 1932 that the midwestern farmers rebelled.

In the 1948 Democratic convention attention was focused on the civil rights plank. In a vain effort to bridge the differences within the party the Truman leadership in the convention developed a plank that the southerners thought too forthright and the northerners regarded somewhat belligerently as too weak. Both the southern and northern factions expressed their dissatisfaction with the resolutions committee's recommendation by proposing their own views on the floor of the convention and defending them with an impressive volume of torrid oratory. The triumph of the northern liberals —and the rejection of the southern plank—contributed to the split in the Democratic party. The entire incident demonstrated, at least negatively, the

[26] *Proceedings*, 1928, p. 150.

uses of platform ambiguity in holding together party groups of divergent views. Again, in 1956, the civil rights question produced a minority report: the dissenters were northern Democrats who were under the necessity of making a demonstration to forestall losses among Negro voters.

NATURE OF THE PLATFORM   No tightly reasoned or succinct manifesto of party doctrine emerges from the convention. The platform tends to be wordy and to be cast in the rhetoric of political declamation.[27] Platforms become objects of cynical regard, yet their qualities mirror the characteristics of the party system itself: the platforms are as they are because the party system is as it is.

The platform may speak with forthrightness on a range of issues, usually settled issues or matters on which the party maintains a traditional position. On such matters, the platforms of the two parties often differ, contrary to general belief. The differences may be in emphasis, degree, detail, or timing, but these are, in the main, the differences of American politics. The contrasts between the party platforms also vary in degree from time to time with the alternating intensification and reduction of conflict between the parties. On a few major current issues the positions of the parties may contrast sharply, though sometimes these differences are camouflaged for the generality by their phrasing in a language clear only to the politically sophisticated.

On some contentious issues intraparty differences dictate an ambiguity in platform pronouncements. The construction of a coalition with a chance to win an election may require the suppression or the subordination of divisive questions. The maintenance of unity in support of a presidential candidate may be facilitated by the platform's escape clauses for some sectors of the party and by its silence on other matters. All this is not to glorify obfuscation, but merely to suggest that the platform is conditioned by the political system as a whole. A desideratum of the system is the maintenance of coalitions inclusive enough to contend for the Presidency; platforms must conform with that necessity. No simpler way exists to destroy an electoral coalition than for its majority to insist on precise, forthright, and advanced policy positions unacceptable to other elements of the coalition.

Platforms are electioneering documents, not blueprints for action. They may indicate the general direction of movement sought by the dominant elements of the party, but from both practical and theoretical necessities they ordinarily leave wide latitude for discretion once the election is won. Lines of action can rarely be spelled out in detail in advance of the time of action. Furthermore, a national convention with power to bind its nominees

[27] The 1960 Democratic platform ran to about 15,000 words; the Republican, 14,000. For platform texts, see K. H. Porter and D. B. Johnson, *National Party Platforms, 1840–1960*, 2d ed. (Urbana: University of Illinois Press, 1961).

for President and the congressional candidates on the party's ticket to specific courses of action would become, in effect, the government. The President and the party in Congress can hardly be reduced to this subordinate
role; they become the government and, for the welfare of the nation as well
as of their party, must act as the government and not as the rubber stamp
of a party organ.

CANDIDATES "AMEND" THE PLATFORM   The generali-
ties of the platform are amplified by the presidential candidate in his speeches
during the campaign. The platform is open to interpretation, and, as Sherman Adams said of General Eisenhower in 1952, the candidate "is the one
who has to interpret it" if he "has a different view as to the shading or meaning of words." Occasionally the candidate proceeds to amend the platform
before the convention has adjourned. In 1904 the Democrats, still suffering
from their espousal of the free coinage of silver in 1896, nominated Alton
B. Parker, a conservative easterner, and said nothing about coinage in the
platform. Parker telegraphed the convention to inform it of his firm attachment to the gold standard and asked that the nomination be declined for him
if this stand was not satisfactory to the convention. The convention stated
that since the platform was silent on coinage, Parker's views should not
preclude him "from accepting a nomination on said platform." In 1928 the
Democratic convention pledged "its nominees to an honest effort to enforce
the Eighteenth Amendment." As the convention was about to adjourn, it received a telegram from Alfred E. Smith in which he made clear his belief
that "fundamental changes" should be made in the "provisions for national
prohibition."

Nominations

After the platform has been disposed of, the convention reaches its main
job: the making of presidential and vice-presidential nominations. Meanwhile, the leaders for each presidential contender have been engaged in interminable conferences, in maintaining the morale and loyalty of the faithful delegations, in trying to induce the wavering to join their ranks, and in
angling for promises of second-ballot support from delegations pledged to
favorite sons and other long-shot candidates. Each campaign manager has
his espionage agents to ascertain the strength of the opposition, to gain
advance knowledge of their strategy, and to avoid being taken by surprise.

PLACING THE CANDIDATES IN NOMINATION   The states
are called in alphabetical order for nominations. A state near the beginning
of the list may yield to a state farther along the line that has a serious contender. For example, Alabama may yield to New York to permit it to place

its candidate in nomination. The nominating speeches traditionally maintain a high standard of extravagance, though connoisseurs of political oratory contend that recent conventions have produced no really fine performances. A noted speech was that of Franklin Roosevelt nominating Alfred E. Smith in 1928 which concluded:

> America needs not only an administrator but a leader—a pathfinder, a blazer of the trail to the high road that will avoid the bottomless morass of gross materialism that has engulfed so many of the great civilizations of the past. It is the privilege of the Democracy not only to offer such a man but to offer him as their surest leader to victory. To stand upon the ramparts and die for our principles is heroic. To sally forth to battle and win for our principles is something more than heroic. We offer one who has the will to win—who not only deserves success but commands it. Victory is his habit—the happy warrior, Alfred E. Smith.

In 1928 John McNab nominated Hoover at the Republican convention:

> I nominate him for his lofty character as a man and citizen; for his broad and kindly human sympathies; for his wholesome heart that rejoices above all things else that he has been useful to the people of his native land.
>
> And now, engineer, practical scientist, minister of mercy to the hungry and the poor, administrator, executive, statesman, beneficent American, kindly neighbor, wholesome human being, I give you the name of Herbert Hoover.

The custom is, as in the quotations, to describe some mythical character, to extol his virtues, to demonstrate that he can be victorious, and at last, to reveal what everybody knew all through the discourse, his name. The naming of the candidate is the signal for bedlam to break loose. Supporters of the candidate start processions through the aisles; bands play the campaign song; delegates and spectators yell themselves hoarse. These demonstrations are, of course, only infrequently spontaneous; they are merely synthesized in varying degrees. The length of the demonstration and the intensity of the applause may give a rough index of the strength and popularity of the various candidates, but no votes are changed by the noise. The pageantry and the demonstrations give the delegates something to do while their leaders are negotiating behind the scenes.[28] And delegates may be relieved of the chore of parading about the convention hall by the employment of professional demonstrators.

After each nominating speech several seconding speeches follow; they

[28] Edward J. Flynn, one-time Democratic national chairman and long-time Bronx leader, concluded that "there are probably considerably less than one hundred men in any convention who really dictate what occurs. These men meet in the so-called 'smoke-filled' rooms." *You're the Boss* (New York: Viking, 1947), p. 97.

are shorter but of the same tenor as the nominating speeches. Politicians highly prize the opportunity to make such a speech before a nationwide television audience, and assignments to make speeches sometimes become counters in the game of politics. State delegations have been delivered in gratitude for an invitation to make a nominating speech.[29]

BALLOTING FOR THE CANDIDATE   With the completion of the seconding speeches the convention is ready to vote, and the roll of states is called. The chairman of each state delegation announces the vote of the state; [30] the announcement may be the occasion for huzzas or boos. Usually the vote is simply announced; in earlier and more flowery days the announcement was the occasion for a short speech more often than now. Thus, in 1868, when Montana was called: "The mountains of Montana, from whence flow the waters of the Columbia and the Mississippi, are vocal with the name of Grant, to whom she gives two votes."

If the first ballot fails to produce a majority, other ballots are taken until a decision is reached. The lack of a majority on the first ballot intensifies efforts by the managers of the leading aspirants to attract additional support on succeeding votes. As the balloting proceeds, state delegations may march out of the hall to caucus to determine what they will do as the political winds shift, or they may go into a huddle on the floor of the convention hall. From time to time the correctness of the chairman's report of a state's vote may be challenged by a member of the delegation, and the convention chairman orders the delegation to be polled. Each delegate from the state then announces his vote. The demand for a poll of a delegation may be a dilatory tactic to play for time as managers negotiate.[31] The switch of a pivotal state in the balloting may mark a turn of the tide toward a particular aspirant. In 1932, when William G. McAdoo cast California's vote for Roosevelt on the fourth ballot, the nomination was in fact made and other states rushed to the bandwagon.

The nomination is often made on the first ballot; the convention merely records the victory of the aspirant who has gathered the support of a ma-

---

[29] The 1956 Republican convention deviated from practice in that its managers arranged for short seconding speeches to be made by nondelegates chosen to suggest that traditionally Democratic groups had allied themselves with Eisenhower. A labor union official, a member of the Farmers' Union, a Jew, a Negro, a southerner, and other such persons made speeches directed more to the television audience than to the convention. The Farmers' Union member, it turned out, had dropped by the Union office to join on the way to the convention.

[30] On the chairmen of state delegations, see D. Marvick and S. J. Eldersveld, "National Convention Leadership: 1952 and 1956," *Western Political Quarterly,* 14 (1961), 176–94. See also J. H. Bunzel and E. C. Lee, *The California Democratic Delegation of 1960* (University, Ala.: University of Alabama Press, ICP Case 67, 1962).

[31] The demand for a poll of a delegation may also be a move to place the face of each delegate in front of the television camera. The Democrats in 1956 adopted the rule that a state's delegation would be polled only upon demand by one-third of its members.

jority of the delegates before the voting started. In the 1944 Republican convention Dewey's managers were able to assemble a majority before the balloting; and when the time came to vote, the other aspirants bowed out of the race. Dewey received all the votes on the first ballot except that of a lone delegate from Wisconsin, who held out for MacArthur. In 1956 Stevenson, in part because of Kefauver's withdrawal shortly before the convention, won on the first ballot in the Democratic convention. In 1960 the first-ballot nomination of Nixon by the Republicans was accompanied by no suspense.

The Republicans have had fewer prolonged convention struggles than the Democrats. Since the Civil War two-thirds of the Republican presidential candidates have been nominated on the first ballot. Only half the Democratic candidates during the same period were nominated on the first ballot. The Democrats set the record in 1924 when they took 103 ballots to break the deadlock between Smith and McAdoo and to nominate Davis. The Republican peak of 36 came in 1880, when Garfield was nominated as a compromise candidate after a deadlock among the supporters of Grant, Blaine, and Sherman.

COMPOSITION OF PARTY DIFFERENCES IN THE NOMINATION The function of the convention is to settle the conflict among factions of the party for the presidential nomination. Yet the task of the convention leaders amounts to considerably more; they must seek to guide the convention toward a decision on a nominee who can be supported by all factions of the party. At times that result comes about by the concentration of strength on a candidate who personifies the terms of consensus among the party factions. At other times the etiquette of political combat operates to sooth the wounds of those who suffer undeniable defeat. At still other conventions, animosities reach such intensity that deadlock ensues and whatever party unity is achieved by the convention is mere façade.

The process of negotiation toward agreement was well illustrated by the Republican nomination of Dewey in 1948. As the delegates arrived in Philadelphia spokesmen for Dewey, Taft, and Stassen issued the routine predictions of victory. It was apparent that Dewey had the largest bloc of delegates but not a majority. The decision rested with the leaders of uninstructed delegations and delegations committed to favorite sons. These leaders made their estimates of the situation, perhaps not without consideration of the probable effect of alternative courses of action on their own political fortunes. Before the balloting began Senator Edward Martin of Pennsylvania withdrew as a "favorite son" to support Dewey. Charles A. Halleck, a Representative from Indiana, took a similar step and his prospects of becoming the vice-presidential candidate were regarded as improved. On the other hand, Governor Green of Illinois plumped for Taft and thereby made himself a possible vice-presidential nominee if Taft won.

With the first ballot, whatever doubt remained about the strength of the principal aspirants was erased: Dewey, 434; Taft, 224; Stassen, 157. On the second ballot the vote stood: Dewey, 515; Taft, 274; Stassen, 149. The convention recessed at about five o'clock to reconvene later. The negotiations of the intervening two or three hours do not appear on the record. When the convention reconvened, Senator Knowland of California read a statement from Governor Warren, California's favorite son, who declared it obvious that Governor Dewey was the favorite and that no useful purpose would be served by prolonging the balloting. Governor Stassen withdrew; the leader of the Michigan delegation withdrew the name of Senator Vandenberg; Senator Baldwin of Connecticut, who had been supported by his delegation for two ballots, announced for Dewey as did the leader of the MacArthur bloc. The convention voted unanimously for Dewey. The leaders who had been engaged for months in mortal combat buried the hatchet, rallied round the winner, and made a great show of unity. Doubtless in the process of negotiation commitments, contingent upon victory, had been made, some expressly and others tacitly.

In a contested convention the groping of leaders toward agreement by no means extinguishes conflict among factions led by determined and ambitious men. The most diverse factions may unite to hold their lines in the balloting in an attempt to "stop" a leading contender for the nomination. At times when contentious issues drive deep fissures through the party, whatever decision the convention yields may leave elements of the party in an abiding mood of dissent. Even so, the etiquette of the old "pros" dictates that even if an opponent is defeated, his nose need not be rubbed in the dirt as well. Amateurs quickly learn the code. In 1952, before the chairman of the Republican convention had announced the results of the final roll call, General Eisenhower had made his way to Senator Taft's hotel to say a word to the vanquished aspirant for the nomination.

PECULIARITIES OF THE CONVENTION CONSTITUENCY
The nomination and the platform represent an attempt to unite the party and to present to the country a ticket that will win the election. The consensus that emerges from the national convention tends to present to the nation an image of the party that diverges notably from the impression built up by its congressional branch. That contrast rests fundamentally on the fact that the convention represents, at times overrepresents, sectors of the party whose views do not find adequate expression in Congress. When the Democrats are the out party, for example, the Democratic congressional contingent tends to be in large degree southern; its votes and the pronouncements of its leaders over time create a picture of a party dedicated in exceptional degree to the peculiar interests of the South. The national convention, on the other hand, includes delegates from districts with substantial numbers of Democratic votes but no Democratic congressional representation. As Westerfield puts it:

"Between 1943 and 1954 the Southerners consistently held around 45 per cent of the Democratic seats in the Senate and around 50 per cent of those in the House—but only about 25 per cent of the votes at national conventions." [32] The conventions nominate a Roosevelt, a Truman, or a Stevenson—men who give the party a policy outlook in contrast with that held by its most conspicuous congressional leaders.

Similarly, the Republican convention gives to the presidential politics of that party a hue quite unlike the policy coloration of its standpat congressional wing. The midwestern areas in recent decades have contributed disproportionately to the party's congressional contingent, and the region's isolationist and conservative spokesmen painted the prevailing picture of the party in the public mind. Yet the national convention in 1952 could nominate Eisenhower rather than Taft, who had unquestioned leadership of the congressional wing of the party. In the convention the coastal states—both Atlantic and Pacific—had a far stronger voice than they had had in the party's congressional councils. [33]

DEMOCRATIC TWO-THIRDS RULE   Two features of nominating procedure peculiar to Democratic conventions need to be mentioned. The national convention follows the unit rule and until 1936 required a two-thirds vote to nominate. In the first Democratic convention, that of 1831, the nomination of Jackson for the Presidency was a foregone conclusion, but the two-thirds rule was adopted to govern the decision on the vice-presidential nomination. In the convention of 1835 the committee on rules recommended that "a majority of two-thirds shall be required to elect the candidates for President and Vice-President." The proposed rule was defended as calculated to produce "a more imposing effect." [34] While its adoption may have assured this "imposing effect," the rule also generated difficulties and stimulated attacks based on the majority principle.

The continuance of the rule was debated from time to time, but not until 1936 was a convention able to consider the rule on its merits. The question of its continuance had always been tied up with the fate of particular aspirants for the nomination. Furthermore, the two-thirds rule was associated with the unit rule by which the entire vote of a state delegation may be cast for the candidate supported by a majority of the delegation. The vote of a few large states, when almost evenly divided but cast as a unit, could give the nomination to a person actually supported by only a minority of the convention. The two-thirds rule made such a result less likely. [35] Moreover, the Solid South

---

[32] H. Bradford Westerfield, *Foreign Policy and Party Politics* (New Haven: Yale University Press, 1955), p. 47.

[33] *Ibid.*, pp. 39–45.

[34] Edward Stanwood, *A History of the Presidency from 1788 to 1897*, p. 182.

[35] Carl Becker, "The Unit Rule in National Nominating Convention," *American Historical Review*, 5 (1899), 62.

regarded the rule as a means by which it could veto candidates displeasing to the region, a view that came to have less and less foundation as the South's proportion (23.1 per cent in 1960) of the convention votes declined.

In 1932 an attack, destined eventually to be successful, was begun against the two-thirds rule by the forces seeking the nomination of Franklin D. Roosevelt. The Roosevelt managers made a hasty retreat when it appeared that their proposal to change the rules of the game to favor their candidate would backfire, and the question was postponed until 1936. In that year the report of the committee on rules, presented to the convention by Bennett Champ Clark, whose father had lost the nomination in 1912 because of the operation of the two-thirds rule, recommended its abrogation. With Roosevelt the certain nominee, the requirement of only a majority to nominate could be adopted without affecting the interests of any aspirant for the nomination. Southern Democrats continued in later years to complain of the 1936 action and from time to time proposed, without much hope of success, a return to the old rule.

DEMOCRATIC UNIT RULE   The Democratic unit rule requires that the entire vote of a state delegation shall be cast as the majority of the delegation desires, if the state delegation has been so instructed by the state convention. For example, if the Virginia state convention instructs delegates chosen by it to abide by the unit rule, the national convention will recognize the instruction as binding upon it. The unit rule, then, is not imposed on the state delegation by the national convention; the convention merely enforces the instruction of the duly empowered agencies of the party within the states. The national convention, however, recognizes state laws that do not subject delegates chosen by primaries to the operation of a unit rule imposed by the state convention.[36] The Republican national convention, on the other hand, does not recognize as valid a state instruction to its delegation to operate under the unit rule.

During this century, with the increase in the number of states failing to instruct their delegations to act as a unit, the importance of the unit rule in Democratic conventions has considerably diminished. As an indication of the practical degree of departure from that rule, it may be noted that on the ballot for the presidential nomination at Los Angeles in 1960, the votes of the delegations from 21 states were divided among two or more candidates. Additional states, too, may not have been bound by the unit rule but merely happened to be unanimous in their choice.

[36] This exception was introduced by the Democratic convention of 1912 at the instance of delegates chosen by presidential primary and pledged to Wilson. The majority of the Ohio delegation, operating under a unit rule, desired to cast the votes of such delegates for Governor Harmon. *Proceedings*, 1912, pp. 59–60.

NAMING THE VICE-PRESIDENTIAL CANDIDATE Energies and enthusiasms are exhausted by the strain of the nomination of the presidential candidate; the convention, in a state of emotional deflation, then proceeds, often hurriedly and without much relish, to finish its business with the nomination of a candidate for the Vice Presidency. The factors governing the selection of the running mate for the head of the ticket are numerous but a few patterns recur. The presidential nominee ordinarily can, in fact, make the choice, though the range of his discretion may differ with circumstances. A limiting consideration frequently persuasive is the supposed necessity of "balancing" the ticket. It is usually thought advantageous to recognize a party faction or a geographical section other than the one represented by the presidential candidate. In 1912 the Democrats nominated Woodrow Wilson of New Jersey and Thomas R. Marshall of Indiana; the Republicans, William Howard Taft of Ohio and James S. Sherman of New York. Considerations of campaign strategy may be influential, as in 1960 when Nixon and his advisers felt that Henry Cabot Lodge would add strength on the foreign policy issue, the issue by which they hoped to beat the Democrats. In the same year the grand problem of the maintenance of party unity made Kennedy's choice of Lyndon Johnson expedient and alternative possibilities inappropriate.

The nomination for the Vice Presidency is occasionally determined by the maneuvers leading to the nomination for the Presidency. In the 1932 Democratic convention the California delegation, pledged to John Nance Garner, swung the presidential nomination to Roosevelt. The convention the next day unanimously placed Garner in second place on the ticket. In the Republican convention of 1944 a similar sequence of events occurred when Governor Bricker yielded the presidential nomination to Dewey without a fight and subsequently received the second place on the ticket.

Commonly the convention ratifies the choice of the presidential candidate or his managers as a matter of routine, but on occasion the vice-presidential nomination sets off a battle. In 1948 the Republican convention cheerfully accepted Dewey's recommendation of Earl Warren.[37] In 1940, in contrast, the Democratic convention reluctantly and with loud manifestations of displeasure ratified Roosevelt's choice, Henry Wallace. In 1944 the Democratic convention had, at first, no clear guidance from Roosevelt; several aspirants believed that he had given them the green light. The right and left wings of the party checkmated each other. The left vetoed James Byrnes of South Carolina but was unable to win for its candidate, Wallace. The nomination of

[37] Senator Vandenberg related that Dewey, after his nomination, assembled about 20 Republican leaders to consider the vice-presidential nomination. The group, in a discussion lasting from 11 P.M. to 4 A.M., arrived at unanimous agreement on Warren. A. H. Vandenberg, Jr. (ed.), *The Private Papers of Senator Vandenberg* (Boston: Houghton Mifflin, 1952), pp. 439–41.

Harry Truman provided a classic instance of the maintenance of party unity by the nomination of a candidate not zealously supported by any wing of the party but also not entirely unacceptable to any major faction of the party.[38]

Conventions depart from their off-hand consideration of the Vice Presidency chiefly when the presidential nominee is obviously not in the best of health. Such a circumstance explained to some extent the warmth of the contest in the 1944 Democratic convention. In 1956 Eisenhower's health made the question of the vice-presidential nomination a potential source of controversy among Republicans, but skillful management by party leaders forestalled effective challenge of Nixon. Adlai Stevenson, the Democratic presidential nominee, sought to make capital of the Republican situation by inviting the Democratic convention to make a free choice for the second place, a step that set off a scramble for delegates among aspirants for the nomination. That an "open" convention on the vice-presidential nomination should have attracted widespread comment serves to mark it as an exception to the more general practice.

NOTIFICATION OF THE NOMINEES   It used to be the custom for the convention to appoint a committee to notify both the presidential and vice-presidential candidates of their nomination. A committee journeyed to the home of the nominee. Its chairman made a speech of notification and the candidate responded with a speech of acceptance. The notification was often an important political ceremony and the speeches were significant campaign documents. In 1932 Roosevelt flew to Chicago to appear before the convention to accept the nomination and broke, as he called it, "the absurd tradition that the candidate should remain in professed ignorance of what has happened for weeks until he is formally notified." Since that time most nominees have followed the precedent Roosevelt set. The old practice nicely complemented the proprieties of yore which demanded that the aspirants stay away from the convention city as the delegates pondered the question of which man they should ask to accept the nomination.

Role and Function of the Convention

How is the national convention to be evaluated? A favorite critique of the national convention is that by Ostrogorski, who called it a "colossal

---

[38] Edward J. Flynn records the survey to find a vice-presidential candidate as follows: "We went over every man in the Senate to see who would be available, and Truman was the only one who fitted. His record as head of the Senate Committee to Investigate the National Defense Program was excellent, his labor votes in the Senate were good; on the other hand, he seemed to represent to some degree the conservatives in the party, he came from a border state, and he had never made any 'racial' remarks. He just dropped into the slot." *Op. cit.*, p. 181.

travesty of popular institutions"; the platform, "a collection of hollow, vague phrases." He quoted with approval the saying: "God takes care of drunkards, of little children, and of the United States!" [39] Other observers, both imported and indigenous, remark on the hilarity and unseemly demeanor of delegates gathered together for the solemn business of nominating a candidate for the Presidency of the United States. It is indeed true that the conventions are rarely august assemblages. They partake of the more robust features of American character. Yet such critiques go only to appearances and do not touch the function of the national convention in the American party system.

In a fairly real sense, the national convention is the national party. When means develop for uniting people in support of a nominee, the essence of party comes into being. When the national convention was contrived to designate presidential nominees, viable national party came into existence. The national convention thus is at the heart of the national party system. Without it or some equivalent institution party government for the nation as a whole could scarcely exist.

The position of the national convention reflects both the strength and the fragility of the national party. The convention casts a net of party unity over party leaders scattered through the counties, the cities, and the villages of the 50 states and brings them to the support of its nominee. The convention provides a means for the contending candidates, factions, and interests within a party to consult and agree upon the terms on which they will work together in the presidential campaign. The resulting concert of interests exerts a formidable power throughout the nation. The national convention, a body unknown to the laws or to the Constitution, brings its affiliated organizations in 50 states to the support of candidates for elector who, if they win in their states, cast their votes without question for the nominees of the convention.[40]

The binding quality of the convention's decision derives more from consent than from any sanction available to the convention or to its agents. The Democratic convention of 1948 demonstrated the limits of the convention's authority when it found itself unable to make a nomination that all the state organizations regarded as binding. The Democratic parties of Mississippi, South Carolina, Louisiana, and Alabama had a "Democratic" candidate other than that of the national convention. Because Mr. Truman's views

[39] See his complete statement in *Democracy and the Party System in the United States* (New York: Macmillan, 1910), pp. 159–60. For a contrary view, see A. B. Wildavsky, "On the Superiority of National Conventions," *Review of Politics*, 24 (1962), 307–19.

[40] The exceptions only "prove" the rule. In 1948 a Democratic elector of Tennessee voted for J. Strom Thurmond, the States' Rights candidate, although Truman had won the popular vote in the state. In 1956 an Alabama elector, despite Stevenson's victory in the state, voted for Walter B. Jones, an Alabama judge. In 1960 an Oklahoma Republican elector voted for Senator Byrd of Virginia. All Mississippi electors also voted for Byrd, but they had won as an unpledged slate rather than as a party slate.

on race policies were unacceptable, these state organizations, in effect, seceded from the party and named a candidate of their own to whom their electors were pledged, J. Strom Thurmond, the Dixiecratic or States' Rights candidate. The 1948 southern bolt had its reverberations in the 1952 Democratic convention when the liberal wing challenged the right of Dixiecratic leaders who had not supported the nominee in 1948 to sit in the convention. After a historic donnybrook, the 1952 convention adopted a rule requiring that all delegates, as a condition of sitting in the convention, give assurance that they would use every "honorable means" to see that the nominees of the convention were placed on their state ballots as the Democratic nominees.[41] Even in the 1952 convention the assurance was not uniformly required.[42] Nevertheless, the convention nominees appeared on the ballots of the southern states in 1952, though not all southern Democratic leaders supported them in the campaign.

In the preliminaries to the 1956 Democratic convention the problem of the "loyalty pledge" arose in a new form. Should the pledge as adopted in 1952 be required of all delegates in 1956? What should be done about those who had participated in the 1952 convention but had campaigned for Eisenhower? Most of the more prominent southern Democrats who had supported the General were not chosen in their states as delegates, and the convention did not have to decide whether to seat such "Republicrats" as Governor Shivers of Texas, James F. Byrnes of South Carolina, or Robert F. Kennon of Louisiana. Moreover, national leaders in an endeavor to heal the breach between the South and the North agreed well in advance of the convention to abandon the loyalty pledge adopted in 1952.[43] The 1956 convention ratified

[41] "No delegate shall be seated unless he shall give assurance to the Credentials Committee that he will exert every honorable means available to him in any official capacity he may have, to provide that the nominees of this Convention for President and Vice President, through their names or those of electors pledged to them, appear on the election ballot under the heading, name or designation of the Democratic Party. Such assurance shall be given by the chairman of each delegation, and shall not be binding upon those delegates who shall so signify to the Credentials Committee prior to its report to this convention."

[42] For an account of the 1952 convention actions on the 1948 bolters, see David, et al., *Presidential Nominating Politics in 1952*, I, 112–42.

[43] The substitute formula adopted by the Democratic national committee in its call for the 1956 convention was: ". . . it is understood that the Delegates to the Democratic National Convention, when certified by the State Democratic Party, are bona fide Democrats who have the interests, welfare and success of the Democratic party at heart, and will participate in the convention in good faith, and therefore no additional assurances shall be required of Delegates to the Democratic National Convention in the absence of credentials contest or challenge." The proviso on contests left open the possibility that the party loyalty of a delegation might be challenged by another delegation claiming to be the true representatives of the state party. For a discussion of the adoption of the formula, see "The Democratic Party's Approach to Its Convention Rules," *American Political Science Review*, 50 (1956), 553–68. See also Abraham Holtzman, "Party Responsibility and Loyalty: New Rules in the Democratic Party," *Journal of Politics*, 22 (1960), 485–501; Abraham Holtzman, *The Loyalty Pledge Controversy in*

the agreed substitute for the loyalty pledge and also the 1955 declaration of the national committee that it was "the understanding that a State Demo‑cratic party, in selecting and certifying delegates" to the national convention, undertook to place on their election ballots "under the Democratic party label" candidates for elector pledged in good faith to support the convention nominees.[44] The 1956 rules were pointedly included in the call for the 1960 convention as some southern leaders were again advocating a bolt from the party. Threats to challenge two or three delegates who had in 1956 served on committees of Democrats for Eisenhower were quelled by contenders for the nomination who preferred to avoid an unrewarding conflict of principle.

Despite the inability of the national party, through the convention, to bind all elements of the party all the time, the total performance of the na‑tional convention as an instrumentality for weaving together the diverse and geographically scattered elements of each party into a national whole consti‑tutes an impressive political achievement. In another respect, the national convention makes a special contribution to the American political system. Had the congressional caucus by some chance survived as the means for nominating presidential candidates, the odds are that Presidents and the presidential system itself would have been radically different. The convention provides a channel for advancement to the Presidency independent of the Congress, a channel that can probably be navigated by men who could not make their way to the top through Congress and that probably is closed to others who can achieve leadership in Congress.

If these estimates are correct, the convention profoundly conditions the character of the American governmental system. It does not limit access to the Presidency to those who climb the ladder within the narrow confines of the inner circles of the representative body; nor does it restrict competition to those who gain the deference of their fellows within any narrowly defined group of party notables. The convention operates flexibly with a range of freedom that enables it to elevate to leadership men it judges to be suited to the needs of the time rather than merely to promote those who have worked their way up the bureaucratic ladder of party status. So broad an avenue to executive authority, it may be argued, leaves the way open to the "man on horseback." Yet, so far the convention system and the associated modes of election have worked within the limits of the basic tenet of party government, namely, that no election shall foreclose the opportunity for another election.

---

the Democratic Party (New York: McGraw-Hill, Eagleton Case 21, 1960) ; A. P. Sindler, "The Unsolid South: A Challenge to the Democratic Party," in A. F. Westin, *The Uses of Power* (New York: Harcourt, Brace & World, 1962).

[44] One of the limits to the fulfillment of this "understanding" was defined in Alabama in 1960. The Democratic candidates for elector were chosen by primary prior to the national convention. Five of the primary victors were loyalists and six were unpledged. Those unpledged ultimately cast their electoral votes for Byrd.

16.

CONGRESSIONAL

NOMINATIONS

An incidental moral of the preceding chapters is that the term "nomination" covers the most diverse phenomena. The grand compromises negotiated in a national convention result in the nomination of presidential and vice-presidential candidates. The spirited primary contest of a pair of fledgling lawyers in a South Carolina county settles, subject to the formalities of the general election, which one will go to the legislature. In a well-organized congressional district, the deliberations of a handful of leaders determine the nomination, whether the formal action is by convention or by direct primary. In another district, the erratic interplay of personal ambitions, pressure-group efforts, and newspaper favor or disfavor eventuates in an unpredictable nomination by a free and unfettered primary. In view of the varied practices in nomination, as well as of the significance of the nominating process in fixing the characteristics of the national parties, the selection of candidates for Congress warrants special attention.

Observation of the nomination of candidates for the House and Senate brings forcibly to attention at least two peculiar characteristics of the American party system. First is the odd mixture of centralization and decentralization in the organization of American parties. The presidential nominating convention makes a decision that is accepted—at least most of the time—as authoritative by the state units of the party. The state's presidential electors, if they win the election, serve as rubber stamps for the party's national con-

434

vention. The most extreme decentralization prevails, too, for each state, and each congressional district enjoys autonomy in the designation of nominees for Senate and House. No national party office, either Democratic or Republican, asserts the right to control nominations made by the party subsidiaries in the states or districts.[1] In the national conventions a consensus is sought among the divergent interests within the party; in the nominations for House and Senate those same interests are free to impose their special policy coloration on the party's local candidates. The differences compromised in the national convention are perpetuated, even accentuated, in the party's congressional slate.

A focus on nominations also brings to the fore another feature of the American system, namely, the fact that much of our politics is intraparty, not interparty, politics. Given the existence of many states and districts strongly attached to one or the other of the parties, the actual choice of Senators and Representatives is often made at the nominating stage. The reality of the nominating process thus differs greatly from district to district and from state to state. "Nomination" may mean precisely that or it may be the equivalent of election.

Senatorial Nominations

Senators are the great panjandrums of American politics. The special role of the Senate elevates its members to positions of great power within the government and among them are to be found conspicuous spokesmen for the chief shades of opinion within each party. Their control—formal and informal—over appointments in the executive branch always gives them great influence in administration and sometimes enables them to become *de facto* heads of departments or agencies—without any of the inconveniences of accountability. Elected to represent their states, Senators often become, in effect, spokesmen for interests spreading across state lines—the steel makers, the shipping interests, the labor unions, a great railroad, an international airline, the Farm Bureau, the China lobby, the National Manufacturers Association, the liberals, the isolationists, even, on occasion, the crackpots. Their long tenure—a couple of re-elections gives them 18 years—aids them in building their power. One Senator can make a nuisance of himself; a handful of them in a wrecking mood can bring the executive branch into a state of paralysis. A President must come to terms with the Senators of his own party—or outmaneuver them. In the minority party, given the lack of an acknowledged national leader, Senators are likely to become the party spokesmen most prominent in national attention. One of them may even become

[1] On British practice in this respect, see Allen M. Potter, "British Party Organization, 1950," *Political Science Quarterly*, 66 (1951), 65–86.

the recognized chieftain of the party, as was the late Senator Taft, though more often a few of them share leadership.

Commonly, nominations for the Senate go to men who have achieved eminence in the party in their state. By their performance in other public offices and by their ascent up the ladder of party status, men make themselves "available" for the senatorial nomination. Of those Senators who served between 1920 and 1956, about a quarter had been state governors and almost a third members of the national House of Representatives. A third of them had been members of state legislative bodies, and about one out of ten had been elected to a statewide office other than governor, such as attorney general. The southern Democratic bloc of Senators included an especially large proportion of former Representatives, while the Republican group from strong Republican states included a much larger proportion of ex-governors than did the entire roster of Senators.[2] These facts suggest that the natural processes of leadership selection tend to narrow the range of eligibles for senatorial nominations. In only a few states can the party organization cast the mantle of its nomination upon an unknown and thereby convert him into a potential Senator.

CONVENTION NOMINATIONS   The parties in the states select their candidates by either direct primary or convention. While only a handful of states retain the convention system, the realities concealed by the direct primary are at times its equivalent. New York, Delaware, Indiana, and Connecticut nominate senatorial candidates by convention. In most southern states the Republican party acts through conventions, but these nominations have been until recently only accolades to Republican worthies and not choices of serious political consequence.

Although the convention system in the states has not been extensively analyzed, the procedure of choice resembles that of the presidential nominating conventions. Often the nomination is settled in advance of the convention by negotiation among party leaders. Since a campaign for the Senate in a populous state is both expensive and strenuous, the problem may be one of drafting a candidate from among the few individuals with sufficient status to make them promising candidates. In New York in 1956, state Democratic leaders, aided by the head of the national ticket, Adlai Stevenson, induced Mayor Robert F. Wagner of New York City to accept the senatorial nomination. In other instances organization leaders are divided and the nomination is settled only when the convention votes are counted.

Senatorial nominations, by whatever method, are made by state author-

[2] Of the southern Democrats, 44 per cent had served in the House. Of the Republicans from a group of 12 strongly Republican states, 40 per cent were ex-governors. Incidentally, Democrats draw a higher proportion of their Senators from the legal profession than do the Republicans, about three-fourths against one-half.

ity without formal interposition of national leaders. Yet the circumstances surrounding the convention procedure permit, when the will is there, a degree of collaboration between national and state leaders. Often New York conventions, both Democratic and Republican, have nominated candidates for the Senate and for the governorship whose designation has been favored by the party's President or presidential candidate. This has been a matter not of coercion by the national party leadership but rather of agreement about lines of action likely to be of mutual benefit.

DIRECT PRIMARY NOMINATIONS: DEMOCRATIC   Most states nominate their senatorial candidates through the direct primary, a formal procedure of popular choice that may conceal the location of real power to designate candidates. The actual choice may be that of a well-knit party hierarchy which is routinely ratified in the primary. Or the primary may involve a genuine test of popular strength between leaders supported by party factions, pressure organizations, newspapers, church groups, or other such centers of influence. Then, too, an aspirant for the nomination may campaign with no asset other than his own belief that he is called to lead the people.

Careful inspection of Table 16.1 will suggest the variety in the reality underlying the forms of primary nominations. That table analyzes only those Democratic primaries of the period 1920–1960 in which no incumbent Senator sought renomination. The nominating process differs radically when the sitting Senator seeks renomination, a matter to be touched on shortly. One broad point the table reveals is that the frequency of spirited primary competition for nomination varies among the states with the strength of the Democratic party. In states with a high probability of Republican victory, most of the time only a single name appears on the Democratic primary ballot. On the other hand, in states in which Democratic nomination virtually assures election, nomination without opposition occurs rarely, and sharply fought contests for the nomination are far more frequent.

Even though the frequency of competition for nomination increases with the expectation of general election victory, not all nominations for sure seats are contested. Nor do all nominations for seats certain to be lost go by default. It is evident that factors in addition to the prospects for victory help determine whether primary contests will occur. Examples pulled more or less at random from the cases hidden away in Table 16.1 will indicate types of nominating situations. About half of the Democratic candidates included in the table who were eventually elected won their primaries in a walk or had been nominated unopposed. Joseph Clark, for example, was unopposed for the Pennsylvania nomination in 1956. Presumably the principal leaders of the Democratic organization of the state concurred in his nomination; at least none of them felt disposed to back a challenger in the primary. Simi-

Table 16.1   Frequency and intensity of competition for senatorial nominations in Democratic primaries involving no incumbents, related to Democratic percentage of general election vote for Senator, 1920–1960 [a]

| Democratic Percentage of General Election Vote | Number and Per Cent of Primaries According to Percentage of Primary Vote to Nominee | | | | Total Number of Primaries |
| | Under 60 Per Cent | | 90–100 Per Cent | | |
	Number	Per Cent	Number	Per Cent	
10–19	0	0.0	5	83.3	6
20–29	3	14.3	15	71.4	21
30–39	12	24.4	32	65.3	49
40–49	53	41.7	40	31.4	127
50–59	33	47.1	21	30.0	70
60–69	9	50.0	3	16.6	18
70 and over	13	52.0	3	12.0	25
Total	123	38.9	119	37.6	316
In South [b]	21	60.0	3	8.6	35
Elsewhere	102	36.3	116	41.3	281

[a] Senators serving under appointment who sought nomination were treated as nonincumbents for the purposes of this table. The coverage of the table is fairly complete for the primaries of the period.
[b] This line includes the Confederate states plus Oklahoma.

larly, the unopposed nomination of Paul H. Douglas in 1948 reflected the fact that his support by the Illinois Democratic organization settled the matter. Some unopposed nominees operated from positions of personal prestige, such as Joseph C. O'Mahoney of Wyoming in 1954. After long service in the Senate, he had been defeated in the Republican landslide of 1952. His unopposed nomination in 1954 came in recognition of his position as a Democratic leader in the state. In 1958 Stephen Young took the Ohio nomination without opposition, probably largely because the Republican incumbent, John W. Bricker, was thought to be unbeatable.

Other eventual winners of the general election had to fight for their nominations. Thus, in Idaho in 1944 Glenn Taylor, the singing cowboy, proved that a wandering minstrel could win the Democratic nomination in that state by polling 33 per cent of the primary vote in a field of four candidates, a fact indicative of the existence of a fractionalized and impotent Democratic hierarchy. Similarly, in 1956 Frank Church won the Idaho nomination, over three other contenders, with 38 per cent of the vote.

The peculiarities of the southern political regime, by now familiar, also affect the figures in the table: fairly close contests for nominations occur about twice as frequently in the South as elsewhere. Only rarely does a southern state nominate a candidate for a Senate vacancy without some sort of primary fight, and often the outcome is close. In these states the primary is the election, and the battles in the primaries tend to resemble those between party candidates in the rest of the country. The southern nominating process —that is, the determination of what two or three persons will contend in the primary—occurs in the combinations of factional and local leaders, in the decisions of those in a position to finance a primary campaign, in the endorsements by major newspapers, and in other informal ways.

DIRECT PRIMARY NOMINATIONS: REPUBLICAN   Variations in the process of nominating Republican candidates for the Senate through the direct primary resemble those demonstrated to exist for Democrats by Table 16.1. Spirited contests for nominations, when no Republican incumbent is seeking renomination, occur more frequently as the probability of Republican victory in the general election increases. Yet even when the chances of Republican victory are high, by no means all Republican senatorial primaries are marked by factional fights for popular favor. In some states some of the time and in others most of the time sufficient unity exists in the Republican organization to bring substantial agreement among party leaders on the nominee in advance of the primary. In New Jersey in 1954 the Republican organization drafted Clifford P. Case to run for the Senate and he was not opposed in the primary. In the same year Colorado Republicans designated Gordon Allott as their candidate without primary opposition. Probably, other things being equal, this organizational solidarity on nominations is most likely to develop either when the chances of election are slight or when the strength of the opposition imposes internal discipline. Nevertheless, about two-thirds of the Republicans elected to the Senate for a first term between 1920 and 1958 had had to win a hard primary fight.

NATIONAL PARTY LEADERSHIP AND NOMINATIONS FOR VACANCIES   Quite apart from the tradition of local autonomy in the determination of nominations, popular participation in the nominating process prevents extensive participation by national party leadership in the designation of senatorial nominees. When nominations are popularly determined, a President or a national chairman cannot very well negotiate with a handful of leaders for a nominee attuned with the national leadership. Moreover, the popular character of nominations itself drastically limits the range of the availables. At times the natural processes of leadership selection make a single individual the "logical" choice before the primary: that is, his standing with the party following is judged by all concerned to make him the strongest man for the nomination. Or perhaps those processes have produced only two or three men sufficiently known to the electorate to be serious aspirants for the nomination. The actual designation of a nominee is only the end point of a process of leadership selection; in only a few states can the controlling clique of the organization settle on a relatively unknown person and, by giving him the party nomination, invest him with sufficient status to make him a strong candidate.

Yet the national party leadership on occasion takes a hand in the choice of senatorial nominees. It can do so advantageously and effectively only under a limited set of circumstances. When a seat is held by the opposition, the national party leadership may help to recruit and support for the nomination a strong candidate to challenge the incumbent. Even this sort of intervention is fraught with hazard. The problems and possibilities are suggested by the role of the Eisenhower Administration in building the Republican slate of senatorial candidates in 1956. In that year the President persuaded John Sherman Cooper, ambassador to India, to run for the Senate in Kentucky, and the Republican state committee, in dire need of a strong candidate, nominated Cooper with cheers. For the second Kentucky seat, the Republicans nominated Thurston B. Morton, who had resigned as Assistant Secretary of State to make the race, apparently with the Administration's blessings. The White House aided Washington state leaders in bringing Arthur B. Langlie into the race against the incumbent Democrat Warren Magnuson. Langlie's position in the state assured him of the primary nomination. In Colorado, ex-governor Dan Thornton, evidently with White House encouragement, was nominated to succeed a retiring Republican, a designation easily arranged because of Thornton's prestige in Colorado, as well as of the comparatively unified status of the Republican organization in that state. Similarly, in 1962 the South Dakota Democratic organization cleared the way for the nomination, with White House approval, of George P. McGovern, an official of the Kennedy Administration and a former Representative, who won over Republican Joe H. Bottum in the election.

When the state party organization itself is fairly united and sees eye to eye with the President, the national leadership may participate in the recruitment of senatorial candidates to fight campaigns against opposition incumbents. A radically different situation presents itself when the choice is made by a wide-open primary campaign. In 1956 Douglas McKay resigned as Secretary of the Interior to seek the Oregon Republican senatorial nomination. He went into the campaign with White House commendation, apparently on the assumption that the national Republican headquarters had paved the way by inducing the other aspirants for the nomination to withdraw from the primary. The way had not been paved and, in consequence, McKay had to campaign vigorously for the nomination against Philip S. Hitchcock, a liberal Republican, to the accompaniment of considerable grumbling about the meddling of national headquarters in Oregon affairs.[3] McKay won the primary. The chances of losing such a contest and of finding on the party slate a candidate who had bested the forces of the national leadership in the direct primary usually suffice to discourage national intervention.

SENATORIAL NOMINATIONS: INCUMBENTS   When an incumbent Senator seeks a renomination, the problem is not one of determining succession to party leadership in the state; it is simply whether to continue the existing leadership. Commonly the Senator holding office has constructed a following that virtually assures him of nomination for another term if he wishes it. Only about 10 per cent of the incumbents who seek renomination in direct primaries are denied it. Yet the regional variations in their degree of success and in the frequency of strong opposition to them point to important characteristics of the party system.

While almost 90 per cent of the Democratic Senators who sought renomination over the period 1920–1954 were successful, only outside the South could a Democratic incumbent expect renomination either with no opposition or with token opposition. (Of course, in prospect any challenge is apt to appear formidable and only in retrospect does it become trifling.) In the South, Democratic incumbents were compelled frequently to fight a strenuous campaign to obtain renomination, an endeavor in which they were by no means uniformly successful. In the South (the Confederate states plus Oklahoma), 42 per cent of the primaries involving incumbents, 1920–1954, gave less than 60 per cent of the vote to the winner. In the remainder of the country only 15 per cent of the primaries were marked by so sharp a contest. In the South, 30 per cent of the incumbent Senators received 80 per cent of the primary vote; in the rest of the country, 55 per cent of the incumbents polled over 80 per cent of the vote. Of the 20 incumbents who lost in their bids for renomination, 18 were southerners.[4] The probability of defeat of a southern incumbent was about 30 out of 100; in the remainder of the country, less than two out of 100.

Given the inclusion of most shades of opinion within the Democratic party of the South, primary campaigns between Democrats tend to take on

---

[3] *The Oregon Statesman*, a Republican journal, objected "to the commissioning of a candidate by the Republican national chairman or by the White House as was done with McKay, to the extent of having a special letter of commendation written by the President. . . . We think Hitchcock should stay in the race both because of his splendid qualifications and to repudiate the notion that Oregon is a province of the GOP GHQ."

[4] In these counts those Senators who were serving by appointment and seeking their first nomination were excluded.

the tone of contests between Democrats and Republicans elsewhere. In 1934, for example, Theodore Bilbo, an heir to the Populist tradition, upset in the primary Hugh Stephens, a southern statesman of the more conservative school. In Florida George Smathers' primary triumph in 1950 over the incumbent Claude Pepper was regarded as the equivalent of a Republican victory. In 1954 John Sparkman, an Alabama liberal, turned back the challenge of Laurie Battle, no adherent of the Fair Deal. In Arkansas in 1954 John L. McClellan, a conservative, won renomination against Sid McMath, former Arkansas governor who had been a prominent partisan of the Truman policies. In the 1962 South Carolina Democratic primary, Governor Ernest F. Hollings attacked Olin Johnston because he was a friend of labor— "a tool of the northern labor goons." Senator Johnston allowed that he could "understand why the working man is for me." He won renomination by a top-heavy majority. Although not all southern senatorial primaries are marked by clear-cut factional alignments, the incumbent southern Democratic Senator may expect, with far higher frequency than his northern colleague, a powerful challenge in the primary.

Incumbent Republican Senators win renomination at about the same rate as the Democrats: about 90 per cent of the time. While the defeated Republican aspirants over the period 1920–1954 were geographically widely scattered, they tended to be, like the defeated Democrats, from states relatively sure for their party. About a third of the Republican upsets were in North Dakota and Wisconsin, states in which a dual factionalism prevailed within the Republican party not unlike that in the Democratic party in southern states.

NATIONAL PARTY LEADERSHIP AND THE RENOMINATION OF INCUMBENT SENATORS   The lack of influence of national leadership in the renomination of incumbent Senators highlights the decentralized structure of the national parties. When the problem is to draft a strong candidate to fight an opposition Senator, the national leadership in a restricted category of situations may take a hand in building the senatorial ticket. Yet when a sitting Senator seeks renomination, the prevailing etiquette demands nonintervention by the national leadership. He has made a record in the Senate either as a supporter of the President or perhaps as a thorn in the side of the Administration. Or, if he is a member of the minority, he has either worked with the party leadership or he has given free play to his own policy eccentricities.

By and large, the sitting Senator who is at odds with the national leadership of his party need fear no attempt by the national party authorities to undercut him in his campaign for renomination at the state party primaries. Nor, if he has gone down the line for the party leadership, can he expect much help if he encounters a serious challenge in the primary. Only infrequently do national party leaders attempt to purge the party of the disloyal, and their success is invariably slight. In 1910 President Taft and the conservative wing of the Republican party attempted to drive the progressive element out of the party by defeating its legislative leaders for renomination in the primaries and conventions that year. Under the leadership of President Taft and Senator Aldrich, the eastern standpat Republicans campaigned against the renomination of western progressive leaders. The Republican campaign committee propagandized the western states against progressives, such as Dolliver, Cummins, and Beveridge, and urged the nomination of true Republicans. Eastern money flowed into these areas to finance the fight, and Taft withheld patronage from progressive Republicans. Patronage referees from the other wing of the party had the distribution of local jobs. Conservative leaders traveled to the West and opened fire against La Follette. Even in some eastern states the insurgent wing of the party was strong enough to merit the opposition of the regular party organization. When the returns were all in, the national party leadership had almost completely failed. State after state renominated progressives, who were as thorns in the flesh of the national party leaders. Taft failed to make the party a simon-pure conservative party.[5]

Republican national leadership failed in efforts to upset state organizations of a progressive tinge; the Democratic national leadership has also failed to upset that party's conservative state machines. In the senatorial primaries of 1938 President Roosevelt sought to exert his influence as the party's national leader. Battles in Congress over his proposal to revamp the Supreme Court, over the administrative reorganization bill, and over the wages and hours bill had indicated sharp cleavages within the Democratic party. The first primary of the year occurred in Alabama, where J. Thomas Heflin was opposed by Lister Hill, a New Dealer, in a contest for a Senate vacancy. "The support of all three branches of labor," Professor Shannon concludes, "and the inferential blessing of the President, who allowed Hill to ride on his train across Alabama, together with the aid of Governor Bibb Graves' political organization seemed to have been decisive in Hill's victory." [6]

In Florida the sitting Senator, Claude Pepper, who had supported the President on all his major measures, was opposed by Representative Wilcox, an anti-New Dealer, and by former Governor Sholtz who professed friendship for the President. James Roosevelt, son of the President, announced that

[5] G. E. Mowry, *Theodore Roosevelt and the Progressive Movement* (Madison: University of Wisconsin Press, 1946), chs. 4 and 5. On the surreptitious attempt by officers of the Republican national committee to defeat George Norris in the 1930 Nebraska primary, see *Fighting Liberal: The Autobiography of George W. Norris* (New York: Macmillan, 1945), ch. 28.

[6] J. B. Shannon, "Presidential Politics in the South: 1938," *Journal of Politics*, I (1939), 150.

"we" desired the return of Pepper to the Senate, and the victory of Senator Pepper was followed by a bold declaration by the President:

> As President of the United States, I am not asking the voters of the country to vote for Democrats next November as opposed to Republicans or members of any other party. Nor am I, as President, taking part in Democratic primaries.
>
> As the head of the Democratic party, however, charged with the responsibility of carrying out the definitely liberal declaration of principles set forth in the 1936 Democratic platform, I feel that I have every right to speak in those few instances where there may be a clear issue between candidates for a Democratic nomination involving principles or involving a clear misuse of my own name.
>
> Do not misunderstand me. I would certainly not indicate a preference in a state primary because a candidate, otherwise liberal in outlook, had conscientiously differed with me on any single issue. I should be far more concerned about the general attitude of a candidate toward present-day problems and his own inward desire to get practical needs attended to in a practical way. We all know that progress may be blocked by outspoken reactionaries and also by those who say "Yes" to a progressive objective, but who always find some reason to oppose any specific proposal to gain that objective. I call that type of candidate a "Yes, but" fellow.

In pursuance of this policy the President intervened in Democratic primaries in Oklahoma, Kentucky, Georgia, South Carolina, and Maryland. The upshot seemed to be that the influence of even so popular a President as Roosevelt could not defeat a Senator running for renomination with the support of the state organization.[7]

Large-scale intervention by the national leadership in senatorial primaries has occurred only at intervals of sharp internal conflict within the party. Usually the national leadership remains silent, even when its staunch supporters face opposition. In 1956, for example, the Wisconsin Republican organization denied its endorsement to Alexander Wiley, a principal spokesman for the Eisenhower Administration, as he sought renomination in the primary. It backed instead Representative Glenn R. Davis, a dissenter from the Administration especially on foreign policy. So far as the record goes, the Administration turned not a hand in support of Wiley in the maneuvers before the action of the Wisconsin organization. Nor did the President in the primary campaign that followed indicate to the Republicans of Wiscon-

---

[7] Jim Farley regarded the purge as a violation of the "rules of the game" which treated nominations as "local matters." He traced all the woes of the "Democratic party, directly or indirectly, to this interference in purely local affairs. In any political entity voters naturally and rightfully resent the unwarranted invasion of outsiders." See *Jim Farley's Story: The Roosevelt Years* (New York: Whittlesey House, 1948), chs. 13–14.

sin a preference for Wiley. The President stood on the view that he should take no "part in any Republican primary." Mr. Wiley won on his own. Intervention almost invariably stirs up recrimination against the national leadership. In 1962 President Kennedy endorsed Senator George Smathers who was running for renomination. The President is, asserted a Smathers opponent, "building up his power at the taxpayers' expense. At this rate, he soon will be known as King John." Another declared: "The people of Florida definitely do not want a presidential rubber stamp in the United States Senate." [8]

Local autonomy in nominations, however they are made, gives a firm anchorage in the grass roots to Senators with views that diverge from the national party line. Moreover, reliance on popular modes of nomination lends special legitimacy and authority to the position of the deviant Senator. He can feel that his renomination amounts to a popular ratification of his views, although it may only reflect the fact that his name is well known. Yet primary nomination may even give advantage to the Senator of unorthodox views. Popular participation in the primary tends to be quite low, and apparently, too, those who vote in the primary tend to be disproportionately persons of a particular shade of opinion within the party. In any event, the sitting Senator who builds popular support often can win renomination over the opposition of a state party organization that would prefer a candidate more in harmony with the national leadership. In the 1920's, for example, Smith W. Brookhart, an agrarian radical of the day, won renomination in Iowa as the state Republican organization, assembled in convention, refused to endorse him for election and declined to invite him to speak to the convention. Few are the state organizations that can deny renomination to a Senator. Yet instances occur. In 1948 the New Jersey Republican organization, under the leadership of Governor Alfred E. Driscoll, decided not to support Senator Albert W. Hawkes for renomination. The Senator's conservative views were out of line with the outlook of the younger, liberal element of the party. Senator Hawkes, probably certain of defeat, did not choose to run in the primary.

These consequences of the decentralization of nominations have been dwelled upon at length by persons interested in contriving ways and means to convert the party groups in Congress into cohesive entities more capable of meeting the tasks of government. Considerably less attention has been given to the fact that the process of nomination also produces those Senators—commonly more than a majority of each party group—who hold together in the advancement of the party's national viewpoint. The conspicu-

[8] In states with strong party organizations (which may really determine primary outcomes) discreet intervention in support of incumbent friends of the Administration may occur without raising a popular outcry. Thus, in 1962 the White House induced Representative William Green, Philadelphia Democratic boss, not to oppose Senator Joseph Clark for renomination in Pennsylvania.

ous deviates from the party line tend to be from the states without sharp interparty competition, though not all Senators from such states are party rebels.

Nominations of Representatives

The process of nominating House candidates resembles in its broad outlines that of senatorial nominations. The choice is made independently within each district. The nomination of Representatives is also often in fact the election, given the existence of many districts comparatively sure for one party in the general election. The predominant mode of nomination is the direct primary; the principal exception consists in southern Republican use of conventions to nominate candidates who still run mainly for glory rather than for office.[9]

NOMINATIONS IN PRIMARIES INVOLVING NO IN-CUMBENTS   As with the nomination of Senators, major differences exist between primaries in which incumbent Representatives seek renomination and those in which the party must select a candidate either to replace a retiring member of the party or to run for a seat the party does not hold. The analysis of primaries involving no incumbents provides clues to the varieties of actual practice under the primary procedure. Table 16.2, in a familiar pattern, relates the frequency of competition among aspirants for primary nominations to the subsequent general election vote.

One broad class of primaries, as may be inferred from the table, consists of those in districts in which the candidate will have only a slight chance of victory in the general election because the district ordinarily goes to the opposition by wide margins. In such districts rivalry for the minority nomination is not ordinarily marked. Close primary contests are relatively infrequent and often only a single name appears on the primary ballot. In such districts the problem may be to seek out a candidate willing to make a hopeless race.[10] At times, however, as the table shows, close primary contests oc-

[9] The states fix the times of primaries; in 1962 primaries fell on 31 different days spread from April to September. The necessary absence of members who are seeking renomination hampers the work of Congress. In 1962 Representative Denton, of Indiana, proposed that Congress set a uniform date for primaries as it had earlier done for general elections.

[10] Newbold Morris relates that Fiorello La Guardia entered politics in a Tammany controlled district. The Republican district leader remarked in the clubhouse as petitions for nomination were being prepared, "We haven't got a candidate for Congress, boys. Who wants to run?" La Guardia immediately volunteered. "O.K. What's your first name?" "Fiorello," he replied. "Hell, let's get somebody whose name we can spell!" By vigorous argument, La Guardia won the nod but he lost the election. *Let the Chips Fall* (New York: Appleton-Century-Crofts, 1955), pp. 75–76.

Table 16.2   *Intraparty competition for House nominations and the prospects of general election victory: Proportions of nominees winning primaries involving no incumbents by wide and by narrow margins related to subsequent general election vote, 1952–1958* [a]

Candidates' Percentage of General Election Vote	Total Number of Primaries		Proportions of Candidates Nominated with Indicated Percentages of Primary Vote			
			Democratic		Republican	
	D	R	Under 60 Per Cent	90–100 Per Cent	Under 60 Per Cent	90–100 Per Cent
0–29	27	73	26%	74%	15%	68%
30–39	170	113	20	65	26	54
40–49	246	127	40	31	39	38
50–59	63	47	40	25	57	11
60–79	11	11	45	9	54	18
100	15	1	93	0	100	0

[a] Excluded for 1956 and 1958 are nominations in California, Connecticut, Delaware, Pennsylvania, New York, and Rhode Island. The coverage for 1952 and 1954 is less complete.

cur in hopeless districts. Even though he has no chance to go to Congress, the winner of a nomination may gain prestige in the party organization and put himself in line for advancement in other directions.

Different circumstances prevail, as the table suggests, when the winner of the nomination has a good chance for general election victory. Broadly, the frequency of warmly fought contests for primary nominations increases with the rise in the certainty that the nominee will be elected.[11] In those districts overwhelmingly committed to one party the winner of the nomination of the chief party ordinarily has had to beat a strong primary competitor.[12]

One type of difference among districts that obtrudes from the table does not explain itself. Among the fairly close districts in the primaries of both parties some nominations result from close popular votes in the primaries,

[11] Table 16.2 employs the general election vote after the primary as a measure of the prospects of victory, a measure not entirely satisfactory. The vote at the preceding election may be a better measure of expectations about the next. Of those seats won by Democrats by from 50 to 55 per cent of the vote, competition within Democratic primaries tends to be more frequent in those districts that had been held by a Democrat than in those districts that had been held by a Republican.

[12] The differences among types of districts in frequency of primary competition that appear in Table 16.2 are greatly narrowed when Pennsylvania and New York primaries are included. In these states party organization is such that even in districts sure for a party its primaries are not frequently contested.

while in other districts candidates are designated without a primary contest. These differences probably reflect, among other things, underlying variations in the organization or structure of party in the constituencies. In some districts, in tightly organized cities, for example, the party organization may be able to crush opposition to its primary slate. The normal road to nomination may be through organization endorsement.[13] The aspirant who does not gain organization support usually regards his cause as hopeless and does not enter the primary. In such districts, if an independent candidate does run, the organization usually piles up an imposing majority against him.

More often the congressional district is so loosely organized that genuine primary competition occurs in those districts fairly evenly balanced between the parties. The congressional district is not ordinarily of much importance as a unit of party organization; congressional district committees, usually provided for by statute or by party rule, are often moribund. Outside of those areas in which strong city or county organizations incidentally encompass congressional districts, the organization tends to be more an informal and personal organization of the incumbent Representative than a party organization. When the incumbent dies or retires, his organization falls to pieces and a free-for-all contest for the nomination may ensue.

To estimate the relative frequency of the occurrence of these differing patterns would require more extensive investigations than have been made. The most clear-cut differentiation that emerges from the available data is between the South and the remainder of the country. In Democratic primaries in the South not involving incumbents, the man who would be a candidate for the House almost invariably has a tough primary fight on his hands. Elsewhere that may be true in only about half of the primaries.[14] This contrast reflects, of course, the peculiar nature of the southern political regime.

Outside the South fewer Democratic than Republican primaries are characterized by sharp competition, and more Democratic than Republican candidates win nomination without even nominal primary opposition. The reasons for this differential are not apparent; it appears, too, fairly consistently in primaries for nomination of candidates for other types of offices.

---

[13] Sol Bloom related the circumstances of his choice for the nomination in a Tammany district in New York: "I knew a lot of people, and I had no serious known enemies. That was one of the reasons for picking me. . . . I was also comfortably situated financially and could afford the expense of the campaign. Briefly, I had been chosen to run because I was an amiable and solvent Jew." *Autobiography of Sol Bloom* (New York: Putnam's, 1948), p. 200.

[14] In the Democratic primaries in the districts in Table 16.2 in which the Democratic candidate subsequently won the election, one-fifth of the nominations outside the South were made without a primary contest; in the South, none. In only half the primaries outside the South did the nominee poll less than 60 per cent of the primary vote; in the South (the Confederate states plus Oklahoma), 94 per cent of the nominees had that small a primary vote.

Possibly the Republican party outside the South simply has a larger supply of persons who combine an ambition for office with the time and means to make primary races.[15]

The process of nomination for the House of Representatives is in some ways more notable for what does not than for what does occur. The high degree of local autonomy in the selection of candidates reflects both the decentralization of national party organization and the popular character of the nominating process. National intervention seems to be limited chiefly to an occasional attempt to induce a potentially strong candidate to run for the nomination for a close seat not held by the party. Unless their tracks are well covered, this limited initiative by national leaders does not extend to all such districts in which the party might have a chance to win a seat from the opposition.

INCUMBENT REPRESENTATIVES AND THE DIRECT PRI-MARY   Once elected, a Representative usually wants to stay in Congress. To remain he must win renomination from his party in his district. Once renominated, an incumbent Representative's fortunes may be governed by the national trend of sentiment in the election. If the drift is against his party and he comes from a marginal district, the odds against his re-election may be high no matter how strenuous his own campaign exertions may be. On the other hand, if the trend favors his party, even though his district is normally close, he is almost certain of re-election.

The existence of a large number of congressional districts sure for one party or the other, coupled with the fact that nominations are commonly made by popular procedures, gives to the nominating process a special importance. In the many sure districts the direct primary becomes the principal occasion on which a Representative may account to his constituency, although the participating primary constituency may be a caricature of the entire constituency. Even when a Representative faces a real threat from the opposition at the general election, he may have to make an electoral campaign against rivals within his own party who challenge him for the nomination. This double jeopardy constitutes one of the oddities of the American party system.

The Representative in office who seeks renomination enjoys great advantage over those who would challenge him. Extremely few Representatives —usually no more than eight or ten—are defeated in the direct primaries at each two-year interval.[16] Furthermore, these primaries involve close con-

[15] For a more detailed consideration of the incidence of competition in House primaries, see Julius Turner, "Primary Elections as the Alternative to Party Competition in 'Safe' Districts," *Journal of Politics*, 15 (1953), 197–210. See also C. A. M. Ewing, "Primaries as Elections," *Southwestern Social Science Quarterly*, 29 (1948–49), 293–98.

[16] In 1962, 12 House incumbents failed to win renomination in the primaries: six Republicans and six Democrats. Eight of the 12 ran in districts that had been reapportioned, and in four districts reapportionment had brought two incumbents into

tests less frequently than do those in which no incumbent seeks renomination. Of the Democrats or Republicans running for renomination, from 5 to 15 per cent may be involved in primary races in which the winner receives less than 60 per cent of the vote. One-half to three-fourths of the Representatives who seek renomination win without primary opposition. Democratic incumbents in the southern states meet formidable opposition more frequently than do Representatives elsewhere in the country.[17]

The relative infrequency of the defeat of incumbents as they run for renomination probably provides no adequate measure of the significance of the popular nominating procedure in sensitizing the Representative to demands within his constituency. While the odds may favor him, an individual Representative never knows when he will be among those who must make a hard primary fight. He must keep his fences mended and to antagonize even the smallest interest within the district may be to encourage it to support an entry against him in the primary, an entry who may be defeated but with some trouble and at some cost.

At the nominating stage the Representative is on his own in marked contrast with his position at the general election when the direction of movement of the national sweep may be determinative. The Representative must fight a lonely battle for renomination. Even if he has supported the Administration regularly, he cannot look to the national party authorities for aid if he is challenged in the primary in his district. He may wheedle from the White House an encouraging word, but neither the national nor the congressional committee can be relied upon for substantial financial aid in his campaign for renomination. If he is not of the Administration party, he is likely to be even more completely on his own resources as he fights for renomination.[18] On the other hand, the incumbent need have little worry that the national leadership will instigate opposition to him in the primary. In

competition for the nomination. In addition, in the Nashville district the Democratic committee had refused to certify a primary nominee because of charges of fraud; the incumbent lost the general election to his challenger at the primary.

[17] These remarks are based on analyses of the primaries of 1948, 1952, and 1954.

[18] The policy of hands off primaries by the national party authorities is violated from time to time, but evidently Representatives, no matter how loyally they support the party line in Congress, may not routinely expect aid when they meet primary challenges. National leaders may steer contributors to beleaguered colleagues. Senator Barry Goldwater, once chairman of the Republican senatorial campaign committee, remarked in the 1956 hearings of the McClellan Committee: "Many, many people come to me, some Democrats even, I am happy to say, and say, 'I would like to get some money into Senator X's campaign.' We tell them that it is a primary problem and we are not interested in the primary, and we keep out of it. But . . . we suggest that he see so-and-so, who will be very glad to handle it. That comes up on both sides of the aisle, and it is one of the ways that money is channeled around into the primaries, and it will happen in general elections, too." How important this routing function is in primary finance and the degree to which it is used by the national leadership to aid those friendly to it remain unknown.

In a pair of celebrated cases in 1950 Senator Owen Brewster, chairman of the Republican senatorial campaign committee, advanced from his personal funds $5,000

a few instances Roosevelt and Truman gave support to primary opponents of incumbents who had been conspicuous dissenters from the party line in the House. Such cases of national intervention are notable by their rarity.

A Representative who manages to stay in office for several terms has the opportunity to become known in his district, to do small favors for many voters, to strengthen his position with the party workers in his district, and in general to crystallize his following. He gains experience and builds up seniority, a fact of which he reminds his constituents, and he ordinarily engages in more or less continuous campaigning for renomination and re-election, partially at public expense. Certainly it makes sense for a party to renominate a Representative who has served his party and his district well. Under these circumstances, explanation of the extent to which incumbents encounter primary opposition may present more of a problem than the explanation of why so many are named without opposition.

Inspection of primaries involving incumbents suggests that certain types of circumstances stimulate primary challenges of incumbents who seek renomination.[19] One type of situation, not uncommon, is that of an aging Representative who, after long years of service, begins to let the reins slip or becomes simply the victim of an aggressive younger candidate not disposed to wait his turn until the old man dies or retires. A first-term Representative who has not had time to establish himself in his district may be regarded as vulnerable by other ambitious politicians who may challenge him in the primary. When district lines are altered in a reapportionment, the structure of support patiently built up by a Representative becomes disorganized, and he often must defend his position against those who judge the new situation to be favorable to themselves.[20] A Representative, too, may come from a state or district in which the battles of politics are normally fought out in the

---

each to the primary campaigns of Richard Nixon of California and Milton Young of North Dakota. The committee had a firm rule not to aid in primaries; for these two men, though, Senator Brewster said, "we had high regard." Nixon and Young won nomination and became entitled to a grant of $5,000 each from the committee, the receipt of which enabled them to repay Senator Brewster.

The Republican congressional campaign committee provides services to Republican incumbents—aid in preparing newsletters, photographic services, and the like—which incidentally help the incumbent who happens to have to fight a primary campaign. In 1954, Hugh Bone records, the Republican committee gave $1,000 to each of 16 Republican Congressmen and $500 apiece to another 36 in April, a date which preceded the primaries, but officials of the committee indicate that they do not provide such aid when there is a primary contest. See Bone, "Some Notes on the Congressional Campaign Committees," *Western Political Quarterly*, 9 (1956), 116–37.

[19] Save for a somewhat higher frequency of challenge in southern primaries, the frequency of close contests in primaries involving incumbents does not vary with the balance of strength between parties as was shown by Table 16.2 to be true for primaries with no incumbents running. The incidence of primary contests is fairly evenly distributed over the range of districts arrayed according to party strength.

[20] The marked lack of enthusiasm of legislators toward proposals to shift the boundaries of their district may stem as often from fear that change would make their lot difficult in the primary as from anxiety that the opposition party might gain advantage.

primaries between well-defined factions of the dominant party. He, more frequently than other Representatives, must defend his position in primary battles, though he does not suffer the inconvenience of a general election campaign. Somewhat similar are the occasional challenges to incumbents in metropolitan districts that arise as an incident to battles for control of the party organization.

An incumbent may be challenged in the primary on broad policy grounds. Given the infrequency of serious contests of any sort, intraparty ideological cleavage cannot often be the basis for a primary challenge against an incumbent. Yet contests so rooted do occur. In 1956, for example, several Republican Representatives had to cope with primary competitors who contended that the incumbent had shown himself to be no Eisenhower Republican.[21] Or an incumbent may have found himself in trouble in the primaries on the charge that he had become too much of an Eisenhower Republican. Similarly, in Democratic primaries at times an incumbent has to meet the charge that he is or is not a Fair Dealer, or a Truman man, or a Kennedy man.

On these matters of intraparty ideological cleavage the party's voters in the primary must ordinarily act on the basis of singularly inadequate information. Only rarely does the national party leadership give the voters guidance by indicating either approval or disapproval of the incumbent's record, which becomes the subject of conflicting assertions more confusing than enlightening to the electorate.[22] The nominating stage is the point at which party discipline can be applied most effectively. Yet the direct primary is a procedure not easily usable, either by the national leadership or by the voters of a district, for that purpose.[23]

---

[21] In 1956 in New York's 27th district Representative Ralph W. Gwinn, 71, faced primary opposition from Christian H. Armbruster, who attacked Gwinn's lukewarmness in support of Eisenhower. Gwinn regarded Armbruster as a "New Deal Republican" too young to comprehend the "evils" of the New Deal and Fair Deal. Similarly, in Massachusetts' Cape Cod district Representative Donald Nicholson, candidate for nomination for a sixth term, had to counter a challenger who asserted that the district needed a Congressman who "acts like a Republican—an Eisenhower Republican."

[22] At times the record of the incumbent presents a policy issue apparent to the primary voters. In North Carolina in 1956 three Representatives who had not signed the "Southern Manifesto" on integration were opposed in the primary on that ground. Only one of them, Harold D. Cooley, won renomination.

[23] It may well be that more disciplining occurs in the primaries than is commonly supposed. In 1954 Republican primaries, those incumbents with quite low scores in support of Eisenhower proposals (under 60 per cent) met fairly stiff primary opposition about three times as frequently as did incumbents with higher scores of party regularity. The numbers involved were small, and the factors stimulative of primary contests are numerous. The question whether Representatives who deviate from the party line, other things being equal, need have special anxiety about primary opposition would be worth further investigation. Julius Turner presents some evidence to indicate that the deviate Representative has a relatively low survival capacity. See his *Party and Constituency: Pressures on Congress* (Baltimore: Johns Hopkins Press, 1952), pp. 174–78.

Legislative Nominations and the National Party System

Focus on the process of nomination of candidates for the House and Senate highlights the decentralized character of each of the major parties. In a sense national party exists only in the nomination of the President and in the campaign for his election. Each of the constituent units, the states and the congressional districts, of the party acts independently in the designation of candidates for Congress. To the extent that they put forward like-minded candidates, the result is a consequence of a parallelism of outlook and interest rather than of a managed articulation of action.

In decentralization of nomination is to be found a basic characteristic of the American party system. Localization of nomination assures both a representation of local peculiarities in the party groups in Congress and, by the same token, a magnification of the difficulties of action by the party as a whole on many types of legislation. That this decentralization of power within the parties should remain, as almost all other facets of American life have fallen prey to centralizing processes, reflects the stubborn persistence of informal political customs.

Signs of centralization in the legislative nominating process are not lacking, but national initiative seems to be effective only within a limited range of circumstances. The presidential candidate and other national leaders may intervene to aid in drafting candidates thought to be strong enough both to win a House or Senate seat from the opposition and to lend strength to the ticket as a whole. Even such limited intervention may be fraught with hazard unless most leaders of the constituency see eye to eye with the national leadership. Moreover, aid and encouragement in the enlistment of a candidate to challenge an incumbent of the opposition party is a far more feasible type of national intervention than is the attempt to defeat or replace a candidate of one's own party who deviates markedly from the legislative policy of the national party. Only infrequently have Presidents attempted to purge their party of such persons and then without notable success.

Reliance on popular nominating procedures in most states and districts may anchor the power of decision in the localities and make difficult the participation of national leadership in legislative nominations. Nomination rests not in the hands of a few leaders with whom agents of the national headquarters might consult and reason; it rests rather in the free and unfettered vote of those who participate in the direct primary and produce its unpredictable results. A national party agent cannot negotiate with a constituency itself susceptible to agitation by the cry of external intervention from candidates opposed to the national leadership.

It is commonly said that the direct primary also tends to increase the frequency of deviation from the national party line by legislative nominees. The argument rests on the assumption that the convention mode of nomination facilitates the maintenance of a degree of consistency of outlook through control of nominations by a self-perpetuating clique. The primary, on the other hand, destroys that consistency and, in so doing, robs the opposition of the opportunity to take advantage of popular dissatisfaction with the stronger party in the state or district. As shifts in outlook occur, the views of the dominant party's nominees may change. Such variability of leadership is thought to be facilitated by the open primary through which Democrats may help nominate a Republican candidate or vice versa. In any event, when the leadership of the stronger party shifts like a weather vane, voters of a state or district are under no compulsion to send a candidate of the lesser party to Congress. Instead they send a man who may deviate from the national line of the stronger party. That the primary procedure facilitates these deviations from orthodoxy seems plausible, although it may well be that they would find expression through whatever nominating procedure happened to be used. It is certain enough that in most districts not much by way of cohesive inner organization exists to serve as guardian, either independently or in collaboration with the national leadership, of the party creed.[24]

A major consequence of decentralization of nominations probably is that neither party mobilizes its maximum potential in legislative contests. Most of the senatorial and congressional incumbents of each party normally seek re-election, but the recruitment and designation of candidates to fight for seats held by the opposition is left mainly to the fortuitous workings of local initiative. The result is that in many districts the minority fails to put up strong candidates even though it has a chance to win. Many districts are unnecessarily conceded to the opposition. National party leaders in quest of a point for leverage to strengthen their party might well give thought to spending a few hundred thousand dollars a year drumming up and supporting able House and Senate candidates for seats held by the opposition. The effects over the long run in the workings of the party groups in House and Senate might be startling.

---

[24] Americans probably on the whole find it more congenial to alter the policy of their party than to shift their party allegiance. The system is so marvelously flexible that this reorientation of party outlook need not involve an overturn of party leadership. In 1950 the Hon. Usher L. Burdick, a Representative from North Dakota, opened a circular to his constituents with these sentences: "The Primary Election will soon be on and I have deemed it advisable to outline some of the issues which I think should be discussed in this campaign. I have outlined my views without equivocation and those views will be my continued views unless the people at meetings and through cards and letters give evidence of the voters' opposition." *Burdick's Magazine*, May–June, 1950.

IV

PARTY AND

THE ELECTORATE

The party apparatus, by posing alternative candidates and programs, arranges the situation to permit the electorate to play its role in the system of party government. Competitive appeals by party spokesmen to the electorate for authorization to govern dramatize the fundamental characteristic of government by the people. Yet it requires, as the preceding chapters have shown, a great deal of party machinery and activity to set the stage for the voters' part in the governmental process.

The question of central interest in the chapters that follow is the nature of the function of the electorate in party government. The great and determinative actions of the voters occur in the presidential and congressional elections. For their treatment it will also be necessary to consider other related or relevant topics, such as campaign management, conditions for the exercise of the suffrage, mechanics of the conduct of elections, and participation of voters in elections.

17.

CAMPAIGN TECHNIQUES

A CRITICAL PHASE of the process of party government is the battle for ballots. Through the national conventions the party system poses for the electorate alternatives in leadership and in policy orientation. At the nominating stage each party attempts to iron out friction among its elements, to reassure the interests traditionally associated with it, and, by other means, to form its battalions for the assault against the opposition. In the campaign the candidates, the activists, and the professionals of each party carry their cause to the electorate as they vie for the popular verdict. In these recurring clashes of electioneering armies in verbal combat is found one of the distinctive processes of popular government. The capacity of its electorate to undergo the tumult of an electoral campaign and still make wise decisions may determine whether a popular government survives.

An American presidential campaign is one of the most awesome spectacles known to man; the fate of a nation may hinge on the outcome of what seems to be a donnybrook among demagogues and Madison Avenue types. Yet our verified knowledge of what goes on in the minds of the voters as they move toward decision is limited; our knowledge of their response to different types of appeals is equally thin. Campaigns are likened to the appeals of opposing counsel to a jury. They are said to be a means of educating and informing the people about candidates and issues. They are classed along with soap-selling operations as systematic manipulations of the mass mind. They are treated as a ceremony by which a party obtains popular consent to govern. They are cynically dismissed as a ritual through which politicians, tools of the interests, profess a love for the people and humbug them. A presidential campaign may contain all these elements, but whatever its precise nature, it moves the electorate to a determination of who shall govern the country.

Campaign Organization and Management

A presidential campaign may be thought to be the work of a tightly knit organization spread over the entire country and directed by cunning men wise in the ways of managing the multitude. In truth, the campaign organization is a jerry-built and makeshift structure manned largely by temporary and volunteer workers who labor long hours amidst confusion and uncertainty. Assignments of responsibility and lines of authority are likely to be hazy. The army of campaign workers is loosely articulated and some of its regiments may be sulky, if not actually insubordinate.

TOP MANAGEMENT OF CAMPAIGNS   A prime necessity in the management of a presidential campaign is the achievement of sufficient unity of command at the top level of the party organization to permit the execution of a coherent campaign strategy. Otherwise, different elements of the party pursue contradictory propaganda lines; ill-considered and off-the-cuff tactics are developed from day to day; resources are dissipated; and disorder prevails. Yet the attainment of a modicum of unity even at the top organizational levels seems to be frustrated by recurring obstacles.

Ultimately, perhaps the presidential candidate must be his own manager, though his effectiveness in that role depends in large measure on his capacity to construct an effective team of top-level associates. No matter what his skill in that respect, he may be either hamstrung or favored by circumstances. Traditionally, the chairman of the national committee has managed the presidential campaign. That pattern prevailed in 1956 when Eisenhower relied principally on Leonard Hall, the national chairman. In 1952, because of the jealousies between old-time Republicans and the Eisenhowerites, considerable backing and filling occurred before Eisenhower settled the rivalries at the top levels by stationing Sherman Adams in Washington as his personal agent to deal with the national committee, a move that left the national chairman in a secondary role. In 1952 Stevenson maintained a personal headquarters at Springfield, Illinois, supposedly to disassociate himself from the Truman Administration, while the national committee operated in Washington. This "two-headed" monstrosity caused much muttering among the professionals. In 1960 the Democratic national chairman, Senator Henry M. Jackson, was a figurehead; the work of the national committee and of other campaign agencies fell under the management of Robert Kennedy.[1]

The tasks of the top-level campaign leadership, in varying degrees of association with or subordination to the candidate, include planning the broad

[1] See D. M. Ogden, Jr., "The Democratic National Committee in the Campaign of 1960," supplement, *Western Political Quarterly*, XIV, 3 (1961), 27–28.

lines of campaign strategy. At this level, too, coordination needs to be achieved among the national committee, the senatorial and congressional campaign committees, and the nonparty committees supporting the candidate. The diverse propaganda activities of the national committee staff must be kept in line with general campaign strategy. An adequate basis of understanding and system of communication must exist so that the candidate, as he tours the country with his own speech-writing entourage, will not conduct a campaign independent of that of the other elements of the organization. To attempt to cope with such problems the national headquarters commonly includes some sort of coordinating committee, board of strategy, or advisory committee. The candidate may or may not pay heed to the headquarters strategists. In 1960 the Republican planning group found itself isolated from Mr. Nixon who made his own strategic decisions without consultation with the national committee staff.

NATIONAL COMMITTEE OPERATIONS   Whatever his relation to the top command the work of the national chairman becomes more onerous as the national committee goes into action for the campaign. The committee must intensify its fund-raising efforts. It must enlarge its permanent staff units and create new, temporary operating units as well. A publicity division may prepare press releases, pamphlets, leaflets, comic books, and other such campaign materials. An advertising agency may be employed to arrange for radio and television time, to advise on the mysteries of these media, and even to prepare substantive campaign materials.[2] A research division may dig up data and write speeches for the candidate and for lesser speakers. A speakers' bureau may recruit orators and route them over the country. Divisions may be created to appeal to groups, such as labor, ethnic minorities, women, Negroes, medical men, or whatever groups seem to deserve, or be susceptible to, attention at the moment. To manage all these and other units so that their work builds into a consistent propaganda campaign strains the administrative capacity of the national chairman; his skills are by no means invariably equal to the task.[3]

The new technology of communications may be laying the basis for a much tighter top control of campaigns. Party propaganda for the entire nation may be fed into a single television camera. This funneling of communications lays the basis for a thoroughgoing enforcement of campaign strategy,

---

[2] Advertising agencies have discovered that they may come under attack for handling a political account (and parties may undergo the same experience for relying on Madison Avenue assistance). In 1960, in an attempt to cope with both problems, a special agency, managed by men on loan from other agencies, was created to handle the Republican national committee account.

[3] A simple device for assuring some adherence to a common line is the "speakers' manual" or "fact book" which the national committees usually make available to their orators, publicists, and workers.

for an insistence upon adherence to common themes, for a complete coordination of party appeals. Instantaneous communication over the nation also makes less tolerable the disunity that often prevails at the top level of party organization. The picturesque professional politician and the hard-bitten newspaperman who predominated around the old-fashioned campaign headquarters may be yielding to the advertising man and to the public-relations expert.[4]

MOBILIZATION OF STATE AND LOCAL PARTY MACHINERY   The integration of state and local party machinery into the national campaign presents its special problems. Given administrative firmness and skill, the top command may fit into a campaign strategy the lines of attack by the candidate, the propaganda themes of the national committee, the efforts of speakers under the control of the national committee, and the work of other elements of the national apparatus. The extension of national leadership and direction to state and local organizations, however, requires both diplomacy and good fortune. These organizations enjoy an indepedence of the national committee and they also have their own fish to fry as they work for their local candidates.

The factor most conducive to effective involvement of state and local organizations in the national campaign is a belief that the head of the ticket will help float local candidates into office. In 1948, for example, all hands expected Mr. Dewey to win the Presidency, and Republican state and local organizations implored him to speak in their localities. At the same time, Mr. Truman was thought to have no future, and many Democratic state and local organizations scarcely exerted themselves on behalf of the man from Missouri. In 1956 Republican state and local organizations could work with zeal for Mr. Eisenhower; they placed a high estimate on the supportive power of his coattails. Some Democratic organizations sat on their hands, for they regarded Mr. Stevenson's cause as hopeless and identification of their candidates with him as injurious. In 1960 some Democratic organizations were remarkably reticent about Kennedy and Johnson; the New Mexico state committee, thus, succeeded in avoiding mention of them in its literature.[5] An

---

[4] In some states and localities the public-relations man has almost completely superseded the professional politician in the management of campaigns. When he accepts a commission to manage a campaign he needs to insist upon complete supervision of campaign propaganda, an insistence that both protects him in his responsibility for his undertaking and produces a far higher degree of unification of campaign management than often prevails under the professional politician. See R. J. Pitchell, "Influence of Professional Campaign Management Firms in Partisan Elections in California," *Western Political Quarterly*, 11 (1958), 278–300; Irwin Ross, "The Supersalesmen of California Politics: Whitaker and Baxter," *Harper's Magazine*, July, 1959. For a handbook by a politically experienced Minnesota advertising man, see Maurice McCaffrey, *Advertising Wins Elections* (Minneapolis: Gilbert, 1962).

[5] F. C. Irion, "The 1960 Election in New Mexico," *Western Political Quarterly*, 14 (1961), 350–54.

incumbent President, of course, has ways and means of encouraging the loyalty of state and local leaders. They are obligated by past favors and, unless the President's prospects for re-election seem slight, they usually have a lively sense of the potential embarrassment of dealing with a President who owes them nothing.[6]

The sense of common cause and the stimuli of common interests that affect dispersed state and local organizations induce a modicum of participation in the presidential campaign; yet the national chairman has few sanctions against the state organization that drags its feet. In an earlier day, before the Hatch Act limited national committee expenditures, the national committee often subsidized state organizations. Now, the national chairman may steer contributors from the financial centers to deserving state organizations. He may advise and encourage. He may hold out hope for reward after victory. He may cut through the organizational layers and provide literature and other campaign aids directly to precinct workers. When worst comes to worst, the national chairman may encourage friends of the candidate to establish a state campaign headquarters separate from those of an inert regular party organization in order that at least a show of activity may be made.

The capacity of the candidate to appeal directly to the voters by radio and television has reduced or at least changed the significance of local party organizations in presidential campaigns. Precinct workers, or so it is supposed, once performed yeoman service in rallying the faithful, in propagating the party gospel, and in converting the wavering. Probably the local organization, when it functions at all, makes its major contribution by getting out to the polls those voters who might be expected to be favorable to the candidate rather than in winning the undecided. Precinct workers can bestir the laggard to register, arrange for absentee ballots, distribute literature, remind the voter that election day has arrived, furnish baby sitters, provide transportation to the voting place,[7] and occasionally win a new vote. These endeavors may, local studies indicate, give an advantage of five percentage points or more to the party with the more active leadership in a precinct.[8] Yet highly active precinct workers are few and do not reach a large propor-

---

[6] Grover Cleveland in 1892 observed that there was "nothing in the world" that would make the New York Democratic organization "hearty and honest in the campaign as surely as the conviction that the country can be carried without them." Allan Nevins (ed.), *Letters of Grover Cleveland, 1850–1908* (Boston: Houghton Mifflin, 1933), p. 296.

[7] A 1940 Gallup poll asked: "Which party usually takes the trouble to see that you get to the polls to vote for President?" Fourteen per cent said Democratic; 12 per cent, Republican; 3 per cent, other; and 71 per cent received no assistance.

[8] Phillips Cutright and P. H. Rossi, "Grass Roots Politicians and the Vote," *American Sociological Review*, 23 (1958), 171–79; Daniel Katz and S. J. Eldersveld, "The Impact of Local Party Activity upon the Electorate," *Public Opinion Quarterly*, 25 (1961), 1–24.

tion of the electorate.[9] Nevertheless, the relative success of the parties in mobilizing their workers to get out the vote may determine the winner of the electoral vote in a close state. Party organizations may play a broader part in the determination of the outcome of party primaries in which voters are few and the candidates relatively unknown.[10]

NONPARTY ORGANIZATIONS   Nonparty organizations supplement the work of the regular party organization. Given the widespread negative attitude toward "politics," these groups can attract the support of prominent citizens not disposed to associate themselves with a purely party endeavor. They can also tap financial support that the party cannot and recruit election-day workers who cannot be readily mobilized under the party banner. The Associated Willkie Clubs, the Volunteers for Stevenson, the Citizens for Eisenhower, and the Citizens for Kennedy and Johnson illustrate the type of nonparty group that can bring to the cause the labors of a candidate's admirers whose amateur status as politicians may be counterbalanced by their zeal and enthusiasm. Such an organization, if prominent in the public prints, may by its existence convey an impression that the candidate's following extends far beyond the party ranks as "plain citizens" of all types spontaneously enlist in the holy cause.

Nonparty groups also create problems in campaign direction. Often these groups grow from the organization that won the nomination for the candidate and are peculiarly his personal organization. As such they are regarded with suspicion by the old-line professionals, and jealousies and discord develop between the amateurs, starry-eyed in their devotion to the candidate, and the professionals, who have seen candidates come and go. Quite practical problems of coordination of effort also arise. Under whose auspices will

[9] Party canvassers reach probably only about 15 per cent of the electorate. After the 1956 election Dr. Gallup's interviewers asked: "In the election just over, did any Republican party worker call upon you personally to try to get you to vote for Republican candidates?" A like question was put about Democratic workers. The following proportions indicated that party workers had called on them:

	Republican worker only	Democratic worker only	Both
Stevenson voters	2%	11%	5%
Eisenhower voters	7	5	4
Nonvoters	4	3	1

In the same survey, the following question was put: "Did anyobdy telephone you to remind you to register or vote?" The "yes" percentages were: Stevenson voters, 8; Eisenhower voters, 9; nonvoters, 3. Of those who had been called, about half remembered their caller as a party worker.

[10] Phillips Cutright and Peter H. Rossi, "Party Organization in Primary Elections," *American Journal of Sociology*, 64 (1958), 262–69. On party organizations in primaries, see Rossi and Cutright, "The Impact of Party Organization in an Industrial Setting," in M. Janowitz (ed.), *Community Political Systems* (Glencoe: Free Press, 1961).

speeches be made in this locality? Who will raise money from whom? How are conflicts in television scheduling to be avoided? How is a division of labor in canvassing to be accomplished? Will the amateurs fight for the local ticket as well as the presidential candidate? And, perhaps more important, who will have the ear of the candidate on patronage matters if he wins? Friction may occur at all levels, from the national headquarters to the precinct.[11] Yet such organizations seem to have become fairly standard adjuncts to the regular party apparatus, and ways and means have to be sought to tie the two together in the campaign. In the 1960 Kennedy campaign, national headquarters placed nonresident representatives in 43 states to mediate between the party machines and citizens' groups.[12]

To be differentiated from the nonparty groups closely associated with the candidate are those committees set up as fronts for the national committee. Most committees of independents, of labor leaders, of farmers, of lawyers, of businessmen, and of others that spring up during the campaign are unacknowledged subsidiaries of the national committee. Propaganda may be issued in the name of such subsidiary organizations, and endorsement and support of the candidate may be gained from persons unwilling to appear under party auspices. The supposition underlying the establishment of these adjuncts to the regular party organization is that their appeal will be more effective with the groups concerned than a party appeal. By the multiplication of such groups the notion may be gotten across that the candidate draws support from a wide range of social groups.

Campaign Strategy

Commentators on politics have borrowed from the military the concept of strategy. A presidential campaign, as a military campaign, may be conducted in accord with a broad strategy or plan of action. That general plan may fix the principal propaganda themes to be emphasized in the campaign, define the chief targets within the electorate, schedule the peak output of effort, and set other broad features of the campaign. The stratgic scheme then provides a framework to guide the detailed work of the party propagandists, the labors of the speech writers, the decisions of those who parcel out the campaign funds, the schedulers of the itineraries of the principal orators,

[11] On the troubles of the Associated Willkie Clubs, see H. O. Evjen, "The Willkie Campaign: An Unfortunate Chapter in Republican Leadership," *Journal of Politics*, 14 (1952), 241–56. For a study of a more effective independent committee, see D. R. McCoy, "The Progressive National Committee of 1936," *Western Political Quarterly*, 9 (1956), 454–69.

[12] T. H. White, *The Making of the President, 1960* (New York: Atheneum, 1961), p. 249.

and the day-to-day endeavors of all the subordinate units of campaign organization.

Often the outlines of a campaign strategy are scarcely visible amidst the confusion of the campaign and, indeed, campaigns often rest on only the sketchiest of plans. The preparation of a reasoned and comprehensive strategy requires more of a disposition to think through the campaign in its broad outlines than often exists around a national headquarters. Once the plan is made, its execution requires an organization sufficiently articulated to respond to general direction in accord with the plan, a requisite that is not always met. And even when a campaign is blueprinted in advance, a flexibility must be built into it to take advantage of the breaks and to meet unexpected moves by the opposition.

SITUATIONAL LIMITATIONS ON STRATEGY   The characteristics of the situations within which presidential campaigners operate set limits on, or condition, the kinds of strategy that may be employed in the battle for the voters' affections. These limitations are not discerned by those who regard campaigns as occasions on which unprincipled men in their quest for power may exploit without limit the prejudices of the masses as they play upon the inherent wickedness and perversity of man. While campaigns have their unlovely aspects, the mores of the democratic order, as well as the particular circumstances of individual campaigns, place bounds on the types of strategy that may be profitably pursued.

The political culture sets continuing, though vague, standards of campaign etiquette.[13] The content of the political culture cannot readily be defined, but it includes the firmly embedded modal expectations of the electorate about what is and what is not proper in the realm of politics. The predominant attitudes, for example, make futile those campaign appeals that extend beyond or deviate clearly from the constitutional consensus. Campaign objectives that would be both feasible and proper in a different political culture would in the United States appear outlandish and to be sought, if at all, by splinter parties not hopeful of gaining power. The drive toward conformity with the basic values and objectives of the society discourages appeals looking toward basic innovation, though it needs to be remembered that the content of these unwritten limitations on political debate change through time.

Other more apparent determinants of broad strategy emerge from the characteristics of the immediate situation in which the campaign occurs and from the candidate's position in it. The candidate of the party out of

[13] The Fair Campaign Practices Committee, a private, nonpartisan group, attempts to spell out the rules of the game and at the beginning of each campaign invites the national chairmen and congressional and gubernatorial candidates to subscribe to its fair campaign code.

power thus tends to follow a strategy of attack upon the record of the party in power. The public-relations specialists who worked out the strategy for the Eisenhower campaign in 1952 concluded their presentation: ". . . the recommended strategy is: *Attack! Attack! Attack!*" [14] The circumstances permitted emphasis upon criticism of the record of the party in power and required no intensive merchandising of an alternative program.

The candidate of the ins, also by virtue of the circumstances of his situation, tends to be driven toward a strategy of defense of his party's record. Adlai Stevenson in 1952 was thrust into a posture of defense of the Truman Administration. In 1956, after four years of Eisenhower, the Republican strategists were denied the simple strategy of attack and had to point with pride to their record. Supposedly a defensive strategy is disadvantageous; whether it is depends on the nature of the ground the candidate is defending. The ins may be able to picture their campaign as a continuation of a great crusade in which they had won only a skirmish at the preceding election, a strategy open to the Democrats in the campaigns after 1932 and to the Republicans in the campaign of 1956. In 1952 the Democrats were still running against Herbert Hoover, and in 1956 the Republicans fired many a barrage at Harry Truman. The ins, unless disaster or ineptitude has overtaken them, enjoy a considerable advantage.

Another broad factor that conditions the strategies of campaigns consists of a bundle of circumstances that might be labeled the temper of the times. In eras of general complacency and economic well-being, assaults against the interests and crusades against abuses by the privileged classes seem to pay small dividends. Periods of hardship and unrest move campaigners to contrive strategies to exploit the anxieties of people—or to insulate themselves from public wrath.

GROUP TARGETS   The customs of American campaigning dictate that the presidential candidate make it appear that he speaks for all the people, all classes, all races, all religions. He seeks to become the embodiment of all aspirations in a grand harmony of interests which denies conflict and even rises above partisanship. Yet beneath the obligatory façade of universality of appeal, party strategists give thought to ways and means to design appeals calculated to inflame, to attract, to enlist particular groups. The contrivance of a group strategy involves the hazard that gains by an appeal to one group may be offset by losses from another group antagonistic to the first.

An important target group consists of the voters traditionally attached to the party. The party's foundation in interest rests among these voters who also provide its most consistent electoral support. Save in exceptional cir-

[14] S. Kelley, Jr., *Professional Public Relations and Political Power* (Baltimore: Johns Hopkins Press, 1956), p. 155.

cumstances, the campaign strategy fixes a course calculated not to strain the loyalties of the party diehards, though they may be relied upon to view tolerantly, at least for a time, gambits antagonistic to them but designed to bring unbelievers to the true faith. The 1952 Republican strategy, for example, assumed that to win the election the party should begin with those who had stuck "with the party through thick and thin." These voters, the campaign strategists asserted, "must not be alienated." High priority was assigned to the task of renewing and maintaining the loyalties of this segment of the party. In 1956 Adlai Stevenson gave sedulous attention to the southern Democrats, a policy not without its offsetting disadvantages, given the composition of the Democratic following.

Early in the 1960 campaign Senator Kennedy adopted the strategy of pinning the Republican label firmly on Vice President Nixon and of emphasizing the differences between the parties. The object was to activate the loyalties of Democrats, an advantageous move because of the preponderance of Democratic identifiers within the electorate. Yet Democratic campaign technicians felt that Kennedy failed to exploit to the full the fact of widespread association in the minds of the people of group interests with Democratic symbolism.[15] Nixon's strategy was to play down Republicanism, for his hope for victory lay in attracting the votes of substantial numbers of Democratic identifiers.

While all ethnic, religious, and economic groups must receive a minimum of ceremonial deference, the party strategy may provide for powerful drives for the support of particular groups or classes within the electorate. These group appeals may be merely a part of the strategy calculated to retain the support of groups long attached to the party. Or they may be designed to draw voters from groups traditionally attached to the opposition. The circumstances may make it probable that such groups have become especially susceptible to special appeals. In 1956, for example, Republicans sought to weaken Negro attachment to the Democratic party—a strategy facilitated by developments in segregation policy that enabled Vice President Nixon to refer to Earl Warren as a "great Republican Chief Justice." In 1948 Mr. Truman, faced by desertion in the South, wound up his campaign with specific commitments and powerful appeals to groups outside the South: Negroes, Jews, and industrial workers.[16] Under some circumstances group appeals do

[15] George M. Belknap, "Motivational Research in the 1960 Presidential Campaign" (Paper prepared for American Political Association meeting, September, 1961).

[16] Commentators on the 1960 campaign assign great weight to Kennedy's telephone call to express sympathy to Mrs. Martin Luther King after her husband had been jailed in connection with participation in a "sit-in" and to Robert Kennedy's interposition to obtain King's release on bail. A million leaflets were distributed among Negroes to extol the humaneness of the candidate "who cares." The effects of such exploits are far less marked than is often supposed. In early October, about three weeks before the incident, Gallup showed Negroes 62 per cent for Kennedy; the estimate for the election was 68 per cent.

not have to be verbalized to be felt; attributes of the candidates constitute the appeal. Kennedy in 1960 did not have to rouse Catholics to his banner; the fact that he was a Catholic served that end. Nevertheless, his forthright confrontation of Protestant critics served incidentally to remind Catholics that one of their co-religionists was a candidate.[17] Nor did Nixon need to say anything to attract anti-Catholic Protestants. Lesser campaigners, to be sure, did not let the realities go unremarked.

GEOGRAPHICAL TARGETS   Another element of strategy consists in schemes for the geographical distribution of campaign effort. The system of voting for President traditionally has encouraged both parties to devote little effort to those states strongly attached to one party or the other and to concentrate campaigning in the close states. Moreover, the fact that the winner in a state takes all its electoral votes makes concentration of effort in the larger, close states rational; a given amount of effort may yield far more electoral votes in one state than in another. The formation of a geographic strategy requires educated estimates of the closeness of sentiment in the various states, as well as judgments about which of the supposedly close states might respond most readily to the appeals open to the party in the particular situation.

Execution of a geographic strategy requires that campaign themes, assignment of major speakers, and concentration of money be handled in accord with the general plan. In the closing days of the 1940 presidential campaign the Democrats sent into Ohio—a state thought to be slipping toward Willkie—President Roosevelt, Henry Wallace, Mayor La Guardia, Senator Norris, and various other Democratic bigwigs. In the same campaign the Democrats-for-Willkie focused a large-scale mail circularization campaign in states that could be converted to Republicanism by a slight shift. In 1960 Kennedy devoted about 57 per cent of his time to the seven largest doubtful states; Nixon allocated 51 per cent of his time to the same states.[18] The principle of concentration of fire is further illustrated by the selective purchase of radio time. In 1952 Republican strategists worked out and executed a plan for "an all-out saturation blitz radio television spot campaign" concentrated in 49 counties in 12 states during the closing week of the campaign.

CAMPAIGN TIMING   An element of campaign strategy is the timing of the output of campaign efforts. The supposition is that if all re-

---

[17] The following estimates of the percentages of 1956 voting groups moving to the opposition candidate in 1960 probably are not remote from the reality: Eisenhower Protestants, 17; Stevenson Protestants, 14; Eisenhower Catholics, 67; Stevenson Catholics, 3.

[18] Stanley Kelley, Jr., in Paul David (ed.), *The Presidential Election and Transition, 1960–1961* (Washington: Brookings Institution, 1961), p. 71.

sources are thrown into the campaign too early, the campaign may reach its peak long before election day and exhaust the campaign chest and the party personnel before the moment when greatest exertion is needed. The campaign should be timed to produce the greatest effect just before the election. Managers of campaigns are by no means completely free in their decisions on timing. They must pay heed to the strategy followed by the opposition. Candidates not widely known may need to conduct a long campaign simply to make their name familiar to the voters, as did Stevenson in 1952. The challenger of an incumbent President may be compelled to begin his attack long before the President feels it necessary to take to the hustings. In 1936, for example, Franklin D. Roosevelt went on a cruise and yielded the stage to the Republicans in the early weeks of the campaign. He resisted pressure from his uneasy advisers to answer Landon's opening volleys and waited until late October to mount his offensive.[19] Richard Nixon expounded and sought to practice a doctrine of campaign "pace" that would produce a "peak" immediately before the voting.

The general notion among the professionals seems to be that a campaign should be managed so as to culminate in a climax of enthusiastic effort a few days before the election, an outburst that generates an impression of confidence, that seems to indicate an overwhelming tide of support for the candidate. On occasion that pattern is approximated as one or the other of the campaigns seems to dominate radio and television, to pre-empt the headlines and the advertising columns, to fill the billboards, as it reaches a shrill intensity that blankets out the opposition in the days just before the voting. How much of an effect all this has on the voting is another question.

CAMPAIGN THEMES   A prime problem in campaign strategy is the creation of a dominant theme or themes for the campaign. This problem goes beyond the simple choice of issues to be emphasized or the selection of aspects of the opposition's record to be attacked. It extends to the creation of a tone or a spirit for the campaign, an aura that envelops the entire operation and gives a distinctive character to the undertaking in all its details. Thus, in 1956 the Republican campaign appeared to be pitched to a lofty line of sincerity, morality, and piety, a theme or tone that seemed to permeate most aspects of the campaign. Or, in 1936 the Democratic campaign evidently was calculated to build a total impression of Roosevelt as the leader of a crusade to crush the selfish interests that had resisted a new deal for the common man. In 1948 Truman created a different sort of total impression, a cocky little man who ran a "give-'em-hell" campaign as he took the fight to the grass roots. In 1952 the Republican attack distilled down to an as-

[19] See J. M. Burns, *Roosevelt: The Lion and the Fox* (New York: Harcourt, Brace, 1956), pp. 271–88. See also H. F. Gosnell, *Champion Campaigner: Franklin D. Roosevelt* (New York: Macmillan, 1952).

sault on the "mess in Washington," a convenient phrase under which all varieties of dissatisfaction might be amalgamated. In the same year Stevenson sought to set a distinctive campaign tone with his proposal "to talk sense" to the people. Kennedy in 1960 attempted to convey a prospect of movement: "While I do not promise an easy future, I can promise you that the United States will move again." Nixon sought to establish an image of mature experience as a pervasive background for his campaign.[20]

POLLS AND CAMPAIGN MANAGEMENT   A tool of growing importance for the management of campaigns is the sample survey conducted by commercial polling organizations. These surveys provide useful intelligence on the state of public opinion as the campaign progresses. While they ascertain, as do the syndicated polls, the estimated division of candidate preferences, they also range more widely in their probes of the public mind. What problems are uppermost in the minds of the voters? In the minds of specific groups of voters? What has been the response of the electors to a policy position taken by the candidate? Was anyone listening? If so, who and how many? What is the extent of popular concern about a particular issue, say, medical care or aid for education? Survey findings do not yield unequivocal guides to campaigners, but they supplement intuitive judgments about mass attitudes. In a sense the surveys create a channel for feedback by which campaigners may learn the responses of the electorate to the stimuli of the campaign.[21]

Art and Artifice in Campaigning

One may speak of grand campaign strategy, rationally formulated and executed with precision, but a great deal of campaign management rests on the hunches that guide day-to-day decisions. The lore of politics includes rules of thumb that are supposed to embody the wisdom of political experience as guides to action. Whether the maxims of the practicing politician have any validity, they do have an interest as an element of the art of politics, an interest frequently capitalized upon by writers for the Sunday supplements.

[20] Hardy souls will find all the 1960 speeches of Nixon and Kennedy assembled in Senate Report 994, 87th Cong., 1st sess. (Washington: Government Printing Office, 1961).

[21] An innovation of the 1960 campaign was the development of a technique for the simulation of electoral response to particular issues. Thus, on the basis of data from past polls the probable response to the religious issue was estimated. See Ithiel de Sola Pool and Robert Abelson, "The Simulmatics Project," *Public Opinion Quarterly*, 23 (1961), 166–83.

FRONT PORCH, SWING AROUND THE CIRCLE, OR WHIS-
TLE STOP   An old problem of campaign tactics is the question of the extent of the speaking and traveling schedule of the head of the ticket. Should the candidate make an extensive swing around the country and speak at as many places as practicable or should he make a "front-porch" campaign? The decision on this question may depend on the qualities of the candidate. In 1920 the Republican strategy was to keep Harding at home in Marion, Ohio. "Keep Warren at home," the Republican leader Penrose is reported to have said. "Don't let him make any speeches. If he goes out on a tour, somebody's sure to ask him questions, and Warren's just the sort of damn fool that'll try to answer them." "The Front Porch campaign," according to Samuel Hopkins Adams, "was determined upon. The role assigned to the candidate was that of the modest, simple, sagacious, home-loving, home-staying statesman. He was to be 'just folks.' To the Mecca of Marion would come the devout, and the Prophet would edify them with the sound doctrine of orthodox Republicanism." [22]

Television has made the vine-clad front porch obsolete. The choice becomes one of whether the candidate is to travel about the country and mingle with the multitude or stay at home near a television camera. In 1956 Mr. Eisenhower's managers intimated in the early stages of the campaign that their candidate would limit himself to a few television speeches from Washington. An appearance or so by the General in a television studio quickly persuaded those concerned that the General's talents could be better employed on the stump.

PICTURING THE CANDIDATE TO THE PUBLIC   Given the bearing of the personal qualities of the candidate on electoral decision, the outcome of an election may be determined by the image of the candidate implanted in the minds of the voters. The nature of the image to be propagated depends on the strategy and circumstances of the campaign. Within limits, skillful propagandists can convert a candidate into a mythical character possessing in distilled form the qualities thought to be advantageous for the campaign. Television, instead of obstructing this process by making the candidate's qualities perceptible to all, may aid in the transformation—so long as the candidate can find his way through the speeches that have been ghosted for him. "In our day," says Mosca, "sects and political parties are highly skilled at creating the superman, the legendary hero, the 'man of unquestioned honesty,' who serves in his turn, to maintain the luster of the gang and bring in wealth and power for the sly ones to use." [23] Before Charles

[22] Samuel Hopkins Adams, *Incredible Era* (Boston: Houghton Mifflin, 1939), p. 170.

[23] *The Ruling Class* (New York: McGraw-Hill, 1939), p. 194.

Michelson became director of publicity for the Democratic national committee, he commented on the process of making imaginary characters of the candidates, thus:

> The American people will elect as President of the United States in November a nonexistent person—and defeat likewise a mythical identity.
>
> They will vote for and against a picture that has been painted for them by protagonists and antagonists in a myriad of publications, a picture that must be either a caricature or an idealization.
>
> Herbert Hoover, the miracle man, the perfect human machine, destitute of error, with a vision beyond cosmic bounds, who resolves every problem into its mathematical elements; who has on tap all the wisdom of the universe; who plots his tasks with unerring curves and discharges them by rule and measure; who has not time for mirth or diversions; no thought but of duty before him.
>
> Alfred E. Smith, the ingenuous child of the New York sidewalks, simple beyond belief, but with that simplicity is combined a knowledge beyond that given in books; a demigod to whom all the complexities of government are clear as day; a paragon of wisdom, gentleness and righteousness, whose facile mind fathoms automatically every depth of economics and politics.[24]

The fictional picture of the candidate expedient to propagate varies with circumstances and, to some extent, with the talents of the candidates. In 1932, for example, Franklin Roosevelt thought it desirable to "dramatize himself as a breaker of custom, a daring, resolute champion of action, establishing a bold contrast with the country's picture of Hoover as timid, hesitant, irresolute." [25] In the 1944 Republican campaign the accent was on youth: Dewey and his entourage were pictured as young, aggressive, forward-looking men; Roosevelt and other Democratic leaders were attacked as tired, old, quarreling men. In 1952 Eisenhower's managers sought to merchandise him as a man who embodied the homely virtues, a simple and sincere man of unmatched integrity, yet possessed of an experience and wisdom beyond compare that would enable him "to go to Korea" and bring peace, order, and security to a troubled world.

The creation of an etched image of the candidate may reduce to a single, appealing symbol the party's position on intricate and complex issues. The candidate may personify a general approach to public questions or a general spirit in public policy. Consider: Jackson, the champion of the common man; Bryan, a fearless crusader attacking the strongholds of special privilege; Harding, the easy-going, pleasant embodiment of the yearning for

[24] Quoted by Ralph D. Casey, "Party Campaign Propaganda," *The Annals*, 179 (1935), 96–105.

[25] Raymond Moley, *After Seven Years* (New York: Harper, 1939), p. 26.

normalcy; Coolidge, the conservative, shrewd, safe, New Englander; Wilson, the militant battler for a new freedom; Franklin Roosevelt, the champion of the forgotten man; Eisenhower, the good and sincere yet superhuman man. To fill such roles requires a modicum of histrionic skill; great politicians must be actors of sorts and politics has its elements of make-believe. Not all candidates succeed in achieving a sharply defined image in the minds of the voters; even when they do, people's perceptions of them may differ from the strategist's designs. Thus, in 1948 a considerable number of voters viewed Dewey as smug, complacent, patronizing, noncommittal, foppish, overdressed, and antagonizing in appearance.[26]

THE LOFTY, NONPARTISAN POSE   If a presidential candidate has attained great popularity, it may be possible for him to assume a position above the battle. His lofty eminence makes attack difficult; it may create an impression of assurance of victory, of a great figure who rises above his petty associates, of a man above politics, of a giant beyond reach of quixotic sallies by the pygmies of the opposition. Perhaps the popular expectation that Presidents should be something more than partisans contributes to the beatification of presidential candidates, but some of them succeed in becoming more saintly than do others. Franklin D. Roosevelt demonstrated some skill in this respect, as various candidates who challenged him learned to their dismay, but Eisenhower undoubtedly demonstrated greater genius in disentangling himself from the ruck and the muck of the political battle. He managed to disengage himself so completely from politics, even from his own Administration, that he provided a target beyond range. From this point he could in the campaign of 1956 look down on the "locust-swarm of partisan orators" in the Democratic ranks; he could belittle the moans of a "few politicians"; he could dismiss criticisms of his farm policy as "drivel" concocted by "partisan orators" and "anguished politicians." This disengagement from politics also permitted him to dissociate himself from the dubious tactics of his allies. Republican literature referring to "Democratic wars" brought from him the indignant comment: "I don't believe when America gets into war we can afford to call it anything but 'our war.' " Democratic tacticians never managed to identify Eisenhower with his party or with his fellow campaigners, so skilled was he in maintaining an image of himself as a sincere man of integrity apart from the wickedness of politics. The most finished partisanship under some circumstances is to appear to be no politician at all.[27]

[26] Angus Campbell and R. L. Kahn, *The People Elect A President* (Ann Arbor: Survey Research Center, 1952), p. 50.

[27] Such poses may have an especial appeal to those most disillusioned about the democratic process. See Murray B. Levin and Murray Eden, "Political Strategy for the Alienated Voter," *Public Opinion Quarterly*, 26 (1962), 47–63. See also Levin's *The Compleat Politician* (Indianapolis: Bobbs-Merrill, 1962).

THE SILENT TREATMENT   Some campaigners are so circumstanced that they may be correct in regarding it as sound policy never to mention the name of the opposing candidate. He may be referred to as "our opponent," as "the gentleman from New York," or he may be completely ignored. Roosevelt explained this policy on the theory that many people could not remember names. They voted for names they knew. To name the opponent was to advertise his name and to impress it on the public mind. Roosevelt knew that there would be no lack of mention of his name by his enemies.

A candidate can give the silent treatment to the opposing standard bearer only under favorable circumstances. Roosevelt could run as if Landon or Dewey were not in the race; Eisenhower could pay little heed to Stevenson. On the other hand, a candidate opposing a popular leader almost of necessity must attempt to cut him down to size. Democratic strategists in 1956, for example, struggled with the question of what to say about General Eisenhower. After the General's heart attack, it seemed advisable to moderate criticism of him lest, by arousing sympathy, more be lost than gained.

DEFENSIVE STRATEGY: REPLY OR IGNORE?   As a presidential campaign moves along, the question of what to do about the opposition's attacks recurs. Should a candidate answer them or should he ignore them? "There's an old bromide in politics that goes something like this: 'If your opponent calls you a liar, do not deny it—just call him a thief.' " [28] The same rule on the proper response to an attack has been put by Murray Chotiner, once a public-relations adviser to Vice President Nixon, in this way: ". . . when you answer it, do so with an attack of your own against the opposition for having launched it in the first place." By far the most adroit handling of a dangerous attack in recent American politics occurred in 1952 as Richard Nixon dealt with the revelation of a fund to which a number of his supporters had subscribed to aid him in paying the incidental expenses of his senatorial office. In the politics of an earlier day the episode would have been regarded as a handful of businessmen buying themselves a Senator. Not so, as Nixon fielded the play under the coaching of his public-relations advisers. A few southern California patriots had contributed to help the Senator get his message to the American people. That message exposed the Democratic Administration, "the Communism in it, the corruption in it." The publicity about the fund had been a smear, "to silence" him, to make him "let up." He dared to continue to fight: "Because, you see, I love my country. And I think my country is in danger." The Senator emerged as a clean-cut young hero, poor but honest, smeared by conspiring Commies

[28] Turner Catledge, "The ABC's of Political Campaigning," *New York Times Magazine*, September 22, 1940, pp. 9, 18, 21.

who sought to block his devastating blows—a recovery acclaimed by connoisseurs of such matters as without equal in the history of humbuggery.

The basic difficulty in answering attacks is that the enemy chooses the terrain of battle that is favorable to his cause. For that reason it may be preferable to ignore an attack altogether. Or an unwise attack by an irresponsible member of the opposition may be chosen for reply. In the 1940 campaign, for example, Roosevelt chose to answer the charge of an obscure Republican campaigner that the President's supporters were "paupers, those who earn less than $1,200 a year and aren't worth that, and the Roosevelt family." The discovery of this remark occasioned high glee on the Roosevelt campaign train; a quick estimate put about half of the American population at the time into this definition of pauper. Roosevelt responded: " 'Paupers,' who are not worth their salt—there speaks the true sentiment of the Republican leadership in this year of grace. Can the Republican leaders deny that all this all-too-prevailing Republican sentiment is a direct, vicious, unpatriotic appeal to class hatred and class contempt? That, my friends, is just what I am fighting against with all my heart and soul."

Campaigners, as they avoid or parry charges, naturally place emphasis on what they regard as their strong points; likewise, they say little about the weaker elements in their record or program. The opposition follows a like policy of speaking endlessly of the popular features of what it has to offer and of minimizing mention of the less attractive aspects. In consequence the issues seem never to be joined in the campaign oratory. Thus, in 1940 the Republicans spoke frequently and vociferously on the third-term issue; the Democrats scarcely mentioned it, but spoke instead of the desirability of an experienced Administration at a critical time in foreign affairs, a proposition difficult for the Republicans to challenge. In 1952 Democrats pointed with pride to the achievements of their foreign policy in Europe; the Republicans did not talk much about Europe but said a great deal about Asia.[29]

DRIVING A WEDGE BETWEEN THE OPPOSING CANDIDATE AND HIS FOLLOWERS   An old campaigning maxim is that "a candidate should always separate his opponent from the rank and file of the party." Willkie in 1940 strove to draw a line between Roosevelt and the Democrats. The "New Dealers" (not the Democratic Administration) had, he argued, departed from the precepts of Democratic heroes and saints. "So if there is any Democratic disciple of Thomas Jefferson in Dubuque he ought to vote for me. Surely any Andrew Jackson Democrat should vote for me and not for my opponent. . . . No Cleveland Democrat should vote against me."

---

[29] For examples, drawn from senatorial campaigns, of the tendency of campaigners to talk past each other, see L. C. Ferguson and R. H. Smuckler, *Politics in the Press* (East Lansing: Michigan State College, 1954), pp. 32–41.

He talked to the Democrats as if they had been betrayed by Roosevelt and the "New Dealers." In turn, Roosevelt avoided attacks against "Republicans" or the "Republican party." Instead, he concentrated his fire on "Republican spokesmen" or "Republican leaders." Republican voters with Democratic inclinations could then say to themselves, or so Roosevelt thought, "he doesn't mean me." [30] Similar is the direction of intense criticism against minor figures rather than the chief of the opposite party. A campaigner may concede the greatness of the rank and file of the opposition, admit that the opposing standard bearer is an honorable man, but, sadly and reluctantly, point to the petty scoundrels who surround him.

RIDICULE: A TWO-EDGED SWORD   A subtle art of campaigning is the use of ridicule, sarcasm, and scorn. Few presidential candidates have been masters of this art. A classic of the type was Roosevelt's speech to the International Teamsters Union in September, 1944, in which he skillfully poked fun at the opposition. In this speech the President rose to the defense of his dog Fala. The President's wife, the President's sons, and the President could ignore attacks on themselves, but Fala's "Scotch soul was furious." Listeners laughed raucously before millions of radios: "I think I have a right to object to libelous statements about my dog." The speech, however, had far-reaching effects. A rip-roaring declamation, it was calculated to arouse the voters from their apathy. Perhaps it was also designed to anger the opposition candidate. The next day Dewey promised "unvarnished candor"; and his next speech, thrown together in haste, did not reflect the same sober consideration as earlier speeches and paved the way for campaign boners, or so the political writers opined.[31]

THE ART OF THE SMEAR   While presidential campaigns may be cleaner than they were a century ago, fine specimens of the smear turn up now and then.[32] A smear is a charge regarded as not quite cricket. Most smears are lies, nothing more, nothing less, but they also include lines of attack that attribute unpatriotic or selfish motives to the opposition or that raise questions no honorable man would raise. A simple falsehood must, of course, be presented in a manner to appear to be the truth. Thus, in 1932 a photograph of a sign before a "Hoover Ranch" reading "No White Men Wanted" was widely circulated; the enterprising photographers had hung a placard prepared for the occasion alongside a sign in front of a California ranch named for Mr. Hoover by one of his admirers. Or, in a Maryland senatorial campaign in 1950 opponents of Millard Tydings published a tabloid

---

[30] Burns, *op. cit.*, p. 286.

[31] On the speech about Fala, see R. E. Sherwood, *Roosevelt and Hopkins* (New York: Harper, 1948), ch. 31.

[32] See Hugh A. Bone, *"Smear" Politics* (Washington: American Council on Public Affairs, 1941).

which included a faked photograph showing Tydings in a friendly conversation with Communist Earl Browder.[33] The supposedly damaging falsehood merges over into the smear that questions the patriotism or motives of the opposition, for example, that Truman carried the nation into the Korean affair to avoid a depression.

In some circles the art of smearing without seeming to smear is regarded with high esteem. That may be accomplished by innuendo, which leaves absolutely no doubt about what is being said, though in cold print the language does not technically say what was attributed to it. Thus, in the campaigns of 1952 and 1954 various Republican orators left the indubitable impression with their auditors that the high Democratic leadership was tinged with treason, communism, and corruption. Yet so nicely worded were these speeches that Democrats who cried "Foul" could not point to the phrase that designated them as traitors.

Obviously the head of a ticket cannot be associated with the dissemination of the more obvious sorts of smears. At times lesser leaders may make a public smear, but the more personal smears travel by word of mouth; sometimes the movement of stories is deliberately expedited; sometimes they originate spontaneously and travel under their own power. The ancestry of a candidate, his extramarital exploits, his meanness, his disposition to rob his fellow man, his association with doubtful characters, his wife's alcoholism, the peccadillos of his children, and a variety of other matters are dealt with in yarns that find their way across the country during a campaign. A few men traveling out of national headquarters can spread a story a long way in a few days.[34] About the only sure defense open to a candidate is a good espionage service to ferret out opposition intentions and the hardihood to threaten to disseminate an equally outrageous tale about his opponent.[35]

Communications Media

The appeals determined upon by the campaign strategists must be gotten to the voters. The candidate in a small rural county may have a word with and shake the hand of every voter in the jurisdiction before election day.

---

[33] Accusations of "softness" on communism have of late been a favorite type of smear. See Frank H. Jonas, "The Art of Political Dynamiting," *Western Political Quarterly*, 10 (1957), 374–91.

[34] An act of Congress of 1944 requires that campaign literature include the names of the persons responsible for its publication or distribution, a requirement calculated to discourage the publication of smears. A New York statute requires that campaign literature carry the name and address of the printer and the name of the person or committee ordering it.

[35] Courts give little aid to those who claim to have lost elections through misrepresentation. See C. M. Kneier, "Misleading the Voters," *National Municipal Review*, 46 (1957), 450–55.

The conditions of national politics differ radically from the suppositions of democratic theorists who see the entire citizenry assembled under a spreading chestnut tree to settle the affairs of state. A presidential candidate, save through the shadows of television, can show himself to only a few voters. Nor can he, given the looseness of national party organization, depend exclusively upon party workers over the nation to carry his message to the people. He must utilize the media of communication—press, radio, and television—to project his image and to transmit his appeals to the people.

CAMPAIGNING AND THE COMMUNICATIONS REVOLUTION   The revolution in communications technology has profoundly altered the character of campaigning and perhaps changed, too, the fundamental bases of political power. These technological innovations began scarcely more than a century ago and multiplied rapidly in recent decades; their full effects have doubtless not yet been felt. In Andrew Jackson's day the facilities for reaching the mass of the people were meager indeed. In the campaign of 1828 Jackson's chief means for circulating his views was the *United States Telegraph,* a partisan newspaper with a circulation of 40,000 weekly. Its successor, the *Washington Globe,* by 1834 had a daily circulation of 12,000. Democratic doctrine proclaimed in the leading articles of this paper was reprinted by local newspapers over the country but only after the Washington newspaper had been conveyed to their offices by the primitive transport of the day.[36]

The communications system of Jackson's time made it essential that the national party have allied with itself local newspapers; it also left a place of great importance for party workers. The trend of technology over a century shortened the lines of communication between the national leadership and the electorate. The invention of the telegraph permitted the simultaneous publication of an item in every city of the land. Parallel improvements in printing machinery and newspaper merchandising brought newspapers within the reach of practically everyone. Later the introduction of movies made it possible for the candidate to be seen and heard by millions of people. The inauguration of network broadcasting after 1920 brought the entire nation within earshot of the campaigner. Television, first used extensively in the campaign of 1952, added another means for the direct linkage of presidential candidate and voter. These developments made it possible for national leaders to reach and influence mass opinion directly without heavy reliance on an intermediate network of party workers or of party newspapers. The same developments probably also tend to elevate to power different persons, those with skills in the use of mass communications; at least they require some mastery of those skills.

[36] E. M. Eriksson, "President Jackson's Propaganda Agencies," *Pacific Historical Review,* 6 (1937), 47–57.

THE PRESS: REPORTER AND PARTISAN   American political parties have fewer and fewer newspapers openly allied with them as partisan journals. The decline of the partisan press, often supported by public advertising or other patronage, has affected the Democratic party far more than it has the Republican party. The independent or nonparty press tends by and large to be Republican in sympathy. Yet the managers of both parties must deal with a press that professes to function as a more or less neutral conduit through which news of events flows. Campaigners must contrive ways and means to inject their propaganda into the channels of the press.

The candidate cannot afford to be ignored by the press; his entourage, as well as the national headquarters, includes men whose job it is to facilitate the work of the newspapermen and to feed materials to the press. The politician believes that unfavorable treatment by the press is better than no coverage. Frank R. Kent put the maxim: "It is better to be roasted than ignored." The late Claude A. Swanson phrased it: "When they stop writing about you in politics, you are dead." [37] Candidates strive to keep in the headlines; every day there must be a story for the press. When the presidential candidate goes on tour, provision is made for correspondents to accompany him; they are furnished advance copies of speeches and facilities to aid them in covering the campaign.

Apart from the coverage of party meetings and speeches, campaign managers funnel their message into the editorial rooms by other means. In the 1936 Republican campaign, for example, the publicity department made arrangements to furnish its press releases in mat, plate, and proof form to weeklies and small dailies. "At their own request 7,000 weeklies and 280 dailies received W.N.U. plate service; 430 weeklies and 557 dailies got mat service, and proof service was supplied to 25 weeklies and 780 dailies." [38] The total number of press releases distributed during the campaign was estimated at 361,000. Column after column in small dailies and country weeklies is filled with material supplied from party headquarters in the form of "editorial suggestions." The foreign language press historically has presented a special problem to party managers, but its decline in importance has doubtless reduced this drain on campaign coffers.

Newspapers, despite their avowal that they are common carriers and little more, may give advantage to one candidate or the other in their news columns by allotting their favorite more space, by prominent placement of stories about him, by misleading headlines, and by other means observed in any campaign. Most newspapers may give fair coverage to both candidates during campaigns, yet the preponderance of editorial support tends to go to the Republican side along with whatever bias prevails in the treatment of

---

[37] Frank R. Kent, *Political Behavior* (New York: Morrow, 1928), 252–53.
[38] Ralph D. Casey, "Republican Propaganda in the 1936 Campaign," *Public Opinion Quarterly*, April, 1937, 27–44.

news. In newspaper editorial support in 1952 Stevenson enjoyed an advantage in only Georgia, Kentucky, and North Carolina, and he "had no daily newspaper support in nine states—Connecticut, Delaware, Maine, New Hampshire, North Dakota, Rhode Island, South Dakota, Utah and Vermont." [39]

About the only weapon a candidate has against newspaper bias is to scream to high heaven about the iniquities of the one-party press, a gambit which may help keep the press a bit more in tune with its professed aim of fair reporting whatever its editorial stand may be. The advertising columns of the newspapers are usually open to party committees but normally at a higher rate than is charged to commercial advertisers. Politicians do not place high value on newspaper advertising, but when one side advertises the other feels that it must do so too. In presidential campaigns the national committees place little newspaper advertising but provide mats for local groups that wish to do so, a means by which national headquarters can maintain some control over what is said in advertisements paid for by enthusiastic local committees.

What of the influence of newspapers? Do people vote as their favorite editors recommend? Do slanted news columns win votes? Do the great publishers swing elections? The evidence on such matters is extremely limited, though it is evident that newspaper influence differs enormously from situation to situation. Roosevelt won four presidential elections over the opposition of most of the press; Truman enjoyed no widespread newspaper support. Eisenhower, on the other hand, had the support of the bulk of the daily press. With newspaper support Roosevelt might have won by wider margins; without newspaper support Eisenhower might have won by narrower margins. The chances are that newspapers exert greater influence in state and local matters than in presidential campaigns. Voters in jurisdictions that elect obscure candidates to fill inconspicuous positions may rely to a greater extent on the press for guidance. In party primaries the press may, other things being equal, exert more influence than in general elections, but in some jurisdictions newspaper opposition is said to be a positive advantage.[40] In turn, newspapers themselves may to some degree be under the same sorts of influences as is the electorate; some newspapers do cross party lines from time to time.

The effect of the press is not to be measured solely by its impact on the fortunes of the candidates during the course of a campaign. By steadily hammering their policy predilections, campaign or no campaign, newspapers over the long pull affect the attitudes of their readers, an influence that may be

[39] N. B. Blumberg, *One-Party Press?* (Lincoln: University of Nebraska Press, 1954), p. 16.

[40] On press influence in local campaigns, see H. F. Gosnell and M. J. Schmidt, "Factorial Analysis of the Relation of the Press to Voting in Chicago," *Journal of Social Psychology*, 7 (1936), 375–85.

reflected in the voting when an election rolls around. The cumulative educational effect of the press in individual communities may become both pervasive and durable. A community dependent, for example, on a Hearst newspaper for a generation or so may develop into a quite different place than one blessed with a more responsible press.

PARTY LITERATURE   During a presidential campaign the national headquarters of the parties publish large quatities of pamphlets, leaflets, and circulars. By such means the party can deliver messages tailored to the interests—and prejudices—of special groups of voters, furnish ammunition to its friends, and present arguments and material that would not be printed by newspapers or transmitted by the radio stations. A 1940 Republican leaflet, "A Third Term?," gave in parallel columns pictures and statements of pro- and anti-third-termers. Among the former were, according to the leaflet, Earl Browder, "Boss Edward J. Kelly," "Boss Frank Hague," and Harold Ickes; among the latter, George Washington, Thomas Jefferson, Andrew Jackson, and Woodrow Wilson. A 1960 Democratic leaflet was entitled, "Why Nixon Is Called the 'Great Pretender.' " The campaign comic book, a relatively new form of campaign literature, lends itself to a most graphic expression of partisanship. Even the most partisan newspaper rarely puts the partisan message as bluntly as it can be stated in campaign literature.

Of the millions of pieces of literature printed in each campaign—some estimates run into the hundreds of millions—a great deal probably never reaches the voters. Its distribution is both a wearisome and costly task. If it is mailed, a large outlay for postage and clerical labor is required. If it is entrusted to party workers for distribution, it may not be distributed, for the party organization is seldom as efficient as it is reputed to be. Shipments of literature in bulk to state committees often stop at state headquarters. Louis Howe, secretary to Franklin Roosevelt, found that only about 3 to 5 per cent of the literature distributed to state committees by national headquarters ever reached the voters. In the 1932 Democratic campaign the national committee sent a few pieces of each kind of literature to each of about 140,000 local committeemen instead of depending on state committees to distribute bulk shipments to precinct workers. In 1952 the Republican national committee distributed to state and local committees catalogs in which items of literature were listed along with indications of where to buy it. In 1960 the Democrats made use of the same technique. If local committees buy their literature, they should be more disposed to exert themselves to distribute it.

RADIO AND TELEVISION   Television and radio have reduced the press to a secondary role in the calculations of the managers of presidential campaigns. These new communications media give the candidate direct access to the people of the nation. He can speak to the voters with no fear that his remarks will be misrepresented by the headline writers or buried on the back pages. If he is a skilled performer and the party war chest allows, he can use television and radio to counterbalance newspaper opposition. Moreover, radio and television, in their capacity as reporters of the news, are under more of a compulsion than the press to give an even-handed account of events.

Television and radio have imposed new requirements upon campaigners and campaigning. Doubtless the radio or television presentation reaches a far larger proportion of the electorate and brings into the political audience a far wider variety of people than ever came within earshot of the old-time political orator. Radio and television speeches must be far more simply put and far shorter than the old-fashioned political speech if the attention of the audience is to be held. The new media also require a mastery of speaking techniques and practices unlike those of the bellowing orator with windmill arms. The persuasive affirmations of the seductive radio voice are more likely to be accepted than are the same words in print.[41] Television has also brought experimentation with propaganda presentations in forms other than the traditional political speech. Spectacles involving the participation of drum majorettes, Hollywood starlets, bogus farmers, and file clerks from the model agencies, with an occasional word by the candidate, are produced for the edification of the multitude. Even the lowly singing commercial has been impressed into the service of politics.

Obviously the new media require at campaign headquarters technical specialists in addition to speech writers. They also pose new problems of tactics as well as new opportunities to reach the people. In 1952, for example, the Democrats made extensive use of television, beginning early in the campaign in order to overcome the handicap from the fact that Stevenson was comparatively unknown. Eisenhower, on the other hand, had not yet developed a television technique, and it was calculated that barnstorming would be advantageous to enable as many voters as possible to see the General's folksy manner at first hand. Beyond such questions that grow out of the circumstances of specific campaigns are numerous problems of technique in the use of television and radio, such as the timing of presentations, the relative emphasis on spot announcements and set speeches, and the minimization of interference with popular programs of entertainment.

Although television by 1960 had had a powerful impact on campaigning for the Presidency, its full effects have not been systematically identified. One consequence that seems indisputable is that individuals can by dramatic

---

[41] Note the comment of an Illinois farmer: "Sometimes when I listen to Roosevelt I even get to thinking he's right and all the time I know he's wrong." Paul F. Lazarsfeld and F. N. Stanton (eds.), *Radio Research, 1941* (New York: Duell, Sloan and Pearce, 1941), p. 267.

television performances attain a national recognition and attract a national following much more rapidly than by reliance on older communications media. Through the televising of his crime investigations, Senator Estes Kefauver became a national figure almost overnight and a contender for the Democratic presidential nomination in 1952 and 1956. Whether television facilitates the manipulation of the electorate by campaigners remains open to doubt; yet its existence compels campaigners to adapt their styles to it.[42] Nor has television supplanted other media as a source of information, though it is regarded as their most important source of campaign information by far more people than is any other medium.

THE ''GREAT DEBATES''   A major innovation in the use of television occurred in 1960 in a series of joint appearances by Vice President Nixon and Senator Kennedy. Of the four broadcasts two were in the form of debates interspersed with questions by reporters, and two consisted of questions put by reporters with answers and comments by each candidate. The "format" of the "debates" left something to be desired. The brevity of the presentations by the candidates prevented adequate development of their positions, and the reporters' questions demonstrated that reportorial interrogation was no way to advance the discussion. Nevertheless, the joint appearances vastly enlarged the size of the public attentive to campaign discussion and enabled each candidate to reach large numbers of persons who would otherwise never have seen him. Both the novelty of the programs and the fact that all networks carried them attracted an extremely large audience —an average of 71,000,000 for each debate. In contrast, paid political broadcasts in 1960 usually attracted an audience less than three-fourths the size of the audience of the entertainment programs they replaced. Probably more important was the fact that the joint appearances changed the nature of the audience. Ordinarily broadcasts reach in larger degree the faithful supporters of a candidate than those he wishes to convert. The joint appearance meant that many Democrats listened to Nixon and many Republicans to Kennedy who would under conventional practice have limited their viewing to their own party's candidate.[43]

POLITICAL RALLIES: THE PERSONAL TOUCH   Radio and television are no substitute for the old-fashioned political rally in which

[42] An analysis of Iowa counties with high television density and of counties with little television coverage in 1952 indicated that no significant difference either in voting turnout or in party division of the vote existed between the two sets of counties. H. A. Simon and F. Stern, "The Effect of Television Upon Voting Behavior in Iowa in the 1952 Presidential Election," *American Political Science Review*, 49 (1955), 470–77.

[43] See Sidney Kraus (ed.), *The Great Debates* (Bloomington: Indiana University Press, 1962) ; Earl Mazo, *et al.*, *The Great Debates* (Santa Barbara: Center for the Study of Democratic Institutions, 1962) ; S. Kelley, Jr., "Campaign Debates: Some Facts and Issues," *Public Opinion Quarterly*, 26 (1962), 351–66.

the candidate can be seen and heard; the tactical problem in campaigning has been to contrive ways and means of combining the personal touch of the rally with the marvels of electronic communication. The psychological evidence indicates that individuals in crowds are rendered suggestible, the applause picking up the doubters in the audience and carrying them along. Listeners to a radio speech, perhaps alone or only a handful of persons, lack the emotional stimulus of the crowd. Television adds the bearing, the gestures, the smiles of the speaker to the voice of radio, but the "personality" of the candidate may not be conveyed through the image on the television screen.

The 1956 campaign provided a test of some of these considerations. Republican campaign planners early hoped to limit Eisenhower to a few high-level speeches from television studios. This sort of presentation turned out to be deadly. A revision of tactics substituted telecasts of the candidate as he spoke to rallies. In this way the cheers of the throng go out over the air and perhaps give televiewers the illusion that they are themselves in the audience, thereby subjecting them to some of the emotional impact of audience participation. Yet the speaker before a great rally must adapt his delivery to the fact that most of his auditors are not in the hall but are in small groups before receivers scattered over the country.

The experience of 1956 confirmed an earlier judgment of James A. Farley who conceded that radio was a "tremendous factor" in the Roosevelt political fortunes, but, who also said, "to my way of thinking, there is no substitute for the personal touch and there never will be, unless the Lord starts to make human beings different from the way he makes them now." The participation of the candidate in parades and rallies permits great numbers of people to see him and probably also helps maintain the zeal and enthusiasm of party workers. At any rate, party managers work on the theory that television has not made barnstorming obsolete. The airplane and television have only modified the conditions of campaigning.

Whatever its effects on the voter, speaking at the crossroads and in the city squares has its values for the candidate. As he travels from place to place and delivers his speech, he samples public response. One line, he discovers, falls flat; another evokes cheers. This phrase commands attention; another seems not to be comprehended. The audience feedback enables the candidate to perfect his appeals and to acquire a sense of the temper of the people; television cameras cannot talk back. When the candidate does go on television, his speeches have been to an extent pretested at the whistle stops.

Effects of Campaigns

Presidential campaigns culminate in the great decisions of the American democratic order. The spectacle of a campaign—with its hullabaloo, its nonsense, its fabrications, its exaggerations—raises doubts among the faint-hearted whether the Republic can long survive, whether the electorate can make its decisions in the national interest. Do clever rhetoricians manipulate and deceive the voters? Do special interests as they work through the parties manage to induce voters to tolerate intolerable privilege, to vote against themselves? Do charismatic candidates flimflam the public? Do appeals to ignorance and prejudice move the electorate to decide on the basis of considerations irrelevant either to its own interest or to the public weal? Are voters swayed by promises of unattainable achievements to be forgotten no sooner than the crowd of glib rascals gets into office?

All such questions go to the heart of the democratic process, and their answers are by no means obvious. Certainly on occasion propaganda artists bunco the voters into electing both scoundrels and incompetents. Privileged groups have successfully defended almost interminably positions seriously detrimental to great numbers of citizens. Reckless campaigners have even poisoned the minds of the people against policies necessary for national security. Such occurrences generate anxieties about the capacity for people for self-government, which are not to be allayed entirely by the observation that despite all these things the Republic has survived. Yet the actions of voters may be better appraised if they are placed in a broader context than the campaign itself. People make the great decisions of self-government by choosing among alternatives put forward by the party system. Those decisions can be no better, no wiser than the choices put to the voters. The record of popular decision may be quite as good as the record of the national leadership, the so-called wiser and better people, in the proposal of alternatives.

Judgments about the nature of the popular electoral decision rest in high degree upon intuitive judgment. The hard knowledge about the interaction between campaigner and the voter is thin, yet enough systematic inquiry has been done to help put the role of campaigning in perspective.[44] A basic fact is that campaigners do not write on a clean slate. They approach an electorate whose group loyalties and policy orientations were fixed rather firmly long before the campaign. Rather than a volatile electorate, we have one not easily moved by the appeals of campaign orators. This quality of the electorate, which may be of fundamental import for the nature of the American polity,[45] manifests itself in the fact that perhaps three-fourths of the voters

[44] Studies that throw light on the matter include Paul F. Lazarsfeld, Bernard Berelson, and Hazel Gaudet, *The People's Choice* (New York: Duell, Sloan and Pearce, 1944); Bernard Berelson, Paul F. Lazarsfeld, and W. N. McPhee, *Voting* (Chicago: University of Chicago Press, 1954); Angus Campbell, *et al., The American Voter* (New York: Wiley, 1960); S. Kelley, Jr., *Political Campaigning* (Washington: Brookings Institution, 1960).

[45] Contrast the French situation as reported by P. E. Converse and Georges Dupeux, "Politicization of the Electorate in France and the United States," *Public Opinion Quarterly*, 26 (1962), 1–23.

remain loyal to the same party's presidential candidate from one election to the next.

The blandishments of the campaigner are also often outweighed in their influence upon the voter by the impact of events. In some presidential elections more votes are won or lost before the campaign begins, even before the nominations are made, than are affected by the campaign itself. In an intensive study of Erie County, Ohio, a sampling of the electorate indicated that the change in sentiment from November, 1936, to May, 1940, accounted for twice as many votes as did the impact of the 1940 campaign. The events that impel the voter in one direction or another may be remote or immediate. People experience or observe immediate events at first hand; remote events have their impact through the mass media. Large-scale economic deprivation, for example, may be immediately perceptible to many people and have its effects on their voting. Remote events are perceived through the mass media, and in such matters the slant given the picture of the world by the media may govern the effects, if any, of events upon voting.

Diehard partisans may remain unmoved by opposition oratory and events may fix many voting decisions, yet campaigns undoubtedly have their effects. Lazarsfeld has identified three of them: re-enforcement, activation, and conversion. Re-enforcement is the effect of the campaign in strengthening the loyalties of the devoted partisans. The campaign helps keep up the courage of those whose minds are already made up. The staunch Republican or Democrat exposes himself largely to propaganda favorable to his viewpoint and thereby reassures himself of the soundness of his judgment. A substantial decline in the number of dedicated partisans in the electorate might, by increasing the proportions susceptible to campaign propaganda, alter the character of American politics. Activation consists in arousing the interest of persons indifferent at the outset of the campaign and in inducing them to vote. They tend to vote in the direction that might have been predicted on the basis of their personal characteristics. Crystallization of the views of the indifferent and undecided may determine the outcome of an election.

The numbers of voters converted by the campaign may be small but sufficient to swing the election one way or the other. Sample surveys provide some measure of the magnitude of shifts in voter affections during campaigns; the essence of the knowledge on the point is that the size of the shifting group of voters differs from campaign to campaign. In 1940, the evidence seems to indicate, the results of the presidential election would have been the same had it been held in August rather than in November. In 1948, on the other hand, the campaign apparently won the election for Truman. The net effect of the shifts of voters during the last weeks of the campaign moved the Democrats ahead of the Republicans, who led in the early stages; possibly the more the voters saw of Mr. Dewey the better Harry Truman looked. In 1952 General Eisenhower led in the sample surveys as the campaign began, and all the ballyhoo had no substantial net effect on the division of the electorate.

These kinds of analyses that identify with fair precision some effects of campaigning may lead to a complacent view of the state of the practice of democracy. It may well turn out that the capacity of people to govern themselves and of popular institutions to shape questions for popular decision will in the future be subjected to far more severe tests than they have been in the past. The increasing salience of problems outside the immediate experience of the voter tends to increase his dependence on the media. The controllers of the media, as well as political campaigners, come to be equipped with both instruments and propaganda techniques more suited to manipulation of the mass from central points of power. These and other tendencies will doubtless make the maintenance of civic intelligence a problem of profound continuing significance.[46]

[46] This chapter has been directed toward presidential campaigns. An additional range of practice and probably sharply differing patterns of electoral behavior prevail in many state and local campaigns. See, for example, Paul F. Lazarsfeld and Morris Rosenberg, "The Contribution of the Regional Poll to Political Understanding," *Public Opinion Quarterly*, 13 (1949–50), 569–86; C. E. Parker, "Polling Problems in State Primary Elections," *Public Opinion Quarterly*, 12 (1948–49), 728–31.

18.

PARTY FINANCE

THOSE RESPONSIBLE for the conduct of campaigns, be they party chairmen, party committees, or candidates, must raise substantial sums to meet the legitimate costs of presenting their case to the electorate. Neither major party possesses an adequate stable income from regular contributions by dues-paying members. Instead, as each campaign rolls around the American party manager must engage anew in heroic efforts to raise large sums. He may be able to tap a goodly number of reliable partisans who contribute from campaign to campaign; he must also search out new prospects who may be responsive to the appeals of his party or candidate under the circumstances of the moment. If he is seeking to finance a campaign for a presidential nomination, he has no list of regular givers to approach. The collection endeavor must be organized *ad hoc* and directed to those potential contributors to whom the would-be nominee may be attractive.

Fund-raisers, whatever worthy cause they promote, share the vicissitudes common to their calling, namely, the difficulties of separating the solvent citizen from his cash. Those who endeavor to fill the party coffers must cope, in addition, with special problems. Though contributing to political parties may be quite as honorable in motive as alms-giving, that fact has not been impressed upon the public consciousness. Political gifts tend to be regarded by many persons as the purchase of a lien on a candidate, a belief that often deprives the party fund-raiser of the leverage that might come from appeals to patriotism and civic spirit. As the fund-raiser seeks to obtain the necessary money without mortgaging his candidate's future actions, he must conform also with laws designed to control the suspect operation of political finance,

486

laws which, if followed literally, would at times make it virtually impossible to finance campaigns.[1]

Magnitude and Nature of Campaign Costs

Although the data on campaign finance suffice to support some observations about trends in total campaign costs, about costs of particular sorts of campaigns, and about the purposes for which the money goes, perhaps the most significant conclusion from the data is that it takes a lot of money to elect the representatives of the people. Large sums are required to meet the costs of presenting on even a modest scale the cause of a presidential candidate to an electorate of a hundred million people. Campaigns for lesser offices cost less, yet the candidates and managers concerned face a formidable task in raising the necessary money.

TOTAL OUTLAYS FOR CAMPAIGNING   So numerous are the committees making campaign expenditures and so incomplete are the reports on their finances that figures on the total cost of political activities in the United States must be estimated rather than compiled. Alexander Heard, after the most thorough examination of the data that has yet been made, estimated that the cash expenditures for nominating and electing all public officials was around $140,000,000 in 1952 and $155,000,000 in 1956. On the same basis, Herbert E. Alexander estimated 1960 political costs at $175,000,000.[2] In addition, campaign managers receive the volunteer services of workers and contributions of other things of value—space, the use of automobiles, and the like. While these overall estimates may be in error by several million dollars in one direction or the other, checks against expenditure reports known to be fairly complete for specific jurisdictions provide the basis for some confidence in them. The 1952 estimate works out to about $1.42 per potential voter; that for 1960, to $1.64. The aggregate expended in the year of a presidential election may seem huge, yet it probably does

[1] The standard work on party finance is Alexander Heard, *The Costs of Democracy* (Chapel Hill: University of North Carolina Press, 1960); also available in condensed form in paperback (Doubleday-Anchor, A288). Congressional Quarterly News Features assembles, after each election, data from reports of expenditures filed by candidates and campaign committees; the resulting analyses may be found in the *Congressional Quarterly Almanac* or in the Quarterly's *Weekly Report*. On party finance in the 1956 campaign, see U.S. Senate, 84th Cong., 2d sess., Subcommittee on Privileges and Elections of the Committee on Rules and Administration, *Hearings on 1956 Presidential and Senatorial Campaign Practices* (1956) and the report of the same committee on *1956 General Election Campaigns* (1957). These items are cited hereafter as Gore Committee, *Hearings* and *Report*.

[2] H. E. Alexander, "Financing the Parties and Campaigns," in Paul T. David (ed.), *The Presidential Election and Transition, 1960–1961* (Washington: Brookings Institution, 1961), pp. 116–49.

not exceed the total of the annual advertising bills of the principal soap companies.

COSTS BY LEVEL OF GOVERNMENT   While the figures on aggregate expenditures tell us something about the magnitude of the problem of party finance, one would like to know what it costs to get elected to a particular office. That question, though, is, given the organization of American politics, if not a nonsense question, a nice problem in cost accounting. The simultaneous conduct of interrelated campaigns for many offices makes it impossible, even if all the expenditures by all campaign committees were known, to allocate costs among the campaigns for individual offices. Expenditures by the national committees are devoted primarily to the presidential campaign, but the presidential candidate may be expected to use a little television time to say a good word about the congressional and senatorial candidates on the ticket. The state committees of the parties usually make substantial expenditures in support of the party slate as a whole. County committees conduct campaigns in support of candidates for national, state, and local office. Individual candidates often spend large sums to get themselves elected, but their activities may benefit their running mates on the party ticket as well.

Though the cost of a particular campaign may be impossible to ascertain, estimates may be made of expenditures by campaign committees and agencies at different levels of government. Professor Heard estimates that 14 per cent of the $140,000,000 spent during the entire year of 1952 consisted of expenditures by the national party committees and other national committees; 48 per cent, by party and nonparty committees operating on a statewide basis; and 38 per cent, for local and district activities. These proportions are for the nation as a whole; among the states the division between state and local costs varies on both sides of the national average.

In the 1960 campaign, outlays by national-level committees amounted to approximately $25,000,000. This sum was about equally divided between Republican and Democratic committees, though the Democrats achieved parity only by incurring a debt of $3.8 million, probably the largest deficit in the history of presidential campaigns. Thus, a party's national committee and its allied committees at the national level need to be able to assemble at least ten or twelve million dollars in the year of a presidential campaign.

Before a man must worry about financing a presidential campaign he must become a nominee and preconvention campaigns are costly, at least in the pecuniary calculus of the average man. Eisenhower supporters spent in the neighborhood of $2.5 million to obtain the Republican nomination for him in 1952, a sum about matched by the war chest of the Taft forces. Estimates that excluded some state and local spending placed the cost of Kennedy's 1960 preconvention campaign at slightly over $1,000,000, while in a cause that turned out to be hopeless, Senator Hubert Humphrey managed to spend $250,000. Expenditures in Nixon's virtually unchallenged quest for the nomination probably amounted to $500,000. When a presidential nomination is contested, a man cannot aspire to be a serious contender unless he can attract well over a million dollars, save under the most exceptional circumstances, such as the 1952 nomination of Stevenson.

"The figure used in any discussion of the cost of campaigning for a Senate seat," says Senator Neuberger, "is usually about $200,000 for an average state, and $1 million for a larger one." [3] Primary campaigns may run up the costs. In 1926 Frank L. Smith won the Illinois nomination for Senator in a primary that involved the expenditure of slightly more than $1,000,000 about equally divided between Smith and his opponent. At the time such sums were thought to be scandalously large, but expenditures of quite imposing totals are now commonplace. The 1952 Massachusetts Senate race by John F. Kennedy cost at least $350,000.[4]

Costs in gubernatorial campaigns are probably of the same general order as senatorial campaign costs, though the high stakes of the game may drive up the costs of the contest for the statehouse. In 1960 in Florida, a state with exceptionally complete reporting, the total expended in the first and second primaries on behalf of candidates for the Democratic gubernatorial nominee was $1,748,000. In 1962 Republicans spent over $2,200,000 to re-elect Nelson Rockefeller as governor of New York, while the weak Democratic efforts on behalf of Robert M. Morgenthau cost over $420,000. Newspapermen estimated that about $2,000,000 went into the 1959 contest for the Kentucky Democratic gubernatorial nomination between Bert T. Combs and Harry Lee Waterfield. In the 1962 California Republican gubernatorial primary, reported expenditures on behalf of Richard Nixon were $453,000; of Joseph Shell, $532,000. Governor Edmond Brown spent $449,000 in his campaign for renomination in the Democratic primary. Costs of mayoralty campaigns in large cities are at times impressive. Reported expenditures on behalf of Robert Wagner in New York City in 1961 were over $1,000,000, while those for Louis J. Lefkowitz, the Republican candidate, were only slightly less.

Given the unsatisfactory state of financial reporting, the costs of campaigns for the House of Representatives are not known with any precision. Outlays by a single candidate of $50,000 or over are not at all uncommon. On the other hand, from time to time a Senator or a Representative avers, probably truthfully, that he has obtained renomination and re-election without the expenditure of more than a few hundred dollars. In one-party areas well-established incumbents may not face a challenge sufficiently serious to require that a real campaign be mounted.[5]

[3] *Congressional Record* (daily ed.), April 12, 1961, p. 5255.
[4] See Hugh Douglas Price, "Campaign Finance in Massachusetts," *Public Policy*, VI (1955), 25–46.
[5] For the most extensive compilation of expenditure data, see Gore Committee, *Report*. Less complete information for 1960 may be found in *Congressional Quarterly Weekly Report*, June 30, 1961.

VARIATIONS IN TOTAL EXPENDITURES   Total expenditures doubtless vary from election to election both within the nation and within individual states and districts. Doubtless also, these differences are associated with varying characteristics of campaigns, though the data are too fragmentary to demonstrate those relationships conclusively. Yet certain factors seem to be responsible for gross differences in outlay. The perceived stakes of an election and the intensity of the feelings it arouses may bear on the level of expenditure. When a popular candidate threatens to upset applecarts, those who are fearful about their applecarts are likely to be generous in their contributions to his opponent. The presidential campaign of 1896, for example, excited both the anxieties and the generosities of the corporate interests. On the other hand, if feelings are not intense or if the outcome of the election seems to be foreordained, party treasurers may have much greater difficulty in raising funds and perhaps not so much will be spent.

The chances are that per capita expenditure varies with the character of campaign organization. In some jurisdictions the party conducts a unified campaign in support of all the candidates on the ticket. In others, it is every man for himself, with each candidate having his own campaign organization and publicity program. The odds are that a common campaign can be carried on at a lower cost than can a series of independent campaigns for every man on the ticket. Whether party committees conducting unified campaigns invariably achieve the economies of scale is another question.

The character of party organization may also bear significantly on the costs of campaign for nomination. In jurisdictions with weak or divided party organizations warm primary contests tend to be the rule and they may be quite costly for the contenders. On the other hand, when the party organization unites behind candidates, whether nominations be by convention or by primary, outlays for campaigns for nomination tend to be less. Nomination costs also differ widely with circumstances. The spirited contest for the Republican presidential nomination in 1952 involved outlays of several million dollars; Mr. Eisenhower's renomination in 1956 was not expensive.

The character of the constituency may affect campaign costs. To reach the voters in a metropolitan district may be more expensive than in a rural district. Urban politicians meet powerful nonpolitical competition for the attention of the public; probably a congressional or senatorial campaign is more salient in the field of attention of a rural than a metropolitan constituency. Or, the candidates for mayor in a small town may have been known for years to most of the voters in the town; the mayoral candidate in a metropolis ordinarily has to spend a good deal of money to make his name, as well as his merits, known to his fellow citizens.

In some instances the availability of funds rather than the necessities of the campaign lead to exceptionally heavy expenditures. At best campaign managers must judge the wisdom of expenditures by hunch and they are beset on every side by proposals to spend. When they happen to have a candidate of great means, or a candidate who has access to large resources, they find ways to spend whatever is available.

OBJECTS OF EXPENDITURE   Though the sums known to have been spent by individual candidates and committees may seem enormous, inspection of the costs of types of campaign activity makes it clear that campaign managers must incur large obligations to meet even the minimum necessities. The chances are also that over the past 50 years changes in the nature of political activity have increased the relative importance of campaign activities that have to be paid for in hard cash.

A major item in the budgets of national and state campaign committees consists of outlays for publicity in its many forms. The long-term trend in the distribution of campaign expenditures has probably been toward the use of a larger and larger proportion of the available funds for publicity. This development has paralleled the rise of new media for propaganda, such as radio and television.

Radio and television expenditures bulk especially large at the national level in a presidential campaign. Almost one-third of the outlays of national level campaign committees in 1956 went for radio and television. It requires little ingenuity to run up a big bill for radio and television time. In 1952 the Citizens for Eisenhower paid $267,000 for an election-eve broadcast that lasted an hour and a half. By 1956, to hire the complete radio and television facilities on NBC for a half-hour would use up most of $100,000. Richard Nixon's four-hour afternoon telethon just before election day in 1960 cost about $200,000. The combined television expenditures of both parties on behalf of their presidential candidates on the day before the 1960 election amounted to over $500,000.

The most complete data on radio and television costs during a campaign were compiled by a Senate committee in 1956. The committee, instead of relying on the reports of campaign committees, obtained reports from the networks and from radio and television stations of their sales of time during the period September 1 through November 6. They sold almost $10,000,000 worth of time during this period to candidates and political committees. This total thus excluded the expenditures in the primaries and in such general election activity as occurred before September 1. The comparable figure for 1960 was slightly over $14,000,000.

State and local campaign committees place heavier emphasis on newspaper advertising than do national committees. A survey of political advertising in 410 newspapers from July 1 to November 30, 1956, produced an estimate that political committees spent $4,280,000 for newspaper advertising during that period. Payments to lesser newspapers are sometimes said to be for editorial support. The foreign language press and the Negro press especially have gained the reputation of susceptibility to offers of advertising in exchange for editorial endorsement.[6]

Other forms of publicity account for smaller proportions of the campaign budget, yet their use requires substantial sums. During the 1956 campaign 25 outdoor advertising companies sold over $500,000 worth of billboard space to campaign committees. Use of direct-mail publicity can become costly. The postage cost alone on a first-class mailing to 100,000 voters would be $5,000. Printing, addressing, and other costs would doubtless be double or triple the postage cost. Lithographs, photographs, and campaign novelties add to publicity costs. In 1940 the Republican national committee spent $48,000 for Willkie buttons.

Overhead expenses include a variety of miscellaneous costs. The staff of the party committee, maintained year in and year out, must be augmented at campaign time. Nonparty committees recruit staffs for the duration of the campaign. Costs of special trains for the presidential candidate, of chartered planes, and of travel for field workers and for speakers must be covered. Postage, rental of quarters, equipment, telephone, telegraph, and express add to the overhead. Seemingly inconsequential items can account for large sums. The cost of preparing and mailing a single printed letter to each registered voter of New York City is said to be $250,000.

Election-day expenses are heavy for city and county organizations. The polls must be manned with watchers; runners are needed to bring out the voters; men and women must be stationed near the polling places to distribute literature and sample ballots; automobiles must be on call to transport voters to the polls. Lavish expenditures for election-day work at times closely approach bribery; the worker traditionally has been expected to vote right and to induce his family, friends, and relatives to do the same. The level of election-day outlays differs widely from place to place. In some communities and neighborhoods the party committee may need $100 or more per precinct for primary or election day. In others, this sort of expense may be negligible. In some types of precincts volunteer workers may readily be enlisted for the chores of election day; in others, greater reliance is placed on paid workers.

The financial transactions of many party and campaign committees include sums that the committee itself does not spend directly but disburses to other committees. These payments from committee to committee usually serve the purpose of transferring money to those points where the need is presumably greatest. State and local committees often make payments to the national committee. A national-level committee will make subventions to state

---

[6] In 1944 practically all expenditures for newspaper advertising by the Democratic national committee went to newspapers of racial groups. The major portion went to the Negro press. C. W. Smith, Jr., "Campaign Communications Media," *The Annals,* 259 (September, 1948), 90–97.

committees, to senatorial committees, or to House candidates. Labor committees usually collect funds and make transfers to party and campaign committees. Some committees, particularly on the Republican side, exist primarily
to collect funds and then parcel out the proceeds among operating committees.

TRENDS IN COSTS   Even though the data on party finance are
too thin to show trends accurately, it seems plain enough that over the past
half-century the problems of financing political activity have changed in nature. The rapid growth of the electorate has brought an increase in outlays.
The rise in the price level has boosted the costs of services that party committees must buy. The managers of campaigns, be they concerned with national, state, or local elections, must raise far larger sums than they did 50
or even 20 years ago. Yet the available information, such as it is, does not
support the notion that aggregate real costs per voter have substantially
increased in recent decades.

Even if costs per voter have not grown markedly, campaign managers
must raise large sums to meet the costs of new styles of campaigning. The
most striking change in the mode of campaigning is the increased reliance
on the media of communication. In an earlier day speeches by presidential
candidates and aspirants for lesser office as well were more noteworthy events
than they now seem to be. Voters assembled from miles around to listen to
the interminable oratory of their political idols. Nowadays the campaign
treasurer still has to finance the travels of his candidate over the country, but
he must also raise the money to put the show on television and radio networks.[7] Probably the communications revolution has had less of an impact
on congressional campaigning than on the budget of presidential campaign
committees. The same probably applies to many campaigns in smaller electoral units. A mayoral candidate in a great city may find television an efficient way to speak to the voters, but the candidate for a state legislative post
from a district within the same city would ordinarily get more for his money
by spending it in other ways.

Other changes have also created new needs even if they do not invariably
create readily identifiable new items in the campaign budget. The long-run
decline of the avowedly partisan press has deprived campaigners of that
assured channel to the electorate; to achieve an equivalent impact on the
voter other species of propaganda need to be used.

Changes in party organization itself have created new problems of cam-

---

[7] Richard L. Neuberger quotes the reminiscence of a former governor of Oregon:
"I was elected with $3,000. All the money came from my own bank account and that of
one friend. Today $3,000 would just about buy you half an hour on a state-wide radio
hookup. Folks once came from miles around by horse and buckboard to attend a political rally. Now they wait for you to go into their homes by radio and newspaper
advertising or direct mail. That takes a lot of money." "It Costs Too Much to Run For
Office," *New York Times Magazine,* April 11, 1948.

paign finance. The odds are that over a half-century the party organizations have declined in vitality. In place after place, the coverage of the city with precinct executives, often supported by the public payroll, has become quite incomplete. While the character of the standing party organizations differs greatly from locality to locality, probably for the country as a whole its functions have come more and more to be performed in ways that require cash outlays.[8] Moreover, the rise of the direct primary has introduced an important new element of cost into politics. Campaigns for delegates to nominating conventions were doubtless at times costly, but certainly the modern primary campaign has made the process of nomination more expensive.

Raising the Money

Few unsolicited contributions arrive at party headquarters. A handful of devoted souls send their checks at campaign time without prompting. Many others who give regularly must be reminded to do so. Still others must be cajoled into doing their financial duty to their party.

The problem of raising money to support political activity is not entirely one of party finance but in large measure one of financing individual candidates. In this county and that, one or the other of the parties may succeed in monopolizing the collection of funds; the party committee conducts a party campaign and doles out funds as it wishes for the separable costs of individual candidates. In substantial degree, however, American politics is atomized and each candidate must in some way or another cover his own campaign expenses. The problem of the individual candidate is most marked in campaigns for nomination; there funds must be raised not to support the party but Elmer Snodgrass in particular. The ability to raise the money to finance a primary campaign thus may become an absolute requisite for a serious fight for a contested nomination. At the general election appeals for funds may be made in the name of the party and that appeal has some effect. Yet so individualized is American politics that in most states each candidate for an important office usually operates a substantial campaign effort independently of that of the party organization.

PARTISAN CONTRASTS IN SOURCES   Given the variety of candidates for whom committees and managers raise funds, many kinds of sources are tapped for contributions. This candidate for the Senate may be able to draw on labor funds; that candidate may have a special appeal to oil

---

[8] The testimony also seems to be that the election-day expenditures that approach bribery, that is, the hiring of "workers" who were expected to deliver their vote and a few others, has declined. Full employment and inflation reduce the persuasive power of a 10-dollar bill.

men. Another may have a following among merchants. One candidate for governor may draw heavy financial support from the liquor interests. One candidate for the House may have banking support; another may have had a wealthy father. Commonly a candidate relies upon many sources. The element of personal friendship may be of great importance in the raising of money for a candidate, especially in primary campaigns.

Little or no systematic information is to be had about the sources of contributions to most campaigns. Considerable analysis has been made of the sources of contributions to national committees. The findings, in essence, seem to be that each party draws heavily on those elements of society traditionally associated with it. Though party spokesmen, both Democratic and Republican, love to discourse upon the universality of the appeal of their party, the hard fact seems to be that the money comes in the main from those whose interests are thought to be tied to the party's cause. While the same general rule probably holds for contributors to the funds of candidates for other offices, the data have not been put together to demonstrate it.

Differences in the sources to which the parties have access appear in a dramatic form from an analysis of the contributions of officers and directors of the great corporations during the 1956 campaign. Gifts of $500 or more known to have been made by such persons aggregated more than $1,900,000, of which more than $1,800,000 went to Republican campaigns and around $100,000 to Democrats, the latter scarcely enough to cover the postage bill of the national committee. Table 18.1 shows the approximate

Table 18.1   Division between Republican and Democratic campaigns of yield of reported contributions of $500 or more in 1956 from officers and directors of types of business enterprises [a]

Type of Enterprise	Republican	Democratic
225 largest corporations	94.6%	5.4%
29 largest oil companies	95.9	4.1
10 leading radio and television stations	97.4	2.6
17 certified airlines	80.7	19.3 [b]
37 advertising agencies	100.0	0.0
47 underwriters of bonds	99.2	0.8

[a] Derived from Gore Committee, *Report.*
[b] Most of the deviation of the airline category from the general pattern was accounted for by Democratic contributions by R. J. Reynolds, a director of Delta Airlines. Air transport is one of Mr. Reynolds' lesser business interests.

percentage division between Democratic and Republican campaigns of the yield of contributions of $500 or over by officers and directors of various types of business enterprises.

Democratic fund-raisers make little headway among the industrial elite as represented by the officers of the great corporations, but this should not be taken to mean that they receive no financial support from business. Their generous givers simply tend to be different from those whose financial affections lean Republican. They are infrequently connected with the great corporations; they are usually associated with smaller business enterprises; and they are likely to be from types of business with a peculiar tie to the Democratic party. These contrasts are brought out by the data of Table 18.2, which

Table 18.2   Percentages of total contributions from gifts of $1,000 or more to Democratic and Republican presidential campaigns from persons identified with various economic pursuits, 1932, 1940, and 1944

| | 1932 [a] | | 1940 [b] | | 1944 [c] | |
Source	D	R	D	R	D	R
Bankers, brokers, manufacturers, oil, mining, utilities, real estate, insurance	45.2	60.6	21.1	57.0	24.3	59.4
Brewers, distillers, soft drinks, contractors, builders, building materials, publishers, radio, advertising, amusements, professions, officeholders, merchants	21.7	11.0	46.8	9.2	46.2	15.6
Others and unidentifiable	33.1	28.4	32.1	33.8	29.5	25.0

[a] Derived from data presented by Louise Overacker, "Campaign Funds in a Depression Year," *American Political Science Review*, 27 (1933), 776. The percentages are based on gifts to the national committees.

[b] Derived from data presented by Overacker, "Campaign Finance in the Presidential Election of 1940," *American Political Science Review*, 35 (1941), 723. In this table the gifts from organized labor included in the original tabulation were omitted to obtain comparability with the 1932 and 1944 figures. The figures for 1940 are based on contributions to the national committees.

[c] Derived from data presented by Overacker, "Presidential Campaign Funds, 1944," *American Political Science Review*, 39 (1945), 916. These figures include gifts of $1,000 or more to the national committees and to certain related organizations as well.

indicates the proportion of the yield of gifts of over $1,000 for each party derived from broad types of contributors. In 1940 and 1944 a far larger proportion of the Republican collections in sums of $1,000 or more came from bankers, brokers, manufacturers, and utility men. Democrats obtained a larger proportion of their funds from a varied array including brewers, distillers, contractors, merchants, officeholders, and men connected with the building materials industry. The metropolitan wing of the Democratic party has long had its affiliations with the liquor business. Any party in power becomes attractive to contractors and it is, of course, in a position superior to that of the outs in the solicitation of officeholders. The table shows, too, the sharp relative decline in Democratic reliance on bankers, brokers, manufacturers, and the like after 1932. Contributions by persons in these categories to the Democratic cause dropped abruptly between 1932 and 1936 as the New Deal drew more clearly the lines of political battle.

Contributions from labor groups go to support Democratic campaign efforts in about the same degree that funds from corporation officials go to the Republicans. Seventeen national labor organizations reported political expenditures of $2,156,000 from January 1 to November 30, 1956. Of this sum, $540,000 was spent directly, chiefly for publicity, and the remainder went as contributions to national, state, and local campaign committees, chiefly Democratic. A Senate committee obtained reports from 171 state and local labor organizations whose expenditures from September 1 to November 30, 1956 amounted to $830,000. About one-half of this sum was spent directly while the remainder was transferred to other campaign committees, most of which were Democratic.[9] In 1960 the gross reported expenditures of national-level labor groups amounted to about $2,300,000. The reports of the principal labor groups indicated that they had contributed to the campaigns of 195 Democratic and 6 Republican House candidates; to 20 Democratic and 2 Republican senatorial candidates.[10]

BIG AND LITTLE GIVERS   Both Democrats and Republicans rely upon large gifts for the bulk of their campaign funds. In 1952, according to Professor Heard's analysis, gifts of over $500 comprised 68 per cent of the receipts of 18 national-level Republican committees and 63 per cent of the funds of 15 national-level Democratic committees. In 1936, 1,945 contributors of over $1,000 furnished almost half the total receipts of the major-party national committees. Probably state and local campaign committees depend to a lesser degree on large gifts, though instances occur in which a handful of donors provide most of the substantial sum required to run for the Senate or for a governorship.

Scraps of evidence suggest that dependence of national campaigns on an extremely few extremely large contributions is not so marked as it once was. Thus, in 1918 Will Hays needed $300,000 to get the Republican congressional campaign under way. He went to New York to have a word with William

---

[9] Gore Committee, *Report,* pp. 45–48.

[10] For contrasts in fund sources in a single state, see J. P. White and J. R. Owens, *Parties, Group Interests and Campaign Finance: Michigan '56* (Princeton: Citizens' Research Foundation, 1960).

Boyce Thompson who, Hays said, responded without hesitation: "Tell Senator Smoot you have the money. I will underwrite the $300,000. I will get two or three others, but I will be responsible for the whole." [11] The Democratic national committee ended its 1904 campaign with a deficit of $900,000, and, it is said, Thomas Fortune Ryan and August Belmont picked up the tab.[12]

Reliance on a few fat cats may be less than it once was, but national-level committees still obtain most of their money from contributors of large sums, that is, if one regards $500 as a large sum. Evidence on the sizes of contributions to other sorts of campaign committees is much less satisfactory. Professor Heard estimated that in 1952 some 20,000 persons contributed at least $500 to one type of campaign committee or another. The Gore committee staff assembled a list of slightly more than 300 individuals, married couples, and firms making political contributions of $5,000 or more during 1956: $2,894,000, to various Republican committees; $860,000, to Democratic committees. The data available to the committee did not include the records of many agencies active during the year in state and local campaigns and was doubtless incomplete for committees concerned with presidential and congressional candidates. In 1960, Herbert Alexander reports, 5,300 contributors of $500 or more accounted for 41 per cent of the gross receipts of committees reporting to the Clerk of the House. Doubtless smaller proportions of the receipts of state and local committees come from large gifts, yet an extremely small proportion of the electorate bears a substantial part of political costs.

Who the little givers are and how much they give are unknown. A sizeable group consists of candidates themselves. Tens of thousands of candidates for town, city, and county offices pay their own campaign expenses, which are nominal or amount to only a few hundred dollars. And a candidate may from time to time move into the ranks of the big givers as he finances his own campaign. A larger number of little givers is accounted for by those public employees who make more or less voluntary gifts. Another numerous group of little givers, perhaps the largest, consists of trade unionists who are tapped for a dollar or more by the political education committees of their unions. Union officials do not themselves know how many individuals contribute. An estimate of 2,000,000 in a presidential election year would probably be high.

On the face of it, the party dinner would seem to be a way of enlarging

[11] *Memoirs of Will H. Hays* (Garden City: Doubleday, 1955), p. 127.

[12] The story goes that Urey Woodson, secretary of the Democratic national committee, told his callers, Ryan and Fortune, the size of the deficit. " 'That's very reasonable,' said Ryan. . . . Then he turned to Belmont. 'Gussie,' he suggested casually, 'you send your check for $450,000 and I'll send mine for $450,000. We'll pay these bills and let Mr. Woodson and the boys go home.' " Belmont protested that he already had $200,000 in the campaign. " 'Yes, Gussie,' Ryan replied quietly. 'I know that. But remember— Parker was your candidate.' Gussie paid, and so did Ryan." Joseph F. Guffey, *Seventy Years on the Red-Fire Wagon* (1952), pp. 30–31.

the base of contributors. The Democratic national committee in the 1930's began systematic use of Jackson Day dinners to raise funds. The Republicans soon took up the $100-a-plate dinner; they made a most spectacular application of the technique in 1956 when they raised $4,000,000 in one evening by dinners over the country which were linked by closed-circuit television to hear the President speak. While dinners may bring in a fringe of new contributors, the chances are that in the main the same people who contribute directly buy the tickets.[13] Ordinarily the party's fund-raising machinery manages the dinners and pushes the sale of tickets. Few people turn up unannounced to buy tickets at the door. The $100-a-plate dinner incidentally has some happy features. The contributor may remain anonymous, at times advantageous both to the party and to the contributor. Probably a good many tickets also appear in one guise or another as items on corporate expense accounts.

All these types of contributors make up a small but apparently an increasing proportion of the electorate. In 1952, 1956, and 1960 the Survey Research Center of the University of Michigan asked its national sample of persons living in households: "Did you give any money or buy tickets or do anything to help the campaign for one of the parties or candidates?" In 1952, 4 per cent of the respondents answered affirmatively; in 1956, 10; in 1960, 11. Thus, in 1960 perhaps 10,000,000 persons made some sort of political contribution. Some party managers believe this to be an overestimate; some respondents may claim to have done their duty when they actually did not. In any case, if the estimate is reasonably accurate, most of the contributors made quite small gifts.[14]

ORGANIZATION FOR FUND RAISING The types of organizations for raising funds are almost as numerous as are campaigns. The candidate himself may have to touch his friends and acquaintances for cash. In another instance a single individual may be given the job of raising money. Usually the larger campaign units create specialized units to solicit contributions—a finance committee or division. Party finance committees follow a pattern of operation characteristic of the financing of nongovernmental collective endeavor ranging from the support of the county fair to the endowment of colleges. That is, a committee of men of prestige in a group

[13] Walter Thayer, finance chairman in 1960 for the Volunteers for Nixon-Lodge, observed that the "people who go to those dinners are ready to be tapped for money. I believe in doing it directly, without all the fuss, incidental expense and use of manpower in setting up the dinners and selling tickets."

[14] The percentages of respondents in occupational groups who claimed to have given money or bought tickets in 1956 were: professional, 19; business and managerial, 18; white collar, 7; skilled, 8; unskilled, 7; farm operator, 6; retired, 6; housewife, 6. Among income groups, the proportions ranged from 1 per cent for the under $1,000 group to 33 per cent for the $10,000 and over group. For analysis of 1960 contributors, see Heard, *The Costs of Democracy* (Anchor ed.), pp. 421ff.

concerned turns a modicum of heat on those able to contribute. For convenience in solicitation, if for no other reason, men of means find themselves the
least neglected target of the fund-raising committee.

The Republican party has developed a far more effective money-raising
apparatus than have the Democrats. The Republicans have attempted to construct a fund-raising organization parallel to the regular party organization.
Though the party has a national finance committee, the state finance committees with their associated local committees carry the brunt of the money-
raising task. These committees, which exist in about two-thirds of the states,
usually are made up of businessmen and others not professionally active in
politics. In some instances the committees operate with the assistance of
experts in the conduct of fund-raising drives. The finance committee seeks,
with by no means universal success, to monopolize the fund-raising function
in its area. It can thereby reduce, if not eliminate, multiple solicitation of
individuals. From the common fund accumulated by the state finance committee, allocations are made to the national committee, the state committee,
county committees, congressional candidates, and other party spending units.
In its broad conception, the scheme is one of specialization: the businessmen
raise the money and the politicians spend it. The relationship is not without
its tensions; the finance committees or their chairmen occasionally encroach
on the sphere of the regular party committees to the annoyance of the professionals.[15]

A finance committee with the proper membership can be most persuasive
with prospective contributors. In 1956, for example, John Hay Whitney
served as chairman of the United Republican Finance Committee of New
York, which had jurisdiction over New York City and environs. "We try to
make all our solicitations personal," Mr. Whitney said, to see to it that "our
fund raisers get out and visit, and talk, and meet the people who contribute." [16] A committee chaired by Mr. Whitney, a man of more than
moderate standing among men of means, could raise money for almost any
cause. In 1952 the chairman of the New York committee was Winthrop W.
Aldrich, chairman of the board of the Chase National Bank. In that year the
committee raised $2,385,000. Committees composed of such persons have
ready access to people with money to give. And people with money to give
may hesitate not to give to such committees. In fact, many of the members
of such committees and their prospects spend a good many days each year
soliciting each other for one worthy cause or another.

[15] Joe Martin records that when he was Republican national chairman, Ernest T.
Weir, chairman of the finance committee, complained that Martin never consulted him.
Martin told him that he consulted people "who know something about politics" and
that he did not regard Weir as "a political expert particularly." In due course, Weir
resigned. *My First Fifty Years in Politics* (New York: McGraw-Hill, 1960), pp. 124–25.
[16] See Mr. Whitney's testimony, Gore Committee, *Hearings*, Pt. I, pp. 38–44.

Democratic fund-raising efforts are more erratic, less systematic, and less effective. The Democratic finance machinery differs from campaign to campaign. It has not acquired the stability of the Republican system which is built around the continuing interest of major businessmen in the party. Instead, the job of raising funds for the national committee tends to be parceled out among individual solicitors who happen to have the capacity to raise money in considerable sums from those who may be favorably disposed to the party under the circumstances of the moment. The solicitors may include the treasurer of the committee, its finance chairman, some national committeemen, and others with no formal party title but with access to financial constituencies with Democratic leanings.

Each national committee is dependent in large measure upon state and local party organizations for funds. Direct solicitation on behalf of the national committee occurs, but each committee also fixes state quotas which it hopes the state organization will meet. In finance, as in other matters, the leverage of the national committee over the state organizations is not notable. Republican state finance committees in the wealthier states appear to attempt in good spirit to meet the levies of the national committee. Democratic national committeemen seem to be more variable in the delivery of their state quotas. In 1960 Paul Butler as national chairman favored states that raised their quotas with better national convention seats and superior hotel accommodations in the convention city.

Neither party is equipped to conduct large-scale canvasses for small contributions. Few county or city organizations can man a community-wide fund-raising drive. If they can, they may be reluctant to share the proceeds with the state committee. The state committee may be equally reluctant to share the proceeds with the national committee. And few state organizations will respond wih enthusiasm to national leadership in the organization of a drive for small contributions. All these problems and more were encountered by Beardsley Ruml when he set out to collect a million $5 contributions for the Democratic campaign in 1952.[17] During several recent campaigns the American Heritage Foundation and the Advertising Council have sponsored propaganda campaigns to encourage people to contribute small sums to party funds. In 1958, according to a survey by Dr. Gallup, 44 per cent read about the "Contribute to Your Party Program," 23 per cent said they would be willing to give $5, but only 5 per cent said they had been solicited. In scattered localities party organizations conduct fairly effective mass solicitation,[18] and the Democratic national committee receives several hundred thousand a

[17] See John Van Doren, *Big Money in Little Sums* (Chapel Hill: Institute for Research in Social Science, 1956).

[18] See Bernard Hennessy, *Dollars for Democrats, 1959* (New York: McGraw-Hill, 1960) and R. F. Schier, "Political Fund Raising and the Small Contributor: A Case Study," *Western Political Quarterly*, 11 (1958), 104–12.

year from its sustaining membership program; yet the parties have made no genuine effort to exploit the potential of the small giver. It is far simpler to rely on large gifts.[19]

INDIRECT CONTRIBUTIONS FROM THE PUBLIC TREAS-URY   Private contributors provide the bulk of political funds, but the government itself, in one way or another, finances a considerable share of campaign activity. This source of support naturally is available only to the incumbent official or party. Sitting Senators and Representatives enjoy perquisites that can be turned to use in campaigns. Their official staffs usually labor diligently in their campaigns for re-election. One of the more innocent aids available to an incumbent is the use of the congressional frank for the distribution of publicity material to his constituents. Members of Congress campaign for re-election continuously, and they can keep their names before the voters by circulation of their newsletters and speeches under the congressional frank. Their right to free postal service is restricted to "official business," a phrase which is interpreted to exclude explicit appeals for political support. Nevertheless, the circulation of reports, reprints of speeches, and other permissible material is advantageous to the incumbent Congressman.

The greatest contribution of the public treasury to party finance is made through the public employment of persons who devote part of their time to the work of the party organization. Although it doubtless runs into millions of dollars annually, the contribution of federal, state, and local governments to the maintenance of party organizations through the patronage system cannot readily be estimated. It is expected, of course, that Presidents, governors, Congressmen, and legislators shall defend and advocate policies before the electorate. On a different plane are the electioneering activities of the lower-ranking administrative employees, some of whom devote a large proportion of their time to precinct work; others may spend only a few days immediately prior to the election. Some are competent and able public employees; others are on the public payroll only because they have special skills in the management of the electorate.

Returns from the assessment of public employees for party purposes may be regarded as an indirect contribution by government itself. Collection of funds from administrative employees of government is a practice almost as old as the Republic. Its present extent cannot be accurately known. At the federal level, outright assessment of classified civil service employees has apparently become negligible. In states and cities assessment seems to occur

---

[19] Some impressive fund-raising has been practiced by right-wing agitational groups led by clerics who bring to their new calling a skill in the extraction of small sums from their auditors. These gentlemen of the cloth retain a connection with the Lord which, tenuous though it may be, suffices to maintain tax deductibility for contributions to some of them, a factor probably helpful in their operations.

more frequently than in the federal service. Given the size of modern government payrolls, systematic collections can yield substantial sums. Assessments of 3 per cent of the annual salaries of Jersey City employees by the Hague organization were said to have netted $174,000 in 1948 and $167,000 in 1949.[20] Somewhat akin to assessment is the collection by party committees of more or less customary amounts from nominees on the ticket to help cover the general costs of the campaign.[21]

Public funds are indirectly channeled into campaigns by such means as have been mentioned. Incumbent officials and parties have at their command the apparatus of government and can shape or time official action for campaign advantage. The incumbent always has the advantage, or the disadvantage, of his record, but some actions seem to be made with an eye to the campaign immediately ahead. Tax reductions tend to occur in election years.[22]

THE NETHER SIDE OF PARTY FINANCE   Campaign finance has its seamy aspects, which create special problems for fund raisers. Finance committees have to work to get most contributions but they need also to fend off some persons eager to give money. Entrepreneurs engaged in economic pursuits on the shady side of the law, as well as others on the edge of trouble with the prosecutor, may approach headquarters hopefully with bags of greenbacks. James W. Gerard, treasurer of the national Democratic finance committee for many years, recorded that he had often declined large "contributions because of their suspicious source." A contribution from

[20] Private employers occasionally "assess" their employees for political contributions. In 1952 persons in the Ford Motor organization raised funds from Ford dealers, though it was insisted that no "pressure" was involved. The same practice occurred in General Motors. Now and then, instances come to light of persuasive solicitation of corporate personnel at the executive and supervisory levels; how widespread the practice is cannot be said. In 1960 Ford initiated a voluntary contribution plan for its managerial and white-collar workers. Each was given an opportunity to contribute in a manner so as not to reveal to his boss the name of the recipient party. Under these circumstances some, but evidently only a few, contributions from this source went to the Democrats.

[21] Expenditures by candidates, incidentally, are not deductible as a cost of doing business in the computation of federal income taxes. McDonald *v.* Commissioner of Internal Revenue, 65 S. Ct. 96 (1944). A Minnesota statute of 1955 permits candidates to charge specified sums as business expenditures under the income tax law of that state.

[22] In 1952 and 1956 Senator John J. Williams, of Delaware, charged that rulings by the Commissioner of Internal Revenue with respect to unpaid loans to the New York State Democratic committee constituted "an indirect way of financing the Democratic campaign of 1948 out of the Federal Treasury." The committee offered to settle its debts at ten cents on the dollar and the 90 per cent loss was held to be a nonbusiness bad debt that could be offset against capital gains in fixing income tax liability. For Senator Williams' charges and the relevant tax rulings, see *Congressional Record* (daily ed.), June 14, 1956, pp. 9357–62. At least two of the lenders whose loans turned sour— Marshall Field and David S. Schulte—did not take advantage of the Treasury ruling. *New York Times* and *New York Herald Tribune*, April 30, 1952.

"a notorious gambler or bootlegger" might, he said, "seriously embarrass the party." [23] R. Douglas Stuart, 1952 Republican treasurer, said: "We guard against unwelcome contributions by requiring that every contribution carry the name of the donor. . . . Where contributions are in cash we require that the contributor be identified." [24] A contribution from a legitimate source may be declined because the candidate wishes to be under no obligation to the donor.[25] Another class of donor whose motives may well be suspect consists of those persons who volunteer to help pay off the deficit of the winning candidate. National committees regularly receive unsolicited contributions after their candidate wins. The flow is especially heavy if the outcome was unexpected. In 1948, for example, an inexplicable delay in the mails brought to Democratic national headquarters in the days after the election a gentle rain of checks dated several days before Truman's unexpected triumph.

One broad type of contribution may result from virtual extortion. From time to time vulnerable persons may contribute under the threat of damaging government action. This kind of collection procedure is most likely to occur in corrupt, bossed communities. Thus, a newspaper comment on advertising in the program of an athletic event sponsored by a Chicago ward club noted that most of the buyers of space were neighborhood saloons. A saloonkeeper never knows when he is violating the law but he does know, it was said, "that violations by those who are not right-minded means license revocation." [26] Contributions may also be exacted from contractors and other sup-

---

[23] *My First Eighty-Three Years in America* (Garden City: Doubleday, 1951), p. 325.

[24] Stories circulate of campaign treasurers who tell bearers of suspect money to bring it back in the name of a respectable donor, a practice that may account for inclusion in the lists of contributors of the names of persons who never in their life had as much ready cash as they are credited with having given to the cause. Stories also abound of campaign treasurers who put dubious money in the safe and return it after the campaign, a gambit that denies the cash to the opposition and avoids antagonizing the giver. Another type of practice appeared from the 1953 testimony of the New Jersey Republican state chairman. He explained that the custom was to report only those contributions in the form of checks; cash was never reported.

[25] A. W. Dunn says that in 1904 the Republicans rejected only one corporation check, one for $100,000 from the tobacco trust. Antitrust proceedings were to be initiated against it, and the Administration wanted to avoid "any entanglements through a contribution from that source." *From Harrison to Harding* (New York: Putnam's, 1922), p. 401.

[26] *Chicago Daily News*, December 5, 1935. In 1936 the Democratic national committee is said to have netted at least $250,000 from its *Book of the Democratic Convention of 1936*. The revenue came principally from the sale of advertising. The Hatch Act amendments of 1940 make it unlawful for any person or corporation "to purchase or buy any goods, commodities, advertising, or articles of any kind or description where the proceeds" directly or indirectly inure to the benefit of candidates for any federal elective office. The awe in which finance committees hold the statute is suggested by a letter from a Massachusetts Democratic committee sponsoring a dinner at $100 a plate in 1961 to help discharge the Democratic campaign deficit. The committee advised businessmen that contributors of $500 or more would be given not only tickets but advertising space in the souvenir program, which would make the cost deductible as

pliers of goods and services to public agencies.[27] Thus, Representative Cramer (R, Fla.) reported that in Delaware the chief engineer of the state highway department approved "huge overruns" by a contractor "who showed his gratitude by contributing $15,000 to the Democratic State Committee." [28]

Regulation of Party Finance

The finances of American party committees, candidates, and campaign managers are regulated by state and federal law. Legislation purports to require publicity of campaign finance, to limit the amounts spent, to prohibit certain types of contributions to campaigns, and to limit the size of contributions. In general, the laws do not in fact limit expenditures, substantially affect the size of contributions, or assure full publicity. The statutory ambivalence reflects a legislative deference to the popular opinion that the power of money ought to be restricted and a simultaneous recognition of the hard fact that rigid limitations probably would be unenforceable. Nevertheless, loopholes in finance statutes are not explicable solely in terms of legislative hypocrisy. The organization of campaign activity presents almost insurmountable technical obstacles to the control of finance. In a federal politics of simultaneous but related campaigns any attempt to limit expenditures is almost inevitably doomed to failure. When the candidate for the Senate, say, approaches his expenditure limit, outlays in the name of the candidate for governor—or for sheriff—may help the cause just as well as expenditures in his name. Yet, as will be shown, the laws regulating campaign finance have had some effects.

REQUIREMENT OF PUBLICITY   A common type of party-finance regulation is the requirement of publicity of the amounts of contributions, the names of contributors, and the nature of expenditures. The underlying assumption is that wrong-doing does not flourish in public. The legislation grew from the belief that secrecy of party finance facilitated

---

an advertising expense in the determination of income tax liability. For the letter, see *Congressional Record* (daily ed.), June 1, 1961, p. 8653.

[27] Fund solicitors can exert leverage over banks with deposits of public funds. A candidate for state treasurer in Illinois, for example, approached a bank with large deposits of public funds but was told he did not have "a Chinaman's chance" to win. The improbable winner won. He withdrew $10,000,000 in state funds from the bank, but he testified that he "tried to be easy with them." He gave 30 days' notice and started withdrawals at the rate of $500,000 a month and then went up to $1,000,000 a month. *Congressional Record* (daily ed.), March 14, 1957, pp. 3301–2.

[28] *Congressional Record* (daily ed.), September 22, 1961, p. 19,600. J. L. Bernd finds that in major statewide Democratic primary races in Georgia at least 50 per cent of the money handled by central headquarters and auxiliary groups comes from highway contractors and liquor dealers. See his *The Role of Campaign Funds in Georgia Primary Elections, 1936–1958* (Macon: Georgia Journal, 1958), p. 3.

purchase of government action. In 1904 Alton Parker, the Democratic presidential candidate, made an issue of the secrecy of funds by the assertion that corporations were furnishing funds to the Republican campaign to purchase the party's favor. The Democratic campaign treasurer of 1904, Perry Belmont, led a movement to obtain appropriate legislation.[29] The first fruits of the work of Belmont and his allies were not publicity laws but laws prohibiting corporate contributions. By 1908, however, public sentiment moved both parties to make their financial records public, and in 1910 Congress required candidates for Congress and political committees to report their campaign receipts and expenditures.

The federal law requires candidates for Senator and Representative and political committees to file at set intervals statements with the clerk of the House of Representatives. The term "political committee" includes organizations accepting contributions or making expenditures to influence the election of candidates "in two or more states," or in a single state if the committee is a branch or subsidiary of a national organization (other than a state or local committee of a political party). The reports must include the name and address of each person who has contributed more than $100, the names and addresses of persons to whom payments of $10 or more have been made, and certain other information. Most states also have legislation requiring candidates, committees, and campaign managers to file similar statements with appropriate public officials.[30]

Although the reports filed under federal and state law make public much information about party finance, that information is both fragmentary and incomplete. The statutes themselves are often defective. The federal law, thus, does not apply to primary campaigns, an omission attributable to the earlier view that nominations were beyond federal purview.[31] Some laws require only that reports be filed after the election. The coverage often does not extend to all who may spend in support of a candidate. Some states require reports by only the candidate and exclude party committees. The federal law requires that a candidate for House or Senate report money received and expended by himself "or by any person with his knowledge." This provision, coupled with the exemption of intrastate committees, assures incomplete reporting.[32] Candidates often manage to have no knowledge of

[29] Perry Belmont, *An American Democrat* (New York: Columbia University Press, 1950), ch. 17.

[30] On technical problems of reporting, see H. E. Alexander, *Money, Politics and Public Reporting* (Princeton: Citizens' Research Foundation, 1960).

[31] A bill passed by the Senate in 1960 but which died in the House would have extended the reporting requirement to costs incurred in campaigns for primary and convention nominations for federal office. Senators and Representatives from one-party areas seem to be especially opposed to this type of extension; as the law stands they are, in reality, exempt from the reporting requirement.

[32] Recent proposals have been to require reports from all committees spending over

sums spent by others in their behalf. Expenditures by lobbying and "educational" organizations may fall outside the statutory definition of reportable expenditures. In 1944 the Committee for Constitutional Government spent $250,000 in the first nine months of the year. A volume it distributed widely began: "This book shows how the New Deal is taking America into national socialism." The inference might have been that the committee opposed Mr. Roosevelt, but it refused to disclose the names of its contributors. It averred that it was exempt from the statute because it supported no candidate or party: "We support the Constitution and free enterprise." [33]

In addition to the defects in the laws, noncompliance and the form of the data submitted help to keep party finance out of the goldfish bowl. Failure to file is rarely followed by prosecution, although the omission of a report in some jurisdictions makes a candidate conspicuous. Reports may put some contributions in the names of dummies: some donors fear reprisals if they have backed the losing candidate. Moreover, the most detailed information may be unrevealing; extensive analysis is required to get at the significance of the data. Hurriedly prepared newspaper stories rarely reveal the inner meaning of the reported facts. Often it requires efforts beyond the capabilities of a newspaperman to ascertain from the reports even so simple a fact as how much money has been spent in a campaign.[34]

---

a specified sum to influence the election of federal officers. A bill passed by the Senate in 1960 fixed that sum at $2,500.

[33] Senate Report No. 101, 79th Cong., 1st sess. (1945), p. 10. Certain constitutional questions concerning the extent of the power of Congress to compel reports were answered in Burroughs v. United States, 290 U.S. 534 (1934). In 1928 the Anti-Smith Democrats, an organization led by Bishop James Cannon, Jr., collected and expended funds in a campaign against Al Smith. In defense against an indictment charging failure to report, Cannon and his secretary, Burroughs, contended that Congress had no power to regulate presidential elections, and therefore no authority over the campaign activities of individuals. (The Constitution provides that presidential electors of each state shall be appointed "in such manner as the legislature thereof may direct.") The Supreme Court held that Congress had acted within its power. The requirement of reports might be said to limit freedom of speech, a contention that has not been authoritatively settled. See the discussion of the point in the note, "Statutory Regulation of Political Campaign Funds," *Harvard Law Review*, 66 (1953), 1259–73. The contention has been made, too, that campaign gifts, just as the ballot, should be secret, an analogy that would be more defensible if contributors were eager to keep the fact of their contributions secret from candidates.

[34] If all funds for each campaign had to be funneled through a single official, responsibility for reporting could be much more clearly fixed. A recent Florida statute requires that all funds go through a single campaign treasurer's hands and be deposited in a bank depository. The terms of the statute made it illegal for a citizen to buy newspaper space or radio time without clearance with the candidate's campaign treasurer. The statute, which has evidently brought about fairly complete publicity, was attacked as an unconstitutional limitation of freedom of expression but was upheld by the Florida Supreme Court. See E. E. Roady, "Ten Years of Florida's 'Who Gave It—Who Got It' Law," *Law and Contemporary Problems*, 27 (1962), 434–54. Massachusetts embodied the depository feature of the Florida law in an act of 1962. The National Municipal League's *Model State Campaign Contributions and Expenditures Reporting Law* (mimeographed, January, 1961) rests on the Florida act.

LIMITATION OF SOURCES OF FUNDS   Contributions from certain types of sources have been prohibited or otherwise limited. The basic explanation for statutes with these purposes has been that the classes of persons affected have been thought to be especially attached to a crowd other than that which controlled the legislature, but other considerations have also been influential. Certain business interests have been thought to be especially prone to the political exertion of their pecuniary power. In other instances the statutes protect those vulnerable to solicitation—for example, public employees.

The federal government and about three-fourths of the states restrict corporate contributions. The federal legislation, enacted in 1907, was an outgrowth of the efficiency with which Mark Hanna assessed corporations for the support of the Republican campaign of 1896 and of the revelations by the "muckrakers" of corporate corruption of state and local politics around the turn of the century. The 1907 act made it unlawful for "any national bank, or any corporation organized by authority of any law of Congress" to contribute "in connection with any election to any political office," or for "any corporation whatever to make a contribution in connection with any election at which presidential and vice presidential electors or a Senator or Representative . . . are to be voted for." The more inclusive limitation on national banks arose from the fact that Congress had broad power over corporations chartered by itself. The narrower limitation on other corporations was based on the authority of Congress over the election of presidential electors and over the election of its own members. In 1947 the prohibition was extended to contributions in connection with nominations for the offices tied by the earlier legislation to the two classes of corporations. Another group of corporations—utility holding companies and their subsidiaries—was brought under federal control by the Public Utility Holding Company Act of 1935, which forbids contributions by such companies to federal, state, or local campaigns.[35]

Although treasurers of campaigns affected by the prohibitions of corporate gifts no longer accept corporation checks, some corporations find ways to spend money in campaigns. Campaign literature may be sluiced through the corporate postage meter; the corporate printing bill may include items that have no relation to the corporate charter; corporate personnel may be assigned to campaign duty. Such resort to indirection, though, suggests that the prohibition of corporate contributions has considerable effect.

[35] The practices that the legislation sought to prevent may be deduced from the case of the Union Electric Company, which was in 1942 found guilty of violation of the act. During the thirties it made contributions to candidates and party committees in Missouri, Illinois, and Iowa. It accumulated a fund of $591,000 for these purposes by obtaining rebates from persons to whom it made payments and by the use of false expense accounts, and thus concealed the political use of its funds. See Egan v. United States, 137 F. (2d) 369 (1943), certiorari denied, 320 U.S. 788.

That effect spills over into those state and local campaigns that are un-
affected by either federal or state prohibitions; some fund raisers indicate
that even in such situations it is difficult to tap corporations for direct contributions. Apart from such concealed contributions, open propaganda may
be conducted to influence elections. Costly campaigns of so-called institutional
advertising and of trade association propaganda have become the fashion in
big business circles. What effect, if any, expenditures for these purposes have
cannot be known, but the outlays have evidently been, if not pro-Republican,
at least anti-Democratic in motive. Moreover, statutes prohibiting corporate
campaign contributions do not extend to expenditures for lobbying or for
propaganda for or against legislation. Corporate influence may work through
these means quite as well as through electoral campaigns.[36]

Congress has placed limitations on trade unions analogous to those
on corporations. In 1936 the United Mine Workers, the Almagated Clothing
Workers, the International Ladies' Garment Workers, and other labor organizations gave $770,000 to the Democratic campaign.[37] For the first time labor
had become a major source of campaign funds and an agitation began for
restrictive legislation, in which Republicans were far more active than
Democrats.

The Smith-Connally Act of 1943 restricted union contributions for the
duration of the war, and in 1947, by the Taft-Hartley Act, Congress placed
corporations and labor organizations permanently on the same footing. It
was made unlawful for

> . . . any corporation whatever, or any labor organization to make a
> contribution or expenditure in connection with any election at which
> Presidential and Vice Presidential electors or a Senator or Representa-
> tive in, or a Delegate or Resident Commissioner to Congress are to be
> voted for, or in connection with any primary election or political con-
> vention or caucus held to select candidates for any of the foregoing
> offices.

The language of the statute is not so restrictive as it may seem.[38] The
most clear-cut effect of the act is to prohibit contributions from union

---

[36] Some discouragement to the expenditure of funds for propaganda to influence
legislation or voting is furnished by the legal provision that such outlays are not deductible as a business cost in the determination of income-tax liability. Determination
of precisely what expenditure falls within the regulatory inhibition presents recondite
questions, and the impression prevails that the Internal Revenue Service is not draconian
in its quest for violations. The Federal Power Commission, through its control of the
accounting of its licensees, may require that political expenditures be charged to surplus
rather than to operating expense and thus compel the stockholders rather than the customers of the utility to pay the cost of propaganda.

[37] Louise Overacker, "Labor's Political Contributions," *Political Science Quarterly*,
54 (1939), 59.

[38] For a treatment of the history and interpretation of the legislation, see Joseph

treasuries—from funds built up from union dues—to campaigns for President, Senator, and Representative. Even that proscription may be violated from time to time, directly or indirectly. Campaign literature can go through union as well as corporate mailing rooms.

A major consequence of the statute has been the use of specially created political affiliates of unions; the funds of these organizations come from contributions solicited from union members for political purposes rather than from dues. The peak labor political committee is COPE—the Committee on Political Education of the AFL-CIO. It represents an amalgamation of the Labor's League for Political Education of the AFL and the CIO Political Action Committee. COPE and its related units in the national unions, the locals, and the state federations are not labor organizations as defined by the federal statute. They are free to solicit funds and to make contributions and expenditures in national elections. Yet the necessity of raising special political funds rather than using regular union revenues limits labor. Collection of large sums in small amounts is no easier for labor organizations than it is for political parties.[39]

The prohibition of union "expenditures" raises a constitutional question that remains unsettled. A statute prohibiting an individual from buying newspaper advertising space to express his views over his own name about the relative virtues of presidential candidates would probably be challenged as a violation of the right of free speech. What of the constitutionality of a prohibition of the same action by a group of men banded together in a union? The Supreme Court skirted the question in a case in which the United Auto Workers was charged with making expenditures to pay for television programs supporting Democratic candidates for Senate and House. The lower court threw out the indictment, but the Supreme Court sent the case back for trial before ruling on the constitutional question. In dissent Justices Douglas and Black argued that the statute as applied was "a broadside assault on the freedom of political expression guaranteed by the first amendment."[40] In the subsequent trial the lower court acquitted the UAW and thereby prevented consideration by the Supreme Court of the constitutional issues posed by the case. The courts, though, have ruled that some types of "expenditures" are not within the statutory prohibition. It was held that the statute did not apply to expenditures in the publication and distribution of

Tanenhaus, "Organized Labor's Political Spending: The Law and Its Consequences," *Journal of Politics*, 16 (1954), 441–71.

[39] Charges that union political education committees extort contributions from unionists recur. That may happen from time to time, but it is doubtful that such coercion is either more effective or more prevalent than the pressure that can be brought by a party finance committee headed by the town's leading banker on businessmen or by the president of a corporation on his vice presidents. For a discussion of practices in raising funds among businessmen, see Duncan Norton-Taylor, "How to Give Money to Politicians," *Fortune*, May, 1956, pp. 113–17.

[40] United States *v.* United Auto Workers, 352 U.S. 567 (1957).

issues of *The CIO News* containing endorsements of candidates for Congress. Purchase of newspaper advertising and radio time by a small union lacking a newspaper of its own has also been held to be beyond the statutory proscription.[41]

Unions interpret the statute to permit expenditures for "educational" purposes from general union funds. Such activities include the conduct of registration drives, the publication and distribution of the voting records of members of Congress, and general education about public affairs. The union contention is that expenditures for such purposes are not in connection with the election of any candidate and thus are not prohibited by the law.

Prohibition of union contributions and expenditures is justified by a regard for the rights of the worker, a part of whose union dues may be used to support a candidate to whom he may be individually opposed, a position espoused far more frequently by Republicans than by Democrats. Union membership is often, in fact whether in law, compulsory. In a case involving the extreme situation, railroad workers who are compelled by the Railway Labor Act to share union costs, the Supreme Court held that unions of these workers could not support their "traditional political activities" against "the expressed wishes of a dissenting employee, with his exacted money." It ordered, in effect, that means be devised by which such dissenters could "contract out." The question of the general federal prohibition of political contributions and expenditures by unions was not raised in the case, and the Court explicitly limited itself to the narrow question of the compulsory support of union political activities under the Railway Labor Act by employees who dissented from the union line.[42]

The federal statute does not reach contributions from union treasuries to campaigns for state and local office. Some states prohibit such use of union funds.[43] In a few states unions have been a major source of Democratic funds for campaigns for state office, and Republicans have sought prohibitory legislation. In 1955 the Wisconsin legislature, by a strict party vote in both

[41] United States *v.* Congress of Industrial Organizations, 335 U.S. 106 (1948); United States *v.* Painters Local Union No. 281, 172 F. (2d) 854 (1949). Similarly, it has been held that the congressional prohibition was not intended to apply to the payment of the salaries of union employees who aided the campaigns of congressional candidates. United States *v.* Construction & General Laborers Local Union No. 264, 101 F. Supp. 869 (1959).

[42] International Association of Machinists *v.* Street, 367 U.S. 740 (1961); International Association of Machinists *v.* Street, 217 Ga. 351 (1961). A lower court decision suggests that union members may "contract in," that is, sign cards authorizing the allocation of a portion of their dues to a union political fund. See United States *v.* Local 688, International Brotherhood of Teamsters, 41 CCH Labor Cases 16, 601. See also United States *v.* Anchorage Central Labor Council, 193 F. Supp. 504 (1961).

[43] The Alabama statute to this effect was held unconstitutional because a like prohibition had not been applied to employers' associations.—Alabama State Federation of Labor *v.* McAdory, 18 So. (2d) 810 (1944).

houses, enacted prohibitory legislation. In the course of the debate it was said that the law would cut off 40 per cent of the revenues of the Democratic party in the state.

Another control of the source of party revenue is the prohibition of the assessment of public employees. Legislation to prohibit assessments is designed to protect government employees as well as to deny this source of revenue to those in power. Defenders—and there are defenders—of the practice of assessment contend that by raising funds in this fashion the party is able to maintain an independence of wealthy contributors and vested interests. The Federal Civil Service Act of 1883 forbade the solicitation or receipt by any officer or employee of the United States of any "assessment, subscription or contribution, for any political purpose whatever" from any other federal officer or employee. Persons not employees of the government may solicit voluntary contributions from employees so long as the solicitation does not occur on government premises; occasionally these collections amount to assessments. Federal legislation also prohibits assessments of state and local employees paid wholly or in part from federal grants or loans, a provision that covers large numbers of state and local workers. Less than half the states prohibit assessments against state and municipal employees generally.

Contractors, suppliers, and other persons having financial transactions with the government have been important donors to campaign funds. In corrupt situations contractors may virtually be compelled to contribute to the party treasury. The 1940 amendment to the Hatch Act attempted to prevent contributions from persons dealing with the federal government. The act prohibits contributions by contractors and the solicitation of contractors for contributions "during the period of negotiation for, or performance" of a contract with a federal agency. This statute is less restrictive than it may seem to be. It does not apply, for example, to a shareholder, even a major shareholder, of a corporation dealing with the government. Technically, he is not, in his personal capacity, negotiating with or performing a contract for the government.

LIMITATION OF AMOUNTS SPENT   A persistent objective of the regulators of party finance has been to limit the amounts spent in campaigns. The electorate may be overwhelmed by extravagantly supported propaganda, or plutocratic elements may prevail—conditions scarcely compatible with popular government. The statutes express the moral judgment of legislators that excessive sums should not be spent in campaigns; yet they do not actually restrict expenditures. If the laws in force have any effect, they probably contribute to the disorganization of the parties, help conceal the size and sources of campaign funds, and bring about a more immediate sense of indebtedness of candidates to donors.

In the Hatch Act of 1940, Congress laid down this rule: "No political committee shall receive contributions aggregating more than $3,000,000 during any calendar year." Before this enactment national committees had on occasion spent more than $3,000,000 in presidential election years. The consequence of the limitation was the creation of committees, more or less independent of the national committee, each of which could raise and spend $3,000,000 and keep within the law. Citizens for Eisenhower-Nixon or Volunteers for Stevenson-Kefauver served to help the parties comply with the Hatch Act as well as to campaign.

A multiplicity of committees has always existed, but often independent committees were only fronts for the party's national committee. The existence of several national-level committees, each with its own funds, complicates the task of campaign management and tends to divide party leadership at the top. Moreover, the limitation on the national committee reduces its earlier importance as a fund-raising agency which disbursed funds to state committees and to individual House and Senate candidates. These national subventions gave some leverage to national headquarters in its leadership of state committees and enabled the national headquarters to do more than is now legally possible to aid its congressional candidates. Central collection incidentally permitted contributions to be pooled in a common fund from whence they flowed to congressional candidates, a procedure that permitted to some degree the creation of an obligation by the candidate to the party rather than to the individual donor.

By the Corrupt Practices Act, which long antedated the Hatch Act, Congress limited the amount to be spent by "a candidate" for the House or Senate in his election campaign, and thereby excluded from the restriction expenditures in the primary campaign and those made by other persons in behalf of the candidate. The federal limits, unless state law sets a lower maximum, are $10,000 for a senatorial candidate and $2,500 for a House candidate. For the larger states and districts the limits are variable, depending on the size of the vote cast in the last election, but in no case may they exceed $25,000 for the Senate and $5,000 for the House. Expenditures for certain purposes, for example, postage, are not included within the limitation. The restraining effect of the federal law is purely illusory.

Most states also have laws placing limits on the size of expenditures in campaigns for state and local offices. Limits set in specified sums are most common although they are sometimes related to the size of the salary of the office or to the number of voters. Whatever their form, the laws ordinarily fix unrealistic limits but contain loopholes commodious enough to permit the business of politics to proceed without violation of the terms of the statute.

Statutes limiting the size of campaign outlays are declaratory of righteous indignation about huge expenditures rather than restrictive of behavior. Yet the technical obstacles to limitation are formidable. What size must campaign funds be to enable candidates and party committees to reach the voters with the minimum essential information? That basic question has never been examined. Instead, nice round figures have been pulled from the air and written into the law. Another major problem arises from the organization of campaigns themselves. Enforcement of a limitation can rest only on a centralization of authority for expenditure in the campaign. With an exception or so, no American legislative body has been able to bring itself to require that all campaign expenditures go through a treasurer or manager designated by the candidate. Such centralization of authority would provide a basis for limiting outlays only in those situations in which individual campaigns are conducted without much relation to other simultaneous races, as in the primaries of some one-party states. When the party committees, committees for federal, state, and local candidates, and other committees campaign side by side for a ticket of candidates whose fortunes are interrelated, restriction of the level of expenditure for specific candidates becomes almost impossible.

LIMITATION OF SIZE OF INDIVIDUAL CONTRIBUTION Large contributions carry the risk that individual campaign donors will provide so large a share of the costs of a campaign that the party committee or the official concerned will be owned by the big giver. In 1940 in the Hatch Act amendments, Congress prohibited gifts of over $5,000 in any one year to the campaign of "any candidate for an elective Federal office" or to any committee campaigning on behalf of candidates for federal office or on behalf of a national party. The law explicitly excluded state and local committees from the restriction. Another sort of big gift not affected by the law is a transfer from one committee to another. A labor committee may pool voluntary collections of a dollar and convert them into gifts that are large proportions of the budgets of some campaigns.

The obvious route for avoidance of the limit has been followed. Persons who wish to give over $5,000 make gifts within that limit to each of several committees or to the campaigns of several candidates for the House and Senate. Or they may make gifts of any size to state committees and keep within the federal law. At times several gifts from the same family, each within the legal limitation, bring the charge that the old patriarch has given sums of legal size in the names of his nieces and nephews. The gift tax probably is more effective in keeping down the size of contributions to particular committees than is the Hatch Act. The tax is complicated but the practical effect for exceptionally wealthy—and generous—individuals is that political contributions of over $3,000 to any single donee in a single year are taxable.[44]

[44] For an analysis of the gift tax, see the testimony of Justin F. Winkle, Assistant Commissioner of Internal Revenue, Gore Committee, *Hearings*, Pt. 2, pp. 352–62.

Statutes that attempt to limit the size of contributions rest on no firm knowledge of how generous a giver must be to gain undue influence. A gift of $5,000 to a presidential campaign may be so small in a total as to command no special attention; a gift of the same size might be far more visible to a congressional candidate. And, perhaps astonishingly enough in this cynical world, a gift of $25,000 or even more is by no means invariably followed by benefits to the donor. In any case, the Hatch Act limitations do not limit. The President's Commission on Campaign Costs in 1962 recommended elimination of the ceiling and the imposition upon contributors themselves of an obligation to report when their aggregate annual contributions exceeded $5,000. Under the practices that have prevailed the determination of who the big givers are and how much they give has been to a degree a matter of chance.

LIMITATION OF PURPOSE OF EXPENDITURES   Expenditures for specified purposes are prohibited chiefly by state legislation. The earlier tendency in legislative drafting was to prohibit expenditures thought to be corrupt. Bribery of voters, for example, is everywhere unlawful. In various states expenditures are prohibited for treating, for conveying voters to the polls, and for election-day workers. The more recent legislative technique has been to specify the objects for which money may legitimately be spent. Well over half of the states have legislation enumerating lawful items of expenditure, which items vary from state to state. Whatever the form of the legislation, the limitations do not hamper campaigning.

What the Money Buys

The cynical view that a campaign contribution is equivalent to a bribe at times indubitably matches the facts. Yet the significance of money in politics can be grasped only by a view that places party finance in the total context of the political process. It is probably fair enough to conclude that men of wealth on the whole use money in politics to protect what they regard as their interests. Their votes are few in a regime of popular government and they build their political defenses by the use of money. Others have votes; they have money. The two are, if not in perpetual conflict, always potentially at loggerheads.

Such statements about the concern of moneyed interests in politics may be generally correct. The difficulty comes in filling in the details, the shadings, the rights and wrongs. That the unbridled dominance of money would run counter to the tenets of a democratic order may be indisputable. On the other hand, a democratic regime that tyrannized men of wealth would both commit injustice and perhaps destroy its instruments of production.

The pragmatic question about the power of money in politics may come down to one of how much power and how that power is used. Abuse of that power may generate disharmonies among the elements of the political order or produce intolerable oppression. On the American scene in some eras the power of wealth has seemed to be without check, but days of reckoning also seem sooner or later to arrive. A considerable body of social and regulatory legislation, enacted over the determined opposition of most men of wealth, serves as evidence of the strength of the counterpoises against wealth. Money has its power in politics but that power has its limits.

Certain practices and customs in campaign finance mitigate or at least gloss over the role of money. Not all the money, not even all the big money, is on the same side. Competition and conflict among those of wealth seep over into the party battle and the general public is sometimes the beneficiary. Moreover, on the national scene the etiquette seems to be that large contributions are made not in expectation of a specific quid pro quo for the individual contributor.[45] The giver rather supports the party whose general outlook seems both most congenial to him and most likely to further his interests. Once the victory is won the contributor can certainly expect to have access to government, to have his views heard sympathetically if not invariably heeded.[46]

The role of contributions in relation to government action must be regarded in a larger context than that of a contributor buying a specific action. Top business leaders may contribute to the Republican party on the assumption that its general policy orientation will turn out to be sympathetic to them. Labor committees may be guided by a similar motivation in their contributions to the Democratic party. In effect, persons with political concerns give to their friends. When the chips are down on specific questions they hope to be treated accordingly. Moreover, the party must so conduct itself as to retain its financial support in the future. Thus, in 1957 the Republican national chairman saw fit to report to the President that the Adminis-

---

[45] At times the etiquette is flagrantly violated. In 1958 H. J. Porter, Texas Republican national committeeman, organized a fund raising dinner honoring Joseph W. Martin, Jr., Speaker of the 80th and 83d Congresses. Porter's letter of invitation to oil and gas men reminded them that Joe Martin had mobilized Republican votes in Congress for legislation of concern to the gas industry and would have to do it again if the bill was to be passed. Eisenhower instructed the national committee to accept none of the $100,000 raised at the dinner. Eisenhower had earlier vetoed the gas bill after it had been revealed that attorneys for the Superior Oil Company had been traveling about the country making gifts of $2,500 (in cash) to Republican state committees. A fair inference from the circumstances of the gifts was that they were not unconnected with the company's interest in recruiting senatorial support for the gas bill.

[46] Consider a statement by Senator John L. McClellan, of Arkansas: "I don't think anybody that gave me a contribution ever felt he was buying my vote or anything like that, but he certainly felt he had an entree to me to discuss things with me and I was under obligation at least to give him an audience when he desired it to hear his views." U.S. Senate, 84th Cong., 2d sess., Special Committee to Investigate Political Activities, Lobbying, and Campaign Contributions, *Hearings,* pursuant to S. Res. 219 and S. Res. 47 (1957), p. 1046.

tration's budget policy was slowing up income from the party's big givers. The pattern of contributions is but one dimension of the structure of interests clustered about parties.

All this is not to deny that from time to time—how often, nobody knows—campaign contributions purchase specific action.[47] A party or a candidate that encounters great difficulty in raising the money absolutely necessary to meet campaign expenses may be under an especially strong pressure to make concrete commitments in exchange for financial support. It may be—and there are scraps of evidence to support the view—that the party or candidate least dedicated to the cause of wealth tends more to put itself under obligation to do specific favors for contributors somewhat beyond the fringe of respectability. Dog-track operators do not let their ideology warp their political judgment; they can do business with either a liberal or a conservative; their chief concern is that they deal with a winner.

No rigorous examination has been made of the bearing of the size of campaign funds on the outcome of popular elections. A census of all races for all offices—congressional, state, and local—would probably show that most, but by no means all, winners had had the longer campaign purses. Even so, the question would remain whether money had turned the trick. Winners have a habit of attracting money. Yet it seems equally clear that in the really great elections, the presidential sweepstakes, the size of the campaign chest does not in itself control the outcome—although big donors may not be neglected after the election. The string of Democratic victories from 1936 to 1948 was accomplished against superior Republican financial resources. Money is not the sole currency of politics; Roosevelt held counters in the game that outweighed money. Nor can it be convincingly argued that superiority in campaign funds had a controlling influence in the Eisenhower victories of 1952 and 1956, though an ample supply of cash was a great convenience to the campaign managers.

The problem raised by the size of campaign funds has not been so much that the longer purse would prevail but that the less well-financed party could not get its case before the public or make an effective challenge. In presidential politics in recent campaigns this has been essentially a problem of Democratic finance. Managers of the Democratic campaigns of 1948, 1952, and 1956 struggled with recurring financial crises. Hours before a scheduled broadcast the money would not be available to pay the bill—which the broadcasters prudently insist was to be paid in advance. Or the till would not contain enough to move the candidate's special train more than a couple of hundred miles up the track.[48] Votes may outweigh dollars, but a tribune of the people who aspires to be President needs enough money

[47] See J. B. Shannon, *Money and Politics* (New York: Random House, 1959), especially chs. 2 and 3.
[48] See Jack Redding, *Inside the Democratic Party* (Indianapolis: Bobbs-Merrill, 1958), pp. 231, 273.

to meet the rockbottom campaign necessities. To some extent labor organizations have replaced the men of means who moved away from the Democrats in 1936, yet the party on the national level has chronic financial difficulties.

NEW DIRECTIONS IN REFORM   For decades legislators approached campaign finance as a problem in the prevention of corruption, either by individual purchase of undue influence or by subversion of the electorate through massive expenditures. Prohibitions of contributions from corporate sources or in excess of specified amounts coupled with publicity of party finance were thus the appropriate remedies. The ineffectiveness of regulatory measures led, especially among students of party finance, to espousal of the removal of limitations and insistence upon the most complete publicity. More recently, the outlook has developed that the basic problem is to make it possible for the parties to raise the large sums legitimately required for campaigning.

Party organizations have themselves made some effort to broaden the base of contributor support. Party finance specialists recognize that the development of a flow of regular contributions from large numbers of relatively small contributors would free parties from the importunities of those who give large sums when the till is empty and also permit more orderly planning and conduct of party activities. The numbers of contributors have increased, yet both parties are still largely dependent upon the big giver. Nevertheless, so long as campaigns are privately financed, the remedy for the financial vicissitudes of the parties rests solely in the hands of the parties themselves. Only they can raise the money to support themselves. It should not be supposed, though, that parties supported by large numbers of small givers would be free from the influence of money. The kinds of people who would contribute to the Republican party or the Democratic party would impose their general policy outlook firmly upon the parties. Yet freedom, especially in state and local politics, from the pressures of the big givers among contractors and other such groups would be a very considerable gain.

To aid the efforts of parties to lift themselves by their bootstraps, tax incentives to givers have been urged. The President's Commission on Campaign Costs in 1962 recommended that a tax credit of up to $20 be available on returns without an itemization of deductions and that an income deduction of up to $1,000 be permitted on returns with itemized deductions. The Minnesota and California state income tax laws grant certain incentives for political contributors.[49]

Tax incentives are worthless unless party organizations have an effective machine for solicitation. Despairing of the prospects for party action, some

[49] See Herbert E. Alexander, *Tax Incentives for Political Contributions* (Princeton: Citizens' Research Foundation, 1961).

persons urge direct government subsidy of campaign activity, a suggestion that raises extremely difficult problems of allocating public funds among party committees and candidates and that also stirs anxieties about the long-run possibility of extensive legislative interference with the internal workings of parties. In Puerto Rico, though, under rather peculiar conditions of party organization, a public subsidy has evidently worked well enough.[50] Short of subsidy for general campaign purposes, the suggestion is made of subsidies for television costs, for postage, and for other such specific objects of expenditure. Similarly, it has been proposed that states issue publicity pamphlets containing information about the candidates, a practice followed in Oregon and North Dakota.[51]

Another type of proposal is that radio and television stations be required to provide free time for candidates as a partial payment for the valuable privileges they gain from their licenses to operate. The radio and television industry resists this proposal with vigor. Apart from such resistance, the proposal raises difficult problems in the determination of the extent of the obligation of each station and in the rationing of time among candidates. The industry has been willing under certain circumstances to donate some time to political campaigners. The Federal Communications Act requires that equal opportunity be accorded to all candidates, a statutory standard which means that if time is given to one candidate, it must also be given to all other candidates. Thus, if a television station gives time to the Republican and Democratic candidates, it must do the same for the Socialist-Worker candidate, the Conservative candidate, and all the other candidates on the ballot. Under a congressional suspension of this requirement for the duration of the 1960 campaign as it applied to presidential and vice-presidential nominees, the television networks provided time worth between four and five million dollars for the "Great Debates" and certain other appearances by the candidates. The President's Committee on Campaign Costs in 1962 proposed that a similar suspension of the statutory requirement be again made for the campaign of 1964.

[50] Henry Wells, *Government Financing of Political Parties in Puerto Rico* (Princeton: Citizens' Research Foundation, 1961).

[51] O. C. Press, *Newspaper Advertising and Publicity Pamplets* (Fargo: North Dakota Institute for Regional Studies, 1955).

19.

PRESIDENTIAL

ELECTIONS

To THE ELECTORATE FALLS a crucial role in the democratic process. The nature of that role is fixed by the choices presented to the electorate by the party leaderships. Thus, the electoral role in a biparty system differs radically from that in a multiparty order. In one instance, the voters decide which party is to govern; in the other, the election may be only a census of shades of opinion within the electorate. In either instance, though, the party system both limits and fixes the nature of the action that can be taken by the electorate, a fact indicative of the basic significance of parties in democratic orders.

The place of the electorate in the political system has been described in many ways. Perhaps only in a biparty regime can the electorate be likened to a jury, and its vote, to a verdict. Less persuasive is the frequent personification of the electorate as a giant of a man who speaks at times in commanding tones, at times in riddles. Again, the electorate is compared to groups of sports fans, to spectators cheering for their favorite teams. Or it is pictured as built of antagonistic groups battling for economic self-interest or for ideological causes. Students of electoral behavior seek to identify factors guiding the individual voter to decision: his political inheritance, his friends, his associates, his group affiliations, his sources of information among the media. All these and other ways of viewing the electorate have their merits—and their limitations. The anthropomorphic conception of the great person of "the people" represents organismic fiction. On the other hand, concentration of attention on the individual voter pulverizes the electorate and diverts attention from its collective role in the process of governance.

Another approach toward an understanding of the function of the electorate is to regard elections as great acts of collective decision. What is the nature of the popular verdict in a presidential election? True, a thousand different "reasons" may explain the votes of individuals. But can a broad meaning be plausibly attributed to the results of a presidential election if it is examined in its total situational context and in its place in the stream of events? By such a view the nature of great popular decisions in presidential elections may possibly be divined. A rough categorization of presidential elections according to the dominant character of the popular decision may be attempted. Each election, to be sure, is unique; elections cannot be grouped neatly into pigeonholes. Nevertheless, an attempt to identify types of elections may suggest clues to the nature of collective electoral decision.[1]

[1] American students are familiar with the mechanics of the election of the President. For others it should be explained that the mode of election is, in form, indirect. The President is chosen by an electoral college for a term of four years. To constitute the electoral college each state appoints, "in such manner as the legislature thereof may direct, a number of electors equal to the whole number of Senators and Representatives to which the State may be entitled in Congress." Constitution, Art. II. The electors meet in each state and vote by ballot. The votes are counted by the President of the Senate. A majority of the electoral votes is necessary for election. In the absence of a majority, the House of Representatives chooses from among the three persons with the highest number of votes. The House votes by states, each state having one vote. Constitution, Amendment XII.

In practice state legislatures have directed that electors be chosen at large by popular vote within each state. Candidates for electors are nominated, through various procedures, by the parties within the states. The voters of a state may have a choice between slates of electors nominated by the Republican and Democratic organizations within the state. Each slate of electors, if it wins, is bound, by custom, to cast its electoral votes for the presidential candidate nominated by the national convention of its party. Violations of the customary obligation are most infrequent. The Supreme Court has held that a state legislature may permit state parties to require of their nominees for elector a pledge to vote for the party's candidate. Ray v. Blair, 343 U.S. 214 (1952). Despite his commitment by a pledge under the statute under which this case arose, one Alabama Democratic elector in 1956 cast his vote not for Stevenson but for Walter B. Jones, an Alabama judge. In 1960 an Oklahoma Republican elector, Henry D. Irwin, cast his vote for Harry F. Byrd rather than for Richard Nixon, the Republican candidate. In 1961 the Oklahoma legislature enacted a statute to require nominees for elector to file an oath that they would, if elected, support the nominee of the national convention of their party. Violation of this oath by an elector was made a misdemeanor punishable by a fine of not more than $1,000. To be differentiated from violators of the customary partisan obligation are "uninstructed" electors. Thus, in 1960 Mississippi chose an "uninstructed" slate of electors in the hope that a close vote in the electoral college might give the state bargaining leverage to advance its peculiar interests. Of Alabama's eleven 1960 Democratic electors, chosen in its party primary prior to the national convention, six were "unpledged" and five were committed to the support of the convention nominee. The "unpledged" electors voted for Byrd as did the Mississippi electors. See Ruth C. Silva, "State Law on the Nomination, Election, and Instruction of Presidential Electors,"

Landslides: Votes of Lack of Confidence

In the quest for an understanding of electoral decision, one category of elections appears quickly from an inspection of presidential elections. On occasion the electorate votes a party out of power in a decisive manner; it expresses clearly a lack of confidence in those who have been in charge of affairs. The mandate to the incoming party may be vague, and, indeed, it may be difficult to read into the vote a bill of explicit dissatisfactions with the party that has been cast out of office. Yet the election clearly expresses a widespread unhappiness with past performance. To this sort of election the term "landslide" may be applied, though that word in common usage means, unhappily, any election won by a large plurality. In those landslides that express a lack of confidence, the party in power, in comparison with the preceding election, loses voting strength in most counties of the nation. Though the data are lacking, the odds are that the decline in strength also permeates most social and economic classes.

In a landslide the might of the electorate in a democratic order appears in spectacular fashion. The people may not be able to govern themselves

American Political Science Review, 42 (1948), 523–29; Robert G. Dixon, Jr., "Electoral College Procedure," _Western Political Quarterly_, 3 (1950), 214–24; Lucius Wilmerding, _The Electoral College_ (New Brunswick: Rutgers University Press, 1958).

Proposals for a modification of the method of election of the President received extensive attention by Congress in the 1940's, 1950's, and 1960's. Among the agitators for change were southern politicians who believed that Negro and labor groups in politically close nonsouthern states with large numbers of electoral votes were able to compel presidential candidates to cater to them. Other groups were moved by a desire to adopt procedures that would make impossible the victory of a candidate with fewer popular votes than another, as well as by other motives. The principal proposals for reform were:

1. To substitute a direct popular vote by a national constituency.

2. To require the choice of those electors corresponding in number to the state's Representatives, from congressional districts rather than by general ticket at large.

3. To retain the present allotment of electoral votes among the states, but to abolish the electors and to provide for the division of the electoral votes of each state among the presidential candidates in the same proportions as the state's popular vote is divided among them.

Various combinations of the second and third proposals, as well as varying formulations of all three proposals, have been considered by Congress. See Ruth C. Silva, "The Lodge-Gossett Resolution: A Critical Analysis," _American Political Science Review_, 44 (1950), 86–99, and her "Reform of the Electoral System," _Review of Politics_, 14 (1952), 394–407. Extensive analyses of the proposals appear in _Nomination and Election of President and Vice President_, being Hearings before a Subcommittee of the Committee on the Judiciary, U.S. Senate, 84th Cong., 1st sess., on S.J. Res. 3 and other resolutions (March, April, 1955). Useful also are the analyses appearing in speeches by Senator Paul H. Douglas in the _Congressional Record_, March 26 and 29, 1956. See also Hearings, Subcommittee on Constitutional Amendments, Committee on Judiciary, U.S. Senate, 87th Cong., 1st sess., on S.J. Res. 1 (and others) Proposing Amendments to the Constitution Relating to the Method of Nomination and Election of the President and Vice President (1961).

but they can, through an electoral uprising, throw the old crowd out and demand a new order, without necessarily being capable of specifying exactly what it shall be. An election of this type may amount, if not to revolution, to its functional equivalent.

THE ELECTION OF 1932   The characteristics of the presidential election of 1932 correspond closely to those of the model of a landslide marking a general withdrawal of popular confidence in the party in power. The Great Depression brought injury not only to farmers and industrial workers but to employers, financiers, merchants, and all classes of people. The Republican Administration floundered as disaster piled upon disaster, and Mr. Hoover became the symbol of the many ills that beset many people. The polling of 1932 unmistakably expressed discontent against Mr. Hoover and his party; his proportion of the two-party vote declined from 58.8 per cent in 1928 to 40.9 per cent in 1932, an exceptionally wide movement of voters.

The shift away from the Republican party between 1928 and 1932 occurred almost everywhere. An analysis by counties according to the increase in the Democratic percentage of the vote appears in Table 19.1. In 99 per

Table 19.1   Landslide elections: Distribution of counties according to percentage point shift in popular vote, 1928–1932 and 1948–1952 [a]

Percentage Point Shift	Per Cent of Counties with Democratic Gains, 1928–1932 [b]	Per Cent of Counties with Republican Gains, 1948–1952 [c]
0–9	8.4	31.3
10–19	28.0	42.0
20–29	36.5	16.6
30–39	17.6	4.9
40–49	4.6	2.6
50 and over	3.9	1.6
Counties moving counter to trend [d]	1.0	1.0
	100.0	100.0

[a] For each election the proportions of counties rest on a sample of every tenth county alphabetically listed by states.

[b] The shift is measured by the difference in the Democratic percentage of the two-party vote.

[c] The shift is measured by the difference between the Republican percentage of the three-party vote in 1948 and the Republican percentage of the total vote in 1952.

[d] The widest movement counter to the trend among the counties in these cells of the samples was six percentage points.

cent of the counties of the country Mr. Hoover's proportion of the popular vote declined from 1928 to 1932; in over one-fourth of them the Republican strength dropped by more than 30 percentage points. Although sample surveys were not then in operation, other evidence suggests that declines in Republican strength occurred in all income and occupational groups. The election was not a revolt of the downtrodden; rather an antipathy toward the Administration and a yearning for something different permeated all social strata.[2]

OTHER LANDSLIDES   The 1932 election may be regarded as a prototype of the electoral decision that expresses a lack of confidence in the party in power. When one seeks to identify other elections that fit nicely into the same category, the limitations of any typology of elections become embarrassingly clear. The presidential election of 1952, however, in certain ways resembled that of 1932 and may be placed in the same general class. While different groups of people were animated by different motives, most classes of people shifted in some degree away from the Democratic party between 1948 and 1952. The total effect was a clear-cut withdrawal of majority support from the Democratic party. The spread of that shift in sentiment over the country is suggested by the data of Table 19.1. In 99 per cent of the counties the Republican proportion of the presidential vote increased between 1948 and 1952. The survey data indicate that the movement to the Republicans occurred also in almost all demographic groups. Republican gains were least marked in upper-income and occupational groups, presumably in part because by 1948 Republicans had enlisted almost their maximum possible support among these categories of people. The data of the Survey Research Center on the partisan divisions of income levels in 1948 and 1952 appear in Table 19.2.

The election of 1952 may have been a vote of lack of confidence in the Democratic party, but the results provided no explicit policy directives for the incoming Administration.[3] The electorate may make unequivocal judgments on past performance or between candidates, but its prescriptions for future action are blurred. The surveys indicated that the new Republicans tended to adhere to Democratic policies; a major foundation of the Repub-

[2] See Roy V. Peel and T. C. Donnelly, *The 1932 Campaign* (New York: Farrar & Rinehart, 1935).

[3] Herbert Hyman and Paul Sheatsley, on the basis of polls in the fall of 1947 and 1948, consider it probable that "Eisenhower could have been elected President on either major party ticket, in either 1948 or 1952." They surmise that "the issues of Communism, corruption and Korea, over which the 1952 campaign was fought, were of decidedly less importance than was the simple candidacy of Dwight D. Eisenhower." "The Political Appeal of President Eisenhower," *Public Opinion Quarterly*, 17 (1953–54), 443–60. See also J. C. Davies, "Charisma in the 1952 Campaign," *American Political Science Review*, 48 (1954), 1083–1102.

Table 19.2 *Partisan divisions in presidential elections of 1948 and 1952 by income levels* [a]

	Voted:			
	Republican	Democratic	Other	Did Not Vote
1952				
Under $2,000	30%	23%	[b]	47%
$2,000–2,999	36	31	1	32
$3,000–3,999	40	35	1	24
$4,000–4,999	41	41	1	17
$5,000 and over	59	28	1	12
1948				
Under $2,000	16%	28%	2	54%
$2,000–2,999	17	38	6	39
$3,000–3,999	35	34	5	26
$4,000–4,999	36	33	6	25
$5,000 and over	53	25	4	18

[a] From Angus Campbell, *et al.*, *The Voter Decides* (Evanston: Row, Peterson, 1954), p. 73.
[b] Less than 1 per cent.

lican victory consisted of persons who had voted Democratic in 1948, who had a Democratic policy orientation, and who continued to regard themselves as Democrats.[4]

The policy shadings of the electoral decision had to be discovered as the new Administration felt its way along diverse courses of action. The Republican party had won a mandate to govern, but the limits of that mandate were fuzzy. Old-guard Republicans gleefully concluded that they had been instructed to repeal the New Deal. As the Administration probed to locate the limits of its mandate it found it prudent in field after field to pull back from positions taken initially and to maintain substantially the status quo in policy. The obstructions encountered in Congress, the congressional elections of 1954 and 1956, the protests of pressure groups, and popular attitudes communicated to government by other means contributed to the definition of the terms of popular support of the Administration.

These remarks suggest some of the limits of the role of elections in the American democratic process. Elections measure only one dimension of public sentiment. The details of the electoral verdict have to be filled in by other

[4] On these points, see Angus Campbell, *et al.*, *The Voter Decides* (Evanston: Row, Peterson, 1954), ch. 12.

modes of consultation of the public. Elections are only one means by which popular influence plays upon government in a democratic order.[5]

Reaffirmation of Support: Votes of Confidence

In another type of presidential election substantially the same coalition of voters prevails as provided the majority in the preceding election. Such an election may be regarded as a vote of confidence in the general course of action the Administration has followed. Not all re-elections of Presidents or all instances in which the President succeeds another of the same party can be placed in this category. In some elections the Administration is returned to power but with substantial losses among one or more groups of voters and perhaps compensating gains among other groups. An ideal type of election as a simple vote of confidence would be one in which the party lines within the electorate had remained stable since the preceding polling.

ELECTIONS OF 1900, 1904, AND 1908   No election completely meets the specifications for a vote of confidence as it has been defined. Invariably from one election to the next some voters cross party lines in both directions. Others become disillusioned and decide to stay at home on election day. Yet in their broad context the elections of 1900, 1904, and 1908 may be regarded as reaffirmations of the vote of confidence won by the Republican party in the decisive election of 1896.

It seems probable that elections that build up social tension to extremely high peaks are followed by a letdown in the intensity of antagonism. The frenzied exertions of campaigners in such an election sharpen cleavages, produce a high turnout of voters on both sides, and perhaps mobilize the maximum strength of the minority. The outcome of the battle clearly establishes the supremacy of the victors, and the vote of the minority sags at the next election as it becomes apparent that all is lost anyway. Even the winning party, confident of its position, may drop strength here and there as its campaign efforts do not suffice to bring out its potential strength.

This sort of pattern seems to fit roughly the elections of 1896 and 1900. The silverites in 1896 fought a losing battle, but in so doing they exerted themselves mightily in their own domain to produce a maximum vote for

---

[5] The election of 1920 probably also belongs in our category of landslide elections. From 1916 to 1920, the Democratic percentage of the two-party vote declined from 51.7 to 36.1. Examination of the 1920 returns also suggests that one might form a category consisting of elections that mark a restoration of an equilibrium established at an earlier, landmark election. The county by county vote in 1920, for example, in some states closely resembled that of 1896, with the notable exception of Republican gains in 1920 in some counties populated by ethnic groups antagonized by Democratic foreign policy.

Bryan, the Democratic candidate. The election statistics make it look as though in the mining states every prospector voted and perhaps twice. The plebiscite of 1896 clearly settled the silver question and in 1900 McKinley easily won re-election. The most marked differences in the voting in 1896 and 1900 were in the western mining states. The mine owners did not pour money into the campaign this time; their cause was clearly lost. McKinley polled a markedly higher vote in the mining states than he had in 1896, while in many of the northeastern and southern states his strength dropped slightly.[6]

The candidacies in 1904 of the picturesque Theodore Roosevelt on the Republican ticket and of the conservative Democrat Alton B. Parker created a set of choices different from those presented to the voters in 1900. Yet the election of 1904 may be fitted into our general category of votes of confidence. The flamboyant Roosevelt with his progressive oratorical flourishes attracted new Republican support west of the Mississippi.[7] Eastern Republicans tolerated the forensics and supported him in slightly higher degree than they had McKinley in 1900. These contrasts in the shifts in the West and in the East between 1900 and 1904 are illustrated in detail for California and Indiana by the scatter-diagrams in Figure 19.1, which compare the Republican percentage of the vote, county by county, in the two elections. In Indiana, a state with a long history of tightly organized two-party politics, Roosevelt made gains over McKinley in most counties, but in California this gain was far more marked.

William Howard Taft in 1908 lacked Teddy Roosevelt's special appeal to the West but he managed to hold together the main elements of the coalition that had supported Roosevelt in 1904. The vote for Taft resembled more closely the 1900 vote for McKinley than it did the 1904 vote for Roosevelt. Most states with marked Republican losses from 1904 to 1908 were western states in which Roosevelt had drawn heavy new support in 1904.[8] By and large in the East Taft held the Republican support of 1904. Comparisons by county of the vote in 1904 and 1908 for the states of New York and Ohio, which appear in Figure 19.2, contrast the situation in a state in which the party lines held with a state in which the Republican strength declined.

[6] From 1896 to 1900 the Republican proportion of the popular vote increased by more than 10 percentage points in Colorado, Idaho, Montana, Nevada, Utah, Washington, and Wyoming.

[7] All the states, save one, in which the Republican percentage of the total presidential vote increased more than 10 percentage points from 1900 to 1904 were west of the Mississippi. They were Colorado, Idaho, Kansas, Michigan, Minnesota, Montana, Nebraska, Nevada, North Dakota, Oregon, South Dakota, Utah, and Washington.

[8] The states in which the Republican proportion of the total presidential vote declined by more than eight percentage points were Colorado, Idaho, Kansas, Minnesota, Nebraska, Nevada, North Dakota, Ohio, Oregon, Pennsylvania, South Dakota, Washington, Wisconsin, and Wyoming.

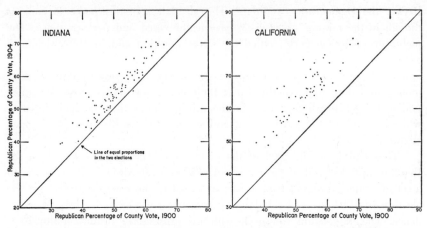

Figure 19.1   Presidential elections of 1900 and 1904 in Indiana and California: Comparisons of Republican percentage of vote by counties

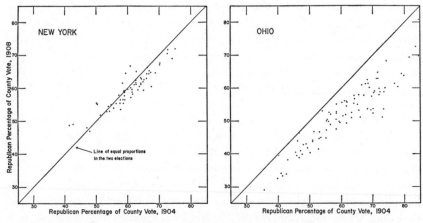

Figure 19.2   Presidential elections of 1904 and 1908 in New York and Ohio: Comparisons of Republican percentage of vote by counties

1948: REACTIVATION OF THE NEW DEAL COALI-
TION   In important aspects of the electoral behavior involved, the election of 1948 deviates from our model of a pure vote of confidence; yet in its
broad context that election amounted to a vote of confidence in the Democratic Administration. Since 1932 the Republican party had been attempting
to crack the new Democratic coalition. That combination held together
against attack with the notable exceptions of the defections of 1940 and
1944 on foreign policy questions. In the congressional elections of 1946

Republicans won majorities of Congress and proceeded to act as if they had a mandate to reverse New Deal policies.

In his forthright campaign of 1948 President Truman unequivocally championed the principal elements of the New Deal under the label of the Fair Deal. In contrast Governor Dewey followed a statesmanlike course; that is, his ambiguous utterances left doubt about his party's position on measures of interest to the component blocs of the Democratic coalition. In the voting, those groups of voters who had constituted the backbone of New Deal support rallied to the Democratic banner and confounded Republican expectations.

Mr. Truman's espousal of civil rights legislation yielded especially strong support among Negroes; the rebellion of the States' Rights Democrats aided in the retention and recruitment of northern Negro support. Industrial workers concurred with Truman's opposition to the Taft-Hartley Act and gave him their vote in high degree. Those Catholics who had been alienated by the wartime alliance with the Soviets found their return to the Democracy simplified by the defection of the Wallaceites. Midwestern farmers, antagonized by Republican congressional policy on agriculture, also made their way back to the Democratic party, a movement facilitated by the end of the war and the temporary lull on the foreign front which enabled farmers to focus on their domestic concerns. Metropolitan consumers were held in line by Truman's defense of controls over rents and prices.[9]

Group Alienation and Attraction: Realignments

A third type of presidential election usually involves a return of the Administration to power and in that sense might be regarded as a vote of confidence. Yet in this sort of election the Administration wins with the support of a coalition different from that comprising its majority at the preceding election. Large numbers of voters have been alienated and the support of others has been gained. The causes of these shifts are various. The Administration's policies may have repelled important groups of voters who desert its candidates in disenchantment; the same policies may well have also attracted new support. Or the movement may be in response to some characteristic of the candidate or feature of the program of the party challenging the ins. Thus, this sort of vote records a realignment among the groups supporting the parties, which may be either transient or durable. A specific policy or event may drive large proportions of a particular group from its traditional party attachment for a single election. Or the impact of policy or events may produce a durable realignment of the party loyalties of particular groups or classes of people.

[9] On the 1948 election, see Angus Campbell and Robert L. Kahn, *The People Elect a President* (Ann Arbor: Survey Research Center, 1952).

Always from one presidential election to the next some voters pass each other as they cross party lines. Hence, all elections might be classified in the category of those that involve an attraction and a repulsion, a realignment. Nevertheless, some elections reshuffle voters on an extremely large scale. In other instances the magnitude of the realignment may not be so great, but the electoral consequences of quite specific policies are readily identifiable and occur on a substantial scale: analysis of the voting makes it clear that fairly large numbers of voters have moved across party lines, apparently in response to the movement of events or to policy actions.

1928: MIXTURE OF DURABLE AND TRANSIENT REA- LIGNMENT   The combination that put Herbert Hoover into office in 1928 differed from that which supported Coolidge in 1924. The issues of the campaign drew heavy new support to the Republican ticket from certain sectors of the population, drove 1924 Republicans to the Democratic banner, and attracted to it also the support of many persons who had not voted in 1924. In large measure the new Republican support was transient in character, while the accretions to the Democratic ranks were far more durable. The election marked the recruitment to the Democratic party of large numbers of voters who were to remain staunch supporters for at least two decades.

The issues of the campaign activated latent animosities that cut across old party loyalties. The candidacy of Alfred E. Smith, a Catholic with a progressive record as governor of New York, drew heavy, new Democratic support in the metropolitan, industrial, foreign-born, and Catholic populations. This growth in Democratic strength was also associated with exceptionally high rates of increase in voter turnout, which suggested that the Democratic appeals tapped elements of the population not politically active in the preceding election. Especially notable were the Democratic gains in the New England states, where Rhode Island and Massachusetts went Democratic. Smith's opposition to prohibition as well as his Catholicism redounded to the advantage of Hoover in the rural, dry, Protestant areas of the nation. While the Republican share of the vote increased over that of 1924 in most rural areas predominantly Protestant, the campaign yielded the greatest Republican dividends in the southern states. Hoover carried several states of the Solid South, and in others the normal Democratic majorities were sharply reduced.[10] Illustrations of these contrasting movements within the electorate from 1924 to 1928 appear in Table 19.3.

[10] By an analysis by partial correlation of the 1928 vote in 173 randomly chosen counties in Massachusetts, New York, Ohio, Illinois, Wisconsin, Colorado, Montana, and California, W. F. Ogburn and N.S. Talbot found that the vote for Smith was more closely associated with antiprohibition sentiment than with Catholicism. "A Measurement of the Factors in the Presidential Election of 1928," *Social Forces*, 8 (1928), 175–83. By a more sophisticated correlation analysis of more comprehensive data, Ruth C. Silva

*Table 19.3   Realignment of 1928: Changes in Democratic propor-
tion of presidential vote, 1924–1928, in selected states*

Roman Catholic States			Protestant States		
State	Per Cent Catholic [a]	Demo-cratic Gain 1924– 1928 [b]	State	Per Cent Catholic	Demo-cratic Loss 1924– 1928
Rhode Island	47.3	13.7	Virginia	1.6	16.5
Massachusetts	38.3	25.5	Alabama	1.4	16.6
Connecticut	34.7	18.3	Tennessee	1.0	8.2
New Hampshire	31.5	6.5	Georgia	0.6	7.6
Vermont	24.9	17.3	S. Carolina	0.5	1.4
Maine	21.8	9.2	N. Carolina	0.2	13.8

[a] Number of Roman Catholics reported by 1926 census of religious bodies as a percentage of total 1930 population.

[b] Percentage point difference between 1924 Democratic percentage of three-party vote and 1928 Democratic percentage of two-party vote.

Although the Republicans triumphed in 1928, the campaign had the significant long-run result for the Democrats of creating abiding Democratic loyalties among metropolitan groups that had been either Republican or indifferent to politics. In its impact especially in the northeastern states, the election might be called a critical election in the sense that it froze into the electorate cleavages that were to prevail, at least in their main outlines, through 1948. The widened differences of 1928 between the cities and the countryside of New England persisted in subsequent presidential elections. On the other hand, over most of the country, the Republican gains of 1928 were wiped out in 1932.

1936: RATIFICATION OF THE NEW DEAL   In the realignments in the voting of 1936 the coalition built by the New Deal jelled. The 1932 voting had been characterized by accessions to Democratic strength among all classes of people. The unfolding of the Rooseveltian legislative program cemented additional support to the Democratic party and

has shown that Smith's 1928 strength (and weakness) had a far closer relation to variations in the population proportions of foreign white stock, that is, persons born abroad or with at least one parent born abroad, than to variations in Catholic population proportions. *Rum, Religion and Votes* (University Park: Pennsylvania State University Press, 1962). See also E. A. Moore, *A Catholic Runs for President* (New York: Ronald, 1956); A. R. Baggaley, "Religious Influence on Wisconsin Voting, 1928–1960," *American Political Science Review,* 56 (1962), 66–70.

simultaneously drove back to the Republican party many who had voted for a change in 1932.

No survey data are available for 1932 and statements about the movements of voters between 1932 and 1936 must necessarily be guarded. Yet, on the basis of extensive analysis of the election returns, educated guesses are possible. The policies of the New Deal brought in 1936 substantial new support from their beneficiaries. Metropolitan, industrial workers turned in heavy Democratic majorities. The unemployed, and those who feared that they might become unemployed, voted Democratic in higher degree. Organized labor moved more solidly into the Democratic ranks. These movements amounted to a continuation and confirmation of the trends that began in 1928.

Defections from the Democratic ranks were most notable in the business groups and in some rural areas. The Republican campaign against the New Deal voiced the resentment of business groups at new government regulations, expressed anxieties about the new role granted to organized labor, and assaulted welfare policies, such as the Social Security Act and unemployment relief. In area after area the voting statistics reveal an upsurge of Democratic strength in 1932 followed by a decline in 1936.[11] The departure of the business elements from the Democratic party manifested itself graphically in party finance. Contributions by manufacturers and bankers to the Democratic war chest in 1936 aggregated less than half the sum from those sources in 1932. The 1936 Republican take from these classes of contributors more than doubled that of 1932.

The return of a party to power under circumstances like those of the 1936 campaign gives such an election a special significance. Drastic innovations in public policy aroused bitter denunciation by the outs; the ins had to stand on their record. The electorate had before it the question whether to ratify these innovations, few of which had been clearly foreshadowed in the 1932 campaign. The result could only be interpreted as a popular ratification of the broad features of new public policy.

1940: ETHNIC RESPONSE TO FOREIGN POLICY   The existence in the United States of large blocs of immigrants and their immediate descendants with ties of sentiment and loyalty to their homelands has provided bases for a type of voting behavior perhaps peculiar among the great democracies. A line of foreign policy favorable to the old country may

---

[11] Gallup poll estimates of the Democratic percentage of occupational groups in 1936 were professional, 49; businessmen, 47; farmers, 59; white-collar workers, 61; skilled workers, 67; semiskilled workers, 74; unskilled workers, 81. See E. G. Benson and Paul Perry, "Analysis of Democratic-Republican Strength by Population Groups," *Public Opinion Quarterly*, 4 (1940), 464–73. On the 1932–1936 shifts in Iowa, see H. F. Gosnell and Norman Pearson, "The Study of Voting Behavior by Correlational Techniques," *American Sociological Review*, 4 (1939), 809–15.

attract the zealous support of those psychologically attached to their fellow countrymen abroad. The same policy may drive from a party other groups whose ancestry runs to nations not favored by the Administration's foreign policy.

Events preceding the 1940 election activated the primeval loyalties and hatreds of various nationality groups, and the 1940 election returns recorded marked Democratic losses among groups that had given Roosevelt strong support in 1936, as well as gains among other groups. The Administration's policy of hostility toward fascist aggression in Europe drove those of Germanic origin into the Republican camp in large numbers.[12] In city after city over the country, wards with large proportions of voters of Italian origin shifted away from the Democratic party. In county after county with large concentrations of persons of German origin, a like response to events occurred. That shift is illustrated by the analysis of the movement of voters from 1936 to 1940 in the counties of North Dakota, which appears in Table 19.4. The higher the proportion of persons of Germanic origin in North

Table 19.4   Foreign policy and ethnic voting: North Dakota counties according to percentage point decline in Democratic percentage of presidential vote, 1936–1940, related to percentage of county population of German or Russian origin, 1930

Per Cent of Population German or Russian [a]	Number of Counties Declining Specified Number of Percentage Points, 1936–1940				
	0–9	10–19	20–29	30–39	40–49
0–9	12	3			
10–19	5	10	2		
20–29		3	2		
30–39		3	3		
40–49			1	2	
50–59				3	1
60–69			2		
70–79					1
Total	17	19	10	5	2

[a] Proportions of county population born in Germany or Russia or of German or Russian parentage. Those of Russian birth or parentage were principally "Volga" Germans.

Dakota counties, the wider was the shift away from the Democratic party between 1936 and 1940. Whether this movement rested on a pacifism, espe-

[12] These shifts have been treated in detail by Samuel Lubell, *The Future of American Politics* (New York: Harper, 1952), ch. 7.

cially notable among the Volga Germans, or a dislike of Roosevelt's strong language about Hitler and the old country may be debatable, but that it occurred there can be no doubt.

The policy of friendship toward Britain and France attracted new support among the voters of areas inhabited by people of British origin. In the rural sections of Maine, New Hampshire, Vermont, and Massachusetts Roosevelt polled a higher proportion of the vote than he had in 1936, and doubtless over the entire country he attracted new support from persons sympathetic to the British cause. Administration criticism of German anti-Semitism renewed and strengthened the Democratic loyalties of Jews.[13]

As these sketchy remarks make plain, a variety of broad electoral decisions are grouped in the category of realignments. Their common characteristic is that blocs of voters move in opposite directions. The kinds of problems that these elections raise for the Administration put in office vary. In some instances the election may mark a stage in the dissolution of an old governing coalition. In another the election may provoke a reconsideration and perhaps a modification of Administration policy. It is as if substantial numbers of people were saying, "When we elected you before, we did not mean for you to do what you have done." In another instance the Administration may regard the election as a ratification of past actions by a new majority so strong that the defections may be viewed with equanimity. In still another the Administration may be alarmed by its losses but believe that the pursuit of its fixed policy course is warranted in the national interest.

ENDURING REALIGNMENTS   If elections are viewed with the advantage of considerable hindsight, another type of realignment may be identified that cuts across the categories we have established to this point. Every polling records the movement of some voters across party lines since the preceding election. These shifts may be minor in size or they may be transient and leave no durable imprint on the gross shape of the party groupings. Other elections may, however, introduce a lasting realignment within the electorate. The losing party loses not only the current election but a

[13] See L. H. Fuchs, *The Political Behavior of American Jews* (Glencoe: Free Press, 1956). From time to time the political orientation of religious groups is influenced by the foreign policy of the administration in power. Thus, in 1914 and 1916 Roman Catholic lay societies waged a campaign of criticism against the Wilson Administration for its policy toward disorders in Mexico that had injured the church in that country. See J. M. Blum, *Joe Tumulty and the Wilson Era* (Boston: Houghton Mifflin, 1951). Such injections of religion in politics are to be differentiated from those resting on simple domestic antagonism among religious groups. Thus, Theodore Roosevelt wrote in 1908 that he had received hundreds of letters from clergymen, "the more narrow-minded evangelical Protestants," protesting against Taft chiefly because he was a Unitarian. Anson Phelps Stokes, *Church and State in the United States* (New York: Harper, 1950), II, 405.

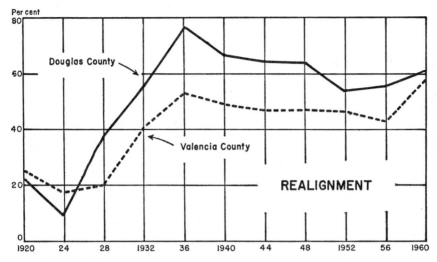

Figure 19.3   Realignment: Democratic percentage of two-party presidential vote, 1920–1960, in Douglas County, Wisconsin, and Valencia County, New Mexico

goodly number of elections in the future. The election of 1928 was in this sense "critical" in the metropolitan and industrial centers, notably in the Northeast. Republican strength in these areas declined abruptly to a lower level that was to prevail for decades.[14] The 1932 and 1936 elections marked the more or less permanent conversion of many more voters to a loyalty to the Democracy. Thus, over the period 1928–1936 a new cleavage was driven through the electorate and the country became normally Democratic. Illustrative of the shift are the graphs in Figure 19.3 which show the Democratic percentage of the two-party presidential vote from 1920 to 1960 in a pair of widely separated counties. To take into account the fact that these basic realignments seem to occur over several elections, MacRae and Meldrum propose that the term "critical period" rather than "critical elections" be employed.[15] An earlier critical election or critical period centered around the presidential election of 1896 when the Republicans formed a new coalition that was to dominate the country most of the time until the Democrats displaced it in the 1930's. Elections that partake of this critical nature are the most striking instances of electoral interposition in the governing process. They clear the way for a broad new direction in the course of public policy.

[14] For a statement of the concept of a "critical" election and for a detailed examination of the 1928 election in New England, see V. O. Key, Jr., "A Theory of Critical Elections," *Journal of Politics*, 17 (1955), 3–18.

[15] Duncan MacRae, Jr., and James A. Meldrum, "Critical Elections in Illinois: 1888–1958," *American Political Science Review*, 54 (1960), 669–83.

ANOTHER CATEGORIZATION OF ELECTIONS   Our categorization differentiates elections according to the nature of the popular decision. To place elections in such a scheme involves a degree of divination to estimate the meaning of the popular verdict. Another system of classification developed by Angus Campbell and his associates differentiates elections according to their relation to the pattern of party identification within the electorate. As has been seen in Chapter 8, the division of party identification between the parties has remained fairly stable over the period for which data are available. Elections may be classified according to the degree to which they reflect this pattern of party loyalties. On that basis, a typology of elections could contain the following classes:

1. *Maintaining elections.* These are elections which reflect chiefly the pattern of party identification within the electorate. They maintain the power of the "normal" majority. The elections of 1900, 1904, 1908, 1924, 1928, 1936, 1940, 1944, and 1948 could be regarded as maintaining elections.

2. *Deviating elections.* In these elections some event, condition, or candidate has the effect of displacing the normal majority from power; the election deviates from the pattern of party identification, though that pattern is itself not basically altered. The elections of 1952 and 1956 were deviating elections in the sense that the pattern of party identification remained predominantly Democratic but the Republican presidential candidate prevailed in the voting.

3. *Reinstating elections.* This category includes elections in which the party dominant in the pattern of party identification is returned to office after a deviating election. The elections of 1920 and 1960 could be so classified.

4. *Realigning elections.* In a realigning election a marked and enduring shift occurs in the division of party identification within the electorate. The minority becomes the "normal" majority.[16]

This system of pigeonholes has its utility in that it focuses attention on the relation of particular elections to the underlying and enduring pattern of partisan loyalties. Thus, the Kennedy victory in 1960 could be regarded as a reinstating election. The deviating elections of 1952 and 1956 had not altered the underlying majority attachment to the Democratic party. The "normal" majority reasserted itself in 1960, although the Democratic vote was somewhat smaller than it would have been had partisan loyalties alone governed the voting. The religious issue attracted to Kennedy a goodly number of Catholic Republicans and probably repelled a larger number of Protestant Democrats.[17]

---

[16] Angus Campbell, *et al., The American Voter* (New York: Wiley, 1960), ch. 19.

[17] See Philip E. Converse, *et al.,* "Stability and Change in 1960: A Reinstating Election," *American Political Science Review,* 55 (1961), 269–80. Converse estimates that the net loss Kennedy suffered by virtue of differences in Protestant and Catholic

Political Cycles and Secular Trends

Our categorization of presidential elections according to the nature of the broad electoral decision may convey the impression that elections are isolated, disconnected, or independent episodes in our political life. On the contrary, presidential elections are but quadrennial readings of the public temper which undergoes continuous change. Each election is a prelude to the next and each bears a greater or lesser resemblance to the preceding election. Each may be affected by gradual changes affecting particular groups of the electorate, changes that proceed steadily over long periods. Systematic knowledge of the processes of alteration of party attachments through time is most limited. Had Mr. Gallup's polling organization been in operation for a half-century or so, one could speak of these processes with greater confidence. Nevertheless, their effects are hidden away in the voting in every presidential election, and over the long run they may change significantly the general framework of attitude pattern and population composition within which individual campaigns occur. Despite the difficulty of identifying these changes, some indication of their probable character is in order.

ACCULTURATION AND PARTISANSHIP   The American political system has absorbed wave after wave of immigration. As each new influx of migrants arrived, peoples of like national origin, language, and culture formed political blocs attached to this or that party as circumstances, immediate self-interest, or a strategy of self-protection dictated. In most eastern seaboard cities the Irish adhered to the Democracy. Scandinavians tended toward the Republican party. Germans in some areas became Democrats; in others, Republicans. These groups were used by the parties and in turn they used the parties.[18]

Although from time to time specific events or issues activate memories linked to the homeland even across several generations, over the long run the cohesiveness of national-origin groups declines. Group ties weaken as English replaces the native language. The public schools place their stamp on the children. The next generation begins to find its way up the business ladder and into the professions. The slums are depopulated as people make their way by stages to the suburbs. A sense of resentment of exploitation of the group by professional Irish, Poles, or Italians develops. The old country

voting tendencies amounted to 2.2 per cent of the two-party vote. That is, if influences of party identification alone had governed the voting, Kennedy would have polled this much larger a vote.

[18] See Oscar Handlin, "The Immigrant and American Politics" in D. F. Bowers (ed.), *Foreign Influences in American Life* (Princeton: Princeton University Press, 1944).

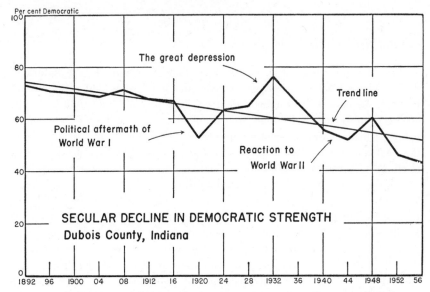

Figure 19.4   Democratic percentage of presidential vote in Dubois County, Indiana, 1892–1956

culture is gradually modified, if not displaced, by the American "culture."

Over the generations the gradual weakening of the cohesion of ethnic groups is paralleled by changes in voting behavior. A secular decline in the partisan solidarity of the group occurs as members of each generation become more susceptible to the political appeals to which people generally respond rather than to group-directed appeals. Individual elections may, to be sure, reactivate the ancient solidarity of particular groups. The secular decline in solidarity by no means follows a smooth curve. The rates of change may differ among different groups and even within the same national-origin group from place to place.

The data on these processes are almost nonexistent, but the evidence on geographically isolated pockets of settlement probably reflects changes that have been taking place in various groups in the electorate. Consider, for example, the record of Dubois County, Indiana, which appears in Figure 19.4. That chart shows the division of the presidential vote of a rural German Catholic community since 1892.[19] Over this period the Democratic proportion of the vote within this county rose and fell with variations in Democratic fortunes nationally, but the fluctuations occurred around a declining trend line over the long term.[20]

[19] See Elfrieda Lang, "German Immigration to Dubois County, Indiana, during the Nineteenth Century," *Indiana Magazine of History*, 41 (1945), 131–51.

[20] For other data on partisan changes through the generations, see Bernard Berelson,

The trend line on Dubois County shows a long-term change affecting a relatively isolated rural community, but the chances are that some such gradual processes of alteration affecting many groups not territorially segregated are hidden away in the election returns. Such secular changes do not, of course, have marked short-term effects on elections. From one election to the next the total change may be quite small, or movements in both directions may offset each other in the presidential voting. Yet over the long run this area or that is gradually transformed from a Democratic stronghold to a competitive area or even into a Republican stronghold, or the movement goes in the reverse direction. The processes of conversion cumulate over the decades and alter the "normal" balance of strength between the parties in cities and in states.

CHANGES IN STRUCTURE OF THE ECONOMY   Over the long sweep of time the gradual changes in the structure of the economy are reflected in the presidential voting as well as in the kinds of problems with which legislators have to wrestle. Exploitation by the Democratic party in this century of the opportunities created by industrialization provides a striking example. Yet even over shorter periods of time than that covered by the industrial revolution drastic alterations occur in particular states and regions. The gradual growth of Republican strength in the South has been principally the response of a growing urban middle class to the issues presented by the party system since 1932.

A long-time Democratic state may abruptly cross the 50–50 line, but that jump may have been preceded by accretions to Republican strength over many years. The chances are that political effects lag behind economic changes. Indeed, those changes do not automatically project themselves into the political arena but await stimulation and exploitation by political leadership. The nature of this temporal process may be inferred from Figure 19.5, which shows the extent to which the Republican and Democratic parties in New Hampshire have relied upon support from the industrial towns and cities since 1888. Before the turn of the century, each party drew about the same proportion of its strength from these areas. After 1896 a secular trend set in by which Democrats came to draw larger and larger proportions of their vote from the industrial towns and cities. The trend undoubtedly reflects factors other than the gradual activation of the Democratic potential among urban mill-workers. Persons of French-Canadian origin increased both in number and in their degree of attachment to the Democratic party. Whatever the factors involved, the chart suggests that many such currents may flow within the electorate over the decades.

---

et al., Voting (Chicago: University of Chicago Press, 1956), ch. 4, and Campbell, *et al.*, *The Voter Decides*, ch. 5.

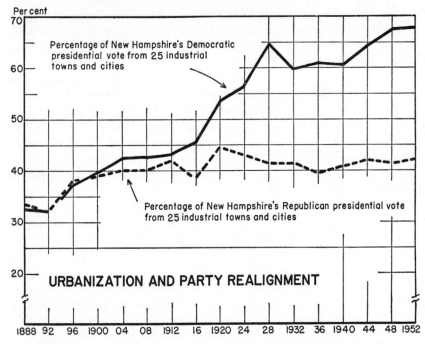

Per cent

Percentage of New Hampshire's Democratic presidential vote from 25 industrial towns and cities

Percentage of New Hampshire's Republican presidential vote from 25 industrial towns and cities

URBANIZATION AND PARTY REALIGNMENT

1888 92   96 1900 04   08 1912 16 1920 24   28 1932 36 1940 44   48 1952

Figure 19.5   Percentages of Democratic and Republican presidential vote in New Hampshire from 25 industrial towns and cities, 1888– 1952

INTERNAL MIGRATION   In the nineteenth century the pattern of distribution of the great streams of internal migration were of basic significance in the fixing of the partisan attachments of newly settled areas. Even now movements of people from place to place alter the politics of individual communities and states. They may not materially affect the balance between the parties in the nation as a whole, but they may make a one-party state a competitive state or otherwise alter the normal partisan division. Though the consequences of these movements cannot be measured with exactitude, the direction of their effects is often clear enough.

The gradual growth of Republican strength in Florida can be traced in large part to the continuing movement to that state of aging Republicans in quest of sunshine. Of the people who have been taking up residence in Arizona in recent years, about one-third, it is estimated, "do not need to earn their living." [21] World War II brought to Oregon shipyard workers from the South and East, and subsequently lumber companies imported woodsmen

[21] N. D. Houghton, "The 1956 Election in Arizona," *Western Political Quarterly,* X (1957), 97.

from the South. The Georgia drawl is heard in the lumber camps and mills. "With the southern accent has come a built-in inclination toward Democratic politics." [22]

Migration of the southern Negro to northern cities has had its consequences for the receiving states and localities in both local and national politics. The exodus of metropolitanites to the suburbs has its effects, though they are somewhat obscure. In some instances Democrats take over the suburbs; in other instances suburban Republicans are re-enforced by new recruits from the city. In still others new suburbanites transfer their allegiance from the Democracy to the Republican party. Probably of greater significance in conversion than physical movement to the suburbs is the fact that many new suburbanites are also ascending the income scale.[23]

POLITICAL CYCLES   The ubiquity of cyclical phenomena in nature has stimulated search for cyclical patterns in electoral behavior. Some speculators opine that the body politic undergoes a pulsating behavior. Movements of sentiment toward one extreme create their own corrective when a weariness of a politics of intensity sets in motion a swing back toward serenity. Arthur M. Schlesinger, for example, finds broad shifts in the nature of governmental policy and parallel changes in the general mood of the nation. The nation alternates between eras of conservatism and liberalism or between eras of emphasis on the rights of property and of emphasis on human welfare. These periods do not coincide with shifts in party control; the predominant mood of an era envelops Presidents and Congresses whatever their party complexion may be.[24]

Others identify cycles in the division of strength between the parties. Elections come to be determined by the stage in the cycle at which they occur. So long as two parties alternate in power a graph of party strength through time must assume a rough cyclical form. Whether the underlying behavior is "cyclical" may be another question.[25] Still others regard voting cycles as derivative of economic cycles. An analysis of presidential elections from 1828 through 1944 shows that the people tend to continue an administration in power during prosperous times and to vote against an administration "when depression marks the approach of election time." Over that period when prices were rising or at a high level of stability, the party in power was returned to power in 16 out of 18 elections. Changes in administration tended to occur when prices were declining or were stable at a low level. Among the exceptions to these general rules were the election of Hayes in 1876,

[22] J. M. Swarthout, "The 1956 Election in Oregon" in *ibid.*, p. 145.
[23] For further discussion of internal migration, see Chapter 9.
[24] A. M. Schlesinger, "Tides of American Politics," *Yale Review*, 29 (1939), 217–30.
[25] See Louis H. Bean, *How to Predict Elections* (New York: Knopf, 1948).

when the official outcome may have differed from the popular verdict, and that of 1912, when Theodore Roosevelt split the Republican party.[26] To picture presidential elections as episodes in a cyclical fluctuation of party divisions dependent on business cycles assigns to economic variations a predominant place in voting. Of their importance there can be no question. Yet on occasion other considerations, such as foreign policy, may offset the effects of a decline or a rise in economic well-being. Moreover, the supposition of derivative cycles assumes a popular disposition after a downswing to put in office whatever party is out of power, Republican or Democratic, an assumption perhaps not so valid as it once was.

A problem in the application of cycle theory to elections and voting is that fluctuations in party strength are not characterized by a neat periodicity. Equilibrium theory resembles cycle theory but it does not insist that peaks and troughs in party strength be equally spaced through time. It attempts to make sense of elections by regarding them as incidents in the life of a system actuated by forces that tend to restore or to maintain an equilibrium or balance between the two parties. The nature of the system is such that a great surge in strength of one of the parties, instead of continuing until the minority is eliminated, tends to set off forces that push toward a restoration of the balance. The least cohesive elements of the top-heavy majority desert; its marginal elements do not obtain what they believe they reserve, for the majority finds it too costly in policy concessions to hold their support; the inevitable errors of the exercise of power disenchant some supporters. From these and other causes the minority regains strength. It eventually becomes a majority and then suffers erosion from the forces that seek to restore the equilibrium. Over the long run the operation of the restoring forces may produce radically different popular foundations for the two parties as the minority recruits new support to replace those battalions it has lost to the majority.[27]

Elections in the Democratic Process

Presidential elections constitute decisions of fundamental significance in the democratic process. The trooping of millions of voters to the polls symbolizes self-rule and legitimizes the authority of governments. But beyond

[26] F. A. Pearson and W. I. Myers, "Prices and Presidents," *Farm Economics*, No. 163 (New York State College of Agriculture), September, 1948, pp. 4210–18.

[27] Donald E. Stokes has tested the hypothesis of the existence of forces tending toward an equilibrium by checking the historical record against a probability model. He finds that the chances are less than four in a hundred that the party division of the presidential vote could have fluctuated within its actual range since 1860 without the operation of forces tending to restore an equilibrium. See D. E. Stokes and G. R. Iverson, "On the Existence of Forces Restoring Party Competition," *Public Opinion Quarterly*, 26 (1962), 159–71.

such mystical functions of the electoral process, elections are pivotal decisions which in turn control many lesser determinations made in the name of the people. Our explorations have been in quest of some understanding of what the electorate does decide or of its role in the democratic process. Obviously the voters decide which party is to govern. That choice tends to bring in its train predictable consequences in direction if not in detail of governmental action, given the contrasting composition and policy orientations of the competing party leaderships. But what beyond the choices of governors do elections decide? Nothing, it may be said. Or a theorist with rationalistic inclinations may picture the party platform as a program of action which the winners are, by their solemn compact with the majority, bound to execute. Neither of these views satisfactorily reflects the reality. Considered in the framework of the flow of events and of the available alternatives, it seems clear that elections decide more than simply who shall govern.

Some elections, it has been argued, express clearly a lack of satisfaction with the performance of the crowd that has been in charge. The possibility of so efficacious an expression of discontent underlies the discipline of a democratic people over its government. Elected officials must live under the threat of defeat or disavowal. Other elections may be plausibly interpreted as a vote of confidence, an occasion when elected officials may happily acknowledge the gratitude of republics. More commonly the electorate may bring in a mixed verdict; some voters are happy with the course of affairs and others are deeply dissatisfied. Even these confused elections may, in their situational context, be meaningful decisions. Other elections may clearly and firmly fix the locus of power and the direction of policy for far more than the four years of a presidential term. Thus, the election of 1896 rejected the upsurge of western silver-agrarian radicalism and gave popular blessing to a coalition that governed until 1912 and returned to power in 1920. The election of 1936 ratified a sharp turn in public policy and successive Democratic victories clinched the reforms of the New Deal. A series of elections may fix the contours that guide the broad flow of public policy. Specific elections may give an unmistakable mandate for a change of direction. Others may approve a newly instituted order of affairs. Still others may record a majority support for the status quo, but the rumblings of the minority may be a portent of a growth of discontent.

Retrospective judgments by the electorate seem far more explicit than do its instructions for future action. An approval of the continuation of the prevailing course of action may be clear enough. Or a rejection of past performance may be resounding. Yet the most acute ear attuned to the voice of the people can sense only the vaguest guidance for innovation to cope with the questions that must be met day by day as an Administration governs. The efficacy of self-government thus depends on party and governmental leadership with the initiative and imagination necessary to meet the public problems that develop and with the courage to assume the political risks involved. The vocabulary of the voice of the people consists mainly of the words "yes" and "no"; and at times one cannot be certain which word is being uttered. On occasion it seems that assiduous but myopic dedication to the doctrine of self-rule brings governmental paralysis as timorous politicians listen vainly for positive instructions from the people. Popular government demands that politicians be accountable but it does not relieve them of the duty of initiative.[28]

These explorations provide a general conception of the limits and nature of the role of the electorate. As one attempts to see national elections in their place in the governing process—in their relation to the party system, in their bearing on the operations of government—it is well to ponder about the mores, the understandings, the customs, the conditions that make feasible these interpositions by the mass of the people in affairs of state. For a political order to withstand periodic electoral clashes, the electorate itself must possess appropriate expectations and inner restraints. Party leaderships in their relationships to the electorate and to each other must keep party warfare within tolerable limits. Governing officials must be bound by an intricate set of norms which, if they do not absolutely limit governmental action, fix procedures and forms of action that maximize acceptance of authority and thereby make contemplation of the consequences of elections bearable, if not invariably comforting.[29]

[28] The prediction of public reaction to new courses of action is so primitive an art that thoughtful politicians remark that the only course to follow is to take the action that seems right, on the assumption that it will be defensible at the next election.

[29] This chapter has been directed solely toward national elections. Elections in smaller jurisdictions reveal a far wider variety of electoral phenomena, much of it of a droll nature. The battles of the Smiths and the Jonses over which clan will name the county supervisor involve matters of a different order than presidential elections. Or a competition of three Irishmen and four Italians for a nomination in a mixed district may combine civic training and a lottery.

20.

CONGRESSIONAL

ELECTIONS

Essential to the American system of separation of powers is the mutually independent election of President and Congress. Vitality is breathed into the constitutional separateness of their positions by the fact that each owes its election and its allegiance, more or less directly, to the voters. Yet the separation of the choice of executive and legislature complicates the task of the electorate as it attempts to make those broad decisions that are its responsibility in a scheme of popular government.

The electorate must choose, not an assortment of unrelated functionaries, but a government. Yet on the day of a presidential election not one but around 500 elections occur. Fifty states choose presidential electors, 435 districts elect Representatives, and a third of the states designate Senators. The problem of choice becomes manageable through the workings of the party system, which allies in common cause candidates for the Presidency and for the Senate and House. By the partisan linkage of candidates, Democratic and Republican, from California to Massachusetts, from North Carolina to Montana, great decisions on the general direction of governmental action can be made by the voters.

Despite the capacity of the party system to confront the nation's electorate with great alternatives, the independence of the choice of executive and legislature assures that elections will produce a mixed mandate. To some extent the affairs of senatorial politics in each state and of congressional politics in each district are governed, not by the great considerations of national politics, but by questions peculiar to the locality. A state may return a Democratic candidate to the Senate on the same day that it gives its electoral vote to the Republican presidential aspirant. A landslide may carry a President and congressional majorities of his party into office. Yet simultaneously, local and parochial considerations may be influential in the choice of individual Senators and Representatives. One Senator may be invincible whatever the direction of movement of the tides of national politics. Another may owe his election indubitably to his unequivocal association with the policies advocated by his party's presidential candidate.

This mixture of nationalism and parochialism in elections contains the roots of the conflicting tendencies of amalgamation and cleavage in executive-congressional relations. That mixture also makes it difficult to discern what a national election decides. Yet, by patient analysis of congressional voting, recurring patterns can be identified, patterns that disentangle to some extent the components of nationalism and parochialism in a national election. The sharper identification of these factors ought as well to promote an understanding of some aspects of the party system that remain obscure when attention centers solely on presidential politics. In this analysis the Senate and the House will receive separate consideration, since the roles and manner of election of these bodies differ.

Electoral Bases of Senatorial Roles

Among parliamentary bodies of the world the American Senate is unique. As it has grown in prestige and authority, other upper chambers have evolved into debating societies or havens for superannuated politicians. The basic circumstance that permits the Senate to flourish is the existence of presidential government which makes possible a genuine bicameralism. Other factors also contribute to the position of the Senate. The freedom of discussion enjoyed by its small membership makes it a forum for full, if not always elevating, debate. The popular election of Senators by constituencies that are often truly great commonwealths endows Senators with an authority not enjoyed by members of upper houses who are designated by appointment or by accident of birth.

Beyond such factors the manner in which the Senate as an institution meshes with the party system profoundly influences its behavior. Forces of localism and of party compete for the loyalty of Senators, and the relative weights of these forces are rooted in the characteristics of the party system. Moreover, the expression of these forces is affected by the electoral calendar. With a six-year term, a Senator may, and at times does, bombastically represent the temper of his constituency as of four or five years earlier. The six-year term also puts many senatorial elections in the off years when the nation seems to speak with a different voice than it does in the years of presidential voting.

SENATORS AND VARIATIONS IN PARTY COMPETITION
Observation of the American Senate may yield an impression of chaos and disorder, of an arena in which strong men—be they honorable men or scoundrels—can construct for themselves positions of great power and influence and indulge in the most eccentric individualistic politics. Yet not all is anarchy within the Senate. Good and sufficient reasons inherent in the situations in which Senators find themselves account by and large for their differences of behavior.

Variations in the degree to which the parties are competitive within their respective states condition the policy inclinations of Senators. Those from one-party states may be untouched by the great tides of national politics. On the other hand, Senators from close states may live under the strongest compulsion to collaborate among themselves in the promotion of the cause of their party nationally. These variations in party competition are an index of other differences among the states. A Democratic Senator from Georgia, secure in his position, works in a different field of influence than does a Democrat from Illinois. A Republican from New York, uncertain in his tenure, confronts a different world than does the Republican from Kansas, almost certain of re-election until dotage or death overtakes him. The conditions of election in sure states tend to separate the Senator from the fortunes of his party nationally. The weakness of party competition often reflects the existence of a regional interest to which the Senator must devote himself undeviatingly.

The proportion of Senators from sure states and from competitive states varies from time to time. For long periods a state may elect Senators by overwhelming majorities and then a major realignment will bring the state's senatorial seats into the contested category. A gross conception of the extent to which senatorial choices result from closely fought battles may be derived from Table 20.1, which groups senatorial elections from 1920 to 1962 according to the closeness of the vote. If an election won by less than 60 per cent of the vote is regarded as contested—a generous definition of contested —about one-half of the elections over the period were warmly fought. A more realistic estimate would be that one-third of the senatorial elections were closely contested. By the same token no overpowering uncertainty existed about the results of perhaps one-half of the senatorial elections.

A larger proportion of Democratic than of Republican Senators is elected without serious challenge. Over the period 1920–1962, more than one-half of the Democratic winners carried their states by more than 60

Table 20.1   Sure and close Senate races: Distribution of senatorial elections, 1920–1962, according to Democratic percentage of two-party vote [a]

Democratic Percentage of Vote	Number of Elections	Per Cent of Elections	Distribution by Winning Party	
			Per Cent of Republicans	Per Cent of Democrats
0–9	5	0.7	1.7	
10–19	6	0.9	2.0	
20–29	28	4.0	9.6	
30–39	55	7.9	18.8	
40–44	81	11.6	27.6	
45–49	118	16.9	40.3	
50–54	108	15.5		26.7
55–59	86	12.3		21.2
60–69	72	10.3		17.8
70–79	35	5.0		8.6
80–89	27	3.9		6.7
90–100	77	11.0		19.0
Total	698	100.0	100.0	100.0

[a] Includes only elections for a full six-year term; excludes eight elections at which independent or third-party candidates won.

per cent of the popular vote, while only slightly over one-third of the Republican Senators polled as large a vote. Around 35 per cent of the Democrats, mostly southerners, won with more than 70 per cent of the vote.

ARTICULATION OF SENATORIAL AND PRESIDENTIAL ELECTIONS   The character of the Senate itself, as well as the nature of the broad decisions made by the electorate, is affected by the constitutional scheme for the election of Senators. A different situation prevails in the election of Senators in presidential years than in off years. In presidential years a fairly close articulation prevails in the voting for President and for Senate. The winning presidential candidate tends to carry into office with himself senatorial candidates on his party ticket. It is absurd to speak of this phenomenon as a pure coattail effect.[1] Both presidential and senatorial candidates are propelled into office by a trend, or a burst, of sentiment favorable to the winning party (or unfavorable to the losing party). Yet the constitu-

[1] Warren E. Miller, "Presidential Coattails: A Study in Political Myth and Methodology," *Public Opinion Quarterly*, 19 (1955–56), 353–68.

tional system also cushions these trends and limits their impact, for only a third of the Senate is renewed at the time of a presidential election. The other Senators remain, if not untouched by the political winds of the moment, somewhat sheltered from their blast.

To understand more precisely the relationship between senatorial and presidential voting in presidential years requires attentive study of Table 20.2, which analyzes the senatorial elections of 1920, 1924, 1928, 1952, and

Table 20.2   Articulation of presidential and senatorial voting in years of Republican presidential victory, 1920, 1924, 1928, 1952, 1956

State Republican Presidential Percentage	Republican Seats [a]			Democratic Seats			All Seats	
	Number	Number Held	Per Cent Held	Number	Number Lost	Per Cent Lost	Number	Per Cent Republican
0–19				5	0	0.0	5	0.0
20–29				4	0	0.0	4	0.0
30–39				8	0	0.0	8	0.0
40–49				13	3 [b]	23.1	13	23.1
50–59	28	21	75.0	33	12	33.4	61	54.1
60–69	32	30	93.8	12	8	66.7	44	86.4
70–79	17	16 [c]	94.1	4	4	100.0	21	95.2
80–100	3	3	100.0	0	0		3	100.0

[a] Republican seats include those for which Republican incumbents sought re-election and those seats to which a Republican had last been elected. The same rule defined the Democratic seats. The tabulation covers only those elections for full six-year terms.

[b] These are the three seats, mentioned in the text, won by Republicans despite the loss of the states by their presidential candidate.

[c] The only Republican seat classified as lost was that of Smith W. Brookhart of Iowa whose 1924 certificate of election was successfully contested before the Senate by his Democratic opponent.

1956, years of Republican presidential victory. Observe, first (from the right-hand column), that the wider the margin of victory of the Republican presidential candidate in a state, the greater were the chances that the Republican senatorial candidate would also carry the state. As the parties within the states become more competitive, the presidential candidate, in years of Republican victory, demonstrates greater popular strength than that of his senatorial running mates. If the winning presidential candidate does not carry a state, the chances that the Republican senatorial candidate will win become slight indeed. In the elections analyzed, only three Republican senatorial candidates won as their states went Democratic presidentially.[2]

Table 20.2 highlights another set of relations between the presidential plebiscite and the senatorial sweepstakes. The capacity of a drift to the Republicans to carry senatorial candidates into office with the presidential candidate depends on whether seats have been held by Republicans or Democrats. Almost certainly a Republican will replace a Republican in those states carried by the winning Republican presidential candidate. In the elections analyzed, only a handful of Republican seats were lost to the Democrats in states carried by the Republican presidential candidate. Most of these losses occurred in 1952 when Republicans Ecton of Montana, Cain of Washington, Kem of Missouri, and Lodge of Massachusetts were defeated as General Eisenhower led in their states. With the exception of Lodge, who met formidable Democratic opposition, these candidates were notable exponents of policies opposed to those supposedly fostered by the General. It may not be politically profitable, in a close state, to be conspicuously out of harmony with the head of a ticket who happens to gauge the popular mood correctly. Other factors, too, may account for loss of a senatorial seat as the presidential candidate wins. In 1956, for example, Democrat Joseph Clark replaced James H. Duff of Pennsylvania as Eisenhower carried the state, a result, among other things, of division in the Republican organization.

In their years of presidential triumph Republicans have greater success in retaining senatorial seats than in wresting seats from Democrats. The wider the Republican presidential margin, the greater are the odds that the Democrats will lose the senatorial seats they occupy. Here again the data of Table 20.2 are instructive. The exact nature of the phenomena underlying the capacity of Democrats to retain seats in the fashion indicated by the table must remain speculative. Perhaps the amassing of popular strength behind a winning presidential candidate may be likened to a tidal wave that destroys those structures nearest the point of initial impact and does less and less damage to other structures as it moves inland. The resistance of Democratic state organizations to the impact of a Republican presidential victory varies similarly among the states. Senatorial posts are lost most frequently in those states in which the Republican presidential candidate is strongest, and as his appeal declines, from state to state, the chances that Democrats will hold senatorial places increase.

Democratic survival of Republican presidential victory appears most marked in the years of Republican landslides. In 1928 Hoover carried state after state in which Democratic Senators retained their posts. Among them were King of Utah, Dill of Washington, Kendrick of Wyoming, Pittman of Nevada, Wheeler of Montana, Ashurst of Arizona, and Copeland of New

---

[2] Pine in Oklahoma in 1920; Hebert in Rhode Island in 1928; and Ernst in Kentucky in 1920.

York. In the same year several southern Democratic Senators, less surprisingly, won re-election as Hoover carried their states. The Eisenhower sweep of 1952 similarly accounted for several of the instances in the table in which Democrats held Senate seats against the Republican tide: Byrd of Virginia, Chavez of New Mexico, Pastore of Rhode Island, Holland of Florida, Daniel of Texas, and Gore of Tennessee. Obviously a factor contributing to the capacity to maintain control of a seat is the political potency of a well-established incumbent Senator with a large personal following.

In years of Democratic presidential victories, the prospects of senatorial candidates, Democratic and Republican, are the reverse of those prevailing in years of Republican triumph. Table 20.3, which analyzes senatorial elec-

Table 20.3   Articulation of presidential and senatorial voting in years of Democratic presidential victory, 1932, 1936, 1940, 1944, 1948, 1960

| State | Democratic Seats [a] | | | Republican Seats | | | All Seats | |
Democratic Presidential Percentage	Num-ber	Num-ber Held	Per Cent Held	Num-ber	Num-ber Lost	Per Cent Lost	Num-ber	Per Cent Demo-cratic
0–29	4 [b]	4	100.0	0	0		4	100.0
30–39	1 [b]	1	100.0	3	0	0.0	4	25.0
40–49	11	6	54.5	32	5 [c]	15.6	43	25.6
50–59	50	46	92.0	28	19	67.8	80 [d]	81.2
60–69	19	19	100.0	13	8	61.5	33 [d]	81.8
70–79	12	12	100.0	1	0	0.0	13	92.3
80 and over	18	18	100.0	0	0		18	100.0

[a] Seats for which Democratic incumbents were candidates for re-election or seats to which a Democrat had last been elected. The tabulation includes only elections for regular six-year terms.

[b] These deviant seats included four southern seats filled, as usual, by Democrats in 1948 as their states went Dixiecratic presidentially and the Mississippi seat won by a Democrat in 1960 as uninstructed electors were chosen.

[c] These are the seats, mentioned in the text, won by Democratic candidates despite the inability of the Democratic presidential winner to carry the states concerned.

[d] These totals include independent and third-party seats.

tions in Democratic years, is almost a mirror image of the preceding table. In Democratic years the chances for election of Democratic senatorial candidates increases, from state to state, as the popular margin of the presidential candidate widens. The exceptions to this rule that appear in the table were elections of Democrats in 1948 in southern states that went Dixiecratic presidentially. If the Democratic presidential candidate does not carry a state, the Democratic senatorial candidate has little chance to win a seat held by a

Republican. Only five instances occurred in the six presidential election years analyzed in Table 20.3.[3]

In their years of presidential triumph, Democrats can expect to retain virtually all those seats they hold in the states their presidential candidate carries. Such seats tend to be lost only under exceptional circumstances.[4] On the other hand, Republicans manage to hold a goodly number of senatorial seats in states that their presidential candidate loses. The stronger the Democratic presidential candidate, from state to state, the smaller is the probability that Republicans will retain their seats. Yet most striking instances of capacity to stand against the Democratic tide occur. The most extreme case among those in the table was the 1932 North Dakota election, when Republican Gerald Nye went back into office with 72 per cent of the vote as 71 per cent of the Dakota voters marked their ballots for Franklin Roosevelt.[5]

These analyses resolve themselves down to the proposition that the fortunes of presidential and of senatorial candidates are fairly closely articulated in presidential years. The party that wins the presidency manages to retain most of the seats it holds from states whose electoral vote it captures. It makes inroads on the seats held by the party losing the Presidency although that party manifests considerable capacity to withstand the presidential tide. Individual senatorial candidates have a keen awareness of these relationships and often choose their campaign tactics accordingly. In Iowa in 1948, when the prospects for Mr. Truman were on the dark side, Guy Gillette, Democratic candidate for re-election to the Senate, sought to avoid a close tie-up with the Truman candidacy. Some of his campaign literature did not identify him as a Democrat. On the other hand, in 1952 in Wisconsin, Joseph McCarthy made energetic efforts to get aboard the Eisenhower bandwagon. In the same year in Massachusetts, Democrat John F. Kennedy, perhaps unimpressed by the chances for Stevenson, did not strive to associate himself sharply in the public mind with the head of the ticket.[6] A presidential candi-

---

[3] In 1932 George H. Moses of New Hampshire lost to Democrat Fred H. Brown, and Hiram Bingham of Connecticut was defeated by August Lonergan. In 1944 John Moses replaced Gerald Nye in North Dakota, and in 1948 J. Allen Frear won over C. Douglass Buck in Delaware.

[4] Illustrative was the 1936 victory of Henry Cabot Lodge, Jr., heir to a famous Massachusetts political name over James Michael Curley, a Democrat strong in Boston but weak elsewhere in the state, who sought to win a seat to which a Democrat had last been elected. In 1960 the Democrats carried Delaware's electoral vote, but the incumbent Democratic Senator, a conservative opposed by labor, fell by the wayside.

[5] Other instances of Republican senatorial survival of the disaster that befell their presidential candidate in their states include the victories of McNary in Oregon in 1936, of Borah in Idaho in the same year, of Norbeck in South Dakota in 1932, and of Saltonstall in Massachusetts in 1960.

[6] In Connecticut in 1952 the percentages of senatorial candidates' advertisements and news items about them that associated the state race with the presidential campaign were for Ribicoff, the Democratic candidate, 7; for Bush, the Republican, 98. L. C. Ferguson and R. H. Smuckler, *Politics in the Press* (East Lansing: Michigan State College, 1954), p. 57.

date, too, may believe it advantageous to separate himself from a senatorial candidate of his party.

OFF-YEAR SENATORIAL ELECTIONS   The victorious party amasses support behind its presidential candidate whose strength its senatorial candidates seem never to match. Yet the direction of the movement of public sentiment tends to be unmistakably clear: it is toward one party—in both executive and senatorial spheres—and against the other. In the off years the conditions of electoral decision are different. Each senatorial race becomes, or at least appears to become, to a degree an autonomous event. Nevertheless, each race occurs within the framework of the balance of power in presidential politics, and the off-year results are closely related to the presidential voting of the preceding presidential year. In senatorial as in House elections, the candidates of the President's party are at a disadvantage in the off years.

Close inspection of Table 20.4, which analyzes senatorial elections in the

Table 20.4   Advantage of the outs in off-year senatorial elections: Results of senatorial elections in off years during Republican presidential administrations, 1920–1958

State Republican Presidential Percentage in Preceding Election	Republican Seats [a]		Democratic Seats [b]	
	Number	Number Lost	Number	Number Lost
Under 40	0	0	15	0
40–49	6	4	8	0
50–59	22	15	31	0
60–69	37	12	11	5 [c]
70–79	20	5 [d]	0	0

[a] Seats to which Republicans had last been elected.
[b] Seats to which Democrats had last been elected.
[c] These are the exceptional instances, mentioned in the text, in which Democrats, from states which had developed extremely strong Republican presidential preferences, lost in the off years of Republican administrations.
[d] Four of these seats were lost in 1922; one, in Maine, was lost in 1958.

off years of Republican administrations, reveals the character of the midterm decision. From that table it is plain that the probability of loss of Republican senatorial seats in the off years of Republican administrations increases, from state to state, as the strength demonstrated by the Republican President in the preceding election declines. Perhaps the less strong the current Republican predisposition of a state, the greater are the chances that general dissatisfaction with the national administration, unpopularity of a particular Senator, or peculiar local factors will result in the loss of a Republican seat in the off years. Whatever the factors producing the outcomes of the individual elections, the total effect is a party-oriented action by the electorate.[7]

In a few instances Democrats lost seats at these midterm elections. Even these losses fit the interpretation of midterm results as party-oriented. Republicans picked up seats at the midterm chiefly in states in which their presidential candidate had shown extremely great strength at the preceding elections. In at least some of these states a sharp shift in presidential preference of the state had occurred since the incumbent Senator of the outs was elected. Thus, 1922, a year of generally good fortune for Democratic candidates, saw the defeat of Gilbert M. Hitchcock of Nebraska who had been elected in 1916 when Wilson drew 57 per cent of the Nebraska vote. By 1920 the Democrats could muster only 33 per cent of the state's vote in the presidential polling, and Nebraskans in 1922 elected Republican Robert B. Howell to bring their senatorial representation into line with their changed presidential preference. Similarly, in 1954, Iowans declined to return to the Senate Guy Gillette, who had won, along with Truman, in 1948. By 1952 Democrats could attract only 35.8 per cent of the Iowa presidential vote and the overwhelming Republican preference persisted sufficiently in 1954 to defeat Gillette.

Yet it should not be supposed that all midterm senatorial elections are precisely alike. The tendency of the President's party to lose a few seats and only under exceptional circumstances to take seats from the outs appears quite uniform. On occasion, however, the reaction against the President's party is so marked as to indicate a sharp loss of public confidence. Such an instance turns up neatly in Table 20.4, which shows a handful of Republican seats lost in 1922 despite the fact that Harding had carried the states concerned in 1920 with over 70 per cent of the vote. So extreme a shift in popular sentiment indicated the depth of discontent generated by the sharp economic downswing early in the Harding Administration. Similarly, in 1958 eight Republican seats in states that had given Eisenhower in 1956 over 60 per cent of their vote were won by Democrats, shifts expressive of an unusual loss of popular confidence by the Administration.

During Democratic presidential administrations the pattern of off-year senatorial elections is, in form, the same as that prevailing in Rpublican administrations: that is, Republicans usually capture some Democratic Senate seats. The chances of an overturn are related to the Democratic presidential strength in the preceding polling. The wider the Democratic margin, the less

---

[7] Senators may attempt to escape retribution when the prospects look bleak by differentiating themselves from their Administration; to what, if any avail, is not clear. Thus, in 1958 Republican Senator Edward J. Thye of Minnesota had been a vigorous critic of Republican farm policies, which were unpopular among Minnesota farmers. Nevertheless, the voters replaced him by a Democrat.

hopefully may a Republican candidate eye a seat occupied by a Democrat. The stronger a Democratic President has shown himself to be in a state, the more confidently may a Democratic Senator from that state expect re-election.

The details of these relationships are set out in Table 20.5, which also contains data to re-enforce the earlier observation that not all midterm elec-

Table 20.5   *Advantage of the outs in off-year senatorial elections: Results of senatorial elections in off years during Democratic presidential administrations, 1932–1950, 1962*

State Democratic Presidential Percentage in Preceding Election	Democratic Seats [a]		Republican Seats [b]	
	Number	Number Lost	Number	Number Lost [c]
40–49	19	7	31	4
50–59	45	20	26	8
60–69	26	3	7	3
70–79	11	0	1	0

[a] Seats to which Democrats had last been elected.

[b] Seats to which Republicans had last been elected.

[c] Of these losses of Republican seats at midterm elections, 10 occurred in 1934; 4 in 1962. The table includes only elections for full terms, and does not cover seats won or lost by extremely wide margins.

tions are alike. Commonly the President's party can have only the most slender hope in its midterm campaigns to capture Senate seats held by the opposition. Yet Table 20.5 turns up a goodly number of instances in which Democratic candidates replaced Republicans at the midterm of Democratic administrations. The largest number occurred in the 1934 elections, when the electorate expressed overwhelming approval of the New Deal by voting Republicans out of office on a large scale, contrary to the usual midterm pattern. In 1962 several Republican Senate seats were lost to Democrats, which suggested that special circumstances existed to strengthen Democrats generally at this off-year election, though peculiar weaknesses of the incumbent Republican candidates contributed to some of the losses.

PATTERNS OF SENATORIAL ELECTIONS AND THE PARTY SYSTEM   The combination of party institutions, patterns of electoral behavior, and electoral procedures that has been described contributes to the powerful resistance of particular areas and interests to the nationalizing tendencies within the parties—that is, to the decentralization, or perhaps the fractionalization, of power within the political system. Mass sentiment that crystallizes in support of a winning presidential candidate cannot be converted into an equivalent control over the Senate. The force of the winning presidential coalition is splintered by the staggering of Senate terms, and even those Senators of the President's party who go into office may owe nothing to him because they come from sure states.

By and large, resistance to the power of the winning presidential coalition expresses itself in party terms, in the capacity of some minority candidates to withstand the surge of the presidential campaign itself, and in the capacity of others to win election in the off years. The minority, Republican or Democratic, fights from bastions of strength not readily reducible by the triumphant majority. Whether the provision of bulwarks for the minority invariably redounds to the general weal may be debatable, but there can be no doubt that our arrangements include such bulwarks. Their significance can perhaps be surmised by consideration of the probable results of electing the entire Senate for four-year terms in the years of presidential elections. Minority representation in the Senate might, in time, be reduced to minuscule proportions. Moreover, the fortunes of the Senators of the President's party would become more closely bound to those of the President and perhaps vice versa. A marked transformation of the character of the Senate would probably occur.

Party, Presidency, and House of Representatives

While the House of Representatives is constitutionally as independent of the executive as is the Senate, the timing and circumstances of its election bring it more strongly under the nationalizing influences of party. The renewal of the entire membership of the House at the time of the presidential election associates the political fortunes of House candidates more closely with their party ticket. Even the midterm elections, a consequence of the two-year House term, tend to reflect shifts in national sentiment toward the parties as a whole, though peculiar local factors often determine the results of individual races.

COORDINATION OF ELECTIONS OF REPRESENTATIVES AND PRESIDENT   The simultaneous election of the President and of all House members enables the electorate to place control of these two organs of government in one or the other of the major parties. Furthermore, it permits, though it does not assure, a maximum unification of party campaign effort behind both presidential and congressional candidates and subjects most races for Representative to the influences that play upon presidential voting.

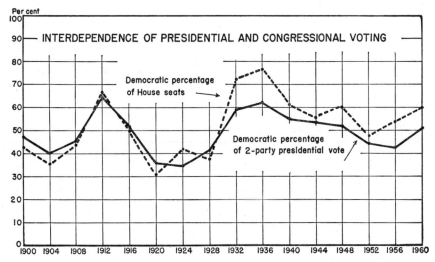

Figure 20.1   Democratic percentage of two-party vote for President and of membership of House, 1900–1960

In consequence of these interrelations, the winning presidential candidate ordinarily carries into office with him a House majority of his own party, and partisan balance in the House fluctuates with variations from election to election in the division of the presidential vote. Figure 20.1 shows this relationship for the elections since the turn of the century. As the figure suggests, the correlation between presidential and congressional voting is by no means exact. A given division of the popular presidential vote is not invariably associated with precisely the same division of House seats. Nevertheless, the figure highlights the broad association of presidential and congressional voting in the years of presidential elections. Even the extraordinary election of 1956, in which Republicans failed to capture a majority of the House as Eisenhower won re-election, fits the pattern of association between presidential and House voting. In that election some Republican House candidates triumphed over sitting Democrats, chiefly in districts Democrats had won by narrow margins in 1954. On the other hand, Democrats replaced enough Republicans to hold their majority. In all the shifting districts save one, the drift of sentiment from 1952 to 1956 was in the same direction in both presidential and congressional voting. In all the districts newly won by Republicans, the General increased his strength over his 1952 percentage of the vote. His vote percentage declined, with a single exception, in the districts his party lost to Democrats.

In 1960 also, despite the fact that the Democratic House bloc declined in size as Kennedy won the Presidency, the shifts in the House elections were connected with the presidential voting. In 1958 Democrats had carried a larger number of House districts than at any election since 1936. In 1960 Republicans captured 29 seats that had been marginally Democratic in 1958. All but three of these districts returned majorities, often substantial, for Mr. Nixon.[8] To offset in part these losses, Democrats picked up eight seats from Republicans. Kennedy carried three of these districts.

Table 20.6   Party shifts of House districts in 1956 related to 1954 vote

1954 Election		1956 Election	
Republican Per Cent of Vote	Number of Districts	Shifted to Republican	Shifted to Democratic
0–34	145	0	
35–39	28	1	
40–44	27	2	
45–49	32	6	
50–54	61		6
55–59	62		3
60–64	56		2
65–100	24		0

The subjection of House elections to the tides of sentiment that govern the outcome of presidential elections helps to account for the fact that the House is often more responsive than the Senate to presidential leadership. The impact of presidential landslides may, in fact, be so great as to reduce the House minority to a corporal's guard. Only 132 House Democrats, about 30 per cent of the membership, survived the Harding victory of 1920, while a mere 89 Republicans, only 20 per cent of the House, went to Washington after Roosevelt's sweep of 1936. Such elections yield embarrassingly large, and at times unmanageable, majorities for the President's party.

Despite the articulation of presidential and congressional elections a goodly number of House members may confidently expect election, once they win nomination, come what may in the presidential plebiscite. A bloc of almost 100 southern seats is ordinarily quite safe for Democratic candidates, and certain metropolitan districts are almost as surely Democratic. Republicans control fewer sure seats. Those districts in which the division of the vote is normally near the 50–50 point are most likely to swing from party to party with the presidential vote. The number of such districts changes from time to time, but from one-third to one-half of the House candidates

[8] One of the three exceptions was the 10th district of Pennsylvania, won by William Scranton, a formidable and attractive young campaigner who became the Republican nominee and winner of the governorship in 1962.

must view the outcome with some uncertainty, though the proportion of districts with extremely close results is ordinarily less.[9]

The fact that a presidential election does not affect the results of campaigns for House seats in the sure districts, Republican or Democratic, does not necessarily mean that an election throws into the House blocs of Representatives unresponsive to the broad verdict of the election. Certainly, Democratic Representatives from sure metropolitan districts in recent Democratic administrations have been loyal supporters of the party program. Even the southerners defected principally on issues of peculiar regional concern. At least on domestic issues Republicans from sure rural districts have tended to be as consistent followers of the party line as have those from closer districts. Yet the fact that a district is sure usually means that its people have a deep concern over an issue or set of issues which will produce dissidence in their Representatives if the national leadership runs counter to that concern. Moreover, Representatives from sure districts acquire seniority in the House and gain the advantage that comes with legislative experience. Hence, the special concerns of the steadfast party areas find especially strong representation in party councils. The disproportionate contribution of sure districts to the contingent of experienced House members is indicated, for a sample election, by the data of Table 20.7.

Table 20.7   Close districts and first-termers: Proportion of Representatives first-termers, according to size of margin in district congressional vote, 1958

District Per Cent Democratic	Total Seats	First-Termers	Others	Per Cent First-Termers
0–39	42	1	41	2.4
40–44	49	7	42	14.3
45–49	61	10	51	16.4
50–54	45	41	4	91.1
55–59	19	8	11	42.1
60–64	40	4	36	10.0
65–69	22	4	18	18.2
70 and over	157	6	151	3.8
Total	435	81	354	8.1

[9] The percentages of seats won by less than 60 per cent of the two-party vote were in 1948, 45; 1952, 37; 1956, 43; 1960, 44. A 60–40 victory is, of course, a victory by a considerable margin. In 1948, 24 per cent of the seats were carried by 55 per cent or less of the two-party vote; in 1956, 20 per cent; in 1958, 27 per cent.

While the House strength of the parties fluctuates with the vote polled by their presidential candidates, the gross relationship, shown in Figure 20.1 can lead to erroneous inferences. The return of House majorities along with presidential pluralities may suggest that the electorate grants a clear mandate of preference for the majority party of the moment. In fact, the voters speak far more equivocally. Despite the apparent correlation between congressional and presidential voting, one popular majority may elect the President and another, the House. The President may owe his election to one constituency and his party's House majority, or at least a goodly number of its members, to another.

Something of the nature of the electoral decision can be discerned if one pushes behind the aggregate relationships shown by Figure 20.1 and compares, district by district, the congressional and presidential vote, as has been done for two presidential elections in Table 20.8. The greater the strength of a party's presidential candidate, from district to district, the greater are the chances that his party's congressional candidate will carry the district. Yet in some districts, the Democratic presidential candidate will have a plurality as Republicans win the House seats, while in others the Re-

Table 20.8   Relation between presidential vote in congressional districts and results of House elections, 1952 and 1956

| District Republican Presidential Percentage | Results of Congressional Races | | | | | |
| | 1952 | | | 1956 | | |
	Total Districts	Number R	Per Cent R	Total Districts	Number R	Per Cent R
15–19	4	0	0.0	5	0	0.0
20–24	4	0	0.0	8	0	0.0
25–29	11	0	0.0	8	0	0.0
30–34	14	0	0.0	14	0	0.0
35–39	36	1 [a]	2.8	20	0	0.0
40–44	33	0	0.0	25	0	0.0
45–49	37	2	5.4	30	1	3.3
50–54	56	17	30.4	63	13	20.6
55–59	87	60	69.0	86	33	38.4
60–64	82	71	86.6	86	70	81.4
65–69	49	47	95.9	58	52	89.7
70–74	21	21	100.0	24	24	100.0
75–79	1	1	100.0	8	8	100.0
Total	435	220		435	201	

[a] Jacob Javits won New York's 21st district.

publican presidential candidate will carry the day as his fellow Republicans go down to defeat in the House races.

The reasons for these divergent results within congressional districts throw light on both the nature of our party system and the character of the electoral verdict. Two broad sets of factors probably account for most instances of deviation from party regularity. First, the elements of strength and weakness in congressional candidates and in district party organizations help to shelter local candidates from national trends. Second, the peculiar policy and personal appeals of the presidential candidates contribute also to their special weakness or strength in particular types of districts. The interaction of these two broad variables produces coincidence and divergence in district voting for President and Representative.

The data of Table 20.8 suggest that within congressional districts the electorate is more strongly attached to local party and perhaps to individual Representatives than to a party's presidential candidates. The party that has become dominant within the congressional politics of a district has a capacity, often remarkable, to withstand the ebb and flow of sentiment in the competition for the Presidency. This ability to hold a district often depends in part on the drawing power of a sitting Representative whose name has become known and who has by favors and services to his constituents, perhaps over a long period, cemented to himself a faithful personal following.[10] Yet often more than personal popularity is involved. The party organization may have a strength quite independent of that of the sitting Congressman; or the voters of the district may lean fairly persistently toward candidates of his party for most offices but now and then split their ticket for the Presidency.

From the capacity of incumbents and local party organizations to resist the general trend it would be expected that a number of districts, Republican and Democratic, would stand steadfast in their customary congressional allegiance in the face of conquest of the district by the opposition presidential candidate. Yet quite apart from this phenomenon, which may be common to many close districts, occasionally individual congressional candidates dramatize an issue peculiar to the district, or themselves, so skillfully that they win even though the opposition polls a huge presidential plurality in the district. For example, in 1952, a Democrat, Howard S. Miller, won election from Kansas' 1st district as Eisenhower drew almost 70 per cent of the vote. Mr. Miller, said to have been the first Democrat elected to Congress from this area, accomplished this feat by opposing the construction of Tuttle Creek Dam, a flood control project that had outraged those whose lands would have been inundated. In the same year, Gracie Pfost of Idaho defeated an incumbent Republican for Congress in a district that went over 60 per cent

[10] In marginal districts, analyses of data such as those of Table 20.8 indicate, a party has a better chance to retain seats against a national tide to the opposition when incumbents seek re-election.

for Eisenhower, and thereby established herself as a formidable lady politician. In New York, beginning in 1946, Republican Jacob Javits won a normally Democratic district by a combination of good luck, strife among the Democrats, and conspicuous espousal of non-Republican policies.

Other elements of the relationship between presidential and congressional voting may be identified if we transfer our attention to the second factor productive of incongruency in presidential and congressional voting —the peculiarities of the presidential contest. Each presidential candidate tends to have a set of appeals, and to attract a following, that does not match precisely the popular congressional support of the party. The peculiarities of his strength may extend the area of his pluralities into congressional districts that his party is unable to carry. On this broad point, the data of Table 20.8 are instructive. Consider the 1952 congressional results in relation to the strength of General Eisenhower, district by district. The popular appeal of the General won for him many congressional districts carried by Democratic congressional candidates. Some of these districts were, to be sure, southern districts. Nevertheless, a presidential candidate may have a strong appeal in a district in which his party, long moribund locally, is simply unable to muster a House candidate who commands much respect. On the other hand, a presidential candidate may also have peculiar weaknesses which assure that he will not carry some districts from which his House running-mates, not tarred with the same brush, emerge victorious. In 1960, for example, Democrats held about 75 seats in districts in which Kennedy trailed Nixon. This discrepancy between presidential and congressional voting probably sprang in considerable measure from Kennedy's vulnerability in these areas on the religious issue.

The divergence between patterns of congressional and presidential electoral support, which differs both in degree and in form from election to election, should not obscure the broader fact that the same people who support a winning President also support in relativly high degree the congressional candidates of his party. Broadly the electorate rallies to the support of a presidential candidate and his fellow partisans, though exceptions occur that contribute to the special character of the American party system.[11] In the great swings of popular sentiment from party to party, the vote for President and that for Representatives move in the same direction, even though some individual Representatives escape the secondary effects of a tide in the presi-

[11] See the analysis of ticket-splitting in 1956 by Angus Campbell and Warren E. Miller, "The Motivational Basis of Straight and Split Ticket Voting," *American Political Science Review*, 51 (1957), 293–312. They found splitting between national and state and local candidates to be more common than between presidential and congressional candidates. In the North 76 per cent of the Eisenhower voters voted straight Republican at the national level in 1956 in contrast with 89 per cent in 1952. In the South the movement was in the opposite direction, 46 per cent against 21 per cent in 1952. In 1956 one out of 10 Stevenson voters split for a Republican Representative or Senator.

dential voting. Pervasive national sweeps of sentiment seem to affect the voters in all congressional districts.[12] Politicians, of course, have their narcissistic traits and often attribute their triumphs to their own sterling qualities when in reality they are the beneficiaries of a general shift of sentiment to their party. The popular decision tends to be in terms of party.[13] Yet there is sufficient looseness in the articulation of presidential and congressional voting to encourage individual Representatives to see their victories (or their defeats) as the result of their own endeavors, a factor probably of basic consequence for the nature of legislative behavior.

PARTY AT MIDTERM: THE MINORITY   Congressional campaigns in presidential years are overshadowed, even swallowed up, by the effort to win the Presidency. The centripetal influence of the fight for the Presidency tends to pull together all factions of the party. Powerful forces operate to bring all good men to the aid of their party to elect a President and a Congress as well. The cohesive drives of the presidential battle are absent in midterm elections. The parties may become fractionalized, for they lack the mechanism, and often the will, to rally their cohorts to disciplined battle.

The problem of presenting a solid front to the electorate may be especially difficult for the minority party. When a deep-seated conflict exists for control of the minority, its latent inner contradictions may materialize in the most glaring form at the midterm campaign. The campaign may be in reality a battle of every man for himself, and there may be no party front presented against the Administration. The extreme situation manifested itself in a declaration by the late Senator Robert A. Taft in 1941: "No Republican National Convention can be held before next year's elections and the party National Committee clearly has no authority to make such declarations. I see no reasons why each Senator should not run on his own foreign policy."

The special difficulties under which the minority may labor are illustrated by the Republican attempt to form a line of battle for the 1950 congressional elections. Soon after the 1948 campaign a struggle developed between the Dewey and Taft wings of the party. Hugh Scott, Jr., chairman of the national committee and a Dewey appointee, proposed to hold a na-

---

[12] The extent to which a congressional election is a "national" election and only partially a set of district elections is indicated by the fact that the proportion of seats won by a party bears a highly regular relation to its proportion of the aggregate or national popular vote. See J. G. March, "Party Legislative Representation as a Function of Election Results," *Public Opinion Quarterly*, 21 (1957–58), 521–42.

[13] Probably well over half of those who vote for Representatives do so as partisans without familiarity with the name of the candidate. In a 1956 survey by the Survey Research Center, 22 per cent gave correctly the name of the party candidate for whom they said they had voted; 43 per cent claimed to have voted for a candidate for Congress on one or the other of the party tickets but could not give his name; most of the remainder did not vote.

tional conference to draft a "fighting and forward-looking" program of "moderation" on which to wage the 1950 campaign. Republican leaders of House and Senate, more disposed toward the Taft wing, had no enthusiasm for "moderation," and Mr. Scott was soon replaced as national chairman by Guy Gabrielson. The new chairman obtained authority from the national committee to create a committee consisting of representatives of the national committee and of the Republican groups in the House and Senate to draft a program for 1950. In due course a policy statement was unveiled "supplementing the Republican platform of 1948." Although it dealt with several questions, it declared that the "major domestic issue today is liberty against socialism." On this slogan it was hoped that the party could unite, but protests swelled up from the ranks. The statement gratified only the Old Guard. The Republican state chairman of New York, a Dewey man, observed that the statement "did not offer enough in specific appeal to all the voters of the nation to make it a lasting, persuasive or overly binding document." A group of dissident Republican leaders met in Philadelphia and adopted a declaration of principles of their own, "a positive" program. They argued for "affirmative and constructive solutions of the tremendously intricate and difficult problems facing the nation." The Republican party thus went forth disunited into the fray.

At midterm the minority lacks the machinery to produce a decision on party policy that will be accepted as binding by all the important segments of the party. Though the pronouncements of the national convention are not necessarily embraced by all elements of the party, in presidential campaigns policy differences may be submerged or their solution may be postponed. At midterm the intraparty discussion must focus on issues and issues alone. Perhaps there is no better way to activate latent differences than to raise issues for discussion.[14]

PARTY AT MIDTERM: THE MAJORITY   The occasional serious tribulations of the minority party in arriving at a midterm program are not to be explained simply by the obstreperousness of human nature. Fundamentally, a different type of leadership tends to develop in the House and Senate wings of the party than among those who focus on winning presidential campaigns. Both parties are plagued by the divergence between the two types of leaders, but it may be especially marked in the minority when its congressional representation has been reduced to the hard core of stand-

[14] The practice seems to be developing for the minority—and on occasion the majority—to issue a midterm manifesto more or less equivalent to a platform. In 1962 a joint House and Senate committee of Republicans prepared, after consultation with Mr. Eisenhower and other leaders, "A Declaration of Republican Principles and Policy." Proposals have been made for a midterm national convention to prepare such documents and to handle other questions, but most "pros" shudder at the thought of a gathering which could, they believe, eventuate only in fruitless wrangling within the party.

patters from sure districts. The image of the minority in the eyes of the country may be formed by the pronouncements of its congressional leaders of an
extreme wing. The sober citizen may well shudder when he wonders whether
the minority will elect a President of the same hue as the more vocal elder
statesmen of the congressional minority.

The vicissitudes of the Administration at midterm are far less trying than
are those of the minority. The Presidency provides an organizing center for
the party whose congressional and presidential elements ordinarily close
ranks for the conduct of the campaign. In truth, the President and his program
create the central issue of the campaign, and the midterm election becomes in
a sense a referendum on the conduct of the government by him and his party.
Yet the role that the President himself should play in the midterm campaign
has not been neatly crystallized. Under some circumstances at least, the
country does not accept it as entirely proper for the President to ask the
country to uphold his policies by electing a Congress of his party.

Woodrow Wilson's 1918 appeal for a Democratic Congress is a notable
illustration of the problem of the proper stance for a President to assume in
the midterm campaign. In his manifesto Wilson declared that the elections of
1918

> occur in the most critical period our country has ever faced, or is likely
> to face in our time. If you have approved of my leadership, and wish me
> to continue to be your unembarrassed spokesman at home and abroad,
> I earnestly beg that you will express yourselves unmistakably to that ef-
> fect by returning a Democratic majority to both the Senate and the
> House of Representatives. . . . The leaders of the minority in the pres-
> ent Congress have unquestionably been pro-war, but they have been anti-
> administration. At almost every turn since we entered the war they have
> sought to take the choice of policy and the conduct of the war out of
> my hands and put it under the control of instrumentalities of their own
> choosing. This is no time either for divided council or for divided leader-
> ship.

Veteran Democratic politicians regarded the issuance of this statement
as a major blunder, however much they may have agreed with its premises.
And to it they attributed the disasters Democrats suffered in the elections of
1918, although doubt may be entertained about the correctness of that interpretation. The late Arthur Mullen, Nebraska Democratic leader, characterized the statement as the "most suicidal document ever sent out from the
White House." He argued that had Wilson's appeal been for the election
of men who had supported his policies, not those of his party, it might have
had contrary effects.[15]

[15] A. F. Mullen, *Western Democrat* (New York: Funk, 1940), p. 182.

When the midterm rolls around, the pundits resurrect the events of 1918 and consider what the incumbent President should do. In 1942, another delicate time politically, Roosevelt met the problem differently than Wilson had. Ed Flynn, the Democratic national chairman, in February, 1942, delivered a rip-roaring partisan speech in which he pointed to the "vast confusion" that would result from the election of a Republican Congress. Only a major military defeat, he thought, could be a greater misfortune. What would the President's comment be? To the reporters he said, "When the country is at war, we want Congressmen, regardless of party, who will back up the Government of the United States and who have a record of backing up the country in an emergency, regardless of party." The President may have believed that few Republicans met the tests he set up, but, if so, he thought it impolitic to say so.

An active role by the President in the midterm campaign is perhaps becoming a more accepted practice of our politics. At any rate, under circumstances different from those of 1918 and 1942, Presidents have exerted themselves to win the election of a Congress of their party at the midterm. In 1950 the Democratic party made a vigorous campaign. President Truman made a straightforward plea for approval of the policies of the Administration by the return of greater majorities in House and Senate. Beset by dissent in his own party, he sought the election of a larger contingent of northern liberal Democrats, lest his program be completely blocked by a combination of the conservative Democratic splinter with the Republican minority.

In the preliminaries to the 1954 elections Eisenhower took a lofty and detached view; he believed that his own participation should be limited to a defense of the Administration's record on a high plane and that the Presidency should not be involved in particular partisan struggles in states and districts. In due course, intelligence from the grass roots indicated that the Republican congressional majority was in peril and the President joined in the fray. He dispatched most of the cabinet to the stump to preach the gospel of Republicanism and he himself made flying trips to states with closely fought senatorial contests. In a broadcast he argued that "you can't have one car with two drivers at the steering wheel and expect to end up any place but in the ditch—especially when the drivers are set on going in different directions. You cannot have efficient Federal government when the Congress wants to follow one philosophy of government and the Executive branch another." He called for the "election of a Republican-led Congress." Even those Republicans who had steadfastly opposed the President's program in Congress echoed these sentiments and strove mightily to get aboard the presidential coattails. Similarly, as the congressional elections of 1958 approached, the Republican national committee and the President bestirred themselves to rouse the faithful to do battle. The national chairman assembled the state chairmen in Washington for a "Campaign School." [16] The President made a few major speeches exhorting the country to elect a Republican Congress, but the brunt of the task of stumping the country was borne by Vice President Nixon.

Whatever role the President chooses to take in the campaign, the majority, by its possession of control of the government, has the means to bring its forces into more or less orderly line for the conduct of the campaign. This accomplishment requires coordination of the endeavors of the party's national senatorial and congressional committees, a task likely to be considerably simpler for the Administration than for the minority. For the majority also, the task of adopting a general policy for the campaign presents no overwhelming difficulty. The performance of the Administration must be the platform, a circumstance that may put the majority on the defensive at the midterm. Yet the record on occasion is supplemented by a more or less formal policy statement. In 1950, for example, the Democratic national committee laid out a statement of party principles which adhered largely to the Fair Deal program as enunciated in 1948. In 1954 the Republican national committee convened at Cincinnati and issued a platform with the theme of "Peace, Progress, and Prosperity."

The nature of the midterm contest encourages a strategy of concentration, since the Administration is most seriously threatened in the close districts —which number from 50 to 100. Campaign resources may be amassed in districts where they will presumably yield the greatest return. Thus, in 1954 the Republicans sent into the 4th district of Missouri, in an effort to hold the seat, the Vice President, the Secretary of Agriculture, the Secretary of Commerce, and the Speaker of the House. All these endeavors, it may be noted, were to no avail. Similarly, the Administration may subject to intensive fire the seats won earlier by the minority by a narrow margin, a tactic which rarely yields results but does compel the minority to exert itself to hold these seats.[17]

NATURE OF THE MIDTERM VERDICT   Since the electorate cannot change administrations at midterm elections, it can only express its approval or disapproval by returning or withdrawing legislative majorities. At least such would be the rational hypothesis about what the electorate

[16] See Philip S. Wilder, Jr., *Meade Alcorn and the 1958 Election* (New York: Holt, 1959).

[17] In the allocation of its campaign resources the Administration to some extent may give priority to those in Congress who have been most ardent in support of Administration policies. This may extend even to half-hearted support of the campaign against an incumbent of the opposition who has gone along with the Administration. On the whole, though, the national party apparatus is not notably effective in rewarding the loyal supporters of the Administration.

might do. In fact, no such logical explanation can completely describe what it does at midterm elections. The Founding Fathers, by the provision for midterm elections, built into the constitutional system a procedure whose strange consequences lack explanation in any theory that personifies the elec-torate as a rational god of vengeance and of reward.

The President's party, whether it basks in public favor or is declining in public esteem, ordinarily loses House strength at midterm—a pattern that, save for one exception, has prevailed since the Civil War. The exception occurred in 1934 when the popularity of the Roosevelt policies was on the ascent. Given the regularity of this pattern, the loss of House strength by the Administration at midterm does not necessarily result from withdrawal of popular favor. An exceptionally heavy loss, however, may reflect the development of a hostile public sentiment and may even portend a defeat in the following presidential election.

Explanation of the Administration's loss at midterm must be sought not so much by examining the midterm election itself as by looking at the pre-ceding presidential election. The stimulation of the presidential campaign brings a relatively large turnout. It attracts to the polls persons of low po-litical interest who in large degree support the winning presidential candi-date and, incidentally, his party's congressional candidates. At the following midterm congressional election, turnout drops sharply. As Figure 20.2 in-dicates, over 10,000,000 persons who had voted in the presidential election stay away fom the polls at midterm. Those who stay home include in spe-cial degree the in-and-out voters who had helped put the President and his

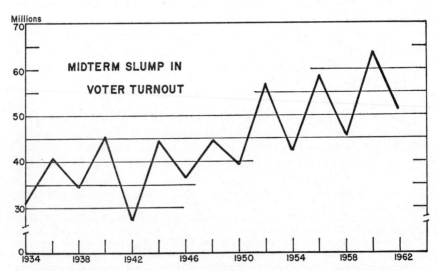

Figure 20.2   Total national vote in elections of members of the House of Representatives, 1934–1962

congressional ticket into office. As they remain on the sidelines at midterm, the President's allies in marginal districts may find themselves voted from office. The coattail vote of the preceding presidential year that edged these Representatives into office simply stays home.[18]

The aggregate result of the election is not the product of a random shifting of districts, some from the President's party to the minority, some from the minority to the Administration. Such movements in both directions would be expected if district results were the chance product of local issues, candidate popularity, and other such matters unconnected with party. The movement is, however, mainly in one direction. The President's fellow partisans lose seats to the outs and only under exceptional circumstances do they capture districts from the outs; the outs retain the seats they have and gain others from the Administration. The significance of a specific midterm result comes not from the simple fact of losses by the President's party. Some loss is to be expected. It is the magnitude of the loss that is important. A sufficiently large loss may indicate a genuine withdrawal of popular favor from the President's party.

Illustrative of the pattern of the midterm shift is Table 20.9, which analyzes the House elections of 1950 in relation to the results by district

Table 20.9   Results of 1950 congressional elections related to 1948 division of major-party vote by districts

Per Cent Democratic, 1948	No. of Districts	1950					
		Districts Unchanged		Shifted to Republican		Shifted to Democratic	
		No.	Per Cent	No.	Per Cent	No.	Per Cent
0–30.0	15	15	100.0			1 [a]	5.3
30.1–35.0	19	18	94.7				
35.1–49.9	133	133	100.0				
50.1–52.5	27	13	48.1	14	51.9		
52.6–55.0	26	15	57.7	11	42.3		
55.1–57.5	18	14	77.8	4	22.2		
57.6–60.0	20	19	95.0	1	5.0		
60.1–100.0	170	170	100.0				
Total	428 [b]	397	92.8	30	7.0	1	0.2

[a] First district of New York. Kingsland Macy was defeated by a Democrat.

[b] Florida districts reapportioned in 1949 were excluded. Also excluded was California's 5th district, where a Democrat had replaced Republican Richard Welch in a 1949 special election.

[18] For evidence, see Angus Campbell, "Surge and Decline: A Study of Electoral Change," *Public Opinion Quarterly*, 24 (1960), 397–418. The percentages of independents

in 1948. The Democrats had virtually no hope of gaining seats they had lost in 1948. They picked up only one such district, one in which a state Republican organization disciplined the Representative by defeating him in the general election. On the other hand, Republicans won 30 seats from Democrats, and of these, 25 had been Democratic in 1948 by less than five percentage points. Usually the Administration at the midterm loses a rather large proportion of the seats it won by narrow margins at the preceding presidential election.

Lest it be thought that the 1950 results represent a unique event rather than a recurring pattern, the findings of a comparison between the outcome of the House elections in 1956 and 1958 are presented in Table 20.10. The

Table 20.10   Results of 1958 House elections related to Republican percentage of 1956 popular vote for Representatives by districts

Republican Per Cent of Vote, 1956	No. of Districts	1958					
		Districts Unchanged		Shifted to Democratic		Shifted to Republican	
		No.	Per Cent	No.	Per Cent	No.	Per Cent
0–9	72	72	100.0				
10–29	30	30	100.0				
30–39	51	51	100.0				
40–44	31	31	100.0				
45–49	51	50	98.0			1 [a]	2.0
50–54	38	17	44.7	21	55.3		
55–59	59	43	72.9	16	27.1		
60–69	87	76	87.4	11	12.6		
70 and over	16	15	93.7	1 [b]	6.3		

[a] Ninth District of Minnesota in which the Democratic incumbent, Coya Knutson, was defeated.

[b] Tenth District of Ohio in which there had been no Democratic candidate in 1956.

1958 election fitted the pattern of the 1950 election but in reverse. The Republicans captured only one 1956 Democratic seat, the ninth of Minnesota. There the husband of Coya Knutson, the incumbent Democrat, had been gulled into uttering the plea, happily echoed by Republicans, "Coya, come home." On the other hand, Democrats made substantial gains, chiefly among seats Republican in 1956 by slender pluralities. The magnitude of the 1958

---

who voted in a series of elections were: 1952, 59; 1954, 22; 1956, 64; 1958, 14. In 1952 and 1956 those calling themselves independents were heavily Republican in their voting. Estimates from Survey Research Center data.

Democratic gains, coupled with the fact that Republicans had been unable to win control of the House in 1956, was interpreted to mean that the Republican party enjoyed extremely low popular esteem.

Reflection about the relationships shown in Tables 20.9 and 20.10 ought to bring some revision of the common assertion that congressional elections are determined by local considerations, by the personality of candidates, all more or less independent of the national party battle. The data of these tables suggest that the balloting represents an episode in the ebb and flow of the fortunes of the parties nationally; the Representatives in the normally close districts are the casualties of battle.[19] Personality and local considerations play a part, but it would require a truly remarkable distribution of attractive personalities to explain why in 1950 only sitting Democrats needed to worry about their fate while in 1958 only sitting Republicans were under a like necessity. The misfortunes of the ins may be attributable to a variety of considerations, but the common denominator of the midterm electoral decision as a whole is a pro-Democratic or a pro-Republican turn.

The outcome of the 1962 House elections moved some commentators to the conclusion that the pattern of Administration loss of House seats in the off years had ceased to operate. That election was about a standoff; Republican net gains amounted to only two seats. Democrats lost a larger number of seats to Republicans, but their gains from Republicans together with the effects of redistrictings made the net loss negligible. The peculiarity of the 1962 outcome was probably related mainly to the oddities of the elections of 1958 and 1960. Democratic success in 1958 brought victory in a goodly number of marginal districts. In 1960, contrary to the usual results in presidential victories, Democrats lost many of these marginal seats and few Democratic representatives came into office on Kennedy's coattails. The 1960 upsurge in Democratic presidential strength was most marked in areas already represented by Democrats. Thus, in a sense, Democrats did not win in 1960 the seats they would have been expected to lose in 1962. Changes in political practice are probably reducing the average size of the midterm swing, though the evidence of 1962 points not so much to basic change as to special factors operative at that time.

---

[19] The analyses in Tables 20.9 and 20.10 simply relate the results of one election to those of the preceding election. E. F. Cox has developed measures of the partisan strength of districts (based on averages of several votes within the districts) to use as a standard against which to appraise the import of a particular election. See his "Congressional District Party Strengths and the 1960 Election," *Journal of Politics,* 24 (1962), 277–302. On an earlier off-year election, see M. Plesur, "The Republican Comeback of 1938," *Review of Politics,* 24 (1962), 525–62.

Constitution, Electoral Practices, and Party System

While the details of the patterns of behavior involved in the interrelationships of constitutional system and party system are intricate, their combined broad effect may be simply stated. They both reflect and contribute to the peculiar nature of the American political system. The basic arrangement that puts teeth into the system of separated powers is the independent election of President, of Senate, and of House of Representatives. The formal electoral autonomy of each of the major organs of government introduces divisive factors into the party system and, in turn, the unifying forces of party react upon the constitutional system and modify the formal separation of the organs of government.

Through the electoral system each major party seeks to extend its control over President, House, and Senate, and to a degree succeeds. Yet, paradoxically, the interworkings of party and electoral system contribute also to the uniqueness and independence of President, House, and Senate. Neither party seems able to mobilize its forces with equal success—or perhaps to mobilize the same forces—in the fight for the Presidency and for Congress. The winning presidential candidate draws support not available to his congressional associates. In part this divergence in sources of support flows from the peculiar appeals of each successful presidential candidate. To some extent it flows from imperfections in the manning and operation of the party apparatus on the congressional level. It results, too, from features of the constitutional system—the staggered terms of the Senate and the off-year elections of the House—which stimulate attempts by legislators to establish themselves within their constituencies independently of party.

One broad consequence of the ensemble of arrangements, formal and informal, is to limit the range of decision made by the electorate in the national polling. Great oscillations of public sentiment and feeling are to some extent blocked or at least damped. Shifts of public attitude seem to be most sensitively and completely reflected in presidential voting; they are obstructed in the congressional voting. The incapacity of the winning party to field a congressional ticket equal in popular strength to its presidential candidate trims the scope of the triumph of the party victorious in the presidential voting. Whether such limitations on popular decision are to the public good presents another question. Doubtless at times they protect the Republic from its foolish whim of the moment; at others, they may form defenses for special interests against public wrath.

In another way the general scheme contributes significantly to the character of the political order by creating points of power that cannot be brought readily under central domination. That is, they assure a dispersion or decentralization of power within the party structures. In the dominant party of the moment the standpat districts provide foundations for party factions not beholden to the national leadership and immune to the depredations of the opposition. The resultant cleavages within the majority are duly recorded on the front pages every day. Less commonly recognized are the consequences of the electoral system for the party of the opposition. The system operates, as we have shown by a variety of analyses, to strengthen the minority within the Congress and thereby to assure the maintenance of points of power with a vested interest in resisting the accumulation of power about the President who leads the current majority. The minority almost invariably places in the Congress, even in years of presidential elections, members who would under a more tightly articulated party system be defeated. The effects of the off-year elections further re-enforce this capacity of the minority to survive.

The effect of all these arrangements in decentralizing and restraining power and in maintaining obstructions to the majority of the moment is congenial to the popular American political philosophy, through which runs a strain of deep distrust of authority. Yet these constitutional virtues may also be defects, in particular the division of authority between the parties, possible because of the midterm elections. In grave circumstances divided partisan control could be disastrous. Even in normal times such elections may place legislative leadership in the hands of those not under the moderating influence of the knowledge that their party is responsible for the administration in all its day-to-day aspects. The fact that our parties are American parties—and not European parties—makes the division of control of the government between the parties less serious than it might be. If the parties were tightly disciplined and doctrinally disparate, midterm elections could result in an intolerable stalemate. As it is, the parties have adapted themselves to the system, and sufficient cross-party collaboration prevails to keep the basic business of government in motion. Yet this division of control has not produced energetic or decisive government, a condition difficult enough for us to achieve without the effects of this oddity of our institutional and electoral system.

The division of governmental control flowing from the midterm elections has led to proposals for constitutional reform.[20] After the Democratic defeat in the election of 1946, Senator J. W. Fulbright of Arkansas proposed that President Truman resign, having first appointed as Secretary of State, who was then in line for succession to the Presidency, a person acceptable to the Republican congressional leadership. He argued that it was desirable to have "at all times, but especially in a time of tense international relations and confusion at home, a government capable of functioning in a definite positive manner." As things stood, he foresaw only stalemate for two years. Acceptance

[20] See W. G. Carleton, "Our Congressional Elections: In Defense of the Traditional System," *Political Science Quarterly*, 70 (1955), 341–57.

of the proposal would have amounted to a step toward a parliamentary government.[21] Others have suggested that the House be elected for terms of four years to run concurrently with that of the President. If both House and Senate were elected concurrently with the President, forces would be loosed which might in the long run alter drastically the relations of President and Congress as well as the character of the party system.[22]

[21] Mr. Truman is said to have remarked, in irreverent allusion to Senator Fulbright's tenure as a Rhodes scholar, that what this country needs is more land-grant colleges.

[22] Congressional elections have been subjected to very little analysis. The chief books are C. A. M. Ewing, *Congressional Elections, 1896–1944* (Norman: University of Oklahoma Press, 1947); Malcolm Moos, *Politics, Presidents and Coattails* (Baltimore: Johns Hopkins Press, 1952); Louis Bean, *The Mid-Term Battle* (Washington: Cantillon Books, 1950); W. M. McPhee and W. A. Glaser, *Public Opinion and Congressional Elections* (New York: Free Press of Glencoe, 1962). An acute analysis of factors in the midterm House elections has been made by Ruth C. Silva, "A Look Into a Crystal Election Ball," *New York Times Magazine,* October 10, 1954.

21.

ELECTORAL

PARTICIPATION

THE EARNEST CAMPAIGNS of the Junior Chamber of Commerce to get out the vote sometimes provoke an amused cynicism or even hostile criticism. Persons with an antidemocratic bent may regard such efforts as stupid endeavors to induce people ignorant of both the candidates and the issues to cast a blind vote. The sophisticates may smile at the work of the JayCees as the harmless antics of humorless activists not likely to affect the political system markedly either for good or for ill. In fact solemn admonitions to the citizenry to go to the polls influence the turnout only slightly if at all. Yet, for the student of politics, the questions raised by a consideration of electoral participation are by no means trivial. Examination of popular participation in the political process may suggest crucial insights into the nature of the political order. Variations in the nature of the act of voting may serve as indicators of fundamental characteristics of the state as may quantitative differences in voting. An extremely small turnout may reflect lack of faith in the democratic process among those who stay at home. It may also result from a widespread belief that affairs are proceeding so well that people need not be deeply concerned.

Political participation by the citizen may involve far more than the simple act of voting. Discussion of public issues, contributions to party causes, work in the chores of campaigns and of election days, the acquisition of information about candidates and issues, and the travail of reflection about public problems are other forms of participation. The varying extent of

these types of participation within electorates may be associated with profound differences in the nature of political systems. A state in which large
numbers of citizens spring to campaign duties as the political conflict warms
up may differ radically from one in which the citizenry regards politics as
a matter for a small official or professionalized political class. A political
order in which the citizen believes that about all he can do is vote yes or
no by no means resembles one in which large numbers of citizens believe
that they can bestir themselves, convert their fellows, and affect the course
of events by their own efforts.

Obviously the full significance of political participation becomes apparent only when nations sharply differing in the character of citizen involvement in the political process are contrasted. While the data for such
contrasts are not available, a good deal is known about the character and
extent of participation in the United States. A summary of that information
will provide a basis for reflection about broad questions associated with participation.

Trends in Presidential Voting

Commonly in the United States popular interest in voting attains its
highest level in presidential elections. The intensity of campaign effort reaches
a peak in races for the Presidency, and the media of communication bring
presidential politics most compellingly to public attention. Yet even in presidential elections participation does not match the levels of interest shown
in the national elections of most other western democracies.

A broad picture of presidential voting since 1896 appears in the graphs
in Figure 21.1. Since 1920 a substantially smaller proportion of the potential
electorate has voted in presidential elections than voted in the 1890's. In
1896 almost 80 per cent of the enfranchised population came to the polls;
in the period 1920–1960, between 49 and 63 per cent. Such a change in
the level of interest may seem, when it appears as a tiny dip in a line on a
chart, to be a small shift. The magnitude of the alteration in voting habits
may be better grasped by noting that if the same proportion of eligibles had
voted in 1960 as in 1896, about 16,000,000 more persons would have gone
to the polls.

PROBLEMS IN MEASURING TURNOUT   Although the graphs
in Figure 21.1 indicate correctly the long-run trend in participation in presidential voting, they do not provide an absolute measure of popular interest
comparable with the figures usually cited for other countries. Editors often
seize upon a figure of around 60 per cent turnout, as in the elections of 1936,
1940, and 1952, compare it with much higher participation figures for

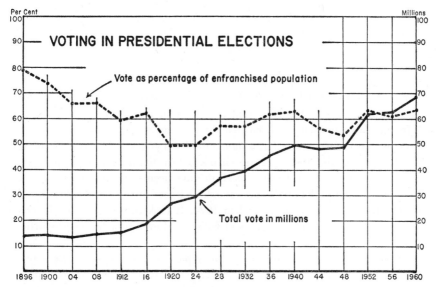

Figure 21.1   Total presidential vote and vote as a percentage of the potential electorate, 1896–1960

Great Britain, Denmark, or Norway, and bemoan the lack of appreciation of the blessings of liberty among our citizenry.

One would obtain a measure of interest in presidential voting more comparable with the figures for other countries, if he drew into Figure 21.1 a graph six or seven percentage points higher than the one that appears there. The percentages shown rest on the proportions of the potential electorate actually voting—that is, in recent decades, of the proportion of citizens 21 and over.[1] Not all such persons possess the technical qualifications for voting. A goodly number cannot meet the requirements for residence. Others may have lost the privilege through criminal conviction. Others may be confined in institutions. Still others may be disqualified because of their inability to meet other suffrage requirements. The participation figures for other countries commonly do not include such disqualified categories in the base from which participation rates are computed. Even after allowance for the shortcomings of our measure of participation,[2] the fact remains that the

[1] In the estimation of the potential electorate for computation of the percentages underlying Figure 21.1, allowance was made for the varying practices among the states before 1920 regarding woman suffrage, as well as for the differing rules on the requirement of citizenship for voting.

[2] Incidentally, not even the number of persons who cast a ballot on the day of a presidential election is known precisely. Some voters either do not mark the ballot for a presidential candidate or they spoil their ballot and it is not counted. The vote for minor-party candidates is certainly incompletely reported. From an analysis of data from states that report the number of persons voting, it is doubtful that the presidential

levels of interest in American national elections are lower than those of other major democracies. Whether that differential indicates that the body politic is in an unhealthy state is another matter.

EXPLANATIONS FOR VARIATIONS IN TURNOUT   A major question posed by the trend of voting is why the decline in electoral interest since the 1890's. The blunt truth is that nobody knows the answer. A frequent explanation has been that the enfranchisement of women in 1920 brought into the electorate large numbers of persons not in the habit of voting. Yet popular interest began to shrink before the adoption of the woman suffrage amendment. A fairly steady decline occurred from 1896 to 1916. Woman suffrage undoubtedly accounted, at least in substantial part, for the drop in turnout rates in 1920 and in 1924. It took some time for women to become initiated into the mysteries of voting and even now larger proportions of women than of men do not vote.

Woman suffrage accounts only for a part of the difference in popular interest at midcentury and in the 1890's. David Riesman has suggested that profound changes in the American character may underlie an increasing apathy toward matters political.[3] Others have surmised that faith in the efficacy of political action has weakened since the fiery political battles of the 1890's. While the trend may reflect some such change in the American polity, its full explanation remains in the realm of speculation.

Some of the lesser fluctuations in turnout revealed by Figure 21.1 find simple but plausible explanation. The climb in turnout from 1924 to 1936 may be attributed in part to the gradual habituation of women to voting. The hotly fought campaign of 1928 probably deserves credit for bringing more voters to the polls, and the campaigns of 1936 and 1940, both of which centered on deeply felt issues, stimulated voter interest to an even higher pitch. The dip in turnout in 1944 resulted from the numbers of persons in the armed services, as well as from the inability of many migrants to war-manufacturing centers to fulfill residence requirements for voting. Turnout remained at a low level in 1948, but in 1952 an upsurge in electoral interest evidently moved the participation level to a new plateau. Though plausible reasons may be conjured up for such fluctuations in turnout, considerable mystery remains about their causes. When a sharp upthrust (or decline) in presidential voting occurs, the same trend appears nearly everywhere over the country in all types of elections whether held at the time of the presidential polling or at another time of the year. It is as if some pervasive and powerful influence were in operation to produce a greater or lesser degree of attention by people to all sorts of political matters.

---

vote exceeds 98 per cent of the turnout. Hence, in 1960 probably on the order of 1,500,000 more persons went to the polls than the number reported as voting for president, 68,839,000.

[3] See *The Lonely Crowd* (New Haven: Yale University Press, 1950).

Variations with Type of Election

Not so many Americans may vote, but those who do work harder at it than do the electors of most other countries. The American voter is marched to the polls far more frequently than are his counterparts elsewhere. In a single year there may be, at different times, municipal primaries, municipal elections, presidential primaries, primaries to nominate candidates for state offices, the presidential election, and perhaps a special election or so. When the voter makes his way to the polling booth, he is confronted, too, by a number of choices unapproached in other countries. A single primary ballot may contain the names of literally dozens of aspirants for nomination for various offices. The general election ballot may require the expression of choices for a dozen or more offices. Moreover, the ballot may include a series of propositions or issues; the elector must act on proposed constitutional amendments, initiated measures, referred questions, charter amendments, bond issues, and other such matters. The American voter, in short, has a formidable task.

PARTICIPATION IN STATE AND LOCAL ELECTIONS Not unexpectedly, electoral participation differs considerably among types of elections, and these variations in interest point to some of the factors affecting turnout. Sharp contrasts exist in campaigns. The salience of the personalities and issues of national politics ordinarily command the attention of far more people than do the less dramatic questions of state politics. These differences appear markedly by comparisons of the vote for candidates for state office in the years of presidential elections and in the off years. Illustrative is Figure 21.2, which indicates the proportion of the potential electorate of Ohio voting for governor during the period 1920–1954. The saw-toothed graph points to the effect of the presidential campaign in drawing voters to the polls. As they vote for President, they incidentally mark their ballot for governor. In the gubernatorial elections held in the off years without benefit of the drum beating of the rivals for the Presidency, the turnout drops sharply. The Ohio pattern occurs uniformly in other states. Thus the total vote in New York's 1962 gubernatorial election dropped about 1.6 million from the 1960 presidential turnout.

When elections of officials of cities, counties, and other local governments occur at a time different from that of the presidential election, turnout tends to be low. Since about 1900, in an attempt to insulate municipal affairs from the influences of national politics, more and more local elections have been scheduled in off years or at times other than the November political season. This timing of local elections has resulted in a reduction in

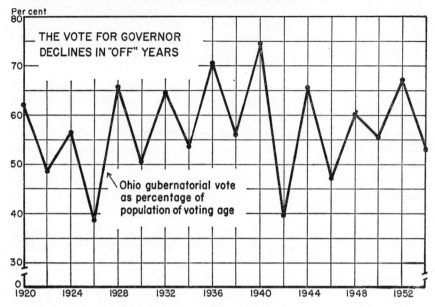

*Figure 21.2   Percentage of citizens 21 years of age and over voting
in Ohio gubernatorial elections, 1920–1954*

turnout. Even when local elections are held in the seasons of national political contests, they excite, on the average, relatively low interest. The information available does not permit an estimate of the modal rate of turnout
in local elections over the country, but the data of Table 21.1 on turnout
in municipal elections in Kansas cities of from 5,000 to 50,000 population
are instructive. Wide variations occur from time to time and from place to
place, but no more than 30 per cent of the eligible voters turned out in about
half of the 880 elections covered. Low-turnout elections often involved no
contest. Even so, the levels of popular concern are persuasive indicators
of the varied circumstances that depress electoral interest at the grass roots:
unchallenged control by local oligarchies, absence of local power to deal with
issues of compelling concern to the citizenry, often a general satisfaction
with the conduct of local government, and doubtless a variety of other factors.

POPULAR INTEREST IN PRIMARIES   Use of direct pri-
maries for the nomination of party candidates gives American voters the
opportunity to vote in a type of election virtually restricted to this country.
Outside the South popular interest in party primaries is far lower than that
in general elections. Comparatively few voters determine who are to be the
candidates in the general election campaign. In about three-fourths of the

Table 21.1 *Low temperature local politics: Distribution of 880 elections in Kansas cities, 1920–1951, according to percentage of estimated eligibles voting* [a]

Per Cent of Eligibles Voting	Number of Elections	Per Cent Distribution of Elections	Cumulative Distribution of Elections
0–9	104	11.8	11.8
10–19	155	17.6	29.4
20–29	179	20.4	49.8
30–39	173	19.7	69.5
40–49	150	17.0	86.5
50–59	91	10.3	96.8
60–69	21	2.4	99.2
70–79	5	0.6	99.8
80–89	1	0.1	99.9
90–100	1	0.1	100.0
	880	100.0	

[a] Tabulation prepared from data presented by C. J. Hein, *Voter Participation in City Elections of Cities with Populations between 5,000 and 50,000 in Kansas* (Lawrence: University of Kansas, Governmental Research Center, 1958), pp. 47–48.

primaries held in a sample of states, analyzed in Table 21.2, less than 35 per cent of the potential electorate voted on the nomination of gubernatorial candidates. On the other hand, in three-fourths of the general elections in the same states more than 50 per cent of the potential electorate went to the polls. In the primary of the weaker party of a state or district, the vote tends to be low in relation to the vote for that party's candidate in the general election. By the same measure, popular interest in the primary of the dominant party usually is considerably higher.[4]

VOTING ON ISSUES   Another type of electoral chore peculiarly American is voting on issues. Some types of questions under American practice are commonly settled by popular vote rather than by the actions of officials. Amendments to state constitutions and to city charters are submitted to the voters for approval. In some jurisdictions bond issues fall under the same rule. In some states voters may, by petition under the initiative procedure, place a proposal for a law or constitutional amendment on the ballot.

[4] Our knowledge of participation in primaries is limited, but it seems evident that certain classes of persons, by voting heavily in primaries, gain special influence at this crucial stage in the democratic process.

Table 21.2   Popular interest in primaries: Distribution of 176 gubernatorial primaries and associated general elections according to percentage of potential electorate voting [a]

Participation Rate	Number of Primaries [b]	Percentage Distribution	Number of Elections	Percentage Distribution
Under 20	31	17.6	0	0.0
20–24	23	13.1	0	0.0
25–29	37	21.0	2	1.1
30–34	39	22.2	5	2.8
35–39	15	8.5	10	5.7
40–44	5	2.8	8	4.5
45–49	10	5.7	17	9.7
50 and over	16	9.1	134	76.2
Total	176	100.0	176	100.0

[a] The primaries and elections included in this tabulation were those held in the period 1926–1952 in the following states: Vermont, North Dakota, Maine, Wisconsin, Michigan, New Hampshire, Pennsylvania, Kansas, Massachusetts, Illinois, Wyoming, Ohio, Colorado, West Virginia, and Missouri.

[b] In this column one primary equals a pair of simultaneous primaries, Republican and Democratic. Thus, in 31 primaries, so defined, less than 20 per cent of the potential electorate voted for Republican or Democratic aspirants for the gubernatorial nomination.

In a similar fashion, in some states acts of the legislature may be suspended and subjected to popular approval or rejection.

On all these types of issues wide variations in voter interest prevail. Proposed amendments to state constitutions excite the interest of relatively few voters. Often they deal with technical questions or with matters that concern few people. In truth, they often must be voted on, not because they deserve popular attention, but because the constitution contains matters which should be handled by statute. On the other hand, when a measure on the ballot deals with a hot issue or with one that affects significantly the interests of important groups in society, a much higher level of voting interest will exist. These differences are illustrated by the data of Table 21.3, which contrasts the proportions of voters who go to the polls that express a choice on different sorts of measures in California, a state whose electors vote on many issues. The proportions voting on constitutional amendments tend to be considerably lower than the proportions voting on initiated and referred measures. The difference flows, not from the form of the issue, but from the substantive differences that usually exist between the two categories of questions. Initiated measures deal with matters in which some organized group has an intense interest and other groups usually are in opposition with equal in-

Table 21.3   *Voter interest in issues: Measures on California ballot, 1948–1954, according to percentage of voters expressing a preference* [a]

Per Cent of Voters Who Cast Ballots for Presidential or Gubernatorial Candidates	Number of Measures Submitted by Legislature	Number of Initiated and Referred Measures	Total
90–94	0	7	7
85–89	3	4	7
80–84	13	5	18
75–79	21	0	21
70–74	15	0	15
65–69	5	0	5

[a] In presidential years, the presidential vote was used as the total number of voters; in the off years, the gubernatorial vote was the base for computation of percentages.

tensity. The spirited campaign efforts by the groups concerned lead far larger proportions of the voters to express a preference on such measures than on questions dealing with technical or relatively unimportant constitutional amendments.[5]

FACTORS INFLUENCING TURNOUT RATES   Several types of elections have been described whose varying character affects the level of popular participation. Other differentiations among elections also bear on participation but they are less readily identified than are those that have been indicated. For example, the closeness of the contest, or the anticipated closeness, seems to be associated with variations in electoral turnout. When the outcome seems to be a foregone conclusion, electoral interest is apt to be low and efforts to get out the vote are likely to be comparatively weak. Perhaps the most striking demonstration of this factor may be found in the variations in participation among the states in the voting for President. Historically, the outcome of the contest for presidential electors in the southern states has not been in much doubt. For that and other reasons, the turnout in the presidential voting in these states has been far lower than in states in which a spirited battle for the electoral vote usually occurs. The differences among the states in presidential voting appear in the map in Figure 21.3, which shows the rates of turnout by states in the 1960 election.

The anticipated closeness of the contest and the associated intensity of campaign effort bear upon the size of the turnout, but it should not be

[5] Similarly, turnout at school bond and tax elections is generally low but becomes greater when proposals arouse enough opposition to bring about their defeat. R. F. Carter and W. G. Savard, *Influence of Voter Turnout on School Bond and Tax Elections* (Office of Education, Cooperative Research Monograph No. 5, 1961).

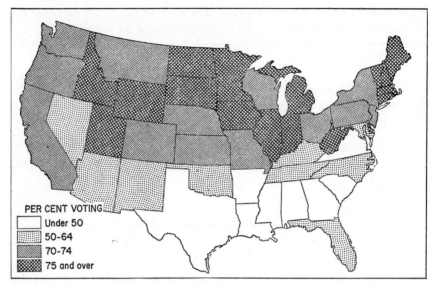

Figure 21.3   Geographical differentials in electoral participation: Percentages of estimated potential electorate voting in presidential election of 1960, by states

supposed that the proportions voting vary uniformly with the closeness of the contest. One race may wind up with a 55–45 division and another with a 51–49 divison and the rate of turnout not differ at all. Rather, it is at the extremes of one-sidedness that the turnout may be most clearly depressed. Moreover, within states habitual levels of participation develop that are not quickly altered when the contest becomes closer or less so.

In addition to the closeness factor, doubtless variations in the intensity of the stimuli to which the electorate is subjected account in a major way for the differences in turnout among the types of elections mentioned. A campaign that evokes enormous efforts by the party organizations to get out the vote, that presents the electorate with dramatic issues, that commands the attention of the media of communication will stir far more interest than a campaign whose outcome seems to the voter to be of slight immediate importance. The clashes of candidates whose personalities engage the emotions of masses of people will pull more voters to the polls than will contests between nonentities. Similarly, when the voter is confronted by issues or questions about which he has no information or which he cannot readily understand, he is likely to pass over those items on the ballot.

These variations in participation among elections have practical consequences that politicians take into account in the scheduling of elections. When the tide of national politics is running in favor of a party, state and local elections may be timed to occur simultaneously with the presidential voting. The greater turnout as well as the pull of the presidential candidate may give advantage to the state and local candidates on his ticket. State and local elections may be scheduled at times other than the presidential election, also on the assumption that the lower turnout at such times will affect the results.

It is a nice question whether the higher turnout in presidential voting tends to make the national government more responsive than state governments to the great surges of sentiment that sweep the country. Or, to put the question in another way, whether a different constituency, a different shade of opinion, may not tend to be dominant in state and local affairs from that which moves the national government. If this should be true, variations in levels of voting may be among the factors conducive to federal centralization on the assumption that a smaller and generally more conservative voting constituency tends to form around state and local governments. The low turnout in municipalities of under 50,000 may be reflective of the special capacity of small penny-pinching oligarchies to capture undisputed control of these communities.[6]

Group Differentials in Political Participation

The character of the general situation in which an election occurs influences the level of turnout. A presidential campaign has greater pulling power than an uncontested municipal election. A fight for the governorship will command the attention of more persons than will a battle for a place on a city council, which, if reported at all, may be hidden back among the classified ads. Probably the differences among such elections are mainly those in the intensity of the campaign stimuli and their distribution over the electorate. If one approaches participation from the standpoint of the individual—rather than from that of the situation—it turns out that persons with specified characteristics, regardless of the nature of the general situation, are more likely to vote than are persons without those attributes. Marked variations exist in the extent to which various types of people vote, and these differentials persist from election to election and occur consistently in all western democracies.

DEMOGRAPHIC CORRELATES OF VOTING AND NON-VOTING   The facts about differentials in voting and nonvoting among various population categories may be stated quite simply. Higher proportions of men than of women vote, although the gap between them in political

[6] See the discussion in V. O. Key, Jr., *Public Opinion and American Democracy* (New York: Knopf, 1961), pp. 116–18.

interest has narrowed since 1920. The percentage of income groups going to the polls increases from step to step up the economic ladder. Electoral interest increases with education. On the educational scale, voting participation occurs least frequently among those with a grade school education, most frequently among those with college training. The young and the old manifest less electoral enthusiasm than do those in the middle years. Metropolitan dwellers turn out in larger proportions in presidential elections than do residents of rural areas. Usually political interest declines from level to level as one goes down the scale of occupational status. Negroes, even in the North, vote in lesser degree than do whites. Persons long resident in a locality are more likely to vote than are newcomers. Persons with strong party loyalties turn out to the polls in relatively larger numbers than do those weakly identified with party or those with independent inclinations. Most of these differences, which have been demonstrated to exist by a large number of inquiries, are shown in detail for a pair of presidential elections in Table 21.4.[7]

Apparently education and income are the demographic characteristics most closely associated with electoral participation. Sharp differences prevail in the participation rates of the highest and lowest income groups, and about the same contrasts exist between the voting interest of those with college and grade school education. Income and education are fairly closely correlated, yet they are independent in their bearing on variations in electoral interest. Thus, among grade schoolers voting particpation increases with income. High-income persons with little formal education vote in about the same proportions as do college persons of equivalent income. Similarly, low-income, college-trained persons show lower rates of electoral participation than do persons of similar education who have managed to make their way into the higher-income groups. Within income categories, voting interest tends to vary with levels of education.

From such data the inference is often drawn that persons with a stake in public affairs and with wider ranges of knowledge and information tend, as one might expect, to show the highest levels of interest in voting. That is perhaps true, but it should be remembered that these facts are drawn from observations of presidential voting and doubtless do not reveal what variations, if any, may exist in behavior in other types of elections. For example, in a municipal primary, city employees, without regard to level of income or education, may vote in extremely high degree and wield a controlling influence.

---

[7] For a systematic and comprehensive synthesis of the extensive literature on electoral participation, see Robert E. Lane, *Political Life* (Glencoe: Free Press, 1959). An earlier summary and analysis is by S. M. Lipset, *et al.*, "The Psychology of Voting: An Analysis of Political Behavior," in Gardner Lindzey (ed.), *Handbook of Social Psychology* (Boston: Addison-Wesley, 1954), II, 1124–75.

Table 21.4   Demographic characteristics in relation to voting and non-voting in presidential elections of 1948, 1952, and 1956 [a]

Characteristics	1948 Voted	1948 Did Not Vote	1952 Voted	1952 Did Not Vote	1956 Voted	1956 Did Not Vote
Sex						
Male	69%	31%	79%	21%	80%	20%
Female	59	41	69	31	67	33
Age						
21–34	56	44	68	32	63	37
35–44	66	34	76	24	75	25
45–54	75	25	79	21	77	23
55 and over	63	37	77	23	78	22
Education						
Grade school	55	45	62	38	60	40
High school	67	33	80	20	74	26
College	79	21	90	10	90	10
Income						
Under $2,000	46	54	53	47	52	48
$2,000–2,999	61	39	68	32	60	40
$3,000–3,999	74	26	76	24	69	31
$4,000–4,999	75	25	83	17	75	25
$5,000 and over	82	18	88	12	83	17
Occupation						
Professional and managerial	75	25	88	12	85	15
White-collar	81	19	81	19	79	21
Skilled and semi-skilled	71	29	74	26	72	28
Unskilled	50	50	60	40	53	47
Farmers	42	58	67	33	74	26

[a] Data for 1948 and 1952 are based on interviews with national samples of voters by Survey Research Center reported by Angus Campbell, *et al.*, *The Voter Decides* (Evanston: Row, Peterson, 1954), pp. 70–73.

MOTIVATIONAL FACTORS IN VOTING AND NON-VOTING   While electoral participation is clearly associated with demographic characteristics such as education and income, the explanation of voting and nonvoting in these terms represents a low order of analysis.

Upper-income people do vote in high degree, but the fact confronts us that a great many poor people also vote. Obviously income is not the sole determinant of voting interest. Some common factor must bring into the active electorate rich and poor, the college-trained and the grade schoolers.

Recent research has gone beyond demographic analysis and sought to identify the motivations that bring people to participate in the political process. From these studies, the most notable of which have been made by Angus Campbell and his associates, it becomes evident that factors other than income, education, and other such characteristics bear on political participation. The intensity of partisan preference, for example, bears significantly on voting. Of those at the highest point on a scale of intensity of partisan preference, 97 per cent voted; of those at the lowest point on the scale, only 65 per cent voted. Similarly, concern about the outcome of the election brings people to the polls. In 1956, of those who "didn't care at all" about the election, 52 per cent voted; of those who "cared very much," 84 per cent voted.

Campbell also attempted to measure the sense of political efficacy, that is, the extent to which the citizen felt that it made a difference whether he voted or participated otherwise in politics. Of those persons with a high sense of political efficacy, only 9 per cent did not vote in 1956. Of those with a low score on this measure, 48 per cent did not vote. In another study, Campbell sought to measure the sense of citizen duty, which represents the degree to which a person feels that he ought to vote as a matter of civic obligation, although he may well believe that his actions will not affect the course of human events. Of those with the highest sense of citizen duty, only 15 per cent failed to vote in 1956 while at the low point of the scale 73 per cent did not vote.

These motivations associated with political participation are positively associated with demographic correlates of participation, but the psychological motivations have a degree of independence from the demographic correlates. That is, intensity of partisan preference, the sense of political efficacy, and the sense of citizen duty become more marked as income increases and as one goes up the educational scale. Yet within each income level, for example, participation varies with the intensity of partisan preference or the sense of political efficacy. Extremely sharp contrasts in voting participation prevail, for example, between persons with a grade school education who have a sense of political efficacy in high and low degree. Similarly, low-income persons with a low sense of citizen duty are far less likely to vote than are low-income persons with a high sense of citizen duty.[8] The inquiries that produced these findings establish the proposition that certain types of attitudes lead to voting; other attitudes are likely to be associated with nonparticipation. Another sort of problem is raised by the question of

[8] See Angus Campbell, et al., The American Voter (New York: Wiley, 1960), ch. 5.

how some individuals come to be equipped with one set of attitudes, others with another. The chances are that these varying attitude patterns are precipitated by the complex of developmental experiences that make a man what he is, such as family influences, formal education, and group associations.

To be differentiated from motivations that bring people to vote are what might be called sociological factors—or relations, direct or indirect, with other people. Of special importance is group affiliation. Persons not affiliated with voluntary groups, such as churches, labor unions, and the like, are less likely to vote than are individuals with several group connections. Persons with strong party attachments are more likely to vote than are independents. Degree of exposure to political discussion and communication affects voter turnout. A person whose immediate group associates have an interest in politics may find himself propelled to the polls even though his own sense of citizen duty is slight.[9] Perhaps the way to put the matter is that the more closely linked with the life of the community a person is, the more likely it is that he will vote. The more numerous these linkages, the odds are, the stronger the stimuli and the social pressures to which he is subjected.

When the analysis of participation shifts from simple demographic correlation to motivational factors, the underlying significance of electoral participation becomes more nearly discernible. If the affairs of the state were so conducted that an extremely large proportion of the population felt that voting was a pointless exercise because things were fixed anyway, the political health of the Republic would not be good. What dire consequences might follow under such circumstances is problematic, but conceivably the populace would be open to the blandishments of men advocating cures by nondemocratic methods. Or a generally depressed civic morale might be an indicator that democratic procedures had already been converted into a farce. The operation of a democratic order may require the existence of a widespread belief among the voters in the reality of their role in the system.[10]

PARTICIPATION DIFFERENTIALS AND THE FORTUNES OF PARTIES   Identification of differentials in electoral participation among groups within the population suggests the mundane question whether they affect the fortunes of parties on the American scene. Those elements of the population with lowest voting rates consist in larger measure of persons with Democratic rather than Republican predispositions. Democratic strength

[9] W. A. Glaser, "The Family and Voting Turnout," *Public Opinion Quarterly*, 23 (1959), 563–70.

[10] Those low on the scale of political efficacy include a large proportion of persons high on the scale of domestic "liberalism." All probably would not be well if a large proportion of the population should come to consist of persons, many of them probably necessitous, yearning for governmental action, yet feeling themselves to be politically helpless.

has been drawn disproportionately from among the lower-income groups, the less well educated, and skilled and unskilled workers.

Democratic candidates would have been strengthened, at least in recent decades, by compulsory voting or by some other means of bringing out substantially the entire electorate. Analysis after analysis has shown a higher preference for the Democratic cause among those who stayed away from the polls than among those who voted. In November, 1940, those who told *Fortune* interviewers that they did not expect to vote were better than four to one for Roosevelt. In 1952 the Survey Research Center found that 54 per cent of the nonvoters in its national sample preferred Stevenson as against the 44.5 per cent of those who voted. The inability of the Democrats to bring their full potential strength to the polls does not result solely from their dependence on groups with generally low voting rates. Democratic businessmen or Democratic college-trained people are less likely to vote than are their opposite numbers among the Republicans.[11]

The fact that Democrats are less inclined to take themselves to the polls than Republicans does not mean that an increase in the total turnout will be accompanied invariably by an increase in the Democratic proportion of the total vote. If at one election the turnout is 55 per cent of the potential vote and at the next 60 per cent, the effect of the increase on the partisan division will depend upon the sectors of the population from which the increment in vote comes. If the additional vote arises largely from groups with a Democratic predisposition, the Democratic proportion of the total vote will increase. Between 1944 and 1948, in some areas the vote in the prosperous wards declined as that in the poorer wards increased. These shifts in participation contributed to the Democratic victory in 1948. Increases in participation, though, do not uniformly work to the advantage of the Democrats. Moreover, the estimation of the effects of shifts in turnout rates is always complicated by their mixture with movements of voters across party lines under the pressure of the issues of the moment.

UPSURGES IN VOTER TURNOUT AND SHIFTS IN PARTY STRENGTH   The relation of differentials in group participation and in percentages of the eligibles voting to party fortunes obviously raises complex problems of analysis. Another kind of change in participation, however, seems to be clearly related to sharp changes in the attractiveness of the parties to the voters. An unusually rapid rate of growth in the total number of voters from one election to the next is accompanied by an exceptionally high rate of increase in the number of supporters of one of the parties but not of the other. At least this relationship has prevailed since 1890. It is as if a huge number of potential voters were waiting in reserve to be brought

[11] See Angus Campbell, "The Case of the Missing Democrats," *New Republic*, July 2, 1956.

into the active electorate and mainly to the ranks of one of the parties by some new set of circumstances.

From 1892 to 1896 the total turnout increased by 14.7 per cent as the Republican vote grew by 35.5 per cent and the Democratic vote declined by 1.1 per cent from the combined Democratic-Populist vote of 1892. The 1916 presidential turnout exceeded that of 1912 by 23.2 per cent, an unusually high quadrennial rate of increase. Wilson's 1916 vote grew by 45 per cent from 1912 while that of Hughes was only 12 per cent over the combined Taft-Roosevelt vote of 1912. Similarly, the period 1948–1952 marked an unusually sharp increase in the total number of voters, accompanied by a Republican rate of growth about four times that of the Democrats.[12] When the national political struggle warms up enough to bring a substantial increase in electoral interest, factors are probably at work to shift voters from party to party as well as to nudge more of them to the polls. Those brought to the polls from the inactive ranks may move predominantly in the same direction as the regular voters are shifting.[13]

Varieties of Participation and the Political System

Most studies of electoral participation have been microscopic: they focus on the individual and attempt to identify the characteristics or the motives that lead him to vote or not to vote. Such analyses, illuminating though they are, throw little light on the larger question of the relation between the extent and nature of citizen participation and the character of the political system in the large. The significance of variations in the nature and extent of participation probably can be grasped only by extensive cross-national analyses, although some tentative speculations may be ventured. They should be read with the probability in mind that the nature of the political order may affect patterns of participation as well as the reverse.

A useful distinction to make is that between electoral participation limited to the simple act of voting and more active types of political participation. The act of voting may have different motivations and different meanings and it may occur in different degrees among national political systems.

---

[12] See Angus Campbell, "Surge and Decline: A Study of Electoral Change," *Public Opinion Quarterly*, 24 (1960), 397–418. In 1840 an outpouring of voters boosted participation precipitously and "engulfed the Jacksonians." R. P. McCormick, "New Perspectives on Jacksonian Politics," *American Historical Review*, 65 (1960), 288–301.

[13] The association of marked boosts in turnout with sharply fought and apparently issue-laden elections gives some support to the argument that our 35,000,000 or so nonvoters consist in large measure of persons left untouched, unreached, and unmoved by the appeals, the alternatives, and the promises projected by the party system. In a sense they do not vote because, given the alternatives, the ritual is meaningless to them. See the discussion by E. E. Schattschneider, *The Semi-Sovereign People* (New York: Holt, Rinehart and Winston, 1960), ch. 6.

Of somewhat greater interest, perhaps because less is known about them, are those types of political participation that go beyond voting. Each man has one vote, but nothing is plainer than that men differ widely in their political influence. Some persons talk up their beliefs, criticize or praise the government, and push their ideas through their membership in this group and that. They may discuss the campaign with their friends and acquaintances and endeavor to persuade them of the error of their ways or to re-enforce them in their sensible agreement with themselves. They may attend rallies, coffee hours, and party dinners. They write to their Congressmen. They serve the party's cause by working at the polls, ringing doorbells, addressing envelopes, or doing other chores. They may even become party functionaries, minor or great, and they may contribute to the campaign chest and solicit others to aid the worthy cause. Such activists may not limit their efforts to campaigns alone; they join the Chamber of Commerce, a trade union, a reform league, and thereby have other avenues for the dissemination of their views. In a sense they may vote many times.

VARIATIONS IN VOTING   Variations in voting participation alone may be either quantitative or qualitative. Such differences may appear by comparisons of the behavior of the same electorate at different times; they may also appear by comparison of the electorates of different nations at the same time.

The question of the significance of quantitative variations in voting has stimulated speculation. The graph of varying proportions of the electorate going to the polls has been likened to a fever chart of the body politic. Social tensions, or so the argument goes, increase with the rate of participation. It seems clear that participation rates provide no measure of the temperature of political conflict either within a single nation or between nations. Turnout rates are affected by many factors, some of which have been touched on in this chapter. Turnout rates do provide a rough measure of the extent of political involvement within the population. An electorate, defined by universal suffrage, that habitually turns out to the extent of 10 per cent is probably associated with a radically different structure of power than one that has a habitual participation rate of 85 per cent. Virginia, where an extremely small proportion of the potential electorate votes in the decisive Democratic primaries, has a radically different sort of political order than New York with its far higher participation rate. Variations in participation do not alone account for differences in the structure of power; the nature of political leadership may affect participation and vice versa. The Virginia political elite maintains sufficient discipline within its ranks to restrain those who might swell political participation by effective advocacy of causes that would agitate the nonvoters.

Qualitative differences in voting, which may not necessarily be correlated with quantitative variations, doubtless are of great significance although that significance can only be surmised. The casting of the ballot may be associated with an intensity of concern that marks this action as but a step toward the manning of the barricades. Nonvoting may be the product of disillusionment and lack of faith in the democratic process. Voting may be a gesture of alliance with a fellow religionist or unionist or Pole, an act almost without political motive and with only fortuitous political consequences. It may be an act performed after careful deliberation about the general weal. It may be an action associated with a belief that it affects the course of events; it may be pure ritual. Obviously the extent of the distribution of varying sorts of attitudes within the electorate about voting itself is associated with important characteristics of the political order, but knowledge of these matters is limited.

VARIATIONS IN OTHER TYPES OF POLITICAL PARTICIPATION   Popular participation in government involves a great deal more than the simple act of voting. Those who wish to influence the course of events must bestir themselves to do far more than vote. The people who pick up the ball and carry it have been labeled as activists, as politists,[14] as opinion leaders. They constitute a small portion of the entire electorate, but the chances are that differences in the size, composition, and behavior of this group are associated with significant variations in the nature of political orders.

The activists may constitute varying proportions of the entire electorate. If the realm of the activists is occupied by a small and exclusive class, perhaps consisting largely of professional politicians, a different sort of system exists than when large numbers of citizens convert themselves into energetic, though amateur, politicians when campaign time rolls around. "Self-government" is a term mainly for oratorical rather than scientific discourse, yet the reality of self-government may be approached as participation becomes more general within the electorate.

Ease of access to the ranks of the activists may be an important index of the nature of the political order. The odds are that in the United States, movement into the ranks of the activists encounters a relatively low level of obstruction. That movement may be observed with special clarity in those endeavors that may have nothing to do with elections but are calculated to influence public policy. A small group of citizens may become exercised about a public problem; it stirs up a noise and pressures the city council into action; it then relapses into inactivity. Another crowd agitates for congressional legislation and a remarkably few people can at times put a bill through Congress.

---

[14] Alfred de Grazia applies the term "politists" to the activists. See his *Elements of Political Science* (New York: Knopf, 1952), ch. 3.

This movement into and out of the ranks of the activists also evidently exists in presidential politics and may be a significant characteristic of the American system. The development of a general concern about the character of the government, the appearance of a popular leader, or the unfolding of a great cause—to be either supported or opposed—may activate the latent amateur politician in millions of citizens. They spring to action and the campaign eventuates in a verdict by the electorate, decisive at least for the moment. At other times, the political activists may be far less numerous. When things seem to be moving along satisfactorily, people may attend to their plowing. When concern arises, however, the ranks of the attentive and active public are swelled, some sort of solution is fought through, and the amateur politicians go back to their callings. At least a look backward at presidential elections suggests that something on this order must occur.

No trustworthy information exists on variations in the size of the politically active sector of the population through time, but a few exploratory analyses have been made of the incidence within the American electorate of types of political participation other than voting. In a study of the 1956 presidential campaign the Survey Research Center asked the respondents in its national sample whether they had given money or bought tickets to help the campaign for one of the parties, whether they had attended meetings or rallies, whether they had worked for one of the parties or candidates, and whether they had talked to others to try to show them how they should vote.

Of the entire sample, only 10 per cent reported that they had given money, bought tickets, or otherwise contributed to the campaign. Seven per cent had attended political meetings or rallies while 3 per cent had done work for one or the other of the candidates. A much larger number, 28 per cent of the sample, reported that they had talked with other people to show them why they should vote for one of the parties or candidates.

While the data indicate that a small proportion of the electorate engages in the more formal types of political participation, the distribution of the high participators within the electorate suggests some inferences about the significance of the American pattern of participation. Generally political activity and participation become more common within the population as one goes up the income scale, up the educational ladder, and up the hierarchy of occupations. The data on variations in extent of political participation by income level appear in Table 21.5. Only 15 per cent of those with incomes under $2,000 and 41 per cent of those with incomes of $5,000 or over ranked as high participators.

From the data of Table 21.5 one might leap to the conclusion that persons in the above-average income brackets constitute most of those who engage in more-than-average political activity. That inference can be checked by another arrangement of the data, which is shown in Table 21.6. The income levels of $5,000 and over account for a share of the high participators

Table 21.5   Division of income classes according to variations in level of political participation in 1952 presidential elections [a]

| Income Bracket | Political Participation Level | | | |
| | Low | Medium | High | |
	Did Not Vote	Voted Only	Voted and Other [b]	N
Under $2,000	47%	38%	15%	315
$2,000–$2,999	31	51	17	255
$3,000–$3,999	24	50	26	364
$4,000–$4,999	17	49	34	233
$5,000 and over	13	46	41	415

[a] Based on a special tabulation of national sample interviewed in 1952 study by Survey Research Center, by courtesy of Angus Campbell, Director of the Center.

[b] Respondents classified as high participators had given money, bought tickets, attended rallies, worked for a party or a candidate, talked to other people to try to influence their vote, or engaged in more than one of these activities.

Table 21.6   Distribution of persons with high levels of political participation in 1952 presidential election among income classes [a]

| Income Bracket | High Participators [b] | | Total Sample | |
	N	Per Cent	N	Per Cent
Under $2,000	49	11.2	315	19.9
$2,000–$2,999	44	10.1	255	16.1
$3,000–$3,999	93	21.3	364	23.0
$4,000–$4,999	80	18.4	233	14.7
$5,000 and over	170	39.0	415	26.3
Total	436	100.0	1,582	100.0

[a] Based on a special tabulation of a sample interviewed in 1952 study by Survey Research Center, by courtesy of Angus Campbell, Director of the Center.

[b] The activities requisite for classification as a high participator are indicated in the note to Table 21.5.

somewhat larger than their proportion of the entire electorate. Nevertheless, persons with more-than-average political activity to their credit are dispersed widely in the population among all income and educational levels. No doubt finer measures of political activity would indicate somewhat sharper differentiations among population classes in particular types of political activity, such as in making political contributions. The chores and debates of politics, however, are by no means the exclusive preserve of any small political caste or class.[15]

This distribution of political activists through the income and occupational hierarchy may be of special significance for the workings of a democratic order. The electorate may be pictured as a system of political strata that are differentiated according to degree and kinds of activity, extent of interest, breadth of information, sharpness of the sense of political efficacy, and other such criteria. These political strata do not coincide with but cut across occupational and income classes, which may give persons of all sorts and classes a sense of sharing in the operation of the system. If this lively sense of participation and of efficacy were limited to a narrow income or occupational group, the tensions that tend to develop along class lines might be accentuated.[16]

[15] These findings are paralleled by another survey reported by J. L. Woodward and Elmo Roper, "Political Activity of American Citizens," *American Political Science Review*, 44 (1950), 872–85. Tables from the Woodward and Roper survey are reproduced in the third edition of this text at pp. 578–79.

[16] For an elaboration of the idea of this paragraph, see Key, *op. cit.*, ch. 8. Also Stein Rokkan and Angus Campbell, "Citizen Participation in Political Life: Norway and the United States," *International Social Science Journal*, 12 (1960), 69–99.

22.

THE ELECTORATE

NOT ALL NATIONS that have universal suffrage are democratic, but all democratic nations have universal suffrage. Even dictatorial regimes are moved to bolster their position by mock election ceremonies and thereby to pay tribute to the potency of the conceptions underlying popular government. Universal suffrage, now regarded as commonplace, did not come about in a day. Popular governments at first allowed only a small part of the populace to vote. In western democratic societies the suffrage has been gradually extended to new groups; each extension has been in response to demands by or on behalf of a group emerging from political subordination and seeking a voice in the management of public affairs. Whether by the acquisition of suffrage these new groups always gained power and influence or merely won a symbol of emancipation may be questioned. Nevertheless, the step-by-step extension of the suffrage has brought with it far-reaching changes in the methods and strategy of politics. In monarchical and aristocratic regimes the gaining of power might be a matter of personal intrigue among a small group of people. Success depended on the possession of qualities and the employment of techniques quite different from those necessary to gain the favor of the electorate under a system of universal suffrage.

A broad popular suffrage is, then, a constant that conditions both the method and the substance of American politics. Its development in the United States is principally of historical interest; the story is nonetheless important for an understanding of American politics. The first great suffrage battle broke down property-owning and taxpaying qualifications for manhood suffrage. The outcome of this struggle marked the decline of the colonial and early American aristocracies and the rise in power and influence of the common man. The question of Negro suffrage was debated and, in the main, settled against the Negro prior to the Civil War. The Fifteenth Amendment was designed to extend the suffrage to the Negro, but its effectiveness was long delayed. The third great dispute over the suffrage turned on the question of its extension to women. While the elimination of property-owning and taxpaying qualifications was accomplished by state action, questions of the vote for Negroes and for women became issues of national politics and raised problems of the expediency of national control of suffrage in the federal system.[1]

Property and the Vote

EARLY PROPERTY QUALIFICATIONS   Until the triumph of Jacksonian Democracy, property-holding and taxpaying qualifications for the exercise of the suffrage were common. The American Revolution had brought no abrupt change in the fundamental nature of suffrage requirements. Changes were made but they were toward lowering, not eliminating, the property qualification.

Suffrage in the colonies rested on the same principles that governed the right to vote in Britain. Generally, the vote was restricted to freeholders or real property owners. Blackstone's justification for this state of affairs was congenial to Americans as well as Britishers. He thought the true reason for the property qualification was to "exclude such persons as are in so mean a situation as to be esteemed to have no will of their own." [2] To grant the vote to urban workers or to persons occupying land under short-term leases would

[1] The federal Constitution adopted state definitions of suffrage for the election of Senators and Representatives. Members of the House were to be chosen by "the people of the several states, and the electors in each state shall have the qualifications requisite for electors of the most numerous branch of the state legislature." Art. I, sec. 2. The same qualifications for voters for Senators were embodied in the Seventeenth Amendment, which made Senators popularly elective. Subject to the federal constitutional prohibitions of denial of the vote on account of race, color, or sex, the states fix the qualifications of voters, but the elector's right to vote for presidential electors, Senators, and Representatives is derived from the federal Constitution, and Congress may take steps to protect this right. The constitutional arrangement results in considerable diversity in the details of suffrage legislation. Dudley O. McGovney summarizes the state laws and argues for uniformity through federal action in *The American Suffrage Medley* (Chicago: University of Chicago Press, 1949). The Constitution originally denied the suffrage to residents of the District of Columbia, but the Twenty-third Amendment, adopted in 1961, granted to them the right to vote in presidential elections. Officials of the District itself, though, are appointed rather than elected.

[2] See Chilton Williamson, "American Suffrage and Sir William Blackstone," *Political Science Quarterly*, 68 (1953), 552–57.

bring into the electorate persons subject to influence or coercion by their employers or landlords. Property owners could be regarded as an independent sector of the citizenry with a stake in the community because of their property ownership and of the fact that they paid most of the taxes.

The colonies and the states after the Revolution differed widely in determinations of the amounts and types of property necessary to establish a right to vote. In some instances the requirement was in terms of value of real estate; the pre-Revolutionary requirement in New York, for example, was ownership of real estate worth 40 pounds. Some states required ownership of a specified acreage. A Virginia act of 1736 limited the vote for members of the legislature to persons with a freehold of 100 acres, "if no settlement be made upon it" or 25 acres "with a house and plantation." A town or city resident might vote as a freeholder "in any house or lot." At times ownership of specified amounts of personal property constituted a means for qualification to vote as an alternative to the real property requirement. During the Revolution eight of the 13 states altered their suffrage requirements, "and the modifications were not such as to indicate that statesmen had abandoned the principle that only property holders should vote. The only tendency manifest was to reduce the amount." [3]

ELIMINATION OF PROPERTY REQUIREMENTS   After the American Revolution the general pattern was, first, to eliminate the property-owning qualification and to substitute a taxpaying requirement, which was, in turn, removed. The actual pattern of change was often more complex than this simple statement suggests, but broadly the electorate was enlarged by stages until universal manhood suffrage became the general custom. South Carolina substituted a taxpaying requirement for the property requirement in 1778; Georgia, in 1789; Delaware, in 1792; Maryland, in 1810; Connecticut, in 1818; Massachusetts, in 1821; New York, in 1821; Rhode Island, in 1842. Vermont granted universal manhood suffrage in 1777, and a few other states later moved directly from property holding to universal suffrage. Virginia, for example, persisted in the property qualification until 1850 when it was removed. At that time the taxpaying requirement was passing out of use, though innocuous remnants remained in various jurisdictions even into the twentieth century. [4]

While the property and taxpaying requirements doubtless at times sharply restricted the suffrage, the fact seems to be that the restrictions were less severe than is often supposed. Brown contends that in Massachusetts the

---

[3] K. H. Porter, *A History of Suffrage in the United States* (Chicago: University of Chicago Press, 1918), p. 10.

[4] For a detailed account, see Chilton Williamson, *American Suffrage from Property to Democracy, 1760–1860* (Princeton: Princeton University Press, 1960).

property qualifications excluded few men because economic opportunity and cheap land "promoted almost universal property ownership." [5] In some areas the property requirements seem to have been ignored in the administration of elections. In New Jersey, it is said, ". . . all serious thought of property qualifications was abandoned long before constitutional reform formally did away with them." [6] The taxpaying qualification itself could often be met by payment of a nominal tax; the poll tax was, thus, adopted in some instances to facilitate fulfillment of the taxpaying requirement. The property and tax standards were in some states not rigorous and whatever they were, their administration in many localities was loose. Nevertheless, in some states they did restrict the electorate and their elimination was accomplished only after bitter dispute.

Defenders of the property qualification regarded themselves as especially threatened by the growth of industrial classes in such cities as Providence, New York, and Philadelphia. Their oratory was correspondingly incandescent. The spectre of ultimate control of the state by the city of New York haunted Chancellor Kent in his famed speech in the New York constitutional convention of 1821 in opposition to a proposal to abolish property qualifications for voters for the state senate:

> . . . The apprehended danger from the experiment of universal suffrage, applied to the whole legislative department, is no dream of the imagination. It is too mighty an excitement for the moral condition of men to endure. The tendency of universal suffrage is to jeopardize the rights of property and the principles of liberty. There is a constant tendency in human society—and the history of every age proves it—there is a constant tendency in the poor to covet and to share the plunder of the rich; in the debtor to relax or to avoid the obligations of contract; in the indolent and profligate to cast the whole burthen of society upon the industrious and virtuous; and there is a tendency in ambitious and wicked men to inflame those combustible materials. It requires a vigilant government, and a firm administration of justice, to counteract that tendency. Thou shalt not covet; thou shalt not steal; are divine injunctions induced by this miserable depravity of our nature.

A similar anxiety was expressed by a member of the Pennsylvania constitutional convention of 1837:

> But, Sir, what does the delegate propose? To place the vicious vagrant, the wandering Arabs, the Tartar hordes of our large cities on the level with the virtuous and good man? . . . These Arabs steeped in crime

---

[5] R. E. Brown, *Middle-Class Democracy and the Revolution in Massachusetts, 1691–1780* (Ithaca: Cornell University Press, 1955), p. 37.

[6] J. R. Pole, "Suffrage and Representation in Maryland from 1776 to 1810: A Statistical Note and Some Reflections," *Journal of Southern History*, 24 (1958), 218–25.

and in vice, to be placed on a level with industrious population is insulting and degrading to the community. . . . I hold up my hands against a proceeding which confers on the idle, vicious, degraded vagabond a right at the expense of the poor and industrious portion of this commonwealth.[7]

If such opposition to the broadening of the suffrage is read through modern eyes, it may be too readily dismissed as only an attempt by the rich and well-born to maintain their special prerogatives. That was certainly a part of the picture, but sincere anxieties existed about the viability of governments grounded on mass suffrage. In part, that fear rested on the actuality of subordination of many men without property to the will of others. In a day with no secret ballot (and no trade unions), employers could often command the vote of their employees, and agricultural landlords could often control their tenants. Apart from such relationships that created predictable difficulties, successive extensions of the suffrage marked steps in the creation of new governmental practices; and moves into the unknown are always fraught with risk. Yet in due course property and taxpaying qualifications were swept away, usually without the dire consequences foreseen by their defenders.[8]

The Negro and the Vote

Proposals to extend the suffrage have invariably generated anxieties among those whose positions might be endangered thereby. That rule has applied with special force to the question of Negro suffrage. The geographical concentration of the Negro population in the South made the grant of the vote to the Negro a threat to the regional political and social system. Not only would the suffrage be extended to the propertyless and the uneducated, but it would be given to blacks not long out of slavery who would, it was feared, gain dominance over their erstwhile masters. Moreover, since the pressure for Negro suffrage came originally almost entirely from outside the South, the debate over the question was a forensic continuation of the Civil War, a factor conducive to the solidification of southern resistance.

[7] Quoted by Porter, *op. cit.*, p. 92.

[8] In North Carolina until 1856 only 50-acre freeholders could vote for state senators but all taxpayers could vote for governor. In New York until 1822 the property requirements to vote for governor were stiffer than those to vote for the state assembly. Richard P. McCormick has shown that the party divisions within the two classes of voters in both states were similar and that the enlargement of the electorate did not significantly alter the balance of strength between the parties. See his "Suffrage Classes and Party Alignments: A Study in Voter Behavior," *Mississippi Valley Historical Review*, 46 (1959), 397–410.

GRANT OF NEGRO SUFFRAGE   The initial grant of Negro suffrage was a phase of the power politics of the post-Civil War period. Negro suffrage had no part in the reconstruction schemes of Presidents Lincoln and Johnson, but the so-called radical group in Congress favored suffrage. Their leaders calculated that the grant of suffrage would enable Negroes, in combination with white union men, to control the southern states. In some northern states, the move would also bring support to the Union party, as the Republicans of the day called themselves.

While the northern states, somewhat reluctantly, granted the vote to the Negro, its extension to the South required coercive measures. The Reconstruction Act of 1867 imposed Negro suffrage upon the former Confederate states. It declared the governments of those states to be provisional until, among other things, new constitutions were formulated by "delegates elected by the male citizens of said states, twenty-one years old and upward, of whatever race, color or previous condition." Another step toward Negro enfranchisement was the Fourteenth Amendment, which became effective in July, 1868. It provided for a reduction of congressional representation of those states that abridged the right of suffrage, a penalty which has never been exacted. The Fifteenth Amendment, adopted in 1870, went more directly to the question of Negro suffrage by forbidding the states to deny or abridge the right to vote "on account of race, color, or previous condition of servitude."

With the enfranchisement of the Negro, rule of the southern states by a combination of Negroes and carpetbaggers ensued for about eight years, a rule that rested ultimately on military force. Southerners are perhaps prone to exaggerate the horrors of reconstruction, but the results were not considered good by even the most sympathetic observers. Extravagance, corruption, and administrative incompetence prevailed.

WHITE CONTROL RE-ESTABLISHED   Federal reconstruction policy united southern whites, formerly divided between the Whig and Democratic parties, who determined to use whatever tactics were necessary to regain control. The activities of the Ku Klux Klan were the most striking example of the methods of intimidation used to discourage Negro political activity. The return of white supremacy in the South was finally sanctioned by the negotiations connected with the Hayes-Tilden contest over the Presidency. The bald and oversimplified version of the deal is that the Presidency went to the Republican, Hayes, and a policy of federal nonintervention in racial matters went to the South. The withdrawal of federal troops from the South by Hayes in 1877 removed the props from the remaining reconstruction governments.[9]

[9] See C. Vann Woodward, *Reunion and Reaction: The Compromise of 1877 and the End of Reconstruction* (Boston: Little, Brown, 1951).

Despite the new disposition to leave the Negro question to the South, the constitutional injunction against state abridgement of the right to vote on account of color remained. Probably private intimidation was the chief means of disfranchisement, but a variety of legal means was also used. Gerrymandering legislative districts against the Negro was a favorite device, as were "elaborate and confusing registration schemes, and devious complications of the balloting process."[10] Some states made conviction for petty larceny a disqualification for voting, on the theory that this infraction of the law occurred more frequently among the blacks.

In the 1890's more refined techniques were developed to deal with Negro suffrage. By this time new political disputes had arisen among southern whites. The new governing combination of business, railroad, financial, and planting classes came to be challenged by the radical agrarians. Each side was tempted to enlist the Negro in its support, a costly sort of campaigning under the political customs of the day. The strongest compulsions existed for the conflicting factions of southern whites to unite on the question of Negro suffrage. Only by effective disfranchisement could political dispute among the whites follow its natural course.

The problem facing the southern constitution-makers was how to circumvent the Fifteenth Amendment in a manner to disfranchise Negroes legally and at the same time leave the way open for all whites to vote. The Mississippi constitutional convention of 1890 was fertile in the invention of contrivances to serve these purposes, and during the following 10 or 15 years its handiwork found imitation in other states. To vote, the elector was required by the new constitution to pay a two-dollar poll tax and, if requested, to present his tax receipt at the polls. The assumption was that Negroes were neither inclined to pay the tax nor habituated to the preservation of records. A two-year residence requirement was imposed, on the theory that Negroes were more migratory than whites. Legislative districts were gerrymandered to discriminate against the sections of the state most heavily populated by Negroes. Conviction for bribery, burglary, theft, arson, obtaining money under false pretenses, perjury, forgery, embezzlement, murder, or bigamy was made a disqualification. If the Negro passed all these bars, there remained the literacy test, to become effective in 1892. With it was coupled an "understanding" clause, the crowning achievement of the Mississippi convention. The clause read that after 1892 qualified voters must be able "to read any section of the state constitution; or to be able to understand the same when read to him, or give a reasonable interpretation thereof." Illiteracy was common among both Negroes and whites, but in the administration of the alternative test—the "understanding" clause—discrimination against Negroes was definitely contemplated.

[10] Paul Lewinson, *Race, Class and Party* (New York: Oxford University Press, 1932), p. 65.

CONSTITUTIONAL   POLITICS   OF   NEGRO   SUFFRAGE

By the turn of the century southern states had generally disfranchised the Negro. Their constitutional forms did not explicitly exclude the Negro from the vote, but their practices ran in direct contradiction to the express prohibitions of the federal Constitution. The political branches of the national government, persuaded that only force could put meaning into the formal right of Negro suffrage in the South, were disposed to let matters rest. Their inertness threw the whole question into the hands of the Supreme Court, which was thus left with the task of its solution.

Litigants were not lacking to bring the question to the attention of the Supreme Court, which in decisions strung out over nearly a half-century dealt first with this and then that aspect of the matter. At times it avoided decision by a convenient disinclination to peer beyond legal form. At other times it struck down obviously unconstitutional practices only for them to be replaced by others. Whether such mundane thoughts entered the minds of the Justices, it was as if the Court were engaged in a delaying action with the hope that time would bring a moment propitious for reconciliation of practice with the Constitution.

Eventually, after many years and after many bouts in the rarefied atmosphere of the chambers of appellate courts, the time came when the possibilities for legal circumvention of the Constitution had been exhausted. The series of cases by which that point was reached provide much fare for the connoisseurs of constitutional interpretation, but here only the high points need be recounted. In Williams v. Mississippi,[11] decided in 1898, the Supreme Court had to examine the suffrage question as it reviewed the indictment of Williams for murder by an all-white grand jury and his conviction by an all-white trial jury. Mississippi law required that jurors be electors. The contention was that the practical administration of the Mississippi constitutional suffrage requirements manifested a scheme by the framers of that constitution to "abridge the suffrage of the colored electors in the State of Mississippi on account of previous condition of servitude." If colored persons could not be electors, they could not, under the state law, become jurors. The coupling of suffrage abridgement with the qualifications for jury duty, it was contended, constituted a deprivation of equal protection of law by the state, a matter prohibited by the Fourteenth Amendment. The Court found that the constitution and statutes of Mississippi did "not on their face discriminate between the races" and that it had "not been shown that their actual administration was evil, only that evil was possible under them."

In 1903, in Giles v. Harris,[12] the Supreme Court had before it the suffrage provisions of the Alabama constitution that permitted permanent registration as a voter before 1903 of all persons "of good character . . . who understand the duties and obligations of citizenship under a republican

[11] 170 U.S. 213 (1898).   [12] 189 U.S. 475 (1903).

form of government," as well as all persons who served in the Revolutionary and certain other wars, together with their descendants. Giles, a Negro, alleged, what everybody knew, that the constitutional provisions were part of a conspiracy to disfranchise Negroes because of their race and, therefore, were void under the federal Constitution. The Court, in an opinion by Mr. Justice Holmes, refused to order the election officers of Alabama to place the name of Giles and other Negroes on the voting lists. He expressed doubt about what the Court could do to enforce such an order if it were issued and concluded that relief against political discrimination would have to come either from the people of the state or from the political departments of the United States government.

In 1915 the Supreme Court held void one technique for discriminating against Negroes in favor of illiterate whites. It invalidated the "grandfather clause" of the Oklahoma constitution.[13] The "grandfather clause" was usually a temporary means for permanently registering as voters all those persons who could vote, or whose ancestors could vote, prior to the adoption of the Fifteenth Amendment. Those whose ancestors could not vote at that time had to clear some other hurdle, such as a literacy test, to establish their right to vote. In conjunction, these two requirements meant that whites who could show that they or their ancestors could vote prior to the adoption of the Fifteenth Amendment could gain registration regardless of their literacy and that Negroes, who were legally barred from the vote prior to the Fifteenth Amendment, were in large measures barred by the literacy test. The court looked behind the form to the intent and held the clause void.

WHITE PRIMARY LITIGATION   The white primary provided the constitutional questions for most of the litigation on the question of Negro suffrage. Circumstances made the white primary an especially effective method for political neutralization of the Negro. Long before the rise of the direct primary method of nomination in the South soon after 1900, Negroes had been excluded from participation in the affairs of the Democratic party. Most Negroes were then Republicans, and the movement of white southerners into the Democratic party, coupled with the adoption of the direct primary, created a situation ideally suited for a solution of the Negro question in a manner satisfactory to the whites. The limitation of participation in the direct primaries to whites, which was in due course formalized in party rules, permitted whites to settle their political disputes in the primary. The state then went through the formality of ratifying the nominees of the Democratic primary at the general election; a few Negroes might vote on that occasion but their vote would be to no avail because the contest had already been settled in the primary.

The litigation over the white primary involved a simple constitutional

[13] Guinn v. United States, 238 U.S. 347 (1915).

principle, but it took two decades to settle the matter. The question was whether a political party in excluding Negroes from its primaries violated the federal constitutional clauses that prohibited discrimination by the state. The Fifteenth Amendment forbids denial of the vote "by the United States or by any state" on account of race or color; the Fourteenth Amendment prohibits denial by "any state" of the equal protection of the laws. Could a political party accomplish by its own rule what the state was forbidden to do?

The judicial merry-go-round was put in motion by an ill-advised action of the Texas legislature. Despite the white primary rule, Negroes commonly voted in San Antonio primaries. A disgruntled candidate, having lost the Negro vote and the nomination, induced the state legislature to pass a law which declared Negroes ineligible "to participate in a Democratic primary election held in the State of Texas." An action so obviously by the state could hardly pass muster with the courts. The Supreme Court in 1927 held the law to be an "obvious infringement" of the equal-protection clause of the Fourteenth Amendment.[14] The legislature immediately repealed the legislation and substituted an act authorizing every political party "to prescribe the qualifications of its own members" through its state executive committee. The Democratic state executive committee then adopted a white primary rule, which was quickly challenged. The Court dodged the question whether a political party, as a private organization, might limit its membership to whites. It based its decision on the view that the party's state executive committee had acted under legislation which made it, in effect, an agent of the state. The exclusion of Negroes by a party committee acting under state authority constituted a denial of equal protection by the state.[15]

The rebuff by the Supreme Court stimulated the juridical imagination of Texas Democrats, and in 1932 another rule limiting participation in the primary to whites was adopted, not by the legislature, not by the state executive committee of the party, but by the party's state convention. Was the convention's action that of a private voluntary association, or was it the action of an instrumentality of a state and as such an infringement of the equal-protection clause? The Court examined the legal nature of parties in Texas and found them to be "voluntary associations for political action" and not "creatures of the state." As a private association the party might exclude Negroes without infringing the equal-protection clause, which applied only to action by a state.[16]

The ingenuity of the constitutional lawyers had not been exhausted, and they eventually raised new questions. Enemies of the white primary took

[14] Nixon v. Herndon, 273 U.S. 536 (1927).
[15] Nixon v. Condon, 286 U.S. 73 (1932).
[16] Grovey v. Townsend, 295 U.S. 45 (1935).

courage from the Supreme Court's 1941 decision in the Classic case.[17] In that decision the Court upset the general belief, based on the Newberry case, that the federal government had no power to regulate primaries held under state authority. The contention in the Classic case was that the constitutional provision directing that the House of Representatives be "chosen . . . by the people in the several States" (Art. I, sec. 2) created a right of the voter under the federal Constitution that might be protected by federal action. The Court accepted this reasoning and upheld indictments of New Orleans election officials charged with fraud in a primary to nominate a United States Representative and, hence, with violation of a provision of the criminal code making it an offense to deprive a citizen of any right or privilege under the Constitution. The Court observed: "Where the state has made the primary an integral part of the procedure of choice, or where in fact the primary effectively controls the choice, the right of the elector to have his ballot counted at the primary is . . . included in the right protected by" Article I, section 2, of the Constitution, just as in an election.

The Classic opinion intimated that the Court might be in a mood to change its mind, and a Texas Negro, who had been excluded from a Democratic primary, brought another suit. In 1944 the Supreme Court, in Smith *v.* Allwright,[18] overruled its earlier decision approving the white primary. The reasoning was that the primary in Texas was an "integral part" of the machinery for choosing officials. Although the state convention had acted on its own authority in excluding Negroes, in other aspects the primary was regulated by state law, and the state provided procedure by which the party certified its nominees for inclusion on the general election ballot. By such action the state endorsed and enforced the discrimination against Negroes. Under these circumstances, discrimination by the party had to be treated as discrimination by the state. The Court held the action to be prohibited by the Fifteenth Amendment.

REACTIONS TO THE ALLWRIGHT DECISION   Smith *v.* Allwright overturned the legal doctrines on which southern states had based white primaries. In one sense the most remarkable consequence of the decision was the degree of its acceptance and the extent to which Negroes came to vote in primaries. In a few states, principally states of the Deep South, reaction to the decision was bitter and their legal lights began to look for loopholes in the decision. The Classic case had laid down two tests for determination whether a primary came under federal control: (1) when it is an "integral part" of the election machinery by law; (2) when it in fact "effec-

---

[17] United States *v.* Classic, 61 S. Ct. 1031 (1941).

[18] 321 U.S. 649 (1944). For a review of the chain of cases, see O. Douglas Weeks, "The White Primary: 1944–1948," *American Political Science Review*, 42 (1948), 500–510.

tively controls the choice." Smith *v.* Allwright turned on the "integral part" test. The test of "control of choice" in the Classic case was dictum and perhaps not good law, the lawyers argued. Possibly a way to preserve the "white primary" would be to repeal all state laws concerning the conduct of primaries and leave the matter entirely to party rule. Exclusion of Negroes from such a private primary by party authorities could not be regarded as a denial or abridgement of the right to vote on account of race or color *by a state* in violation of the Fifteenth Amendment.

To determine whether the "control of choice" test of the Classic case was mere dictum or law, the South Carolina legislature in 1944 repealed all laws relating to the conduct of primaries and left nominations subject solely to management by party authorities. A Negro, denied the right to vote in the 1945 primaries, sued for damages. In the suit it was stipulated that since 1900 every governor, member of the General Assembly, United States Representative, and United States Senator for the state had been a nominee of the Democratic party. If 47 years was enough, the Democratic primary indubitably controlled the choice. The only question was whether that control brought a privately conducted primary within the constitutional prohibition against racial discrimination.

United States District Judge J. Waties Waring, a Charlestonian of impeccable South Carolina connections, found that the South Carolina plan fell before the Constitution. The primary controlled choice. He dismissed the contention that the Democratic party should be regarded as a private club: ". . . private clubs and business organizations do not vote and elect a President of the United States, and the Senators and members of the House of Representatives of our national congress; and under the law of our land, all citizens are entitled to a voice in such selections." The federal circuit court upheld the district court and the Supreme Court declined to review the decision.[19] South Carolina Democratic party authorities did not comply with the decision with alacrity. The party, in essence, limited membership to whites but permitted Negroes to vote in the primaries, provided that they met various requirements including an oath to support the principles of the Democratic party. It required another suit to compel admission of Negroes to party membership.[20] In 1950 South Carolina, more or less reconciled to the proscription of the white primary, sought to keep Negro voting to a minimum by the requirement that voters, black or white, be able to read and write or, alternatively, own property assessed at $300 or more.

Alabama rejected South Carolina's strategem of attempting to get around Smith *v.* Allwright by repealing the primary laws. Without state regulation

[19] Elmore *v.* Rice, 72 F. Supp. 516 (1947), 165 F. 2d 387 (1947), 68 S. Ct. 905 (1948).
[20] Brown *v.* Baskin, 78 F. Supp. 933 (1948).

of the primaries, Gessner T. McCorvey, chairman of the state Democratic executive committee, said that he did not "know how such elections could be properly policed." There would be no punishment for fraud. "My own idea," he said, "is that the way to handle the situation with which we are confronted is to see that only properly qualified persons are permitted to register." To limit registration to "properly qualified persons," Alabama in 1946, by a narrow popular margin, amended its constitution to require as a condition for registration ability to read and write, to "understand and explain" any article of the United States Constitution, "good character," and an understanding of "the duties and obligations of good citizenship under a republican form of government." The effectiveness of the Alabama scheme necessarily depended on systematic discrimination against Negroes in its administration by the county boards of registrars. In January, 1949 a federal district court saw what everyone knew: ". . . that this amendment was intended to be, and is being used for the purpose of discriminating against applicants for the franchise on the basis of race or color." It was, therefore, "both in its object and the manner of its administration," unconstitutional. The Supreme Court declined to overrule the lower court decision.[21]

A special session of the Mississippi legislature in 1947 considered ways and means of avoiding the consequences of the Allwright case. Leaders of a move to follow the South Carolina precedent and leave nominations to the unregulated actions of party authorities were blocked by sober citizens sensitive to criticism from outside the state. Nonparticipation by Negroes flowed largely from social inhibitions other than statute anyway. The legislature limited itself to the adoption of a scheme declaring ineligible to participate in party primaries persons not in "accord with the statement of the principles of the party holding such primary." The "principles" adopted by the Democratic party under this authority included propositions thought to be unacceptable to Negroes, such as opposition to fair employment practices legislation. In 1954, after the agitation of the segregation question had stirred up concern, Mississippi tightened its voting requirements.

Arkansas had earlier developed the scheme of prescribing a requirement of adherence to party principles repugnant to Negroes as a means of discouraging Negro participation in primaries. The Democratic party convention of 1944 limited party membership to whites but permitted nonmembers to vote in the primary provided they met tests of allegiance to party principles. Among the principles was the "preservation of existing laws relating to the segregation of races in schools, public conveyances and other lawfully designated places." Exclusion of blacks from party membership

---

[21] Davis *v.* Schnell, 81 F. Supp. 872 (1949), 69 S. Ct. 749 (1949). In 1951 Alabama, again by a narrow margin, adopted another constitutional amendment calculated to give boards of registrars leeway to reject Negro applicants for registration.

made them ineligible for party posts and ineligible to run as candidates in the primary, clearly unconstitutional limitations. In 1950 the restriction of party membership to whites was removed.[22]

It might be supposed that every conceivable mode to circumvent the decision in Smith v. Allwright had been tried and found wanting, but in 1953 the Supreme Court considered another means of evasion in the Jaybird case. The Jaybird Democratic Association of Fort Bend County, Texas, had since 1889 conducted a primary of its own before the official nominating primary. The winner of the Jaybird primary entered the regular Democratic primary and ordinarily won the official party nomination without opposition. No legal bar existed to voting by Negroes in the official primary although the nominations had, in effect, been settled earlier in the Jaybird primary. This set of circumstances gave the Supreme Court some difficulty. How could it be contended that the action of the Jaybird Association was action by the state in abridgment of the Negro's right to vote? Justice Black's opinion characterized the practice: "For a state to permit such a duplication of its election processes is to permit a flagrant abuse of those processes to defeat the purposes of the Fifteenth Amendment." [23]

TECHNIQUE IN DEFUSING POLITICAL EXPLOSIVES
While the United States was not completely out of the woods on the question of Negro suffrage after Smith v. Allwright, that decision both marked and stimulated substantial progress toward bringing practice into accord with formal constitutional doctrine. The long and tortuous path the Supreme Court followed to reach that decision suggests some reflections on the art of handling difficult political issues. In truth, in 1900 the constitutional provisions on Negro suffrage could have been given reality in the South only by powerful measures of coercion. The Supreme Court had not the instruments of power and the political arms of government had no disposition to intervene.

Instead of making decisions that would have been only empty exhortations the Court followed a delaying tactic for decades. Never for long, however, did it completely foreclose opportunity for litigants to raise the consti-

---

[22] Oklahoma sought to deal with Negro candidates by prescribing that they should be identified as such on the primary or election ballot. In 1955 the statute was held to deny equal protection. See McDonald v. Key, 224 F. 2d 608 (1955).

[23] Terry v. Adams, 345 U.S. 506 (1953). In 1960, again relying on the Fifteenth Amendment, the Supreme Court held invalid an Alabama statute redefining the corporate limits of Tuskegee. The city had included about 400 Negro voters; the void statute fixed its boundaries so as to exclude from the city all save four or five Negroes. Gomillion v. Lightfoot, 364 U.S. 339 (1960). For the background, see Bernard Taper, *Gomillion Versus Lightfoot* (New York: McGraw-Hill, 1962). The decision raised hope that the Supreme Court would strike down state legislative gerrymanders in which racial discrimination was not involved, and that question was opened to litigation in Baker v. Carr, 82 S. Ct. 691 (1962). On the extent of partial disfranchisement by gerrymander, see Paul T. David and Ralph Eisenberg, *Devaluation of the Urban and Suburban Vote* (Charlottesville: Bureau of Public Administration, University of Virginia, 1961).

tutional question in another form. Negroes faced, not an absolute blockage of hope, but rather a long, a painfully long, series of provisional barriers. Meanwhile, in spite of delay in the legal sphere, social changes were taking place to give the question a different political reality. Urbanization in the South created circumstances radically different from the rural plantation society—circumstances under which many whites feared far less the probable consequences of Negro suffrage. As the generations went by, the educational and economic status of Negroes improved. Within the South itself, many whites began to agitate for civic rights for Negroes. At times their concern was that of a political leadership that hoped to enlist Negroes on its side, but more generally it was a concern over the conflict of principle and practice or a response to external criticism.

Alteration in the objective circumstances paved the way for constitutional decisions that might have some reality. In fact, even before Smith *v.* Allwright, the white primary was dying. More and more Negroes were voting in Democratic primaries. A rapid increase in Negro voting followed the decision. Generally, the freest exercise of Negro suffrage occurred in the cities and in the states around the rim of the South with relatively few Negroes in their population. The most marked informal resistance and the most marked increase in the rigor of the application of literacy tests and other such limitations took place in the states and areas with the highest proportions of Negro population. In such areas resistance hardened further in the mid-fifties as the debate on school desegregation developed. Yet the constitutional doctrines on Negro suffrage had far greater reality than they had had even 20 years earlier.[24]

Changes in the political position of the Negro in the nation as a whole presently made it feasible for Congress to exercise its power in an effort to enforce the constitutional right to vote. Until 1957 the principal way to enforce the right was by private litigation, a costly and unsatisfactory procedure, though the Attorney General could, and occasionally did, act under laws penalizing conspiracies to deprive persons of their constitutional rights. The 1957 Civil Rights Act authorized the Attorney General to institute civil suits for injunctive relief where the vote was denied or threatened. It also forbade intimidation, threats, and coercion for the purpose of interfering with the vote and authorized suits for relief by both the Attorney General

[24] The question of the vote for Indians raised constitutional issues similar to those of Negro suffrage. Not until the Nationality Act of 1924 did all Indians possess United States citizenship. Before that time about two-thirds of the Indians had acquired citizenship by treaties and by legislation applicable to particular tribes. The laws of various western states, however, continued to deny the vote to Indians until invalidated in the late 1940's by decisions of state courts and inferior federal tribunals. The extent to which Indians exercise the suffrage varies greatly from place to place. On the legal background, see Felix S. Cohen, *Handbook of Indian Law* (Washington: Government Printing Office, 1942) ; N. D. Houghton, "The Legal Status of Indian Suffrage in the United States," *California Law Review*, 19 (1931), 507.

and private persons. The Civil Rights Act of 1960 provided for the appointment of voting referees by the federal courts to apply the state requirements for voting when discrimination has prevailed "pursuant to a pattern or practice." In fact, the satutory procedure for the designation of a referee is complicated and difficult to traverse. The potency of this tool probably will rest mainly in its threat rather than its application, though it must be applied occasionally to be threatening. In July, 1962 in Louisiana's East Carroll parish a federal judge found a pattern of discrimination to prevail and registered a few Negroes in the first action of this type.

By the Civil Rights Act the government lent its authority and dignity, as well as its resources, to efforts to make effective the constitutional prohibition against denial of the vote on account of color. The burden of legal action had been earlier borne chiefly by private organizations such as the NAACP. Cases instituted by the Attorney General under the new legislation encountered the resistant legal ingenuity of southerners, though here and there intimidation was restrained and discriminatory practices checked. Legal pressures under the new law re-enforced trends long under way to constrict the area in which discrimination against Negroes in voting occurred. By 1961 the Commission on Civil Rights could conclude that Negroes encountered no "significant racially motivated impediments to voting" in Arkansas, Oklahoma, Texas, and Virginia. In Florida, North Carolina, and Tennessee such discrimination was found to prevail only in a "few isolated counties." Even in the remaining five states important breaches had been made in the bars to Negro voting.[25]

Woman Suffrage

The crusade for woman suffrage in its beginning was closely related to the abolition movement. Woman, because of her extensive legal disabilities under the common law, was compared with the slave. And, in truth, the legal rights of the married woman were closer to those of the slave than to those of free white men. The movement for the removal of legal disabilities of women and for the right of suffrage gained headway prior to the Civil

[25] The factors associated in localities with restraints on Negro voting include the presence of relatively large numbers of Negroes in the population, ruralism, and an agrarian economy that rests on relations of notable dependency on the part of its Negro segment. Conversely, resistance to Negro voting seems to be weaker in localities with diverse economies, with urbanization, and with small proportions of their population Negro. Yet these relations are by no means uniform. Other factors enter into local variations. In Louisiana, for example, Roman Catholic counties seem less resistant than Protestant to Negro voting. See J. H. Fenton and K. N. Vines, "Negro Registration in Louisiana," *American Political Science Review*, 51 (1957), 704–13. See also Harry Holloway, "The Negro and the Vote: The Case of Texas," *Journal of Politics*, 23 (1961), 526–56.

War and kept under way until the adoption of the Nineteenth Amendment to the Constitution in 1920. This long campaign produced an immense quantity of literature from both advocates and opponents of suffrage. Eventually the case for suffrage came to rest on variations of the doctrine of equality and freedom. An early formulation by an advocate of woman suffrage before the Massachusetts constitutional convention of 1853 was as follows: [26]

> I maintain first that the people have a certain natural right, which under special conditions of society manifests itself in the form of a right to vote. I maintain secondly that the women of Massachusetts are people existing under those special conditions of society. I maintain finally, and by necessary consequence, that the women of Massachusetts have a natural right to vote.

RATIONALIZATIONS OF OPPONENTS OF WOMAN SUFFRAGE   The rationalizations of the opponents of woman suffrage were of a low order, and at this late date it is difficult to see how they could have been uttered with such sobriety and piety. A few extracts from a statement by Senator Joseph E. Brown of Georgia in 1884 will illustrate the tone of the argument. He argued that "the Creator intended that the sphere of the males and females of our race should be different." Man, he contended, was "qualified for the discharge of those duties that require strength and ability to combat with the sterner realities and difficulties of life." Among these duties were military service, road construction, labor in the fields, and government. The management of government he thought, was "a laborious task, for which the male sex is infinitely better fitted than the female sex." "On the other hand," the argument continued, "the Creator has assigned to woman very laborious and responsible duties, *by no means less important* than those imposed upon the male sex, though entirely different in their character. In the family she is a *queen*. She alone is fitted for the discharge of the sacred trust of wife and the endearing relation of mother." And, the good Senator said, "when the husband returns home weary and worn in the discharge of the difficult and laborious tasks assigned him, he finds in the good wife solace and consolation which is nowhere else afforded." How could the wife, he asked, with all the "heavy duties of citizen, politician and office-holder resting upon her shoulders, . . . attend to the more sacred, delicate, refining trust . . . for which she is peculiarly fitted by nature? Who is to care for and train the children while she is absent in the discharge of these masculine duties?" The Senator could not bear to visualize the burden of public duties thrust upon women.[27]

---

[26] Quoted by Porter, *op. cit.*, p. 141.

[27] The argument is quoted in full by Susan B. Anthony and Ida Husted Harper, *The History of Woman Suffrage* (New York: the Authors, 1902), IV, 93–100.

The Senator's argument embodied the stock objections to woman suffrage, and it amounted to little more than saying, "Woman's place is in the home." But women were everywhere coming out of the home. Women were beginning to enter the professions; they were working in factories, shops, and stores; in the West they were laboring in the fields; they were making their way into colleges and universities; and some of them came to control great wealth. And as these changes progressed, the demand for woman suffrage became louder and more insistent.

What of the opposition to woman suffrage? Although much of it was simply inertia and resistance to change, a part was based on a belief that substantial interests would be endangered by the extension of the franchise to women. One of the official historians of the suffrage movement states that following 1896 the

> . . . Republican party was in complete control of the Government at Washington and was largely dominated by the great financial interests of the country, and this was also practically the situation in the majority of the States. The campaign fund controlled the elections and the largest contributors to this fund were the corporations, which had secured immense power, and the liquor interests, which had become a dominant force in State and national politics, without regard to party. Both of these supreme influences were implacably opposed to suffrage for women; the corporations because it would vastly increase the votes of the working classes, the liquor interests because they were fully aware of the hostility of women to their business and everything connected with it.[28]

The liquor interests foresaw correctly the attitudes of women voters, who have tended to favor restrictions on the liquor traffic in higher degree than do men. Corporate interests, however, had less reason to become exercised: nonvoting has been especially marked among women of working-class families.

WOMAN SUFFRAGE IN STATE AND LOCAL ELECTIONS
The earlier victories for woman suffrage were in connection with school elections. Kentucky in 1838 granted school suffrage to widows and unmarried women with property subject to taxation for school purposes; Kansas in 1861 was the first state to give the vote on school questions to all women. Michigan, Utah, Minnesota, Colorado, New Hampshire, and Massachusetts followed by 1880; by 1890 school suffrage had been gained by women in 14 states and territories. Wyoming was the first state to grant women the privilege of voting in all elections. It did so as a territory in 1869, and when

---

[28] Ida Husted Harper, *The History of Woman Suffrage* (New York: National American Woman Suffrage Association, 1922), Vol. V, p. xviii.

it was admitted to the Union in 1890 its constitution put men and women on the same plane regarding the suffrage. Three other western states soon followed Wyoming: Colorado in 1893, and Utah and Idaho in 1896. After 1896 the suffrage movement began to encounter stiffer opposition, and no state was brought into the suffrage fold until the Progressive movement was fully under way. Here again, western states were more receptive to the idea of woman suffrage. Equal suffrage was granted by Washington in 1910; California in 1911; Arizona, Kansas, and Oregon in 1912; and Montana and Nevada in 1914.

MILITANT MOVEMENT FOR NATIONWIDE SUFFRAGE FOR WOMEN   The progress toward nationwide suffrage through action by individual states had been slow, and during the period from 1913 to 1919 more militant tactics were adopted by one set of suffrage advocates. Influential in the change of method was Mrs. O. H. P. Belmont, who had observed the activities of the English suffragettes. Mrs. Belmont, a sympathetic commentator writes, "was practically the only leader formerly associated with the conservative forces who had the courage to extricate herself from the old routine propaganda and adventure into new paths. She always approached the struggle for liberty in a wholesome revolutionary mood." [29] The leader of the fight in the field, however, was Alice Paul, an able and resourceful woman. The activities of these and other women in leadership of the militant campaign for the adoption of nationwide woman suffrage constitute one of the most instructive chapters in agitation in American politics.

The militant suffragettes began with mild tactics in the 1914 congressional elections. By that time women had been enfranchised in several western states, and their campaign was concentrated in those states. The Democratic party, as the majority party, was to be held responsible for the failure to propose a constitutional amendment granting woman suffrage. All Democratic candidates for Congress in the woman suffrage states were opposed regardless of their individual stand on the suffrage question. Only 20 of 43 Democratic candidates in the nine suffrage states won. "It was generally conceded," Miss Stevens says in her excellent primer on agitation, "that we had contributed to these defeats." [30] Congressmen and other politicians began to accord a more respectful ear to the suffrage advocates; and in their platforms of 1916 both parties advocated the grant of woman suffrage by state action. This was not satisfactory to the militant suffrage leaders, who organized in the election of 1916 a protest vote against the Democratic party.

When Congress and President Wilson temporized, new tactics were adopted. Early in 1917 the women began to picket the White House and won acres of newspaper space over the country. Day after day, in both good

---

[29] Doris Stevens, *Jailed for Freedom* (New York: Boni & Liveright, 1920), p. 32.
[30] *Ibid.*, p. 36.

weather and bad, the women carried their banners before the White House. The routine was varied by the occasional march of a delegation to present a petition to the President; sometimes the delegations were received, sometimes not. The militant tactics of the Woman's party aroused criticism, and the government played into the hands of the suffragettes by adopting a policy of suppression. After six months of picketing, the demonstrators were arrested for "obstructing traffic." Others took their place; they were arrested; still others took their position on the picket line.

At their trials the women either stood mute or made speeches for liberty and woman suffrage; they refused to pay their fines on the ground that to do so would be an admission of guilt; they insisted on serving their terms in jail: "As long as the government and the representatives of the government prefer to send women to jail on petty and technical charges, we will go to jail. Persecution has always advanced the cause of justice." [31] Thus spoke one of the defendants. To the workhouse went the suffragettes. Martyrdom had the desired effect; a stream of telegrams in protest began to reach the President and Congressmen. Other women went on the picket line and thence to jail. This tactic generated publicity for the cause and created a housing problem for the District of Columbia penal authorities.

A dramatic touch was added to the campaign by the prisoners' claim to treatment customarily accorded political prisoners. In all civilized nations, the contention was, persons imprisoned for political offenses were accorded different treatment from that given the ordinary criminal. To reenforce their claim for this status, the prisoners went on a hunger strike. This tactic, Miss Stevens says, brought "the Administration face to face with a more acute embarrassment. They had to choose between more stubborn resistance and capitulation." The Administration unwisely resorted to forced feeding of the prisoners, not pleasant for the prisoners and productive of horrendous newspaper stories. But women continued to come to Washington from all over the nation and added to the prison population. The trials furnished glorious opportunities for propaganda for the cause.

In January, 1918 the House passed the proposed suffrage amendment, but the necessary two-thirds majority was lacking in the Senate. A great demonstration was arranged by the women before the White House. Additional arrests occurred; as each speaker rose to talk, she was dragged away to the waiting patrol wagons. Another hunger strike ensued and, finally, the prisoners were released. But additional demonstrations occurred; more women were sent to prison; and those released went aboard a "Prison Special" to tour the country and enlist support.

The President was finally won over to the cause of nationwide woman suffrage. In 1919 the newly elected Republican House passed the proposed amendment, and Wilson turned enough pressure on the Democratic Senators

[31] *Ibid.*, p. 102.

to win a two-thirds majority. By August, 1920 the necessary three-fourths of the state legislatures had ratified the amendment, which provided that "the right of citizens of the United States to vote shall not be denied or abridged by the United States or by any State on account of sex."

Militant tactics won the battle, but it need not be concluded that any sort of political agitation may be carried on solely by picketing the White House, going to jail, and indulging in hunger strikes. The women leading the movement had the backing of local associations and societies over the entire country, and the ordinary strategy of propaganda and pressure went on while the more spectacular acts were being committed in Washington. Moreover, many of the leaders of the movement were persons of high social and economic standing. One of the imprisoned women, for example, had a short time earlier been a guest at the White House. They were women who could not be thrown in jail without regard to the political consequences.

The movement also illustrates the problem of government in handling a determined agitation. Mrs. Belmont quoted Wilson who had written: "Governments have been very successful in parrying agitation, diverting it, in seeming to yield to it and then cheating it, tiring it out or evading it. But the end, whether it comes soon or late, is quite certain to be the same." Mrs. Belmont drew a parallel: "While the government has endeavored to parry, tire, divert, and cheat us of our goal, the country has risen in protest against this evasive policy of suppression until today the indomitable pickets with their historic legends stand triumphant before the nation." [32]

The Regulation of the Suffrage

The states establish specific requirements to vote subject to federal constitutional limitations contained chiefly in the Fourteenth, Fifteenth, and Nineteenth Amendments. The equal protection clause of the Fourteenth Amendment has been construed to prohibit discrimination by a state along lines of color in the definition of the electorate. The Fifteenth Amendment explicitly forbids denial of the right to vote "by the United States or any state on account of race, color, or previous condition of servitude." The Nineteenth Amendment prohibits denial "on account of sex." While a catalog of suffrage rules state by state would serve no useful purpose, an indication of the principal types of qualifications fixed by state constitution and law is in order.

[32] Quoted in *ibid.*, p. 246. The suffragettes may not have had a steamroller, but the steady din of their agitation must have been about as soothing as the rattle of a pneumatic hammer. Senator Boies Penrose, Pennsylvania boss and foe of woman suffrage, the story goes, was taunted by a suffragette and told that he might as well be for woman suffrage because it was coming anyway. The Senator's retort was: "So is death, but I don't have to go out and meet it halfway."

POLL TAXES   The poll tax, a head tax as a prerequisite for voting, by 1962 remained in use in only five southern states: Alabama, Arkansas, Mississippi, Texas, and Virginia. Under this type of suffrage requirement an annual tax of from one to two dollars must be paid before one becomes eligible to vote. In Alabama, Mississippi, and Virginia liability for the poll tax is cumulative; that is, a person may not pay the poll tax for the election year only and gain the suffrage; he must either pay the tax annually for several years before the election or in the election year pay the delinquent taxes for the period of cumulation prior to the election. Until 1953 in Alabama the tax liability could cumulate to $36, but a constitutional amendment of that year reduced the period of cumulation to two years at $1.50 per year.

An important motive in adoption of the poll tax in the southern states was the disfranchisement of the Negro, the supposition being that whites would pay the tax and that Negroes would not. In operation, however, the poll tax together with some of its incidental features, such as the requirement of payment long in advance of the election, disfranchises a substantial number of whites as well as blacks. It is charged, although the case is not well established, that the adoption of the poll tax in southern states was connected with a desire to disfranchise the poorer whites as well as the blacks. The timing of the adoption gives a plausibility to this view, for the tax, save in Georgia, went into effect after other methods had made the blacks timid about approaching the polling places. The tax came at about the time the Populists, the Farmers Alliance, and other political dissenters were threatening the ruling oligarchies.

Dissatisfaction with the "tax on voting" has led to movements for its repeal both by state and federal action. Six states—North Carolina, Louisiana, Florida, Georgia, South Carolina, and Tennessee—have abandoned the poll tax and proposals for repeal have been agitated in other states. In the 1940's Congress considered bills to eliminate the poll tax by statute, but advocates of this type of federal action were handicapped by doubts about its constitutionality. Leadership in this early agitation rested mainly in the hands of liberal groups outside the South; they worked on the theory that the poll tax restricted the southern electorate so drastically that conservative southerners had great advantage in campaigns for southern seats. More recently the proposal has been to eliminate the tax by constitutional amendment. In 1962 such an amendment, sponsored by Senator Holland of Florida, was submitted by Congress to the states for ratification. Advocacy of the amendment by Senator Holland is a measure of the recognition that the poll tax has been only one of many factors in the peculiar political order of the South and probably a relatively unimportant one.[33]

[33] For a detailed analysis, see Frederic D. Ogden, *The Poll Tax in the South* (University, Ala.: University of Alabama Press, 1958). In 1962 Texas voters, in an advisory referendum conducted in the party primaries, favored repeal of the poll tax.

LITERACY TESTS   Literacy tests have been used to exclude from the suffrage classes of persons thought not to possess the qualities necessary for responsible citizenship and, incidentally, to protect the position of those established in the seats of power. Recent immigrants and Negroes have been the principal targets of the literacy tests. Connecticut in 1855 and Massachusetts in 1857 were the first states to adopt a literacy test. In both states the older groups were challenged in their hegemony by the waves of new immigrants. In Connecticut the Know-Nothing representatives in the legislature brought about the submission of the literacy amendment to the state constitution. In Massachusetts the Irish had aligned themselves with the Democrats, and the native American and Whig members of the legislature combined to propose the literacy amendment to the constitution. In 1890 Mississippi adopted a literacy test as one of a battery of expedients to exclude the Negro from the franchise; other southern states soon followed the Mississippi precedent.

About one-third of the states retain the literacy test in one form or another. Usually its administration is by registration officials in whose hands the requirements often become meaningless save when the test is arbitrarily applied to exclude Negroes from the vote. In New York the educational authorities administer the test, and a substantial number of those tested fail.[34]

In several southern states in which the literacy test was designed chiefly to exclude Negroes, alternative means were developed to permit illiterate whites to vote. Mississippi in 1890 contrived the arrangement by which a person unable to read a section of the state constitution might be registered if he could "understand" any section when read to him and give a "reasonable interpretation" thereof. The assumption was that registrars would find that illiterate whites had the capacity to "understand" and "interpret" the constitution. Several states adopted the Mississippi plan, and others also established property ownership as an alternative to literacy.

In a few instances the "understanding" alternative has been converted into a requirement in addition to literacy. In Louisiana the constitution requires, *inter alia*, that a person be able to read any clause in the state or national constitution *and* to "give a reasonable interpretation" of any such clause. Discriminatory administration of such requirements along racial lines has been held unconstitutional in a case arising in Alabama. Nevertheless, with the object of coping with a growing Negro vote, Mississippi in 1954 amended its constitution to require, as a supplement to the literacy test, that an applicant for registration be able to interpret any section of the state constitution "to the satisfaction" of the county registrar, a provision whose constitutionality was challenged by litigation instituted by the Department

---

[34] When there is no showing of discrimination in its application, a state literacy requirement violates no federal constitutional provision. See Lassiter *v.* Northampton County Board of Elections, 360 U.S. 45 (1959). In 1961 a three-judge federal court upheld New York's English-language literacy test in litigation to test its application to Spanish-speaking persons.

of Justice in 1962. Georgia requires ability to read and write or "good character and an understanding of the duties and obligations of citizenship." [35] Literacy tests and related franchise requirements took on more importance in the South after the judicial invalidation of the white primary. Widespread discrimination against Negroes in the application of these tests led to agitation for the abandonment of the literacy requirement. The United States Civil Rights Commission in 1961 recommended congressional legislation to require that any state test for literacy or for capacity to "interpret" could be met by six grades of formal education, a proposal that rested on the assumption that such a requirement could not be applied in the same discriminatory manner as the existing state literacy and "understanding" or "interpreting" requirements.[36] In 1962 the Senate killed the President's proposal that the Commission's recommendation be effectuated.

CITIZENSHIP   All states now require United States citizenship as a prerequisite to the exercise of the suffrage. "For the first time in over a hundred years, a national election was held in 1928 in which no alien in any state had the right to cast a vote for a candidate for any office—national, state or local." [37] During the nineteenth century at least 22 states and territories gave aliens the right to vote, provided, of course, that they met other requirements, such as that of residence. Often it was required that aliens should have taken the first steps in the naturalization procedure. About 1875 the elimination of alien suffrage began. By 1900 only 11 states continued the right; by 1925 the privilege remained only in Arkansas. In that state a 1926 judicial decision declared effective a constitutional amendment voted in 1920 but theretofore held inoperative, and thereby wiped out the last voting privilege of aliens.

AGE   In 1960 all states, except Georgia, Kentucky, Hawaii, and Alaska, required that a person be 21 years of age to vote. Agitation to lower the voting age to 18 developed during World War II. In 1943 Georgia lowered the voting age to 18 years. The campaign slogan was "Fight at 18, vote at 18." Legislative consideration in many other states at about the same time led to no action. In 1946 the Democratic party in South Carolina adopted the 18-year rule for participation in its primaries, but this liberalization was later abandoned. In 1954 President Eisenhower supported a proposal to amend the federal Constitution to fix the age qualification at 18, but the Senate de-

[35] See J. L. Bernd and L. M. Holland, "Recent Restrictions Upon Negro Suffrage: The Case of Georgia," *Journal of Politics*, 21 (1959), 487–513; Margaret Price, *The Negro and the Ballot in the South* (Atlanta: Southern Regional Council, 1959).

[36] U.S. Commission on Civil Rights, *Voting* (Washington: Government Printing Office, 1961), p. 141.

[37] L. E. Aylsworth, "The Passing of Alien Suffrage," *American Political Science Review*, 25 (1931), 114–16.

feated the plan. In 1952 South Dakota voters, by a 700-vote margin, rejected a constitutional amendment to set the age qualification at 18 years, and in 1955 Kentucky voters adopted such an amendment to their constitution. Alaska entered the union with an age requirement of 19 and Hawaii with one of 20. In 1961 Congress had before it proposals to amend the Constitution to make 18 the voting age, but none was submitted to the states for ratification.[38]

RESIDENCE   Every state requires a minimum period of residence in the state, most commonly one year, as a voting qualification. Most states also have a supplemental requirement of a minimum residence in the county and voting district. In Alabama, for example, a person must have resided two years in the state, one year in the county, and three months in the voting district. Michigan, Oregon, Idaho, Indiana, and certain other states require only six months' residence in the state. Mississippi requires two years' residence in the state and one year in the voting district, but reduces the latter period to six months for ministers of the gospel, a recognition of the itinerant character of their calling.

The geographical mobility of the American population gives the residence requirement a greater significance than might be supposed. In the 1950's, annual census surveys showed that about 3 per cent of the people lived in a different state than they had one year earlier; roughly the same proportion lived in a different county of the same state than it had one year earlier. Residence requirements thus probably exclude about 5 per cent of the potential electorate from the ballot.[39] In 1954 Wisconsin adopted a law to permit voting for presidential electors, but not for state and local officers, by persons who had been residents of the state for less than a year but who would have been qualified to vote in the state from which they came had they remained there. California, Missouri, Ohio, and Oregon have similarly waived normal residence requirements. Connecticut in 1953 coped with the problem by permitting a person who had moved from the state to vote for presidential electors by absentee ballot within a 24-month period after he had moved, provided he had not become a qualified voter in the state to which he had moved. Vermont in 1957 adopted a similar measure.[40]

[38] For a compilation by Walter Kravitz of proposals to lower the voting age, see *Hearings*, Subcommittee on Constitutional Amendments, Committee on the Judiciary, U.S. Senate, 87th Cong., 1st sess., on S.J. Res. 1 and others, Pt. 4 (1961), 859–65.

[39] Ralph M. Goldman estimates that 5,000,000 persons were prevented from voting in 1954 by residence requirements. "Move—Lose Your Vote," *National Municipal Review*, 45 (1956), 6–9. W. Ross Yates, by a state-by-state analysis of residence requirements, estimates that they disfranchise 4.3 per cent of the potential electorate. See his "The Functions of Residence Requirements for Voting," *Western Political Quarterly*, 15 (1962), 469–88.

[40] See M. S. Ogul, "Residence Requirements as Barriers to Voting in Presidential Elections," *Midwest Journal of Political Science*, 3 (1959), 254–63; also the analysis

DISQUALIFICATIONS   The constitution and laws of each state exclude certain categories of persons from the suffrage. The disqualifying factors vary from state to state. Most states exclude the insane, idiots, and incompetents from the suffrage. In a few states "immoral" persons are not entitled to vote; in some states inmates of prisons are explicitly excluded from the vote. A similar end is achieved in other states that deny the suffrage to persons convicted of certain crimes. The crimes that disqualify in most states are felonies and election bribery. In some states disqualification follows conviction for treason, bigamy, defalcation, perjury, larceny, forgery, arson, embezzlement, and other specified acts. In South Carolina, for example, an imposing list of felonies and misdemeanors operates to wipe out the right to vote. It includes burglary, obtaining money or goods under false pretenses, robbery, adultery, wife beating, house breaking, receiving stolen goods, breach of trust with fraudulent intent, fornication, sodomy, incest, assault with intent to ravish, miscegenation, and crimes against the election laws. Louisiana, in its efforts to restrict Negro voting, in 1960 made conviction for most misdemeanors evidence that a person failed to meet the state's requirement of "good" character for registration. Thus, conviction for participation in a "sit in" demonstration might deprive a person of the right to vote.[41]

Suffrage and Political Power

Broadening of the suffrage over the centuries has been associated with a radical change in the nature and distribution of political power. The discussion and decision of matters of state formerly rested with a comparatively small proportion of the population, an aristocracy, oligarchy, or ruling class. Leadership—and, perhaps, the power of decision—continue to be vested in a comparatively small proportion of the population. Yet the conditions of exercise of power have radically changed. The wishes and probable actions of a vast number of people at the polls must be taken into consideration in the exercise of public power.

An odd feature about the expansion of the suffrage calls for reflection by those seeking to comprehend the nature of political power. Disfranchised groups have gained the right to vote without being able to exert the power of the suffrage. If political power rested on the vote alone, groups enjoying that right could merely have refused to share it with others. But the disfranchised have had power enough to demand and to obtain the vote. On the other hand,

by Walter Kravitz in *Congressional Record* (daily ed.), February 22, 1961, pp. 2389–93. In some states intrastate movers who do not meet the precinct or town residence requirement at their new address may return to vote in the precinct of their original residence.

[41] Louisiana also made parentage of illegitimate children and participation in common law marriage indicators of "bad" character.

a group such as the Negroes, who received the legal right to vote through the gift of others, has not been powerful enough to make the legal right universally effective in the southern states.

Obviously it is difficult to conclude that the suffrage is the sole cause either of legislation enacted for the benefit of formerly disfranchised classes or of the power enjoyed by these groups. Movements for the broadening of the suffrage have ordinarily gone hand in hand with movements for substantive legislation. Before 1850 agitators for legislation for the benefit of the workingman often also fought for the repeal of property and taxpaying qualifications on voting. The woman suffragists were not interested in the suffrage alone; they were also concerned with the removal of the legal disabilities of women and with such matters as the regulation of the liquor traffic and the promotion of general civic decency. Once a group has gained the suffrage it is in a more powerful position to promote and to protect its cause, but it first must gain, without the ballot, enough power to win the vote. Perhaps the doctrine and practice of popular government contain an inner logic that leads inevitably to the expansion of the suffrage. Once voting is initiated, it is a most troublesome problem to justify in principle the suffrage for one class and not for another. Moreover, if competition for power prevails, invariably some of those within the privileged circle will hope for allies by the admission of their friends from without.

2 3 .

REGISTRATION,

ELECTIONS,

BALLOTS

O<small>NCE IT IS DETERMINED</small> that persons possessing specified qualifications shall be entitled to vote, it is necessary to establish machinery and procedures to effectuate that policy. Although the machinery of elections may be a matter of administrative detail, it is a singularly important one. Implementation of the principle of popular elections should require only simple procedures to permit qualified electors, and no others, to express their choice and to assure an honest and expeditious count of the ballots. Yet the laws governing elections are intricate, and many election procedures are bitterly disputed because different parties or factions believe their fortunes will be affected thereby. The conclusion of a student of the history of voting legislation in New Jersey could be applied more widely. He reviewed scores of legislative acts, all but a few of which "were intended for no other purpose than to insure the supremacy of the temporarily dominant party."[1] The leading authority on American elections observed in 1929 that "little progress has been made in the technique of elections in this country. Probably no other phase of public administration is so badly managed. Our elections have been marked by irregularities, slipshod work, antiquated procedure, obsolete records, inaccuracies, and many varieties of downright

[1] R. P. McCormick, *The History of Voting in New Jersey* (New Brunswick: Rutgers University Press, 1953), p. 163.

fraud." [2] Despite improvements in many jurisdictions, the conclusion would not have to be changed materially today.

The conduct of elections, even for presidential electors, Senators, and Representatives, is a responsibility of the states, which usually regard their duty as discharged when they have enacted bulky volumes of election laws to guide the work of officials in the voting precincts. A mastery of the minutiae of these laws is an essential for the grass-roots political worker; this discussion, however, can touch only the broadest problems in the management of elections, which turn principally around the process of registration and the actual conduct of the election.

Registration Systems

The function of a registration system is the preparation of a list of names of persons who meet the suffrage requirements of the jurisdiction. On election day the officials in charge of voting permit those persons to vote whose right to do so has been established through the registration procedure. Party affiliation may also be indicated at the time of registration and the registration records thus become the means for limiting primary participation to party members in states with closed primaries.

The development of registration systems furnishes an illuminating illustration of the factors underlying administrative formalities. Originally, in small rural communities individuals presenting themselves at the polls were usually known to the election officials, to the watchers at the polls, and to their neighbors. The officials knew of their own knowledge whether the person requesting a ballot met the suffrage requirements. This fact could be established on election day, if, indeed, any attention was given to the matter at all. With the development of urban society, more formal procedures became necessary to identify those entitled to vote.

The impersonality of urban relationships greatly facilitates certain types of election-day frauds, such as the colonization of voters, personation, and the use of repeaters. It is not to be inferred that voting frauds have been, or are, limited to urban communities; conditions there merely faciliate types of frauds that involve voting by legally unqualified persons. Consequently, with the growth of cities legislatures began to adopt registration laws, particularly in the post-Civil War period. Formalized procedures came into use under which individuals might establish in advance of the election those facts, such as residence, age, citizenship, and other matters, necessary to qualify them to vote. The inclusion of a name on the resulting list of registrants constitutes evidence on election day that the person named is en-

[2] J. P. Harris, *Registration of Voters in the United States* (Washington: Brookings Institution, 1929), p. 3.

titled to vote. Thus administrative formalities arise to replace the common knowledge of the smaller community. The influence of urbanization is evident in many registration laws that apply only to large communities or fix more rigorous requirements for larger cities.[3] In southern states registration systems were not a product of urbanization but were established to enforce the literacy tests and other voting qualifications peculiar to the region.[4]

Registration systems of a variety of types are used in the states to prepare voting lists. Registration may be permanent or periodic: that is, an elector may be enrolled on the lists permanently, or there may be a complete reregistration at intervals. Registration may be personal or nonpersonal: that is, for registration, personal application by the elector may be required, or the authorities may prepare a voting list from their own knowledge or from information at their disposal. Registration may be compulsory or noncompulsory: that is, either a person's name must be on the list to qualify him to vote, or he may be permitted on election day to establish by appropriate evidence that he possesses the voting qualifications if his name is not on the list.

PERIODIC AND PERMANENT REGISTRATION   In recent years the chief technical controversy over registration has turned on the issue of periodic versus permanent registration. The older form of periodic registration is being gradually displaced by permanent registration. About three-fourths of the states use some form of permanent registration either on a statewide basis or in designated cities or counties. Under periodic registration completely new lists of voters are prepared annually, biennially, or quadrennially. The customary procedure provides for the decentralized preparation of the lists by registration boards sitting usually at the polling place in each precinct. During specified days the boards sit and receive the requests of individuals for the inclusion of their names on the lists. Such is

[3] Urban political leaders at times attribute the greater stringency of laws applying to cities to a rural desire to reduce the urban vote. If city voters are required to go to the polls once to register and again to vote and rural people do not have to make a special trip to the polls to register, the contention is that popular participation in voting in the cities is reduced.

[4] Registration authorities in the southern states apply the suffrage requirements in a manner to meet whatever the local situation demands, subject to suit instigated by the NAACP or the Department of Justice, a hazard which has made it difficult in some localities to fill the post of registrar. For an account of discriminatory practices against both whites and blacks which would set off a civil commotion almost anywhere else in the United States, see Donald S. Strong, *Registration of Voters in Alabama* (University, Ala.: Bureau of Public Administration, 1956). See also O. H. Shadgett, *Voter Registration in Georgia* (Athens: University of Georgia, 1955). Data on Negro registration in the South are untrustworthy, but 1960 estimates indicated the lowest proportions registered in Alabama, Mississippi, South Carolina, and Georgia, less than 15 per cent, and the highest proportions in Arkansas, Florida, and North Carolina, probably in the range of 35–40 per cent. See U.S. Commission on Civil Rights, *Voting* (Washington: Government Printing Office, 1961).

the more general practice under systems of periodic registration, though not all such systems fit this pattern. Louisiana, for example, requires a quadrennial registration of all voters in most of its parishes, but the voter may register at any time at a central place in each parish rather than only on certain days at the polling places.[5]

Its defenders contend that periodic registration produces clean lists. When all would-be voters must come to the registration places shortly before the election to get their names on the list, presumably those who have died since the last registration, those who have moved from the precinct, and those disqualified in other ways will not be included on the new lists. This plausible assumption appears to be unsupported by experience. Certain cities notorious for registration and election frauds have employed periodic registration; the decentralized and more or less irresponsible conduct of registration in the polling places throughout a city facilitates the padding of the lists. Understandings between registration officials of different parties (who supposedly police each other) may result in the falsification of the lists; the name of a nonexistent person on the registration lists permits that name to be voted in the party primaries. Even if the registration officials are honest, the conditions of urban society are such that precinct registration officials have no personal knowledge of the residence or identity of many of those applying for registration.

Permanent registration involves a single appearance by the applicant for registration before the registration officials. His name remains on the register until he dies, changes his residence, or becomes otherwise disqualified. This convenience to the voter is the strong justification for permanent registration. The absence of periodic reregistration, however, requires the substitution of other means to purge the rolls of disqualified persons. In the newer permanent systems a continuous revision of the lists occurs. Changes may be made on application of the voter, who has, let us say, moved from one precinct to another. Or the registration officials may act on the basis of information available to them. The central registration staff may examine death certificates and strike names from the voting lists. From court records may be obtained the names of persons adjudged insane or convicted of crimes that disqualify them from voting. In some instances corrections are made on the basis of information on removals provided by utility com-

---

[5] The scheduling of times at which registration may occur can have untoward consequences. If, for example, registration is limited to specified days, persons who happen to be ill at the time are unable to register. One local analysis revealed that about one-quarter of the nonregistrants had been either ill or absent from the locality on registration day. See P. Bradley and A. H. Cope, "A Community Registration Survey," *American Political Science Review*, 45 (1951), 775–78. Labor leaders occasionally complain that registration offices are open only at times when workers have to lose a half-day's pay to register. Such an administrative practice affects, at times deliberately, the balance of partisan strength.

panies. The Post Office in 1961 agreed to make available to registrars, at a charge of five cents per name, change-of-address cards filed with it.

In areas where transiency is high or fraudulent registration is suspected a house-to-house canvass may be conducted to check the lists. Commonly registrations are canceled because of failure to vote in a specified number of elections. To keep the permanent lists current is no mean task, for within a year as much as 20 per cent of the population may move into a different residence. The central staff in charge of the revision of the registration records is usually also vested with the responsibility of accepting the applications of new electors for registration. Except for a short interval prior to elections, the acceptance of new registrations is continuous rather than restricted to a few days during the year as under the periodic system.

On the issue of fraudulent registration (and hence potential fraudulent voting) neither system is foolproof. Permanent registration creates an administrative situation in which it is possible to bring about less fraud in registration. The decentralized preparation of the rolls by temporary employees (generally recruited because of their loyalty to the party organization), characteristic of periodic registration, results in administrative machinery impossible of supervision by the city or county registration authorities. Precinct registration officials are usually not disinterested individuals; their ward organization may even be eager to have fictitious names on the lists. With a small permanent staff in charge of the continuous revision of the permanent lists, it is more nearly possible to avoid these influences through supervision. Furthermore, it is possible in a central office to have access to more trustworthy evidence pertaining to residence, removal, or loss of voting privilege than is usually available to the precinct officials. It does not follow, to be sure, that the lists under permanent registration will be freer of names of persons unqualified to vote. Yet if the political and administrative will is present, it is more feasible to maintain clean lists under permanent registration than under the periodic system. If that will is absent, fraud and error may be as prevalent under permanent registration as under other systems.

From the standpoint of cost, permanent registration appears to be preferable to periodic registration. Once a system of permanent registration has been installed, the principal items of cost are for the support of a small central staff to accept new registrations and to revise the records and for special canvasses. In periodic registration, on the other hand, personnel to accept registrations in every precinct from the entire electorate is necessary, and an entirely new set of records must be purchased at each registration, a characteristic that endears the periodic system to printers who cater to election officials. Jurisdictions with permanent registration also tend to use more modern record-keeping and filing systems than is customary under periodic registration.[6]

[6] See Joseph P. Harris, *Model Voter Registration System*, rev. ed. (New York: National Municipal League, 1957).

PERSONAL AND NONPERSONAL REGISTRATION   Registration may be personal or nonpersonal. The systems that have been described, under which the elector must make personal application to have his name placed on the registration list, are personal systems. Under a nonpersonal system the lists are prepared by official agencies from information at their disposal. In the United States the nonpersonal scheme generally involves an annual revision by the precinct registration board, which meets to revise the list of the prior year and to add names of new electors in the precinct. The list is usually then posted for the information of the electors of the precinct, and a second meeting of the board is held to permit the appearance of those persons whose names have been omitted and to hear challenges against names incorrectly included in the list. Party workers often keep a close watch over the work of the registration board to assure that their members are registered. In the United States this form of registration is limited in the main to rural or semirural areas, since in only the smaller communities do the precinct registration officials possess the necessary knowledge to maintain the lists.[7] In European countries greater reliance on nonpersonal registration prevails. On the Continent elaborate continual censuses of the population make it possible to keep the registration records up to date without personal application for registration by the electors.

COMPULSORY AND NONCOMPULSORY REGISTRATION   Classification of registration systems as compulsory or noncompulsory is determined by whether it is mandatory that a person's name be on the list before he is permitted to vote. Under the noncompulsory system it is possible for a voter to be "sworn in" at the polls; that is, he makes an affidavit that he meets the suffrage requirements and is supported in this statement by witnesses. The noncompulsory system exists primarily as a concession to those groups that originally opposed registration in any form. The possibility of "swearing in" voters leaves a loophole for fraud.[8]

Two states have no formal system of registration. In Texas and Arkansas lists of those entitled to vote are prepared from the records of those who have paid poll taxes or established their eligibility to vote under provisions

---

[7] Nonpersonal registration is used in over half the election districts in upstate New York. In 1950 registration in 10 of the 57 upstate counties of New York exceeded the numbers of citizens 21 and over as reported by the census. In another 11 counties registrants numbered between 90 and 100 per cent of the citizenry of voting age. In New York City, with personal registration, only 53.5 per cent of the citizens 21 and over were registered; in the state outside the city the percentage was 79.8. Upstate Republicans have usually expressed great anxiety about the dangers of padded voting lists in New York City, but most of the deadwood is on the upstate rolls.

[8] It is recorded, how correctly one cannot say, that in Chicago's ninth ward on April 3, 1883, among those "sworn in" were George Washington, Thomas Jefferson, John Hancock, James Madison, and Abraham Lincoln. Each of these distinguished men, the story goes, voted the straight Democratic ticket. See Bruce Grant, *Fight for a City* (Chicago: Rand McNally, 1955), p. 67.

of law exempting them from the tax. These arrangements constitute, in effect, periodic systems of registration.

In debates over the form of registration systems, the National Municipal League and the League of Women Voters have advocated permanent registration, while most party organizations have favored periodic registration. The party position has been in the main dictated by the petty patronage connected with the employment of precinct registration officials rather than by any refined estimate of the effects of different registration systems on the outcome of the party battle. Those effects, if any, are difficult to appraise. Certainly any administrative hurdle in the path to the polling booth reduces the total turnout, and periodic registration is more of an obstacle than is permanent registration. Cities are probably handicapped in state politics when their voters must register periodically while the outstate operates under permanent registration. The chances are also that administrative obstacles to voting have more severe effects in the lower reaches of the educational and economic scale, a factor which may tip the scales one way or another when cleavages along such lines prevail in the voting. Since party organizations must devote great quantities of energy to registration campaigns, they should themselves benefit from registration systems that make it simple for the voter to register and stay registered.

Elections

In the United States, state and local governments conduct elections, even for federal elective officials. And within the states, elections, though governed by state legislation, are administered by local governments, with usually little or no supervision by state agencies.[9] In the consideration of election administration, therefore, attention must be concentrated on counties, cities, or whatever unit of local government is responsible for the conduct of the balloting.[10] Commonly those officials charged with the conduct of the general election are also responsible for the direct primaries, though in several southern states party organizations manage the primaries.

[9] The only comprehensive treatment of election management is by J. P. Harris, *Election Administration in the United States* (Washington: Brookings Institution, 1934). For a guide through the legal maze in one state, see Judith N. Jamison, *Local Election Administration in California* (Los Angeles: Bureau of Governmental Research, University of California, 1952). For a study illustrative of the role of state election authorities, see G. A. Schubert, Jr., *The Michigan State Director of Elections* (ICP Case Series, No. 23, University of Alabama Press, 1954).

[10] Federal power is exerted in elections through the Corrupt Practices Act and the Hatch Act. Occasionally fraud in elections of federal officials is reached obliquely through prosecution under a section of the Federal Criminal Code punishing conspiracy to deprive persons of rights guaranteed by the Constitution.

ELECTION ORGANIZATION   The task of conducting an election involves preparation of ballots; designation of polling places; making of arrangements for quarters for the polls; selection, instruction, and supervision of precinct officials to conduct the voting; preparation and distribution to the polling places of booths, ballots, voting machines, and supplies needed on election day; identification of voters as they come to the polls; presentation of ballots to the voters; general management of the polling place on election day; and counting of the ballots after the voting. Conduct of elections is, then, a large and tedious but relatively simple administrative task. It is, moreover, a highly seasonal operation. The dates of elections are fixed by statute. The peak load on the election machinery falls quadrennially on the first Tuesday after the first Monday in November, the date set by Congress for the choice of presidential electors, at which time Senators and Representatives are also chosen. The midterm elections of Senators and Representatives also occur with similar uniformity, thanks to an act of Congress. State constitutions and statutes generally set elections for state officials on the same date as the presidential and congressional polling, although this practice is not universal. Furthermore, the widest variation prevails among the states in the scheduling of direct primaries and local elections.

In the more populous cities and counties a board of election commissioners is usually responsible for the conduct of elections. In other places the county board may be the chief local election authority; or the city clerk or the county clerk may be the responsible official.[11] It is the duty of the central county or city authority to select precinct officials, to procure and distribute election equipment and supplies to the precinct polling places, to make arrangements for polling places, and to supervise (generally ineffectively) the work of the precinct election officials who manage the polling places on election day. Control of the city or county election machinery is a prize eagerly sought by the party organizations. Its control gives the organization the patronage of the election machinery and also, at times, can be used to obstruct embarrassing inquiries into the conduct of elections.

The city or county is divided into precincts of various sizes, each of which usually includes a few hundred voters. The polling place in each precinct is manned on election day by a group of precinct officials. Their titles, which vary from jurisdiction to jurisdiction, may be "judge of elections," "election inspector," or "clerk." They determine whether persons presenting themselves at the polling place are entitled to vote; give such persons ballots or access to the voting machine; count the ballots and report the results to the central election authority.

In form, precinct officials are appointed by the central election com-

---

[11] A compilation, by the Library of Congress, of state statutory provisions covering the appointment of local election officials appears in *Congressional Record* (daily ed.), June 18, 1962, pp. A4526–A4534.

mission or agency of the city or county, but in most jurisdictions they are, in fact, named by the party organizations. The law usually prescribes that precinct officials shall be divided between the two major parties; in practice, the precinct captain or committeeman of each party has the privilege of naming the election officials to which his party is entitled in his precinct. These election-day jobs are a part of the patronage at the disposal of the precinct captain and are used by him to reward his followers in the precinct. It hardly needs to be observed that the method of appointing precinct officials has never resulted in election machinery notable for efficiency, but the procedure has gotten a thankless job done. In piping days of full employment the attractiveness of a one-day job with long hours and small pay declines and manning the polls often becomes a problem of positive recruitment, not one of fending off eager applicants for picayune political plums.[12]

In the conduct of the polling, the first step is to determine whether the register of voters contains the name of the person who applies for a ballot. If the name is on the list the person is usually given a ballot without further ado. At this stage, however, the right of a person to vote may be challenged. Challenges are infrequent, but, if a challenge is made, various types of evidence may be offered to establish the right of the person in question to vote. Comparison of the voter's signature with that in his application for registration furnishes a means of identification in those jurisdictions using this registration practice. Some registration systems include in the records a description of the voter: height, color of eyes, color of hair, and the like. Such descriptions are practically worthless as a means of identification.

As votes are cast, a list is prepared of those who have voted. The party watchers also check off on their lists the names of those who have voted; as the day wears on, they dispatch runners to bring in the laggards. An incidental but important feature of the voting in machine-controlled precincts is the provision for assistance to the voter in marking his ballot. Persons incapable of marking the ballot may usually request assistance in this task; the reasons justifying a request for assistance vary from state to state, but they include illiteracy (in those states without a literacy test), blindness, and other physical infirmities. Under this provision the secrecy of the ballot may be destroyed, and bargains between party workers and voters may be carried out.

---

[12] Reluctance to undertake the tiresome chore of manning the polls have appeared from coast to coast. In Oakland, California, in 1954 the elderly and infirm persons who could be recruited to man the precincts could cope with the paper work only with difficulty; one hardy 80-year-old woman remained on duty as her three associates fell ill. In Bristol, Rhode Island, party leaders were dismayed to discover that they could not find enough people in their organizations to meet the needs of the election authorities. And in some localities officials had to invoke long-unused laws that permitted them to compel persons to serve.

COUNTING THE BALLOTS   At the proper time (in some jurisdictions before the closing of the polls) the counting of the ballots begins.
The procedure for counting is often prescribed in minute detail. The statute
may require one election official to read from each ballot the choices expressed, while two other election officials (one from each party) watch. The
choices are supposed to be tallied independently by two clerks, and both
counts are supposed to check at the conclusion of the process. In practice
these statutory provisions tend to be ignored, for the simple reason that to
follow them slavishly would make the count almost interminable. The laws,
for example, often prescribe that the vote on each ballot on all offices shall
be recorded at one time. In practice, often the count is made on a single office at a time. The law usually requires that the tally sheet shall actually be
made as the count proceeds, but in practice the count is often made and then
the official tally sheets are filled in. Otherwise the clerks run into difficulty
in making their tallies match. Apart from outright fraud, error is likely to
creep into the count. The long ballot, the weariness of election officials, and
often their indifferent clerical capacities lay the basis for considerable honest
error in the count.[13]

After the completion of the count, the precinct election officials prepare
a certificate indicating the number of votes received by each candidate and
the number of votes cast for and against each proposition on the ballot. This
certificate, together with the ballot box, is sent to the central election authority—election commissioners, city council, county clerk, or whatever agency
is vested with authority—and the results are "canvassed"; that is, the returns from all the precincts are added and the outcome of the election is pro-
nounced. In some jurisdictions the canvassing authority "canvasses" the
voting machines—that is, checks the readings of the counters on the machines against the reports by the precinct officials. For state offices the county
and city results are certified to some state authority—usually the secretary
of state—who totals the results from all the counties of the state. The process
of canvassing is a simple exercise in arithmetic; and the results have been
known long before the official canvass through tabulations made unofficially
by newspapers, television chains, party officers, and others.

ELECTION CONTESTS   Provision is generally made to permit
a contest of the result of an election as declared by the official canvassing
authorities. The contest is sometimes heard by the election officials, some-

---

[13] The hours during which the polls are open tend to be long in order to accommodate
persons who wish to vote before or after work. About half the states have laws requiring
employers to give time off for voting, in some instances without deductions from wages.
On the antidocking clauses, see Day-Brite *v.* Missouri, 342 U.S. 421 (1952), and Illinois
Central R.R. Co. *v.* Commonwealth, 305 Ky. 632 (1947). For a summary of legislation,
see *Labor Law Journal*, 3 (1952), 719–21.

times by the courts, and, if legislators are involved, usually by the legislative body, which is generally the sole judge of the qualifications of its members. The ease with which a recount may be brought about varies from jurisdiction to jurisdiction. In some instances a recount may be had as a matter of right; in others, proof must first be made of misconduct or errors by election officials. In some states recounts are discouraged by the requirement that the petitioner for a recount finance the work—a rule that may nip in the bud frivolous requests for recounts but which also ignores the public interest in both competent and honest election administration. When a recount is not improbable, precinct election officials might be expected to strive for ac· curacy in their work.[14]

CIVILIAN ABSENTEE VOTING   An aspect of election administration of some importance is provision for voting by those persons who are unable to appear at the polling place on election day. Absentee-voting laws originated during the Civil War to permit voting by military personnel, but the extension of the absentee-voting privilege to civilians occurred principally after 1900. By 1955 all states except New Mexico and South Carolina had adopted some form of absentee-voting legislation for the benefit of civilians. Even by 1936, according to an estimate by Paul G. Steinbicker, about 2 per cent of the votes cast in the presidential election were absentee votes.[15]

State laws on the subject of absentee voting by civilians are characterized by almost infinite variation. One point of difference pertains to the geographical limits on absentee voting. In a few instances the voter must be outside the state before he may exercise the absentee-voting privilge. In others, he qualifies to vote absentee if he is home ill or bedridden. Some states specify rather narrow ranges of causes of absence to qualify, as, "in the usual course of business"; others merely specify absence. Another point of difference concerns the elections to which absentee-voting provisions apply. New Hampshire, for example, permits absentee voting only in general elections; Tennessee, in "any election for any purpose whatsoever."

To cast an absentee ballot an elector must apply to the appropriate elec-

---

[14] Two recent gubernatorial elections in Michigan have been followed by recounts. In 1950 the initial tabulation gave G. Mennen Williams a plurality of 1,301 in a total of over 1,800,000 votes. His lead grew to 4,157 after a partial recount. In 1952 Williams' initial plurality of 8,618 (in a total vote of over 2,800,000) increased to 9,978 after a partial recount. For an exhaustive study of these recounts, see S. J. Eldersveld and A. A. Applegate, *Michigan's Recounts for Governor, 1950 and 1952: A Systematic Analysis of Election Error* (Ann Arbor: University of Michigan Press, 1954). Either house of Congress may order a recount in election contests involving its members. For example, in 1960 the House recounted the ballots in Indiana's 5th district and gave the seat to Democrat J. Edward Roush instead of to Republican George O. Chambers who had been certified as the winner by Indiana authorities.

[15] "Absentee Voting in the United States," *American Political Science Review*, 32 (1938), 898–907.

tion officials within a prescribed period preceding the election. When he mails his ballot to the election officials, it must be accompanied by an affidavit showing compliance with the legal requirements, which vary but include such matters as a certificate by a notary public or other officer that the person entitled to the ballot actually marked it—a precaution against abuse of the absentee-voting privilege.

Absentee-voting procedures are said to be especially susceptible to fradulent manipulation. The bases for such charges are suggested by North Carolina's experience. In that state, absentee voting is permitted in the general election but not in the primary. The local gossip is to the effect that the Democratic legislature made this arrangement to give a little leeway to Democrats, who control the election machinery, in the state's western counties in which the outcome of the battle between Republicans and Democrats is close. In the election of governor in 1944 the absentee vote (military and civilian) constituted 6.7 per cent of the state total, and in 25 of the 100 counties the absentee vote exceeded the plurality of the winning candidate. The absentee vote was highest in the western counties; it exceeded 15 per cent of the total vote in seven counties. In one county 25.7 per cent of the total ballots were absentee. Generally the percentage of absentee ballots increased with the closeness of the contest from county to county. One hypothesis would be that fraud had occurred; another, that when the contest is close greater efforts are made to get out the vote.[16]

SOLDIER VOTING   Considerable legislation has developed to facilitate absentee voting by military personnel. The problem of voting procedures for the military became of special importance in World War II. In the evolution of federal legislation on soldier voting the issue has arisen over the extent to which Congress should, or could constitutionally, go in protecting the right of soldiers to vote in view of state control of registration and voting. In the Federal Voting Assistance Act of 1955 Congress took a restricted view of its responsibility and limited itself to a recommendation to the states to enact legislation to facilitate absentee voting by servicemen, members of the merchant marine, civilian employees of the United States abroad, members of welfare or religious organizations attached to the armed services, and their spouses and dependents. The Department of Defense maintains a staff with the duties of collecting information about state laws on the topic, of stimulating state legislation to simplify soldier voting, of making available to troops information on voting procedures, and of expediting the transmission of ballots. Most states have enacted legislation to permit soldier voting but some of the laws are severely limited in their workability. Some states, for

[16] Those most likely to be away from home on election day and also most disposed to take the trouble to vote absentee tend to be more often Republican than are voters generally. Thus, in 1960 the absentee vote gave Nixon his popular margin in California.

example, permit absentee voting but persist in requiring registration in person; others make ballots available too late to permit them to be received in remote places in time to be returned before election day; still others do not extend absentee voting to primaries.

The spread of large numbers of American military personnel over the world makes the problem of absentee voting one of an entirely different magnitude than when the principal concern was to make it possible for the occasional traveling salesman or locomotive engineer away from home to vote. In 1960 the armed forces included 1,866,000 persons of voting age, of whom 735,000 voted. Their dependents and employees of civilian agencies abroad added to the potential absentee vote, though the states have not simplified absentee-voting procedures for these classes of persons so generally as they have for members of the services.[17]

FRAUD   The American election system has gained an unenviable reputation for fraud, although electoral fraud occurs far less frequently than is commonly supposed. Often a day or so before the voting, candidates charge that the wicked opposition is conspiring to steal the election, and on the day after the election the losers may claim that they have been robbed. Sometimes indictments for electoral fraud amount to nothing more than political persecution. Charges and rumors of election irregularities are displayed prominently in the press. The truth about the incidence of electoral fraud cannot readily be discovered. If it could be, the findings probably would indicate that fraud has declined over the long term. Yet fraud has occurred on a large scale and votes are still stolen from time to time. The publicized records of shady practices in the big cities are matched by relatively unpublicized stolen elections in the country.[18] In corruptly ruled localities the psychological effect of fraud may contribute more than do the stolen votes to the power of the machine. Opposition is likely to falter if the belief prevails that elections are fixed whatever the actual vote may be. A hair-raising volume descriptive of electoral frauds could be compiled; space permits here only the indication of the nature of a few broad types of irregularities.

Fraud and error in registration lay the basis for electoral fraud. When the lists of voters contain false names or the names of persons who have moved away, the party organization may readily find persons to vote those names, provided that the precinct election officials are willing to connive in

---

[17] See B. A. Martin, "The Service Vote in the Elections of 1944," *American Political Science Review*, 39 (1945), 720–32; "Findings and Recommendations of the Special Committee on Service Voting," *American Political Science Review*, 46 (1952), 512–23; Federal Voting Assistance Program, *Third Report* (1961).

[18] Communities develop, or so it seems, their own peculiar customs and attitudes toward electoral bribery and fraud. In one county, elections may be really as clean as a hound's tooth while an adjacent county over long periods maintains a record of consistent crookedness. See A Kentucky Legislator, "How an Election Was Bought and Sold," *Harper's Magazine*, October, 1960.

such an arrangement. How do such names get on the registration lists? The lists may be padded with imaginary names by the registration officials in keeping with a plan to vote the names later. Superfluous names may be on the list merely because of failure to purge the lists of names of persons who have died, moved from the precinct, or otherwise lost their eligibility to vote. When the names of persons who die are left on the lists, the basis is laid, as the argot runs, for "voting the cemetery."

Lists with superfluous names are a condition precedent to a simple and easy type of fraud. On election day fictitious names on the registration lists may be voted in various ways. Sometimes the machine employs repeaters to go from precinct to precinct to vote under false names already on the list in each precinct. To organize and manage a squad of repeaters is expensive, and the task of voting the names on the registers may be left to the precinct election officials, aided by the precinct party workers. A Philadelphia precinct official testified, for example:

> We didn't record a man as voting unless he actually voted, or unless we knew he could be depended on. For example, I was sure my mother wouldn't come to the polls, so it was quite safe to cast her ballot for her. The people who live next door to us are the right sort, but they're lazy and like to stay at home. So I told them I would cast their votes for them. But we played the game fair.[19]

When a person votes under the name of some other person, the act is called "personation." When there is no attempt at deception but a wholesale voting of names on the registers (or not on the registers) by the election officials, the practice is known as "ballot-box stuffing." This practice is cheaper and easier than the organization of repeaters and personators. Cruder practitioners of fraud make no effort to give an appearance of legality to their work and duly record as having voted persons whose names do not appear on the registration lists.

Another point at which fraud may occur is during the counting of the ballots. Occasionally the count is a farce: the vote is determined arbitrarily or by agreement among the election officials and the attendant party workers. This type of fraud is most likely to occur at primaries, when the only persons with an interest may be the machine workers for each party organization, and at general elections in precincts where the minority party is either powerless or a subsidiary of the majority. During the count ballots may be altered or removed and substitutions made. Alterations may have several objects. A long ballot may be marked for only a few offices. The counting official may take up the burden where the elector stopped and finish the laborious exercise of the suffrage. The purpose of alteration may be to change the vote

---

[19] A. F. Macdonald, "Philadelphia's Political Machine in Action," *National Municipal Review*, 15 (1926), 28–35.

completely. For example, in Chicago investigators for the Citizens Association reported that "after the polls closed many 'straight' Republican ballots were converted into 'straight' Democratic ballots by the simple expedient of erasing the cross in the Republican party circle and putting a cross in the Democratic party circle." [20] Alteration of the ballot may have as its object the spoiling of a ballot so that it will be thrown out. A cross may be altered, for example, to make it appear to be an identifying mark, invalidating the ballot.[21]

Sometimes fraud or trickery occurs in the certification of the results. The ballots may be accurately counted and recorded on the tally sheets but the certificate reporting the results of the precinct doctored. An old trick is the transposition of figures. The candidate receives, for example, 49 votes; in certifying this item it may be written 94. Or perhaps the report is prepared without even this sort of attempt to camouflage fraud as error.

The cruder practitioners of electoral fraud leave a trail as plain as that of a bleeding black bear trodding freshly fallen snow. If one precinct reports no votes for a candidate while the surrounding precincts give him a substantial vote, an odor of fraud or error is in evidence. Or if a precinct board reports more votes than the precinct has voters, a fair presumption may be raised that the election code has been transgressed. The annals are replete with such instances of patent irregularity. Yet to pin the guilt on crooked election officials in a court of law is not always easy. In truth, the well-managed political machine sees that the election records are, on their face, in meticulous accord with the niceties of electoral jurisprudence. The young assistant district attorney trying to make a reputation by the prosecution of an election fraud case against such an organization should steel himself against disappointment.

Ballots

Certain additional features of election management are connected with the ballot and the voting machine. These may be regarded as fairly humdrum matters of administrative detail, but some questions of ballot form are still the subject of spirited disputes. These matters of form, like others connected with the voting process, may have effects that give advantage to one party or the other in particular situations.

SECRECY OF THE VOTE   Although the secrecy of the ballot has become commonplace, the general use of secret methods of voting is a

[20] Quoted by Harris, *Election Administration in the United States*, p. 352.
[21] A recondite jurisprudence defines precisely what constitutes a valid crossmark. See Spencer Albright, "Legislation on Marking Ballots," *Southwestern Social Science Quarterly*, 21 (1940), 221–26. Irregularities, it should be noted, may give effect to the intent of the voter. Precinct officials may, for example, count choices indicated by a checkmark even though the law prescribes the use of a crossmark.

relatively recent development in American politics. In the colonial period and in the early history of the United States the more prevalent form of voting was the oral, or viva-voce, method. Under this arrangement each voter would appear before the election officials and announce orally the candidate whom he desired to support. Oral voting gradually gave way to a system of voting by ballots, which by no means assured secrecy of voting. At first, ballots were printed privately rather than by public authority. The parties or candidates furnished separate ballots to the voters. The Democratic ballot might be of pink paper; the Republican, white. Such characteristics of privately printed ballots enabled observers at the polls to know which ballot an elector dropped into the box.[22]

Serious concern over the absence of secrecy in voting arose soon after the Civil War when intimidation and bribery of voters became rife. It will be recalled that the groups benefiting from the earlier restricted suffrage clung desperately to their privileged status and, as they were compelled to yield to the demands for a broader suffrage, predicted dire results for those of property and substance from the enfranchisement of the masses. After the Civil War the full effects of the broadened suffrage began to be felt, and concerted attempts were made to neutralize these effects by bribery and intimidation. The lack of voting secrecy facilitated bribery, since a person was not inclined to purchase a commodity of whose delivery he was not assured. Similarly, the lack of secrecy enabled those in a position to intimidate to apply their sanctions. Without secrecy of the ballot, employers might control the votes of their workmen; landlords, the votes of their tenants; creditors, the votes of their debtors.

Many states, to ensure secrecy, enacted regulatory legislation to govern the private printing of ballots; but these measures were uniformly ineffective, and those desiring a truly secret vote turned toward the Australian ballot. This ballot, so named because of the place of its origin, was printed by public authority. It contained the names of the candidates of all parties and was coupled with methods of election administration designed to ensure voting secrecy. Agitation for the new type of ballot originated in large measure from labor and other minority groups that believed their political strength to be diminished by the intimidation and bribery prevailing under the existing system of balloting. They were joined in their advocacy in some states by urban reform groups and on occasion by the minority political party. Thus, the early agitation for the Australian ballot was led by people outside the governing cliques; eventually the reform gained broader support.[23]

In the United States the first Australian-ballot law was enacted by the

[22] E. C. Evans, *A History of the Australian Ballot System in the United States* (Chicago: University of Chicago Press, 1917), pp. 6–7.

[23] See John H. Wigmore, *The Australian Ballot System*, 2d ed. (Boston: Boston Book Company, 1889). For a defense of nonsecret voting, see John Stuart Mill, *Representative Government*, ch. 10.

Kentucky legislature in 1880. This measure applied only to municipal elections in Louisville; the state constitution explicitly required viva-voce voting at elections of state officers. By 1900 a large proportion of the states had adopted the Australian ballot. By 1942, 45 states used this type of ballot; action by South Carolina in 1950 brought the Australian ballot to all the states, though in some states procedures under which secrecy of the ballot might be violated continued to prevail.[24] By and large, ballot reformers have attained their objectives. Yet ballot secrecy has had its unforeseen consequences. It enables, for example, a worker as he votes to ignore the pressures of his fellow workers as well as the importunities of his employer.

Irregularities remain but not to the degree that existed before the introduction of the Australian ballot. Secrecy of the ballot may be destroyed, as we have seen, by statutory provisions to permit "assistance" to illiterate, blind, or otherwise incapacitated voters.[25] Another device sometimes used to destroy the secrecy of the vote and to facilitate purchase is the "endless chain" or "Tasmanian dodge." Under this scheme it is necessary to obtain an official ballot; the purchaser of the vote marks the ballot as he desires it to be voted, then delivers it to the bought elector who enters the polling place and procures a ballot. In the booth the voter substitutes the marked ballot for the fresh one, inserts the marked ballot in the ballot box, and delivers the fresh ballot to the party worker. This ballot is marked and given to another voter who repeats the process; the chain goes on unbroken. To check this practice over half of the states number the ballots. When a voter receives a ballot, the number is recorded opposite his name; before he is permitted to deposit the ballot he must show the numbered stub (the ballot is folded so as to show only the number) to the election officials who tear it off. In some instances a venal voter may mark his ballot so as to identify it to the election officials and those watching the count; in this way the purchaser may assure himself that he has received delivery. Identification of an individual ballot in this way is illegal; ballots signed plainly fall within the proscription, but other types of symbols designed to identify are more difficult to deal with.

CONSEQUENCES OF PUBLIC PROVISION OF BALLOTS
Australian-ballot laws constituted an entering wedge for the detailed regulation of party activity. When it was decided that public authorities should print ballots containing the names of the candidates of all parties, it became

---

[24] In several southern states a number is written on the ballot as it is cast which corresponds to a number alongside the name of the voter on the polling list. The practice has been defended on the ground that it permits, when an election is contested, the ballot boxes to be opened and the ballots cast by disqualified persons to be thrown out.

[25] One aspect of ballot secrecy for which no solution is apparent is suggested by the warning of ecclesiastical authorities to their parishioners as they instructed them how to vote in a recent election: "The Australian ballot is not secret to God."

necessary to define "party" by law and to fix the procedure that the party should follow in certifying its nominations for inclusion on the ballot. Otherwise the agency in charge of ballot preparation might be faced with the problem of deciding which of several lists of nominees should be printed as the Democratic list, for example, without having any legal standard for its decision. It was also necessary to require that nominations be made far enough in advance of an election to give time to print the ballot.

Their power to decide, at least in the first instance, whether particular names shall be placed on the ballot is another factor that makes the control of election authorities of value to party organizations. This power is of special significance with respect to the primary ballot. Where party organizations actively support a slate in the primary, the elections board often enforces a meticulous observance of the election laws on anti-organization candidates who present petitions to gain a place on the ballot. When such a petition can be thrown out on a technicality, the anti-organization candidate rarely receives the benefit of the doubt.

Minor parties often face legal obstacles in getting their candidates on the general election ballot. A party is sometimes defined in terms of the number of votes cast for its candidates at the preceding election. In Ohio, for example, "when any political party fails to cast 10 per cent of the total vote cast at an election for the office of governor it shall cease to be a political party within the meaning of this act." By raising the percentage required to keep party candidates on the official ballot, legislatures sometimes discriminate against minor parties. Usually, however, provision is made to permit a new party to place its candidates on the ballot by petition. In Oklahoma, for example, any "political party presenting a petition of 5,000 names of voters . . . shall have the names of its candidates for state and local offices placed on a ballot."

The fixing of the number of signatures at a high figure frustrates the desire of minor parties to have the names of their candidates on the ballot. In Illinois a petition with 25,000 signatures is required to put the candidates of a new party on the ballot. Moreover, the petition must contain the signatures of 200 registered voters in each of at least 50 counties. In 1948 Illinois Republicans sought unsuccessfully to have this act declared void in order that Henry Wallace's Progressives might get on the ballot and divert support from the Democrats. Often the time of petitioning for a place on the ballot is fixed to discourage splinter candidacies. If minor-party petitions must be filed before the primaries or conventions, those disgruntled by major-party actions on nominations cannot put an independent or third-party candidate on the ballot. Such a rule in Oklahoma kept both the Wallace Progressives and the Thurmond Dixiecrats off the 1948 ballot of that state.

BALLOT FORMS   Once it is decided that the ballot shall be provided by public authority, it must be determined how the names of candidates shall be arranged on the ballot. Two principal types of ballot forms have developed, though variations on these forms also exist. They are the office-block ballot, in which all candidates for each office are grouped together, and the party-column ballot, in which all the candidates of each party for all offices are grouped together in parallel vertical columns.

The party-column ballot, used in about 30 states, is sometimes called the Indiana-type ballot because the Indiana law of 1889 has served as a model for other states.[26] In most states using the party-column ballot, it is possible to vote for the candidates of a single party for all offices by making a single cross in the circle at the head of the column containing the party's candidates. In some states the party emblem is carried at the top of its column, a feature which, in less literate days, was of some utility in guiding the voter to the right column on the ballot. To vote a split ticket on a party-column ballot usually requires the recording of a choice for each office, a path the voter will presumably hesitate to follow when he has the alternative of making a single crossmark. Professional party workers generally favor the use of the party-column ballot because it encourages straight-ticket voting. A sample party-column ballot is reproduced in Figure 23.1.

In contrast with the party-column ballot is the office-block, or, as it is sometimes called by virtue of its origin, the Massachusetts ballot. Names of all candidates, by whatever party nominated, for each office are grouped together on the office-block ballot, usually with an indication alongside each name of the party affiliation. The supposition is that the voter will be compelled to consider separately the candidates for each office, in contrast with the encouragement given to straight-ticket voting by the party-column ballot. Pennsylvania uses a variation on the office-block ballot: the candidates are grouped according to office but provision is made for straight-ticket voting by a single mark.[27]

Expectations of short-term partisan advantage often underlie changes in ballot forms. In Ohio in 1949, for example, friends of Republican Robert A. Taft spent over $85,000 in successful advocacy of an initiated proposal

[26] For a tabular analysis prepared by Spencer Albright of the ballot laws of all the states, see *Book of the States, 1954–1955* (Chicago: Council of State Governments, 1954), p. 82.

[27] Another classification of ballots is partisan and nonpartisan. The partisan ballot includes either party symbols or other identification of the party affiliation of the candidates. The nonpartisan ballot, which lacks such identification, is used in the attempt to take certain kinds of elections "out of party politics," chiefly judicial and municipal elections. Still another ballot classification is the consolidated and nonconsolidated ballot. A consolidated ballot includes all offices and questions being voted on at an election on a single ballot. In some jurisdictions, candidates for federal office may be listed on one ballot, candidates for state office on another, and constitutional amendments and propositions on still another. In some instances the consolidated ballot has been divided to deprive a party's state and local candidates of the strength from a popular presidential candidate or vice versa. For a collection of facsimiles of ballots, see C. O. Smith, *A Book of Ballots* (Detroit: Bureau of Governmental Research, 1938).

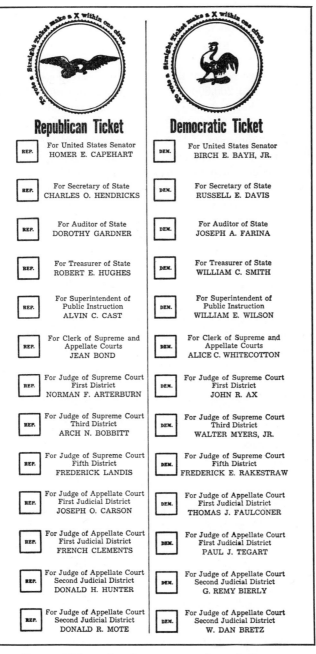

Figure 23.1   Specimen party-column ballot

to substitute the office-block ballot for the party-column form. They believed that such a change would aid Taft in the 1950 senatorial election. Frank Lausche, a popular Democratic candidate would, it was thought, lend strength to the entire Democratic ticket through the party-column ballot. After his 1950 victory Taft guessed that the new ballot was responsible "for something between 100,000 and 200,000" of his total plurality of 430,000.[28]

While these short-term maneuvers for partisan advantage interest the knave in all of us, the issue of ballot form has implicit within it larger considerations about the roles of both the electorate and the party system. The party-column ballot would seem to be the appropriate accompaniment of a party system under which the party leaderships could nominate candidates more or less in accord with the party program. With the party as an active and integrating element in the electoral and governing process, the voter can sensibly vote a straight ticket. The rise of the office-block ballot, however, represents in a sense a change in the role of the party system, or at least a lowering of expectations of its capacity to screen aspirants for nominations. The nominating processes often place on the party ticket the most varied assortment of individuals. To vote consistently at the general election the voter may need to split his ticket. By the same token, the emphasis on the individual associated with the office-block ballot tends perhaps further to weaken party as each candidate attempts to attract attention to himself, and only incidentally to his party, in the campaign.[29]

LONG VERSUS SHORT BALLOT   Whether the ballot is in form a party-column or an office-block ballot, it is usually a long ballot containing a large number of names and perhaps constitutional amendments and other propositions on which the voters are asked to express an opinion. In 1932 the "average party-column ballot consisted of 565 square inches of paper, on which were printed over 102 names and three propositions." In the office-block states the ballot averaged 349 square inches and contained the names of 77 candidates and four propositions. In the off year of 1934 the average ballot had an area of 398 square inches, and the average voter was

[28] The position of a candidate's name on the ballot or voting machine may give advantage or disadvantage. A careful analysis has been reported by D. S. Hecock and H. M. Bain, Jr., *The Arrangement of Names on the Ballot and Its Effect on the Voter's Choice* (Detroit: Wayne State University Press, 1956). Some jurisdictions rotate the order of names on the ballot from precinct to precinct; some leave the assignment of order on the ballot to a lottery by the election authorities. In the drawing of names from hats some remarkable departures from the laws of chance occur; in Jersey City the Democratic slate won top place in nine consecutive city elections.

[29] A study of voting in the 1956 presidential election throws light on the effects of ballot form. About the same proportions of persons strongly identified with parties voted straight tickets in multiple choice states and in single choice states. The office-block form was associated with a higher degree of ticket splitting among weak identifiers and independents. See Angus Campbell and W. E. Miller, "The Motivational Basis of Straight and Split Ticket Voting," *American Political Science Review*, 60 (1957), 293–312.

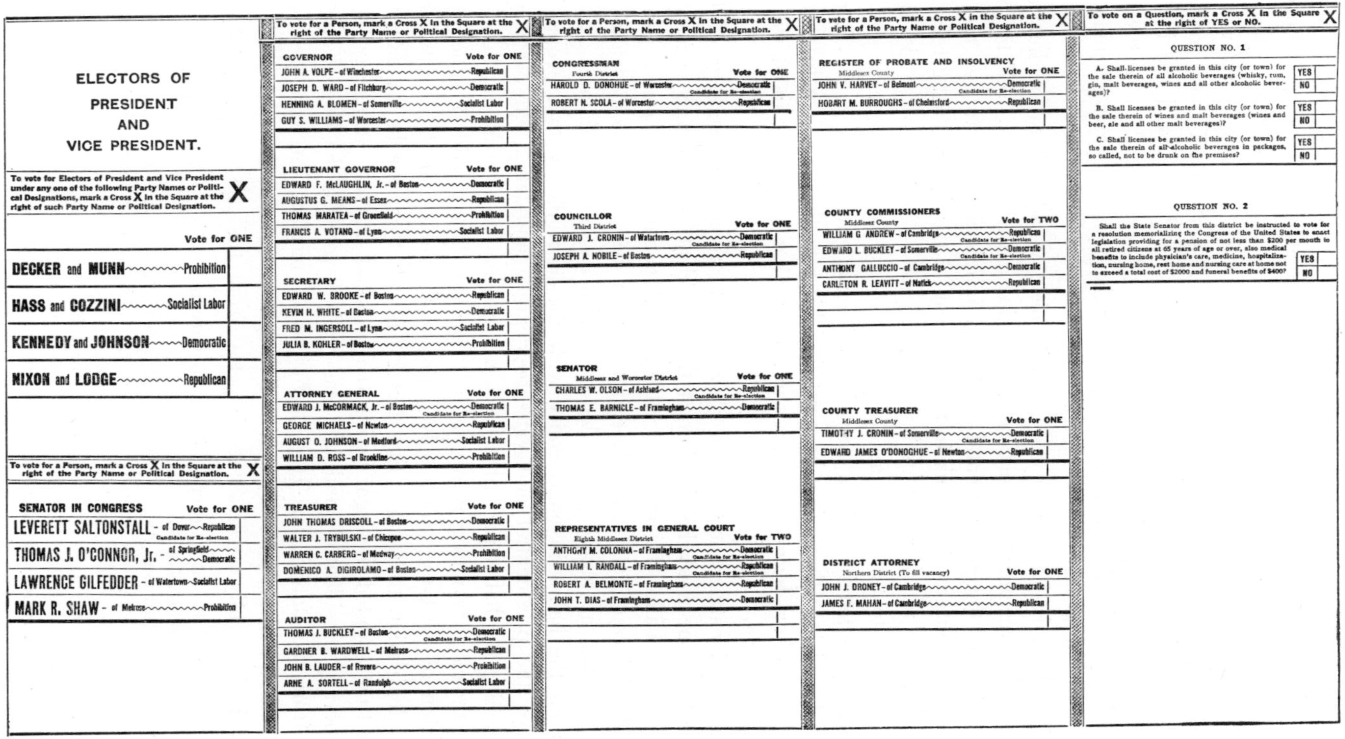

Figure 23.2 Specimen office-block ballot

asked to express 22 choices.[30] The number of expressions of opinion demanded of the American voter constitutes a greater burden than is borne by any other voter in the world. The ballot is so long, in fact, that the voter wearies and often refrains from voting on offices or measures toward the bottom. Not uncommonly, as many as 25 to 30 per cent of those voting fail to mark a choice on obscure constitutional amendments, and the less conspicuous offices almost invariably attract a far lower vote than do the offices at the head of the ticket. In the larger states these partial nonvoters may number in the hundreds of thousands.

The long ballot is a problem not in election administration but in the design of governmental structure. The ballot merely adapts itself to the requirements of the governmental system. It is relevant to note that the short ballot has been a major plank in the platform of the governmental reformers. To reduce the number of popularly elective state and local offices is, the argument goes, to tailor the task of the electorate to a manageable size. The voter, confronted by only a few choices, could presumably make more informed decisions than when he must find his way through long lists of candidates of whom he never heard who are running for offices about which he knows nothing.

An incidental aspect of the movement to reduce the acreage of ballot paper has concerned the election of the President. The custom once was to place on the ballot the names of all the presidential electors pledged to each presidential candidate. Of course, for over a century the presidential electors have had no function save that of a rubber stamp, yet their names have been on the ballot in comformity with the legal theory that people vote, not for the presidential and vice-presidential candidates, but for electors. Shortening the ballot presented the legal problem of determining how to remove the electors' names from it and at the same time provide for the popular selection of electors.[31] Iowa solved the legal problem in 1919 when it enacted legislation to remove the electors' names from the ballot and at the same time adopted the legal fiction that a ballot marked, let us say, for the Democratic presidential candidate was really a vote for the Democratic electors from the state.[32] The Iowa technique of meeting the legal problem is the method generally used. Spencer Albright points out that the presidential short ballot really received its impetus from the use of the voting ma-

[30] Spencer Albright, "General Election Ballots in 1934," *Southwestern Social Science Quarterly*, 16 (1936), 85–95.

[31] The Constitution, Art. II, sec. 2, provides: "Each state shall appoint, in such manner as the Legislature thereof may direct, a number of electors equal to the whole number of Senators and Representatives to which the State may be entitled."

[32] L. E. Aylsworth, "The Presidential Short Ballot," *American Political Science Review*, 24 (1930), 966–70; Ruth C. Silva, "State Law on the Nomination, Election, and Instruction of Presidential Electors," *American Political Science Review*, 42 (1948), 523–29.

Figure 23.3   Face of voting machine. Photograph courtesy of Automatic Voting Machine Corporation.

chine, which, because of its limitations, required a vote for all the presidential electors of a party at one stroke of the lever. In the 1956 election over half of the states used the presidential short ballot. Since most states now permit a vote for all electors by marking a single cross, the presidential short ballot does not reduce the burden of the electorate materially, but it does reduce the sheer size of the ballot.

V O T I N G   M A C H I N E S   Since 1892, when the city of Lockport, New York, made the first use of voting machines, the voting machine has been gradually taking the place of the paper ballot.[33] In 1898 Rochester, New York, adopted the machine as the sole method of voting, and several other New York cities followed during the next year. Laws in over three-fourths of the states permit the use of machines in all or some localities of the state. Most of these laws, however, merely authorize the local govern-

[33] On voting machines, see Harris, *Election Administration in the United States,* ch. 7; Spencer Albright, *The American Ballot* (Washington: American Council on Public Affairs, 1942). ch. 4.

ments, which usually administer elections, to install voting machies. Hence the degree of their use varies greatly among the states with permissive legislation. The Automatic Voting Machine Corporation estimates that in the 1960 presidential election about 50 per cent of the votes were cast by machine.

In essence the voting machine is a mechanical device for recording and counting automatically the choices registered by the voter. It is provided with a face equipped with levers corresponding to each candidate or proposition to be voted upon. On its face, adjacent to each lever, is a printed paper indicating the candidate for whom a vote will be recorded if that lever is pulled down. In operating the machine, the voter pulls a lever to close the curtains to conceal himself. This movement clears the machine for operation; unless the curtain is closed the machine cannot be operated. The voter then pulls the levers to indicate his choices. Machines are manufactured with a single lever to vote a straight ticket, corresponding to the party-column ballot. If the law of the state concerned prescribes the office-block ballot, the machine is designed to require the movement of a lever for each office. After lowering the levers to indicate his choices, the voter pulls the lever to open the curtain, which movement also actuates the counters to record his choices. At the close of the polls a panel on the back of the machine covering the counting devices is removed, and the election officials read off, record, and report the total vote indicated for each candidate.

Advocates (and manufacturers) of the voting machine are voluble in its praise. It prevents certain types of fraud and error in the conduct of elections. The "Tasmanian dodge" for example, cannot be worked on a voting machine. It prevents, too, the fraudulent spoiling of ballots by election officials during the count. Fraud and error in the count are impossible. The danger of fraud in reporting the precinct results is minimized, since it is a simple matter to compare the machine with the report of the vote by the precinct election officials. The machine makes the results available quickly after the closing of the polls, for it is not necessary to count ballots. The machine speeds up the voting process itself.

The manufacturers contend that substitution of the machine for the paper ballot reduces election costs. The Automatic Voting Machine Corporation concludes that it is generally possible to amortize the cost of the machines over a period of from 10 to 12 years through savings over paper ballots. The use of the machine permits a reduction in the number of precincts, with a consequent reduction in the number of election officials. Nor are so many election officials necessary. The machine, however, carries with it new costs, such as the expense of storage and of being set up for use. It is plain enough that election authorities, if they have the will, can bring about savings to offset some, if not all, costs of the machines. Even if machines increased election costs, the assurance of a quick and accurate count and other desirable features of the machines might be worth the cost.[34]

[34] Several recent innovations in mechanical voting have yet to find much acceptance. In 1960 the Ohio secretary of state approved for use in that state Coyle's voting machine, an adaptation of the punched card to voting. The special but low cost apparatus permits the voter to punch holes alongside the names of candidates whose names are printed in ballot form on an IBM card; counting can be accomplished rapidly on standard office machines. A Tulsa firm, Seismograph Service Corporation, has developed a new machine not radically different in appearance or function from the older machines but considerably less costly. The Norden Division of United Aircraft has contrived an electronic device for counting paper ballots at a rate of up to 1,200 per minute. Ballots would be brought from the precincts to a central place for counting by this equipment, which was designed to meet the special needs of Los Angeles County. None of the older mechanical voting machines has the capacity to accommodate the large number of candidates and issues on that county's ballot. For imaginative comments about the technical possibility of voting by dial telephone, see R. M. Goldman, "Public Elections in An Electronic World," *Telephony*, January 28, 1961.

V

PARTY AND

THE GOVERNMENT

The oratorical theory of democracy has it that like-minded people, Republicans or Democrats, manage to form a majority in support of a set of candidates committed to a program of action who, when elected, proceed as officials to carry out that program. Such a view vastly oversimplifies the linkage between popular will and governmental action.

The party that runs the government is, in a sense, a party different from the one that won the election. To win elections requires machinery for the designation of candidates and for drumming up voter support—the electioneering apparatus. To manage governments requires another type of party, a grouping of parliamentarians and administrators bound together in common cause under common leadership. The "party-in-the-government" must have an independence of the electioneering machinery outside; otherwise, it would be unable to fulfill its constitutional responsibilities. The party's national committee would be, in fact, the government. Nor can it be irrevocably bound by promises or commitments made by national conventions; other-

651

wise, it would not be free to cope with problems as they developed. Indicative of these necessities is the existence of governmental party organs separate from the electioneering machinery. These are most visible in the party machinery in House and Senate, but the President and the partisans clustered about him in the executive branch of the government could be regarded as a party group comparable to a House or Senate party caucus.

24.

PARTY LEADERSHIP

IN LEGISLATION

E L E C T I O N S are dramatic episodes in the struggle for power. The high visibility of party activity in campaigns screens the fact that there are two radically different kinds of politics: the politics of getting into office and the politics of governing. The machinations of the outs as they struggle to gain control stem historically from virtual conspiracies to overthrow the government; a successful challenge at the polls against a party in power amounts to a legitimized coup d'état. When a party gains power it is transformed; once challenger and critic, it becomes the government—and it hopes to remain the government.

The art of winning office differs from that of governing, but the politics of governing is a continuation of the politics of winning office. In campaigns a high premium goes to skills in swaying the multitude. Harvesting the fruits of victory requires deftness in the politics of governance, and these skills in maneuver, in compromise, in persuasion are not those of mass electioneering. Preservation of the winning combination demands a nicely balanced recognition of the claims of factions and interests associated in the victorious party; a sense of decent restraint lest rapacity hasten the day of defeat; an adequate magnanimity toward the vanquished; a capacity to transmute partisan triumph into an advance of the general interest; as well as prowess in the rough in-fighting that occurs as the opposition seeks to discredit those in power.

A distinction can be made between the functions of parties in campaigns and in the conduct of government. In a sense, the two functions are performed by two different parties. The party has its organization outside the government to nominate candidates and to campaign for their election. On the other hand, the party members occupying legislative and executive posts have responsibility for conduct of the government. The party group within the representative body has its own organization and identity quite independent of the party outside the government. In nations with parliamentary governments, a clear line is drawn between the parliamentary party and the party outside the government. In the United States the notion of a dual personality of party is not so commonly recognized. Nevertheless, the distinction serves to emphasize the importance of adequate attention to the two functions of party.

Governmental Structure and Party Government

Party performance in the conduct of government is conditioned by the nature of governmental institutions, a proposition of peculiar importance in the comprehension of the role of party in American government. It has been the fashion to assert that the structure of government is a matter of indifference: whatever its character may be, the dominant social forces will express themselves through it. Such reasoning may be valid if one is concerned with broad social movements over long periods of history. Nevertheless, in the day-to-day conduct of government the nature of the governmental mechanisms is of great significance. Structure and procedure influence what can be accomplished and the way it is accomplished. In the long run, party forces also influence the form and nature of institutions, though changes so induced are usually gradual. More clearly perceptible is the fact that, in the everyday business of governing, the institutional tools that party leaders work with modify, divert, and distort as well as reflect the political forces of the moment.

PARTY AND GOVERNMENT IN BRITAIN   The problems of the formulation and execution of a party program under the presidential form of government are thrown into bold relief by a comparison of that system with the British system of responsible cabinet government. Under the latter scheme undisputed and undivided party leadership is vested in the cabinet, a body formed of the leaders of the majority party in the House of Commons. Cabinet members steer the course of legislation in the House, and individually they head the administrative departments of government. Thus there is unified in the hands of the cabinet both legislative leadership and executive power. The cabinet governs and is, appropriately, referred to as the Government.

The cabinet governs, but it governs subject to the approval of the House of Commons and ultimately of the nation. Approval by the House, however, means the support of the majority within the House, from which cabinet members are generally recruited. Although the cabinet, in its power to dissolve parliament and call an election, has a weapon with which to discipline its followers, maintenance of party unity depends fundamentally on the enunciation by the cabinet of a program that will satisfy the party in the House. The members of the Commons tend to reflect, in turn, the attitudes and opinions of their constituents. Cabinet measures that arouse intense criticism may be modified to quell discontent in the party ranks and in the country. The cabinet may even withdraw a measure that threatens party unity. In some situations a minister may be "thrown to the wolves" to satisfy the party or the public. In extreme instances the majority party may change party leadership and, hence, the cabinet, to retain the confidence of the House and of the country. If the party majority in the Commons cannot be satisfied, at least according to the literary theory of the British constitution, the cabinet may lose its majority and thereby lose office, an event that would precipitate a general election. In practice, by the mysterious usages of the British constitution, elections come about by other means.

The machinery of cabinet government thus facilitates the formation and execution of party policy. Party leadership and governmental leadership are in the same hands. The cabinet itself is recruited from among the legislators, and its members are those who have proved themselves in the Commons and have gained the support of their fellows. Consequently, it is probable that most shades of opinion within the party will be represented in the government and will, in turn, be reflected in the measures the government proposes. The convention of collective accountability of the cabinet—all members share blame for a sour policy or for the ineptness of a colleague—doubtless brings a variety of views to bear on decisions on individual policy proposals.

Party discipline in the House of Commons flows in part from the nature of party operations in nominations. A high degree of centralization prevails within the party on candidacies. A local Conservative or Labour association nominates persons approved by the national leadership and, at times, persons suggested by the party's central office. The mandate of the member of Commons is in a sense not to represent his constituency but to collaborate with and to support the leadership of his party in the conduct of the government. The institutional context of the election of Commoners thus imposes upon them a different type of obligation than is supposed to rest upon the American legislator.

SEPARATION OF POWERS AND THE SPLINTERING OF PARTY LEADERSHIP By contrast, the major features of the cabinet system enable us to obtain a better understanding of the effects of the structure of American government on the formation and execution of party policy. The unity of party in government is too often regarded as the result of the disciplinary effect of individual penalties and sanctions. More fundamentally, party unity rests on consensus on programs and policy. The structure of American government impedes the formation of a party policy that would reconcile the differences within the party in control of the government. In the absence of such a policy, party unity is likely to be disrupted. Although the most prolonged consultation and negotiation would not produce party programs on which all Republicans or all Democrats would unite on all questions, the governmental structure makes difficult the unification of party within the limits of what is feasible.

The obvious structural feature that handicaps party government is the separation of powers, which splinters party leadership. The President, as the head of his party, occupies the premier position in the definition of party policy. But there is no assurance that his program will meet with the approval of all factions of his party in the House and Senate. The machinery of government does not routinely assure consultation with all factions of the party in the formulation of the presidential program. The independence of executive and legislature creates institutional jealousies and misunderstandings.

In short, British government is party government. The prime minister is the party boss and the cabinet members are his lieutenants. The American system, on the other hand, creates three independent centers of party and governmental power: the House, the Senate, and the Presidency. Even if the same "party" controls all three, the majority "parties" of the House, the Senate, and the Presidency are separate entities with no acknowledged obligation to work together and no satisfactory routine procedure for doing so. "At Westminster," says Holcombe, "party government is the essence of constitutional government, but at Washington there is both party government and constitutional government." [1] Yet, for government to function, the obstructions of the constitutional mechanism must be overcome, and it is the party that casts a web, at times weak, at times strong, over the dispersed organs of government and gives them a semblance of unity.

Presidential Leadership

"A President," as Merriman Smith has said, "is many men." [2] He is the symbolic head of the nation, the President of all the people, the constitutional

---

[1] "The Changing Outlook for A Realignment of Parties," *Public Opinion Quarterly*, 10 (1946–1947), 455–69.

[2] *A President Is Many Men* (New York: Harper, 1948).

monarch of the Republic. He must also be a workaday executive who directs the administration and exercises leadership in the solution of contentious issues. But first of all he must be a politician, a politician who has bested all other politicians to climb to the top of the heap within his own party and to triumph over the opposition at the polls. In the fulfillment of his role as leader in the legislative process, he may act on one occasion as President; at another moment he may operate as leader of his party; or he may play both roles simultaneously as he seeks to obtain enactment of his legislative program. Whether he is acting in one capacity or in the other is not always obvious, but that he tends to be the chief legislator there can be no doubt. Nor is there much doubt that his effectiveness as chief legislator depends on his success in building and managing party support. "There have been," observes Holcombe, "Presidents who have tried to govern without benefit of any organized partisan support, but they have never succeeded well enough to make their methods a model for imitation." [3]

EXECUTIVE INITIATIVE IN LEGISLATION　The position of the President, as Chief Executive and as leader of his party, makes of his office the only point about which leadership of the party in the conduct of the government may be established. Most of the great legislative issues are posed by the President. He advocates action and sets the terms of the debate on great questions. He must also concern himself with the mass of minor legislation necessary to keep the wheels of government turning: appropriations, amendments to existing legislation, developments and modifications of government operations. In this range of matters, legislative initiative falls peculiarly within the province of the President and his administrative associates. These legislative proposals emerge mostly from the experience of the administrative departments from which detailed innovations in public policy must mainly come, albeit not without nudging and needling by Congressmen.

By and large, the Presidency, not Congress, is the center of legislative initiative. It is the President who determines the major issues on which Congress acts; and it is the President who attempts, with or without success, to bring his party colleagues in the House and the Senate to the support of his policy. As Professor Ford pointed out:

> It is the rule of our politics that no vexed question is settled except by executive policy. Whatever may be the feeling of Congress toward the President, it cannot avoid an issue which he insists upon making. And this holds good of presidents who lost their party leadership as with those who retain it. Tyler, Johnson, and Cleveland, although repudiated

[3] A. N. Holcombe, "Presidential Leadership and the Party System," *Yale Review,* 43 (1954), 321–35.

by the parties which elected them, furnished the issues upon which party action turned.[4]

At one stage the President's role may be characterized by powerful advocacy of a new substantive program; at another his role may appear to be more one of leadership in strategy, timing, and the fixing of priorities on fairly routine matters. In either role the President does not "think up" all the laws. Most major new policies have behind them a long and persistent agitation, which may have had its leadership among members of Congress; and a significant statute may rest on the accumulated findings of a generation of congressional committees.[5] Yet it remains for the President to pull the proposal out of the ruck of mere discussion, to elevate it to the stature of a party issue, and to support its passage with the strength of his Administration.

PARTISAN FOUNDATIONS FOR COLLABORATION AND CONFLICT   Both collaboration and conflict characterize the relations of the President with Congress. Those ingredients occur in different proportions from time to time, but invariably they have a foundation in the enduring nature of the party system. Republican (or Democratic) Senators and Representatives, like the people who vote them into office, are not a homogeneous lot in their philosophies of government. Democratic (and Republican) Senators and Representatives tend to divide into factions; the nature of the President's problem of party leadership depends partially upon the division of strength among the different factions of his party.

Commonly, when a President goes into office a substantial number of the legislators of his party stand committed to the broad policy orientation of the President. Such legislators, though they may quibble on matters of detail, respond generally to presidential leadership. On the other hand, his party commonly has also another group of legislators who, on a range of issues, deviate from the presidential outlook. If they are to follow the President, they have to be wheedled or bought. Eisenhower came into office, for example, along with a number of Republicans who professed to be attached to the new Republicanism and also with others, perhaps more numerous, who adhered to the old-style Republicanism. Roosevelt, Truman, and Kennedy could rally northern, metropolitan Democratic legislators to the support of their legislative programs; the conservatives of the southern wing often broke party lines on economic questions, while southerners of all political hues resisted presidential leadership on race questions.

[4] H. J. Ford, *The Rise and Growth of American Politics* (New York: Macmillan, 1898), pp. 283–84.

[5] See L. H. Chamberlain, *The President, Congress, and Legislation* (New York: Columbia University Press, 1946).

These broad differences within the majority party fundamentally condition the task of presidential leadership and fix limits on party action. They rest, of course, not so much on the personal beliefs of legislators as on the fact that the legislators reflect shadings of view within the mass of the party. The contingent of isolationists with which Eisenhower had to cope, for example, spoke for an ancient stream of attitude within the party. Nor are these ideological cleavages within parties new.

Apart from these cleavages which may control on a cluster of issues, a President holds or loses the support of his fellow partisans on individual issues for other reasons. The legislator remains extremely sensitive to the peculiar needs and desires of his constituency, a factor that may move him from the party ranks when constituency interest conflicts with the party program. At times the conflict may not be so much between a constituency interest and the party program as between a pressure group and presidential leadership. A legislator may have to decide whether to follow the lobbyists of the American Farm Bureau Federation or his party leadership, and not infrequently the lobbyists win.

VARYING CONCEPTIONS OF PRESIDENTIAL ROLE IN LEGISLATION The presidential role of legislative leadership varies among Presidents with their conceptions of the proper role of the office. In this century Democratic Presidents have subscribed to the doctrine that the Chief Executive should provide forceful presidential leadership, while Republican Presidents have, with the exception of Theodore Roosevelt, leaned toward a more restricted view of their role. Woodrow Wilson pictured himself as something of a prime minister with an obligation to lead his party in the fulfillment of its program, and he proceeded accordingly to act vigorously and effectively.[6] Franklin D. Roosevelt exerted a leadership in legislation hardly matched by any other President, while Harry Truman, if not invarably successful in his dealings with Congress, never left the solons in doubt about the legislative objectives of the White House.

Warren G. Harding, a man not given to theorization, evidently believed that the business of legislation should be left to Congress. A handful of Senators had been active in bringing about his nomination in part because they hoped to take the initiative in legislation from the White House. Nor did Calvin Coolidge provide firm legislative leadership. Herbert Hoover says that on coming to the Presidency he "felt deeply that the independence of

---

[6] "The President," said Wilson, "is expected by the nation to be the leader of the party as well as the chief executive officer of the Government, and the country will take no excuses from him. He must play the part and play it successfully, or lose the country's confidence. He must be Prime Minister, as much concerned with the guidance of legislation as with the just and orderly execution of law; and he is the spokesman of the nation."

the legislative arm" should be "respected and strengthened." He had, he says, "little taste" for forcing action by Congress.[7] Eisenhower also brought to office a restricted notion of the duties of the President with respect to legislation.

These partisan differences in executive roles have been neither a matter of chance nor the result solely of the personal qualities of the Chief Executives. They emerge, rather, from the differing characteristics of Republican and Democratic parties. The Democratic party has been the party of reform and innovation; reform and innovation must inevitably be driven through Congress by aggressive executive leadership. The Republican party, on the other hand, has been far less a party of innovation; its policy commitments in the main could be fulfilled either by legislative inaction or by comparatively modest modifications of existing law.

Even when Congress is not confronted by the divisive issues of reform and innovation, the manner in which it conducts the normal flow of legislative business may be mightily affected by the manner in which the President operates. When the President is unable to lead, the party in power tends toward a policy of drift. When the President abdicates his legislative leadership, there is no place for the mantle to fall.

INSTITUTIONAL   RIVALRIES   AND   JEALOUSIES   No matter what party is in power or what President is in office, a deep antipresidential sentiment permeates Congress and exists even among members of the President's own party. Representatives and Senators develop a loyalty to Congress as an institution and a regard for its place in the constitutional system. Legislators rather encourage the notion that the assertion of presidential leadership somehow violates our constitutional commandments and is a governmental sin to be committed, if at all, surreptitiously. The dignity of Congress is redressed by an occasional setback to the President. He may be reversed and rebuked for apparently no reason save an assertion of congressional power. But congressional enunciation of the rights and privileges of the legislative branch may be a mere cloak for allegiance to substantive policies in conflict with those of the President. "It is traditional that those who, yielding to other pressures, fail to ratify presidential proposals should disguise their opposition as an endeavor to maintain the integrity and independence of the legislative branch of the government." [8]

EXECUTIVE LEADERSHIP AND POPULAR RULE   People with a yearning for orderliness would like to see developed a state of affairs under which a President could rally his party in Congress to his support

[7] *Memoirs, 1920–1933* (New York: Macmillan, 1952), p. 217.
[8] O. R. Altman, "First Session of the Seventy-fifth Congress, January 5, 1937, to August 21, 1937," *American Political Science Review*, 31 (1937), 1083.

with a minimum of pyrotechnics. Yet a President may not be doing his job unless he gets into a fight with Congress now and then. Congress, by the nature of its composition, becomes the stronghold of particular interests—and the special interests certainly ought to be represented. As the bulwark of particularism, Congress is a center of resistance to actions in the general interest and an initiator of actions to benefit partial interests. The President may attempt to block special group pressures or to divide and placate by proposing more moderate measures. His proposals may clash with the narrower and more parochial interests that bring their influence to bear upon the individual Senator and Representative. Ford commented many years ago:

> The situation is such that the extension of executive authority is still the only practical method of advancing popular rule. This disposition of American politics to exalt executive authority causes some critics of our institutions to infer that democracy tends towards personal rule. Appearances seem to corroborate this theory; but all that it really amounts to is that at the present stage of our political development American democracy, confronted by the old embarrassments of feudalism, compounded from new ingredients, instinctively resorts to the historic agency for the extrication of public authority from the control of particular interests—the plentitude of executive power.[9]

These observations, written over a half-century ago, retain their fundamental validity. The country perhaps could not tolerate an unending warfare between the President and Congress. On the other hand, long-continued peaceful relations between Chief Executive and Congress would probably indicate that all was not well with the Republic.

Each President must deal with a party representation in Congress that includes shadings of attitudes and factions of greater or lesser cohesiveness. The extent to which the President can carry along with him his fellow partisans of the Congress depends in part on the measures that he chooses to promote. By avoidance of divisive issues, he may maintain the fullest support of his party for those matters on which substantial agreement prevails. It might be possible for a President, through consultation, to submit legislative programs that would command virtually unanimous agreement within the party. Such a program would, however, have been formed to exclude contentious matters, and many of the measures included would have had their sharp corners rounded off.

The most careful formulation of presidential legislative recommendations undoubtedly facilitates lawmaking, but it may be fortunate that Presidents can urge projects that may even not be well matured and that are certain of defeat. Campaign promises and presidential recommendations at times represent objectives that are unattainable in the short run. The enactment

[9] *Op. cit.*, pp. 356–57.

of great public measures is not a matter of a moment. Agitation, discussion, and consideration may occur over long periods before great aims are achieved. If parties and Presidents were limited in their programs to those objectives capable of immediate enactment, the energetic advocacy of great causes would be handicapped. It may be a happy feature of the constitutional system that the President can urge, without risk of overthrow of the government by parliamentary vote, the adoption of proposals certain to be defeated in the short run. Presidents, to achieve greatness, must perhaps have in them a strain of evangelism and utopianism as well as the knack of keeping the governmental routines in operation.

SANCTIONS FOR PARTY DISCIPLINE   The President's greatest resource in rallying legislative support is the fact that he and a substantial block of the Congressmen of his party stand for broadly the same program. Concurrence of view, not command, underlies their agreement. Genuine Kennedy Democrats generally work together on legislation. The unity of policy consensus, however, can be re-enforced by weapons at the President's disposal, which may also be used to bring to his support other individuals, either generally or on particular measures.

The major formal means for putting the presidential program before Congress are the message on the state of the union, the budget, and the economic report. The message on the state of the union carries out the President's constitutional duty to "give to the Congress information of the state of the Union," and to "recommend to their consideration such measures as he shall judge necessary and expedient." The budget embodies the President's financial program. The economic report, made under the terms of the Employment Act of 1946, reviews the state of the economy and may contain recommendations for legislation. In addition, the President makes specific recommendations in special messages to Congress and may indicate his views in communications to individual members of Congress.

These communications put the President's legislative program on the record, but unless the President follows through with unceasing negotiation and persuasion his recommendations may die with the echo of the voice of the reading clerk. In some instances the President may appeal over the heads of Congress to the public for support of his measures.[10] By this means a President who advocates popular measures may direct varying degrees of pressure upon Congress. That pressure may induce legislators to seek to be known as supporters of a popular President. Obviously the supposed advantage to a legislator of such an identification varies enormously from time to time as does the skill of Presidents in mobilizing popular support. At the

[10] Of course, every time the President makes a public statement about legislation, he is appealing for public support although he may not explicitly ask the voters to "write their Congressman."

first congressional session after his inauguration, Pendleton Herring comments that Franklin Roosevelt

> displayed remarkable skill in manipulating the attention of Congress and of the public. His messages to Congress were strategically timed and positive and specific in character. Disagreement with his proposals was interpreted by the general public as obstructionism. . . . His radio talks to the nation served the double purpose of reassuring the people and breaking down resistance in Congress. Legislators were made only too well aware of the temper of their constituents.[11]

Another weapon is patronage. The President by the control of appointments may reward or punish, but the bargaining power does not rest exclusively on his side. Legislators, too, have votes with which to bargain. Nevertheless, a judicious deference to legislative patronage recommendations may build party solidarity in Congress. Woodrow Wilson, thus, had his troubles with the conservative and progressive elements of his party, but from a realistic utilization of patronage there resulted, says Link, "the establishment of the President's nearly absolute personal mastery over the Democratic party and the Democratic members of Congress." [12] Patronage has its limits. A Democratic President scarcely expects to obtain southern senatorial support for civil rights legislation by allocating a few jobs. Nor would a Republican President expect to manage his reactionary wing so cheaply. Yet a systematic correlation of patronage allocation and legislative performance has its utilities in maintaining the loyalties of the faithful. Patronage also has its uses in indemnifying legislators whose services to the Administration may seem to have contributed to their failure of re-election. The possibility of the loss of his job may be a grim prospect to an aging Congressman; administrative appointments of lame ducks, by the promise they hold for others, serve more than a compassionate purpose.

A patronage of policy also has its uses in specific situations. Senators and Representatives, of necessity, must concern themselves with questions of local and individual concern. White House support may clear the way for a special measure of interest to a Senator; a word from the same source may initiate a project in a Representative's district. The administrative departments have their own axes to grind with Congress and they make their own deals, but in a significant legislative battle sufficient centralization of policy

[11] "First Session of the Seventy-third Congress, March 9, 1933, to June 16, 1933," *American Political Science Review*, 28 (1934), 67.

[12] A. S. Link, "Woodrow Wilson and the Democratic Party," *Review of Politics*, 18 (1956), 156. The Postmaster General had a list of Senators who were the "real friends" of the Administration and "entitled to priority" in patronage; a group of less zealous supporters could claim only "secondary consideration." J. M. Blum, *Joe Tumulty and the Wilson Era* (Boston: Houghton Mifflin, 1951), p. 157.

patronage may develop at the White House to sway the votes necessary to carry the day.[13]

Consultation between the President and his party leaders in Congress may aid in the development of programs and strategies likely to attract maximum party support. Legislative leaders can advise the President on the temper of Congress; they can warn of obstacles. The President may enlist the leaders in his cause or he may be enlisted in their cause.[14] Consultation between congressional leaders and the President can do no harm and may on occasion expedite the march of legislative business. At any rate, Presidents find it desirable to schedule frequent, usually weekly, conferences with the legislative leaders of their party. These sessions serve, to some extent, to link legislature and executive and to develop agreement on party program and strategy.

From time to time, President Truman caused the Democratic national chairman to ask national committeemen and state chairmen to attempt to bring Democratic Senators and Representatives to the support of Administration recommendations. It cannot be said that these attempts had much effect. In truth, national party authorities seem to be unable either to help or to harm congressional candidacies. Without some demonstration that support of the party leadership has a bearing on his own political fortunes, the individual Senator or Representative is not likely to be deeply moved by the requests of party functionaries.[15] On the other hand, when the state chairman, national committeeman, or other such party official has a powerful position in his own bailiwick, he can, if he is so disposed, see that his Congressmen regularly support the Administration.[16]

---

[13] Given the impact of federal projects and contracts in almost every congressional district, the potential for pressure on legislators by pulling into the White House the discretion to grant or withhold federal largesse is impressive indeed. Occasionally, enough of this policy patronage is centralized to whip a few legislators into line on a critical measure. Yet the weapon is limited by technical considerations applicable to each program, by the desire of administrative agencies to use discretion for their own benefit, and, perhaps more fundamentally, by the fact that this weapon, if used to its full capacity, would turn out to have an earth-shaking recoil.

[14] Jack Garner reported that Roosevelt "talked the legislative leaders into a lot of things and we seldom talked him out of anything permanently." Bascom Timmons, *Garner of Texas* (New York: Harper, 1948), p. 228.

[15] An extreme instance of independence of partisan ties is indicated by these remarks of the late Senator Langer, of North Dakota: "I want to make it plain that the people of North Dakota do not care whether I am here as a Democrat or Republican. . . . I may say that after I received the Republican nomination for United States Senator the first time, the Republican National Committee donated money to my opponent in the primary.

"Mr. President, I owe the Republican Party in North Dakota absolutely nothing. Not only that, the Republican nominee for President refused to travel on the same train with me. He had my opponent in the primary on the train with him and introduced him to the people of North Dakota." *Congressional Record* (daily ed.), January 11, 1950, p. 331.

[16] Blocks of Representatives from boss-ridden cities sometimes provide sure votes

All these instruments employed in the relationships between President and Congress are, of course, expedients rather than a formalized battery of means for bridging the gap between the executive and legislative departments. They are brought into play as circumstances and presidential preferences dictate rather than in any regular or predictable way. Their existence reflects the fact that the American constitutional system is not designed to be a party government but that its operation requires at times that it approximate party government.[17]

Mechanisms of Party Government in Congress

The majority party must fulfill its responsibility for the management of legislation through a complex institutional apparatus. Its chief spokesman, the President, participates in the work of Congress only from the other end of Pennsylvania Avenue. Unlike its British counterpart, the American majority must manage two legislative houses, each of which regards itself as more than the equal of the other. Within each chamber, the majority must bring an intricate organizational apparatus under its control. Since the American Congress is a creative legislative body and not an organ solely for the registration of approval or disapproval of measures originating elsewhere, its management requires a high order of leadership, a mastery of the arts of diplomacy, and patience in intrigue.

The fundamental characteristics of the American parties—their diversity of composition, their dominant policy orientations, their inner contradictions—manifest themselves in bold relief in the membership of the party groups in the House and Senate. Moreover, as the majority grasps control of the machinery of the House and Senate, all its shadings of interest and ideology also find lodgment at points of power in the legislative organization. The organization of legislative direction becomes a mixture of centralization and decentralization, with factions of the majority, often minorities of the majority, in control of critical points in the legislative machinery. This circumstance starkly exposes to public view the problems of maintaining sufficient majority cohesion to control the significant legislative decision.

---

for the leadership but not much other contribution to the legislative process. Hardworking Congressmen have disdain for their brethren of the Tuesday-to-Thursday Club who spend long weekends nursing their constituencies or keeping their law practices alive.

[17] On the Presidency, see E. S. Corwin, *The President* (New York: New York University Press, 1940) ; Pendleton Herring, *Presidential Leadership* (New York: Farrar and Rinehart, 1940) ; Harold Laski, *The American Presidency* (New York: Harper, 1940) ; W. E. Binkley, *President and Congress* (New York: Knopf, 1947) ; Sidney Hyman, *The American President* (New York: Harper, 1954) ; Clinton Rossiter, *The American Presidency* (New York: Harcourt, Brace, 1956) ; Richard E. Neustadt, *Presidential Power* (New York: Wiley, 1961).

The basic instruments of party control of the legislative machinery are the House Democratic caucus, the House Republican caucus, and the comparable groups within the Senate. It is through these groups, which are unknown to the formal rules of Congress and which meet in private, that the majorities in House and in Senate agree upon persons to staff the formal and informal organization of the respective houses. The party caucus produces party solidarity on the question of who is to manage the legislative machinery, but only infrequently does the caucus even attempt to solidify the majority on questions of what shall be put through the machinery.

LEGAL AND EXTRALEGAL MECHANISMS FOR PARTY CONTROL OF THE HOUSE   For the guidance of the deliberations of each House of Congress, the majority party establishes extralegal machinery and uses in an extralegal way the formal machinery of Congress. The broad features of the machinery in both houses are similar, and in both the party mechanism has arisen to meet the need for leadership and direction common to all large decision-making bodies. As James Madison said in *The Federalist,* "in all legislative assemblies, the greater the number composing them may be, the fewer will be the men who will in fact direct their proceedings." And control of the party organization in the House, with its 435 members, is much tighter than it is in the Senate with its mere 100 members.

The House majority is led and directed by a set of party leaders who, though they are agreed upon by the party caucus, gain leadership by proving in the day-to-day work of Congress that they possess the qualities to command the deference of their colleagues. The major posts of formal authority brought under party dominion are the Speakership, the Rules Committee, and the standing committees of the House. Next in importance to the Speaker is the majority leader, an official not of the House but of the party group; the majority whip serves as a lieutenant of the majority leader. The minority also has its floor leader and its whip. Both the majority and minority parties in the House have a "steering committee." Of these committees, it was said in 1946, they "seldom meet and never steer," a characterization that may be less true than it once was, though the committees are not leadership organs of major significance.[18] Each party caucus also has a com-

[18] Joint Committee on the Organization of Congress, Senate Report No. 1011, 79th Cong., 2d sess. (1946), p. 12. Of late the House Republicans have called their steering committee the policy committee. It consists of the holders of the principal posts of party leadership plus representatives from regions of the country. In 1962 it met weekly and from time to time formulated the Republican view on issues before the House. In 1962 the Democrats revived their steering committee, which had fallen into disuse during the era of Speaker Rayburn, in a move to create a body that would be more heavily weighted with members of the northern liberal wing than was the leadership. The committee included the principal leaders plus members elected by Democratic representatives from each of 18 geographic areas. Speaker Rayburn had feared that such a body would dilute the power of the leadership; the new committee was explicitly given only a role

mittee on committees which nominates the majority and minority members of each of the standing committees of the House.

If the holders of all these posts constituted a cohesive inner clique of the majority, the leadership could readily determine the course of legislative action. The practices of the House, however, result in a representation of most of the factions of the majority in the roster of officials and leaders of the House. On those routine questions on which the leadership is not divided —and there are many of them—the House acts expeditiously and with a minimum of friction and fuss; on those questions that divide the leadership of the majority, party management often falters.

SPEAKER OF THE HOUSE   First among the leaders of the House majority is the Speaker. He achieves his position by working his way to the top of the heap during years of service in the House and ordinarily moves to the Speakership from the floor leadership of his party group. He occupies a place of power in the party as well as among his colleagues in the House. The eminence and influence of the Speaker are made clear by mention of such men as Sam Rayburn, Joseph W. Martin, Jr., John Nance Garner, and Nicholas Longworth.

Before a drastic revision of House rules in 1910–1911, the Speaker, as an agent of the majority, dominated the House. In addition to his power as presiding officer to grant recognition and to decide points of order, he appointed committees and sat as a member of the Rules Committee. Speaker Cannon, a standpat Republican, did not exercise his power in a manner to hold the confidence of all factions of his party. The progressive wing joined with Democrats to divide and disperse the Speaker's authority. Stripped of the prerogative of appointment and of membership on the Rules Committee, the Speaker remains with his diminished powers a leader and agent of the majority caucus. He acts as a party agent in guiding the conduct of House business, but as Hasbrouck has observed, the rules of the House "have so developed as a vehicle for the program of the majority that the Speaker need only apply them, to serve, on the whole, the ends of his own party. There is seldom need for him to discriminate as a moderator in order to promote his aims as a political leader." [19] Yet when he has discretion he does not hesitate to use it to the advantage of the majority, and he collaborates with his associates in the inner circle in planning majority strategy.

MAJORITY LEADER   The majority floor leader plays a role in the direction of the work of the House second in importance only to that

---

"advisory" to the leadership. Its promoters hoped that it would serve as a channel of communication between leaders and rank and file and generate a wider sense of participation in the affairs of the party group.

[19] P. D. Hasbrouck, *Party Government in the House of Representatives* (New York: Macmillan, 1923), p. 85.

of the Speaker. The floor leader is elected by the party caucus, and his duties are so onerous that he serves on no legislative committee.[20] He functions as a sort of field commander who leads and guides the majority in the legislative battle. He keeps in close touch with the chairmen of legislative committees and, in consultation with other important party figures, guides the course of party action in the House. Subject to his responsibility to his party followers, he arranges the work schedule of the House; and in this task he consults frequently with the minority leader to assure, insofar as practicable, a mutually acceptable schedule of debate.[21]

The majority leader and the Speaker usually serve as links between the President and the House, at least when the Administration has a House majority. In varying degrees the majority leader is an organ of the Administration as well as of the party in the House. He may have obtained his post with Administration support, and commonly he leads the legislative battles of the Administration on the House floor and helps to defend the work of the administrative departments against their critics.

PARTY WHIP   Another agent of the party leadership is the party whip, a functionary who is, in the case of the Democrats, appointed by the majority leader and, in the case of the Republicans, elected by the caucus. He serves as a sort of top sergeant for the leadership. One of his duties

[20] The selection of the floor leader by the caucus may become a test of strength between factions of the majority. In 1962 the Democrats elevated John W. McCormack of Massachusetts from the majority leadership to the speakership, despite misgivings by southerners who thought him to be too sensitive to the wishes of the Catholic hierarchy and by northerners who feared that he would be ineffective in legislative management. The caucus then unanimously elected the whip, Carl Albert of Oklahoma, as majority floor leader. Before the caucus met, Richard Bolling of Missouri, a leader in the liberal wing of the party, had withdrawn his name from consideration. He had concluded that he could not muster the votes necessary to win. In such situations decisions are often made without a formal vote to avoid exacerbation of intraparty differences. Relative strengths can be appraised without the drawing of swords.

[21] Illustrative are these extracts from a statement of the legislative program for the following week by Majority Leader Albert on July 13, 1962:

"Monday is Consent Calendar day. The gentleman from Georgia, chairman of the Committee on Armed Services, will call up the conference report on the military construction authorization bill, H.R. 11131. . . . There are also two suspensions programmed for Monday: S. 1824, providing an additional judicial district for Florida; and Seashore Park.

"Tuesday is Private Calendar day. Also on Tuesday we will consider H.R. 11974, the Atomic Energy Commission authorization bill, with 2 hours of general debate.

"On Wednesday there will be the conference report on the bill S. 167, the Antitrust Civil Process Act. Also H.R. 12135, the Federal Highway Act of 1962, with 2 hours of general debate.

"On Thursday there will be H.R. 12391, the general farm bill, with 2 hours of general debate.

"On Friday we will take up the State, Justice, Commerce, and the judiciary, and related agencies appropriations bill for 1963." *Congressional Record* (daily ed.), July 13, 1962.

is to keep in close touch with the members: to communicate the wishes of the party leaders to the rank and file, and to attempt to keep them in line with the party program. He informs them of the schedule of the House and scours Washington to bring absent members to the floor when their attendance is imperative.[22] He canvasses the members to determine their attitude on questions that endanger party unity. In all this work each party's whip is aided by assistants who deal with members from specific regions.

RULES COMMITTEE   The formal instrumentality for control of the procedure of the House is the Rules Committee. The majority party, but not necessarily its majority faction, holds a majority of the seats on this committee which exercises powers crucial to the management of the House. Consideration of major measures is governed by special rules that it recommends to the House. It may kill a bill by refusal to recommend a rule; it may expedite legislation by recommending appropriate rules; it may limit debate drastically; it may limit the amendments to be offered to bills; it may, in effect, determine the form of the question to be voted on by the House.[23] The committee may even control the substance of the measures submitted to the House by declining to grant a rule until the legislative committee modifies the bill to meet its wishes.[24]

On those measures on which substantial agreement exists within the majority, the Rules Committee facilitates the work of the House leadership. The committee's actions that excite comment, however, bear on contentious bills that divide the majority. Almost inevitably on the committee are members at odds with the Administration on at least some of its program. Thus,

[22] The Republican whip's notice prior to the vote on the Brannan farm plan included this exhortation: "Every Republican member who is on his feet and breathing, or shows any signs of life and is free from doctor's orders must be accounted for on the above-mentioned dates, and be ready to vote on this important and far-reaching legislation. We must defeat the Brannan farm bill. It can be done if all Republicans are on the job."

[23] Illustrative is the rule for the consideration of the Housing Act of 1956: "*Resolved*, That upon the adoption of this resolution it shall be in order to move that the House resolve itself into the Committee of the Whole House on the State of the Union for the consideration of the bill (H.R. 11742) to extend and amend laws relating to the provision and improvement of housing. . . . After general debate, which shall be confined to the bill, and shall continue not to exceed 2 hours . . . , the bill shall be considered as having been read for amendment. No amendments shall be in order to the said bill except that it shall be in order for any member of the Committee on Banking and Currency to move to strike out all after the enacting clause of the bill H.R. 11742 and insert as a substitute the text of the bill H.R. 12328, and such substitute shall be in order, . . . but shall not be subject to amendment." *Congressional Record* (daily ed.), July 25, 1956, p. 13131. In a less restrictive form the special rule sets the time for debate but places no limitation on the amendments to be in order.

[24] See J. A. Robinson, "The Role of the Rules Committee in Arranging the Program of the U.S. House of Representatives," *Western Political Quarterly*, 12 (1959), 653–69, and his "The Role of the Rules Committee in Regulating Debate in the U.S. House of Representatives," *Midwest Journal of Political Science*, 4 (1961), 59–69.

in 1954 Speaker Martin had to enlist the AFL to re-enforce Administration pressure on the committee to obtain a rule to permit the House to vote on an Eisenhower public housing proposal; most of the Republicans on the committee opposed public housing. On the other hand, in the same year the committee expedited action on a bill to cut taxes which the President opposed. During recent Democratic Administrations the committee has often been at odds with the House leadership and with the President. Right-wing Democrats on the committee have joined with Republicans to obstruct the Administration program.

While power on the order of that of the Rules Committee needs to be exercised to guide the flow of House business, whether it should be in the hands of an irresponsible body raises another question. After their 1948 victory, Democrats cast about for ways and means to circumvent the committee in order that they might enact, or at least attempt to enact, their campaign promises into legislation. The solution, adopted in 1949 over opposition of the right wing of the southern wing of the party, was the 21-day rule which empowered the Speaker to recognize chairmen of legislative committees to bring directly to the floor of the House, bills which the Rules Committee had sat on 21 days. In 1950 Administration forces beat off a proposal, supported by a bloc of southern Democrats and Republicans, to repeal the rule. In the 81st Congress, the Speaker permitted eight Administration measures to come to a vote under the rule, each of which the House passed. After the elections of 1950, newly elected Republicans joined with dissident Democrats to repeal the 21-day rule.

In 1961 the Kennedy Administration, fearful that its major measures would be bottled up in the Rules Committee, supported a proposal to enlarge the committee for the duration of the 87th Congress and thereby to permit the addition of enough Democrats favorable to the Administration to prevent control of the committee by a combination of Republicans and conservative Democrats. Only the most determined efforts—plus the assistance of liberal Republicans mainly from the Northeast—carried the proposal in the House by a vote of 217–212. While the packing of the committee expedited some measures, in due course coalitions developed in the committee to kill some types of bills, as, for example, the 1962 Kennedy proposal to create a Department for Urban Affairs. In January, 1963 the House made permanent the temporary enlargement of the committee, an action that did not touch the root of the problem of the role of the committee but at least preserved the new status quo.

There are defenders of the power of the Rules Committee to make decisions perhaps contrary to the ostensible will of the majority of the House. Faced by an insistent and irresistible clamor, the House, by the inaction of the committee, may be saved the embarrassment of a vote. Or the members, hell bent for election, may be denied an opportunity to pass an unwise but apparently popular measure. Others argue that the legislative machinery should, as a matter of principle, contain within itself means by which minorities may block action on irreconcilable questions. Whatever the rationalizations, in practice the Rules Committee hampers as well as facilitates party control of the House.[25]

STANDING COMMITTEES   The majority claims for its members the chairmanship and a majority of the members of each of the House committees, but the manner of assignment to committee posts often obstructs the work of the majority leadership. The majority (through its committee on committees selected by the caucus) controls assignments of members to committees, but once on a committee a member moves upward by seniority until he becomes chairman (or ranking minority member). Committee chairmen are thus designated by the fortuitous coincidence of political and biological longevity.[26] They may or may not be in harmony with the dominant faction of the party in the House; they may or may not belong to the President's faction of the party. The seniority rule has the virtue of avoiding the squabbles that would arise under other methods of choice; it also often weakens majority control. The rule propels into committee chairmanships members from those districts most firmly attached to the majority, and sure Democratic districts or standpat Republican districts often diverge from the presidential policy orientation.[27]

Committees exercise great powers over legislation through their capacity to report or not to report bills and through their prerogatives in the amendment and rewriting of measures. The committees "form miniature legislatures with a high degree of autonomy," and their chairmen can ordinarily prevent committee action even though they may not be able invariably to control the committee affirmatively. When committee chairmen work in harmony with the House leadership, they may exercise their powers to accomplish the party program. When the chairman does not see eye to eye with the Administration or the House leadership, he can cause trouble by his power to bottle up in committee measures whose passage is desired by the leadership. Doubtless, at times what appears to be capriciousness on the part of a committee chairman may really be action in accord with the will of a majority of the House, which permits the glory—and the heat—to accrue to the credit of the chairman. The chairman is always under some compulsion to take into ac-

[25] While the seniority rule seems to be about as durable as the Constitution, it would be an interesting experiment to except the Rules Committee from it.

[26] George Goodwin, Jr., "The Seniority System in Congress," *American Political Science Review*, 53 (1959), 412–36; Nicholas A. Masters, "Committee Assignments in the House of Representatives," *American Political Science Review*, 55 (1961), 345–57.

[27] In the 86th Congress, only 23 per cent of the Democratic members of the House scored less than 40 per cent on a scale of legislative positions favored by the ADA. The comparable figure for Democratic committee chairmen was 50 per cent; for southern Democratic committee chairmen, 75 per cent.

count in his work his sense of the mood of the House as a whole. Nevertheless, he possesses a range of discretion and he does not uniformly exercise that discretion as a member of a leadership team dedicated to the enactment of a party program.[28]

The powers enjoyed by committees and by committee chairmen point to a basic problem in legislative management. The accomplishment of the work of the House demands a division of labor and a delegation of functions to committees. Yet the fulfillment of the responsibility of the House as a whole requires that it not be a rubber stamp for its committees. House committees enjoy prerogatives that few great legislative assemblies permit their committees to arrogate unto themselves. The tendency of committees to become special pleaders for particular interests, quite apart from the political idiosyncracies of committee chairmen, militates against the leadership in the execution of a general program of legislation. A first essential in the execution of a program in the general weal is the power to batter down the more outrageous demands of narrow interests. The strategic advantages enjoyed by committee chairmen handicap efforts in that direction.

MECHANISMS OF PARTY CONTROL: SENATE   Superficially, the formal apparatus of party control in the Senate resembles, in the main, that of the House. The majority group designates majorities on each legislative committee; it has its floor leader, its whip, and its caucus. The Senate also adheres to the rule of seniority in the designation of committee chairmen, although Lyndon Johnson, as Democratic leader, induced his colleagues to waive their right to vacancies on desirable committees in order to give good committee assignments to freshman Democratic Senators. Unlike the Speaker of the House, the Vice President, as presiding officer of the Senate, has been, over the long run, more likely to be tolerated than looked to as a legislative leader, although both John N. Garner and Richard Nixon played active roles in the politics of the Senate. The House and Senate, despite their mechanical similarities, are not alike. Given the greater looseness of party ties in the Senate and its higher visibility, the intraparty factional battles for control of the party apparatus usually reveal more starkly the fissures within the party groups than does the struggle for control of the House.

In the maneuvers for control of leadership of the Republican Senate group, a recurring pattern is a struggle between Old Guard and so-called modern Republicans, usually won handily by the Old Guard. In the organization of the Senate after the 1952 election, the announcement by Senator Robert A. Taft that he would be available as majority leader stilled talk of other candidacies for the post. The Administration had to deal with a Senate leadership that included no Eisenhower enthusiasts in posts of great im-

[28] See R. F. Fenno, Jr., "The House Appropriations Committee as a Political System: The Problem of Integration," *American Political Science Review*, 56 (1962), 310–24.

portance and consisted mainly of men distinctly cool toward the General's foreign policies. After the death of Senator Taft, William F. Knowland was moved up to the majority leadership, an action regarded as favorable to Eisenhower since the possible alternatives were men irrevocably opposed to the Administration's foreign policy. Senator Knowland opposed only parts of it.[29] As majority leader, the Senator was given to public expression of disagreement with the Administration program as well as to public expression of his views of the direction in which it should go.[30] In 1959, after Knowland's retirement, a rerun of the drama of the Old Guard versus the modern wing occurred as Senator Everett M. Dirksen of Illinois won the minority leadership over John Sherman Cooper of Kentucky. The liberals received a consolation prize in the designation of Thomas H. Kuchel of California as assistant minority leader.

The Democratic Senate group, since it is even less homogeneous than the Republican group, must seek leaders who can bridge the gaps within the party rather than leaders who typify the dominance of one wing of the party. Thus, in 1951 the Senate Democrats chose a new majority leader in a contest between Senator E. W. McFarland of Arizona and Joseph C. O'Mahoney of Wyoming. O'Mahoney represented the Fair Deal wing of the party. McFarland, on the other hand, had not gone along with the Truman program on civil rights, although on other legislation he had been regarded as an Administration follower. The southerners and the moderates united on McFarland, who, at least to some degree, straddled both factions. Similarly, in 1953 the Democrats chose Lyndon Johnson of Texas as floor leader. A tumult would have been stirred by an attempt to install a deep-dyed southerner, such as Russell of Georgia; nor would the South have taken kindly to a man of the views of Lehman of New York. The post fell to a man so located on the political spectrum that he could seek to maximize party unity, relatively unembarrassed by demands of his own constituency save on petroleum questions. Mike Mansfield of Montana, chosen as Johnson's successor in 1961, had some of the qualifications of a middleman in that he had ties, but not too intimate ties, with both the southern and northeastern wings of the party.

THE FILIBUSTER AND PARTY GOVERNMENT   A special feature of Senate procedure is the absence of an effective cloture rule. De-

---

[29] In accord with his hands-off policy toward the affairs of Congress, Eisenhower, though, expressed no preference for a successor to Taft and also instructed his cabinet to stay on the sidelines. R. J. Donovan, *Eisenhower: The Inside Story* (New York: Harper, 1956), p. 112.

[30] Knowland opined that the majority leader has a dual responsibility. "One is to represent the views of his party in the Senate, and in a kind of broad sense of the Senate itself, to the White House. Secondly, he is to interpret the views of the Administration to his party, and where he finds that there are differences between the two, try to work out areas of agreement with regard to those differences."

bate may be shut off only by concurrence of two-thirds of those present and voting.[31] In the absence of a readily imposed cloture, a determined minority can talk a bill to death by holding up the business of the Senate until the majority yields. The major beneficiaries of the practice have been southerners who invoke the right to filibuster, or threaten to do so, to kill bills proposing federal action on the rights of the Negro, though on occasion other minorities also indulge in dilatory debate. The right of filibuster is defended on the ground that legislation with drastic consequences should not be enacted over the determined opposition of a numerous minority in the country. To that prudent principle great deference is accorded, even in the absence of its formalization in such practices as the filibuster. The right of minority veto of Senate action means that some types of legislation could be enacted, no matter how numerous a party's majority might be, only under the spur of a more determined and more intense popular sentiment than has yet been aligned in their support.

PARTY POLICY AND PARTY UNITY   The majorities of both House and Senate maintain a high degree of cohesiveness on questions of the organization of their respective chambers. They take control of the instruments to guide the legislative process, yet they do not maintain sufficient unity to determine the outcome of all substantive issues. To a degree, party groups split because of inadequate machinery and insufficient use of existing machinery to develop party programs and to hold the party members in line, but party disunity rests more fundamentally on the divergence of the outlooks of the elements within each party.

The classic means by which a majority may predetermine the results of a representative assembly is a caucus, a private session of a majority whose members commit their votes in advance of action in the assembly. Democratic and Republican caucuses of the House and Senate convene to agree upon slates of officials, and in the chambers the party groups cohere in opposition to each other on these organizational matters. Only most infrequently are caucuses convened to decide the party position on legislative questions; nor does the caucus attempt to fix the vote of its members on such matters as do the caucuses in some state legislatures.

Whatever party discipline prevails in the Congress comes from the exertions of the Administration and the House and Senate leadership rather than from imposition by the party caucus of its will. The caucus has, to be sure, certain disciplinary powers, but they are exercised only rarely and then against recalcitrant members for actions outside the Congress. Professor Berdahl's careful survey of the record suggests that the sin most likely to bring caucus displeasure is bolting the party in a presidential campaign.[32]

[31] In 1961 the Senate defeated a proposal to reduce the requirement from two-thirds to three-fifths. See Alan Rosenthal, *Toward Majority Rule in the United States Senate* (New York: McGraw-Hill, Eagleton Case 25, 1962).

[32] C. A. Berdahl, "Some Notes on Party Membership in Congress," *American Po-*

Western insurgent Republicans supported La Follette for the Presidency in 1924. The Republican Senate conference adopted a resolution to exclude the "disloyal" Senators (La Follette, Ladd, Brookhart, and Frazier) from the conference and not to name them to "fill any Republican vacancies on Senate Committees." Within two years, however, the conference relented.[33]

The caucus does not, and perhaps cannot, serve as a means of hammering out a party program on which its members can unite to push through the House or Senate. The reason is simply that to bring together partisans with irreconcilable disagreements is more likely to exacerbate than to compose their differences. Moreover, to attempt to control by caucus action the vote of the deviant members would run counter to the political mores which place a high value on independence. The late Senator William E. Borah for decades was a thorn in the side of the Republican leadership. A constituent chided him for opposing the Republican Administration: "What would you have a Senator do?" he replied. "Sincerely represent his views, however inadequate they may be, or act as an intellectual prostitute for some party organization?" It is one of the glories of the American system of legislation that it has enough play in it to allow room for courageous and righteous men to rise above their party. One of the drawbacks is that by the same token the machinery gives considerable license to the scoundrel.[34]

The belief persists, correctly enough, that the roots of party disunity rest in the lack of agreement on party program. The cure is said to be the contrivance of means for the development or negotiation of agreement on party programs to which most party members can subscribe or be induced to support. The Joint Committee on the Organization of Congress in its 1946 report proposed the creation of "policy committees" by both parties in both houses. The committees would formulate legislative policy programs to be made public. The Joint Committee proposed no means of party discipline; each member would be "free to vote as he saw fit, but the record of his action would be available to the public as a means of holding both the party and

---

litical Science Review, 43 (1949), 309–21, 494–508. See also his *Our Two-Party System* (Bureau of Public Administration, University of Mississippi, 1951).

[33] In 1960, after Senator Harry F. Byrd had refused to support the Kennedy-Johnson ticket, there was talk, apparently not regarded seriously, of displacing him as chairman of the Senate Finance Committee.

[34] The notion that the legislator should form his views by the exercise of his free and unbossed judgment has an emotional appeal, but something can also be said for the view that the party caucus should be able to bind its members to the caucus position. The Congressman tends to be elected, not because of the peculiar lilt of his golden-throated oratory, but—at least in the competitive districts—because he is a Republican or a Democrat. Why should a party group permit its control of the chamber to be endangered by the voting idiosyncrasies of some of its members? Or when party splits occur, the party abdicates its function of aggregating sufficient power to govern and to a degree makes a mockery of popular government by its failure to fulfill expectations aroused in the campaign. All of which may be true, but since the last effective use of the caucus—in Wilson's first term—Congress has come to face issues capable of breaking the bonds of any caucus decision. Moreover, Congressmen have developed new ideas and habits of action appropriate to their role of independence.

the individual accountable." [35] These committees would have funds "for the maintenance of a high-grade secretariat to assist in study, analysis, and research on problems involved in policy determination."

The House struck from the congressional reorganization bill the provision for policy committees. The Speaker and other Democratic leaders feared that such a committee would encroach upon their traditional sphere of authority. The Senate, however, adopted the policy committee proposal. It provided funds "for the maintenance of a staff for a majority policy committee and a minority policy committee in the Senate, consisting of seven members each, for the formulation of over-all legislative policy of the respective parties, the members of such staffs to assist in study, analysis, and research on problems involved in policy determinations." The practical result of this provision was the transformation of the party steering committees of each party in the Senate into policy committees.[36]

Two impressions emerge from the records of the Senate policy committees. One is that the minority policy committee, other things being equal, can more easily be developed into an instrument of policy formation and leadership than can the policy committee of the majority, at least when Senate majority and Administration are in the hands of the same party. Under the leadership of Senator Taft the Senate Republican committee before 1952 became a fairly effective instrument for the expression of majority policy and for leadership. The Democratic Senate policy committee evidently became more significant after the Democrats lost the Administration. The main reason for this difference is that the President remains the chief spokesman for the majority; a Senate policy committee will be overshadowed by him.

Another equally plain proposition is that mere creation of a party policy committee is not in itself likely to have consequences of much import one way or another. For the committee to be effective it must be the instrument of a leader or a handful of leaders who have risen to positions of command. By his qualities as leader rather than by his formal post as chairman of the policy committee (and later leader), Senator Taft managed the Republican Senate group. After his death, the Senate policy committee declined sharply in influence.[37] Similarly, Lyndon Johnson, as majority leader and chairman of the policy committee, used the committee to supplement his own not in-

[35] Joint Committee on the Organization of Congress, *op. cit.*, pp. 12–14.
[36] The Democrats retain a steering committee which functions as a committee on committees.
[37] The bibliography on Congress is voluminous and only a few titles can be cited: Ernest Griffith, *Congress: Its Contemporary Role*, 3d ed. (New York: New York University Press, 1961); G. H. Haynes, *The Senate of the United States* (Boston: Houghton Mifflin, 1938); G. B. Galloway, *The Legislative Process in Congress* (New York: Crowell, 1953); J. M. Burns, *Congress on Trial* (New York: Harper, 1949); Bertram Gross, *The Legislative Struggle* (New York: McGraw-Hill, 1953); W. S. White, *Citadel* (New York: Harper, 1957); Roland Young, *The American Congress* (New York: Harper, 1958); G. B. Galloway, *History of the House of Representatives* (New York: Crowell, 1961); H. N.

considerable powers of persuasion and management, though it could scarcely be said that his was a collective leadership.[38]

PARTY COHESION AND THE GOVERNMENTAL SYS-
TEM   The fact that the American Congress has to be managed by an extraordinary amount of pulling and hauling, maneuvering and compromising, rather than by the quiet and orderly registration of party majorities, gives rise to criticism, to proposals for party reform, and to no little bewilderment among our allies around the world.[39]

The painful fact probably is that the characteristics of the party groups in Congress reflect fundamental features of our party system, not readily susceptible to alteration. The accidents of history and the necessities of forming a following large enough to elect a President bring discordant elements under each party umbrella. No institutional contrivance within the party groups in Congress can close their deeper cleavages. Beyond this, monolithic party groupings within Congress could very well alter in a fundamental way the character of the constitutional system. Disciplined majority groups in House and Senate could be antipresidential as well as pro-Administration. The balance moves between "presidential" and "congressional" government. The solidification of party groups in the Congress might well turn the balance against the President under some circumstances. It is not certain that tightly disciplined legislative partisanship would be compatible over the long run with a strong Presidency, at least without the most radical alteration of the party system.

The Place of Party in Legislation

The members of the majority unite to control the machinery of Congress, but on substantive matters they often break ranks. So imperfect is the

---

Carroll, *The House of Representatives and Foreign Affairs* (Pittsburgh: University of Pittsburgh Press, 1958); Stephen K. Bailey, *The Condition of Our National Parties* (New York: Fund for the Republic, 1959).

[38] The Democratic policy committee had enough importance to become the subject of a fracas when Mike Mansfield succeeded to the majority leadership in 1961. The policy committee had consisted of appointees of the floor leader; the assumption was that it should include men the leader wanted to advise and work with in his leadership role. The liberal wing failed to obtain larger representation on the committee, but succeeded in obtaining adoption of a caucus rule that members of the committee would be elected by the caucus on nomination of the leader. See Ralph K. Huitt, "Democratic Party Leadership in the Senate," *American Political Science Review*, 55 (1961), 333–44; M. E. Jewell, "The Senate Republican Policy Committee and Foreign Policy," *Western Political Quarterly*, 12 (1959), 966–80; Hugh A. Bone, "An Introduction to the Senate Policy Committees," *American Political Science Review*, 50 (1956), 339–59; D. B. Truman, *The Congressional Party: A Case Study* (New York: Wiley, 1959).

[39] The classic critique is Woodrow Wilson's *Congressional Government*, available in a paperbound edition (New York: Meridian Books, 1956).

mobilization of party strength that some commentators dismiss party as irrelevant to the business of legislation. In fact, appraisal of the place of partisanship in Congress presents perplexing questions to which there are no pat
answers. The role of party in Congress differs from decade to decade, from
session to session, from issue to issue, and even from legislator to legislator.
The most plausible path toward a comprehension of the place of party is to
identify some of these variations in the behavior of the party membership in
Congress.

PARTY UNITY AND DISUNITY   In most parliaments a high
degree of unity prevails in the party groups. In Congress, party solidarity
on roll calls is exceptional, yet party appears to be the strongest and most
persistent factor associated with the actions of Senators and Representatives.
Party considerations, however, exert a far more powerful influence on some
types of questions than on others, while on some matters partisanship is
virtually nonexistent.

One large segment of the business of Congress remains largely outside
the field of party warfare. Much of its work consists of private bills or measures of local or particular application, and they are commonly passed without floor discussion. In the 1961 session of the Senate, for example, most of
the debate concentrated on 94 of the 1,133 bills and resolutions passed by
the Senate. In the House the debate was directed to 133 measures as the House
passed 1,234 bills and resolutions.[40]

The majority fulfills its duty when it sees that these measures not of
general import receive thorough and rational consideration. That duty is met
through committee management and through some monitoring of measures
by the leadership. In each house the party leaders designate "official objectors" who are obligated to post themselves on measures on the private and
consent calendars and to raise objection when they deem it advisable.[41] The
mode of handling these measures indicates the live-and-let-live character of
the American party system. If the majority asserted full control of these matters, the party system would be something other than what it is. If only majority members could sponsor local or special bills with any hope of passage,
a partisan capture of the Congress would be much more of a "total" victory than it is.

On those questions settled by a roll-call vote in House or Senate,[42] party

[40] F. M. Riddick, "The Eighty-Seventh Congress: First Session," *Western Political
Quarterly*, 15 (1962), 254–73.

[41] For a statement of policy by House majority and minority objectors on the consent calendar, see *Congressional Record* (daily ed.), April 12, 1961, p. 5320. Their
policies were calculated to assure that certain types of measures, because of their importance, should receive some discussion rather than pass by unanimous consent and that
other types of legislation should be adopted from the consent calendar only if reviewed
by the department concerned and by the Bureau of the Budget.

[42] In the 1961 session the Senate passed 1,133 bills and resolutions and had 204 roll
calls; the House passed 1,234 bills and resolutions and had 116 roll calls.

affiliations of legislators have a bearing on their vote although the degree to which the division of the vote parallels the party division varies greatly from roll call to roll call. In the 1940's, according to Turner's findings, about 15 per cent of the House roll calls were party votes—that is, at least 90 per cent of the Democrats opposed at least 90 per cent of the Republicans. In contrast, in the era of McKinley about half the roll calls were party votes.[43]

While roll calls with the parties almost solidly opposed to each other are fairly infrequent—about one out of six in the 1940's—on a high proportion of roll calls there are significant differences in the voting behavior of Republicans and Democrats. That is, the bulk of the Democrats, although less than 90 per cent, will oppose the bulk of the Republicans. Or party differences may be marked even though majorities of both parties vote on the same side of the issue. Of the Republicans, for example, 80 per cent might vote aye along with 55 per cent of the Democrats.

Given these characteristics of group behavior, ascertainment of the relationship between party affiliation and voting becomes a matter of the measurement of degrees of party unity and loyalty. Once a technique of measurement is contrived, the problem remains of estimating the significance of party as party in the legislative process. On these matters great effort and considerable ingenuity have been expended, but it must be said that the number of incontroverted general propositions that can be made on the subject is not large.

Obviously the extent to which majority legislators support the Administration program is a critical determinant of the role of the party group. A rough measure of this dimension of party loyalty is the percentage of the roll calls on which the legislator votes for the President's recommendations. An impression of the behavior of the party groups in the House based on such a measure appears in Figure 24.1. That chart rests on scores assigned to each Representative on the basis of his record in the session of 1961, that is, the percentage of 65 roll calls involving recommendations of President Kennedy on which he voted in agreement with the position of the President.

The chart makes it plain that, on the average, a substantial difference existed between Democrats and Republicans on this set of issues. Democrats had, far more frequently than Republicans, records of high consistency in concurrence with Kennedy. Yet, within each party group the voting scores were spread over a wide range. Most frequently Democrats supported the President on from 80 to 90 per cent of the roll calls. Democrats low in their support scores were mostly from the South, although not all southerners had low scores. The chart also shows clearly the existence of substantial ranges of agreement between the parties on this set of questions. Support of the President's recommendations between 30 and 50 per cent of the time was common among Republicans. Only three Republicans had sufficiently sen-

[43] Julius Turner, *Party and Constituency: Pressures on Congress* (Baltimore: Johns Hopkins Press, 1951), p. 28.

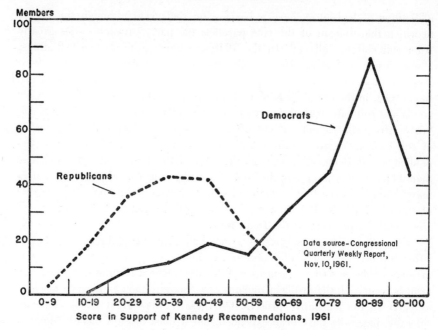

Figure 24.1   Partisan differences in voting in the House of Representatives: Distribution of Democratic and Republican Representatives according to their score in support of Kennedy legislative recommendations, 1961

sitive antennae and strong senses of partisanship to avoid agreement with the President on less than 10 per cent of the roll calls.[44] Commonly the party groups cohere more tightly on some types of questions than on others. Of 116 House roll calls in 1961 reported by the *Congressional Quarterly,* a majority of the Republicans opposed a majority of the Democrats on 58.

A House or Senate leadership without a substantial bloc of regular partisan supporters would be mightily handicapped, but the fact remains that the majority seems never to be cohesive enough to prevail on all issues. The leadership must always solidify its own forces as well as it can and then, if necessary, try to pick up enough votes from across the aisle to carry the

[44] Although scores constructed on the same principle as those underlying the chart are widely used, the student should be warned of their limitations. The essence of the trouble is that two men with different voting records may have identical scores. One man could be pro-Administration on one-half of the roll calls and another pro-Administration on the other half and each would have a score of 50. The figure is based on scores compiled by the *Congressional Quarterly Weekly Report,* a publication with which students of American politics should be familiar. The *Weekly Report* includes reports and analyses of the work of Congress along with information on other aspects of American politics. Annually, much of the information of the *Weekly Report* is brought together in the *Congressional Quarterly Almanac.*

day. Among the controverted issues in any session of the House or the Senate there may be found a goodly number that the majority could not have won without some opposition support and others that it would not have lost in the absence of defections from its own ranks. And these roll calls productive of intraparty cleavage are likely to include those on substantive programs regarded as of the greatest importance.

ROOTS OF PARTY UNITY AND DISUNITY   Party groups at times cohere; at other times they fly apart. These variations result not from the whim or caprice of the legislator. On some matters powerful forces operate to unite each party group in opposition to the other. On others, equally impelling forces operate to pull splinters or factions away from the position of the party group. These behaviors of legislators have roots in their constituencies. The determinism of the representative relationship both contributes to the tendencies toward party unity and to the desertions of the leadership.

The diverse elements comprehended within each party make almost every roll call unique in the way it divides the legislative chamber and the party groups. Yet durable factional elements within each party can be relied upon to bolt the party on certain categories of issues. Perhaps the best advertised factional group within a party is the Democratic southern wing. The members of that faction may be the most regular of the regular on the routine run of legislation, but they uniformly bolt on proposals for federal action with respect to the Negro.

Southern solidarity is restricted to the racial question. On other matters southern Democrats vary. Like their constituents, southern Democratic legislators range from the reactionary to the liberal. The outlook of a state's Senator depends on what faction of the state's Democratic party he represents. These remarks are supported by the data in Figure 24.2, which shows the distribution of Senators, Republican and Democratic, according to their stands on 10 issues of major concern to the AFL-CIO in the 1959 and 1960 sessions of Congress. Northern Democrats tended to rank high on a scale of support of the AFL-CIO position, while on the average Republicans ranked low. Southern Democrats, however, are scattered, as may be seen from the chart, all along the measuring rod. Their modal position was low on the scale but some southerners ranked relatively high. Republicans, too, as the chart shows, had members scattered all across the political spectrum.[45]

A cleavage on foreign policy has plagued the Republican congressional groups. The impact of events from 1916 to 1952 and the positions of the

[45] The Republicans ranking highest were Smith of Maine, Javits of New York, Cooper of Kentucky, and Fong of Hawaii. The lowest ranking northern Democrat on the scale, Frear of Delaware, failed of re-election in 1960, perhaps an indication of the proposition that a legislator who deviates too markedly from the line taken by legislators from comparable constituencies places his political future in peril.

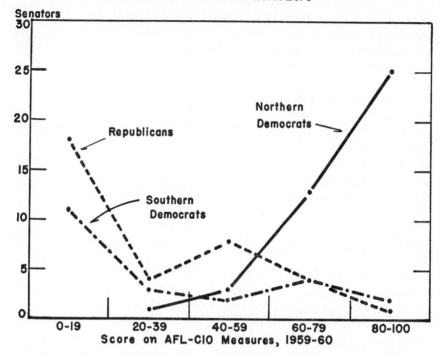

Figure 24.2   Republican and Democratic Senators according to their degree of support of major legislative positions favored by AFL-CIO, 1959–1960

parties during this period attracted one type of political activist into the Republican ranks, another to the Democratic. Those resentful of American participation in "Democratic wars," those isolationist by belief, and those dubious of international cooperation found the Republican position more congenial. Faithful Democrats found themselves committed to a more internationalist position, and the party drew to its ranks many who gave a high priority to internationalism. This process of polarization continuing over the decades profoundly affected the policy orientation of the two parties, although it did not neatly divide all voters into two camps. Partisan differences must be described in terms of modalities, not dichotomies.

These differences appear in the behavior of the party groups in Congress, with the consequence that the Eisenhower Administration found it difficult to muster sufficient congressional support to govern. Republican members of the House, for example, gave fairly consistent support to orthodox Republican domestic policies; on the other hand, the largest group of consistent supporters of the Administration on foreign policy issues was among the Democrats. A goodly proportion of the Republican members could be relied upon to oppose the Administration, although the Republican group included men of all shadings of view on foreign policy. At times the Republican Senate group acted as if it were in opposition to the Administration; in 1956 the major challenges to Eisenhower's foreign policy measures were led by the late Senator Styles Bridges, chairman of the Republican policy committee.

To indicate the problem of the Eisenhower Administration in building Republican support for both its foreign and domestic measures, Figure 24.3 compares Democratic and Republican House members according to their scores in support of the General's 1955 requests in the foreign and domestic categories. Almost 40 per cent of Republican House members opposed the Administration foreign policy position at least 40 per cent of the times they voted; a bit more than 40 per cent of the Democrats supported the Administration on at least 80 per cent of their votes. The hard core of the isolationist Republican wing is usually said to be midwestern, but the data suggest that Republican isolationism may not be so much a product of sectionalism as it is a reflection of ruralism. Republicans from rural districts in all sections of the country are on the average more isolationist than their colleagues from the urban districts. Many of the rural districts happen to be in the Midwest.[46] Sample surveys of popular attitudes regularly demonstrate

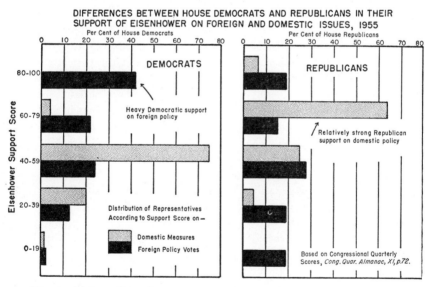

Figure 24.3   Distribution of Republican and Democratic Representatives according to their scores in support of Eisenhower requests on domestic and foreign policy matters, 1955

[46] In 1955 Republicans from the most rural districts had an average score of 40 in support of Eisenhower foreign policy requests while their colleagues from the most urban districts average 63. Variation in support existed among regions, but within each region the rural-metropolitan difference held. Within the Democratic group, the average

the existence of a higher degree of isolationism on the farms than in the metropolis. The positions of rural Representatives may be only a reflection of the views of their constituents.

The foregoing analyses identify the constituency foundations of the broad and recurring cleavages within the party groups in Congress. Often southern Democrats depart from their party line. Republicans from northeastern and far western urban districts frequently dissent from their partisan colleagues on issues of both foreign and domestic policy. Some legislators are, thus, pulled from their party position by what they perceive to be the interests or the outlooks of their constituencies. Focus of attention on these well-known types of policy deviants, though, oversimplifies the reality. Issues cut across party groups in many ways. On one vote this set of legislators may be under conflicting pressures; on the next vote a different group will be similarly affected. The most diverse sorts of constituency interests may militate against party solidarity.[47]

Constituency interests may disrupt party solidarity; the same forces may unify the party group. Given the issues of recent decades, it might be expected that Democratic Representatives from northern, urban, working-class districts would vote alike in high degree. Such, indeed, turns out to be true. Julius Turner demonstrated in great detail the association between constituency characteristics and the voting records of Representatives. The essence of his analysis was that variations in the voting records of Representatives were associated with partisanship and such constituency characteristics as metropolitanism or ruralism, native-born or foreign-born population, and the sectional location of the district. For the period he analyzed, Democratic representatives from northern, metropolitan, foreign-born districts had, on the average, the highest loyalty to the Democratic House group in voting on roll calls; that is, they voted with the majority of the party group most consistently. Among the Republicans, those from rural, native-born districts in the interior of the country had on the average the highest records of loyalty to their party group. Other combinations of constituency characteristics were associated, on the average, with lower records of party loyalty.[48]

---

for the Democrats from the most rural districts was 59; for those from the most urbanized, 75. These averages are of *Congressional Quarterly* scores, the data underlying Figure 24.3.

[47] Illustrative is the 1956 Senate vote on a measure to end federal control of natural gas prices. Democratic Senators from gas-producing states were pulled from the party position by constituency considerations; northern liberals were re-enforced in their party loyalty by the interests of their constituencies. Republican Senators who happened to be from gas-consuming states were drawn from their party position to the support of governmental regulation of private enterprise. In a 1954 House vote on flexible farm prices, Democrats from metropolitan districts veered from the general party position of support for rigid prices. Republicans from midwestern farm districts were similarly drawn away from the Eisenhower line of flexible prices.

[48] For comparisons of the records of Representatives from many categories of dis-

Turner found that if constituency characteristics are held constant—that is, if the records of Representatives from similar districts are compared—a difference persists between Republican and Democratic legislators. Perhaps the moral is that party unity, to the extent that it exists, rests in large measure on similarities of district characteristics and, inferentially, similarities of attitudes and interests.[49] Were there enough metropolitan working-class districts to elect a majority of the House, that majority could readily be molded into a disciplined and cohesive majority at least on domestic economic questions. Or if the rural, native, interior districts were numerous enough to elect a majority, it could be shaped into a united working Republican majority. The obdurate facts of the geographical distribution of our population prevent either party from putting together a majority of Representatives from districts with similar characteristics. Although more assiduous work by party leadership could doubtless produce a higher degree of party unity, for the foreseeable future the varying qualities of the constituencies will place limits on party unity in Congress.

One should not overstate the significance of correlations between constituency characteristics and Representatives' voting records. Undoubtedly the legislator's estimates of the attitudes of his district control his vote on some measures. Nevertheless, sufficient looseness remains in the tie between legislator and constituent to enable him, without endangering his political future, to exercise over a considerable range of questions a discretion so as to support the party program, to express his own good or capricious judgment, or even to vote for some causes that conflict with the interests of most of his constituents.[50]

---

tricts, see Julius Turner, *op. cit.* For an analysis technically far more advanced than Turner's pioneer study, see Duncan MacRae, Jr., *Dimensions of Congressional Voting* (Berkeley: University of California Press, 1958). For a bibliography citing other relevant studies, see Norman Meller, "Legislative Behavior Research," *Western Political Quarterly*, 13 (1960), 131–53.

[49] Most studies of the relation of legislator and constituency rest on inferences about the attitudes of voters. For example, a district with a high percentage of industrial workers in its population would be presumed to have different attitudes than one with a low proportion of such persons. In a pioneer analysis, W. E. Miller and D. E. Stokes have compared directly attitudes of constituents (as determined by a sample survey) with attitudes of Representatives (as determined both by interview and from their roll-call votes). The most marked correlation between Representative and constituency occurred on civil rights questions. A lesser correlation existed in the area of social welfare, but it rose sharply when it was limited to the comparison of the attitudes of Representatives and the popular majorities that elected them. Scarcely any correlation existed between Representative and constituency in the policy area of foreign involvement. A finding of some significance was that variance in Representatives' outlooks was more completely accounted for when their perceptions of constituency attitudes, as well as actual attitudes as determined by sample surveys, were included in the reckoning. See "Constituency Influence in Congress," forthcoming.

[50] See V. O. Key, Jr., *Public Opinion and American Democracy* (New York: Knopf, 1961), ch. 19.

BIPARTISANSHIP IN FOREIGN AFFAIRS   In domestic affairs the erraticism introduced into government action by the weakness of party ties may not be disastrous for the Republic. Delay for a year or two or longer may merely mean that things have to go along as they have been. Incapacity to act may have more grave consequences in external affairs. A stability of policy when stability is required, a flexibility of policy when flexibility is in order, a firmness in adherence to commitments, a point of manageable power from which to negotiate—all these and other characteristics are requisite to the conduct of foreign relations.

To organize internal politics in a manner to support our external politics an ostensible departure from partisanship has occurred in the practice of a bipartisan foreign policy. In practice collaboration between the parties has included participation of important minority leaders in negotiations, consultation of minority leaders, understandings between presidential candidates to restrict campaign debate on foreign policy, and a deliberate appeal across party lines in the Congress by the Administration for support on foreign policy questions. Given the two-thirds rule for consent to ratification of treaties as well as the looseness of majority discipline, a substantial and strongly led minority can immobilize the United States in its external politics. A major fruit of bipartisan collaboration in the 1940's was the reversal of the isolationist policies of the 1920's and 1930's and the greater involvement of the United States in world politics. Roosevelt had seen at first hand Wilson's failure as he attempted to execute such a policy on partisan lines, and he strove to avoid that fate by enlisting support from the Republican minority.

Probably what successful bipartisanship amounts to is the capacity of the President to hold most of his own party together and to command, as well, the support of a substantial splinter of the opposition. Thus, Roosevelt and Truman managed to hold the northern and southern Democrats together on foreign policy questions, a unity induced in part by the rewards and penalties available to the Administration. They recruited Republican support mainly in the East, although the great Republican foreign policy leader was Senator Vandenberg of Michigan. Republicans from the interior could be relied upon to provide the principal opposition to the Administration's foreign policy.[51] With the Eisenhower Administration pursuing a generally similar foreign policy, the same cleavages remained. A Republican President could command some support from Republican legislators that a Democratic President could not, but the General enjoyed the cordial distrust of the isolationist wing of his party and had to recruit Democratic support for his measures. That support, while often decisive, was less complete than would

[51] See H. Bradford Westerfield, *Foreign Policy and Party Politics* (New Haven: Yale University Press, 1955), and George L. Grassmuck, *Sectional Biases in Congress on Foreign Policy* (Baltimore: Johns Hopkins Press, 1951).

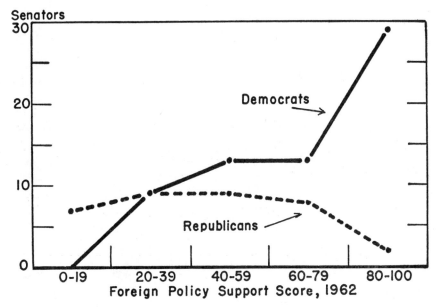

Figure 24.4 Distribution of Republican and Democratic Senators according to score in support of Kennedy foreign policy requests, 1962

have been accorded to a Democratic President. In turn, in 1962 Eisenhower exhorted Republican legislators to support Kennedy's foreign trade legislation. The pattern of support constructed by the President's maximization of solidarity within his own party and recruitment of allies from the opposition appears for 1962 in Figure 24.4, which rests on *Congressional Quarterly* data.

SPLIT PARTISAN CONTROL   The common objectives of partisan allies in the House, the Senate, and the Presidency provide, or so the theory runs, the basis for collaboration among the organs of the government in the achievement of national purpose. Even when the nominees of the same party control both the Presidency and the Congress, as the foregoing discussion makes clear, partisan coordination of the independent organs of government lacks perfection. When one party controls the Presidency and another the House or Senate, the normal rivalry between executive and legislature is aggravated by party differences.

The occasional existence of division in partisan control of the Presidency and Congress points both to some of the characteristics of the party system and to the importance of party in the governing process. If the parties were disciplined groups dedicated to divergent programs, a division of partisan control would hamstring the government. In fact, sufficient comity prevails between the parties so that an opposition Congress, although it may heckle and harass, at least provides appropriations and enacts the necessary legislation to keep the government in operation.

In a negative way the eras of divided control underline the significance of party in the total governing process. Presidents have rarely been able to carry through notable legislative proposals with Congress in the hands of opposition majorities. On the other hand, opposition congressional majorities are themselves unable to assume the leadership in great affairs against the wishes of the President. They may block the President; they may, if they can muster enough votes to override a veto, repeal or whittle down existing legislation. But they can initiate no great undertaking that requires executive collaboration in its fulfillment. Common partisan control of executive and legislature does not assure energetic government, but division of party control precludes it.

LONG-RUN IMPACT OF PARTY ON PUBLIC POLICY   In these pages the emphasis has been on the solidarity and disunity of party groups in the short run and on the consequent necessity for ceaseless maneuver to form combinations to govern. Another way to speculate about party and public policy is to look at the course of governance over a far longer period of time. The long-run view may yield an estimate of the role of party far different from that which emerges from the microscopic examination of yesterday's votes in the House or Senate.

At intervals a new majority wins control of the Presidency and Congress and its ascent to power marks a reorientation of legislative action. The program may or may not be solidly opposed by the minority legislators; some of the majority may grudgingly support or even oppose. Yet, that the party system in its totality is the vehicle for these shifts in direction and tempo of legislation there can be little doubt. Wilson's New Freedom and Roosevelt's New Deal illustrate surges of party strength associated with new directions in legislation. Harding's "normalcy" had its repercussions in congressional action. Eisenhower's victory brought a new tone in domestic legislation.

The new majority party is the vehicle for the expression of these great shifts in public sentiment that become perceptible as we look backward. It perhaps becomes such, not necessarily through the attractiveness of its program or the adroitness of its campaigners, but because it was, as the minority, an instrument conveniently at hand for use when the need arose. Yet when the workings of party in legislation are examined microscopically rather than through the broad sweep of history, the party group appears as a most cumbersome and imperfect piece of machinery.

Parliamentary Party and Presidential Party

From these excursions into the workings of party in legislation there should emerge a sharper recognition of the contrast between the presidential party and the parliamentary party. As it appears in the struggle for the control of the Presidency, the American party is relatively highly disciplined. The process of presidential nomination brings most of its factions and splinters to the support of the candidate, and its presidential electors, if they win their states, cast their votes in support of the party's nominee.

It could almost be said that we have one party system for the purposes of the Presidency; another, for the Congress.[52] The necessities of presidential politics conceal the reality of a multiplicity of parliamentary parties concealed behind the labels of Republican and Democratic. The lines separating these subparties do not appear in the organization of the party in the country for electoral purposes; they become apparent only in the workings of the party in the House and Senate; even there the lines dividing them are blurred. Southern Democrats unite against their northern brethren only on some issues; the Republicans of the interior at times make common cause with their colleagues from the coastal regions.

The institutional apparatus accommodates itself to the interplay of centripetal and centrifugal forces within each major party, permitting expression to both, yet permitting neither to triumph completely. Within each party the drives toward unity, the common denominator of shared interests of all factions, the solidarity contrived of compromise find expression in the presidential candidate or in the President. In the workings of Congress, the forces of particularism, of section, of class, of all types of subgroups within the party enjoy comparatively free play—a luxury made tolerable by the stability introduced into the government by an executive whose tenure is beyond reach of mercurial parliamentary majorities. At times, though, the paralysis induced by the internal discordancies of the majority party in Congress lends credibility to the charge that the function of Congress is to see to it that the people do not get what they vote for.[53]

---

[52] For a spirited argument that the congressional, rather than the presidential, majority should prevail, see Willmoore Kendall, "The Two Majorities," *Midwest Journal of Political Science*, 4 (1960), 317–45.

[53] See J. M. Burns, *The Deadlock of Democracy* (Englewood Cliffs: Prentice-Hall, 1963).

25.

ADMINISTRATION

AS POLITICS

T HE VICTORIOUS political party has responsibility for the formulation of a legislative program and for the leadership and guidance of legislative operations. It has a responsibility, too, for the direction of the work of the administrative departments of the government. It executes its lawmaking duties by organizing the legislative bodies and by leading the majority as best it can. On the administrative side it is enabled to carry out its program by presidential designation of secretaries and assistant secretaries and like officials in charge of administrative departments and agencies. They, in turn, have, within limits, authority to designate their principal assistants. A relatively small number of persons, politically loyal to the President and to the party in power and presumably attached to its program, has the function of guiding the machinery of government in fulfillment of the party's responsibility to the electorate.

In some respects control of administration is even more difficult than fulfillment of party responsibility for legislation. Often party leaders in the legislative body come to their tasks better equipped than do the partisans at the head of departments. They have had experience in the House or Senate on the minority side, whereas cabinet members often approach their tasks innocent of experience in federal administration. Furthermore, the President and department heads do not enjoy undisputed sway in the management of administration. Their fellow partisans in Congress usually like to take a hand in the matter and consider that they have a responsibility for the control of administration. The administration, like the majority in Congress, contains within itself centrifugal forces that strain the capacity of the President, in his role as chief administrator, to prevent special interests from dominating particular administrative agencies, at least on some questions.

Administration consists of more than management of routines. In some respects it is, like the legislative process, between-election politics; it must cope with similar problems and its practice requires similar skills. Great administrative decisions, like legislative acts, may involve a reconciliation of conflicting interests and must be made with an alertness to their general public acceptability. Nor is the task of the President in the leadership of federal administration simply one of the issuance of directions to subordinates: the arts of compromise, of negotiation, of persuasion have as great a relevance in the White House as in Congress.

Administrative Agencies: Actors in the Political Process

The majority party must control the administrative apparatus if it is to impress upon the government its conception of the public interest. Under the laws they administer most executive agencies have wide discretion, the exercise of which may touch party policy. Moreover, administrative agencies are originators of proposals for legislation and often exert an influence in the making of new policy. These drives toward new policy and alterations in old policy must at least not run counter to the dominant inclinations of the party in power. The President acts both as Chief Executive and as party leader in the direction of administration.

ADMINISTRATIVE AGENCIES NOT CIPHERS   Administrative agencies are not as clay in the hands of the President and his partisan associates. They tend to have a tradition, an outlook, and a policy inclination of their own. To budge them from their predetermined paths is not always easy. Vast aggregations of public servants, military and civil, organized into well-knit hierarchies and animated by common aims and spirit have a potency in the political process that is often underestimated or even ignored. Government departments and agencies at times act as spokesmen or representatives before legislative bodies and the public for segments of society that they serve. Through the prosecution of research that reveals public needs and points toward public action, administrative agencies often initiate movements leading to new public policy. In the management of programs of procurement and expenditure, agencies may affect significantly the fortunes of great industries. In the politics of appropriations almost every administrative bureau or department seeks to maintain or enlarge the scope of its operations.

In one respect administrative agencies are like pressure groups: they operate continually, in Republican and Democratic administrations alike, to advance their interests; indeed, often the closest working relations are maintained between a pressure organization and the governmental agencies in which it is interested. Pressure groups and administrative departments are elements in the pattern of politics that may be jarred and realigned by the results of an election but are seldom completely thrown from power. The administrative organization exerts its strength through transient department heads and Presidents, no matter what party is in power. With close relationships between its headquarters personnel in Washington and Congress it is able to make its wishes known to Congress either through the department head or through unofficial channels. Often with a personnel distributed over the nation, it is sometimes able to stir up, by discreet measures, pressure from home to bear on Congress. With almost a monopoly of information in its sphere of interest, the administrative organization is able to release or withhold data in such a fashion as to influence the course of legislative action.[1]

REPRESENTATIVE ROLE OF ADMINISTRATIVE AGEN-CIES   A factor that conditions the task of the President in the direction of administration is the representative role of administrative agencies. Pressure groups and administrative agencies themselves often contend that the agency has a duty to act in furtherance of the interests of the group it serves. This is a doctrine of bureaucratic representation: that the Department of Labor should speak for and represent the interests of labor in making recommendations for new legislation; that the Department of Agriculture should promote vigorously the interests of the farmer and ignore those of other groups; and so on. A characteristic statement of this notion is one made in 1943 by the National Co-operative Milk Producers' Federation:

> Eleven months from now the people will go to the polls. They will decide many important issues. One of the greatest issues which farmers will help decide will be on the question of who controls the Department of Agriculture. We believe that the organized farmers of America will demand of both political parties that they will provide a reconstituted Department of Agriculture to serve agriculture. Other Departments of Government serve the groups for which they are named. The Department of Agriculture today is not being permitted to function for the farmers. We call for definite pledges on this great fundamental issue.[2]

With agency after agency attached to the interests of particular groups and under pressure to promote partial interests, the President as administra-

---

[1] See J. L. Freeman, "The Bureaucracy in Pressure Politics," *Annals*, 319 (September, 1958), 10-19.

[2] National Co-operative Milk Producers' Federation, *A Daily Policy for 1944*, p. 7.

tive leader has no little difficulty in bringing about the operation of the government in accord with a party program dedicated to the general welfare. The prevailing practice is that the administrative agencies represent the interests they serve.[3] Many of them owe their existence to the groups they serve. As new groups or classes rise to power and influence they are recognized through the establishment of governmental departments. The creation of the Department of Agriculture was the first recognition of an economic class in the administrative structure; later the departments of Commerce and Labor were established.

The degree to which an administrative agency becomes an attorney for its constituency varies with circumstances. The Veterans' Administration is rarely in a position to oppose the interests of the veterans. On the other hand, when an agency is subjected to pressure from conflicting interests, it may enjoy a greater freedom in formulating and advocating its recommendations. The Department of Agriculture cannot satisfy completely the beet-sugar growers, the beet-sugar refiners, the Louisana cane-sugar growers, and the seaboard cane-sugar refiners. When different interests play on an administrative agency, it may seek to work out a program of legislative recommendations appeasing divergent demands insofar as practicable.

ADMINISTRATIVE AGENCY AND ITS CONGRESSIONAL ALLIES   By their close communion with interests in society administrative agencies may gain a certain independence of presidential direction. By the same token they become beholden to those groups upon whose support they depend. These group relations often extend over into alliances involving the administrative agency, the pressure group, and Congress. Administrative agencies develop friends in Congress whose policy interests parallel those of the agency. At times a bureau or agency may become virtually independent of the President, so powerful is its support in Congress. These relationships make it difficult to bring the work of such agencies into line with the President's program, and insofar as it is a party program they tend to vitiate party responsibility. To the extent that a President fails as a legislative leader he is also likely to fail as chief administrator; when Congress has the whiphand in legislation, it also tends to undercut the President as Chief Executive.

A POLITICS OF SELF-PRESERVATION   In the objectives they seek, administrative agencies are almost as varied as they are numerous. Yet most agencies seek to maintain, if not to expand, their activities and to assure the retention of administrative arrangements they regard as satisfactory. Every bureau is eager to obtain appropriations to carry out its program on an adequate scale, and few bureau chiefs believe that last year's

[3] See Charles Wiltse, "The Representative Function of Bureaucracy," *American Political Science Review*, 35 (1941), 510–16.

appropriation was enough. An organization's prestige is measured in part by the size of its appropriations and the number of its employees; aside from such considerations, in seeking appropriations the personnel of an agency is animated by a faith in the worth of the work that is being done and by a belief that the public interest will be advanced by the appropriation of the amount requested. Persons employed by the government, like those employed elsewhere, are likely to have enthusiasm about what they are doing.

The administrative agency usually exerts its strength to defend itself and its program from attack in legislative bodies. Administrators tend to have a vested interest in the law they enforce; and, when its enemies attack, the agency is quick to line up its legislative friends in defense. A special type of legislative proposal that arouses intense interest of administrators is a reorganization bill. Comprehensive schemes to reorganize the administration through legislation have invariably been defeated in Congress in large measure through pressure exerted by the bureaucracy. Only with the greatest of difficulty did Franklin D. Roosevelt obtain passage of a reorganization measure delegating to the President the power to shift administrative units from one department to another; yet certain agencies succeeded in bringing about the adoption of amendments excepting them from the operation of the act. The Army Corps of Engineers, for example, which has been one of the most persistent opponents of administrative reorganization, has succeeded in maintaining the status quo for itself.[4] Fights on questions of administrative organization are sometimes battles between two federal agencies for jurisdiction over a particular matter, such as the dispute between the Department of Agriculture and the Department of the Interior over the Forest Service. The Forest Service, with its far-flung field service closely knit into the life of the communities served, has gained strong public support and has successfully resisted efforts to transfer it to the Department of the Interior.[5]

INSTITUTIONAL   INERTIA   AND   POLICY   DIRECTION
From the public prints it might be supposed that administrative agencies ceaselessly seek to enlarge their functions and to advance their cause. Such drives for power exist, but quite as prevalent is an institutional inertia almost gyroscopic in its effect. The responsibilities of political direction may require that an agency be jolted from its ancient ruts. Some political heads of agencies impress their views on the organization they direct, but at times the de-

---

[4] See Arthur Maass, *Muddy Waters* (Cambridge: Harvard University Press, 1951). The capacity of administrative agencies, often in association with their pressure-group allies and congressional friends, to resist reorganization suggests the limitations of presidential control over administration. See Avery Leiserson, "Political Limitations on Executive Reorganization," *American Political Science Review*, 41 (1947), 68–84.

[5] On rivalry among the Forest Service, the Bureau of Land Management, and the National Park Service in the area of recreation policy, see Julius Duscha, "The Undercover Fight Over the Wilderness," *Harper's Magazine*, April, 1962.

partment as an institution has a momentum and a pattern of action that escape direction.[6] "The department" over a long period builds up a tradition, a policy, and, one could almost say, a "personality" of its own. A point of view comes to permeate the organization; and, if new recruits do not have the departmental attitude, they acquire it in time. These departmental traditions are difficult to bring to life on paper, but they are of enormous importance in the determination of the direction in which the department will exert its influence in the legislative process. Moreover, departmental policy tends to harden into a tradition that resists alteration. The institutional pattern of ideas comes to be set in a certain fashion, and it tends to stay that way.[7] In consequence, chief executives and legislative bodies often have to seek advice on public policy from outside existing administrative services to offset the force of tradition. Under extreme conditions about the only way to get a job done may be to establish a new agency.

EXPLOITATION OF ADMINISTRATIVE RESOURCES Partisan control of administration may be regarded as a simple exercise of command. If it is that and nothing more it is apt to be both sterile and futile. Few political heads of departments know enough to tell their staffs what to do; their task is to use the resources of their departments in the public interest. From the permanent staffs of government agencies emerge ideas for action and plans for improving the efficiency of administration. From the same source may come judgments, informed by experience, on the wisdom or probable repercussions of contemplated courses of action. The thinking and planning of the civil servant may approach the intelligent and informed exercise of a trusteeship of the public welfare. The effective political head of an agency finds ways to blend the resources of his department with his own skills in political maneuver and to accommodate the mandates of his party and the creative capacities of the permanent service.

Politicians cannot think up all the laws; a skillful administrative politician may be the midwife who brings to fruition the ideas of his staff. In some spheres administrative officials possess what amounts to a sovereignty of competence. Since a large proportion of legislation consists of modifications of old policy, those in charge of the administration are in possession of

---

[6] Consider the widespread public astonishment generated by President Kennedy's Secretary of Defense, Robert McNamara, when he proceeded to operate on the assumption that it was really his job to run the Department of Defense.

[7] Public lands, including forested lands, were at one time in the custody of the General Land Office of the Department of the Interior. After considerable political pyrotechnics forests were assigned to the Department of Agriculture for protection and management. "The national forest idea ran counter to the whole tradition of the Interior Department," said Gifford Pinchot, who was chief of the Bureau of Forestry of the Department of Agriculture in Theodore Roosevelt's Administration. "Bred into its marrow, bone and fiber, was the idea of disposing of the public lands to private owners." "How the National Forests Were Won," *American Forests and Forest Life*, October, 1930.

information and experience basic to the formulation of changes. For example, in the application of tax laws the Internal Revenue Service discovers loopholes facilitating evasion and suggests remedies to Congress. A crusading Food and Drug Administration urges changes in the law in order to broaden its coverage to protect the public and to make effective enforcement more feasible. Scientists of the Department of Agriculture discover means to control a pest and recommend suitable measures. The Children's Bureau calls attention to high rates of infant mortality and agitates for a program to bring about a reduction. In every sphere of governmental activity the influence of the knowledge and experience of the administrative official makes itself felt in new legislation.[8]

BROAD PROBLEMS OF POLITICAL DIRECTION   These remarks pose in general terms the problem of political direction of administration. Scores of administrative entities, if we observe the reality that some departments are units only in name, constitute a vast and cumbersome apparatus the victorious party must bring under its control. Each of the major agencies enjoys the support, and perhaps opposition, of organized interests. Each has its friends in Congress. Each may be of particular concern to some faction or group within the party. A party can meet the requirements of accountability only if it can bring under control those actions of the administrative apparatus most likely to touch party policy or to produce party embarrassment. The nature of that problem of control may be illuminated by an examination of the modes of action of administrative agencies and the techniques of direction by the President.

Administration and Public Policy: Methods

Embedded in the administrative agencies are powerful particularistic drives that at times threaten to fragment the government. The President presides over the unruly assemblage of administrative institutions and attempts to maintain within it a semblance of order and a harmony with party policy on at least the major questions. Hierarchical etiquette makes the President the boss of the administrative apparatus, but by custom, and on occasion by a bit of insubordination, administrative agencies enjoy considerable freedom in the promotion of their objectives.

PUBLIC-RELATIONS ACTIVITIES OF ADMINISTRA-TIVE AGENCIES   The techniques of administrative agencies in pre-

[8] On the administrative origin of reforms of the Progressive era in California, see G. D. Nash, "Bureaucracy and Economic Reform: The Experience of California, 1899," *Western Political Quarterly*, 13 (1960), 678–91.

senting their case to the public and to the lawmakers are fundamentally similar to those employed by private lobbying groups. Almost every governmental agency conducts some sort of public-relations program, but only a small proportion of the publicity issued by administrative agencies is concerned with the promotion of proposed courses of public policy. The objectives of the bulk of governmental publicity are the performance of a function, such as the dissemination of information on improved farming methods by the Department of Agriculture, or the furnishing of information to the public on the course of public affairs, such as the news releases issued by the Department of State.

Administrative agencies are concerned with the creation of a reservoir of good will among the general public that can be drawn on when specific legislative proposals are under consideration by the legislative body. A "good" press and a "good" name are of great value in convincing Congress of the necessity for an increased appropriation or for other legislation requested by the agency. On the other hand, a "bad" press can make the agency's relations with Congress difficult. Sometimes the public-relations strategy is to dramatize the agency through publicizing its chief. The Federal Bureau of Investigation furnishes an excellent example of this technique. Other agencies do not build up a single personality but seek to create a public opinion favorable to the service as an institution. Still other agencies seek to propagate an idea.

None of the types of public-relations activities cited involves an appeal for public support for any particular policy advocated by the agency; rather, they are calculated to establish a favorable general attitude toward the personalities, services, and ideas concerned. If this type of generalized publicity is effective, an underlying sentiment is formed that is likely to help when specific legislation is under consideration by Congress.

A different type of publicity—a sort of administrative guerilla warfare —flows from the informal and often surreptitious relations of administrators with journalists. Information is fed to these persons who report it "on high authority" or as from "informed sources." By this means Congress may be needled, the President nudged, a fire lighted under a superior, or officials in another department may be stirred to action or to anger. The most spectacular examples of this practice occur when the Navy, the Air Force, and the Army engage in psychological warfare through the press. Bitter debates among the bureaucrats tend to spill over into the press.[9] The services, too, engage in extensive publicity calculated to improve their public image. If, by some miracle, all the public-relations men of the services could be transformed into militarily useful manpower, our striking power would be given an impressive boost.

While there are critics of the public-relations activities of administrative

[9] See S. P. Huntington, "Interservice Competition and the Political Roles of the Armed Services," *American Political Science Review*, 55 (1961), 40–52.

agencies, in truth, an agency, if it is to function effectively, must develop support in Congress, from its clientele, and from the public generally. An act of Congress is not enough to establish it firmly, particularly if its operations affect some powerful group adversely. As an agency recruits sufficient support to assure a degree of stability, however, it thereby gains a degree of autonomy which may limit presidential direction. Agencies may, in rare instances, completely escape presidential control.

ADMINISTRATIVE AGENCIES AND THE LEGISLATIVE PROCESS   Since a large proportion of the legislative output either originates in administrative experience or affects administrative operations, administrative agencies play an extremely important role in the process of lawmaking as a whole. They originate legislative proposals; they attempt, at times, to defeat proposals originating from other sources; and, at other times, they seek to bring about alterations in proposals pending in the legislative bodies. To carry out these activities the agency must have facilities for drafting and for responsible consideration of proposals. It must also watch the course of legislation to keep informed on proposals that might affect its work; otherwise, legislation might be enacted that would be either difficult to administer or would tie the agency in knots.[10]

Most legislation is routine and arouses no controversy. It seeks to accomplish objectives that, by common consent, are wise and necessary for the conduct of public business. Congress routinely requests the advice of administrative agencies on legislation. Representatives of agencies appear before the committees of Congress and present information indicative of the need for action or the advisability of inaction. The relation of the agency to Congress is often not so much one of advocacy as of consultation with committeemen who have a responsible concern about the administrative operation in question.

Administration bills that propose a major change in public policy are likely to arouse opposition and to call for a vigorous presentation of the department's case. Under these circumstances the department may call on its allies among the pressure groups for assistance in dealing with Congress. When the objectives of the Department of Agriculture, for example, are coincidental with those of the American Farm Bureau Federation, the lobbyists of the Federation will appear, present testimony, buttonhole members of Congress, and perhaps focus upon Congressmen pressure from their constituencies. Or if the Farmers' Union is with the Department and the Federation against it, the Department may plan its legislative strategy in

---

[10] To be differentiated from legislative proposals by administrative agencies are bills initiated by organizations of public employees. Such groups are prolific sources of bills on retirement, leave, compensation, and related matters. For an analysis of their activities in one congressional session, see R. L. Frischknect, "Federal Employee Unions and the First Session, Eightieth Congress," *Western Political Quarterly*, 1 (1948), 183–85.

consultation with Union officials. Connections exist between nearly every administrative unit and private associations, which are of great importance in the promotion of legislation. There is a deep-seated congressional jealousy of "bureaucrats," and the bureaucracy is restricted in the methods that it may use in dealing with Congress. If it seeks to stir up popular pressure on Congress in support of specific legislation, it is likely to arouse criticism and resentment in Congress; but its allied private pressure groups may turn the pressure on Congress more freely.[11]

It is chiefly in political disputes involving questions of high policy that the Administration attempts to focus a supporting public sentiment on Congress. And the important figures in these affairs are not petty bureaucrats but the principal leaders of the Administration. On these great questions the President or cabinet members may appeal to the country for support in coping with Congress.

ADMINISTRATION, PARTY, AND PRESIDENCY   Fulfillment of party responsibility and achievement of party purpose require that the administrative agencies be brought under party control. In this endeavor the role of the President is crucial. Two broad methods are at his disposal to impress upon the machinery of government his party's policies: the power of appointment and removal; the authority to review and superintend operations of administrative agencies.

The relevance of the power of appointment for party policy becomes most evident when control of the Presidency shifts from one party to another. Republican cabinet officers ordinarily have a different policy orientation from that of Democratic department heads. Appointments and removals of officials of subcabinet rank will also be tinged by policy considerations as well as by patronage factors.[12] The affiliations of appointees often parallel the obligations and commitments of the incoming party and foreshadow the course of its actions.[13] Undoubtedly an incoming party tends to replace a

---

[11] A 1959 investigation disclosed that the Army had induced one of its major contractors to put on an advertising campaign extolling the merits of the Nike missile at a moment when Congress was confronted with the problem of choice among types of missiles sponsored by different military services.

[12] Consider the impact of Republican laissez-faire policy on the role of the Bureau of Standards as reported by S. A. Lawrence, *The Battery Additive Controversy* (ICP Case No. 68, 1962).

[13] The early Eisenhower appointments included officials who had been strongly on record as opposed to the programs they were to administer: "The new head of the Rural Electrification Administration is regarded in his home state of Minnesota as an opponent of REA projects; the new head of the Housing and Home Finance Administration fought hard and consistently in Congress against the program he is now to administer; an arch protectionist who voted against the Reciprocal Trade Program when he was in the House has been appointed to the Tariff Commission; an Assistant Secretary of Interior appears to oppose conservation and has testified that the public lands should ultimately be turned over to private citizens; the new general counsel of the

higher proportion of the upper levels of the bureaucracy than is necessary to gain effective control of the administrative apparatus. After the election of 1952 this result came about in part from the demands for patronage from a party long out of power and in part from the unfamiliarity with governmental practice of many of the top-level Republican appointees. Victims of their own propaganda, they believed themselves to be surrounded by New Deal bureaucrats engaged in a conspiracy to sabotage the Eisenhower crusade, a point of view that became less marked as the businessmen learned their way around Washington.

While the power to appoint the heads of agencies is essential, it does not solve the problem of direction of the administrative apparatus. The President has a continuing task of guiding and coordinating the work of the adminis-trative agencies which, left to their own devices, go off in all directions. In this task he has the assistance of the White House staff. The Bureau of the Budget serves as a staff aid to the President in the review of budget requests; it is bad form for an agency head to seek from appropriations committees a greater sum than is recommended in the President's budget. Agency legislative proposals are required to be cleared through the Bureau of the Budget for advice on their conformity with the President's program.[14] The Council of Economic Advisers aids in the coordination of economic policies of the government departments, while the President has at his disposal the National Security Council to simplify the task of riding herd on those responsible for diplomatic and military policies.[15]

As the President seeks to maintain control over the unwieldy administrative system, he may act at times as party leader; he also acts as chief executive. Were there no parties or elections, the chief executive would have to be equipped with machinery to aid in coordinating and directing the administrative system. Yet in his role as principal administrator the President must look to the achievement of the aims of his party, and he himself makes a substantial proportion of the record upon which his party must stand at the next election.

Department of Health, Education and Welfare is a former Congressman who voted to restrict social security coverage; the new chairman of the Federal Trade Commission previously made his living representing interests who did battle with the Commission; and the President's original appointee to head the Bureau of Mines was so articulate in his opposition to the Mine Safety Law he was to administer that the congressional committee forced the White House to withdraw his name." H. M. Somers, "The Federal Bureaucracy and the Change of Administration," *American Political Science Review*, 48 (1954), 138–39.

[14] See R. E. Neustadt, "Presidency and Legislation: The Growth of Central Clearance," *American Political Science Review*, 48 (1954), 641–71; Arthur Maass, "In Accord with the Program of the President?" *Public Policy*, IV (1953), 77–93.

[15] These remarks give only the faintest notion of the enormity of the President's task in directing administrative agencies, each with its own traditions, its own connections with pressure groups, its peculiar alliances in Congress, its habits and conceptions of the public interest.

Limitations on Administrators

By various means Congress has sought to limit the activities of administrative agencies designed to influence public opinion and legislative action. In these endeavors it has been motivated in part by congressional jealousy of the growing power and influence of the bureaucracy, in part by adherence to the theory that administrative agencies should have no place in the initiation of legislation, and in part by congressional resentment of the actions of particular administrative agencies in specific situations.

PROHIBITION OF EMPLOYMENT OF ''PUBLICITY EXPERTS''   The first statutory limitation on public-relations activities applicable to all administrative agencies was enacted in 1913. It grew out of the announcement of a civil service examination to select a "publicity expert" for the Office of Public Roads. The duties of this position were to "consist of the preparation of news matter relating to the work of the Office of Public Roads and securing the publication of such items in various periodicals and newspapers, particularly in country newspapers." The desire was to obtain the services of a man "whose affiliations with newspaper publishers and writers is extensive enough to insure the publication of items prepared by him." The phraseology of the announcement could not have been better calculated to arouse animosity in Congress. Congressman Gillett observed: "The different departments of the administration certainly are not very modest in finding men and means to put before the country in the press the duties and purposes of their administration." And Congressman Fitzgerald agreed "that there was no place in the Government Service for an employee whose sole duty was to extol and to advise the activities of any particular service of the Government." The outcome was the following enactment: "No money appropriated by this or any other act shall be used for the compensation of any publicity expert unless specifically appropriated for that purpose." [16]

Congress has made no specific appropriation for the employment of publicity experts. Consequently, there has resulted, says McCamy, the "evasive hiring of publicity experts under such titles as 'Director of Information,' 'Chief Division of Information and Education,' 'Chief Informational Officer,' 'Editor-in-Chief,' 'Assistant to the Director' or 'Assistant to the Administrator,' 'Supervisor of Information Research,' 'Assistant to the Chairman,' or 'Director of Publication.' " [17] The fact is, however, that many laws authorize

[16] 38 Stat. L. 212.
[17] J. L. McCamy, *Government Publicity* (Chicago: University of Chicago Press, 1939), p. 7.

administrative agencies to carry on educational work or to inform the public, and expenditure of funds for publicity work can be legally justified under these authorizations. The principal effect of the legislation of 1913 has been to outlaw the title "publicity expert."

PROHIBITION OF EXPENDITURES TO INFLUENCE CONGRESS   In 1919 Congress enacted the following legislation:

> No part of the money appropriated by any act shall, in the absence of express authorization by Congress, be used directly or indirectly to pay for any personal service, advertisement, telegram, telephone, letter, printed or written matter, or other device, intended or designed to influence in any manner a member of Congress, to favor or oppose, by vote or otherwise, any legislation or appropriation by Congress.[18]

Indicative of the practices toward which the legislation was directed is the statement in congressional debate that this clause would "prohibit a practice that has been indulged in so often, without regard to what administration is in power—the practice of a bureau chief or the head of a department writing letters throughout the country, for this organization, for this man, for that company to write his Congressman, to wire his Congressman, in behalf of this or that legislation." The law does permit executive employees to communicate with members of Congress at the request of Congressmen through "the proper official channels" on legislation or appropriations.[19]

Further statutory limitations on publicity by governmental agencies were imposed in 1939. By an act effective July 1 of that year, Congress prohibited administrative agencies from sending through the mail free of postage, books, documents, pamphlets, and the like materials unless a request had been received. This limitation was adopted as the result of the objections of some Congressmen to the practice of New Deal agencies of transmitting large volumes of publicity matter through the mails. A statute of 1961 prohibited the use of any appropriated funds "for publicity or propaganda purposes designed to support or defeat legislation pending before Congress."

ENFORCEMENT OF PROHIBITIONS BY CRITICISM In practice the principal sanction for the enforcement of these limitations on

---

[18] 41 Stat. L. 68.

[19] The quoted statutory language is broad in its coverage, but other statutes make it the duty of agency heads to make recommendations to Congress and, in effect, exempt their policy advocacy from the general prohibition. A commotion developed in 1962 over the meaning of the prohibition as applied to career employees. The Civil Service Commission issued a ruling in which it called attention to the limitations on the use of public funds for the support of or opposition to new legislation but continued: "Aware of these implications, however, the career official may explain the position of the administration in the proposed legislation before interested public groups." After Senator John J. Williams began an agitation against the ruling, the Civil Service Commission rescinded its interpretation.

administrative agencies is the possibility of adverse criticism in Congress, to which the executive officers of the government are extremely sensitive. The absence of a body of case law interpreting the statutes as applied to different kinds of situations makes it difficult to say precisely what is prohibited. The law does not prevent recommendations of new legislation through proper channels—the President and the heads of departments. The chief effect of the regulatory legislation seems to be to discourage administrative agencies from openly organizing support throughout the country for or against specific bills.

The kinds and tenor of congressional criticism of administrative activity in relation to public policy may be illustrated by a few examples. In 1940 Congressman Smith of Ohio assailed Nathan Straus, administrator of the United States Housing Authority, and members of his staff for "gumshoeing about the Capitol and offices of Congressmen lobbying for the passage of the housing bill." He described the activities of Mr. Straus and his staff as "perfidious action" and announced that "every bureaucrat should be put in jail for lobbying to put his schemes through Congress." In 1953 members of the House Committee on Ways and Means talked ominously of referring the matter to the Department of Justice when the Secretary of the Treasury sought to persuade the NAM and the Chamber of Commerce not to oppose a short-term extension of the excess-profits tax.

Similarly, in 1945 Senator Robert A. Taft made an extended criticism of the Treasury Department for its "information" activities in support of the Bretton Woods agreements. The Senator showed that the department had circulated hundreds of thousands of pamphlets and that its staff had spoken at many meetings and to many organizations in support of the agreements. He contended that such action violated the statute of 1919 and that it also subverted the normal constitutional process by enabling the administration to organize and direct public pressure upon Congress. Such practices raise genuinely important constitutional issues, but congressional attitudes seem to be grounded more on the particular issue than on the principle involved. A legislator seems more likely to become critical if he opposes a particular measure that is being aided by the administrative propaganda than if he favors it. Thus, in 1946, when President Truman instructed the admirals to refrain from lobbying against the establishment of a Department of National Defense, the congressional opponents of service consolidation objected vociferously that the experts were being muzzled and other high crimes and misdemeanors committed.

Administrative agencies are also subjected to criticism from private sources for their efforts, alleged or real, to influence congressional action. In the battle over medical care for the aged in 1962, the American Medical Association garnered a good deal of publicity from its demand that the Attorney General determine whether Secretary Abraham Ribicoff had committed a criminal act by publishing a booklet on the topic. The AMA charged that the

Secretary had used tax funds "to propagandize for a bill which many people and many groups have vigorously opposed." It cited the prohibition of the use of public funds in any attempt to influence Congress. The Secretary retorted that the AMA was only making "silly charges," for the law explicitly obligated him to make recommendations to Congress for changes in the social security system.

Outbursts such as those cited have a common origin. They come from critics, inside and outside Congress, of the policies fostered by the administrative agency concerned. Attacks on administrative action are usually part of a campaign against a specific piece of legislation. Phrased in extravagant language, they are designed to discredit the administrative agency by branding it as a lawbreaker. These attacks may keep administrative agencies within legal bounds, but, within the sphere of legality, there is large scope for administrative lobbying. The President and other policy-forming officials have a responsibility to recommend to Congress courses of action; Congressmen, in turn, rely on administrative officials and employees for advice and assistance. The administration remains one of the most important influences on the course of legislative action.

Legal limitations of the sort discussed are likely to be ineffective in stemming the tide of administrative publicity calculated to influence public opinion and the course of legislative action. In some respects, the growth of administrative publicity reflects a profound change in the nature of our governmental arrangements. To executive agencies has shifted in considerable measure the initiation of legislative policy. A corollary of this change is the development of administrative propaganda and education to aid in the crystallization of public sentiment concerning new policies. In another respect, administrative agencies have themselves become lawmakers through congressional delegation of authority. To make administrative rules and regulations publicly acceptable, propaganda or education has to be carried on as a substitute for the discussion and debate that earlier served in a more exclusive degree to manufacture public consent to governmental action. Yet there remains a serious problem in the definition of the sphere of permissible official propaganda that is in keeping with the theory of representative government.[20] The capacity of governmental agencies to manipulate public

[20] There is no denying, says Arthur Macmahon, "that the public-relations activities of governmental agencies may be dangerous for democratic society. Especially when large resources are involved, an agency should not be more interested in perpetuating itself than in enlightening public opinion. The eagerness to win public support may pass beyond the boundary of cultivating consent into demanding obedience. The formula of public relations for modern administration is elusive. The kind of advocacy that prejudices responsible government must be avoided. Yet administrators must be left adequately equipped to fulfill their responsibilities. Careful and continuous scrutiny by legislatures and citizens is the best guarantee that the limits of desirable administrative informational activity will be observed." *The Administration of Federal Work Relief* (Chicago: Public Administration Service, 1941), p. 292.

opinion must be restrained if the authority of the politically accountable policymakers is to be preserved.[21]

Independent Commissions and the Party Program

The party in power has the responsibility and the means for controlling the ordinary government departments and agencies. Its appointees head these agencies, and departmental policy is expected to be in accord with the Administration program. The independent commissions, however, have broad policymaking power and are beyond the ready and effective control of the government of the day. Their independence is justified on the ground that in their quasi-judicial activities the commissions must impartially determine private rights in relation to law. By that independence, however, the commissions come to determine political or policy questions with only a tenuous political accountability. An Administration may come into power pledged to adopt altered policies in important spheres, but it may find itself blocked by the fact that the regulatory commissions are controlled by men appointed by prior Presidents of a different policy persuasion.

The situation may be illustrated by a report by David F. Houston, then Secretary of Agriculture, covering a cabinet meeting early in Woodrow Wilson's first Administration:

> The matter of railway rates was considered at some length. It was agreed that the situation ought to be met squarely and promptly. One of the members (Lane) said that some of the rates on certain goods were too low. They had been made in the interest of owners of industries along the line: Those he said should certainly be raised, but those on all competing roads would have to be raised also. . . .
>
> It was agreed that the matter was one for the Interstate Commerce Commission and that it should either raise or reclassify rates or insist on greater efficiency in management. It was agreed that no pressure of any sort could be brought to bear on the Commission. The impropriety of approaching it or its members was recognized.[22]

Here the President and the cabinet, with political responsibility for the conduct of government, agreed that the situation "ought to be met squarely and promptly." But they also agreed that the matter was one for the Interstate Commerce Commission, and that it was improper to suggest action by the commission.

When President Coolidge in 1925 appointed William E. Humphrey to

[21] See F. E. Rourke, *Secrecy and Publicity* (Baltimore: Johns Hopkins Press, 1961).
[22] From *Eight Years with Wilson's Cabinet* (New York: Doubleday, Doran, 1926), I, 86–87.

the Federal Trade Commission, that body came to be dominated by a Republican majority, and its policy in the enforcement of the prohibition of "unfair methods of competition" in interstate commerce was drastically softened. Yet for the previous five years the commission had not been in accord with the policy of the Republican Administration. The shift in the commission's attitude with the appointment of Humphrey is indicated by a speech that he made:

> Under the old policy of litigation it [the commission] became an instrument of oppression and disturbance and injury instead of a help to business. It harassed and annoyed business instead of assisting it. Business soon regarded the commission with distrust and fear and suspicion —as an enemy. There was no cooperation between the commission and business. Business wanted the commission abolished and the commission regarded business as generally dishonest.[23]

It is difficult to see how a commission that attempted to prevent "unfair methods of competition" could be "a help to business," except to those businesses injured by unfair competition. When Franklin D. Roosevelt came into office, his conception of the role of the Federal Trade Commission was more nearly in accord with the ideas of the Wilsonian period and he requested the resignation of Humphrey in the following terms: "I do not feel that your mind and my mind go along together on either the policies or the administering of the Federal Trade Commission, and, frankly, I think it best for the people of this country that I should have a full confidence." Humphrey resisted the removal order, and the Supreme Court decided that Congress could limit the President's power to remove members of commissions exercising quasi-judicial powers. The decision made more difficult the harmonization of the policies of the independent regulatory commissions with the objectives of the party in power.

Harding and Coolidge had their troubles with the Tariff Commission, a body with only power to advise on tariff rates. In 1923 Harding wrote to Culbertson of the Tariff Commission:

> I only venture to say at this time that I think it is altogether desirable to hold up a declaration of broad policy until I can sit down and go over the entire situation with the commission. As I understand it, the commission is the agency of the President in dealing with the tariff problem, and my intimate association and final responsibility in all matters lead me to believe that it is highly essential for a thorough understanding before embarking on any definitely defined course.

When the question of reappointment of one member of the commission arose, Coolidge offered the appointment on condition that an undated letter of resig-

---

[23] Quoted by Edward P. Herring, *Public Administration and the Public Interest* (New York: McGraw-Hill, 1936), p. 125.

nation be signed by the appointee. Refusal to accede to the condition resulted in failure to receive reappointment. While the Tariff Commission occupies a position different from that of the ordinary regulatory commission, these incidents illustrate the difficulties of bringing about a congruity of political power and responsibility in the areas carved out for the independent commissions.

Limitations on the President's power of removal often mean only that a new Administration is delayed in gaining a majority of the members of an independent commission. That delay may be brief or it may be extended. Only eight months elapsed, for example, before the Eisenhower Administration obtained control of the National Labor Relations Board and introduced a narrower conception of the board's functions.[24] On the other hand, over four years passed before it had a majority of the TVA board. Yet even when an Administration names the personnel of an independent agency, the mode of operation of such agencies places them to a degree beyond Administration direction. That end was sought by the architects of the independent agencies, but it has its vexing consequences for Presidents.

What has happened in the creation of the independent commissions is that Congress, unable itself to deal with specific problems, has handed over to the independent commissions power to arbitrate differences between divergent social and economic interest. The standards to govern the commissions have been extremely vague guide lines, such as "fair," "just," "reasonable," "the public interest," and "the public convenience and necessity." [25] In settling these differences the commissions have adopted a procedure of impartiality, with many features and appearances of the judicial process; but in reality they are declaring policy as Congress does when it decides like issues. Then, too, mixed with these lawmaking functions is the duty of deciding the rights of individuals, which may be more or less purely judicial in nature.

The commissions' assumption of an independent posture and their tendency to isolate themselves from the administration's planning and contriv-

[24] The AFL-CIO concluded that, though the language of the Taft-Hartley Act had remained unchanged, the new board had given the act "a new, and almost anti-labor meaning" on many important issues. See Seymour Scher, "Regulatory Agency Control through Appointment: The Case of the Eisenhower Administration and the NLRB," *Journal of Politics*, 23 (1961), 667–88.

[25] Given such discretion, appointments are the basic actions in the determination of the policy of regulatory commissions, and they are, hence, often the subject of warm contention. Thus, in 1960 President Eisenhower decided not to reappoint William Connole to the Federal Power Commission. Mr. Connole had earned the outspoken enmity of the natural gas industry by his regulatory outlook; by the same token he had the vociferous support of mayors and other officials of gas consuming areas, but their clamor was not enough to save him. Earlier, in 1949, the gas industry had induced the Senate to deny confirmation to the appointment to the Federal Power Commission of another person dedicated to effective regulation, Leland Olds. Probably the general rule is that regulated industries succeed more often than they fail in blocking the appointment of commissioners hostile to their interests.

ing to meet new situations limit their usefulness in an important way. Impartiality and the judicial viewpoint—no matter how essential they are in settling individual cases under established law—are likely to be incompatible with the exercise of leadership in the formation of new policies, in the anticipation of problems, and in the preparation of policies to meet problems as they arise. The Interstate Commerce Commission apparently had something of this sort in mind when it reported:

> There is need for readjustments between and within the different branches of the transportation industry, for the consideration of present tendencies and their probable results, for the avoidance of uneconomic and wasteful practices, and in general for the determination, creation, and protection of the conditions most favorable to the development of a transportation system which will best serve the public interest. There is a field here both for continuing study and research and for active, aggressive, and consistent leadership on the part of Government which has never been occupied. The real problem is to fill that void in the best possible way.[26]

With one important governmental agency dealing with certain aspects of the transportation problem, however, it is virtually impossible for another, such as is suggested by the remarks of the commission, to undertake with success the function of research and aggressive leadership.[27]

The problem of working out the proper relationship of the independent regulatory commissions to the government as a whole remains unsolved. It seems obvious that a more suitable *modus operandi* will have to be devised, but how it will be done is unclear. Herring states the dilemma:

> The President has certainly no right to intervene on behalf of any private party who may come before a commission, but this does not mean that he has no concern with its general interpretation of the law. Can some way be found for admitting his influence upon policy without causing interference with the commission's judicial activities? How can the chief executive, for example, be given a means of exerting his influence in national transportation problems without disrupting the work of the Interstate Commerce Commission? [28]

[26] Interstate Commerce Commission, *52d Annual Report* (1938), pp. 24–25.

[27] Thus, in 1955 the Eisenhower Administration proposed, on the basis of the report of a cabinet committee, a revised transportation policy. The Interstate Commerce Commission unanimously took exception to the Administration's recommendations in a statement to the congressional committees considering them. Public policy toward railroads in the 1950's and 1960's provides a scandalous illustration of the paralysis produced by the dispersion of the power to govern among many agencies.

[28] *Op. cit.*, p. 224. See Marver Bernstein, *Regulating Business by Independent Commission* (Princeton: Princeton University Press, 1955), and S. P. Huntington, "The Marasmus of the ICC: The Commission, the Railroads, and the Public Interest," *Yale*

Friction will exist until the question is worked out. The urgency of the need for a satisfactory solution increases as the breadth of governmental regulation grows. Since the various aspects of the economic system dealt with by different independent commissions and ordinary government departments are interrelated, a coordinated government policy becomes more and more essential. It is the responsibility of the party in control to devise and execute such a program, but an Administration is limited in the fulfillment of that responsibility by the independence of the regulatory commissions.[29]

The Place of Bureaucracy in a Democracy

The administrative services are not inert mechanisms that translate the will of the legislature into action. These services themselves are a significant force in the state and play an important role in the determination of what is to be done in the name of the state. Yet their importance in this respect is not so great as might be inferred from the more extravagant diatribes against the bureaucracy.

The trend of events, however, suggests inquiries into the shape of things to come for administrative services and parliamentary institutions. The growing volume and complexity of public functions have reduced to a fiction the theory of separation of powers and the parallel doctrine of the separability of politics and administration. Representative bodies, the institutional embodiment of democratic ideology, have by the compelling force of events lost both power and prestige. Their role in the initiation of public policy has been diminished by losses to pressure groups and administrative agencies; their authority to decide many issues has, of necessity, been delegated to the administrative services. They have been driven toward a role of futile and uninformed criticism, at its worst motivated either by partisan or picayune considerations.

The administrative services have, in terms of the distribution of both formal governmental power and informal political influence, been the chief heirs of the declining representative bodies. In a culture whose traditional theory has been that political issues should be decided by popularly elected representatives, what are the dangers and problems of the growing importance of the administrative service? Charles E. Merriam pointed out that as we

---

Law Journal, 61 (1952), 467–509; Bernard Schwartz, *The Professor and the Commissions* (New York: Knopf, 1959).

[29] Independence from the President comes in practice to mean dependence upon the regulated industry and on interested members of Congress. Both are consistent defenders of agency "independence." Thus, in 1961 the broadcasting industry opposed a presidential plan to inject a bit more energy into the management of the Federal Communications Commission. Members of Congress, all of whom either had had or hoped for favored treatment from broadcasters, stood firmly against the President.

emerge from the era of corruption, incompetence, and ignorance in administration

> . . . the new possibilities are those of arrogance and indifference to the public, lack of sympathy approaching harshness and cruelty, devotion to inflexibility and routine, grumbling at theory and change; procrastination, quibbling and delay; or the opposite of too great and rash speed without adequate preparation of the public for the change.
>
> Above all there is the ever impending danger of the desire for personal self-perpetuation and expansion of power, bureaucratic parochialism of the pettiest type; the sabotage of the ends of office by placing the machinery or the person above the function he is there to serve; or the effort of the administrator to take over the role of the policy maker, by various devices, direct or otherwise.[30]

Although tendencies in these directions are discernible, there are offsetting factors. In the initiation and formation of public policy the power of group and class drives, as has been shown, is fundamental. Yet private groups find it difficult, even when the best of intentions are granted, to exert their strength for the general welfare. The legislative programs of administrative agencies, however, tend to incorporate the objectives of private groups and to temper and to modify them in the public interest. Indeed, in many situations of policy parturition it seems that the bureaucracy is the only participant animated by a devotion to the common welfare. In this connection Gaus and Wolcott inquire:

> At what point in the evolution of policies in the life of the community shall the process take place of transforming a specialist point of view and program, through compromise and adjustment, into a more balanced public program? Much of this process must take place in the administrative agencies through the selection of personnel, their continued in-service training, the content and discipline of their professions, researches, and responsibilities, the attrition of interbureau and interdepartmental contact and association, and the scrutiny of their work, by the over-all administrative staff and auxiliary agencies and by Congress. If there is the proper attention to these matters, the viewpoint of the civil service will differ from the surrogacy that one expects from the officials of a pressure group.[31]

A possible line of development, then, would be the direction and harnessing of the power, knowledge, and skills of the administrative services

---

[30] "Public Administration and Political Theory," *Journal of Social Philosophy*, 5 (1940), 305–6.

[31] *Public Administration and the U.S. Department of Agriculture* (Chicago: Public Administration Service, 1940), p. 283.

so that they might constitute a force in the initiation of public policies calculated to promote the common weal. Development of an administrative corps of this character depends in large measure on the further development of techniques of organization and supervision whereby the political heads of administrative services may better overcome the parochialism of the permanent staffs and liberate their talents. This problem of the overhead organization of governmental departments and of the government as a whole is of prime importance in the determination of the direction in which the powers of the bureaucracy will be exerted. Politically responsible officials in collaboration with Congress have the task of orienting public policy, but in the absence of effective techniques for organizing and directing the administration their efforts are likely to be either obstructed or ineffectively carried out by the administrative services.

The danger of the rise of a bureaucracy aggressively grasping for unwarranted power is probably much less than the danger of drifting into a condition in which the bureaucracy is a purely negative force. A seasoned bureaucracy, without heroic measures to the contrary, tends to become attached to the time-honored ways of doing things, hostile toward innovation, lacking in initiative, and timid. These qualities are admirable at the right time and place, but the next few decades in the United States will hardly be the time and place for pleasant habituation to the customary.

This is not to argue for a bureaucracy that will usurp the functions of Congress and the President; the contention is, rather, that present conditions demand a bureaucracy that will minimize the magnitude of the tasks of Congress and the President. How may that be done? The pressure on Congress may be reduced by the development of procedures within administration for the satisfactory settlement of matters unworthy of the attention of Congress; by the eradication of parochialism within administrative agencies and the consequent submission of legislative recommendations that are more likely to meet the desires of Congress; and by the development of internal controls that would reduce the task of congressional surveillance of administration. The task of presidential direction of administration increases in difficulty with the growth of the number of administrative agencies; the impression of the President's policy on particularistic administrative agencies becomes an almost impossible job (yet that is the President's responsibility and duty). To make the functions of Congress and the President actual as well as nominal, it is essential to have a bureaucracy dedicated to seeking out the general welfare, yet mindful of the final authority of Congress and the President in defining how the general welfare shall be promoted.

The problem of bureaucracy is in part not a problem of bureaucracy at all. It is rather a question of attracting into party service an adequate supply of men competent to manage and control the bureaucracy from their posts as the transient but responsible heads of departments and agencies. Publicists have been greatly exercised about making the civil service attractive enough to draw able men to it as a career. Of no less importance is the attraction of even abler men to the service of parties to direct and carry responsibility for the direction of the career staffs. It is through such persons who owe their posts to the victorious party that popular control over government is maintained.

INDEX